Don't Waste Your Time® in the

Canadian Rockies

The Opinionated Hiking Guide

Boot-tested and written by Kathy & Craig Copeland

Heading outdoors eventually leads within.

The first people on Earth were hikers and campers. So today, when we walk the land and bed down on it, we're living in the most primitive, elemental way known to our species. We're returning to a way of life intrinsic to the human experience. We're shedding the burden of millennia of civilization. We're seeking catharsis. We're inviting enlightenment.

First edition March 1994; Second edition June 1998;
Third edition March 2000; Fourth edition August 2001;
Fifth edition July 2004; Fifth edition updated July 2006;
Sixth edition July 2009: Sixth edition reprinted January 2011

Cover and interior design by Matthew Clark, www.subplot.com

Maps & production by C.J. Poznansky, giddyupgraphics@mac.com

Printed in China by Asia Pacific Offset

All photos by authors except page 26 by Tim Rhodes
Inside front cover: Route to Caldron Lake (Trip 9)
Inside back cover: Helmet Falls (Trip 89)

Published in Canada by hikingcamping.com, inc.
P.O. Box 8563, Canmore, Alberta T1W 2V3 Canada
fax: 403.678.3343 nomads@hikingcamping.com

Authors of opinionated guidebooks always welcome readers' comments.

Library and Archives Canada - Cataloguing in Publication

Copeland, Kathy, 1959-
Don't waste your time in the Canadian Rockies: the opinionated hiking guide / Kathy and Craig Copeland. — 6th ed.

Includes index.
ISBN 978-0-9783427-5-3

1. Trails—Rocky Mountains, Canadian (B.C. and Alta.)—Guidebooks.
2. Hiking—Rocky Mountains, Canadian (B.C. and Alta.)—Guidebooks.
3. Rocky Mountains, Canadian (B.C. and Alta.)—Guidebooks.
I. Copeland, Craig, 1955- II. Title. III. Series.

GV199.44.C22R64 2009 796.52209711 C2009-902266-4

YOUR SAFETY IS YOUR RESPONSIBILITY

Hiking and camping in the wilderness can be dangerous. Experience and preparation reduce risk, but will never eliminate it. The unique details of your specific situation and the decisions you make at that time will determine the outcome. This book is not a substitute for common sense or sound judgment. If you doubt your ability to negotiate mountain terrain, respond to wild animals, or handle sudden, extreme weather changes, hike only in a group led by a competent guide. The authors and the publisher disclaim liability for any loss or injury incurred by anyone using information in this book.

CONTENTS

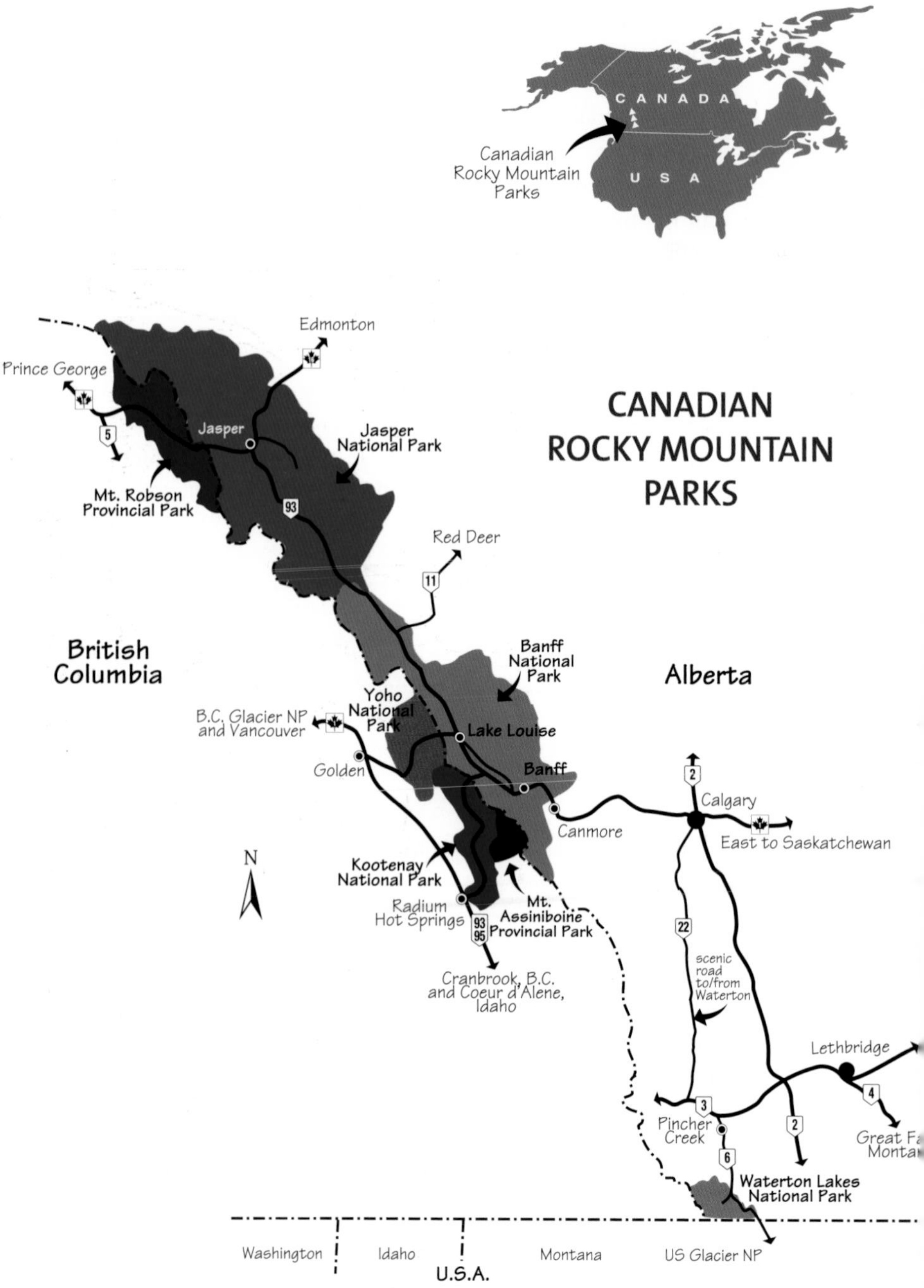

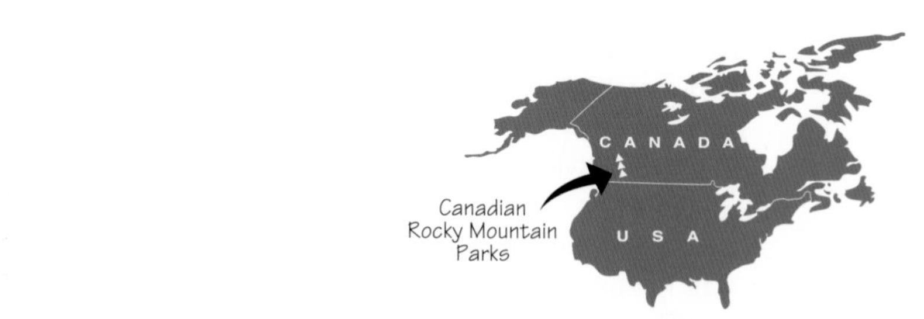

CANADIAN ROCKY MOUNTAIN PARKS

Edmonton
Prince George
5
Jasper
Jasper National Park
Mt. Robson Provincial Park
93
Red Deer
11
British Columbia
Banff National Park
Alberta
Yoho National Park
B.C. Glacier NP and Vancouver
Lake Louise
Golden
Banff
2
Calgary
Canmore
East to Saskatchewan
N
Kootenay National Park
Radium Hot Springs
93
95
Mt. Assiniboine Provincial Park
22
scenic road to/from Waterton
Cranbrook, B.C. and Coeur d'Alene, Idaho
Lethbridge
4
3
Pincher Creek
2
Great Fa
Monta
6
Waterton Lakes National Park
Washington
Idaho
Montana
US Glacier NP
U.S.A.

WATERTON LAKES NATIONAL PARK

1 Akamina Ridge / Wall & Forum lakes

2 Rowe Lakes / Lineham Ridge

22 Crypt Lake

23 Carthew Summit / Alderson Lake

37 Bertha Lake

38 Goat Lake

59 Vimy Peak

60 Blakiston Creek Valley

100 Avion Ridge / Twin Lakes

106 Tamarack Trail

116 Lineham Creek Falls

119 Waterton Lakeshore

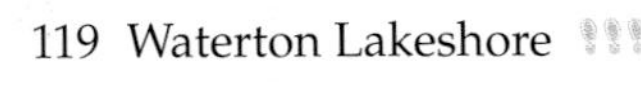

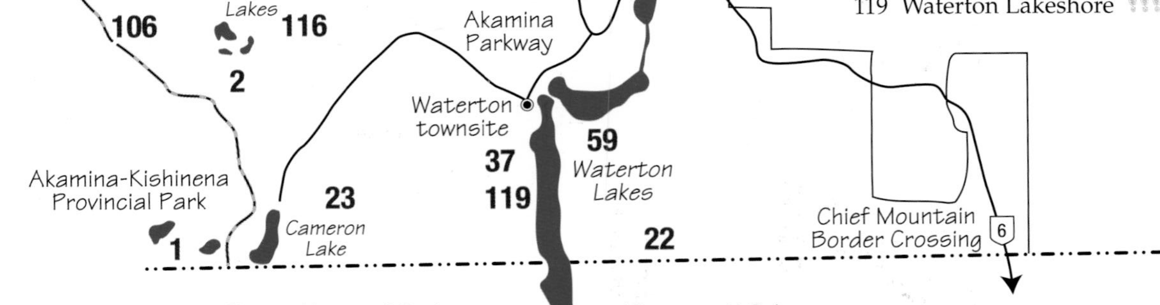

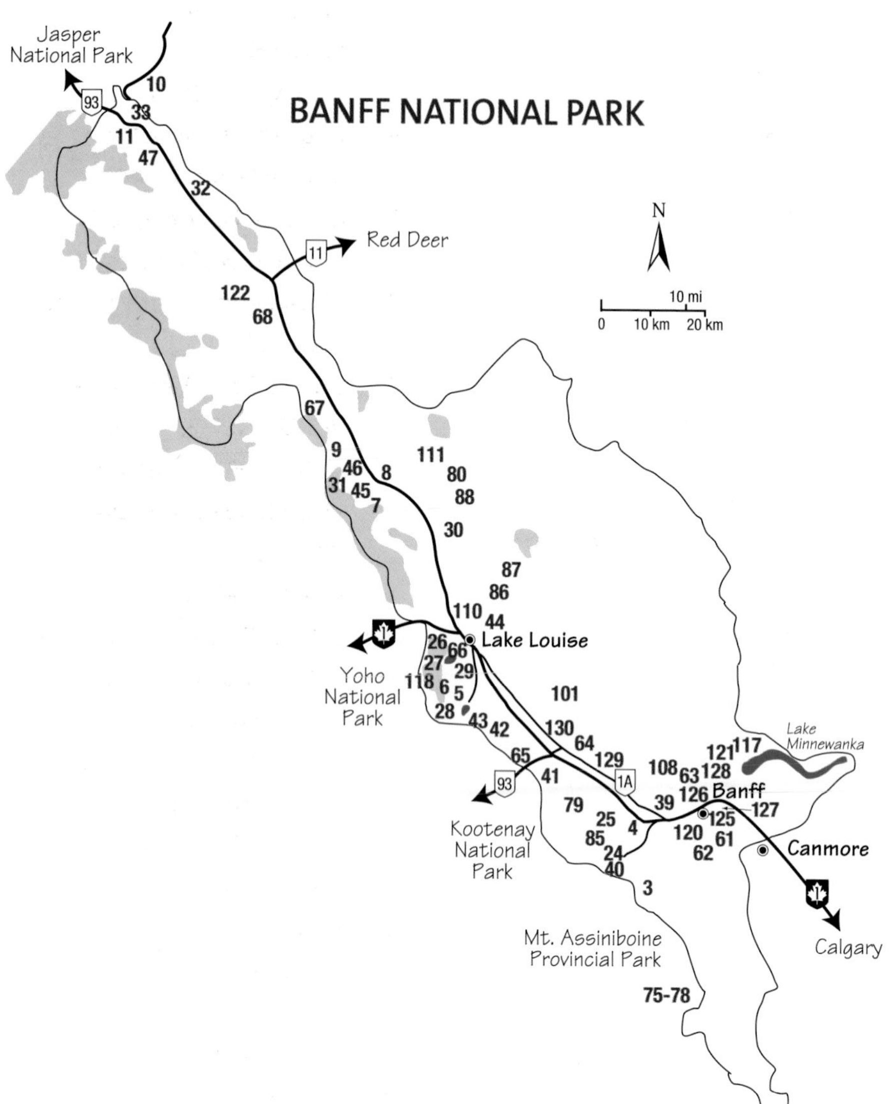
BANFF NATIONAL PARK
Jasper National Park
Red Deer
Lake Louise
Yoho National Park
Kootenay National Park
Lake Minnewanka
Banff
Canmore
Calgary
Mt. Assiniboine Provincial Park
N
10 mi
0 10 km 20 km
93
11
1A
10
33
11
47
32
122
68
67
9
46
8
31
45
7
111
80
88
30
87
86
110
44
26
66
27
29
118
6
5
28
43
42
101
130
64
65
41
129
108
63
121
117
128
126
39
125
127
120
61
62
79
25
4
85
24
40
3
75-78

BANFF TRIP LOCATIONS

Trip	Location
3	Citadel Pass
4	Bourgeau Lake / Harvey Pass
5	Sentinel Pass
6	Paradise Valley
7	Bow Peak
8	Helen Lake / Cirque Peak
9	Caldron Lake
10	Cataract Pass
11	Parker Ridge
24	Healy Pass
25	Egypt & Shadow lakes via Redearth Creek
26	Mt. Saint Piran
27	Devil's Thumb
28	Eiffel Lake
29	Saddleback/ Fairview Mtn
30	Molar Pass
31	Bow Hut
32	Sunset Pass
33	Nigel Pass
39	Cory & Edith passes
40	Rock Isle & Grizzly lakes
41	Twin Lakes
42	Taylor Lake
43	Consolation Lakes
44	Boulder Pass
45	Bow Glacier Falls
46	Bow Lookout
47	Saskatchewan Glacier
61	Mt. Rundle
62	Sulphur Mtn (gondola trail)
63	Cascade Amphitheatre
64	Rockbound Lake
65	Boom Lake
66	Lake Agnes / Beehives
67	Cirque & Chephren lakes
68	Sarbach Lookout
75-78	Mt. Assiniboine Region
79	Gibbon & Healy Passes
80	Pipestone Pass / Devon Lakes
85	Egypt Lake
86	Skoki Valley / Merlin Lake
87	Red Deer & Baker lakes
88	N. Molar Pass / Fish Lakes
101	Pulsatilla & Badger Passes
108	Elk Lake
110	Pipestone River
111	Siffleur River / Dolomite Creek
117	Aylmer Lookout & Pass
118	Plain of Six Glaciers
120	Sulphur Mtn (Cosmic Ray)
121	Lake Minnewanka
122	Glacier Lake
125	Tunnel Mtn
126	Stoney Squaw
127	Bow River
128	C-Level Cirque
129	Johnston Canyon
130	Castle Lookout

KOOTENAY NATIONAL PARK

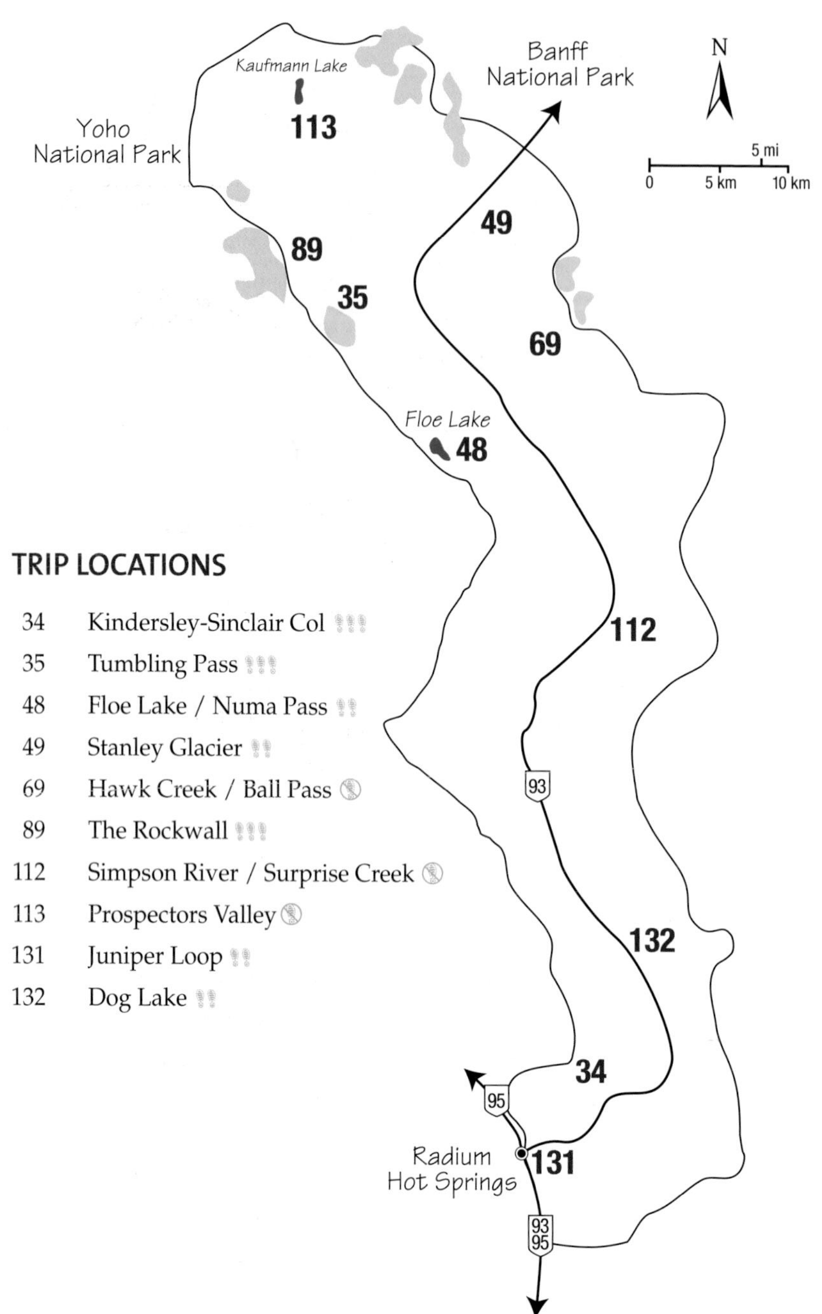

TRIP LOCATIONS

34 Kindersley-Sinclair Col
35 Tumbling Pass
48 Floe Lake / Numa Pass
49 Stanley Glacier
69 Hawk Creek / Ball Pass
89 The Rockwall
112 Simpson River / Surprise Creek
113 Prospectors Valley
131 Juniper Loop
132 Dog Lake

YOHO NATIONAL PARK

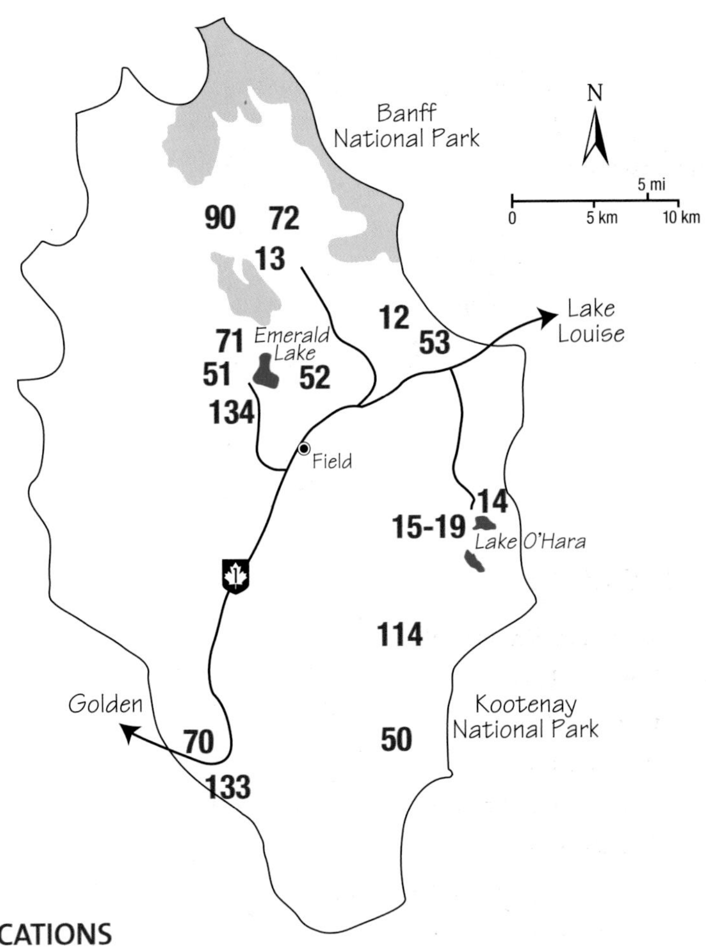

TRIP LOCATIONS

12	Sherbrooke Lake / Niles Meadow
13	Iceline
14	Lake O'Hara Alpine Circuit
15-19	Lake O'Hara Region
50	Goodsir Pass
51	Hamilton Lake / Emerald Col
52	Emerald Triangle
53	Paget Lookout & Peak
70	Mt. Hunter Lookout
71	Emerald Basin
72	Yoho Valley
90	Kiwetinok Pass / Whaleback
114	McArthur Creek
133	Wapta Falls
134	Emerald River

JASPER NATIONAL PARK

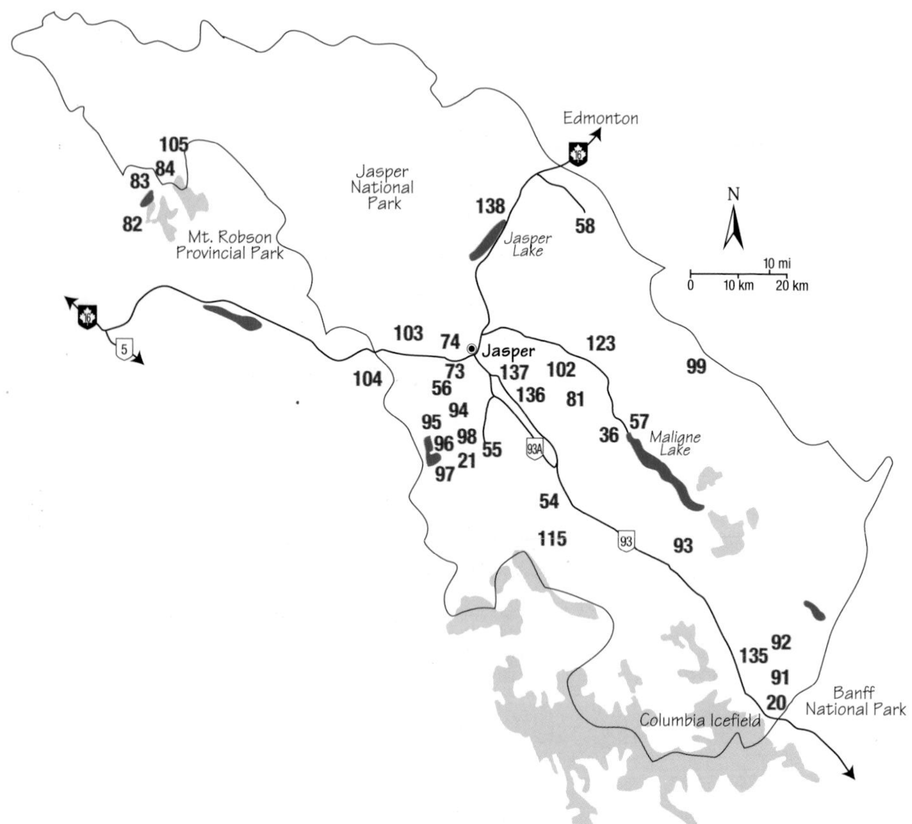

JASPER TRIP LOCATIONS

Looking southeast from Paget Peak (Trip 53) at the massif between Lake Louise and Lake O'Hara

TIME IS PRECIOUS

A disappointing trip leaves a psychic dent. Sometimes it can't be helped. But often it can, by knowing where to go instead of guessing. Too many hikers toil up scenically deprived trails to lackluster destinations when they could be savouring one of North America's consummate mountain panoramas. That's been our motivation: to save you from wasting your precious time. Even in this glorious mountain kingdom, not all scenery is created equal. Some places are simply more striking, more intriguing, more inspiring than others. Now you can be certain you're choosing a rewarding trail for your weekend or vacation.

These are our boot-tested opinions on which are the best hikes in the Canadian Rocky Mountain parks, which ones you should avoid, and why. We rate each trip *Premier, Outstanding, Worthwhile,* or *Don't Do.*

This kind of advice, available only from a *Don't Waste Your Time®* guidebook, is what you'd expect if consulting an honest friend who has vast hiking experience and wants you to enjoy a memorable adventure. It's also like eating an energy bar, because your stamina is affected by your attitude, and your attitude is boosted by exhilarating sights.

With other guidebooks, deciphering which trails offer superior scenery, then choosing one, can be a slow, difficult process. We've made it fast, easy and enjoyable. Our opinions are strong, but they're based on widely shared, common-sense criteria. **To help you understand our commentary, here are our preferences:**

• A hike isn't emotionally rewarding solely because of the destination. We want to be wowed along the way by stately trees, profuse wildflowers, plunging gorges, rocky escarpments. Watching a stream charge on its journey is a delight. Trails carved into rugged mountainsides are enthralling. Solitude is a sustaining necessity of life. Observing wild creatures is a primal joy. The closer we get to gleaming glaciers and piercing peaks, the more ecstatic we feel. High, airy, eye-stretching, soul-expanding perches thrill us most of all.

• Spending an entire, sunny, summer day below treeline doesn't appeal to us. Plodding for hours through disenchanted forest (scrawny, scrubby) is depressing. We soon lose interest in rubble-pile mountains devoid of sharp definition or sheer walls. When the scenery is monotonous and the trail cantankerous, it's trudgery. Although we'll push ourselves far and high for a grand sight, we're disappointed by an unengaging approach.

This is the guidebook we needed when we moved to Calgary. We both worked in the city and had only weekends to explore the nearby Canadian Rockies. There are 3400 kilometres (2100 miles) of trails in the mountain parks. Where would our limited time be best spent? None of the credible sources of information stated bold opinions. You now hold in your hands the solution to this problem. Our boot-print ratings and discerning trail reviews will warn you away from inferior trips and empower you to choose worthier ones. Our complete directions will tell you precisely where to find the mountain magic that distinguishes this wondrous range.

We hope our suggestions compel you to get outdoors more often and stay out longer. Do it to cultivate your wild self. It will give you perspective. Do it because the backcountry teaches simplicity and self-reliance, qualities that make life more fulfilling. Do it to remind yourself why wilderness needs and deserves your protection. A deeper conservation ethic develops naturally in the mountains. And do it to escape the cacophony that muffles the quiet, pure voice within.

Ascending moraine above Peyto Lake, en route to Caldron Lake (Trip 9)

TRAIL-RATING SYSTEM

PREMIER

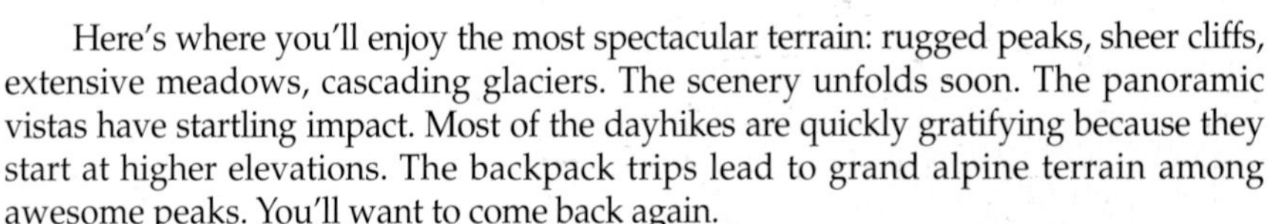

Here's where you'll enjoy the most spectacular terrain: rugged peaks, sheer cliffs, extensive meadows, cascading glaciers. The scenery unfolds soon. The panoramic vistas have startling impact. Most of the dayhikes are quickly gratifying because they start at higher elevations. The backpack trips lead to grand alpine terrain among awesome peaks. You'll want to come back again.

OUTSTANDING

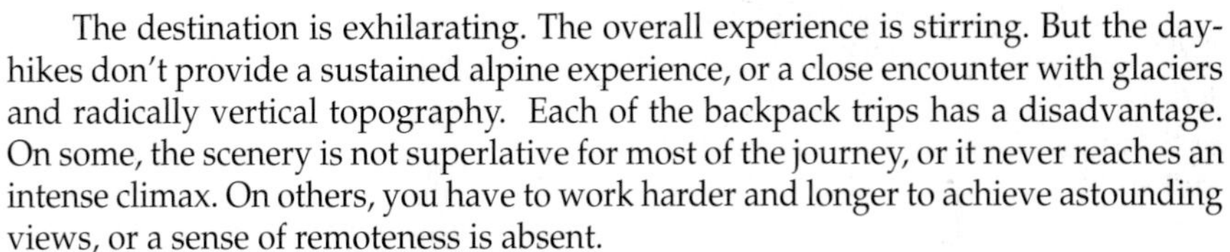

The destination is exhilarating. The overall experience is stirring. But the dayhikes don't provide a sustained alpine experience, or a close encounter with glaciers and radically vertical topography. Each of the backpack trips has a disadvantage. On some, the scenery is not superlative for most of the journey, or it never reaches an intense climax. On others, you have to work harder and longer to achieve astounding views, or a sense of remoteness is absent.

WORTHWHILE

You'll see beautiful scenery here, just not the kind that leaves an image blazed in your memory. The dayhikes are enjoyable, revealing a special aspect of the area. On the backpack trips, you'll trek a long way before it's obvious why you came, but you'll be glad you did.

DON'T DO

The sights are easily shrugged off on these tedious trails, or the time-and-energy demand overwhelms the scenic reward. Hike here only after you've thoroughly explored the range. Repeating a *Premier* or *Outstanding* trip would be more fulfilling.

SHOULDER-SEASON HIKING

Shoulder-season is a travel-industry term referring to the months before and after the popular, main season. We use it to describe early-summer and late-fall trips that allow you to start hiking by mid-May, and continue hiking perhaps into November. Low elevation or sun exposure ensures these trails are snow-free sooner and longer than others. You'll generally be hiking through forest, but hey, you'll be hiking.

Remember: shoulder-season ratings are not equivalent to ratings for prime hiking season. A shoulder-season *Premier* might be merely *Worthwhile* in mid-summer. A shoulder-season *Worthwhile* could be a *Don't Do* in mid-summer.

Shoulder-season: Premier means the trip is exciting overall. Compared to other choices in early summer or late fall, these trails are more enjoyable and the scenery more rewarding.

Shoulder-season: Outstanding means the trip is pleasing, though not in its entirety. These trails are longer and feel wilder than other early-summer or late-fall options.

Shoulder-season: Worthwhile means the trip is simply an opportunity to hike in early summer or late fall. Several of these trails lead to viewpoints or unique geographic features.

The shoulder-season trips rated *Premier* and *Outstanding* (117, 119, 121, 122, and 123) are long enough to be short backpack trips.

The following summer-season trips are too significant to be listed as shoulder-season, but they might be hikeable by mid-June or into November. Dayhikes: Sunset Lookout (Trip 32), Cory and Edith passes (Trip 39), Sulphur Skyline (Trip 58), Lake Agnes (Trip 66), and Yoho Valley (Trip 72). Backpack trips: Mt. Robson / Berg Lake (Trip 82), the Snowshoe Trail to Twin Lakes (Trip 106), and Elk Lake (Trip 108).

WILDFLOWER HIKES

To see a chaotically colourful flush of alpine wildflowers, hike these trails between early July and early August. Lower-elevation meadows, like those near the Summit Lakes (Trip 123), can begin blooming in mid June. Some spring blossoms appear in early May on slopes that receive intense sun exposure, like the one below Castle Lookout (Trip 130).

- Citadel Pass (Trip 3)
- Helen Lake (Trip 8)
- Niles Meadow (Trip 12)
- Verdant Pass (Trip 21)
- Healy Pass (Trip 24)
- Molar Pass (Trip 30)
- Rock Isle Lake (Trip 40)
- Numa Pass (Trip 48)
- Cavell Meadows (Trip 55)
- The Skyline (Trip 81)
- Jonas Pass (Trip 92)
- Maligne Pass (Trip 93)
- Elysium Pass (Trip 103)
- Moose Pass (Trip 105)
- Summit Lakes (Trip 123)

DAYHIKING OR BACKPACKING?

To help speed your decision making, we've separated the trips roughly according to round-trip distance. Most backpack trips are longer than 26 km (16 mi). Most dayhikes are shorter than 18 km (11 mi).

Don't necessarily limit yourself to our guidelines. Many backpack trips are hikeable in a day, if you're swift. Some dayhikes make excellent backpack trips if you want or need a short option; for example, Lake Annette / Paradise Valley (Trip 6), Bow Hut (Trip 31), Tumbling Pass (Trip 35), or Waterton Lakeshore (Trip 119).

TRIPS AT A GLANCE	*Trips in each category are listed according to geographic location: starting in the south and moving roughly from west to east, then north. After the trip name, the round-trip distance is listed, followed by the elevation gain.*

DAYHIKES AT A GLANCE

PREMIER

1	Akamina Ridge Circuit	18.3 km (11.3 mi)	985 m (3230 ft)
2	Lineham Ridge	17.2 km (10.7 mi)	960 m (3150 ft)
3	Citadel Pass	18.6 km (11.5 mi)	700 m (2296 ft)
4	Bourgeau Lake / Harvey Pass	19.2 km (12 mi)	1046 m (3431 ft)
5	Sentinel Pass	11.6 km (7.2 mi)	726 m (2381 ft)
6	Lake Annette /	11.4 km (7.1 mi)	245 m (804 ft)
	Paradise Valley	19.6 km (12.2 mi)	450 m (1476 ft)
7	Bow Peak	12.6 km (7.8 mi)	970 m (3182 ft)
8	Helen Lake / Cirque Peak	14 km (8.7 mi)	550 m (1804 ft)
9	Caldron Lake	16 km (10 mi)	1025 m (3362 ft)
10	Cataract Pass	26 km (16.1 mi)	640 m (2100 ft)
11	Parker Ridge	11 km (6.8 mi)	593 m (1945 ft)
12	Niles Meadow	19.6 km (12.2 mi)	717 m (2352 ft)
13	Iceline	12.8 km (8 mi)	690 m (2265 ft)
14	Lake O'Hara Alpine Circuit	9.8 km (6 mi)	495 m (1625 ft)
15	Lake Oesa	6.6 km (4.1 mi)	240 m (787 ft)
16	Opabin Plateau	7.2 km (4.5 mi)	250 m (820 ft)
17	Lake McArthur	7 km (4.3 mi)	413 m (1355 ft)
18	Little Odaray	8.4 km (5.2 mi)	930 m (3050 ft)
19	Cathedral Prospect	14.9 km (9.2 mi)	340 m (1115 ft)
20	Wilcox Pass	8 km (5 mi)	335 m (1100 ft)
21	Verdant Pass	22.5 km (14 mi)	665 m (2180 ft)

OUTSTANDING

22	Crypt Lake	17.4 km (10.8 mi)	690 m (2263 ft)
23	Carthew Summit	20.1 km (12.5 mi)	651 m (2135 ft)
24	Healy Pass	18.4 km (11.4 mi)	655 m (2150 ft)
25	Whistling Pass via Redearth & Pharaoh Creeks	26.4 km (16.4 mi) plus 21 km (13 mi) by bike	900 m (2952 ft)
26	Mt. Saint Piran	13 km (8 mi)	920 m (3018 ft)
27	Devil's Thumb	10.4 km (6.4 mi)	778 m (2552 ft)
28	Eiffel Lake	11.2 km (7 mi)	405 m (1328 ft)
29	Saddleback / Fairview Mtn	10.6 km (6.6 mi)	1014 m (3326 ft)
30	Molar Pass	20.4 km (12.6 mi)	540 m (1775 ft)
31	Bow Hut	14.8 km (9.2 mi)	500 m (1640 ft)
32	Sunset Pass	16.4 km (10.2 mi)	725 m (2380 ft)
33	Nigel Pass	14.4 km (8.9 mi)	365 m (1197 ft)
34	Kindersley-Sinclair Col	17.7 km (11 mi)	1055 m (3460 ft)
35	Tumbling Pass	24.6 km (15.2 mi)	770 m (2526 ft)
36	Bald Hills	12.6 km (7.8 mi)	610 m (2000 ft)

WORTHWHILE

37	Bertha Lake	10.4 km (6.4 mi)	471 m (1545 ft)
38	Goat Lake	13.6 km (8.4 mi)	525 m (1722 ft)
39	Cory & Edith passes	12.9 km (8 mi)	1000 m (3280 ft)
40	Rock Isle & Grizzly lakes	7.9 km (4.9 mi)	180 m (590 ft)
41	Twin Lakes	16.4 km (10.2 mi)	1065 m (3493 ft)
42	Taylor Lake	17 km (10.5 mi)	730 m (2395 ft)
43	Consolation Lakes	6 km (3.8 mi)	60 m (197 ft)
44	Boulder Pass	17 km (10.5 mi)	645 m (2116 ft)
45	Bow Glacier Falls	9 km (5.6 mi)	148 m (485 ft)
46	Bow Lookout	6 km (3.7 mi)	235 m (770 ft)
47	Saskatchewan Glacier	13.6 km (8.4 mi)	340 m (1115 ft)
48	Floe Lake / Numa Pass	27.5 km (17 mi)	1000 m (3280 ft)
49	Stanley Glacier	11.2 km (6.9 mi)	484 m (1587 ft)
50	Goodsir Pass	21.4 km (13.3 mi) plus 29 km (18 mi) by bike	1110 m (3642 ft)
51	Hamilton Lake / Emerald Col	14.2 km (8.8 mi)	1088m (3569 ft)
52	Emerald Triangle	19.7 km (12.2 mi)	868 m (2847 ft)
53	Paget Lookout & Peak	7.4 km (4.6 mi)	520 m (1705 ft)
54	Geraldine Lakes	10.5 km (6.5 mi)	407 m (1335 ft)
55	Cavell Meadows	6.1 km (3.8 mi)	420 m (1378 ft)

56	Indian Ridge	7 km (4.3 mi)	585 m (1920 ft)
57	Opal Hills	8.2 km (5.1 mi)	460 m (1500 ft)
58	Sulphur Skyline	8 km (5 mi)	636 m (2086 ft)

DON'T DO

59	Vimy Peak	25.6 km (16 mi)	1095 m (3592 ft)
60	Blakiston Creek Valley	4 km (2.5 mi)	55 m (180 ft)
61	Mt. Rundle	10.8 km (6.7 mi)	993 m (3255 ft)
62	Sulphur Mtn (gondola trail)	5.6 km (3.5 mi)	660 m (2165 ft)
63	Cascade Amphitheatre	14.8 km (9.2 mi)	685 m (2247 ft)
64	Rockbound Lake	16.8 km (10.4 mi)	770 m (2526 ft)
65	Boom Lake	10.2 km (6.4 mi)	175 m (575 ft)
66	Lake Agnes / Beehives	7 km (4.3 mi)	390 m (1280 ft)
67	Cirque & Chephren lakes	13.2 km (8.2 mi)	140 m (460 ft)
68	Sarbach Lookout	10.6 km (6.6 mi)	570 m (1870 ft)
69	Hawk Creek / Ball Pass	19.4 km (12 mi)	862 m (2827 ft)
70	Hunter Lookout	13 km (8 mi)	825 m (2705 ft)
71	Emerald Basin	9.2 km (5.7 mi)	248 m (813 ft)
72	Yoho Valley	17 km (10.5 mi)	290 m (950 ft)
73	The Whistlers	19.4 km (12 mi)	1216 m (3990 ft)
74	Saturday Night Lake	25.3 km (15.7 mi)	770 m (2525 ft)

BACKPACK TRIPS AT A GLANCE

PREMIER 

75	Mt. Assiniboine via Citadel Pass	29 km (18 mi)	520 m (1706 ft)
76	Nub Peak	11.4 km (7.1 mi)	558 m (1830 ft)
77	Wonder Pass / Bryant Creek	27.5 km (17 mi)	230 m (754 ft)
78	Windy Ridge	20.4 km (12.6 mi)	585 m (1919 ft)
79	Gibbon & Healy passes	40.4 km (25 mi)	1730 m (5670 ft)
80	Pipestone Pass / Devon Lakes	60 km (37.2 mi)	1768 m (5800 ft)
81	The Skyline	44.5 km (27.6 mi)	1205 m (3952 ft)
82	Mt. Robson / Berg Lake	42 km (26 mi)	786 m (2578 ft)
83	Mumm Basin / Hargreaves	12 km (7.5 mi)	505 m (1656 ft)
84	Snowbird Pass	21.2 km (13.2 mi)	758 m (2486 ft)

OUTSTANDING 

85	Egypt Lake	24.8 km (15.4 mi)	990 m (3247 ft)
86	Skoki Valley / Merlin Lake	31.4 km (19.5 mi)	1110 m (3640 ft)
87	Red Deer & Baker lakes	15 km (9.3 mi)	355 m (1165 ft)
88	N. Molar Pass / Fish Lakes	29.6 km (18.4 mi)	1128 m (3700 ft)
89	The Rockwall	55 km (34 mi)	2260 m (7416 ft)
90	Little Yoho Valley / Whaleback	28.8 km (17.9 mi)	1050 m (3444 ft)
91	Tangle Pass / Beauty Lakes	16 km (10 mi)	1175 m (3855 ft)
92	Jonas & Poboktan passes	79.3 km (49.2 mi)	1830 m (6002 ft)
93	Maligne Pass	30.4 km (18.8 mi)	691 m (2265 ft)
94	Tonquin via Maccarib	43 km (26.7 mi)	905 m (2970 ft)
95	Tonquin Hill	12 km (7.4 mi)	576 m (1890 ft)
96	Amethyst Lakes	10.5 km (6.5 mi)	100 m (328 ft)
97	Eremite Valley	8.6 km (5.3 mi)	240 m (787 ft)
98	Tonquin via Astoria	20 km (12.4 mi)	315 m (1033 ft)
99	Rocky & Cairn passes	56.6 km (35.1 mi)	1037 m (3400 ft)

WORTHWHILE 

100	Avion Ridge	24 km (14.9 mi)	945 m (3100 ft)
101	Pulsatilla & Badger passes	62.2 km (38.6 mi)	1549 m (5081 ft)
102	Watchtower Basin	25.6 km (16 mi)	1000 m (3280 ft)
103	Elysium Pass	29 km (18 mi)	1340 m (4395 ft)
104	Fitzwilliam Basin	27 km (16.7 mi)	951 m (3120 ft)
105	Moose Pass	78 km (48.3 mi)	1230 m (4034 ft)

DON'T DO 

106	Tamarack Trail	36.4 km (22.6 mi)	1440 m (4723 ft)
107	Marvel Pass	46 km (28.5 mi)	730 m (2394 ft)
108	Elk Lake	27 km (16.7 mi)	830 m (2722 ft)
109	Mystic pass & lake	36 km (22.3 mi)	1190 m (3903 ft)
110	Pipestone River	37 km (23 mi)	905 m (2970 ft)
111	Siffleur River / Dolomite Creek	69.2 km (43 mi)	595 m (1952 ft)
112	Simpson River	32.2 km (20 mi)	1325 m (4345 ft)
113	Prospectors Valley	30 km (18.6 mi)	568 m (1863 ft)
114	McArthur Creek	10.3 km (6.4 mi)	730 m (2395 ft)
115	Fryatt Valley	44 km (27.3 mi)	810 m (2657 ft)

SHOULDER-SEASON TRIPS AT A GLANCE

PREMIER 

116 Lineham Creek Falls	8.4 km (5.2 mi)	375 m (1230 ft)
117 Aylmer Lookout & Pass	23.4 km (14.5 mi)	570 m (1870 ft)
118 Plain of Six Glaciers	13.8 km (8.6 mi)	464 m (1522 ft)

OUTSTANDING 

119 Waterton Lakeshore	12.8 km (7.9 mi)	145 m (475 ft)
120 Sulphur Mtn (Cosmic Ray)	8.5 km (5.3 mi)	880 m (2886 ft)
121 Lake Minnewanka	15.6 km (9.7 mi)	100 m (328 ft)
122 Glacier Lake	18 km (11.2 mi)	475 m (1558 ft)
123 Summit & Jacques lakes	9.6 km (6 mi)	77 m (253 ft)

WORTHWHILE 

124 Bear's Hump	2.4 km (1.5 mi)	238 m (780 ft)
125 Tunnel Mtn	4.8 km (3 mi)	240 m (787 ft)
126 Stoney Squaw	4.5 km (2.8 mi)	184 m (604 ft)
127 Bow River	6.2 km (3.8 mi)	110 m (361 ft)
128 C-level Cirque	8.4 km (5.2 mi)	455 m (1495 ft)
129 Johnston Canyon / Inkpots	11.8 km (7.3 mi)	215 m (705 ft)
130 Castle Lookout	7.4 km (4.6 mi)	520 m (1705 ft)
131 Juniper Loop	7.2 km (4.5 mi)	227 m (745 ft)
132 Dog Lake	6.9 km (4.3 mi)	195 m (640 ft)
133 Wapta Falls	4.8 km (3 mi)	45 m (150 ft)
134 Emerald River	8.2 km (5.1 mi)	170 m (558 ft)
135 Beauty Creek	3.6 km (2.2 mi)	40 m (130 ft)
136 Wabasso Lake	6.4 km (4 mi)	110 m (360 ft)
137 Valley of Five Lakes	4.3 km (2.7 mi)	80 m (262 ft)
138 Devona Lookout	19.2 km (11.9 mi)	330 m (1082 ft)

Wapta Icefield, from summit of Mt. Niles

Trails Not in this Book

We excluded many trails we would have rated *Don't Do*. It seemed a waste of your time, as well as ours, to fully describe all the undesirable options. You're unlikely to be drawn to them anyway. Most are too punishing, tedious, or sketchy to be enjoyable for the vast majority of people. A few are long-distance trails requiring a big time commitment but yielding little high-impact scenery. It's a rare hiker who endures any of these. The following are representative examples.

(1) The Brewster Creek trail is way too long compared to others leading to Mt. Assiniboine and is often traveled by horse outfitters. Branching off it is the Fatigue Creek trail, another old outfitters' route and the worst possible approach to Fatigue and Citadel Passes. It's steep, rough, and entails numerous fords.

(2) Castleguard Meadows is a prized destination for mountaineers who can safely travel the Saskatchewan Glacier. But entering via Alexandra and Castleguard valleys requires hikers to endure the extremes of boredom and danger. Too much road-walking and too many hazardous fords make it an inadvisable trip.

(3) For several reasons, this book covers little of Banff Park's front ranges. They're prime grizzly habitat. They lack the high concentration of alpine scenery that most visitors seek in the Canadian Rockies. Scarce and distant trailheads necessitate extended backpack trips. Commercial horse outfitters frequent the region. Few hikers possess route-finding skills, or the mental and physical toughness to bushwhack very far, which some front-range trails require, like those along the Upper Panther and North Cascade rivers.

(4) A trail's historical significance means nothing to most hikers. Fur traders once plied Howse Pass, but you won't see them today, nor will you see much else. Viewless forest, wearisome detours around flooded river flats, and a root-bound track lead to the unexceptional pass.

(5) The trail from Sunwapta Falls to Fortress Lake is a one-view proposition. It's a long, uninspiring hike to the lakeshore, beyond which only intrepid explorers can continue. Though impressive, the sight at trail's end doesn't justify the trip. En route, a challenging ford of the Chaba River adds further discouragement.

(6) The South Boundary Trail is more than 165 km (102 mi) long. We describe trips at each end: Jacques Lake (Trip 123), and Nigel Pass (Trip 33). We also describe the Heart of the South Boundary (Trip 99): Rocky Pass to Cairn Pass. But we've omitted the rest of this lengthy trail. Too many days of uneventful hiking disqualifies it from a book whose emphasis is efficient use of limited time. For the same reason, we've also omitted most of the North Boundary Trail. It stretches across northern Jasper for more than 170 km (105 mi). We describe only the scenic climax: the west end, near Mt. Robson (Trips 82-84) and Moose Pass (Trip 105).

Rainy-Day Trips

Though it's possible to hike most trails in a rainstorm, the peaks you came to see will likely be shrouded. Above treeline, you risk death by thunderbolt. (Read our *Lightning* section.) But with the right attitude, on certain trails, a rainy-day hike is a revelation.

Mist cloaking mountains creates a mysterious atmosphere. New waterfalls appear, ever-present ones swell. Forest understory brightens, and the fragrance is headier. When sunlight bursts through tattered clouds, or a rainbow arches suddenly overhead, it's rousing.

So don't sit out the storm. Hike it out. The trails below are good choices for a little wet-weather exercise. Some are rated *Don't Do*. But superior scenery is invisible during a downpour. That's when these low-elevation trips shine.

- Consolation Lakes (Trip 43), near Lake Louise
- Bow Glacier Falls (Trip 45), north of Lake Louise
- Cavell Meadows (Trip 55), south of Jasper townsite
- Blakiston Creek (Trip 60), in Waterton
- Boom Lake (Trip 65), west of Castle Junction
- Lake Agnes (Trip 66), near Lake Louise
- Yoho Valley (Trip 72), near Field
- Saturday Night Lakes (Trip 74), southwest edge of Jasper townsite
- Lineham Creek (Trip 116), in Waterton
- Waterton Lakeshore (Trip 119), in Waterton
- Lake Minnewanka (Trip 121), near Banff townsite
- Jacques Lake (Trip 123), between Jasper townsite and Maligne Lake
- Dog Lake (Trip 132), in south Kootenay
- Wapta Falls (Trip 133), in southwest Yoho
- Beauty Creek (Trip 135), in Jasper
- Wabasso Lake (Trip 136), south of Jasper townsite
- Valley of Five Lakes (Trip 137), south of Jasper townsite
- Celestine Lake (Trip 138), north of Jasper townsite

Elk beside Jasper Lake

Wilderness Ethics

We hope you're already conscientious about respecting nature and other people. If not, here's how to pay off some of your karmic debt load.

Let wildflowers live. They blossom for only a few fleeting weeks. Uprooting them doesn't enhance your enjoyment, and it prevents others from seeing them at all. We once heard parents urge a string of children to pick as many different-coloured flowers as they could find. Great. Teach kids to entertain themselves by destroying nature, so the world continues marching toward environmental collapse.

Give the critters a break. The mountain parks are not zoos. The animals are wild. Recognize that this is their home, and you are an uninvited guest. Behave accordingly. Allow all of them plenty of space. Most are remarkably tolerant of people, but approaching them to take a photograph is harassment and can be dangerous. Some elk, for example, appear docile but can severely injure you. Approaching any bear is suicidal. Read our *Bears* section.

Stay on the trail. Shortcutting causes erosion. It doesn't save time on steep ascents, because you'll soon be slowing to catch your breath. On a steep descent, it increases the likelihood of injury. When hiking cross-country in a group, soften your impact by spreading out.

Roam meadows with your eyes, not your boots. Again, stay on the trail. If it's braided, follow the main path. When you're compelled to take a photo among wildflowers, try to walk on rocks.

Leave no trace. Be aware of your impact. Travel lightly on the land. At campgrounds, limit your activity to areas already denuded. After a rest stop, and especially after camping, take a few minutes to look for and obscure any evidence of your stay. Restore the area to its natural state. Remember: tents can leave scars. Pitch yours on an existing tentsite whenever possible. If none is available, choose a patch of dirt, gravel, pine needles, or maybe a dried-up tarn. Never pitch your tent on grass, no matter how appealing it looks. If you do, and others follow, the grass will soon be gone.

Avoid building fires. Prohibited in many backcountry areas, they're a luxury, not a necessity. Don't plan to cook over a fire; it's inefficient and wasteful. If you pack food that requires cooking, bring a stove. If you must indulge in a campfire, keep it small. Use the metal firebox provided at the campground, or an existing fire ring made of rocks. If there are no boxes or rings, build your fire on mineral soil or gravel, not in the organic layer. Never scorch meadows. Below a stream's high-water line is best. Garbage with metal or plastic content will not burn; pack it all out. Limit your wood gathering to deadfall about the size of your forearm. Wood that requires effort (breaking, chopping, dragging) is part of the scenery; let it be. After thoroughly dousing your fire, dismantle the fire ring and scatter the ashes. Keep in mind that untended and unextinguished campfires are the prime cause of forest fires.

Be quiet at backcountry campgrounds. Most of us are out there to enjoy tranquility. If you want to party, go to a pub.

Pack out everything you bring. Never leave a scrap of trash anywhere. This includes toilet paper, nut shells, even cigarette butts. People who drop butts in the wilderness are buttheads. They're buttheads in the city too, but it's worse in the wilds. Fruit peels are also trash. They take years to decompose, and wild animals won't eat them. If you bring fruit on your hike, you're responsible for the peels. And don't just pack out *your* trash. Leave nothing behind, whether you brought it or not. Clean up after others. Don't be hesitant or oblivious. Be proud. Keep a small plastic

The western wood lily is increasingly rare due to picking.

bag handy, so picking up trash will be a habit instead of a pain. It's infuriating and disgusting to see what people toss on the trail. Often the tossing is mindless, but sometimes it's intentional. Anyone who leaves a pile of toilet paper and unburied feces should have their nose rubbed in it.

Poop without impact. Use the outhouses at trailheads and campgrounds whenever possible. Don't count on them being stocked with toilet paper; always pack your own in a plastic bag. If you know there's a campground ahead, try to wait until you get there.

In the wilds, choose a site at least 60 m (66 yd) from trails and water sources. Ground that receives sunlight part of the day is best. Use a trowel to dig a small cat hole—10 to 20 cm (4 to 8 inches) deep, 10 to 15 cm (4 to 6 inches) wide—in soft, dark, biologically active soil. Afterward, throw a handful of dirt into the hole, stir with a stick to speed decomposition, replace your diggings, then camouflage the site. Pack out used toilet paper in a plastic bag. You can drop the paper (not the plastic) in the next outhouse you pass. Always clean your hands with a moisturizing hand sanitizer, like Purell. Carry enough for the entire trip. Sold in drugstores, it comes in conveniently small, lightweight, plastic bottles.

Urinate off trail, well away from water sources and tent sites. The salt in urine attracts animals. They'll defoliate urine-soaked vegetation, so aim for dirt or pine needles.

Keep streams and lakes pristine. When brushing your teeth or washing dishes, do it well away from water sources and tent sites. Use only biodegradable soap. Carry water far enough so the waste water will percolate through soil and break down without directly polluting the wilderness water. Scatter waste water widely. Even biodegradable soap is a pollutant; keep it out of streams and lakes. On short backpack trips, you shouldn't need to wash clothes or yourself. If necessary, rinse your clothes or splash yourself off—without soap.

Respect the reverie of other hikers. On busy trails, don't feel it's necessary to communicate with everyone you pass. Most of us are seeking solitude, not a soiree. A simple greeting is sufficient to convey good will. Obviously, only you can judge what's appropriate at the time. But it's usually presumptuous and annoying to blurt out advice without being asked. "Boy, have you got a long way to go." "The views are much better up there." "Be careful, it gets rougher." If anyone wants to know, they'll ask. Some people are sly. They start by asking where you're going, so they can tell you all about it. Offer unsolicited information only to warn other hikers about conditions ahead that could seriously affect their trip.

Backcountry Permits

Upon entering the Canadian Rocky Mountain national parks, everyone must pay a user fee. In addition, Parks Canada charges a per-person, per-night fee for backcountry camping. If you plan to backpack at least six nights, it's economically wise to buy a Wilderness Pass allowing you unlimited backcountry camping for an entire year. Even with a Wilderness Pass, you must reserve space at your intended campsites. And Parks Canada charges a fee for reserving more than one day in advance.

Returning to Little Yoho Valley, from Kiwetinok Pass (Trip 90)

Backcountry campsites in the national parks are 100% reservable. You can make reservations up to 90 days in advance by writing or calling the appropriate park info centre. If reserving for just one night and only a couple people, the fee seems disproportionately high. You can change your reservations by phone or mail, but Parks Canada will re-inflict the reservation fee each time. Campgrounds on popular trails are booked full early, so making reservations is a necessary form of trip insurance.

Plan your itinerary before calling a park info centre, so you can ask for specific campgrounds along your intended route. The info centre will mail you the permit if you purchase it at least two weeks in advance. Otherwise, you must pick it up at the info centre the day you begin hiking. The info centres do not call permit holders about bear warnings or trail closures, so check the park's website for trail reports. And, when you arrive at the trailhead, look at the kiosk before you start hiking. If there's a bear warning or trail closure, it will be posted there.

Leave Your Itinerary

Even if you're hiking in a group, and especially if you're going solo, it's prudent to leave your itinerary in writing with someone reliable. Agree on precisely when they should alert the authorities if you have not returned or called. Be sure to follow through. Forgetting to tell your contact person that you've safely completed your trip would result in an unnecessary, possibly expensive search. You might be billed for it. And a rescue team could risk their lives trying to find you. Can't leave your itinerary with friends or family? The national parks have a voluntary registration system. Ask the appropriate info centre for details.

Hiking with Your Dog

"Can I bring Max, my Pomeranian?" Yes. All the Canadian Rocky Mountain parks allow dogs in the backcountry with the stipulation that they be leashed the entire time. Bringing your dog, however, isn't simply a matter of "Can I?" Ask yourself, "Should I?"

Consider safety. Dogs infuriate bears and are thus a danger to themselves, their owners and other hikers. If a dog runs off, it might reel a bear back with it.

Consider the environment. Many dog owners blithely allow their pets to pollute streams and lakes. Every time Maxie craps on the trail, will you dispose of it properly?

Consider the rest of us. Most dog owners think their pets are angelic, but other hikers rarely agree. A curious dog, even if friendly, can be a nuisance. A barking dog is irksome. A person continually yelling unheeded commands at a disobedient dog is infuriating, because it amounts to *two* annoying animals, not just one. An untrained dog, despite the owner's hearty reassurance that "he won't hurt you," can be frightening.

This isn't a request to leave your dog at home. We've backpacked with friends whose dogs we enjoyed immensely. This is a plea to see your dog objectively.

Physical Capability

Until you gain experience judging your physical capability and that of your companions, these guidelines might be helpful. Anything longer than an 11-km (7-mi) round-trip dayhike can be very taxing for someone who doesn't hike regularly. A 425-m (1400-ft) elevation gain in that distance is challenging but possible for anyone in average physical condition. Very fit hikers are comfortable hiking 18 km (11 mi) and ascending 950 m (3100 ft)—or more—in a single day.

Backpacking 18 km (11 mi) in two days is a reasonable goal for most beginners. Hikers who backpack a couple times a season can enjoyably manage 27 km (17 mi) in two days. Avid backpackers should find 38 km (24 mi) in two days no problem. On three- to five-day trips, a typical backpacker prefers not to push beyond 16 km (10 mi) a day. Remember: it's always safer to underestimate your limits.

Crowded Trails

The Canadian Rockies attract an unceasing onslaught of tourists. Banff Park is besieged by nearly five million visitors annually. The nation's coast-to-coast highway blares through Banff and Yoho parks. The entire range is within easy striking distance of Alberta's two big cities: Calgary and Edmonton. It makes solitude elusive.

Ascending Eiffel Peak. Moraine Lake below in Valley of the Ten Peaks (Trip 5)

To avoid the throngs, you have several choices: (1) Go midweek. (2) Schedule your visit in fall, after the flood of vacationers subsides. (3) Probe deeper into the wilds than most people dare, for example beyond Fish Lakes, over Pipestone Pass, to Devon Lakes (Trip 80), or through Badger Pass (Trip 101) into the Sawback Range. (4) Wander cross-country, by veering off trail in areas like Poboktan Pass (Trip 92). (5) Hike the loneliest of the trips rated *Don't Do*: Vimy Peak (Trip 59), Siffleur River (Trip 111), or Simpson River / Surprise Creek (Trip 112).

Most hikers, however, rather than negotiate more challenging terrain or endure less inspiring scenery, prefer sharing *Premier* trails with other people. Generally, it's only at night, in backcountry campgrounds, that a solitudinous soul might be annoyed by a sense of enforced conviviality.

Try not to let the presence of other hikers quash your joy. Be glad they're out there. People who commune with nature develop reverence—an attitude that could help solve a lot of the world's problems. And the more hikers, the more of us who'll be working together to protect wild lands from development and resource extraction.

Maps

The maps in this book are for general orientation only. Our *On Foot* directions, however, are elaborate and precise, so you shouldn't find topographical maps necessary. Yet we do recommend them, for several reasons:

(1) On a long, rough hike, a topo map makes it even easier to follow our directions. (2) A topo map is safety equipment, because it can help ensure you don't get lost.

Bighorn sheep, Deception Pass (Trip 86)

(3) If the terrain through which you're hiking intrigues you, a topo map can contribute to a more fulfilling experience. (4) After reaching a high vantage, a topo map enables you to interpret the scenery.

The Surveys & Mapping Branch of the Department of Energy, Mines and Resources (DEMR) publishes 1:50 000 topo maps of the Canadian Rockies. They're sold at outdoor shops, bookstores, and park info centres. In the trips for which you might want them, we list the applicable DEMR topo maps. Example: Southesk Lake 83 C/11. Bear in mind, DEMR does not update its maps frequently or thoroughly. Some DEMR maps do not indicate minor trails, even though they're distinct on the ground. DEMR maps are also expensive, and several might be necessary for a single backpack trip.

Gem Trek Publishing (www.gemtrek.com) prints 1:50 000 and 1:100 000 topo maps of the Canadian Rockies. They're ideal for most hikers. They indicate all trails, distances, and significant elevations. Buying one Gem Trek map saves you the expense of several DEMR maps. You can purchase Gem Trek maps online (maps@gemtrek.com), at outdoor shops and bookstores in and near the Canadian Rockies, and at park info centres.

Distances and Elevations

There is no definitive source for accurate distances and elevations in the Canadian Rockies. Park offices, brochures, books, government maps, publishers' maps, and trail signs often state conflicting figures. But the discrepancies are usually small, and most hikers don't care whether a trail is 8.7 km (5.4 mi) or 9 km (5.6 mi), or whether an ascent is 715 m (2345 ft) or 720 m (2362 ft). Still, we made a supreme effort to ensure accuracy.

Carry a Compass

Left and *right* are relative. Any hiking guidebook relying solely on these inadequate and potentially misleading terms should be shredded and dropped into a recycling bin. You'll find all the *On Foot* descriptions in this book include frequent compass directions. That's the simplest, most reliable way to accurately guide a hiker.

What about GPS? Compared to a compass, GPS units are heavier, bulkier, more fragile, more complex, more time consuming, occasionally foiled by vegetation or topography, dependent on batteries, and way more expensive.

Keep in mind that the compass directions provided in this book are of use only if you're carrying a compass. Granted, our route descriptions are so detailed, you'll rarely have to check your compass. But bring one anyway, just in case. A compass is required hiking equipment—anytime, anywhere, regardless of your level of experience, or your familiarity with the terrain.

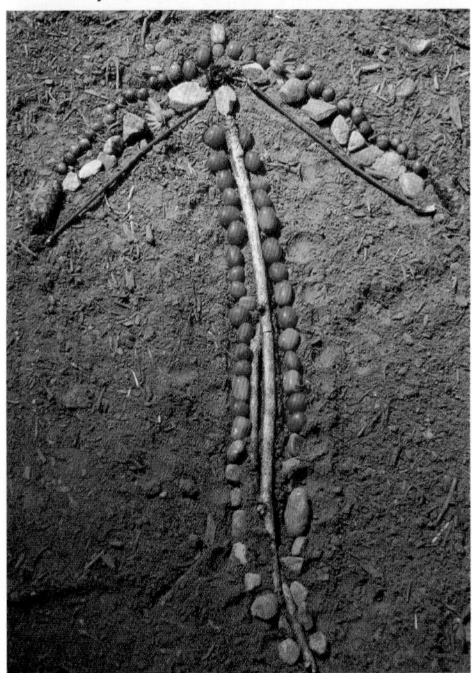

Their friends must have been very slow.

Clip your compass to the shoulder strap of your pack, so you can glance at it quickly and easily. Even if you never have to rely on your compass, occasionally checking it will strengthen your sense of direction—an enjoyable, helpful, and conceivably life-saving asset.

Keep in mind that our stated compass directions are always in reference to true north. In the Canadian Rockies, that's 19° left of (counterclockwise from) magnetic north. If that puzzles you, read your compass owner's manual.

Placate the Weather Gods

The volatile Canadian Rocky Mountain climate will have you building shrines to placate the weather gods. Conditions change quickly and dramatically. Summer is pitifully short.

Bow Lake

Most trails aren't snow-free until June. Alpine passes can be blanketed in white until late July. Snowfall is possible any day of the year and likely at higher elevations after August. Above treeline, the annual average temperature is below freezing, and most precipitation is snow.

That's why this book includes 23 shoulder-season trips. Some enable you to hike as early as mid-May and as late as November. These trails are snow-free sooner and longer than others, because they're at lower elevations and are exposed to ample sunlight.

Park info centres post weather forecasts and trail-condition reports. Recorded weather forecasts are available by phone: (403) 762-2088. When the snowpack is melting in late spring and early summer, just one week of sunny weather can greatly increase trail accessibility.

Regardless of the forecast, prepare for heavy rain, harsh winds, plummeting temperatures, sleet, hail... the whole miserable gamut. Scorching sun and soaring temperatures are always possible too. The weather can change drastically, with alarming speed. Though the sky is clear at dawn, it might be boiling with black clouds by afternoon. Storms can dissipate equally fast.

Statistics indicate that, throughout the Canadian Rockies, you should expect rain one out of every three days in summer. Even many rain-free days are cloudy. So don't squander a blue sky. Celebrate it: hike fast and far on a *Premier* trail.

Charts showing the mountain parks' average monthly precipitation during hiking season are of little help. June is likely to be wettest, October driest. The figures for July, August and September are too close for anyone to reliably recommend when your hiking trip is least likely to be rained out. Locals, however, will tell you we usually get a snowstorm in early September, followed by a couple weeks of clear skies, pleasantly cool daytime temperatures, and nighttime lows around freezing.

Charts showing the average monthly maximum and minimum temperatures in the mountain parks reveal the following. By May, the highs reach about 16°C (61°F), the lows stay just above freezing. In June, the highs and lows are roughly 4°C (7°F) warmer than in May. July is usually the hottest month, with highs around 24°C (75°F), lows averaging 7°C (45°F). August can be almost as hot as July, but generally isn't. September tends to be slightly warmer than May. In October, the highs top out near 12°C (54°F), the lows drop just below freezing.

Many hikers say fall is their favourite time in the Canadian Rockies. Bugs are absent, crowds diminish, larch trees are golden. But shorter days restrict dayhiking, and colder nights make backpacking less comfortable. We prefer the long days of mid-summer.

Typically, the Canadian Rocky Mountain climate will grant you two-and-a-half months of optimal high-country hiking. That's only 20% of the year. At the end of June, however, you'll have 16½ hours between sunrise (5:30 a.m.) and sunset (10 p.m.).

Carpe diem.

Mountain goat

Wildlife

The readily visible presence of wildlife surprises travelers in the Canadian Rocky Mountain parks. It's possible to see all kinds of animals—big and small—at any time, even when you're driving the Icefields Parkway. Deer, chipmunks, squirrels, raccoons, skunks, bats, owls, and other birds, you might expect. But also be on the lookout for eagles, mountain goats, bighorn sheep, caribou, moose, coyotes, black bears, and grizzlies. Elk as tall as pickup trucks frequent Banff townsite. In the evening, watch for porcupines waddling out of the forest and beavers cruising ponds. On alpine trails, you're likely to see pikas and marmots. It's a rare and fortunate hiker who glimpses a wolf, wolverine, or cougar.

Shadow Lake (Trip 25)

Ticks

Ticks are vile, insidious creatures, but slow and easily thwarted if you're vigilant. In the Canadian Rockies, they're active from early April to mid-June.

Look at your pinky fingernail. Rocky Mountain wood ticks are generally smaller than that. They have dark, reddish-brown bodies with eight legs. Their protruding mouths have barbs too small to see. Ticks are arachnids but lack the speed and seeming intelligence of spiders. They climb onto grass and shrubs. When an animal or a hiker brushes past, the tick slides off the vegetation and clings to its victim. It spends three or more hours crawling upward, searching for moist flesh. Upon choosing a drilling site, it secretes a kind of glue, then bites—painlessly, unnoticed—and begins sucking blood. It drops off when gorged.

A tick bite can cause Rocky Mountain spotted fever or tick paralysis. Neither has been reported in the Canadian Rockies for many years. Lyme disease is not yet evident here. Ticks don't transmit disease immediately upon biting; it takes hours.

Spotted fever is potentially fatal. Symptoms include fever, headache, chills, muscular pain, coughing, and a spreading rash. Symptoms of tick paralysis are numbness, drowsiness and loss of coordination, all of which can disappear soon after the tick is removed. If you suspect either malady, see a doctor fast. With early detection, antibiotics are highly effective.

Learn to recognize tick habitat. They thrive on sunny, grassy slopes below 2000 m (6560 ft), especially those frequented by large mammals such as deer, elk or bighorn sheep. To sprawl or even sit in ticky terrain is to offer yourself for dinner. Inspect your clothing and your body occasionally while hiking. Do it again thoroughly at day's end. Ticks will favour your groin, armpits, neck and scalp, but can bite almost anywhere. Ask a companion to check your head and back. If you're hiking with a dog, inspect it as well. Dogs can transfer ticks to people.

Finding and removing ticks before they bite is easy. If you discover one burrowed into your skin, the sooner you detach it, the safer you are. Let a doctor do this. If you attempt it yourself, forget about suffocating the tick with Vaseline, or burning its butt with a match. You'll only make the tick regurgitate and defecate, increasing the likelihood of disease transmission. Don't use normal tweezers; they're too big and might crush the tick, spurting its gut contents into your wound. And don't use your fingers, or you might contaminate whatever else you touch. If you do touch it, wash your hands afterward.

You want to remove the entire tick—mouth and all. Use fine-pointed sliver grippers, or a specialized tick-removal tool. Gently hold the tick by its mouth without grabbing or squeezing the body. Lightly, steadily, pull it directly back until your skin "tents." Hold it there, perhaps several seconds, until the tick lets go. If its mouth breaks off and remains attached, pull it out like a splinter. Drop the tick into an empty film canister along with a damp scrap of paper to keep it hydrated, in case your doctor wants a laboratory analysis. Clean your tick removal tool. Wash your wound with soap and water, rub it with an antiseptic wipe, then bandage it. Record the date and time you were bitten. Monitor yourself for signs of disease.

Watch for moose in boggy, marshy areas.

Grizzly bear

Bears

Bears are rarely a problem in the Canadian Rockies. But oblivious hikers often endanger themselves, other people, and the bears. If you're prepared for a bear encounter and know how to prevent one, you can hike confidently, secure in the understanding that bears pose little threat.

Only a couple hundred grizzly bears roam the Canadian Rocky Mountain national parks. The black-bear population is comparable. You're more likely to see a bear while driving the Icefields Parkway than while hiking most backcountry trails. Park info centres post trail reports that include bear warnings and closures. Check these before your trip; adjust your plans accordingly.

Grizzlies and blacks can be difficult for an inexperienced observer to tell apart. Both species range in colour from nearly white to cinnamon to black. Full-grown grizzlies are much bigger, but a young grizzly can resemble an adult black bear, so size is not a good indicator. The most obvious differences are that grizzlies have a dished face; a big, muscular shoulder hump; and long, curved front claws. Blacks have a straight face; no hump; and shorter, less visible front claws. Grizzlies are potentially more dangerous than black bears, although a black bear sow with cubs can be just as aggressive. Be wary of all bears.

Any bear might attack when surprised. If you're hiking, and forest or brush limits your visibility, you can prevent surprising a bear by making noise. Bears hear about as well as humans. Most are as anxious to avoid an encounter as you are. If you warn them of your presence before they see you, they'll usually clear out. So

Black bear

use the most effective noisemaker: your voice. Shout loudly. Keep it up. Don't be embarrassed. Be safe. Yell louder near streams, so your voice carries over the competing noise. Sound off more frequently when hiking into the wind. That's when bears are least able to hear or smell you coming. To learn more, read *Bears & People* at www.pc.gc.ca/pn-np/ab/jasper/natcul/natcul5_e.asp, or download the *Bears Beware!* MP3 at hikingcamping.com.

Bears' strongest sense is smell. They can detect an animal carcass several kilometres (miles) away. So keep your pack, tent and campsite odor-free. Double- or triple-wrap all your food in plastic bags. Avoid smelly foods, especially meat and fish. On short backpack trips, consider eating only fresh foods that require no cooking or cleanup. If you cook, do it as far as possible from where you'll be sleeping. Never cook in or near your tent; the fabric might retain odor. Use as few pots and dishes as you can get by with. Be fastidious when you wash them. At night, hang all your food, trash, and anything else that smells (cooking gear, sunscreen, bug repellent, toothpaste) out of bears' reach. Use the storage cables provided at backcountry campgrounds. Elsewhere, a tree branch will suffice. Bring a sturdy stuffsack to serve as your bear bag. Hoist it at least 5 m/yd off the ground and 1.5 m/yd from the tree trunk or other branches. You'll need about 12 m/yd of light nylon cord. Clip the sack to the cord with an ultralight carabiner.

Backpackers who don't properly hang their food at night are inviting bears into their campsite, greatly increasing the chance of a dangerous encounter. And bears are smart. They quickly learn to associate a particular place, or people in general, with an easy meal. They become habituated and lose their fear of man. A habituated bear is a menace to any hiker within its range.

If you see a bear, don't look it in the eyes; it might think you're challenging it. Never run. Initially be still. If you must move, do it in slow motion. Bears are more likely to attack if you flee, and they're fast, much faster than humans. A grizzly can outsprint a racehorse. And it's a myth that bears can't run downhill. They're also strong swimmers. Despite their ungainly appearance, they're excellent climbers too. Still, climbing a tree can be an option for escaping an aggressive bear. Some people have saved their lives this way. Others have been caught in the process. To be out of reach of an adult bear, you must climb at least 10 m/yd very quickly, something few people are capable of. It's generally best to avoid provoking an attack by staying calm, initially standing your ground, making soothing sounds to convey a nonthreatening presence, then retreating slowly.

What should you do when a bear charges? If you're certain it's a lone black bear— not a sow with cubs, not a grizzly—fighting back might be effective. If it's a grizzly, and contact seems imminent, lie face down, with your legs apart and your hands clasped behind your neck. This is safer than the fetal position, which used to be recommended, because it makes it harder for the bear to flip you over. If you play dead, a grizzly is likely to break off the attack once it feels you're no longer a threat. Don't move until you're sure the bear has left the area, then slowly, quietly, get up and walk away. Keep moving, but don't run.

Arm yourself with pepper spray as a last defense. Keep it in a holster, on your hip belt or shoulder strap, where you can grab it fast. Many people have successfully used it to turn back charging bears. Cayenne pepper, highly irritating to a bear's sensitive nose, is the active ingredient. Without causing permanent injury, it disables the bear long enough to let you escape. But vigilance and noise making should prevent you from ever having to spray. Do so only if you really think your life is at risk. You can buy pepper spray at outdoor stores. *Counter Assault* is a reputable brand.

Remember that your safety is not the only important consideration. Bears themselves are at risk when confronted by people. Whenever bears act aggressively, they're following their natural instinct for self preservation. Often they're protecting their cubs or a food source. Yet if they maul a hiker, they're likely to be killed, or captured and moved, by wildlife management officers. Protecting these beautiful, magnificent creatures is a responsibility hikers must accept.

Merrily disregarding bears is foolish and unsafe. Worrying about them is miserable and unnecessary. Everyone occasionally feels afraid when venturing deep into the mountains, but knowledge and awareness can quell fear of bears. Just take the necessary precautions and remain guardedly alert. Experiencing the grandeur of the Canadian Rockies is certainly worth risking the remote possibility of a bear encounter.

Lake Louise Hiking Restrictions Due to Bears

To grant grizzly bears the habitat they need, and to protect people, Banff Park restricts hiking on many trails in the Lake Louise / Moraine Lake area. At times, hiking is permitted only in groups of four or more. When a bear is known to be staying in a particular place, nearby trails might be closed and hiking prohibited until the bear leaves. So, before hiking here, call or visit the Lake Louise Info Centre: (403) 522-3833. Ask if the trail you intend to hike is closed or has restrictions due to bears.

Cougars

You'll probably never see a cougar. But they live in the Canadian Rockies, and they can be dangerous, so you should know a bit about them.

Elsewhere referred to as a *puma, mountain lion*, or *panther*, the cougar is an enormous, graceful cat. An adult male can reach the size of a big human: 80 kilos (175 pounds), and 2.4 metres (8 feet) long, including a 1-metre (3-foot) tail. In the Canadian Rockies, they tend to be a tawny gray.

Nocturnal, secretive, solitary creatures, cougars come together only to mate. Each cat establishes a territory of 200 to 280 square kilometres (125 to 175 square miles). They favour dense forest that provides cover while hunting. They also hide among rock outcroppings and in steep canyons.

Habitat loss and aggressive predator-control programs have severely limited the range of this mysterious animal that once lived throughout North America. Still, cougars are not considered endangered or threatened. Cougars appear to be thriving in western Canada.

Cougars are carnivores. They eat everything from mice to elk, but prefer deer. They occasionally stalk people, but rarely attack them. In folklore, cougars are called ghost cats or ghost walkers, and for good reason. They're very shy and typically avoid human contact. Nevertheless, cougars have attacked solo hikers and lone cross-country skiers in the Canadian Rockies.

Cougar sightings and encounters are increasing, but it's uncertain whether that's due to a larger cougar population or the growing number of people visiting the wilderness. If you're lucky enough to see a cougar, treasure the experience. Just remember they're unpredictable. Follow these suggestions.

Never hike alone in areas of known cougar sightings. Keep children close to you; pick them up if you see fresh cougar scat or tracks. Never approach a cougar, especially a feeding one. Never flee from a cougar, or even turn your back on it. Sudden movement might trigger an instinctive attack. Avert your gaze and speak to it in a calm, soothing voice. Hold your ground or back away slowly. Always give the animal a way out. If a cougar approaches, spread your arms, open your jacket, do anything you can to enlarge your image. If it acts aggressively, wave your arms, shout, throw rocks or sticks. If attacked, fight back. Don't play dead.

Lightning

Many of the trails in this book lead to meadows and ridges where, during a storm, you could be exposed to lightning.

Storms tend to develop in the afternoon, so you can try to reach alpine destinations early in the day. But it's impossible to always evade violent weather. You hike to commune with nature, the power of which can threaten your safety.

Even if you start under a cloudless, blue sky, you might see ominous thunderheads marching toward you a few hours later. Upon reaching a high, airy vantage, you could be forced by an approaching storm to decide if and when you should retreat to safer ground.

The following is a summary of lightning precautions recommended by experts. These are not guaranteed solutions. We offer them merely as suggestions to help you make wise choices and reduce your chance of injury.

If your hair is standing on end, there's electricity in the air around you. A lightning strike could be imminent. Get outa there! That's usually down the mountain, but if there's too much open expanse to traverse, look for closer protection.

A direct lightning strike can kill you. It can cause brain damage, heart failure or third-degree burns. Ground current, from a nearby strike, can severely injure you, causing deep burns and tissue damage. Direct strikes are worse, but ground-current contact is far more common.

Avoid a direct strike by getting off exposed ridges and peaks. Even a few metres (yards) off a ridge is better than on top. Avoid isolated, tall trees. A clump of small trees or an opening in the trees is safer.

Avoid ground current by getting out of stream gullies and away from crevices, lichen patches, or wet, solid-rock surfaces. Loose rock, like talus, is safer.

Look for a low-risk area, near a highpoint at least 10 m/yd higher than you. Crouch near its base, at least 1.5 m/yd from cliffs or walls.

Once you choose a place to wait it out, your goal is to prevent brain or heart damage by stopping an electrical charge from flowing through your whole body. Squat with your boots touching one another. If you have a sleeping pad, put it beneath your boots for insulation. Keep your hands away from rocks. Fold your arms across your chest. Stay at least 10 m/yd from your companions, so if one is hit, another can give cardiopulmonary resuscitation.

Deep caves offer protection. Crouch away from the mouth, at least 1.5 m/yd from the walls. But avoid rock overhangs and shallow depressions, because ground current can jump across them. Lacking a deep cave, you're safer in the low-risk area below a highpoint.

Hypothermia

Many deaths outdoors involve no obvious injury. "Exposure" is usually cited as the killer, but that's a misleading term. It vaguely refers to conditions that contributed to the death. The actual cause is hypothermia: excessive loss of body heat. It can happen with startling speed, in surprisingly mild weather—often between 0 and 10°C (30 and 50°F). Guard against it vigilantly.

Cool temperatures, wetness (perspiration or rain), wind, or fatigue, usually a combination, sap the body of vital warmth. Hypothermia results when heat loss continues to exceed heat gain. Initial symptoms include chills and shivering. Poor coordination, slurred speech, sluggish thinking, and memory loss are next. Intense shivering then decreases while muscular rigidity increases, accompanied by irrationality, incoherence, even hallucinations. Stupor, blue skin, slowed pulse and respiration, and unconsciousness follow. The heartbeat finally becomes erratic until the victim dies.

Avoid becoming hypothermic by wearing synthetic clothing that wicks moisture away from your skin and insulates when wet. Read *Prepare For Your Hike*, in the back of this book, for a description of clothing and equipment that will help you stay warm and dry. Food fuels your internal fire, so bring more than you think you'll need, including several energy bars for emergencies only.

If you can't stay warm and dry, you must escape the wind and rain. Turn back. Keep moving. Eat snacks. Seek shelter. Do it while you're still mentally and physically capable. Watch others in your party for signs of hypothermia. Victims might resist help at first. Trust the symptoms, not the person. Be insistent. Act immediately.

Create the best possible shelter for the victim. Take off his wet clothes and replace them with dry ones. Insulate him from the ground. Provide warmth. A prewarmed sleeping bag inside a tent is ideal. If necessary, add more warmth by taking off your clothes and getting into the bag with the victim. Build a fire. Keep the victim conscious. Feed him sweets. Carbohydrates quickly convert to heat and energy. In advanced cases, victims should not drink hot liquids.

Behind Mt. Edith Cavell, near Verdant Pass (Trip 21)

Dayhikes

TRIP 1

Akamina Ridge / Wall and Forum Lakes

LOCATION	Akamina-Kishinena Provincial Park
ROUND TRIP	8.8 km (5.5 mi) to Forum Lake 11.2 km (6.9 mi) to Wall Lake
CIRCUIT	18.3 km (11.3 mi) for Akamina Ridge
ELEVATION GAIN	355 m (1165 ft) to Forum Lake 115 m (377 ft) to Wall Lake 985 m (3230 ft) for circuit
KEY ELEVATIONS	trailhead 1665 m (5460 ft) Forum Lake 2020 m (6626 ft) Wall Lake 1780 m (5838 ft), ridge 2565 m (8413 ft)
HIKING TIME	3 to 8 hours
DIFFICULTY	easy hiking to moderate scrambling
MAPS	page 492; Gem Trek *Waterton Lakes National Park*

OPINION

You scramble to attain views from the top. But if the going gets dicey, as it might on the way up Akamina Ridge, it can have the exhilarating effect of making you look inward as much as outward. While you probe the terrain, it probes your psyche. Though you stand on the summit, it's with the realization that you, not the mountain, have been overcome.

Challenging as Akamina Ridge is, however, the approach trail is for everyone. Toddlers, waddlers, hardened hikers, or serious scramblers can set out at the same trailhead and, within a few hours, all will be elated.

It's easy for parents to chase their energetic kids to Forum Lake, a gorgeous liquid disc at the base of a sheer cliff. Wall Lake is slightly farther, but it's more impressive because the surrounding walls are higher yet. And atop those walls is Akamina Ridge, stretching between Forum and Wall Lakes. Clamber up the rocky spine of this sleeping brontosaurus and your reward is an airy ridgewalk with views into Waterton and U.S. Glacier national parks.

Wall Lake's stunning cirque screams "camp here!" but due to an alarming number of hiker / grizzly-bear encounters, camping is now verboten. You can camp at the Ashman Cabin site along Akamina Creek, but don't. It's dismal, devoid of scenery, not worth the nightly fee or the trouble of hauling your gear. Better to dayhike and spend all your time at the lakes or on the ridge, then car camp in Waterton Park.

Intrigued by Akamina Ridge? To complete the loop, start at Forum Lake and ascend to the obvious, low saddle. The scrambling here is moderately difficult. It's the only demanding portion of the trip. Overcome this and the rest is a cinch.

Wall Lake, from the east end of Akamina Ridge

The inadvisable alternative is to start your loop trip at Wall Lake. Attaining the ridge that way is a steep-though-straightforward hike, but you won't face the rugged, trailless descent to Forum Lake until near the end of the journey. If it's too steep for you, bad news: you'll have to retrace your steps all the way back around, a hairy ordeal in gathering gloom.

If eggs are the only thing you like to scramble, but you're keen to attain the ridge, make it an out-and-back trip ascending via Wall Lake. Going this way, you'll hike through a luxuriant, stream-fed basin above the lake—pretty enough to be enjoyable again on the way down. After reaching the highpoint on the ridge, you can about face, skipping the trailless descent to Forum.

Finally, a warning: Akamina Ridge can be fiercely windy. That's why nothing grows over an inch high on the crest. Even if the sky is clear, the sun hot and the air calm, be prepared for a big blow atop the ridge. Imagine a flea on the snout of a sneezing bear. That's you up here in a gale. Pack windproof clothing.

FACT

By Vehicle

From the junction just north of Waterton townsite, drive Akamina Parkway 14.6 km (9.1 mi) to the Akamina Pass trailhead, at 1665 m (5460 ft). The parking area is on the left side of the highway, the trail on the right.

On Foot

Initially ascend west on an old road through unremarkable forest. In about 20 minutes, after gaining 115 m (125 yd) in 1.5 km (0.9 mi), reach the provincial park **boundary** and a kiosk with a topo map. A sign says Wall or Forum lakes are still an hour away, but fast hikers can reach either in 45 minutes.

From the next signed **junction** at 2.2 km (1.4 mi), left leads to the park ranger cabin and, 2 km (1.2 mi) beyond, Forum Lake. Straight leads to a campground and another signed junction in 5-8 minutes. There, left leads 2.7 km (1.7 mi) to Wall Lake.

Heading to Forum, after passing the ranger cabin, bear left for a couple-minute sidetrip to small Forum Falls. Then ascend about 150 m (500 ft) to the bridged crossing of the outlet stream at 3.5 km (2.2 mi). Follow a boardwalk spanning a boggy area and soon reach **Forum Lake**, at 4.4 km (2.7 mi), 2020 m (6626 ft). Even in late summer, the steep slopes cupping it are emerald green. Larch forest flanks the north shore.

If continuing to Akamina Ridge, look right (west). See the low saddle? That's your immediate goal. From where the trail ends at Forum Lake, go right about 5 m/yd along the shore, then veer right onto a bootbeaten path. You'll soon be crashing through tall grass, krummholz (stunted fir trees) and deadfall. The 2105-m (6900-ft) **saddle** offers only a precarious perch, but an awesome view of Wall Lake directly below. You can also see a trail on the far side of Wall Lake cirque, to the right of steep scree slopes. That's how you'll descend from Bennett Pass, after traversing the ridge. It looks formidable from this vantage, but it's actually not.

What can be difficult, depending on your scrambling ability, is the route left (south), from the saddle onto Akamina Ridge proper. You'll have to surmount a 5-m/yd rock band. If you're hesitant, turn back now. If you're comfortable proceeding on this very steep, grassy, slippery slope, contour south, staying beneath the rock. Use the worn patches as footholds. About 20 m/yd along, look for a silver log that might still be braced vertically against the broken rock band. The ascent is slightly less steep through this tiny draw.

Favouring the Forum Lake side of the crest, continue working your way up. After pulling yourself over another escarpment, you'll be on the **ridge** at 5.3 km (3.3 mi), having left the trailhead about three hours ago. The rest of the route requires no scram-

Akamina Ridge

bling. But figure on spending three hours atop the ridge, taking photos and absorbing the views.

Ahead, you can see the ridge has four bumps. Each requires about a 100-m (330-ft) gain. The second bump (2515 m / 8250 ft) is way easier than it looks. From 2565 m (8413 ft) on the **third bump**, drop 130 m (420 ft), then traverse the west slope of the fourth bump, beneath its summit. A faint path is discernable here. It's a gentle descent from the fourth bump to the end of the ridge.

Watch for a cairn marking the **intersection** of the Akamina Ridge route with the Bennett Pass trail at 10.2 km (6.3 mi), 2230 m (7314 ft). Below here, you can see the trail dropping southwest below **Bennett Pass**. You, however, should turn right (southeast) and begin the long descent through a lush basin, to Wall Lake. Yellow and red paintbrush are profuse. Farther down, near the stream, look for fuchsia monkeyflower, white Sitka valerian, purple fleabane, and blue forget-me-nots.

At 12.7 km (7.9 mi), 1780 m (5838 ft), reach a signed junction at **Wall Lake**. Turn left (northeast) on a broad, smooth trail following the shore. The forest is surprisingly verdant—more so than in adjacent Waterton. Huge spruce add interest. Eager foliage crowds the trail. After leaving the lake, stay right at a junction with a horse trail. It's a cakewalk back to the Akamina road-trail at 15.8 km (9.8 mi), where you turn right (southeast). Within 5-8 minutes, reach the Forum Lake junction. Continue straight to reach the trailhead at 18.3 km (11.3 mi).

TRIP 2

Rowe Lakes / Lineham Ridge

LOCATION	Waterton Lakes National Park
ROUND TRIP	17.2 km (10.7 mi) to Lineham Ridge 19.6 km (12.2 mi) including Upper Rowe Lakes
ELEVATION GAIN	960 m (3150 ft) to ridge 1120 m (3675 ft) including lakes
KEY ELEVATIONS	trailhead 1600 m (5248 ft) ridge 2560 m (8397 ft)
HIKING TIME	5½ to 6 hours for ridge, 7 including lakes
DIFFICULTY	moderate
MAPS	page 492; Gem Trek *Waterton Lakes National Park*

OPINION

May beauty be before me. May beauty be behind me. May beauty be below me. May beauty be above me. It's an ancient, aboriginal incantation, and an apt description of how it feels to stand on Lineham Ridge.

Lineham Ridge

The beauty begins at the trailhead, as you set out beside cascading Rowe Creek, whose streambed consists of dazzling red argillite. After ascending lightly treed slopes that allow views across the Rowe and Cameron creek valleys, the trail enters a pleasing, mature forest.

Both lower and upper Rowe Lakes are lovely, set beneath steep cliffs. But the panorama awaiting you on Lineham Ridge is astounding. So, on the way up, bypass the spur trails to the lakes. Visit them on the return, if you have time and energy. You'll look down on the lakes as you climb.

From the stream-fed greenery of Rowe Basin meadow, in the upper valley, the trail cuts an elegant, sweeping traverse across the headwall. The mauve and rouge talus slopes are themselves alluring. So is the promise of superior views. Where you've been and where you're going are always in view. You're continually rewarded for upward effort.

Lineham Ridge, mid-September

You'll top out in an ocean of peaks bounded on the northeast by prairie. Lineham Ridge boosts you to eye level with many of the mountains on the horizon. The Lineham Lakes are visible in the valley north of the ridge. The jagged skyline to the south is in U.S. Glacier National Park.

Hiking in Waterton, we feel more trepidation than usual, because bear encounters are more likely in this relatively small refuge. Be sure to make noise often. At least this trail passes through semi-open forest until reaching the meadow and talus slopes, so you can usually survey your surroundings.

FACT

By Vehicle

From the junction just north of Waterton townsite, drive Akamina Parkway 10.5 km (6.5 mi) to the Rowe Lakes trailhead parking area, on the right, at 1610 m (5280 ft).

On Foot

Head upstream along the north side of Rowe Creek. As you ascend Rowe Creek valley, Buchanan Ridge is visible southeast across Cameron Creek valley. Gain 355 m (1165 ft) on pleasant, moderately-graded trail until reaching a junction at 3.9 km (2.4 mi). The left spur leads 200 m (220 yd) to tiny, Lower Rowe Lake. For Lineham Ridge, continue straight. The ascent is gentle.

At 5.2 km (3.2 mi), 2020 m (6626 ft), reach a junction in verdant **Rowe Basin**. There is no longer a campground here. Left (south) are the Upper Rowe Lakes. For Lineham Ridge, go straight (west) and begin a 540-m (1770-ft) ascent. Traverse the valley head-

Festubert Mtn, from the Tamarack Trail

wall, then switchback, cresting **Lineham Ridge** at 8.6 km (5.3 mi), 2560 m (8397 ft). Lineham Lakes are visible 365 m (1200 ft) below, in the valley north of the ridge.

Continue east, climbing along the **crest**, but turn back before the long, switchbacking descent into forest. The Tamarack Trail (Trip 106) drops 550 m (1805 ft) to the south fork of Blakiston Creek, then proceeds northwest to Lone Lake.

From Rowe Basin junction, it's 1.2 km (0.75 mi) and a gain of 160 m (525 ft) through alpine larch to Upper Rowe Lakes. Drop to the smaller of the two upper lakes for a view over the edge of this hanging valley. You can peer 180 m (590 ft) down to Lower Rowe Lake.

TRIP 3

Citadel Pass

LOCATION	Banff National Park
ROUND TRIP	18.6 km (11.5 mi)
ELEVATION GAIN	700 m (2296 ft)
KEY ELEVATIONS	trailhead 2195 m (7200 ft), pass 2360 m (7740 ft)
HIKING TIME	6 to 7 hours
DIFFICULTY	moderate
MAPS	page 493; Gem Trek *Banff & Mt. Assiniboine*; Banff 82 O/4

OPINION

The impact of skimming a heli-hiking brochure is double-barreled. First the photos. Then the price list. Both are breathtaking. But for those of us lacking hockey socks full of money, there's an alternative. An affordable way to be whisked up a mountain and begin hiking above timberline, in a see-forever alpine meadow. Simply catch the shuttle up to the ski area at Sunshine Village, where the trail to Citadel Pass offers maximal scenery in return for minimal elevation gain.

It's an idyllic hike through country that does a believable imitation of heaven, unless you're here during a thunderstorm. The meadows sprawl for 15 km (9 mi) near the crest of the Continental Divide. Mid-July through mid-August, you'll likely witness a vast array of wildflowers, which can make this an enjoyable outing even on a drizzly day. But tempestuous weather is no fun at this elevation, and could be dangerous, because you're totally exposed to whatever the sky throws at you. Besides, good visibility is essential for appreciating distant views of mighty Mt. Assiniboine and other impressive peaks including The Monarch—a massive mountain whose dominant appearance justifies its name.

Don't zero-in on Howard Douglas Lake as a dayhike destination. It's in a shallow bowl that limits views. And you needn't climb Quartz Hill for an improved panorama. Follow the trail beyond it and the lake. Southeast of Quartz Hill, you can see the mountains it previously blocked. You'll face plenty of ups and downs just staying on the trail; adding cross-country exploration to your effort will make it exceedingly difficult to reach Citadel Pass and make it back to Sunshine Village in time to catch the last shuttle down to the parking lot. Though this trip begins in the alpine zone, your accumulated ascent by day's end will be substantial. The elevation gain stated above is a conservative estimate only.

Swift dayhikers, taking advantage of the gentle terrain, can stride out, reaching Citadel Pass in 2½ hours—if they're not detained by a brilliant flower display. The benefit of a fast pace is that you can extend the trip beyond Citadel, to Fatigue Pass.

Western chaliceflower and fireweed. Quartz Hill in background.

Just 15 minutes beyond, the magic of a little ascent will reveal itself. Distant peaks seem to leap into the foreground. Mt. Assiniboine is south/southeast. U-shaped Wonder Pass is left (northeast) of Mt. Assiniboine. Nasswald Peak and Og Mtn are southeast. Fatigue Mtn is nearby, northeast. Even Mt. Temple is visible, northwest. Simpson Ridge is southwest. Try to allow an extra hour for this additional scenery splurge.

If you balk at the cost of riding the shuttle, it's possible to hoof it from the Sunshine parking lot up to Sunshine Village. The distance: 6.5 km (4 mi). The ascent: 520 m (1706 ft). It takes at least 1½ hours. It's boring, too. Just a rocky road switchbacking up through trees. And remember, you'd have to hike back down as well. Even if you're very fit, it's worth paying for the shuttle. Think of all the long, sweaty ascents you've cursed. This is a rare opportunity to skip one. Take it.

FACT

The convenience of shuttle service to these extraordinary alplands assures you won't be alone. But a choice of destinations, people's widely varying hiking speeds, and the sheer vastness of the terrain will allow you more solitude than you might expect.

The Sunshine Meadows / Rock Isle Lake area draws an average of 60 visitors on a sunny, summer day; sometimes as many as 130. But 60% mosey no farther than Rock Isle or Grizzly lakes (Trip 40), so you won't see too many trekking to Citadel Pass, or Healy Pass (Trip 24). A mere 10% of visitors are backpackers heading to Assiniboine.

If you're here to hike (as opposed to walk), you can leave most people behind at or before Howard Douglas Lake.

The profusion of wildflowers belies the harshness of this sky-high environment. It provides only 45 growing days per year. Some plants struggle 20 years to produce a single flower. Help preserve these hardy-yet-delicate beings by not plucking them or crushing them under foot. Stay on the trails.

By Vehicle

Drive the Trans-Canada Highway east 21 km (13 mi) from Castle Junction, or west 9 km (5.6 mi) from Banff townsite. Turn south onto the signed Sunshine Village road. Proceed 8.3 km (5.1 mi) to the parking lot at the gondola station. The gondola does not operate in summer.

By Bus

White Mountain Adventures shuttle service is available June 20 through September 30. Reservations are not necessary. In the past, departure times have been every hour on the hour beginning at 9 a.m., with the last bus up at 4 p.m. Return times have been every hour on the half hour, with the last bus down at 5:30 p.m. White Mountain also offers shuttle service from Banff townsite. If you ride the first bus up, then hike like a demon, it's possible to reach Fatigue Pass and return to the village in time to catch the last bus down. If the shuttle schedule is too restrictive for you, ask about one-way prices.

On Foot

From Sunshine Village ski lodge, at 2195 m (7200 ft), walk south past the left (east) side of the saloon. Go uphill 200 m (220 yd) to the Parks Canada cabin. Fifteen metres past it, turn left (east-southeast) onto the well-groomed gravel path. It ascends gently. Reach the first junction at 2290 m (7510 ft). Go right (south) and continue the easy ascent. In another 5-7 minutes, reach the next junction, 1.2 km (0.7 mi) from the village. Right (west) leads to Rock Isle Lake (Trip 40). Go left (south-southeast) on the narrower path for Quartz Hill and Citadel Pass.

The north end of Quartz Hill is visible south. Wedgwood Peak and other giants in the Assiniboine area are south-southeast. Lookout Mtn is the gray peak northeast with a ski lift on its bare chest. Mt. Howard Douglas looms above it. Behind it is Brewster Creek Valley.

About 45 minutes from the village, the trail descends—one of many downs and ups. Soon regain 145 m (480 ft). Much of the narrow path is deeply-eroded through here. If the wildflower show hasn't slowed you, reach a 2393-m (7850-ft) shoulder of **Quartz Hill** in about 1½ hours, having hiked 5 km (3 mi) from the village. The 3618-m (11,867-ft) horn of Mt. Assiniboine is visible ahead. The first lake beneath you is Howard Douglas (labeled Sundown on some maps). Citadel Pass is the cleft way left (east-southeast)—not the lower, forested saddle south-southeast.

Descend to reach the shore of **Howard Douglas Lake** at 2280 m (7480 ft). The **campground** is in trees, behind the lake's northeast corner. The lake is not visible from the three tentsites or cooking area. The #1 site is somewhat separate. The #3 site is near the creek.

After the deeply rutted, narrow trail to Howard Douglas Lake, the path improves through meadows with a scattering of alpine fir and larch. Ascend

100 m (330 ft) and pass another lake before reaching **Citadel Pass** at 9.3 km (5.8 mi), 2360 m (7740 ft). Citadel Peak is right (southwest). Fatigue Mtn is left (northeast). A big sign here indicates you're about to enter Mt. Assiniboine Provincial Park. Another sign by the Banff Park kiosk has ridiculously varying distances. Magog Lake, at the base of Mt. Assiniboine, is 19.6 km (12.2 mi) southeast, though one sign says 17 km.

If proceeding to Fatigue Pass, ascend left (east) from the Assiniboine sign. Fatigue is only 2.5 km (1.6 mi) beyond Citadel Pass, and if all you want is a better view you don't even have to go that far. Though you can initially pick up a faint path, it peters out. Look southeast and you'll see where it resumes, switchbacking up a rounded, grassy mound. Continue in that direction, over heather, through a draw, and across a rockslide. Shortly after tagging onto the trail you saw from Citadel Pass, it too disappears. But there are now widely spaced cairns to guide you. Rise to 2470 m (8100 ft), then drop into **Fatigue Pass**. Along the way, a sign on a cairn states the elevation of the pass: 2390 m (7840 ft). It also says Brewster Creek is 10.7 km distant.

Ambitious scramblers can choose a route from just north of Citadel Pass, to the summit of 2959-m (9707-ft) Fatigue Mtn.

If continuing from Citadel Pass to Lake Magog and Mt. Assiniboine, descend gradually southeast through meadows for 1.2 km (0.75 mi) before dropping more steeply through forest into Golden Valley and Valley of the Rocks (Trip 75).

Howard Douglas Lake below Quartz Ridge

TRIP 4

Bourgeau Lake / Harvey Pass / Mt. Bourgeau

LOCATION	Banff National Park
ROUND TRIP	19.2 km (12 mi) to pass 24 km (14.9 mi) to summit
ELEVATION GAIN	1046 m (3431 ft) to pass 1530 m (5018 ft) to summit
KEY ELEVATIONS	trailhead 1401 m (4596 ft) lake 2150 m (7052 ft) pass 2447 m (8025 ft) summit 2931 m (9615 ft)
HIKING TIME	5 to 7 hours for pass, 6 to 8 for summit
DIFFICULTY	moderate to pass challenging to summit due only to elevation gain
MAPS	page 493; Gem Trek *Banff & Mt. Assiniboine*; Banff 82 O/4

OPINION

Bourgeau Lake is merely the box office. Harvey Pass is the warm-up act. Mt. Bourgeau is the headliner. Most people pay for a ticket, then leave without seeing the show. What they miss is astounding.

Atop Mt. Bourgeau's broad summit, you'll appreciate much of Banff National Park: sprawling meadows beneath you, icy peaks parading over distant horizons. Though the panorama is comparable to that afforded by Mt. Temple (the mammoth peak towering above Lake Louise), scrambling is not required here. A discernible trail ascends from Harvey Pass, all the way up Bourgeau's west ridge. Given fair weather and sufficient daylight, you simply need the will and energy to keep walking. From the pass, robust hikers storm the peak in just 45 minutes.

The only obstacle that might foil your intent to summit Mt. Bourgeau is the superlative view from Harvey Pass. It's tempting to stop here. Mt. Assiniboine and the knot of burly bodyguard peaks surrounding it are an awesome sight; on clear days Harvey Pass offers a premier vantage of this stellar massif. The expansive Sunshine and Healy Pass meadows are also visible from Harvey Pass and will keep your eyes happily roaming while you savour your Ryvita and smoked wild salmon.

Okay, you've finished lunch. Can't muster the resolve to continue ascending Mt. Bourgeau? How about a small burst of energy propelling you up the slope west-northwest of Harvey Pass? Minimal gain at a moderate grade soon grants an improved prospect. It might entice you to keep wandering the alplands toward

Healy Pass—an off-trail excursion for which a map and compass are helpful. And if that sounds too demanding, try departing Harvey Pass as if aiming for Mt. Bourgeau. Within minutes, at the first broad saddle, veer left. You'll quickly top out on the gentle knoll above Harvey Lake's northeast shore.

Just can't pry your posterior off that comfy perch in Harvey Pass? Fine. But make sure you get at least that far. Bourgeau Lake, beneath the massive, soaring northwest wall of Mt. Bourgeau, is impressively beautiful, yet even a swift hiker will plod nearly two hours through forest to get there and see nothing memorable en route. So take a break at the lake, then continue. Just above are lovely lakelets in an alpine basin. Between them is a cascading stream, where you'll enjoy the optimal, aerial view of Bourgeau Lake. And minutes above the second lakelet is Harvey Lake in Harvey Pass, where your sense of accomplishment, and the scenic reward for your effort, will increase exponentially.

FACT

By Vehicle

Drive the Trans-Canada Hwy west 2.8 km (1.7 mi) from the Sunshine Village turnoff, or east 44 km (27.3 mi) from the Lake Louise turnoff. The trailhead is on the southwest side of the divided highway. If driving east, simply turn off right. If driving west, slow down, turn left, then stop before carefully crossing the eastbound lane. The trailhead parking lot is at 1401 m (4596 ft).

On Foot

The trail departs the west end of the paved parking lot. A fence (built to prevent animal deaths on the highway) requires you to step up to a gate, then step back down to the trail. Pass the trailhead sign and head west.

In about 12 minutes, the trail approaches **Wolverine Creek canyon**, where the sound of rushing water drowns out the noise of vehicles on the highway. Your general direction of travel is now southwest and will remain so all the way to Bourgeau Lake.

About 35 minutes from the trailhead, having ascended 230 m (754 ft), attain the first view: northwest into Wolverine Creek canyon and north-northeast across Bow Valley. The ascent eases. Views temporarily open.

After hiking about an hour, cross a bridge over a tributary stream at 3.7 km (2.3 mi). The gentle grade continues for about another half hour, until the trail reaches cascading **Wolverine Creek**, at 5.5 km (3.4 mi), 1850 m (6068 ft). Rockhop across, then begin ascending steeply.

About 15 minutes farther, just above the cascade, attain your first glimpse upward into **Bourgeau Lake basin**. Behind you, the view across Bow Valley has also expanded. The trail continues tilting skyward. You'll ascend another 10 minutes before it levels at 2108 m (6915 ft) then rolls into the subalpine zone. You've entered the basin. The wall of Mount Bourgeau looms ahead, south-southwest.

Expect mucky sections of trail here. (Stay on the main path. Mud won't hurt your boots, but straying off the trail will permanently widen it to an unsightly road-width.) Reach the northeast shore of **Bourgeau Lake** at 7.4 km (4.6 mi), 2150 m (7052 ft). Near the shore, a sign indicates the trail to Harvey Pass.

The lakeshore is home to pesky, obese chipmunks who've learned that hikers are easy marks. If you take your pack off, keep it zipped shut. And steel yourself to

Mt. Bourgeau, from the shore of Bourgeau Lake

the begging antics of these ravenous rogues. Processed food is even less nutritious for animals than it is for you. Feeding them erodes their ability to survive in the wild by fostering dependence on humans. Besides, feeding wild animals is illegal in the Canadian Rockies National Parks.

Proceeding to Harvey Pass? Good on you. From the sign near where you arrived at the lakeshore, follow the trail right (west-southwest). After rounding the lake's northwest shore (usually mucky), the trail improves as it ascends the right (north) side of the **inlet cascade**. Do not ascend the steep, narrow, slippery path above the cascade's south bank.

About 30 minutes after departing Bourgeau Lake, crest the lip of the upper basin and arrive at the **first lakelet**. Elevation: 2332 m (7650 ft). The trail continues around the north shore. Maintain a brisk pace and within five minutes you'll be rockhopping the creeklet draining the **second lakelet**. Follow the trail southeast now—above the first lakelet, just east of the second lakelet, up a short, steep, compacted scree slope—and another five minutes will bring you to the third lakelet, called **Harvey Lake**, in 2447-m (8025-ft) **Harvey Pass**, at 9.6 km (6 mi). Looking back, a tarn is now visible below, just above the second lakelet. But even this improved aerial view of the picturesque alpine basin doesn't compare with the wondrous vision ahead (south-southeast): the Mt. Assiniboine massif.

The trail rounds Harvey Lake's east shore. Within a couple minutes, reach the south side of Harvey Pass, where you have two options: (1) ascend left (east) for Mt. Bourgeau, or (2) follow a diminishing path right (southwest) onto heathery slopes. The trail up Mt. Bourgeau's west ridge is visible from the pass.

At an aggressive pace, it takes 45 minutes to hike from Harvey Pass to the top of 2930-m (9610-ft) **Mt. Bourgeau**. Distance from the trailhead: 12 km (7.5 mi). The day's total elevation gain: 1530 m (5018 ft). Though a small communications structure crowns the mountain, the summit is spacious and the panorama is unmarred. On a clear day, you can spend an hour identifying significant Canadian Rockies landmarks. A sampling of the spectacle includes Banff townsite (east-northeast), Mt. Joffre and the big peaks in Kananaskis Country (distant southeast), Mt. Assiniboine (south-southeast), Sunshine Meadows and Ski Area (south), Healy Pass (southwest), the Bugaboos (distant southwest), Mt. Ball (west-northwest), Mt. Temple and the big peaks between Lake Louise and Lake O'Hara (northwest). Strong, determined hikers can return to the trailhead within three hours of departing the summit.

Mt. Bourgeau, from meadows west of Harvey Pass

TRIP 5

Valley of the Ten Peaks / Sentinel Pass

LOCATION	Banff National Park
ROUND TRIP	11.6 km (7.2 mi)
ELEVATION GAIN	726 m (2381 ft)
KEY ELEVATIONS	trailhead 1885 m (6183 ft), pass 2611 m (8564 ft)
HIKING TIME	4 to 5 hours
DIFFICULTY	moderate
MAPS	page 495; Gem Trek *Lake Louise & Yoho*; Lake Louise 82 N/8

OPINION

The mundane-existence-shredding Ten Peaks loom above resplendent Moraine Lake. With faces as striking as their names—Wenkchemna, Neptuak, Deltaform, Tuzo—the ten distinct alps form a sublime bulwark rising 1340 m (4400 ft) from the turquoise lake. The trees in Larch Valley, whether green in summer or gold in late fall, are a soft, colourful counterpoint to the austere valley walls. But Sentinel Pass is where you'll feel the full impact of this glorious scene and can also peer into Paradise Valley.

Go all the way to Sentinel Pass, where the views down both sides cheapen superlatives. Switchbacks, and the constant tug of rapidly-improving scenery, enable even the once-a-summer hiker to gradually make it.

Though the trail attracts herds of tourists, don't miss this gift-of-the-gods hike. Avoid the stampede by starting after 2 p.m. In summer, you'll have plenty of light until 9 p.m. When you reach the pass, 2½ hours at a moderate pace, many hikers will have left.

Returning from the pass, extend the hike by going right at the junction below Larch Valley and heading west 3.2 km (2 mi) to Eiffel Lake (Trip 28). Fewer people visit Eiffel, though the contouring trail is easy and the Ten Peaks are directly across the valley.

If you can arrange a shuttle, it's worth continuing from Sentinel Pass northwest into Paradise Valley (Trip 6). The route is initially steep and rugged, descending a rockslide, but is well marked and maintained in the valley. This one-way shuttle-trip is 17 km (10.5 mi). It ends at the Paradise Valley trailhead, on the Moraine Lake Road, 10 km (6.2 mi) below the Larch Valley trailhead.

Experienced scramblers who start early can proceed from Sentinel Pass, up the southwest ridge of Mt. Temple, to witness an explosion of mountain scenery from the 3543-m (11,621-ft) summit. A narrow, rough trail departs the pass but quickly deteriorates as it aims for the sky. The route is dangerously exposed. To attempt it, you must be confident on steep scree slopes and capable of climbing on all fours through gullies that split the sheer rock bands. Wait until early August, when the route should be snowfree. Be careful not to rain rocks on scramblers below you. Watch out for rocks raining down on you.

The Sentinel Pass trail also grants access to 3084-m (10,118-ft) Eiffel Peak (see page 27). Experienced scramblers turn left (south)—above the Eiffel Lake trail, but below Larch Valley—onto a bootbeaten route. It quickly drops to an unbridged creeklet, then ascends the broad ridge curving northwest, then north to the peak. The way forward is obvious, but only to those who are up to the navigational challenge. Above treeline, several routes are evident in the scree. They eventually funnel to where the ascent steepens dramatically. Follow gullies through the rock bands—usually snowfree after mid-July—then negotiate rubbly slabs to attain the summit. If you need more detailed directions, you're in over your head and are courting injury. Though Eiffel Peak is a slightly less demanding goal than Mt. Temple, the panorama it affords is comparably spectacular. The 70-m pillar immediately northwest of the peak is called Eiffel Tower.

FACT

By Vehicle

From Lake Louise village, drive uphill, southwest, on Lake Louise Drive. Turn left on Moraine Lake Road and follow it 12.5 km (7.8 mi) to the huge parking lot at road's end. Elevation: 1885 m (6183 ft).

Before your trip

Read page 37 about possible hiking restrictions due to bears.

A few of the Ten Peaks, beyond Minnestimma Lake

Pinnacle Mountain, above Sentinel Pass

On Foot

Walk south through the parking lot to the shore of Moraine Lake, then past the lodge to the trailhead sign. The wide, well-maintained path switchbacks as it ascends moderately through forest. After gaining 360 m (1180 ft) in 2.4 km (1.5 mi), reach a junction. Left leads to Eiffel Lake and Wenkchemna Pass (Trip 28). Turn right. The ascent is more gentle now, the trail gradually curving north. Pass through subalpine larch to arrive in the open meadows of **Larch Valley** near 3.5 km (2.2 mi). Snow-cloaked 3234-m (10,607-ft) Mt. Fay (southeast of the valley lip) is the most prominent of the Ten Peaks.

Continuing north to Sentinel Pass, within 10 minutes reach the tiny Minnestimma Lakes (meaning *sleeping water*).Where the trail passes between them, Eiffel Peak is left (west). The craggy notch of Sentinel Pass is visible ahead, between Pinnacle Mountain (left) and Mt. Temple (right). The trail climbs tight switchbacks on open talus slopes to gain 176 m (577 ft) in its final surge. Crest **Sentinel Pass** at 5.8 km (3.6 mi), 2611 m (8564 ft). Unusual rock spires give the pass its name.

North of the pass, a trail descends 500 m (1640 ft) into Paradise Valley, intersecting the upper valley trail in 2.3 km (1.4 mi). From there, detour left 0.7 km (0.4 mi) deeper into the valley for a view of Horseshoe Meadow. Then return to the junction and hike northeast out of the valley, passing splendid Lake Annette en route.

TRIP 6

Lake Annette / Paradise Valley

LOCATION	Banff National Park
ROUND TRIP	11.4 km (7.1 mi) to lake
CIRCUIT	19.6 km (12.2 mi) through upper Paradise Valley
ELEVATION GAIN	245 m (804 ft) to lake 450 m (1476 ft) for circuit
KEY ELEVATIONS	trailhead 1720 m (5642 ft) lake 1965 m (6445 ft) highpoint on valley's southeast wall 2115 m (6937 ft) lowpoint at Giant Steps 2025 m (6642 ft)
HIKING TIME	2¼ hours for lake, 5 hours for circuit
DIFFICULTY	easy to lake, moderate for circuit
MAPS	page 495; Gem Trek *Lake Louise & Yoho;* Lake Louise 82 N/8

OPINION

Lake Annette is to the Canadian Rockies what espresso is to coffee: a small serving, but highly concentrated. It ranks among Banff Park's most impressive, easy-to-reach destinations.

A short distance from the trailhead, magnificence looms above. The valley walls are phantasmagoric wedding cakes of rock and ice. Cornices occasionally crack off ridges and shatter into snow cones. Frothy clouds, snagged from the sky, frequently soften the craggy crests.

The enormity of it all can be wonderfully overwhelming, especially from the shore of Lake Annette, directly beneath the sheer, 1200-m (3936-ft) north face of Mt. Temple. Many hikers turn around here, their spectacle levels topped-up for weeks to come.

Beyond Annette, the trail leads to a rockslide where you can overlook Paradise Valley's upper reaches and see Horseshoe Glacier clinging to the headwall. A bit farther, you can choose to boost the day's challenge/reward quotient by ascending the short, steep, rugged route to Sentinel Pass (Trip 5). You can even extend this option by proceeding through the pass, then descending to Moraine Lake and completing a hitchhike- or shuttle-assisted loop. Total hiking distance: 17 km (10.5 mi).

Should you decline the Sentinel Pass option and continue your tour of Paradise, you'll drop to the valley floor and cross Horseshoe Meadow. Here you can swerve toward home or add a pinch more distance and scenery to your day by visiting the Giant Steps—an unusual cascade, where Paradise Creek pours over enormous, blocky slabs of quartzite.

Throughout your stay in Paradise, be alert for bears. This valley, particularly the lush avalanche paths swooping down the northwest wall, is a seasonal home for

North face of Mt. Temple towers over Lake Annette.

bruins. Female grizzlies in particular rely on it for summer habitat. Their survival, and that of their offspring, affects the viability of the region's endangered bear population. They need to be here. People appreciate the valley scenery but do not depend on it. So bears deserve deference. Still, Banff Park has thoughtfully modified trails and continues to vigilantly monitor bear activity, enabling thousands of hikers each year to enjoy this rapturous enclave.

FACT

Before your trip

Contact the park office. Whenever a bear is likely present in Paradise Valley, the park allows only groups of four or more to hike here (see page 37), and it closes the backcountry campground. For your safety, as well as that of the bears, please obey these restrictions.

By Vehicle

From Lake Louise village, drive uphill, southwest, on Lake Louise Drive. Turn left on Moraine Lake Road and follow it 2.5 km (1.6 mi) to the trailhead parking area on the right, at 1720 m (5642 ft).

On Foot

Ascend steeply left from the kiosk into the forest. Stay on the main trail paralleling Paradise Creek, heading upstream. In about 13 minutes, ignore a faint, left fork. At 15 minutes, curve right (north), away from the creek, following the sign for Paradise

Upper Paradise Valley, from above Sentinel Pass

Valley. Shortly beyond, reach a signed junction at 1.3 km (0.8 mi). Right continues northwest to Lake Louise. Go left (west) to enter Paradise Valley.

Ascend slightly, then descend south. Cross a bridged tributary, then cross two bridges spanning **Paradise Creek**: first to the east bank, then back to the west. Here, about 50 minutes from the trailhead, Mt. Temple is in full view directly south.

Nearly an hour from the trailhead, reach a signed junction at 4.2 km (2.6 mi), 1836 m (6022 ft). Right (west) enters Sheol Valley, climbs to Saddleback (Trip 29), then descends to Lake Louise. Proceed straight (south), following the creek upstream.

After hiking just over an hour, cross yet another bridge spanning Paradise Creek, this time to the southeast bank. Looking downstream, Lake Louise ski area is visible across the Bow Valley. Ascend southeast. Five minutes farther, reach **Lake Annette** at 5.7 km (3.5 mi), 1965 m (6445 ft).

Continuing into Paradise Valley? Ascend southwest on the trail signed for Sentinel Pass. Endure a short stretch through viewless, ugly forest. Soon rockhop a stream, exit the trees, and attain a grand view from a huge **rockslide** at 2085 m (6839 ft), about 20 minutes from Lake Annette. Numerous cascades are visible (right / northwest) spilling off Mt. Aberdeen.

Proceed southwest, traversing the **southeast wall of Paradise Valley** among larch and fir. Hop a creeklet, attain a view, then continue through forest another 10 minutes to a vantage where you can survey the west side of Mt. Temple (left / east) and the boulder-strewn slope beneath Sentinel Pass (left / south).

Reach a signed junction at 8.4 km (5.2 mi), 2115 m (6937 ft), about 1¾ hours from the trailhead. Right descends west, offering the most direct route to Paradise Valley campground and the Giant Steps. For a slightly longer but more scenic circuit of upper Paradise Valley, bear left and continue contouring southwest. Regardless which way you proceed, unless you exit the valley via Sentinel Pass, you'll return to this junction on your way back to the trailhead.

If you continue contouring southwest from the 8.4-km (5.2-mi) junction, reach another signed junction at 8.8 km (5.5 mi), 2111 m (6926 ft). Total hiking time: just under two hours. Left (east) ascends 2.3 km (1.4 mi) to Sentinel Pass (Trip 5), then drops through Larch Valley to reach the Moraine Lake trailhead parking lot. Skip below for details. To complete a circuit of upper Paradise Valley, go right (west-southwest) and descend among boulders into **Horseshoe Meadow**.

On the floor of upper Paradise Valley, pass an old, wood sign among larches indicating the route left (south) to Wasatch Pass. Cross a bridge to the north bank of **Horseshoe Creek**. Four minutes farther reach a signed junction at 10 km (6.2 mi), 2070 m (6790 ft), about 2¼ hours from the trailhead. Proceed straight (north) to complete the upper-valley circuit. Go left (northwest) to reach either Paradise Valley campground or the Giant Steps in 0.8 km (1.3 mi).

Heading straight (north) from the 10-km (6.2-mi) junction, the trail parallels the creek, following it downstream. Two minutes farther, reach a signed junction at 10.1 km (6.3 mi), 2060 m (6757 ft). Sharp left (northwest) detours 0.7 km (1.2 mi) back to the Giant Steps. To complete the upper-valley circuit, continue straight (east), descend to a bridged crossing of Horseshoe Creek, then ascend east to a junction at 11.2 km (6.9 mi), 2115 m (6937 ft). You're now on familiar ground, having previously traversed the valley's southeast wall via this trail. Turn left and retrace your steps northeast, past Lake Annette, then down to the trailhead—an 8.4-km (5.2-mi) final leg that takes about 1¾ hours.

The Giant Steps

PARADISE VALLEY TO SENTINEL PASS

From the junction at 8.8 km (5.5 mi), 2111 m (6926 ft), on Paradise Valley's southeast wall, you'll gain 500 m (1640 ft) in 2.3 km (1.4 mi) to reach Sentinel Pass (Trip 5). Initially on trail, ascend left (east) among larch trees on a rocky, grassy slope. The 2611-m (8564-ft) pass is soon visible ahead. Defined trail quickly ends. Curving right (south), pick your way across boulders. Initially favour the left (east) side of the basin. The moderate grade steepens dramatically. The final ascent is via bootbeaten route on the talus slope to the right.

TRIP 7

Bow Peak

LOCATION	Banff National Park, south of Bow Lake
ROUND TRIP	10 km (6.2 mi) to Crowfoot Pass 12.6 km (7.8 mi) to Bow Peak 14 km (8.7 mi) to Balfour Prospect
ELEVATION GAIN	456 m (1496 ft) for Crowfoot Pass 970 m (3182 ft) for Bow Peak 641 m (2102 ft) for Balfour Prospect
KEY ELEVATIONS	trailhead 1939 m (6360 ft), pass 2355 m (7724 ft), peak 2869 m (9410 ft), prospect 2270 m (7446 ft)
HIKING TIME	2½ to 3 hours for pass, 4 to 4½ hours for peak, 3½ to 4 hours for prospect
DIFFICULTY	moderate for pass and/or prospect challenging for peak
MAPS	page 494; Gem Trek *Bow Lake & Saskatchewan Crossing*; Hector Lake 82 N/9

OPINION

Rarely is it so easy to sign your name in a Canadian Rockies summit-cairn register. Strictly speaking, Bow Peak is a scramble, because the final ascent is off trail. But it demands none of the skill or daring that makes most scrambles formidable for the average hiker. If you have the juice to boulder hop your way up a steep, 514-m (1686-ft) slope, you can scribble a nugget of wisdom or humour in the register atop Bow Peak. You can also admire mountains and glaciers galore while gloating in a greater sense of achievement than is possible on most trails.

You'll face only two minor challenges en route to the final ascent: a sketchy beginning, and a ford. There's no trailhead, and initially no trail. But if you proceed according to the simple directions below, you'll pick up a bootbeaten path through comfortably open forest. And your immediate goal, though not visible from the start, is only a short distance away and will be obvious when you arrive: the Bow Lake outlet, which is usually an easy, calf-deep ford. On the far bank, a forgotten but still serviceable trail climbs to Crowfoot Pass and the base of Bow Peak.

For so few difficulties, the rewards are immense. Among them is solitude, because the lack of a formal trailhead flummoxes most people. Then there's Crowfoot Pass, a premier destination even if you don't continue up the peak. The pass is a broad, alpine saddle between Crowfoot Mtn and Bow Peak. Two tarns, like golf-course hazards, guard its north edge. Pierce them, crest the pass, and you'll attain superb views north and south. From there you can scramble up the peak or continue hiking south to Balfour Prospect, where you'll see the eastern visage of Mt. Balfour—a startling sight. The glaciers oozing off it look like the Great Carpenter went crazy

Crowfoot Pass

with a caulking gun. Meltwater cascades crash into the canyon below. Braided streams rage across the flats to feed Hector Lake.

FACT

By Vehicle

From the Num-Ti-Jah Lodge / Bow Glacier turnoff at the north end of Bow Lake, drive the Icefields Parkway (Hwy 93) southeast 4.4 km (2.7 mi).

Or, from its junction with Hwy 1, just north of Lake Louise, drive the Icefields Parkway (Hwy 93) north 34.3 km (21.3 mi). (From Mosquito Creek Bridge drive the Parkway 10.5 km / 6.5 mi north.)

From either approach, turn into **Crowfoot Glacier viewpoint**, on the southwest side of the Parkway. (If you were heading northeast, you must turn around.) The southeast end of Bow Lake is visible below. The Helen Lake trailhead (Trip 8) is across the Parkway.

Reset your trip odometre to 0. Slowly drive southeast. In 0.9 km (0.55 mi) reach a gravel pullout on the right (southwest) side of the Parkway. On the left (northeast) side are exposed black rocks in the dirt slope. Park here, in the gravel pullout, at 1939 m (6360 ft).

On Foot

From the gravel pullout, walk the Parkway east-southeast, away from the main body of Bow Lake. Count your paces, so you'll know precisely where to leave the pavement. It's about 230 paces to a culvert.

Continue 140 paces beyond the culvert. Stop here, turn right (south), and descend off the Parkway. There might still be flagging on low trees marking this spot, which is 1.3 km (0.8 mi) from Crowfoot Glacier viewpoint.

After negotiating the roadside boulders, reach a dirt depression in a clearing, near a stand of willows and trees. Follow the bootbeaten path generally south-southeast, through a natural opening in the forest. Bear left where a path joins from the right. Proceed to the **Bow Lake outlet**, where the Bow River originates. From the Parkway to the outlet, you'll descend 20 m (65 ft) in 1 km (0.6 mi). Bow Peak is visible southeast. The saddle right of it is your next goal: Crowfoot Pass.

Ford the outlet precisely at the lake, where it's shallowest and has the least current. (The water level varies. In midsummer, you can expect an easy, calf-deep ford. But if it's significantly deeper, it might be dangerous; abort the trip.) On the south bank, pick up an unmaintained but defined trail through the forest. It curves east, following the **Bow River** downstream.

Rockhop a couple creeklets. Though the trail remains distinct, expect to negotiate lots of deadfall. At 2.5 km (1.6 km) rockhop a **tributary stream**. The trail then ascends right, generally south, up the tributary drainage, into the alpine zone. Just after passing two tarns (left and right), crest **Crowfoot Pass** at 5 km (3.1 mi), 2355 m (7724 ft). Mt. Temple is visible south-southeast. On a clear day, you can also see Mt. Assiniboine (Trips 76-78) distant south-southeast. Cirque Peak (Trip 8) is north. Right of it and slightly closer is Dolomite Peak, north-northeast.

BOW PEAK

From Bow Pass, turn left (east) off the trail and freelance your way up the large, chunky boulders. Reach the **summit** at 6.3 km (3.9 mi), 2869 m (9410 ft). The panorama includes Bow Lake northwest, Mosquito Creek valley northeast, Mt. Hector southeast, Hector Lake south, and the glacier-encrusted Waputik Range south and southwest.

BALFOUR PROSPECT

Follow the trail descending south from Crowfoot Pass. The view ahead, down the Bow Valley, includes Hector Lake below. Cross a creeklet in a ravine. Proceed south-southeast through flowery meadows and among stunted trees. The path diminishes but remains evident. Rockhop across a broad, shallow creek and bottom-out at 2220 m (7282 ft). Then ascend south-southwest through a larch-lined corridor to reach 2270-m (7446-ft) **Balfour Prospect** at 7 km (4.3 mi), on a subalpine ridgecrest, about 30 minutes from Crowfoot Pass. Despite the trees, the panorama (right/west to left/southeast) is grand, dominated by 3273-m (10,735-ft) Mt. Balfour and its namesake glacier on the Alberta-B.C., Banff-Yoho boundary.

TRIP 8

Helen Lake / Cirque Peak

LOCATION	Banff National Park, east of Bow Lake
ROUND TRIP	12 km (7.4 mi) to Helen Lake, 14 km (8.7 mi) to ridge above lake, 16 km (9.9 mi) to Cirque Peak
ELEVATION GAIN	422 m (1384 ft) to Helen Lake 550 m (1804 ft) to ridge above Helen Lake 1043 m (3421 ft) to Cirque Peak
KEY ELEVATIONS	trailhead 1950 m (6400 ft) Helen Lake 2372 m (7780 ft) ridge above Helen Lake 2500 m (8200 ft) Cirque Peak 2993 m (9817 ft)
HIKING TIME	4 hours for Helen Lake, 6 hours for Cirque Peak
DIFFICULTY	easy for Helen Lake, moderate for Cirque Peak
MAPS	page 494; Gem Trek *Bow Lake & Saskatchewan Crossing*; Hector Lake 82 N/9

OPINION

His T-shirt read, "Get a life! A hiking life! It's the only one that matters!" He was loping down the trail from Cirque Peak and Helen Lake, his face a mask of wild-eyed elation.

Someone more zealous about hiking than we are? Apparently. We laughed at the preposterous, myopic message on the man's chest. Yet we had to admit, if *he* endorsed this trail, it must be extravagantly rewarding. And it is.

The summit of Cirque Peak affords a vast panorama. Here, at the elevation of a low-flying cloud, you'll see peaks, glaciers, valleys, meadows and lakes swirling around you. Yet Cirque Peak is, incredibly, within reach of the average hiker.

To be precise, Cirque Peak is a scramble, because it's off trail and quite steep. But there's nothing technical about it. The route is obvious. Keep slogging up shifting scree and, with a little help from your hands near the top, ta da! Suddenly you're looking down the remnant glacier that swoops off the sheer north face. Lift your eyes westward, and there's the Wapta Icefield—as good a view of it as you'll get from any hiker accessible destination.

Cirque Peak's panorama ranks among the best a mere hiker can attain in the Rockies. But failure to top out isn't a total loss. Ascend as far as you feel comfortable. Every 30 m (98 ft) of upward progress allows a more commanding view. You don't even have to set foot on Cirque Peak for this to be a premier hike. Helen Lake basin has high-caliber flower power. The area is among our favourites for meadowland beauty.

Hiking to Helen Lake, you'll spend blessedly little time in trees before emerging into the subalpine zone, where you can appreciate distant scenery. Another bonus is the return-trip entertainment: views of glacier-mantled mountains lining the Icefields Parkway.

A half-day is all it takes for strong hikers to visit Helen Lake. So if the rain doesn't stop until afternoon, you can still pull it off. Less ambitious hikers seeking a gentler outing should allow a full day.

The keeners in your group can clamber up and down Cirque Peak in 1½ to 2 hours while the others relax at the lake. From the lake, the sitters can watch the scramblers ascend. Everyone should (our friend, the hiking-life firebrand, would say "must!") continue to the ridge above Helen Lake for an improved view.

FACT

By Vehicle

From the junction of the Trans-Canada (Hwy 1) and the Icefields Parkway (Hwy 93), drive the Parkway northwest 33.2 km (20.6 mi) to the Crowfoot Glacier viewpoint. Or, from Bow Summit, drive the Parkway southeast 7.7 km (4.8 mi). From either approach, turn into the trailhead parking lot on the north side of the Parkway. It's across from the viewpoint, at 1950 m (6400 ft).

On Foot

Heading generally east, ascend through Engelmann spruce and alpine fir for the first 3 km (2 mi). Views soon open west to the end of Bow Lake and southwest to Crowfoot mountain and glacier. Bow Peak (Trip 7) is directly south across the Parkway. Mt. Hector is southeast.

Helen Lake (right), from Cirque Peak ascent

Ascending Cirque Peak

On subalpine slopes, the trail works around a southeast-jutting ridge. About 45 minutes after setting out, turn the corner left (north) near 2134 m (7000 ft) and switchback briefly. Then contour through heathery alplands, high above **Helen Creek canyon**. Ahead is Cirque Peak, rising above (north of) Helen Lake. Dolomite Peak is east across the valley. A rough stretch of trail briefly wiggles down and around the foot of a rockslide. At 5 km (3.1 mi) hop across Helen Creek.

At 6 km (3.7 mi), 2372 m (7780 ft) reach **Helen Lake**. Moderate-paced hikers will be here in 1½ hours. The trail skirts the right (east) side of the lake, then switchbacks up to crest a ridge at 2500 m (8200 ft), 7 km (4.3 mi). This is the **highpoint** of the trip, unless you continue up Cirque Peak. East, below you, is skinny Lake Katherine in a desolate basin (skip below for directions). Dolomite Pass is northeast. The Waputik Mountains and Wapta Icefield are southwest.

Aiming for Cirque Peak? From Helen Lake, switchback up toward the ridge, as described above. Where the trail bends right (southeast), ascend straight up a rough route leading directly to the ridgetop. Turn left (north) to face the peak. You can see two ways of reaching the main scree slope that leads to the summit: (1) Angle left, then scramble up the rock band to the middle of the ridgeline; (2) Detour right, around the rock band, past a tarn, to the southeast-facing scree slope and slog up the bootbeaten track. This second option appears easier but is more tedious. Stick to the ridgeline.

Lake Katherine

Either way, from the ridge above Helen Lake, it takes about one hour to surmount the main scree slope and reach the 2993-m (9817-ft) summit of **Cirque Peak**. Total distance from the trailhead: 8 km (5 mi). Southwest, turquoise Bow Lake is 1052 m (3452 ft) below you. The Wapta Icefield is draped above and beyond Crowfoot Mtn. To the north, you can survey much of Dolomite Creek valley. Rugged, grey, unnamed peaks are east and northeast. Southeast is ice-capped 3394-m (11,132-ft) Mt. Hector. The Helen Lake basin and meadows are south.

Hikers who crest the ridge above Helen Lake but decline to continue the ascent to Cirque Peak have another option. The trail beyond initiates a rough, wild backpacking adventure into the Dolomite Creek and Siffleur River valleys, which are linked to the Fish Lakes (Trip 89) by Pipestone Pass (Trip 81). You can, of course, simply follow it a short distance. From the ridgecrest, the trail descends generally east. It skirts the north shore of **Lake Katherine** at 8 km (5 mi), 2387 m (7829 ft), where you'll likely enjoy the solitude that you perhaps didn't find at Helen Lake.

TRIP 9

Caldron Lake

LOCATION	Banff National Park
ROUND TRIP	16 km (10 mi)
ELEVATION GAIN	685 m (2247 ft) going in 340 m (1115 ft) coming out
KEY ELEVATIONS	trailhead 2070 m (6790 ft) highpoint 2400 m (7870 ft), lake 2350 m (7708 ft)
HIKING TIME	7 hours
DIFFICULTY	moderate
MAPS	page 494; Gem Trek *Bow Lake & Saskatchewan Crossing*; Blaeberry River 82 N/10

OPINION

Eye of newt, tail of yak, make these hikers burn to come back. Imbibe of Caldron Lake, and you're under its spell. You'll find this powerful alpine brew hidden among the Waputik Mountains, near the Wapta Icefield, beneath striking peaks and glaciers, in a seldom-visited rock-and-tundra basin, at the end of a sketchy but discernable route. Later, you'll find it deep in the folds of your memory.

This journey into the wild begins at a viewpoint visited daily by waves of tourists. They come and go, unaware of what they've missed. Caldron Lake's bewitching atmosphere is preserved because this is not an official trail, the route is unannounced by signs, and the trip immediately requires a sharp, long descent forbidding to camcorder-toting tourists. Be glad of it.

From the Peyto Lake viewpoint, the route drops you into another world, or at least the post-apocalypse era of this one. Water, both frozen and gushing, has cleansed and simplified the valley. It's chaotically beautiful. You'll cross glacial outwash flats and hike beside a raging stream whose infancy you can sense in its rambunctious eagerness. Then you'll climb the snaking spine of a moraine and brave a precipitous traverse; both demand focused awareness. Finally, you'll ease into the hanging valley of Caldron Lake and fall under its alchemic influence.

Come here after late July, when the traverse is likely to be snowfree. Acrophobes will recoil at this final obstacle even when it's dry. For a comprehensive view of Caldron Lake and its soaring, icy backdrop, allow a couple hours to continue around the north shore.

Peyto Glacier, from route to Caldron Lake

FACT

By Vehicle

Drive the Icefields Parkway 16.5 km (10.2 mi) south of Waterfowl Lakes campground, or 4.9 km (3 mi) north of the Num-ti-jah Lodge / Bow Glacier turnoff on the north side of Bow Lake. At Bow Summit, turn southwest and follow the paved access road 0.5 km (0.3 mi) to the Peyto Lake viewpoint main parking lot, at 2070 m (6790 ft).

On Foot

Walk the signed, paved path about 0.4 km (0.25 mi) to the **viewing platform** overlooking Peyto Lake. Stop here, at 2135 m (7000 ft), to see Peyto Lake and survey the route to Caldron Lake. It's all visible. After dropping to Peyto Lake, the route heads up-valley southwest across the outwash flats and over the forested ridge toward Peyto Glacier. It then ascends the moraine on the right (west) side of the valley and traverses above the double waterfall to enter the Caldron Lake basin. The lake remains hidden from view until shortly before you reach it.

From the viewing platform, return to the paved path and turn right. Go 40 m/yd along the fence at the edge of the slope, then turn right onto a rough trail descending steeply into forest. Where the trail departs the paved path, there might be a sign urging glacier travelers to make hut reservations. The trail drops 290 m (950 ft) in 2.4 km (1.5 mi) via switchbacks to the broad outwash flats at the south end of **Peyto Lake** (1845 m / 6050 ft). The descent takes about 30 minutes.

Angle southwest across the flats. Aim for the **forested ridge** that juts toward the stream. Cross the ridge on a cairned path. South of the ridge, cross narrower, rocky flats. Stay on the left (east) side of the stream. Head upstream (generally south) following a few cairns. Clamber along the canyon wall, just above the roaring water. A cable might still be in place to assist you on a particularly steep, smooth slab.

At 5.4 km (3.3 mi) cross to the west bank on a **bridge** with a hand cable. Turn right (north). About 300 m (328 yd) downstream, the route begins climbing through boulders. It soon hooks back south onto the **lateral moraine**. Ascend the narrow path along its spine, which curves southwest. Views improve as you rapidly gain elevation. Peyto Glacier is south. Dragonback Glacier, on 3065-m (10,053-ft) Mt. Thompson, is southeast.

Two cairned routes split near the top of the moraine. One proceeds south toward Peyto Glacier. Follow the other one right, gradually curving northwest. Where the route is not evident, continue ascending on rock and heather, approaching the precipice to your right. Then traverse the path bootbeaten into the ochre-coloured scree just above the cliff band. (This is the cliff that the double waterfall spills over. You saw it from the Peyto Lake viewing platform.) The path, if not obscured by snow, is obvious. But it's narrow and on a steep slope. Be careful. Though the traverse takes only a few minutes, a stumble could be fatal. If the path is snowcovered, do not proceed without an ice axe and experience using it. This is the **highpoint** of the route: 2400 m (7870 ft). North is 2917-m (9570-ft) Caldron Peak.

At about 7.5 km (4.6 mi), glimpse Caldron Lake northwest. Beyond the lake is 3095-m (10,154-ft) Mistaya Mtn. As you continue, the glacier on Peyto Peak reveals itself above the headwall south of the lake.

To fully appreciate the **Caldron Lake** environs, including the north face of 2970-m (9742-ft) Peyto Peak, descend through boulders to the east shore at 8 km (5.1 mi), 2350 m (7708 ft), then proceed right, around the north shore. From here on, wandering is fruitful in all directions.

Caldron Lake

TRIP 10

Upper Brazeau Canyon / Cataract Pass

LOCATION	Banff National Park
ROUND TRIP	26 km (16.1 mi) to pass
ELEVATION GAIN	370 m (1214 ft) to Cataract Lake 640 m (2100 ft) to pass
KEY ELEVATIONS	trailhead 1860 m (6100 ft) lake 2215 m (7265 ft), pass 2485 m (8150 ft)
HIKING TIME	7 to 9 hours for lake, 8 to 10 for pass
DIFFICULTY	moderate
MAPS	page 496; Gem Trek *Columbia Icefield*; Columbia Icefield 83 C/3

OPINION

Striding into Cataract Pass adds an exhilarating climax to this journey. But it's upper Brazeau canyon, en route, that earns the *Premier* rating. It's like no place else in the range.

Long ago, near the canyon mouth, a massive chunk of the northeast wall sheered off and came crashing down. The chaotic boulder debris, much of it a striking salmon colour, rests alongside soft, lush, green grass, on the utterly flat banks of the Brazeau River headwaters. Here, freshly liberated from ice, the river is a shallow, languidly hypnotic, milky turquoise stream. It's this bizarre juxtaposition of elements, colours, textures and angles that makes upper Brazeau canyon a unique, transfixing sight.

Cataract Lake, as we call it, is unnamed on maps. Along with two other lesser lakes, it rests in the barren uppermost reaches of the canyon, beneath a glacier-mantled headwall. The setting is austerely beautiful. But if you have time and energy, carry on—up the steep route to Cataract Pass. Your reward will be two aerial views: (1) of the enthralling upper Brazeau canyon and its surrounding peaks, and (2) far down the other side of the pass, into forested Cataract Creek canyon. What you probably won't see are people. With no established trail traversing it, Cataract Pass is lonely indeed. The solitude here is as stirring as the vista.

The mouth of upper Brazeau canyon virtually swallows Nigel Pass. After enjoying the scenic hike to Nigel, you'll turn off the main trail, onto the upper Brazeau route. It's initially obvious but is infrequently cairned through several huge piles of mammoth boulders. Not that you'll get lost, even if you make your way independently of the directions below. The canyon is narrow and short. Just keep working your way southeast, along the canyon's northeast side. Near Cataract Lake, a route reappears—spurting up the scree slope to Cataract Pass.

Upper Brazeau River canyon

After a winter of normal snowfall, wait until late July before striking out for Cataract Pass. By then, enough snow should have melted to reveal the final ascent route. If it's visible, you'll be walking on dry scree, which is safer and easier than on snow. Should the steepest pitch be icy, you'll be scrambling on all fours.

From the Brazeau River crossing immediately below Nigel Pass, moderate-paced hikers reach Cataract Lake, at the foot of Cataract Pass, in about two hours. They ascend from the lake to the pass in about 30 minutes. Regardless of pace, most people will want at least 1½ hours along the way to sit and appreciate their good fortune at being here.

FACT

By Vehicle

Follow the directions in Trip 33 to the Nigel Pass trailhead, at 1860 m (6100 ft).

On Foot

At a glance, such detailed directions might seem to suggest that hiking to Cataract Pass is a complex endeavour. It's not. If you have even a little experience navigating cross-country, directions might be superfluous. Just make your way up-canyon to the obvious pass. Simple. But if you're less than supremely confident and would appreciate some help, no worries. That's what all these details are for.

Start by hiking 7.2 km (4.5 mi) to **Nigel Pass**, as described in Trip 33. Here, at 2195 m (7200 ft), you'll leave Banff National Park and enter Jasper National Park. Dominating yet unnamed, the anvil-shaped, 3035-m (9951-ft) peak left (northwest) above the pass will remain visible as you probe upper Brazeau canyon. From the pass, the trail drops to a crossing of the **Brazeau River**, at 2180 m (7150 ft). The unbridged river is shallow—easily forded, usually rockhoppable. (Cool word, huh?)

On the northeast bank, the main trail—indicated by a yellow blaze on a tree—ascends left (north). That's the way to Jonas Pass (Trip 92). For upper Brazeau canyon, follow the Brazeau upstream by forking right (southeast) onto a path bootbeaten into grass and heather. You might see grass-of-Parnassus here (five white petals with lime lines), as well as shrubby cinquefoil. Your general direction of travel all the way to the pass will remain southeast, following a route that stays on the northeast side of this drainage.

Several minutes upstream from the crossing, the river is slower, deeper, and the water is a milky turquoise due to glacial silt. Uniform, grassy banks give the appearance of a canal. Soon angle left (east), away from the water. Follow cairns through a **bouldery gap**. You're now at the bottom of an enormous slide, where a massive chunk of the canyon wall sheered off and came crashing down. You'll be negotiating slide debris much of the way into **upper Brazeau canyon**.

After the second boulder pile, drop to the water's edge and proceed upstream on a faint path. Elephant's head and yellow paintbrush grow in the wet grass here. After the third boulder pile, arrive at a small, flat, strip of grass. At the fourth boulder pile, avoid rough rocks by walking 150 m (165 yd) along the water's edge, on a narrow (20 cm / 8 in) band of dirt and grass. Then cross the stream to willow-and-grass flats. You've hiked about 45 minutes since crossing the Brazeau River beneath

Cataract Lake, just below Cataract Pass

Looking toward Nigel Pass, from mouth of Upper Brazeau River canyon

Nigel Pass. Despite all the ups and downs through the boulder piles, you're now at 2219 m (7278 ft)—a mere 39 m (128 ft) higher than the river crossing.

Pass a **confluence**. The main stream pours through a rocky cleft here, and a small tributary joins it. Stay in the vegetation, left of the tributary, north of the cleft. Look for a cairn on a small rise. A faint path resumes east-southeast. A gentle ascent ensues. Aim for the gap 0.4 km (0.25 mi) up-canyon. In another five minutes, negotiate boulders to reach a level streambed lined with broad, flat, shingle rocks. If the water is shallow, hop up the streambed.

Cross mud flats left of the main stream. The steep route to the pass starts at a patch of heather and dryas. It climbs southeast, up the left side of the tan scree. Reach the route by crossing a **moraine** composed of striped sedimentary rocks. Go right briefly to the top of the rocks to overlook **Cataract Lake** (unnamed on maps). It's at 2215 m (7265 ft). The route to the pass is northeast of it. On the ascent, you'll glimpse two smaller lakes in the upper reaches of the canyon; one is above the cascades west of Cataract Lake.

The route to the pass, cairned the whole way, gains 270 m (885 ft). In the middle, where the grade steepens to 45° and the route narrows to the width of a single boot, caution and concentration are necessary. Crest 2485-m (8150-ft) **Cataract Pass** at 13 km (8.1 mi). A sign here indicates the boundary partitioning Jasper National Park from the White Goat Wilderness Area.

After descending back into upper Brazeau canyon, swift hikers can return to Nigel Pass in 1¼ hours, and from there to the trailhead in 1½ hours.

TRIP 11

Parker Ridge

LOCATION	Banff National Park
ROUND TRIP	4 km (2.5 mi) to saddle, 11 km (6.8 mi) up ridgecrest
ELEVATION GAIN	272 m (892 ft) to saddle 593 m (1945 ft) up ridgecrest
KEY ELEVATIONS	trailhead 2010 m (6560 ft) saddle 2282 m (7485 ft) ridgecrest 2550 m (8364 ft)
HIKING TIME	1 to 2 hours for saddle, 4 to 5 for ridgecrest
DIFFICULTY	easy
MAPS	page 496; Gem Trek *Columbia Icefield;* Columbia Icefield 83 C/3

OPINION

The tall, slender towers on a mosque are called minarets. Their needlepoint shape was intended to pierce the sky, allowing the prayers of faithful Muslims to rise heavenward to Allah. Mountain devotees might attribute a similar spiritual purpose to the peaks they worshipfully hike and climb. If so, here's a fitting place to loft your reverent thoughts into the firmament: Parker Ridge. Though nearly as accessible as a church, it's in the heart of the Canadian Rockies, overlooking the Saskatchewan Glacier and surrounded by 3000-m (9840-ft) peaks.

Talk about peaky. The nearby Columbia Icefield, which feeds the Saskatchewan Glacier, is ringed by eleven of the twenty-two highest peaks in the range. Parker Ridge is a shoulder of one of them—3493-m (11,452-ft) Mt. Athabasca—so you'll certainly see it, because you'll be on it. With minimal scrambling, you can attain a gratifying height, as well as solitude. Simply continue beyond the saddle where the trail ends.

Even if you're driving the Icefields Parkway with no intention of hiking, stop at the Parker Ridge trailhead and amble up to the saddle for a walloping view of pure, raw wilderness. High in the tundra, above the upper North Saskatchewan River valley, you'll have a parapent pilot's view of the Saskatchewan Glacier flowing off the colossal Columbia Icefield. You also might see white, fluffy puffballs—mountain goats—along the ridge or below its south side.

Unless you're here early or late in the day, you won't be alone. Parker Ridge is painfully popular. From the highway, you can see hikers atop the saddle. From the trail, you can see and hear vehicles on the highway. Tentative, novice hikers will find that comforting. The rest of us must contain our annoyance. Evade others by hiking before 9 a.m. Starting after 4 p.m. also works, but not for photography; you'll be aiming your camera into the sun. Only if you keep hiking up the ridgecrest, past trail's end in the saddle, are you guaranteed no obligation to chirp "hello" every few minutes.

Parker Ridge

Though you won't be far from your vehicle, pack windproof clothing, warm gloves, and an insulating hat. Otherwise a chilly wind atop the ridge could force you to descend too soon. After wandering the valley below with your eyes, you might want to explore it on foot; check out Saskatchewan Glacier (Trip 47).

FACT

By Vehicle

Drive the Icefields Parkway north 41 km (25.4 mi) from Saskatchewan River Crossing, or south 4.2 km (2.6 mi) from the Banff-Jasper boundary at Sunwapta Pass. The trailhead parking lot is on the south side of the highway, just east of Hilda Creek Hostel, at 2000 m (6560 ft).

On Foot

Starting between the avalanche-warning sign (left) and the alpine-info sign (right), the broad trail leads south into open forest. After bending east, it begins switchbacking—among scattered alpine fir, through heather, and eventually across open tundra. Initially you might see paintbrush, fleabane, and deep-pink willow-herb. Hilda Peak, a glacier-draped satellite of Mt. Athabasca, is visible west-northwest.

Roaming Parker Ridge, high above the Icefields Parkway

Reach the **saddle** on Parker Ridge at 2 km (1.2 mi), 2275 m (7462 ft). The ascent is steep, so hiking times vary: 30 minutes to one hour. Views en route are grand.

Atop the saddle, the panorama explodes. The Saskatchewan Glacier is southwest, far below. To quickly attain a better view of it, follow the trail left (southeast) about 0.5 km (0.3 mi), descending slightly along the south side of the ridge. Mounts Athabasca and Andromeda are west, rising above the north side of the glacier. East-southeast, across the highway, is Cirrus Mtn.

The other option, from where you first reached the saddle, is to go straight (southwest), following a wide path up a knoll. In seven minutes, the path divides. Right is less steep; both forks rejoin shortly. Even in this climatically brutal environment, wildflowers survive. Look for moss campion (tiny fuchsia flowers in a green cushion), saxifrage (purple), alpine forget-me-nots (baby blue), mountain avens (white), and alpine cinquefoil (yellow). Where the path fades among the rocks, follow cairns several minutes farther to a crude wind-shelter crowning the 2305-m (7560-ft) **knoll**. Wilcox Pass (Trip 20) is visible northwest. Wilcox Peak rises on its left (west) side, Nigel Peak on the right (east). Nigel Pass (Trip 33) is north-northeast.

Want to proceed up the ridgecrest toward Mt. Athabasca? From the wind shelter, drop southwest—sans trail—off the knoll. Cross heather and scree, heading generally southwest, into a **depression**. Bottom-out at 2252 m (7388 ft). Then begin ascending again, mostly on heather. Go right (west) and pick up a bootbeaten route along the narrow, rocky **ridgecrest**. After a dip, start the final, moderate ascent. About 5.5 km (3.4 mi) from the trailhead, reach 2550 m (8364 ft). Further progress is more arduous, requiring you to drop then re-ascend on steeper terrain.

The view here is splendid. South, across the headwaters of the North Saskatchewan River, a long cascade plummets off the 610-m (2000-ft) canyon wall. Southwest, past the Saskatchewan Glacier, you can see Castleguard Meadows—reached by a long plod through the Alexandra and Castleguard river valleys, or by traveling up the glacier tongue. Beyond the meadows is hulking Mt. Bryce. Northeast, visible above Nigel Pass, is the distinctive, sheer wall at the mouth of Cataract Canyon (Trip 10). Return the way you came. The saddle where you first crested Parker Ridge is one hour distant.

TRIP 12

Sherbrooke Lake / Niles Meadow

LOCATION	Yoho National Park
ROUND TRIP	6 km (3.7 mi) to lake 19.6 km (12.2 mi) to meadow
ELEVATION GAIN	197 m (646 ft) to lake 717 m (2352 ft) to meadow
KEY ELEVATIONS	trailhead 1615 m (5297 ft) lake 1812 m (5942 ft) meadow 2332 m (7650 ft)
HIKING TIME	2 hours for lake, 7 to 8 for meadow
DIFFICULTY	easy to lake, moderate to meadow
MAPS	page 500; Gem Trek *Lake Louise & Yoho*; Lake Louise 82 N/8

OPINION

Cascading water thunders over boulders. Your ear funnels the sound waves to three nearly microscopic bones. They begin throbbing. The vibrations resound on a fine membrane, causing fluids to tremble. Filaments respond, firing electric charges into your brain and—most mysteriously of all—sparking rapturous emotion. It's a physiological, psychological marvel, and you'll enjoy it repeatedly en route from Sherbrooke Lake to Niles Meadow. The trail is creekside much of the way. And, depending on time of year, you'll hike within earshot of ten or more cascades, several impressively big and thrillingly close.

But first you'll hike to Sherbrooke Lake. The trail is well maintained, the distance short, and the ascent gently graded, making this a sensible destination for parents wrangling children. The turquoise lake is pretty. But the setting isn't postcard material by Canadian Rockies lofty standards, and the vegetated shoreline begrudges visitation. So continue north, along the east shore. The trail hugs the water's edge, allowing you to appreciate the lake and gaze at the mountains ringing it.

As for those boisterous creeks and cascades, they begin just minutes beyond the lake's north shore. It's a short, moderate ascent through big timber, past the first crashing cascade, into an expansive meadow immediately above. Don't hike to Sherbrooke Lake without continuing at least this far. Visiting the meadow—an easy 1¾ hours from the trailhead—adds a scenic climax and a hint of adventure to a short outing. The views here outshine those at the lake. Small cascades will likely adorn the basin walls, enlivening the atmosphere with water music.

A little more than an hour from the spacious meadow, or a little more than three hours from the trailhead, you'll arrive at Niles Amphitheatre. Plan to drop your pack, pull up a rock, and break bread here. Seated on the grassy amphitheatre's west side, you can study the trail switchbacking up the southeast shoulder of Mt. Niles then traversing toward Niles Meadow.

Though it's tempting, don't turn around after lunching at the amphitheatre. It's only a 30-minute ascent to Niles Meadow, where the panorama explodes, as will your sense of accomplishment and fulfillment. You'll be high in the alpine zone, overlooking Sherbrooke Valley, with a view of southern Yoho's monster peaks.

Right. Now you can stop. But do so only if you must. A 40-minute ramble through alpine rubble will earn you the penultimate perch atop the saddle southwest of Mt. Niles. It overlooks the Daly Glacier—a tongue of the Waputik Icefield and the source of Takakkaw Falls. Or consider the 20-minute scree-slog up the southeast shoulder of Mt. Niles, for an aerial view of Niles Meadow and neighbouring Niles Creek basin.

FACT

By Vehicle

From Field, drive the Trans-Canada Hwy east 11.5 km (7.1 mi). Or, from the Alberta-B.C. boundary at the Great Divide, drive the Trans-Canada west 5.5 km (3.4 mi). From either approach, turn north—across from the west end of Wapta Lake—into the Wapta Lake Picnic Area, at 1615 m (5297 ft). It's 0.4 km (0.25 mi) west of West Louise Lodge.

On Foot

From the parking lot, walk east, into the picnic area. The trailhead is immediately north of the covered picnic shelter. Wapta Lake is visible across the highway. Follow the trail north, past the outhouse.

Within two minutes reach a signed **junction** at 1629 m (5344 ft). Right (east) descends to West Louise Lodge. Go left (west) for Sherbrooke Lake, Niles Meadow, and Paget lookout and peak.

About 25 minutes from the trailhead, reach a signed **junction** at 1.4 km (0.9 mi), 1771 m (5810 ft). Right (north-northeast) ascends to Paget Lookout in 2.2 km (1.4 mi) and Paget Peak beyond. Bear left (north-northwest) on the now level trail for Sherbrooke Lake (1.6 km / 1 mi farther) and Niles Meadow. Paget Peak is partly visible right (north-northeast) above the forest.

Pass the south end of **Sherbrooke Lake** after hiking about 50 minutes. Though the lake is within view, it's not yet easily accessible. Stay on the trail. Cross a series of footlogs bridging creeklets and runoff drainages. At 3 km (1.9 mi), an unmarked left (west) spur drops a few feet to the lake's southeast shore. Elevation: 1812 m (5942 ft).

Sherbrooke Lake usually offers hikers little or no room to relax on the shore. If the water level is low, you might find a sliver of sandy, rocky beach, but don't count on it. Expect the water's edge to be crowded with vegetation. The trail continues north, however, frequently grazing the east shore, affording unobstructed views across the turquoise lake and of the surrounding peaks. North-northwest, lording it over the head of the valley, is pointy, 2972-m (9748-ft) Mt. Niles. Rising abruptly from the west shore is 2695-m (8839-ft) Mt. Ogden. South-southwest, behind you, across the highway, are the 3073-m (10,082-ft) Cathedral Crags.

Sherbrooke Lake, Mt. Niles distant center

To Sherbrooke Lake, the trail is excellent. Continuing up-lake, the trail is rougher, more overgrown, but it's adequate and poses no obstacles. Near the lake's north end, cross a couple streams via footlogs. Round the **northeast shore** within 30 minutes of leaving the southeast shore. Here the panorama begins expanding south-southeast to include the multi-peaked, glacier-laden massif between Lake O'Hara and Lake Louise. These striking mountains will be increasingly visible as you hike up-valley.

Departing Sherbrooke Lake's northeast shore, the trail heads generally north. Enter a beautiful, mature forest and begin a moderate ascent beside the rushing inlet stream. Within five minutes, pass a thundering **cascade**. Above it, the trail levels at 1887 m (6188 ft) and soon enters a **spacious meadow**. Anyone hiking to Sherbooke Lake should continue this far; the extra distance and effort are nothing compared to the scenic reward. The view is 360°. Seasonal cascades plummet down the mountain walls, filling the meadow with water music. After crossing footlogs bridging the two streams in the meadow, re-enter forest at the meadow's north end. Hiking time from Sherbrooke Lake: 25 minutes.

Ascending gently, the trail is soon creekside again. Pass right of a second picturesque **cascade** about ten minutes from the spacious meadow. Just ten minutes farther, the forest reopens along the margins of the creek, granting views from the trail.

At 2000 m (6562 ft), about 25 minutes from the spacious meadow, rockhop a tributary streamlet. Just beyond, the trail veers left to a fallen log serving as a bridge to the creek's south bank. The trail then climbs slightly, turns right (west) and proceeds upstream.

Entering Niles Amphitheatre

After rockhopping another tributary streamlet, reach a bridge (broken but usable) conveying you back to the creek's north bank. Hiking time: about 40 minutes from the spacious meadow. The trail ascends upstream, west-northwest, at a moderate grade. Soon pass right of a third **cascade**, then re-enter forest.

Nearly an hour from the spacious meadow, pass a fourth exhilarating **cascade** that bounces down big rock slabs left of the trail. Mountains are again visible here. West is the ridge separating Sherbrooke Valley from popular Yoho Valley. East is the ridge separating Sherbrooke Valley from trackless Bath Creek Valley.

The trail steepens—for the first time so far—as it switchbacks above the fourth cascade. But it quickly pops out of the trees at 2155 m (7067 ft) revealing a **grand view** south-southeast back down Sherbrooke Valley. To the north, Niles Peak looms large.

After a brief level stretch, the trail curves north, eases into **Niles Amphitheatre**, and temporarily vanishes. The amphitheatre—2131 m (6990 ft) at its lowest point—is an attractive enclave, roughly the size of five football fields. A cascade graces the headwall, keeping the grassy floor moist. Hiking time: a little more than an hour from the spacious meadow; a little more than three hours from the trailhead.

Though enticing, the amphitheatre is not the day's objective. Niles Meadow is above treeline—on the chest of Mt. Niles. Strong hikers who depart the amphitheatre rested and eager can reach the alpine meadow in 30 minutes. The vastly improved panorama is well worth the additional effort. Follow the directions below.

The grassy, natural entryway, which you descended north into the mouth of the amphitheatre, leads to a flat, denuded area of scattered rocks. Stop here. Look right (northeast) at the forested shoulder of Mt. Niles. It's scarred with several gullies, the most prominent of which starts at a big, bald patch and drops almost to the amphitheatre floor. Go right (northeast), across the amphitheatre, toward that prominent gully.

Hop over the streams. Step through the squishy grass. Approaching the **prominent gully**, you'll see it's marked with a big cairn. From that cairn, ascend north-northeast through the gully. One minute up, reach a second, smaller cairn, where the gully has been crudely blocked off ahead. Turn right (east) here, exit the gully, and proceed onto a discernible trail. It climbs east briefly, then begins switchbacking generally northeast. The switchbacks soon end and the trail continues ascending north, out of the trees, toward Mt. Niles. It steadily dwindles to a path, then, having completed its service, fades altogether. Keep aiming for Mt. Niles.

Near 2287 m (7500 ft) expect to encounter a snowfield or, if it's receded, a stream draining one. Carefully kickstep or rockhop across and continue upward. The slope gradually eases, becoming nearly level at 2332 m (7650 ft). You've arrived at **Niles Meadow**. In addition to seeing more of everything you previously glimpsed en route, Mt. Temple now punctuates the horizon south-southeast.

Given sufficient daylight and the energy for further exploration, inquisitive hikers will find the **saddle southwest of Mt. Niles** an irresistible goal. It overlooks the Daly Glacier—a tongue of the Waputik Icefield and the source of Takakkaw Falls. For a shorter foray, zip up to the **southeast shoulder of Mt. Niles** and peer into Niles Creek basin.

At a moderate but steady pace, it takes three hours to hike from Niles Meadow back to the trailhead at the Wapta Lake Picnic Area on the Trans-Canada Hwy.

The Vice President presides over the Iceline (Trip 13)

TRIP 13
Iceline

LOCATION	Yoho National Park
ROUND TRIP	12.8 km (8 mi) to 21.1 km (13.1 mi)
ELEVATION GAIN	690 m (2265 ft)
KEY ELEVATIONS	trailhead 1520 m (4985 ft) highpoint 2210 m (7250 ft)
HIKING TIME	5 to 8 hours
DIFFICULTY	moderate
MAPS	page 497; Gem Trek *Lake Louise & Yoho*

OPINION

"One day's exposure to mountains is better than a cartload of books." John Muir said it. Yoho proves it. The park is smaller than others in the Canadian Rockies yet has the heaviest concentration of high-impact scenery. You'll survey a big chunk of it from the Iceline.

After a stiff climb past treeline, the trail undulates over rugged glacial moraine. Daly Glacier and 380-m (1246-ft) Takakkaw Falls are visible across the valley. *Takakkaw*, by the way, is a Stoney Indian word meaning *magnificent*. Emerald Glacier and the 800-m (2625-ft) west face of The Vice President are beside you. Fred Flintstone chaise lounges—rock slabs—invite you to sprawl and stare.

The Iceline's quick access to postcard scenery is no secret, so you won't be alone here. And, like most trails aiming for the alpine zone, this one's steep, but you might not notice. Bombardment by dazzling sights is a natural pain reliever.

Many people hike the Iceline out and back, as far as the highpoint. It's a 12.8 km (7.9 mi) round trip. Others about-face earlier, satisfied with the vantage beneath Emerald Glacier. You can also choose one of two loops. Neither includes any "must see" sights, but both reveal more of the area:

(1) Drop past Lake Celeste on the old Highline trail, then descend to Yoho Valley (Trip 72) for the return. You'll quickly exit the realm of rock and ice, pass through meadows, and enter forest. This loop is 4.2 km (2.6 mi) longer than a round trip to the highpoint.

(2) Continue northwest on the Iceline into Little Yoho Valley, then descend to Yoho Valley for the return. You'll see another tarn, the pyramids of The Vice President and President from their north sides, and the pretty subalpine meadows of Little Yoho. This loop is 8.3 km (5.1 mi) longer than a round trip to the highpoint, yet adds only 30 m (100 ft) of elevation gain. A further extension—detouring from Little Yoho up to Kiwetinok Pass (Trip 90)—is also possible for swift dayhikers, but few include that unless backpacking.

The Iceline

FACT

By Vehicle

From the Yoho Park Visitor Centre, in Field, B.C., drive the Trans-Canada Hwy northeast 3.7 km (2.3 mi). Or, from the Alberta-B.C. boundary, drive the Trans-Canada southwest 12.5 km (7.8 mi). From either approach, turn north onto Yoho Valley Road. In 12.5 km (7.8 mi) pass the trailhead on the left, near the Whiskey Jack youth hostel, at 1520 m (4985 ft). Hikers must park in the Takakkaw Falls lot at 13.2 km (8.2 mi). Walk the trail from the south end of the parking lot, paralleling the road, back to the Yoho Pass trailhead by the hostel.

On Foot

Ascend switchbacks through forest. Keep right at the 1-km (0.6-mi) and 1.2-km (0.7-mi) forks. At 2.5 km (1.6 mi) turn right again, onto the Iceline trail. Left leads south to Yoho lake and pass.

The Iceline ascends northwest, soon emerging from trees. Traverse rocky slopes with Emerald Glacier left (west) above you. Hop across a couple streams. The trail undulates over moraine, ascending steadily to a **junction** at 5.7 km (3.5 mi). Left continues northwest over the Iceline highpoint, then into Little Yoho Valley (Trip 90). Right (north) descends past Lake Celeste.

ICELINE HIGHPOINT: 12.8-KM (8-MI) ROUND TRIP

From the 5.7-km (3.5-mi) junction, stay left and proceed northwest to the 2210-m (7250-ft) **highpoint** on a moraine at 6.4 km (4 mi). Having climbed 690 m (2265 ft) from the trailhead, you're now in a rocky amphitheatre beneath Emerald Glacier. The 3066-m (10,059-ft) Vice President is visible southwest. Northwest, across the Little Yoho Valley, are Whaleback Mtn (right) and Isolated Peak (left). Return the way you came.

ICELINE / LITTLE YOHO VALLEY / YOHO VALLEY: 21.1-KM (13.1-MI) LOOP

From the 6.4-km (4-mi) highpoint, descend to a blue tarn chilled by ice slabs. The trail heads generally northwest. Enter subalpine forest near 8.5 km (5.3 mi). The north side of the President Range is visible south.

Reach a junction at 10.5 km (6.5 mi), 2075 m (6805 ft), just south of the **Little Yoho River**, in **Little Yoho Valley**. The faint trail left (southwest) heads upstream to Kiwetinok lake and pass (Trip 90). For now, bear right, cross the **bridge** at 11 km (6.8 mi), and arrive at **Stanley Mitchell Hut**. Proceed left (west) 0.3 km (0.2 mi) for **Little Yoho campground**.

From the hut, the trail exiting Little Yoho Valley descends east, staying above the river's north side. At 14 km (8.7 mi), the right fork ascends past Lake Celeste. Stay straight. Only 100 m (110 yd) farther, at 1905 m (6250 ft), the left fork ascends the Whaleback (Trip 90). Stay straight again. At 14.7 km (9.1 mi), the left fork leads past Marpole Lake to Twin Falls Chalet. Stay straight again.

Intersect the **Yoho Valley trail** (Trip 72) at 16.3 km (10.1 mi). Left leads to Twin Falls campground. Right heads down-valley southeast to the Takakkaw Falls trailhead at 21.1 km (13.1 mi).

ICELINE / LAKE CELESTE / YOHO VALLEY: 17-KM (10.5-MI) LOOP

At the 5.7-km (3.5-mi) junction, turn right and descend into subalpine forest. Round the east side of small **Lake Celeste**. Immediately after crossing the bridged Little Yoho River, intersect the **Little Yoho River trail**, above the north bank, at 9.9 km (6.1 mi). Left (west) ascends into Little Yoho Valley. Turn right. In 100 m (110 yd), the left fork ascends the Whaleback (Trip 90). Stay straight. At 10.6 km (6.6 mi), the left fork leads past Marpole Lake to Twin Falls Chalet. Stay straight again.

Intersect the **Yoho Valley trail** (Trip 72) at 12.2 km (7.6 mi). Left leads to Twin Falls campground. Right heads down-valley southeast to the Takakkaw Falls trailhead at 17 km (10.5 mi).

TRIP 14
Lake O'Hara Alpine Circuit

LOCATION	Yoho National Park
LOOP	9.8 to 12.4 km (6 to 7.7 mi)
ELEVATION GAIN	495 m (1625 ft)
KEY ELEVATIONS	trailhead 2035 m (6675 ft) Wiwaxy Gap 2535 m (8315 ft) Opabin Lake 2285 m (7495 ft) All Souls' Prospect 2475 m (8118 ft)
HIKING TIME	6 to 7 hours
DIFFICULTY	moderate
MAPS	page 498; Gem Trek *Lake O'Hara*

OPINION

"So what's your favourite hike in the Canadian Rockies?"

It's a question that makes us cringe and squirm as if we'd just walked face first into a spider web.

Anointing *the* trail seems to belittle a range whose distinctive attributes include a wealth of superlative hiking options.

But if pressed by someone who insists on an answer and is willing to tolerate our elaborate equivocations, we'll eventually state one of our ten or so front runners—a list that continues evolving but always includes the Lake O'Hara Alpine Circuit.

Yoho National Park's Lake O'Hara region is achingly beautiful, which is why there's a locked gate on the access road, a shuttle bus, and a restriction on the number of visitors. Otherwise popularity would have destroyed it.

You're a solitudinous soul? You'll still find O'Hara too crowded. You want to experience the quintessence of the Canadian Rockies within eight hours? Hike the O'Hara region's most ambitious and gratifying trail: the Alpine Circuit.

An acrophobe's nightmare, the Alpine Circuit links high-elevation routes to create an alpine-zone loop clinging to the walls of towering mountains. After the initial, taxing grunt up to Wiwaxy Gap, however, the minimal-but-adequate trail makes no serious demands. Ups and downs are few, so you can appreciate nonstop marvelous scenery: cascades, pocket meadows, turquoise lakes, and thousand-meter cliffs creased with snow-filled fissures.

The Alpine Circuit showcases the art of trail building. The cliffside paths were lovingly crafted by the Italian stonemason and zealous alpinist Lawrence Grassi. He was the Park warden at O'Hara for many years. His Old World heritage and his passion for these New World mountains moved him to create a remarkable walkway for all who love wilderness. An American botanist, Dr. George Link, also deserves gratitude for his extensive mapping and trail building in the O'Hara region. He spent most of his summers here—exploring, absorbing, and making it easier for the rest of us to do the same.

You can shorten the Alpine Circuit, but don't do so by eliminating Wiwaxy Gap, Huber Ledges, or Yukness Ledges. That would eviscerate the venture. Ascend to Wiwaxy, descend to Oesa, then follow Yukness Ledges to Opabin Plateau. At the plateau, you can shorten the trip by descending northwest, directly back to Lake O'Hara, thus skipping Opabin Lake and the All Souls' route on Mt. Schaffer. Ideally, include both in your itinerary. If you must cut one, make it Opabin Lake. All Souls' is longer and more arduous, but grants new, aerial views of the entire region.

Though cairns and paint-blazes on rocks mark the Alpine Circuit, bring a good map to keep yourself oriented. The trip is not inherently dangerous unless snow obscures the trail or visibility is poor due to weather or sunset. No scrambling is required, but you'll often be a step away from sharp drops. Because it's above tree-line, pack for all possibilities: hot sun to freezing rain. Sturdy boots are a must.

The Alpine Circuit sounds too demanding for you? Consider a shorter, easier, O'Hara introduction. Hike directly to Opabin Plateau or Lake Oesa. These trails are less spectacular, more crowded, but both destinations are on the Alpine Circuit. We describe other O'Hara region trails in Trips 15 through 19. None is as challenging or rewarding as the Alpine Circuit, but you'll want to hike several if you're here for a few days.

Fit, experienced hikers can complete the Alpine Circuit on a daytrip into O'Hara. The trick is to catch the first bus in and the last bus out: 8:30 a.m. and 6:30 p.m. A better plan is to stay overnight at the campground, hut, or lodge. Two days here ensures you can also hike to Lake McArthur—another premier trail that will further inhibit your ability to answer that vexing question: "So what's your favourite hike in the Canadian Rockies?"

FACT

Before your trip

To protect the Lake O'Hara region, Yoho Park restricted visitation and excluded private vehicles. Hence the locked gate on the access road, and the advent of the shuttle bus. Skip below for details about riding the bus.

Want to stay at Lake O'Hara Lodge? For current prices and reservations, call (250) 343-6418, or (403) 678-4110 in winter. By mid-March, the lodge is usually booked full for July, August, and September.

Want to stay at Elizabeth Parker Hut? Check the current price and make reservations with the Alpine Club of Canada. See *Information Sources.*

Intend to camp? For the current price and reservations, call the Yoho Park Visitor Centre: (250) 343-6433. The campground is open mid-June to early October. Don't have a campsite reserved? Every day, at the Visitor Centre in Field, three to five camping permits are allotted for the following day: first come, first served. So, go there the day before you want to enter O'Hara. The Visitor Centre opens at 9 a.m. (mountain daylight savings time), but arrive by 8 a.m. to get in line.

Camping at O'Hara is no guarantee of a tranquil night, for several reasons. The campground is big. It's usually full. Everyone arrives by bus, without schlepping their gear. And most of the trails, though highly scenic, are not overly taxing. That means lots of happy, energetic campers who, if unaware, are likely to violate your right to silence. Please keep your own volume low. Be quiet after 10:30 p.m. In search of serenity, choose a campsite higher up the slope, away from the communal area.

Yukness Ledges, Alpine Circuit

By Bus

Shuttle bus service to and from Lake O'Hara is available mid-June to early October. For current fares and schedules, or to reserve a seat (up to three months in advance), call the Yoho Park Visitor Centre: (250) 343-6433. Inbound buses depart the parking lot at 8:30 a.m., 10:30 a.m., 4:30 p.m., and 7:30 p.m. Outbound buses depart Lake O'Hara Lodge at 7:30 a.m., 9:30 a.m., 3:30 p.m., and 6:30 p.m. That's mountain daylight savings time. Daytrippers should catch a morning bus, preferably the first one. Dogs are not allowed.

Don't have bus reservations? Every day, at the Visitor Centre in Field, six bus seats are allotted for the following day: first come, first served. So, go there the day before you want to enter O'Hara. The Visitor Centre opens at 9 a.m. (mountain daylight savings time), but arrive by 8 a.m. to get in line. The purchase limit is two bus tickets per person.

As a last resort, try standby. Cancellations are filled the day of departure. So, by 7:30 a.m. on the morning you want to enter O'Hara, go to the bus-stop shelter, near the parking lot, and hope you get lucky. The worse the weather, the better your chance.

Maps

Buy a detailed map of the Alpine Circuit. They're available at the Yoho Park Visitor Centre, in Field, and at Le Relais day-use shelter, across from the warden cabin, near the northwest end of Lake O'Hara.

By Vehicle

From the Trans-Canada Hwy, between Field and Lake Louise village, turn south onto Hwy 1-A. If you're driving northeast, the turnoff is 1.6 km (1 mi) east of the lodge at Wapta Lake, which is atop Kicking Horse Pass. If you're driving southwest, the turnoff is 3 km (2 mi) west of the signed Continental Divide.

From either approach, cross the railroad tracks then turn right (west). Proceed 0.8 km (0.5 mi) to the parking lot. The 11-km (6.8 mi) dirt road to Lake O'Hara leads south from here; access is restricted by a locked gate. This is where you catch the shuttle bus. The Cataract Valley hiking trail to Lake O'Hara starts here too. Mountain bikes are prohibited on the road and the trail.

Arriving

See Lake O'Hara Region (Trips 15 to 19).

On Foot

Start where the outlet stream departs the northwest corner of Lake O'Hara, at 2035 m (6675 ft). Here's how to get there. From the lodge, hike the lakeshore trail north. From the campground, cross to the east side of the road and follow the trail heading southeast, along the right (west) side of the outlet stream, 0.5 km (0.3 mi) toward the lake. From the hut, head east to the road and continue past the warden cabin.

Cross the bridged outlet stream. Head generally east. In 300 m (328 yd) fork left (northeast) toward Wiwaxy Gap. For the next 1.6 km (1 mi) climb steeply 500 m (1640 ft) on a narrow path to emerge above treeline. Reach **Wiwaxy Gap** at 2 km (1.2 mi), 2535 m (8315 ft). It hunkers between the Wiwaxy Peaks (west) and 3368-m (11,047-ft) Mt. Huber (east-northeast). From this aerie, you can survey most of the Lake O'Hara region. North of the gap, you can see Cataract Brook valley and the peaks above Kicking Horse valley.

From the gap, the route drops gradually southeast, along the cliff ledges of Mt. Huber, 1.7 km (1.1 mi) to Lake Oesa. You'll see the lake as you descend. At 3.7 km (2.3 mi) reach a rocky knoll overlooking **Lake Oesa**. The shore is 200 m (220 yd) farther east, at 2275 m (7462 ft). The Alpine Circuit crosses the Lake Oesa trail (Trip 15) at this knoll.

North is Mt. Huber. Behind it is 3464-m (11,362-ft) Mt. Victoria, her spine arching southeast to join 3423-m (11,227-ft) Mt. Lefroy. Just over the ridge (out of sight) Victoria Glacier rumbles down toward Lake Louise. Due east is 3283-m (10,768-ft) Glacier Peak. Yukness Mtn forms the cliffs on the south side of Lake Oesa.

Leaving Oesa, the Alpine Circuit drops to cross the outlet stream, then

Huber Ledges, en route to Lake Oesa

ascends right (west). It curves around Mt. Yukness and heads south. Contour the rock slabs and catwalks of the **Yukness Ledge route**, then descend to meadowy Opabin Plateau. Reach the east side of Hungabee Lake at 6.4 km (4 mi). Proceed southeast to reach **Opabin Lake** at 6.8 km (4.2 mi), 2285 m (7495 ft).

Yukness Mtn is north, Ringrose Peak east, Hungabee Mtn southeast, Opabin Glacier south, and Schaffer Ridge southwest. From Opabin Lake, follow the trail right (southwest), curving northwest and gently descending. Bear left (northwest) at the fork as you pass Hungabee Lake again, this time on its west side.

Reach a junction at 7.7 km (4.8 mi). Straight (north) descends 1.4 km (0.9 mi) directly back to Lake O'Hara. Left on the lakeshore trail leads to Lake O'Hara Lodge, for a total loop distance of 9.8 km (6.1 mi).

Want to continue the Alpine Circuit to additional lofty viewpoints? Go left at the 7.7-km (4.8-mi) junction. Cross a creek and immediately turn right (north) on a spur. Reach **Opabin Prospect** at 8.4 km (5.2 mi). It overlooks Mary Lake and Lake O'Hara. The Wiwaxy Peaks are north. Mt. Huber is northeast.

From Opabin Prospect, curve south to a **junction** at 8.8 km (5.5 mi), 2210 m (7250 ft). Right descends steeply north on the West Opabin trail. In 1 km (0.6 mi) it reaches another junction just north of Mary Lake. Right leads to Lake O'Hara in a few minutes. Left on the lakeshore trail leads northwest to Lake O'Hara Lodge, for a total loop distance of 10.2 km (6.3 mi).

Want to continue the Alpine Circuit to additional lofty viewpoints? Proceed straight (southwest) at the 8.8-km (5.5-mi) junction, onto the **All Souls' alpine route**. It curves northwest, traversing the nose of Mt. Schaffer. It's a rugged, rocky route providing yet another perspective of the Lake O'Hara region. Ascend 275 m (900 ft) in 1 km (0.6 mi) to **All Souls' Prospect**, at 2475 m (8118 ft). The route then descends steeply to reach Schaffer Lake at 10.9 km (6.8 mi), 2215 m (7265 ft).

Still have energy to pursue views? Just before **Schaffer Lake**, turn right (northeast) on the rocky Big Larches trail. In 1.1 km (0.7 mi), turn left. Soon after, go right to reach Le Relais day-use shelter, across from the warden cabin, near the northwest end of Lake O'Hara. Total loop distance: 12.4 km (7.7 mi).

Had enough views? Here's a more pastoral return that's a few minutes shorter. Ignore the Big Larches trail and continue the final 100 m (110 yd) to **Schaffer Lake**. Turn right and follow the Alpine Meadows trail north. At Elizabeth Parker Hut, go right (east). Soon after, bear left to reach Le Relais day-use shelter, across from the warden cabin, near the northwest end of Lake O'Hara.

TRIPS 15-19

Lake O'Hara Region

LOCATION	Yoho National Park
ROUND TRIPS	6.6 km (4.1 mi) to 14.2 km (8.8 mi)
ELEVATION GAINS	240 m (787 ft) to 495 m (1625 ft)
KEY ELEVATIONS	trailheads 2035 m (6675 ft) Lake Oesa 2275 m (7462 ft) Lake McArthur 2252 m (7387 ft) Odaray Grandview 2525 m (8282 ft) Linda Lake 2090 m (6855 ft)
HIKING TIME	3 to 7 hours a day, for 2 to 5 days
DIFFICULTY	moderate
MAPS	page 498; Gem Trek *Lake O'Hara*

OPINION

You can sweep up around the ashram all you want. If it's a thunderbolt of enlightenment you're seeking, you're as likely to find it in the mountains. Especially if the mountains are those ringing Lake O'Hara and comprising the most celebrated massif in the Canadian Rockies. It's a spectacle that can liberate us from the shabby little world we humans habitually skulk around in, and awaken us to the state of exalted wonder that is our birthright.

Spiritual jubilance often manifests itself in physical celebration, and here you can give it free reign, lighting out in the most concentrated, rewarding network of trails outside the Swiss Alps. Choose from a wealth of destinations, including a dozen alpine lakes, from minutes to hours away. All are rated *Premier*. And all are dayhikes. So you'll be striding freely, fluidly, unburdened by the weight of a full backpack.

Your choice of accommodation is varied, too. At O'Hara, you can pitch your tent, bunk in an alpine-club hut, or splurge on the comforts of a lodge. And the campground is no grotty hikers' ghetto. It's front-country quality, well organized, with comfortably-spaced tent pads, two sheltered cooking and eating areas, outdoor tables, food lockers, fire pits with benches, plus a regularly topped-up supply of firewood.

The O'Hara region has five hiking areas: Lake Oesa cirque (Trip 15), Opabin Plateau (Trip 16), Lake McArthur cirque (Trip 17), Odaray Grandview (Trip 18), and Duchesnay Basin (Trip 19) containing Linda and Cathedral lakes. You're a fit, experienced hiker, up for a little challenge? Your priority should be the lofty, thrilling, Alpine Circuit (Trip 14), which includes Lake Oesa and Opabin Plateau. You're not that robust? You can visit Oesa and Opabin separately or together, without linking them via the Alpine Circuit. The second goal for most hikers? Combine Lake McArthur with Odaray Grandview.

Clearly, you'll want at least three days in this awe-inspiring enclave. If you hike slowly, or prefer to limit your trail-time to five hours a day, allow four days to fully appreciate the region. Along the way, practice your Stoney. The region bristles with intriguing, poetic place names from the Stoney Indian language—exotic to ears steeped in English. Oesa (owe-EE-suh) means *ice*. Wiwaxy (wih-WAX-ee) means *windy*. Hungabee (HUNG-uh-bee) means *chieftain*. Opabin (oh-PAY-ben) means *rocky*. Yukness (YUCK-ness) means *sharpened*. And Odaray (OWE-duh-ray) means *cone*, as in the shape of a mountain.

TRIP 15 LAKE OESA

Lake Oesa is a turquoise treasure, clutched by colossal peaks on the Great Divide: Yukness Mtn, Ringrose Peak, Glacier Peak, and Mounts Lefroy, Huber, and Victoria. The most impressive view of Oesa is an aerial one, from the Alpine Circuit, before it descends to the shore. But even if approached from below, via the less adventurous trail leading directly from Lake O'Hara, Oesa is an extraordinary sight, one that every first-time O'Hara visitor should witness.

TRIP 16 OPABIN PLATEAU

Adorned with small meadows, stands of alpine larch, and picturesque tarns, Opabin Plateau is in a hanging valley beneath Yukness Mtn and Schaffer Ridge. Ideally, drop to the plateau after a clockwise trip around the Alpine Circuit. For a more thorough, relaxed exploration, hike here directly from Lake O'Hara. Opabin has an intimate, pastoral charm. It's lovely, but less spectacular than the rugged Lake Oesa cirque.

TRIP 17 LAKE MCARTHUR

The half-day hike to Lake McArthur should be number two on your to-do list, after the Alpine Circuit. This 1.5-km (1-mi) long lake is an opulent blue jewel resting in the buxom cleavage of Mt. Biddle, Mt. Schaffer and Park Mtn. Their sheer cliffs rise more than 600 m (2000 ft) from the water. The lake's 85-m (280-ft) depth creates the intense blue colour. If you can join a group hiking to Odaray Grandview, swing by McArthur Lake en route. Forget this whole area, however, if you see a posted bear warning. Even when there are no warnings, stay alert. This is prime grizzly habitat. Make noise. Hike in a group. The louder you are, the bigger your group, the safer you'll be. Read the *Bears* section for further suggestions.

TRIP 18 ODARAY GRANDVIEW

Odaray Grandview is the only trail-accessible vantage where you'll see Morning Glory Lakes, Linda Lake, Lake McArthur, Lake O'Hara and Lake Oesa, all at once. And the panorama to the east, crowded with peaks of the Great Divide, is as magnificent a view as any in the range. Experienced scramblers can continue above Odaray Grandview to Little O, a southeastern outlier of Odaray Mtn. It affords a tremendous view of the Goodsir Towers (south-southwest, Trip 50). If you encounter ice or snow, however, you'll need skill and confidence to surmount the summit ridge and complete the final ascent.

Hungabee Lake, beneath Yukness and Hungabee mountains

TRIP 19 DUCHESNAY BASIN / CATHEDRAL PROSPECT

Duchesnay Basin, harbouring Morning Glory, Linda and Cathedral lakes, is less compelling than other areas in the Lake O'Hara region, because it's lower—more forested, less alpine. Scrutinized on its own merits, the basin rates no higher than *Outstanding*, so hiking only here wouldn't justify the time and expense of busing into O'Hara. If staying in the region for several days, however, *do* hike here. You'll enjoy solitude—a rarity in this hikers' holy land. You'll earn yet another unique, indelible, O'Hara perspective: east over Linda Lake, to Mounts Huber and Victoria. Above the basin, Cathedral Prospect grants a memorable view southeast over the entire region, including the Alpine Circuit ledges. Duchesnay is especially beautiful the last couple weeks of September, when the bountiful alpine larches are golden.

FACT

Before your trip

Make reservations to ride the shuttle bus into the Lake O'Hara region, as well as to stay at the campground, hut, or lodge. For details, see Lake O'Hara Alpine Circuit (Trip 14).

Be aware that grizzly bears frequent the region, particularly the southwest corner. Bear encounters have increased as visitation has risen. Consequently, the Odaray Highline trail to Odaray Grandview has voluntary restrictions: Only four groups are allowed on the trail per day, with each group comprising no more than six people. The goal is to disturb bears as little as possible. Check the current status of O'Hara trails by calling the Yoho Park Visitor Centre: (250) 343-6433. After you arrive, ask at Le Relais day use shelter. Caught violating trail closures or restrictions, you could be fined up to $2000.

Speaking of money: bring some cash. You can buy maps, beverages, snacks, even baked goods, at Le Relais. Cross your fingers and hope for their scrumptious carrot cake. Campers are also welcome at the lodge for afternoon tea (juices, fresh fruit and baked goods) from 3 to 4 p.m.

Maps

See Lake O'Hara Alpine Circuit (Trip 14).

By Vehicle and Bus

See Lake O'Hara Alpine Circuit (Trip 14).

Arriving

If you're tenting, get off the bus at the campground. It's 0.6 km (0.4 mi) before Lake O'Hara.

If you're staying at Elizabeth Parker hut, get off the bus at Le Relais day-use shelter: across the road from the warden cabin, near the northwest end of Lake O'Hara, shortly before the lodge. Walk the signed trail departing the west side of the road. A gentle ascent southwest leads to a junction at 0.3 km (0.2 mi). Stay right to reach the hut at 0.5 km (0.3 mi).

If you're staying at Lake O'Hara Lodge, it's at road's end. The bus will take you all the way there.

Lake O'Hara, from the Huber Ledges. Schäffer Ridge beyond. Mt. Biddle distant left.

TRIP 15 LAKE OESA

ROUND TRIP	6.6 km (4.1 mi)
ELEVATION GAIN	240 m (787 ft)
HIKING TIME	3 hours
DIFFICULTY	easy

On Foot

Start where the outlet stream departs the northwest corner of Lake O'Hara, at 2035 m (6675 ft). Here's how to get there. From the lodge, head north on the lakeshore trail. From the campground, cross to the east side of the road, pick up the trail heading southeast, and follow it along the right (west) side of the outlet stream 0.5 km (0.3 mi) toward the lake. From the hut, head east to the road and continue past the warden cabin.

After any of these approaches, cross **Lake O'Hara's bridged outlet stream**. Head generally east. In 300 m (328 yd) the Wiwaxy Gap trail forks left (northeast). Continue straight, along the lakeshore. At 0.8 km (0.5 mi) turn left (north) onto the Lake Oesa trail. Ascend 65 m (70 yd) before the trail turns east again and the grade eases.

Pass small **Lake Victoria** and the shortcut to the Yukness Ledge route, both on your right, at 2.7 km (1.7 mi). Proceed straight (southeast) deeper into the cirque. At 3.1 km (1.9 mi) reach a rocky **knoll overlooking Lake Oesa**. The shore is 200 m (220 yd) farther east, at 2275 m (7462 ft). The Alpine Circuit route (Trip 14) crosses the Lake Oesa trail at the knoll.

North is 3368-m (11,047-ft) Mt. Huber. Behind it is 3464-m (11,362-ft) Mt. Victoria, her spine arching southeast to join 3423-m (11,227-ft) Mt. Lefroy. Out of sight, just over the ridge, Victoria Glacier rumbles down toward Lake Louise. Due east is 3283-m (10,768-ft) Glacier Peak. Yukness Mtn forms the cliffs on the south side of Lake Oesa.

Instead of returning directly to Lake O'Hara, if you're up for a challenge and a few more hours of hiking, read the Alpine Circuit description then ascend the Yukness Ledge route (right, south-southwest from the knoll). Your return trail from there would be through Opabin Plateau.

TRIP 16 OPABIN PLATEAU

LOOP	7.2 km (4.5 mi)
ELEVATION GAIN	250 m (820 ft)
HIKING TIME	3 hours
DIFFICULTY	easy

On Foot

Start in front of **Lake O'Hara lodge**, at 2035 m (6675 ft). Head southeast on the lakeshore trail. In 0.7 km (0.4 mi), a trail forks right (south). Proceed straight along the shore for the more moderate ascent to Opabin Plateau. At 1.1 km (0.7 mi) turn right (southeast) on the East Opabin trail and start climbing.

At 2.1 km (1.3 mi) the trail forks. Go left (southeast) and soon enter the east side of the plateau. Pass the first of the tiny **Moor Lakes**. At 2.9 km (1.8 mi), near the northeast end of **Hungabee Lake**, you might notice the Yukness Ledge route intersecting from the left. It's part of the Alpine Circuit (Trip 14). To sample it and attain broader views,

Lake Oesa

turn left and ascend. After about 0.5 km (0.3 mi) the route contours on the ledge. Continue another 0.5 km (0.3 mi) if you're comfortable doing so.

Beyond where the route intersected your trail, proceed southeast. Reach **Opabin Lake** at 3.5 km (2.2 mi), 2285 m (7495 ft). Yukness Mtn is north-northeast, Ringrose Peak east, Hungabee Mtn southeast, Opabin Glacier southeast, and Schaffer Ridge southwest. From Opabin Lake, follow the trail right (southwest), curving northwest and gently descending. Bear left (northwest) at the fork as you pass **Hungabee Lake** again, this time on its west side.

Reach a junction at 4.4 km (2.7 mi). Straight (north) descends 1.4 km (0.9 mi) directly back to Lake O'Hara, rejoining the trail you originally ascended to Opabin Plateau. To vary your return and attain a viewpoint, go left at this junction, cross a creek, then immediately turn right (north) on a spur trail leading 0.6 km (0.4 mi) to **Opabin Prospect**. It overlooks Mary Lake and Lake O'Hara. The Wiwaxy Peaks are north-northwest. Mt. Huber is northeast.

From Opabin Prospect, curve south 0.4 km (0.25 mi) to a junction. Turn right and descend steeply north on the West Opabin trail. In 1 km (0.6 mi) you'll be just north of Mary Lake, at another junction. Turn right to reach **Lake O'Hara** in a few minutes. Then turn left, onto the lakeshore trail, and follow it northwest back to **Lake O'Hara Lodge**, where your total loop distance is 7.2 km (4.5 mi).

TRIP 17 LAKE MCARTHUR

ROUND TRIP	7 km (4.3 mi)
ELEVATION GAIN	413 m (1355 ft)
HIKING TIME	3 hours
DIFFICULTY	moderate

On Foot

Start on the signed trail, on the west side of the road, across from the **warden cabin**. It's near the northwest end of Lake O'Hara, at 2035 m (6675 ft). A gentle ascent southwest leads to a junction at 0.3 km (0.2 mi). Stay right and soon enter alpine meadows. At the junction beside **Elizabeth Parker hut**, turn left (south) and begin ascending through forest. At 1.5 km (0.9 mi), 2180 m (7150 ft), reach **Schaffer Lake** and many junctions.

Round the right (west) side of Schaffer Lake. At its south shore the trail forks. Right leads southwest to McArthur Pass in 0.4 km (0.25 mi). Go left (south) onto the high cutoff trail, ascending south-southeast through larch forest toward Lake McArthur.

Ascend steeply to another junction at 2.3 km (1.4 mi), 2310 m (7577 ft). Right descends to McArthur Pass and the Odaray Highline trail. Go left again, continuing the ascent around Mt. Schaffer's west shoulder. The stone steps traversing the cliff bands on this trail were built by Lawrence Grassi, who created the Alpine Circuit. The grade eases as the trail curves southeast into the lake basin.

Reach the trail's 2350-m (7710-ft) **highpoint** at 3 km (1.9 mi). Lake McArthur is visible ahead. The glacier beyond the far (southeast) shore is on sheer-faced, 3319-m (10,886-ft) Mt. Biddle. Descend to reach the north shore of **Lake McArthur** at 3.5 km (2.2 mi), 2252 m (7387 ft). The lake bottom is 85 m (280 ft) below the surface, making this Yoho Park's deepest body of water.

TRIP 18 ODARAY GRANDVIEW AND LITTLE O

ROUND TRIP	7 km (4.3 mi) to Grandview, 8.4 km (5.2 mi) to Little O
ELEVATION GAIN	495 m (1625 ft) to Grandview, 930 m (3050 ft) to Little O
HIKING TIME	3 to 4 hours for Grandview, 6 to 7 for Little O
DIFFICULTY	moderate to Grandview, challenging to Little O

Voluntary restrictions

In the early 1990s there were too many encounters between grizzly bears and hikers in the Odaray area. For wary animals to continue using this corridor with little disturbance, it was necessary to limit human visitation. So, the Odaray Highline trail—starting between Schaffer Lake and McArthur Pass, then climbing generally northwest to Odaray Grandview—now has voluntary restrictions. Only four groups are allowed on the trail per day, with each group comprising no more than six people.

So, upon arrival at the Highline trail junction, check the logbook to see how many groups have ascended that day. If there are four groups ahead of you, don't go; try again the next day. Obviously, the earlier you arrive, the better your chances of being one of the four. But obey any signs superseding the voluntary restrictions. If the trail is closed due to bear activity, don't even think about hiking it. You can check the trail's current status at Le Relais day-use shelter before your hike.

Lake McArthur

On Foot

Start on the signed trail, on the west side of the road, across from the **warden cabin**. It's near the northwest end of Lake O'Hara, at 2035 m (6675 ft). A gentle ascent southwest leads to a junction at 0.3 km (0.2 mi). Stay right and soon enter alpine meadows. At the junction beside **Elizabeth Parker hut**, turn left (south) and begin ascending through forest. At 1.5 km (0.9 mi), 2180 m (7150 ft), reach **Schaffer Lake** and many junctions.

Round the right (west) side of Schaffer Lake. At its south shore the trail forks. Left (south) is the cutoff trail ascending to Lake McArthur. Go right, ascending southwest, to reach a junction in **McArthur Pass** at 2.2 km (1.4 mi), 2230 m (7315 ft).

Left leads generally southeast to McArthur Lake. Right (west-northwest) is the **Odaray Highline trail**, leading to Odaray Grandview. Before continuing in that direction, check the **logbook**. Have four groups preceded you on the Highline today? If not, you're good to go. Begin the gentle ascent, soon on loose rock, up the slopes of Mt. Odaray.

At 3.3 km (2 mi), the trail jogs left (west) and deteriorates in talus. A steep, rough ascent ensues. Established route ends at 3.5 km (2.2 mi), 2530 m (8300 ft), where a large cairn signifies your arrival at **Odaray Grandview**. North-northwest, across forested, lake-splashed Duchesnay Basin, is Cathedral Mountain. Nearby northwest is the 1150-m (3772-ft) east face of Odaray Mtn. Lake O'Hara is east-northeast.

West-southwest is the Odaray Mtn outlier known as **Little O**. Capable scramblers will have no difficulty finding a route up the steep, loose talus to its 2965-m (9725-ft) summit. The ascent is on an east-facing slope that retains snow into late summer, so it's likely easiest and safest in September.

TRIP 19 DUCHESNAY BASIN / CATHEDRAL PROSPECT

ROUND TRIP	14.9 km (9.2 mi) from O'Hara campground
ELEVATION GAIN	340 m (1115 ft)
HIKING TIME	4 to 5 hours
DIFFICULTY	easy to Cathedral Lakes, moderate to Cathedral Prospect

Caution

You're entering the most remote, least travelled area in the Lake O'Hara region. Make noise frequently to warn bears of your presence.

On Foot

Starting at Elizabeth Parker hut

Facing west at the junction beside the hut, turn right and cross the bridged stream. In a few minutes reach another junction. Go right (northwest). After a gentle ascent to a highpoint, drop southwest to a junction at 2.2 km (1.3 mi), on the west shore of the second **Morning Glory Lake**. Right leads 0.7 km (0.4 mi) generally north to intersect the trail from the campground. Go left (north-northwest) and ascend.

Reach a T-junction at 3 km (1.8 mi), on the southeast shore of **Linda Lake**. Right rounds the east shore. Go left 0.5 km (0.3 mi) to a junction, where you'll bear left. Now skip the next three paragraphs. Resume following the directions from the **southwest corner of Linda Lake**.

Ascending Little Odaray

Starting at Lake O'Hara campground

From the north end of the campground, at 2010 m (6593 ft), follow the trail north-northwest 1.9 km (1.2 mi) through forest to a junction. Right (east) leads to the road. Turn left (southwest).

At 2.7 km (1.7 mi), reach a 4-way junction. Left (south) leads to Morning Glory Lakes in 0.7 km (0.4 mi). Right (north) is the Cataract Brook trail, leading 6.7 km (4.2 mi) north to the parking lot near the Trans-Canada Hwy. Proceed straight (west).

Reach a T-junction at 3.7 km (2.3 mi), 2090 m (6855 ft), near the northeast side of **Linda Lake**. You can turn left or right to circle the lake. Go right (north), around the north shore. Soon attain a view south to 3159-m (10,362-ft) Odaray Mtn.

After rounding the north shore, reach a junction at 4.5 km (2.8 mi), near the **southwest corner of Linda Lake**. Mt. Victoria is visible north-northeast. Hiking from the campground? Turn right. Hiking from the hut? Bear left.

From either approach, head northwest on the Cathedral Lakes / Duchesnay Basin trail, through tree-lined, subalpine meadows. Pass between the lower **Cathedral Lake** (left) and **Vera Lake** (right) at 6.1 km (3.8 mi). (If you started at the hut and insist on precision, subtract 1 km / 0.6 mi from this and subsequent distances.) Crossing the bridge over Cathedral's outlet, you'll see Vera downstream.

The trail curves west-southwest, then ascends northwest toward Consummation Peak. Ten minutes past Cathedral and Vera lakes, ignore the overgrown route forking left (west-southwest) to Duchesnay Pass. Continue right (north-northwest) to Cathedral Basin.

Odaray Mountain, from northwest end of Lake O'Hara

The Cathedral Basin trail deteriorates to a rough, rocky route, soon requiring you to clamber over small boulders. At 2235 m (7330 ft) ascend left of a rockslide. Blazes (red and orange paint) offer guidance. Proceed among alpine larch trees. About 30 minutes beyond the Duchesnay Pass fork, hike northeast on a heathery slope. Rockhop a creeklet and ascend. Reach 2350-m (7700-ft) **Cathedral Prospect** at 7.4 km (4.6 mi), beneath Cathedral Mountain.

North, deeper in **Cathedral Basin**, is tiny **Monica Lake**. South, below, are the Duchesnay Basin lakes, which you hiked past to get here. Above them is Odaray Mountain. Most of the Lake O'Hara region, including the Alpine Circuit route and Opabin Basin, is visible southeast.

The shortest way back to the hut is to retrace your steps. Hikers returning to the campground can vary the trip slightly by going right at the southwest end of Linda Lake and curving around its south shore. Bear left at the next fork to reach the T-junction where you first saw Linda Lake. Turn right (east) and you're again on familiar ground.

TRIP 20

Wilcox Pass

LOCATION	Jasper National Park, near Icefield Centre
ROUND TRIP	8 km (5 mi)
ELEVATION GAIN	335 m (1100 ft)
KEY ELEVATIONS	trailhead 2040 m (6690 ft), pass 2375 m (7790 ft)
HIKING TIME	3 hours, 2 more for rambling
DIFFICULTY	easy
MAPS	page 501; Gem Trek *Columbia Icefield*

OPINION

Hike to Wilcox Pass and you'll be disappointed—in subsequent hikes. This will become the benchmark. Few trails anywhere are so instantly and extravagantly gratifying. (See main photo, back cover.)

The ascent is brief and enjoyable, through a 400-year-old forest—remarkably grand for the Canadian Rockies. Then, suddenly, the Columbia Icefield looms over your left shoulder. Ahead, a sweeping meadow summons you onward through the pass where bighorn sheep, nibbling at the tundra, are a common sight. You've now witnessed the quintessence of the Canadian Rockies.

The Columbia Icefield is a 325-square-kilometer frozen sea feeding the Saskatchewan, Columbia and Athabasca rivers. Barely visible from the Parkway below, the icefield inspires exuberant outbursts from passing motorists. Yet what they glimpse is a mere sliver of the icy vastness you'll see from Wilcox Pass, where the view comprises the Athabasca and Dome glaciers between two prodigious peaks: 3491-m (11,450-ft) Mt. Athabasca and 3451-m (11,319-ft) Snow Dome.

The problem with Wilcox Pass is people. Too many of them. The premier scenery here is no secret, so expect to share it with a dozen other hikers, perhaps more. To spice your day with a pinch of adventure and a dash of solitude, you have three options:

(1) Proceed through the pass. Cross tussocky tundra, then descend the forested Tangle Creek drainage to the Parkway. It's an 11.2-km (7-mi) through-trip. Hitchhiking back to your vehicle should be easy.

(2) Ascend to the ridgecrest on the south shoulder of Wilcox Peak. Altitude greatly expands your view of the icefield and the pass.

(3) Hike cross-country to Nigel Lake. It's visible from Nigel Peak's northwest ridge, just 45 minutes beyond the pass. The setting looks like the land Creation forgot.

FACT

By Vehicle

Drive the Icefields Parkway southeast 2.8 km (1.7 mi) from the Icefield Centre, or northwest 1.9 km (1.2 mi) from Sunwapta Pass. Turn northeast toward Wilcox Creek Campground. Trailhead parking is on the left, shortly after exiting the Parkway. Elevation: 2040 m (6690 ft).

On Foot

Ascend steeply northwest through an ancient forest of alpine fir and Engelmann spruce. Soon attain views of the peaky, icy, western horizon. Heading generally northwest, enter **meadows** at 2 km (1.2 mi). The Columbia Icefield's Athabasca Glacier is visible left (southwest) at 2.5 km (1.6 mi). The ascent eases about 45 minutes along, where the trail skirts a **ravine**. Detour left (west) above the ravine for an improved glacier view. Reach the **Wilcox Pass** monument cairn at 2375 m (7790 ft). You've hiked 4 km (2.5 mi) and gained 335 m (1100 ft) in about one hour. From here, the trail maintains an effortless grade through the pass. Tread lightly in these fragile alplands. Avoid the spongy tussocks; step on rock wherever possible. Don't create new, unnecessary routes: walk abreast of companions, not single file.

TANGLE CREEK

The trail proceeds northwest through the long, broad, alpine pass. Near the north end, at 7.2 km (4.5 mi), begin descending into forested **Tangle Creek valley**. The trail curves left (southwest), staying south of the creek. Reach the **Icefields Parkway** at 11.2 km (7 mi), 1860 m (6100 ft). Via the pavement, you're now 10 km (6.2 mi) north of Wilcox Pass trailhead.

WILCOX PEAK

From the Wilcox Pass monument cairn, a distinct trail forks left (southwest) across rolling meadow toward Athabasca Glacier. Follow it about ten minutes to the **highest knoll**, at 2435 m (7987 ft). (Do not continue to the next knoll, about six minutes farther.) From the cairn atop the knoll, look right (northwest). A route is visible in the scree on the right (east) side of Wilcox Peak's south shoulder. Proceed cross-country to that **route**, then follow it upward until you attain a superior view from the **ridgecrest**. Hiking the crest is easy to where it flattens at 2705 m (8872 ft). Soon after, the crest steepens and becomes more rugged. Only experienced scramblers should continue up 2884-m (9460-ft) Wilcox Peak. The ascent route, favouring the right (east) side of the mountain, is rated "moderate," requires hands-on work, and is mildly exposed near the summit.

Bighorn sheep near Wilcox Pass

NIGEL LAKE

Allow 1½ hours for a round trip from Wilcox Pass to the crest of a low ridge where you can overlook Nigel Lake within the embrace of Nigel Peak.

Athabasca Glacier from near Wilcox Pass

The lakeshore is about 45 minutes beyond the ridge.

Heading northwest into Wilcox Pass, observe the right (east) wall of the pass. That's a ridge of Nigel Peak. The ridge drops northwest. That's where you want to ascend it.

From the Wilcox Pass monument cairn, go right (east) cross-country. Beyond the **wet meadows**, turn left (north). Following traces of sheep track, contour the base of the ridge.

About 15-20 minutes along, having gained only about 20 m (70 ft), pick up a **route**. The view northwest reveals the full length of Wilcox Pass with its tarns, tussocky meadows, and rock ribs.

Proceed north at about 2470 m (8100 ft). As the route fades, look for **another route** about 30 m (100 ft) above. Angle up to it and resume north. You're now about a third of the way up the slope. Visible below is the rocky depression you avoided by moving higher.

At a mossy spot, scramble the final 30 m (100 ft) right (east) to the **ridgecrest**. You're now about 45 minutes from the pass, and 100 m (330 ft) above it. The cirque harbouring Nigel Lake is visible below (southeast). The rocks in the basin are sharp, rough, free of lichen and moss, as if freshly hatched. For a full view of the lake and Nigel Peak, scramble a bit farther south up the ridge.

TRIP 21

Verdant Pass

LOCATION	Jasper National Park
ROUND TRIP	22.5 km (14 mi)
ELEVATION GAIN	665 m (2180 ft)
KEY ELEVATIONS	trailhead 1730 m (5680 ft) pass 2110 m (6920 ft)
HIKING TIME	7 to 8 hours
DIFFICULTY	moderate
MAPS	page 502; Gem Trek *Jasper & Maligne Lake;* Amethyst Lakes 83 D/9

OPINION

Nature massages your brain. Caressing your cortex with sunshine, kneading your cerebrum with beauty, it softens your stentorian intellect, so you can hear the quiet, pure voice within.

At Verdant Pass, you'll witness nature at her most grand and feral. Hiking here on a fine day is a soothing brain massage that will ensure you give your whispering soul the attention it deserves.

The Verdant Pass meadows are a lavish expanse, bigger than some airports: 2.5 km (1.5 mi) long, 1 km (0.6 mi) wide. Lakes, tarns and creeks shimmer in the green vastness. The horizon is splashed white by the distant Hooker Icefield. Rampart peaks rise all around, including maelstroms of rock hardened into whirlpool images. You're in virgin alplands here. Please leave no trace of your passage.

Climbers forged this trail up the east side of Verdant Creek valley. It leads to an ascent route on the back of Mt. Edith Cavell. The pass is between Edith, which towers above you at neck-craning height, and Chevron Mtn—especially striking when its swirling striations are accentuated by a dusting of snow. Be sure to ascend the hillock guarding Edith's second cirque, where you'll see a teal lake at the base of sheer cliffs.

Though seldom used, the narrow, rooty trail is easy to follow. The ascent is initially moderate, but steepens during the final rough stretch to Edith's first cirque. Beyond here, there's no trail. Your explorations will be cross-country, but because you're above treeline, navigating should be no problem. Still, bring a topo map and compass. None of this trip, even the portion on trail, can you walk absentmindedly. Be especially attentive crossing the meadows, so you don't kerplunk into a bog, or wrench an ankle in the tussocks.

Preserve the unsullied majesty of Verdant Pass by hiking abreast of your companions. Single file causes more damage. Wherever possible, walk on rock. Even stepping on hard tussocks is better than on the fragile alpine flora.

Verdant Pass and the peaks above Whirlpool Valley

FACT

By Vehicle

From the junction of Hwy 16 and the Icefields Parkway, at the southwest edge of Jasper townsite, drive the Parkway south 7.2 km (4.5 mi). Turn right (west) onto Hwy 93A and follow it south 5.3 km (3.3 mi). Turn right onto Mount Edith Cavell Road and follow it 12.2 km (7.6 mi) to the Tonquin Valley (Astoria River) trailhead parking area, just past the youth hostel. Elevation: 1730 m (5680 ft).

On Foot

From the north end of the parking area, descend the old dirt road. Cross the bridge spanning the Cavell Lake outlet stream. Go up the hill and turn right to avoid a horse corral. You're now on the Astoria River trail, gradually descending southwest. This is the expressway to Tonquin Valley. The broad, smooth path allows fast striding.

After hiking 4.5 km (2.8 mi) in about one hour, look for a narrow, **unsigned trail** branching left (south) at 1705 m (5592 ft). There are two large boulders across from it, on the right side of the Astoria River trail, which continues descending. If you miss the Verdant Pass trail, in 0.4 km (0.25 mi) you'll reach a wood bridge spanning Verdant Creek. Turn back.

The narrow, rooty trail to Verdant Pass ascends moderately through forest. After gaining 158 m (520 ft) from the junction, a level stretch grants you a respite. Soon, about 7.5 km (4.7 mi) from the trailhead, the path deteriorates, climbing steeply into sub-

Southwest face of Mt. Edith Cavell

alpine meadows. Below you (right / west) is a deep gorge. Angle left, up the lower slopes of Mt. Edith Cavell. Follow the dwindling path across a creeklet, then over the top of a gentle rise at the mouth of **Edith's first cirque**. You're now just over 2200 m (7200 ft), having gained 500 m (1640 ft) from the Astoria River trail.

A sketchy route continues left (east) into the cirque. It dead-ends in talus, above a tiny tarn. Ignore it. Verdant Pass is visible below you, south. Edith's second cirque is southeast. From this point on, you're exploring cross-country, choosing your own route. Stay aware of the terrain, so you can find your way back. The following guidelines might help.

Head southeast across the heather. Descend 15 m/yd down a rockslide. Continue along the bottom edge of the rocks for a few minutes, to a green basin. As you approach a large tarn, there's a heathery hillock on your left (east), at the mouth of **Edith's second cirque**. You're now on the north edge of Verdant Pass. The northeast-facing crags of 2879-m (9446-ft) Chevron Mtn are west, across the creek drainage. The Hooker Icefield is visible south.

Before proceeding into the pass, scramble 50 m (160 ft) up the hillock to see the teal lake at the base of sheer cliffs. Afterward, descend the hillock by veering left toward the smaller tarn and creeklet in the green basin below. Crest **Verdant Pass** at 11.3 km (7 mi), 2110 m (6920 ft).

Proceeding deeper into the pass, weave through stunted trees and cross tussocky meadowland. Descending the south side of the pass, angle right (southwest) to stay on the edge of a meandering stream and boggy meadows. A boulder field provides the easiest and most eco-sensitive route. The Whirlpool peaks are obvious, southeast. A grassy ridge southwest is the optimal vantage and logical turnaround point for a dayhike. From there, you can survey the Whirlpool River valley, and the Divergence Creek valley between Mt. Lapensee (left / northeast) and Divergence Peak (right / southwest).

TRIP 22

Crypt Lake

LOCATION	Waterton Lakes National Park
ROUND TRIP	17.4 km (10.8 mi)
ELEVATION GAIN	690 m (2263 ft)
KEY ELEVATIONS	trailhead 1280 m (4200 ft) lake 1970 m (6462 ft)
HIKING TIME	5½ to 7 hours
DIFFICULTY	moderate
MAPS	page 502; Gem Trek *Waterton Lakes National Park*

OPINION

If you learn about Crypt Lake after you've left Waterton Park, you'll be on your knees, eating dirt, shaking your fists at the heavens, crying "Why? Why did I miss it?"

Justifiably famous, this protean journey begins with a boat ride across Upper Waterton Lake. You'll then hike up Hell Roaring Valley on a roller-coaster trail, pass four waterfalls, enjoy constant views much of the way, crouch through a dark tunnel, and cling to a safety cable as you round an airy mountainside. Ultimately you'll behold Crypt Lake in its looming cirque. The walls surrounding the emerald water soar a neck-craning 600 m (1970 ft) above the shore.

A crowd often snakes along the entire route, creating a carnival atmosphere, but that's easy to overlook when you're witnessing such grandeur. Hoping for serenity, come after mid-September.

It's possible to hike here by late June, but you should expect to cross snowfields. Sturdy boots (for kicking footholds) and trekking poles are essential then. If you doubt your ability to negotiate steep snow, wait until mid-July. The Crypt Lake trip is exciting enough without an impromptu luge run.

FACT

By Vehicle

Drive to Waterton townsite. Park in the large paved lot by the tour boat landing.

By Boat

The tour boat that makes stops operates from early June to mid-September. Catch the 9 a.m. or 10 a.m. boat, crossing Upper Waterton Lake to Crypt Landing. In June there's only a 10 a.m. departure. The 9 a.m. departure is scheduled July through August. Returning to Waterton townsite, the boat departs Crypt Landing at 4 p.m. and, only in June, 5:30 p.m. Confirm current schedules and prices with the Waterton Inter-Nation Shoreline Cruise Company: (403) 859-2362.

Several waterfalls are visible en route to Crypt Lake.

On Foot

From Crypt Landing, at 1280 m (4200 ft), the trail climbs southeast via moderately graded switchbacks, through Douglas fir, lodgepole pine and spruce. At 0.4 km (0.25 mi), a spur forks right, passing **Hell Roaring Falls** in 1 km (0.6 mi), rejoining the main trail in 1.8 km (1.1 mi). Staying on the main trail, bear left at 3 km (1.9 mi) where the spur merges. Gain 244 m (800 ft) before twice crossing a tributary of Hell Roaring Creek. A few minutes later, a long cascade is visible in the rocky gorge.

At 3.7 km (2.3 mi), reach **Twin Falls** with its huge pool. The trail continues undulating southeast through forest. Cliffs are visible periodically on the right. At 5.6 km (3.5 mi), 1600 m (5250 ft), reach Burnt Rock Falls, which drops 15 m (50 ft). Soon after, you'll see stupendous Crypt Falls. The ascent now tilts skyward, across open slopes allowing views of cliffs and cascades.

After crossing a stream and a talus slope, the trail leads to a **ladder**. Climb it, then crouch and waddle through a 20-metre **tunnel**. It was blasted through the shoulder of the mountain to ease access to the lake. Exiting the tunnel, the trail diminishes to an airy route strung with a safety cable. Ascend another ten minutes among whitebark pine to attain the lip of **Crypt Lake cirque**, at 8.7 km (5.4 mi), 1970 m (6462 ft).

Descend 20 m/yd to the lakeshore. Or stay high and proceed right (west) among open forest for another ten minutes, to a viewpoint where you might have less company. Another option is to hike along the east shore to the Canada-US border at the far (south) end of the lake.

If you're strong, hiking to Crypt Lake is a 3-hour task; allow 2½ hours for the descent to Crypt Landing. Average hikers take 3½ to 4 hours up, 3 hours down.

Ascending to Crypt Lake

TRIP 23

Carthew Summit / Alderson Lake

LOCATION	Waterton Lakes National Park
SHUTTLE TRIP	20.1 km (12.5 mi)
ELEVATION CHANGE	651-m (2135-ft) gain, 1016-m (3332-ft) loss
KEY ELEVATIONS	Cameron Lake trailhead 1660 m (5445 ft) summit 2311 m (7580 ft) Alderson Lake 1860 m (6100 ft)
HIKING TIME	6 to 7 hours
DIFFICULTY	moderate
MAPS	page 503; Gem Trek *Waterton Lakes National Park*

OPINION

Bound over the mountains. Top-out high above treeline. See peaks, glaciers, cirques, lakes. And never retrace a step on this one-way dayhike made possible by a convenient shuttle.

You'll feel you're truly exploring, because from start to finish, it's all new terrain. The trip climaxes on the mauve-and-rouge alpine slopes of Mount Carthew, with a holy-moly view of U.S. Glacier National Park. But the other summits visible on this hike aren't screamers. You'll see a lot of prairie, which, to a mountain mind, is a curious but unmoving sight. You're on the edge of the Rockies here, not deep in their midst. It's like watching a movie romance, instead of wooing a lover. And you'll chug through forest half the trip. For these reasons, it fails to earn a *Premier* rating.

Carthew Summit (actually a pass, not a summit) is desolate, south facing, sun blasted. On a hot day, it'll bake your enchilada. So carry plenty of water; there's none between Summit Lake and upper Carthew Lake. Also bring sunglasses, a broad-brimmed hat, and a gauzy, longsleeve shirt. Be thankful for a lightly overcast sky, but don't hike this trail under threatening clouds; it's too high and exposed.

The final 7 km (4.3 mi) beyond Alderson Lake are through dense forest. You'll dispatch that stretch faster going down than you would coming up, because monotony kills motivation.

FACT

By Vehicle

You have three options for the one-way hike: (1) Arrange a two-car shuttle, with one vehicle waiting for you at the finish. (2) Leave your car at the Cameron Falls trailhead in Waterton townsite. Walk to the sports shop in Tamarack Village Square and

Descending across 1.5-billion-year-old Kintla argillite, from Carthew summit

pay Tamarack Shuttle Service to drop you at Cameron Lake. The shuttle usually departs the townsite at 8 and 9 a.m. Call (403) 859-2378 for current schedules and prices. (3) Hitchhike from the townsite to Cameron Lake, then hike back.

To reach the Cameron Lake trailhead, drive the Akamina Parkway 15.7 km (9.7 mi)—from the junction just north of Waterton townsite, to the large parking lot at road's end. Elevation: 1660 m (5445 ft).

To leave a car at the Cameron Falls trailhead, drive Evergreen Avenue south along the west side of Waterton townsite. Immediately after crossing the bridge below Cameron Falls, turn right into the parking area.

On Foot

From the Cameron Lake parking lot, walk toward the lake. Go left past the boat rental office. Cross the bridge over Cameron Creek, ascend east a bit, then south on the well-engineered trail.

Climb 275 m (900 ft) on moderately-graded switchbacks beneath 300-year-old spruce and fir trees. Through the forest, glimpse Cameron Lake, Herbst Glacier on Mt. Custer (south), and Forum Peak (west). At 3 km (1.9 mi) reach open, subalpine forest. The trail now heads southeast. At 4.3 km (2.7 mi), 1935 m (6347 ft), reach **Summit Lake**. Expect wildflowers here in season. Summit Lake makes a fine rest stop, but the best scenery is higher. Push on.

Reach a junction 100 m (110 yd) past Summit Lake. Right drops southeast to Boundary Creek, in a forested valley just south of the Canada / U.S. border. Ascend left (north) on the Carthew-Alderson trail. Climb 376 m (1233 ft) in 3.6 km (2.2 mi) from

Carthew Lakes

Summit Lake, across scree slopes, to the trail's highpoint: 2311-m (7580-ft) **Carthew Summit**. Total distance from Cameron Lake trailhead: 7.9 km (4.9 mi).

Fuchsia moss campion, mountain dryas, and lavender sky pilot punctuate the desolate slopes. You can see south into the cirques of Nooney and Wurdeman lakes, at the base of 2867-m (9406-ft) Chapman Peak, in U.S. Glacier National Park. Northeast is flat, yellow-gray, Alberta prairie. From Carthew Summit, a 15-minute scramble left (northwest) will earn you a perch on Mt. Carthew's lower peak, where the panorama is wider.

Continuing from Carthew Summit, don't get sidetracked by game trails. Follow orange markers. Descend a steep talus slope northeast into **Carthew Lakes basin**—reached at 9.3 km (5.8 mi). The trail rounds the lakes' left (northeast) shores, passing the larger, second lake at 2160 m (7085 ft). It then re-enters subalpine forest, leading you over rock escarpments. Below the basin, pass a 120-m (394-ft) cascade. Lose elevation quickly via short switchbacks.

At 12.7 km (7.9 mi), 1860 m (6100 ft), enter **Alderson Lake** cirque. The 860-m (2820-ft) north face of Mt. Alderson rises from the south shore. A campground, cooking shelter and outhouse are above the north shore.

Leaving Alderson Lake, cross the natural dam formed by a moraine. It's another 7 km (4.3 mi) to Waterton townsite. Descend northeast into **Carthew Creek valley**, through a mature forest. The trail stays south of the creek, not beside it. Buchanan Ridge is left (northwest), Bertha Peak right (south). The trail meets Cameron Creek just before reaching the townsite. You lose most of the elevation the last 2.4 km (1.5 mi). Complete the one-way trek upon reaching Cameron Falls trailhead, at 20.1 km (12.5 mi), 1295 m (4248 ft).

TRIP 24

Healy Pass / Monarch Ramparts

LOCATION	Banff National Park
ROUND TRIP	18.4 km (11.4 mi), plus 8.4 km (5.2 mi) for Ramparts
ELEVATION GAIN	655 m (2150 ft) from Sunshine parking lot to pass 360 m (1180 ft) from Sunshine Village to pass
KEY ELEVATIONS	Sunshine parking lot 1675 m (5495 ft) Sunshine Village 2195 m (7200 ft) pass 2330 m (7642 ft) Ramparts 2410 m (7905 ft)
HIKING TIME	6 to 7 hours
DIFFICULTY	moderate
MAPS	page 493; Gem Trek *Banff & Mt. Assiniboine*, Gem Trek *Kootenay National Park*; Banff 82 O/4

OPINION

Wildflower meadows, like coral reefs, have an enchanting power to rivet your attention to the present moment. In a culture preoccupied with the past and future, hiking or snorkeling can be therapeutic. So hike to Healy Pass during full bloom—late July to mid-August—when the meadows are a riot of colour, as brilliantly and variously hued as a reef teeming with tropical fish. Your eyes will swim through bold splashes of red, pink, yellow, purple and white.

Even if the flower display is less than full strength, Healy Pass pleases. The view is grand, encompassing a 70-km length of the Continental Divide—from Mt. Assiniboine (southeast) to Storm Mtn (northwest). The Ball Range, the Pharaoh Peaks, and the Massive Range are prominently visible. You'll also see Egypt, Scarab, and Pharaoh lakes (Trip 85) in context—more impressive than from their shorelines. In autumn, the pass again makes a spectacle of itself, sporting a brilliant gold beard of alpine larches.

Compared to most passes, Healy is generous. It offers hikers a sensational yet easy way to extend the day's exploration: continue along the 4.2-km (2.6-mi) alpine crest of the Monarch Ramparts. From the pass, the elevation gain is piddling. And views are constant. You can go out and back, or create a circuit by returning on the Eohippus Lake trail.

There are several ways to reach Healy Pass. The optimal ways are described here: (1) Ride the shuttle bus up to Sunshine Village, effortlessly gaining 520 m (1705 ft), then hike to Healy Pass via Simpson Pass. (2) From the Sunshine parking lot, hike to Healy Pass via Healy Creek. Both approaches are virtually the same length. The ascent is four times greater on the Healy Creek trail, but the grade is moderate overall. The Healy Creek trail is also viewless, but the trail is periodically close to the creek. Stretches of the trail from Sunshine are often muddy. If you're fit, hike up Healy Creek. You won't be restricted to the shuttle schedule, and you'll save money. If you don't mind the expense, ride the shuttle, hike in via Simpson, out via Healy Creek.

Backpacking to Egypt Lake? Enter via Healy Pass. It's shorter and more scenic than via Redearth and Pharaoh creeks (Trip 25). But dropping from Healy Pass to Egypt Lake is worthwhile only on an overnight trip. Dayhikers with extra time should devote it to hiking the Monarch Ramparts. Read Trip 85 for directions to Egypt Lake.

Trying to decide between Citadel Pass (Trip 3) and Healy Pass? Go to Citadel. You'll spend the entire day in open, alpine country, and you'll hike through more extensive meadows.

FACT

Before your trip

Visit whitemountainadventures.com to learn more about the White Mountain Adventures shuttle bus from the Sunshine parking lot to Sunshine Village. Check current prices and make reservations by calling (403) 760-4403 October through June 14, (403) 762-7889 June 15 through September, or (800) 408-0005.

By Vehicle

Drive the Trans-Canada Hwy east 21 km (13 mi) from Castle Junction, or west 9 km (5.6 mi) from Banff townsite. Turn south onto the signed Sunshine Village road. Proceed 8.3 km (5.1 mi) to the parking lot at the gondola station, at 1675 m (5495 ft). The gondola does not operate in summer.

(1) To reach Sunshine Village, at 2195 m (7200 ft), you must hike the restricted-use access road (starting on the south side of the gondola station), or ride the White Mountain Adventures shuttle bus. For details read the *By Bus* section in Trip 3.

(2) To hike the Healy Creek trail, walk around the right (north) side of the gondola station. Enter the smaller parking lot behind. The trail, initially a road, starts left of the info kiosk. Elevation: 1675 m (5495 ft).

On Foot

Starting at Sunshine Village

From the north end of the lodge, at 2195 m (7200 ft), turn left on the road. Proceed onto the gravel path. Go past the staff lodging to the trail sign at the bottom of Wawa Ridge ski lift. Follow the Meadow Park trail northwest uphill through subalpine forest. Bear right at the 1.6-km (1-mi) junction. Crest Wawa Ridge at 2 km (1.2 mi), 2360 m (7740 ft). From here you can see southeast to Sunshine Meadows, the Citadel Pass area, and Mt. Assiniboine.

From Wawa Ridge, the trail drops west back into forest. After curving southwest, the descent steepens as you approach **Simpson Pass**. Reach the pass at 5.6 km (3.5 mi), 2135 m (7003 ft). It's a small meadow surrounded by forest. Pay attention at this potentially confusing junction:

• Right leads north 1.3 km (0.8 mi) to the Healy Creek trail, where you could descend right (northeast) 5.9 km (3.7 mi) to the Sunshine parking lot. That would spare you the 225-m (738-ft) ascent back to Wawa Ridge.

• For Healy Pass, bear left (west), climbing steeply. At 6 km (3.7 mi) ignore the left spur. It leads south 3.2 km (2 mi) to small Eohippus Lake. Your trail levels, then drops slightly to a junction with the Healy Creek trail at 7.6 km (4.7 mi). Bear left (northwest) and ascend into the tarn-sequined, flower-rich meadows north of the Monarch Ramparts. Crest 2330-m (7642-ft) **Healy Pass** at 9.1 km (5.6 mi).

Skip below for a description of the pass and directions to the Monarch Ramparts.

Monarch Ramparts and The Monarch, from Healy Pass

Starting at Sunshine parking lot

Behind (west of) the gondola station, the Healy Creek trail (initially a road) starts left of the info kiosk. Cross the culvert and begin ascending. For the first seven minutes, your road is beneath and parallel to the Sunshine Village access road. Healy Creek is below (right).

At 0.8 km (0.5 mi), 1765 m (5790 ft), a road ascends left. Descend right (southwest) on trail. A minute farther, cross a bridge over Sunshine Creek. The trail remains wide.

At 3 km (1.9 mi) cross a bridge to the north bank of **Healy Creek** and continue southwest. An hour from the trailhead, begin a noticeable but easy ascent. Fifteen minutes farther, a meadow of willow and shrubby cinquefoil breaks the forest.

At 5.4 km (3.3 mi) **Healy Creek campground** is on the left. The creek, 30 m/yd distant, is audible. The open forest of predominantly spruce is interspersed with willows and grassy meadow.

Reach a fork at 5.9 km (3.7 mi), 1982 m (6500 ft). Bear right (west) for Healy Pass. The ascent steepens. Left crosses a bridge over Healy Creek and leads south to Simpson Pass. You'll return to this fork from Simpson Pass if you complete the Monarch Ramparts / Eohippus Lake circuit.

At 7.7 km (4.8 mi) enter another **meadow** and reach a junction 20 m/yd past a bridge. Left leads south to Simpson Pass. Go right, heading northwest into the tarn-sequined, flower-rich meadows north of the Monarch Ramparts. The trail levels at 2134 m (7000 ft).

Crest 2330-m (7642-ft) **Healy Pass** at 9.2 km (5.7 mi). Fast hikers will be here 2½ hours after departing the trailhead. Southeast is 3618-m (11,867-ft) Mt. Assiniboine—30 km (19 mi) distant. South, at the far end of the Monarch Ramparts, is the 2904-m (9525-ft) pyramid called The Monarch. West-northwest are Egypt and Scarab lakes. Northwest is Pharaoh Lake, beneath the Pharaoh Peaks. Northeast is the Massive Range, including Mt. Brett left and Mt. Bourgeau (Trip 9) right.

Healy Pass, the **Monarch Ramparts** extend southeast 4.2 km (2.6 mi) to the base of The Monarch. A bootbeaten route runs along the crest of this 2410-m (7905-ft) high ridge. Fast hikers can dispatch it, out and back, in 2¼ hours. But with a little cross-country experience and preferably a map in hand, you don't have to turn around. Keep going. Descend the southeast end of the Ramparts to the tarn-dotted meadows below and complete a 25.2-km (15.6-mi) circuit via Simpson Pass.

If hiking the circuit, don't bail off the Ramparts too soon. The left (northeast) side of the ridge is forbiddingly steep for most of its length. Only near the end, beneath The Monarch, is the descent comfortably gradual. Here, a path among the larch and boulders invites passage to the meadows below. Expect to see a profusion of glacier lilies if you come in early July.

Glacier lilies below Monarch Ramparts, early July

Having successfully dismounted the ridge, you'll find the route fades in the meadows. Proceed southeast about 1 km (0.6 mi) to intersect a trail above the north shore of **Eohippus Lake**. Turn left and follow it north.

Reach a junction in 3.2 km (2 mi). Left (west) leads to Healy Pass. Go right. A 7-minute descent east leads to a signed junction in 2135-m (7003-ft) **Simpson Pass**. Straight (east) goes to Sunshine Meadows via Wawa Ridge. Turn left (northeast).

A steep, 1.3-km (0.8-mi) descent north ensues. Within 15 minutes, cross a bridge over **Healy Creek** and intersect the Healy Creek trail at 1982 m (6500 ft). You're now on familiar ground. Turn right. Descend the Healy Creek trail generally northeast 5.9 km (3.7 mi) to the Sunshine parking lot.

TRIP 25

Whistling Pass via Redearth and Pharaoh Creeks

LOCATION	Banff National Park
CIRCUIT	21 km (13 mi) by bike, plus 26.4 km (16.4 mi) on foot, 47.4 km (29.4 mi) total
ELEVATION GAIN	340 m (1115 ft) by bike plus 560 m (1837 ft) on foot, 900 m (2952 ft) total
KEY ELEVATIONS	trailhead 1400 m (4592 ft), Redearth/Pharaoh junction 1740 m (5707 ft), Shadow Lake 1852 m (6075 ft), Haiduk Lake 2067 m (6780 ft) Whistling Pass 2300 m (7544 ft), Egypt Lake shelter 1995 m (6544 ft)
TRAVEL TIME	10 to 11 hours
DIFFICULTY	challenging
MAPS	page 506; Gem Trek *Banff - Egypt Lake*

OPINION

"My life is better than your vacation." They don't say it, but that's what many residents of Canmore and Banff think when they see people, obviously on holiday, streaming into Banff National Park.

It's smug. Presumptuous. Dismissive. It's also—judging by the envy visitors express to locals, and the gratitude locals feel about living here—plausible. Case in point: Whistling Pass. It's remote, wild, lonely, exciting, beautiful. As impressive as any vantage accessible by trail in the Canadian Rockies. Yet from Canmore or Banff, it's a daytrip. A wake-up-in-the-comfort-of-your-own-bed and be-back-home-for-a-late-dinner excursion. And if you live here, it's just one of countless, stirring, backcountry destinations on the whadya-wanna-do-today? menu.

Of course, Whistling Pass can also be a daytrip if you're a visitor. But only if you're hardy mountain folk, as experienced and capable as those whose permanent basecamp is Canmore or Banff. Otherwise this journey likely presents more mental and physical challenge than you can safely handle.

It begins with a 10.5-km (6.5-mi) approach via mountain bike, in which you'll ascend 340 m (1115 ft) through Redearth Creek Valley. The terrain—a former road—isn't technical, but you'll be climbing steadily through forest without motivation from notable views. Do not consider approaching on foot. Swiftly entering and exiting the region by bike is what makes this trip feasible in a day.

You'll then dismount, lock or stash your bike, and hike a 26.4-km (16.4-mi) loop trail gaining 560 m (1837 ft) over 2300-m (7544-ft) Whistling Pass—named after the resident marmots (whistlers).

From Egypt Lake shelter, you'll hike down Pharaoh Creek Valley. Here the striding is easy, but the distance will probably seem long given how much energy you've already expended. Arriving back at your mountain bike is both a relief and a thrill. The 10.5-km (6.5-mi) descent to the trailhead is a grinning, whooping, pedal-only-to-gain-speed affair that makes you wish every mountain venture ended like this.

Early summer is your window of opportunity here. You want the snowpack on Whistling Pass to have melted enough so it doesn't impede hiking, but you want to go as close to the summer solstice as possible, for maximal daylight. Try the last week of June through the first week of July. Pick a blue-sky day when a high-pressure zone has applied for permanent residence in southern Alberta. If the weather's questionable, you don't want to be out, exposed, so far from civilization, with so little on your back, for such a long time.

Start early. Pace yourself but keep moving. Take only short rest breaks. Endeavour not to rely on that headlamp that's in your pack. The downhill ride at day's end is no fun in the dark. Traveling 47.4 km (29.4 mi) in a nonstop push through backcountry Banff is an exhilarating, athletic accomplishment, especially worthwhile because of the stellar scenery en route between Shadow Lake and the basin south of Whistling Pass (See images on pages 32 and 299.)

FACT

By Vehicle

Drive Trans-Canada Hwy 1 southeast 10.5 km (6.5 mi) from Hwy 93 at Castle Junction, or west 20 km (12.4 mi) from Banff townsite. From either approach, turn south into the Redearth Creek trailhead parking lot, at 1400 m (4592 ft).

By Bike

Depart the far end of the trailhead parking lot, right of the toilets. A fence (built to prevent animal deaths on the highway) requires you to step up to a gate, then step back down to the trail, which for the first 10.5 km (6.5 mi) is a former road.

The trailhead sign is on the far side of the fence. Ignore the steep trail (blocked by deadfall) ascending left. Go right and begin a moderate ascent west-northwest.

After briefly paralleling the highway, the trail curves left into **Redearth Creek Valley**, high above the creek's southeast bank. Your general direction will remain southwest all the way to Shadow Lake.

A steady climb ensues. The grade is efficient: it rarely relents, but neither is it severe. Moderately-strong cyclists might feel compelled to walk their bikes on only a couple, short pitches.

At 6.9 km (4.3 mi) cross a bridge to the creek's northwest bank and pass **Lost Horse Creek** campground (right). Proceed up-valley.

Reach **Redearth/Pharaoh junction** at 10.5 km (6.5 mi), 1740 m (5707 ft). Cycling is prohibited beyond. Left leads generally south, following Pharaoh Creek upstream. Right abruptly ascends north, then continues southwest, past Shadow Lake Lodge, to Shadow Lake.

If you brought a lock, secure your iron horse to the bike rack near the fork. If you're lock-less and must therefore stash your bike and cycling gear, continue left (southwest) a couple minutes to the bridge spanning **Redearth Creek**. Immediately beyond is a cabin and corral in a **grassy clearing**. Hidey-holes are plentiful in the surrounding forest.

On Foot

From Redearth/Pharaoh junction at 10.5 km (6.5 mi), ascend right (north) to begin our recommended counter-clockwise circuit.

The trail skirts **Shadow Lake Lodge** at 1825 m (5986 ft). Shortly beyond, reach a fork at 12.9 km (8 mi). Go left. Right (north) climbs over Gibbon Pass to Twin Lakes (Trips 41 and 79).

The trail forks again on the northeast shore of **Shadow Lake**, at 13.9 km (8.6 mi), 1852 m (6075 ft). Right parallels the lake's north shore for another 2 km (1.2 mi). Go left (south) and cross a long bridge over the outlet. The bridge affords an unobstructed view west to glacier-mantled Mt. Ball.

Beyond the bridge, resume generally south on rough, often muddy trail. Soon cross a bridge over Whistling Creek. Haiduk Peak dominates the southern horizon. At 18.2 km (11.3 mi), 1921 m (6301 ft), reach **Ball Pass Junction campground** (right) and bridges spanning Ball Creek. The trail forks here. Right climbs southwest over Ball Pass (Trip 69). Go left.

The trail momentarily veers north before curving right and ascending southeast into **Whistling Valley**. Enter an open, marshy basin, pass right of a pond, and approach the southeast shore of **Haiduk Lake** at 21 km (13 mi), 2067 m (6780 ft). Haiduk Peak rises 852 m (2795 ft) directly above the southwest shore, Whistling Pass is visible southeast, and the Pharaoh Peaks form the upper valley's east wall.

After grazing Haiduk Lake, the trail rises southeast into the alpine zone. Crest 2300-m (7544-ft) **Whistling Pass** at 24.5 km (15.2 mi). In terms of scenery as well as elevation, this is the apex of the trip. Behind you (northwest) is a sublime view: over Haiduk Lake to Mt. Ball. The vista ahead (southeast) is equally marvelous: over Scarab Lake to The Monarch.

The trail gently drops into the flowery basin south of the pass and bends left (east). Soon enter forest, where a sharp descent on rugged trail ensues. At 26.3 km (16.3 mi) bear left, passing a right spur that descends south, skirts the east shore of Scarab Lake, then ends above, on the east shore of Mummy Lake.

Switchbacks plunge generally east-northeast. Pass a right (south) spur accessing the north shore of Egypt Lake. Reach level ground at 1995 m (6544 ft). Pass **Egypt Lake campground** tentsites (right). Reach a fork in front of **Egypt Lake shelter** at 28.2 km (17.5 mi). Continue straight (north) and begin the long, gradual descent of **Pharaoh Creek Valley**.

At 28.7 km (17.8 mi) ignore a left (west) spur ascending to Pharaoh, Black Rock, and Sphinx lakes. Proceed generally north for the next two hours. The trail remains close to **Pharaoh Creek**, crossing it repeatedly via bridges.

Pass **Pharaoh Creek campground** (left) at 32.7 km (20.3 mi). Cross the final Pharaoh Creek bridge and enter a **grassy clearing** at 36.8 km (22.8 mi). There's a cabin and corral here. If this is where you stashed your bike, you're now on familiar ground.

Immediately right (north) is a bridge spanning **Redearth Creek**. Just beyond (northeast), at 36.9 km (22.9 mi), 1740 m (5707 ft), is **Redearth/Pharaoh junction** and the bike rack where you began hiking. If you locked your bike here, you're now on familiar ground.

Mount your steed, bear right, and enjoy the long descent northeast back to **Redearth trailhead** on the Trans-Canada Hwy, where the bike-hike circuit ends at 47.4 km (29.4 mi).

TRIP 26

Mt. Saint Piran

LOCATION	Banff National Park
ROUND TRIP	13 km (8 mi)
ELEVATION GAIN	920 m (3018 ft)
KEY ELEVATIONS	trailhead 1730 m (5675 ft) summit 2650 m (8692 ft)
HIKING TIME	4½ to 5½ hours
DIFFICULTY	moderate
MAPS	page 497; Gem Trek *Lake Louise & Yoho*; Lake Louise 82 N/8

OPINION

The philosopher William James believed addiction expresses a yearning for the divine. It's an illuminating insight into why many of us crave mountain adventure and pursue it with unflagging zeal. We ascend thirstily, at every opportunity, not just for the vistas or the sense of accomplishment, but for the bliss, the rapture, the ineffable ecstasy that well up within us during intimate communion with mountain wilderness. Often, those feelings are hard won, requiring an exhaustive effort. But not on Mt. St. Piran, an easily-attained yet spectacular summit where mountain addicts can feed their obsession and initiates might acquire a healthy addiction.

The initial 3.7 km (2.3 mi) is on a cloyingly crowded trail from Lake Louise to the teahouse at Lake Agnes. At least it's moderately graded and easy to stride. Just before the teahouse, the trail to St. Piran veers off, and the sense that you're participating in a human migration will subside. You'll ascend onto subalpine slopes with not a single teahouse pilgrim in sight. Shortly beyond, you'll turn onto a spur and evade most of the remaining hikers bound for the Little Beehive (Trip 66).

Though missing from most maps, this spur quickly reveals itself to be a narrow but distinct trail. Switchbacks make the ascent comfortably gradual. The views, which began near the teahouse, have expanded to a panoramic vista that continues improving. The final 15 minutes to the summit require you to negotiate loose, ragged rock on the mountain's steep, upper spine. Tread mindfully. A saddle just below the summit is a gratifying consolation prize.

Atop St. Piran, high above Lake Agnes and the Little Beehive, you'll behold a big swath of Banff Park's best scenery. This is one of the most impressive hiker-accessible perches in the area. Many of the dozen or so mammoth peaks ringing Lake Louise are in view. Even the Waputik Icefield is visible, far above Kicking Horse Pass. Allow yourself 45 minutes to sit and absorb.

Mt. Temple, Haddo Peak and Mt. Aberdeen, from St. Piran trail

FACT

By Vehicle

From Lake Louise village, go south-southwest on Lake Louise Drive. Continue uphill 5.3 km (3.3 mi) to the actual *Lake* Louise. About 200 m (220 yd) before the road ends at Chateau Lake Louise, turn left into the bi-level parking lot, at 1730 m (5675 ft).

Before your trip

Read page 37 about possible hiking restrictions due to bears.

On Foot

From the west end of the lower parking lot, walk the paved path west to **Lake Louise**, at 1731 m (5678 ft). Bear right. Follow the path around the end of the lake. Pass the **Chateau**. On the northeast shore is a trail sign (starting point for distances below). Go right (northwest), away from the lake. Proceed into the **forest** on a well-maintained trail. A break in the trees soon grants a view south, across the lake, to 2744-m (9000-ft) Fairview Mtn.

At 2.4 km (1.5 mi) bear left (west) where a horse trail goes right to Lake Louise village. A few minutes farther, at 2.6 km (1.6 mi), 2025 m (6642 ft), reach a junction at **Mirror Lake**. Go right (north-northwest) on the main trail to Lake Agnes. Begin a switchbacking ascent. About 40 minutes from the parking lot, strong hikers will attain the first of many grand views over the Bow Valley. Castle Mtn is east-southeast. Larches are increasingly prevalent as you ascend.

Five minutes farther, reach a junction at 3.1 km (1.9 mi), 2082 m (6830 ft). The **Lake Agnes teahouse** is visible ahead (west), above and beyond a headwall cascade. For Mt. St. Piran, fork right (northeast) toward Little Beehive.

Within ten minutes, reach the next junction, at 3.6 km (2.2 mi). Left (straight) descends southwest 0.3 km (0.2 mi) to the teahouse. Detour that way while returning from St. Piran, then descend to rejoin the main trail at Mirror Lake. For now, go right (north-northeast) and ascend toward Little Beehive.

The next turn (12 minutes farther if you're fast, 15 if you're slower) is obscure; stay alert. Enter the subalpine zone (stunted trees), attain views over Lake Louise and the Chateau, and proceed onto an open slope. Two minutes after trees again encroach on the trail, reach a fork at 3.8 km (2.4 mi), 2191 m (7186 ft). There's a big boulder on the left, by a sign. The main trail rounds a small point and proceeds north-northeast 0.5 km (0.3 mi) to Little Beehive. Turn left and ascend north-northwest on a distinct, yet easily-overlooked spur.

Doubting you'll make it to the summit? Follow the spur just ten minutes farther (75 m / 245 ft higher) for a terrific, 180° view. You'll see several icy peaks, including 3464-m (11,362-ft) Mt. Victoria (southwest), and 3543-m (11,621-ft) Mt. Temple (south-southeast).

Determined to summit? Good. Continue ascending moderately graded switchbacks on open slopes. Attain increasingly splendid views. Behind you (south) are Mt. Aberdeen (right) and Haddo Peak (left).

Reach a **saddle** at 2526 m (8285 ft), just 15 minutes below the summit. The Waputik Icefield is visible northwest. Hector Lake is distant north-northwest. Broad, forested Pipestone River Valley is north-northeast. From the saddle, ascend the rough route over boulders and loose slabs. Step carefully. Attain the summit of 2650-m (8692-ft) **Mt. St. Piran** at 6.5 km (4 mi).

Nearby, west-southwest, just across Goat Pass, is 2976-m (9761-ft) Mt. Niblock. The Devil's Thumb (Trip 27) is also nearby, south. Beyond the Thumb, appearing to loom above it, are ice-crusted Mt. Lefroy and The Mitre.

To overlook Lake Agnes, Mirror Lake and Lake Louise all at once, walk southwest a few minutes, down the rounded crest of the summit ridge, to a nearly flat spot. Abbot Pass is also visible south-southwest, between Mounts Victoria (right) and Lefroy (left).

Devil's Thumb shadow in Lake Agnes. Teahouse above far shore.

TRIP 27

Devil's Thumb

LOCATION	Banff National Park , above Lake Louise
CIRCUIT	10.4 km (6.4 mi)
ELEVATION GAIN	778 m (2552 ft)
KEY ELEVATIONS	trailhead 1731 m (5678 ft) summit 2458 m (8062 ft)
HIKING TIME	3 to 4 hours
DIFFICULTY	easy until challenging final approach
MAPS	page 497; Gem Trek *Best of Lake Louise*

OPINION

Human beings exist on the thin seam of extremes: earth, and atmosphere. Most of us are never aware of it. Atop a mountain, it's obvious.

An exalted perspective helps us see we're a fortunate bunch, we humans, a unique miracle in this vast universe. And it reminds us: life on earth is precarious; to sustain it, we must restore the balance immediately.

These realizations—one exhilarating, the other sobering—make summiting a heady experience. So let's climb. A thrilling place to do it is Devil's Thumb.

As the name suggests, it's not actually a mountain. Calling it a *peaklet* would be generous. It's just a promontory. Yet its location is astounding: overlooking Lake Louise, on the edge of a glaciated cirque, among a coterie of 3000-m (9840-ft), ice-encrusted goliaths comprising the most celebrated massif in the Canadian Rockies.

In summer, thousands of tourists visit Lake Louise each day and gasp at what they see. The view from the lakeshore is stirring. But topping out on Devil's Thumb dials it up to paint-shaker intensity. Plus it's a tranquil summit. You'll likely be alone.

The crowds of lakeshore gawkers? So far away, they appear no bigger than the dot at the end of this sentence. The lakeshore hotel? A mere Chiclet beside the water.

The probability of solitude on Devil's Thumb is not due to distance from the trailhead. This is a short hike, mostly on an exceptionally well-maintained path. But the Thumb is a detour. The route deteriorates, narrows, contours a precipitous slope, then points you at the final, trail-less, skyward pitch and says, "Good luck."

This climactic passage is very short. Strong hikers accustomed to off-trail rambling pound up it unconcerned and would testify in court it doesn't qualify as scrambling.

The footholds, however, are small and shallow. This alone might disorient the little elves, responsible for balance, who reside in your head. If so, back off. Leave the satanic digit on your someday list. Though shy of the summit, you'll have achieved a gratifying panorama and will enjoy the rest of this otherwise easy circuit.

While Devil's Thumb itself is lightly visited, the trail to and from, especially near Lake Agnes (Trip 66), can be buzzy as a shopping mall. To enjoy any semblance of peace, start hiking before 9 a.m. or after 4 p.m.

FACT

By Vehicle

Drive Hwy 1, 1A, or 93 to Lake Louise. From Lake Louise Village, drive uphill (southwest) on Lake Louise Drive. Continue to the actual *Lake* Louise. Near road's end, 200 m (656 ft) before the Chateau Lake Louise, turn left into the multilevel parking area.

On Foot

From the west end of the lower parking lot, walk the paved path west to **Lake Louise**, at 1731 m (5678 ft). Bear right. Follow the path around the end of the lake. Pass the **Chateau**. On the **northeast shore** is a trail sign (starting point for distances below). Go right (northwest), away from the lake. Proceed into the **forest** on a well-maintained trail.

A break in the trees soon grants a view south, across the lake, to 2744-m (9000-ft) Fairview Mtn. At 2.4 km (1.5 mi), bear left (west) where a horse trail goes right to Lake Louise Village. A few minutes farther, at 2.6 km (1.6 mi), 2025 m (6642 ft), reach a junction at **Mirror Lake**.

Turn left and, in 100 m (328 ft), turn right for the direct ascent to Lake Agnes (Trip 66). Left is the Highline trail, which you'll return on to this junction. Reach the **Lake Agnes teahouse** at 3.1 km (1.9 mi), 2135 m (7003 ft), above the lake's northeast end. The Big Beehive rises above the southeast shore.

From the teahouse, follow the trail southwest along the **northwest shore of Lake Agnes**. Curve around the lake's southwest end, then ascend generally southeast to a four-way junction atop the ridge, at 4.4 km (2.7 mi), 2261 m (7416 ft). This is **Big Beehive saddle**. Left follows the ridgecrest northeast five minutes to the gazebo atop Big Beehive. On the return, descend south from here, to the Highline trail.

For Devil's Thumb, go right (southwest) on the unmarked, initially broad path. It ascends gradually through larches. Within five minutes, encounter the one obstacle where you'll likely use your hands: a **rock outcrop** about 3 m (10 ft) high. Above it, follow the narrow route curving around the southeast side of the promontory.

Fifteen minutes from Big Beehive saddle, the path curves right (north) and deteriorates. Ascend the slope (dirt, grass, scree) following others' bootprints. A 20-m (66-ft) section is steep and challenging.

Above that, you'll find solid purchase on grassy ledges. Reach a **small saddle** immediately west of and below your objective. Go right, working your way over rock slabs, to the 2458-m (8062-ft) summit of **Devil's Thumb** at 5.2 km (3.2 mi).

Ceiling of gazebo atop Big Beehive

Lake Agnes (northeast) is visible 338 m (1109 ft) below. Lake Louise (east) is 727 m (2385 ft) below. Mt. Victoria is west-southwest. Abbot Pass is southwest, with Mt. Lefroy towering above its east side. The Mitre is south-southwest, Haddo Peak is south-southeast, and Mt. Aberdeen is between them.

Mt. Victoria, en route to Devil's Thumb

Retrace your steps to the junction in **Big Beehive saddle**. Go right (south). Descend steeply for 1.1 km (0.7 mi) to a T-junction with the **Highline trail**, at 2010 m (6593 ft). Your total distance here is 6.9 km (4.3 mi). Turn left and follow the Highline trail generally north. It ascends to, then undulates near, 2050 m (6724 ft) to reach a junction immediately south of **Mirror Lake**.

You're now on familiar ground. Turn right. In 100 m (328 ft), turn right again. Descend south, then switchback down to reach the northeast shore of **Lake Louise** at 10.4 km (6.4 mi).

TRIP 28

Eiffel Lake / Wenkchemna Pass

LOCATION	Banff National Park
ROUND TRIP	11.2 km (7 mi) to lake 19.4 km (12 mi) to pass
ELEVATION GAIN	405 m (1328 ft) to lake 725 m (2378 ft) to pass
KEY ELEVATIONS	trailhead 1885 m (6183 ft) lake 2290 m (7510 ft) pass 2610 m (8560 ft)
HIKING TIME	5 to 6 hours
DIFFICULTY	moderate
MAPS	page 495; Gem Trek *Lake Louise & Yoho*; Lake Louise 82 N/8

OPINION

It's the ultimate art gallery. Ten supernal peaks are lavishly displayed so close across the valley you can almost hear your oohs and ahhs come echoing back.

This is the Valley of the Ten Peaks, best appreciated from the higher vantages of Larch Valley and Sentinel Pass (Trip 5). But the trail to Eiffel Lake, while lower, has the benefit of being even closer to the peaks. And the contouring trail allows you to devote full attention to them instead of boot placement or muscle strain.

En route to Wenkchemna Pass, Eiffel Lake is impressive enough to warrant destination status. It's spectacular in bright sunlight, shimmering from sapphire to cobalt. The lake is named after the peak above its northeast shore. But it's Neptuak Mtn, above the southwest shore, that hikers marvel at from the trail while gazing at the lake. *Neptuak*, which means *nine* in the Stoney Indian language, is the ninth peak in the celebrated ten. So, to fully appreciate all the peaks, hike at least as far as the lake. The Stoney word for *ten*? *Wenkchemna*.

Wenkchemna Pass doesn't qualify for the gallery showing. Views south and west are disappointing. Sentinel Pass is vastly superior. And hiking to Wenkchemna Pass is longer and more taxing than it appears from Eiffel Lake. But it can be worthwhile. The trail is through intriguingly desolate moraine. And the pass is, after all, atop the headwall of arguably the grandest valley in the Rockies. Go for the going's sake, not with any expectation of ultimate reward.

Keep in mind, the first 2.4 km (1.4 mi) from the trailhead are not level, as is the subsequent stretch to Eiffel Lake. And this initial leg of the trip is the same as for Trip 5. So it's possible to visit Sentinel and Wenkchemna passes on a long dayhike.

Wenkchemna Peak above Eiffel Lake. The pass is left of the peak.

FACT

By Vehicle

From Lake Louise village, drive uphill, southwest, on Lake Louise Drive. Turn left on Moraine Lake Road and follow it 12.5 km (7.8 mi) to the huge parking lot at road's end. Elevation: 1885 m (6183 ft).

Before your trip

Read page 37 about possible hiking restrictions due to bears.

On Foot

From the shore of Moraine Lake, walk past the lodge to the trailhead sign. The wide path switchbacks as it ascends moderately through forest. After gaining 375 m (1230 ft) in 2.4 km (1.5 mi), reach a **junction**. Right ascends to Sentinel Pass. Bear left for Eiffel Lake.

The trail contours west across flower-speckled subalpine slopes at the base of Eiffel Peak. At 5.6 km (3.5 mi), 2290 m (7510 ft), reach small **Eiffel Lake** set in sharp, angular boulders. Soon after, the trail ascends gently west-northwest and crosses boulder fields. It steepens during the last several switchbacks over scree to reach **Wenkchemna Pass** at 9.7 km (6 mi), 2610 m (8560 ft). The pass environs can retain snow all year, but even if the trail is obscured near the top, it's easy to find your way.

Looking south-southwest from the pass, you'll witness the devastation of the summer 2003 fire that swept up Tokumm Creek valley, all the way to the pass. What remains of the once lush and dense forest are charred snags and blackened earth.

TRIP 29

Saddleback / Fairview Mtn

LOCATION	Banff National Park
ROUND TRIP	7.4 km (4.6 mi) for Saddleback 10.6 km (6.6 mi) for Fairview
ELEVATION GAIN	600 m (1970 ft) to Saddleback plus 414 m (1358 ft) to Fairview
KEY ELEVATIONS	trailhead 1730 m (5674 ft) Saddleback 2330 m (7642 ft) Fairview 2744 m (9000 ft)
HIKING TIME	4 to 5 hours for Fairview
DIFFICULTY	moderate
MAPS	page 497; Gem Trek *Lake Louise & Yoho;* Lake Louise 82 N/8

OPINION

Fairview is a hands-in-your-pocket summit. No scrambling required. But this burly mountain takes a brash stance, cheek-by-jowl with the monster peaks of Lake Louise. So the panorama packs a punch. You'll also see Lake Louise from a startling perspective: 1000 m (3280 ft) below you.

The trail up Fairview is the highest in the Canadian Rockies. (Routes like the one up Temple don't count.) On the way is Saddleback, a meadowy pass between Fairview and Saddle Mtn. With a rifle-shot view of Mt. Temple, meadows rich with wildflowers in summer, and larch trees brilliant gold in fall, Saddleback is a destination in its own right. You won't be here alone—it's often crowded—but you'll be glad you came. If you join the larch march in late September, don't stop where the trail arrives at the pass. Hikers collide here like bumper cars. Continue right (north) a little to find seclusion among the trees.

Just reaching Saddleback is steep. It's short though, and avalanche swaths break the forest, allowing motivational views across Bow Valley. If you've got the get-up-and-go to climb Fairview, jump up and do it. The additional 45 to 60 minutes (one way) doubles the value of the hike.

Though Fairview is the primo viewpoint on this trip, there's another: Saddle Mountain. This minor summit is 90 m (295 ft) above Saddleback and takes about 30 minutes to bag. On top is a pulse-pounding precipice, a hang glider's dream launch into Paradise Valley.

FACT

By Vehicle

From Lake Louise village, go south-southwest on Lake Louise Drive. Continue uphill 5.3 km (3.3 mi) to the actual *Lake* Louise. About 200 m (220 yd) before the road

On Fairview Mtn summit. Left to right: Mounts Aberdeen, Lefroy, and Victoria.

ends at Chateau Lake Louise, turn left into the bi-level parking lot. If you park in the lower lot, walk to the canoe-rental building at the northeast end of Lake Louise. The trailhead is here, at 1730 m (5674 ft). If you park in the upper lot, a spur trail from the west edge of the pavement joins the trail 100 m (110 yd) beyond the trailhead.

Before your trip

Read page 37 about possible hiking restrictions due to bears.

On Foot

Head southeast up the forested slope of Fairview Mtn. In 300 m (330 yd), keep straight. The right fork goes 1 km (0.6 mi) to a lookout 100 m (330 ft) above the lake. Stay straight again at 0.4 km (0.25 mi). The left fork contours southeast around the base of Fairview Mtn to join the Paradise Valley trail.

Continue ascending steeply southeast among ancient spruce. Avalanche paths grant Bow Valley views left (east). At about 1.6 km (1 mi), the trail bends southwest. Stay on the main trail if you notice a steeper route right. Switchback up through larches to subalpine meadows. Reach the **Saddleback** at 3.7 km (2.3 mi), 2330 m (7642 ft). Fairview Mtn is right (northwest). Saddle Mtn is left (east). The 1200-m (3940-ft) north face of glacier-capped Mt. Temple is south, across Paradise Valley. The sheer wall of Sheol Mtn is nearby south-southwest. Haddo Peak is southwest.

Straight ahead when you arrive at Saddleback, you might notice a faint trail descending south through larches. It plunges deep into Sheol Valley to join the Paradise Valley trail in 4.1 km (2.5 mi). From there, it's a long way through forest back to Lake Louise. It's better to return the way you came.

Mt. Aberdeen, from just below Fairview Mtn summit

Sheol Mountain, from Saddleback

If proceeding to **Fairview Mtn**, don't follow the bootbeaten shortcut up steep talus on your right as you enter Saddleback. It's easier and equally fast to continue into the pass, then go right (northwest). From the upper larch fringe, a distinct trail switchbacks steeply 1.6 km (1 mi) up Fairview's southeast slope. You'll climb 414 m (1358 ft) from Saddleback to the 2744-m (9000-ft) **summit**. Total distance from the trailhead: 5.3 km (3.3 mi). Glacier-crowned Mt.Victoria is southwest. You'll want a topo map to identify all the other peaks.

TRIP 30

Molar Pass

LOCATION	Banff National Park
ROUND TRIP	20.4 km (12.6 mi)
ELEVATION GAIN	540 m (1775 ft)
KEY ELEVATIONS	trailhead 1830 m (6000 ft) pass 2370 m (7775 ft)
HIKING TIME	6 to 7 hours
DIFFICULTY	easy
MAPS	page 514; Hector Lake 82 N/9

OPINION

Life unraveling in a frenzied blur? Here's where to slow down. Groove on the simple but soulful pleasure of walking. Move through the world at a humane, awareness-sharpening, life-lengthening pace. And what a beautiful sliver of the world this is.

The rooty and muddy-when-wet trail saunters through open forest—not the typical claustrophobic chore—with lively Mosquito Creek and its tributaries for company. An easy to moderate ascent leads to meadows within a couple hours. A short wander into Molar Pass reveals greenery spangled with wildflowers from mid-July to early August. Views of peaks include Molar Mtn and glacier-chested Mt. Hector.

With a little extra time and energy, say two hours, you can extend your walk toward North Molar Pass (Trip 88). You'll have walked 60% of the way there already. The Mosquito Lake environs reprise the alpine wonders you witnessed at Molar Pass. Pad through the gently sloping tundra as far east as you please.

Walking becomes work southeast of Molar Pass, on the rough, wet trail descending into the long, dull Pipestone River valley. Go there only in search of solitude. You'll find little else. The sensible way to visit Pipestone Pass is via North Molar Pass and the highline route from Fish Lakes.

FACT

By Vehicle

Follow directions for Fish Lakes (Trip 88) to the parking lot, at 1830 m (6000 ft).

On Foot

Just past the trailhead kiosk, begin a brief climb north above **Mosquito Creek**. The trail gradually returns creekside and continues upstream (north). All the crossings of Mosquito and its tributaries are bridged. The ascent is gentle, the tread rooty and rocky. Proceed through open, coniferous forest, often on the creek's level, broad, boulder-strewn bank.

Molar Pass.

Reach **Mosquito Creek campground** at 5.5 km (3.4 mi), 2015 m (6610 ft). Just past the campground, cross to the creek's south bank. The trail gradually curves east, remaining creekside for another 1 km (0.6 mi). The ascent is moderate. Cross back to the north bank at 6.7 km (4.2 mi), now curving southeast.

Reach a **junction** at 7.3 km (4.5 mi), 2195 m (7200 ft). Bear right (southeast) for Molar Pass. Left (northeast) leads to North Molar Pass (Trip 88). On a foray in that direction, you'll gain 115 m (375 ft) to Mosquito Lake (unlabeled on the topo map).

Proceeding toward Molar Pass, the trail rapidly approaches timberline. The pass is in view about 15 minutes beyond the junction. The trail soon deteriorates, then temporarily vanishes in muck. Keep tromping southeast, following what appears to be the logical route, until the trail reappears on a higher, drier slope. Behind you (northwest) is an impressive sight dominated by 2972-m (9748-ft) Dolomite Peak on the left and unnamed 2988-m (9800-ft) peaks on the right.

Above and east of Molar Pass

Near 9.7 km (6 mi) the trail steepens, traversing southwest up the grassy, rocky headwall. Visible north are the vast meadowlands crossed en route to North Molar Pass. Crest **Molar Pass** at 10.2 km (6.3 mi), 2370 m (7775 ft).

The trail proceeds southeast through the pass. The next 0.8 km (0.5 mi) offer easy, scenic hiking across a rolling meadow. Molar Mtn (3022 m / 9912 ft), distinguished by its twin buttes, is visible southeast. The icy, north aspect of Mt. Hector is south.

TRIP 31
Bow Hut

LOCATION	Banff National Park
ROUND TRIP	14.8 km (9.2 mi)
ELEVATION GAIN	500 m (1640 ft)
KEY ELEVATIONS	trailhead 1940 m (6365 ft), hut 2440 m (8000 ft)
HIKING TIME	5 to 6 hours
DIFFICULTY	moderate
MAPS	page 494; Gem Trek *Bow Lake & Saskatchewan Crossing*; Hector Lake 82 N/9

OPINION

Earth's raw, naked body is fully displayed here. You'll hike the trail nearly to Bow Glacier Falls, then follow a well-trod route up a rough-and-tumble canyon to a spacious hut perched near the edge of the 40-sq-km Wapta Icefield. Light scrambling is briefly necessary only where a limestone boulder bridges a precipitous gorge. Acrophobes might recoil, but most hikers will be unfazed. Beyond, the route is gnarlier than most national park trails but won't deter experienced hikers. The hut's easy accessibility is unusual, allowing non-climbers a safe glimpse into the mountaineers' fantastic realm of rock and ice. A daytrip is sufficient to visit the hut and absorb the sights.

FACT

Before your trip

If you want to stay in the Bow Hut, check the current price and make reservations with the Alpine Club of Canada. The contact numbers are listed under *Information Sources* in the back of this book.

By Vehicle

Drive the Icefields Parkway to Bow Lake—36 km (22.3 mi) northwest of where the Parkway departs the Trans-Canada Hwy near Lake Louise village, or 5 km (3 mi) southeast of Bow Summit. From either approach, turn west onto the Num-ti-jah Lodge / Bow Glacier road and continue 0.4 km (0.25 mi) to the trailhead parking area on the left at 1940 m (6365 ft).

On Foot

Walk past the lodge and onto the level trail gradually curving southwest around the northwest shore of **Bow Lake**. South (left) is 3050-m (10,004-ft) Crowfoot Mtn. Reach the lake's west end in 20 minutes. Proceed south across gravel flats. The trail beside the inlet stream is cairned. If the water's too high, follow the parallel, alternate trail 30-60 m/yd to the west, undulating over terminal moraines (now forest-and-brush-covered lumps).

Bow Hut, beneath Mt. Nicholas

Reach the **gorge** at 3.3 km (2 mi). A reinforced trail steeply ascends the north edge. Here at 1997 m (6550 ft), about 45 minutes from the trailhead, arrive at a **limestone boulder** bridging the gorge. Heading for Bow Glacier Falls (Trip 45)? Don't cross; continue ascending right. For Bow Hut, cross the limestone boulder. Solid hand-and-footholds are plentiful, and the top is broad and flat, but be careful. Turn back if hesitant.

Across the boulder, on the east side of the gorge, follow the lower, rockier, boot-beaten path right. It soon curves left, rises through trees, then drops sharply to the creek. Proceed south, upstream. Negotiate a steep rockslide, then resume a gradual ascent on the canyon-edge path. Shortly after exiting the forest and rock-hopping a tributary creek, reach 2207 m (7240 ft) on a moraine. You're now entering a bouldery **cirque**. The hut is visible above (right / southwest).

At 6.8 km (4.2 mi), near the head of the cirque, the route turns right (west). It gets steeper and rougher. Reach **Bow Hut** at 7.4 km (4.6 mi), 2440 m (8000 ft). Mt. Olive (3130 m / 10,269 ft) is south. Though you can pick your way a little farther, up to the Wapta Icefield, don't venture onto the ice without the knowledge and equipment to do it safely.

TRIP 32
Sunset Pass and Lookout

LOCATION	Banff National Park
ROUND TRIP	16.4 km (10.2 mi) to pass plus 3.2 km (2 mi) to lookout
ELEVATION GAIN	725 m (2380 ft) to pass plus 201 m (659 ft) to lookout
KEY ELEVATIONS	trailhead 1440 m (4723 ft) pass 2165 m (7103 ft) lookout 1993 m (6537 ft)
HIKING TIME	5 to 7 hours
DIFFICULTY	moderate
MAPS	page 509; Gem Trek *Bow Lake & Saskatchewan Crossing*

OPINION

A steep ascent through trees will buy you an equal distance of meadow wandering in Sunset Pass. It's a bargain. The beauty of the meadows, the possibility of enjoying them in early summer, and the option of a side trip to a superb valley-viewpoint, more than compensate for the effort you'll expend.

En route to the pass, detour to Sunset Lookout. It commands an exceptional vista of Banff Park's northern reaches, including nearby ice-capped summits and the braided channels of the Alexandra River. But if you don't have time for both the pass and the lookout, push on to the pass. The highway is an inescapable feature of the lookout panorama. Sunset Pass is 2.5-km (1.6-mi) long and utterly wild. Peaks surrounding this hidden, hanging vale are far apart, more scree than cliff, but the scene is impressive nonetheless.

The trail to the pass has a southwest exposure, and the meadows are broad, giving the sun every opportunity to melt the snowpack and clear the way for you by mid- to late June. The meadows could be saturated with water, however, until the end of July. (Gaiters keep boots drier in the soggy, willowy meadows.) Still, it's worth proceeding through the pass. Though the initial view of the meadows is rewarding, the scenery opens up as you go, revealing the surrounding mountains, climaxing with an aerial perspective of Pinto Lake far below the north end of the pass.

Strong hikers who start early can detour to Sunset Lookout, traverse Sunset Pass to the Pinto Lake overlook, and return to the trailhead, all in a day. If you're pressed for time, probe the pass but stop short of the overlook, so you can visit the lookout on your way back. The other option is to spend a night on the edge of the pass, at Norman Lake campground—one of Banff's more appealing backcountry sites. The lake, really just a pond, is distant, but the tentsites are comfortably spaced among large spruce trees and afford views of the pass environs.

Sunset Pass is grizzly habitat. Be wary and make noise. Bring binoculars if you have them. The open terrain makes it possible to spot large mammals at a distance, but unaided you might have difficulty identifying them. A deer and a bear can both look like brown blobs when they're 2 km (1.2 mi) away and you're squinting into the sun.

FACT

By Vehicle

Drive the Icefields Parkway (Hwy 93) north 16.5 km (10.2 mi) from Saskatchewan Crossing, or south 28.5 km (17.7 mi) from the Banff-Jasper boundary at Sunwapta Pass. The trailhead parking lot is at the base of a forested slope, on the north side of the parkway, just west of the Norman Creek bridge, at 1440 m (4723 ft).

On Foot

From the info kiosk, the trail climbs into forest. Switchbacks moderate the ascent. Within 15 minutes, at 1 km (0.6 mi), a right (northeast) spur allows a glimpse into Norman Creek gorge. Ten minutes farther, at 1598 m (5240 ft), is a better overlook, again on the right. The ascent soon steepens. Half an hour up, at 1677 m (5500 ft), attain a view west over the braided channels of the Alexandra River Valley.

At 2.9 km (1.8 mi), 1860 m (6101 ft), having gained 420 m (1378 ft) in about an hour, reach a **junction**. Right (north-northeast) continues to Sunset Pass. Left (northwest) leads to Sunset Lookout; see description below.

Proceeding to Sunset Pass, the ascent remains stiff for another seven minutes or so before easing. The undergrowth is more complex and lush now. At a low, exposed rock shoulder, turn east and descend. Ignore the overgrown, defunct path straight ahead. A shallow, seasonal pond is below. Descend slightly for several minutes, then ascend steeply through yet more forest.

At 3.8 km (2.4 mi), 1960 m (6430 ft), you've vanquished most of the ascent. Relax. Large boulders beneath the trees provide seating from which you can survey the Sunset Pass environs ahead. East is the stark massif of an unnamed peak. North-northwest is 3135-m (10,283-ft) Mt. Coleman. The trail enters a rolling field of willows, then crosses a footbridge over Norman Creek.

While crossing the gentle hill to the campground, look back to Norman Lake—the small, teal pond that feeds the creek. The meadow mostly comprises thickets of difficult-to-negotiate willows; stay on the path to skirt it.

At 4.2 km (2.6 mi), 1966 m (6450 ft), reach **Norman Lake campground**. It's on the edge of the meadow, beneath large spruce trees. It has a fire pit, outhouse, and bear-proof food storage. The tent pads are level and well separated. Just beyond the campground is a fine view (especially in morning light) southwest to the icy summit of Mt. Amery and south to the striated cliffs of its outlier.

To proceed north into Sunset Pass, go left (north-northeast) from the first tentsite. The trail is immediately left of the tree bearing the campground sign. It rounds the east side of a marshy, willowy meadow. Undulating, it rises and dips about 7.5 m (25 ft) along the way. The meadows continue 300 m (328 yd) before the trail enters a stand of trees. Ascend among scattered trees to reach the north edge of **Sunset Pass** at 8.2 km (5.1 mi), 2165 m (7103 ft), on the Banff Park boundary. This is the highpoint of the trip.

North Saskatchewan River Valley, from Sunset Lookout

Sunset Pass meadows

The trail continues into the White Goat Wilderness. Follow it 0.5 km (0.3 mi) northwest onto a flank of Mt. Coleman, where deep-blue Pinto Lake and the Cline River valley are visible northeast, 415 m (1360 ft) below you. From the park boundary, it's 6 km (3.7 mi) to the campground just north of **Pinto Lake**. From there, a muddy, horse-trodden trail descends the Cline River valley 30 km (18.6 mi) to the David Thompson Highway.

SUNSET LOOKOUT

At the 2.9-km (1.8-mi) junction described above, go northwest. The former fire lookout is 1.6 km (1 mi) distant. After gaining 143 m (470 ft) in 20 minutes, the grade eases, virtually contouring north-northwest at 2027 m (6650 ft). This easy stretch lasts about seven minutes before plunging 34 m (110 ft) to the **Sunset Lookout** site at trail's end. Elevation: 1993 m (6537 ft). You're on an overhanging escarpment here; be cautious.

A huge expanse of the North Saskatchewan River valley is visible. The Parkway is 553 m (1814 ft) below. West-northwest is 3342-m (10,962-ft) Mt. Saskatchewan. West is the Alexandra River Valley. Southwest is 3329-m (10,923-ft) Mt. Amery. Southeast is the glacier-bearing massif of 3261-m (10,696-ft) Mt. Wilson, whose soaring cliffs loom above the Icefields Parkway north of Saskatchewan Crossing.

TRIP 33

Nigel Pass

LOCATION	Banff National Park
ROUND TRIP	14.4 km (8.9 mi)
ELEVATION GAIN	365 m (1197 ft)
KEY ELEVATIONS	trailhead 1860 m (6100 ft), pass 2195 m (7200 ft)
HIKING TIME	4½ to 6 hours
DIFFICULTY	easy
MAPS	page 496; Gem Trek *Columbia Icefield*; Columbia Icefield 83 C/3

OPINION

Nigel Pass asks little and gives generously. It turns nobody away. Even wobbly hikers with blown knees find comfort and joy on this gentle, merciful trail. The word *steep* does not apply here.

A high-elevation trailhead ensures the trees en route are too few to obscure views for long. Probing the refreshingly open Nigel Creek valley, the trail slices through avalanche paths and subalpine meadows. Wildflowers are rife in summer. You'll enjoy big scenery the whole way. South is the icy vastness of northern Banff. North is the remote wilderness of southern Jasper.

The pass is a humble, unremarkable, but very accommodating ridge. Surrounding it are nameless, starkly beautiful mountains. The trail drops off the pass to an easy though unbridged crossing of the Brazeau River. There you have a choice. The main trail climbs through boulders and scree. It eventually leads to Jonas Pass (Trip 92)—highlight of a premier multi-day loop—but dayhikers should definitely continue 0.8 km (0.5 mi) in that direction, where a grand view of the Brazeau River valley awaits them. The other option after the unbridged river crossing is to head upstream on a sketchy route into upper Brazeau canyon (Trip 10). By following it all the way to Cataract Pass, you can stretch the moderate Nigel Pass dayhike into a full day of rewarding exploration.

FACT

By Vehicle

Drive the Icefields Parkway (Hwy 93) south 8 km (5 mi) from the Banff-Jasper boundary at Sunwapta Pass, or north 37 km (23 mi) from Saskatchewan River Crossing (junction of Hwys 93 and 11). The trailhead parking area is on a dirt access road, below the northeast side of the Parkway, at 1860 m (6100 ft).

Nigel Pass

On Foot

From the trailhead kiosk, descend the gated access road. About 50 m (65 yd) past the gate, turn right (north) onto the south end of the historic South Boundary Trail. It descends to a bridge over **Nigel Creek**. After admiring the water-sculpted boulders, cross to the northeast bank and begin a gentle ascent through a pleasant forest of Engelmann spruce and alpine fir.

Soon curve northwest, contouring above the creek. The forest is broken by avalanche paths that grant views. Yellow-orange Sitka columbine, red paintbrush, purple fleabane, cobalt larkspur, and white yarrow thrive here in summer. Fifteen minutes along, cross a rocky gully. The trail then plows through waist-to-head-high willows. The creek below helps muffle the still audible highway noise.

At 1905 m (6248 ft), about 40 minutes from the trailhead, reach a fork. Left is blocked. Bear right on the main trail. Enter historic **Camp Parker** at 2.1 km (1.3 mi), among large Engelmann spruce. The trail forks again. Left leads to a corral, descends to footbridges spanning Nigel and Hilda creeks, then ascends to a warden cabin, which is accessed via the gated trailhead road. Go right (north-northeast) following the signed, main trail. It stays east of Nigel Creek to ascend the valley. Hilda Peak, a satellite of Mt. Athabasca, is soon visible south.

About an hour from the trailhead, curve right (north) into **Nigel Creek valley**. The sound of vehicles on the highway finally vanishes. Willowy meadows allow 360° views. You can glimpse Parker Ridge (Trip 11) southwest. Gray, scree-laden mountains surround you.

Brazeau River, near Nigel Pass

After hopping a tributary creeklet and making a short, steep ascent, Nigel Pass is visible north, distinguished by lumpy, orangish-tan rock. It's about an hour distant. Two minutes farther, at 4.7 km (2.9 mi), pass a horse trail forking left. Proceed straight (north). Enter open meadows at 5 km (3.1 mi).

Hop another tributary creeklet and begin the final ascent to the pass. The trail climbs earnestly for ten minutes, then levels. The eroded, multi-trenched path is lined with purple fleabane. Step over another creeklet and resume the ascent—moderate with steep sections—until the trail levels at 7.2 km (4.5 mi) atop 2195-m (7200-ft) **Nigel Pass**. You're now astride the Banff-Jasper parks boundary. Hiking time: about 2½ hours, but strong hikers might beat that by 30 minutes or more. The White Goat Wilderness is east, beyond the next ridgecrest. The Brazeau River valley is north-northwest. Nigel Peak (3213 m / 10,539 ft) is directly west. South, across the Parkway, beyond Parker Ridge, is 3344-m (10,968-ft) Mt. Saskatchewan and various glaciers.

To fully appreciate the Nigel Pass environs, hike through the pass and drop to the Brazeau River. It's unbridged but easy to ford or rockhop. On the northeast bank, the main trail—indicated by a yellow blaze on a tree—ascends left (north). It eventually leads to Jonas Pass (Trip 92), but dayhikers should continue 0.8 km (0.5 mi) in that direction to overlook the Brazeau River valley and see a cascade plummeting off the north end of Nigel Pass. This **viewpoint** is just before the descent steepens dramatically.

Immediately after crossing to the Brazeau River's northeast bank, there's another option: follow the Brazeau upstream by forking right (southeast) onto a path bootbeaten into grass and heather. This is the route into **upper Brazeau canyon** (Trip 10). Hike it all the way to **Cataract Pass**, and you'll extend the Nigel Pass dayhike into a nine- or ten-hour adventure.

Cascade in upper Brazeau River Valley

TRIP 34

Kindersley-Sinclair Col

LOCATION	Kootenay National Park
LOOP	17.7 km (11 mi)
ELEVATION GAIN	1055 m (3460 ft)
KEY ELEVATIONS	trailhead 1340 m (4395 ft) col 1055 m (3460 ft)
HIKING TIME	6 to 7 hours
DIFFICULTY	moderate
MAPS	page 505; Gem Trek *Kootenay National Park*

OPINION

In response to his father's invitation to go hiking, a precocious child we know said, "Hiking? Isn't that just walking for the hell of it?"

You've got to admit, the kid's right. That's what we hikers do. So a loop hike—walking for hours in a big circle just to end up exactly where we started—is especially absurd. Yet we love doing it.

A loop, where you never retrace a step, where every stride propels you into the unknown, is the ideal dayhike, absurd or not. But loops are rare. Don't miss this one through Kindersely-Sinclair Col.

Stupendous views of surrounding ranges will reward you for persevering the long approach and substantial climb. A well-constructed trail and adequate switchbacks make it less onerous than the numbers might suggest.

A liberal sprinkling of larches just below the col adds a photogenic, golden flourish to the trip's climax should you be here in late September. The cooler weather then is also appealing, because this isn't the heart of the Rockies. It's the southwest edge, where summer is noticeably hotter.

If you keep hiking while approaching the col, you'll pop over it and be descending the other side within minutes. You'll be above treeline, enjoying the trip's scenic climax, for no more than half an hour. So don't rush it. After toiling through the forest, relish your reward. Start by sitting at the col and gazing like an owl. Let the beauty stream into your soul through wide, appreciative eyes. Then stride out on one of the optional alpine explorations described below. One takes 30 minutes, the other an hour.

FACT

By Vehicle

Drive Hwy 93 to the Kindersley Pass trailhead. It's 9.5 km (6 mi) northeast of Kootenay Park's west gate at Radium Hot Springs. The small parking area is on the southeast side of the highway. The signed trail starts across the highway, on the northwest side, at 1340 m (4395 ft). The Sinclair Creek trailhead is 1.2 km (0.75 mi) farther northeast on Hwy 93. You'll reach it after hiking the clockwise loop described below. Then walk the highway back to your vehicle at the Kindersley trailhead.

On Foot

You'll hike generally northwest all the way to Kindersley Pass. Within seven minutes start ascending long switchbacks. The trail climbs at a moderate grade through a forest of lodgepole pine, white spruce, and Douglas fir. At 2.7 km (1.7 mi), 1660 m (5440 ft), ascend steeply along the edge of a lush **avalanche swath**. It allows the first view up the drainage to the pass.

Within 1½ hours, at 1905 m (6250 ft), Mt. Sinclair is visible southeast, across the highway. Half an hour farther, continue along a couple boardwalks, then cross a bridged stream.

At 6 km (3.7 mi), 2012 m (6600 ft), crest a forested ridge west of **Lookout Point**, which juts into Sinclair Creek canyon. The trail drops a bit, leads to a footlog spanning a stream, then resumes climbing moderately.

Traverse more slopes where avalanches have swept away the trees. Enter the narrow, grassy cleft of **Kindersley Pass** at 8.4 km (5.3 mi), 2210 m (7249 ft), just below treeline. Mt. Kindersley is north. You're on the Kootenay Park boundary here.

From the pass, follow the trail right (northeast, then southeast). For the next ten minutes, ascend steeply among scattered stands of alpine larch. At 8.7 km (5.5 mi), encounter an errant Kindersley Pass sign. Ascend steeply again, then contour across open slopes strewn with krummholz (stunted alpine fir).

Surmount **Kindersley-Sinclair Col**, a gentle alpine saddle, at 10 km (6.2 mi), 2395 m (7846 ft). The northeast horizon bristles with peaks of the Mitchell Range. East, below you, is upper Sinclair Creek canyon. Before plunging into the canyon and continuing the loop, consider these optional detours from the col.

(1) Hike southeast, along the ridge, to the nearby 2520-m (8270-ft) outcrop. The 125-m (410-ft) ascent takes just 15 minutes and will earn you a terrific panorama, including a view of the Bugaboos (west). You can be back to the col in half an hour. If you don't want to go all the way, at least ascend 60 m (197 ft) for an improved vantage.

Lichen

Easy summit above Nixon Creek

(2) Hike north-northeast on the faint path contouring around the head of Sinclair Creek canyon. At 2385 m (7820 ft), where the path descends, bear left (north-northwest) across a rockslide, onto a grassy slope. Then ascend to the 2480-m (8130-ft) ridgecrest overlooking Nixon Creek canyon. Elevation gain from the col: 85 m (279 ft). From there, you can proceed right, along the crest, about another 10 minutes to a knob, beyond which the ridge plummets to Nixon Pass. The ridgecrest panorama is well worth the one-hour round trip from the col.

From Kindersley-Sinclair Col, strong hikers can reach the highway via Sinclair Creek canyon in 1½ hours. At a moderate pace, you'll be there in 2¼ hours. Departing the col, follow the narrow trail east-northeast. It descends through rock, then grass and heather. Five minutes down, larches appear and the creek is audible. Fifteen minutes down, enter forest. Soon rockhop to the east bank of **Sinclair Creek**. From here on, the trail is well defined. Proceed south-southeast.

About an hour below the col, pass a bushy, trailside clearing. You're still near the creek. Mt. Sinclair is visible ahead. The sense of wilderness in this canyon belies how close you are to the highway.

At 15 km (9.3 mi), cross a log bridge to the creek's west bank. Where the trail intersects an old, abandoned road, go right another 150 m (164 ft) to intersect the **highway** at 16.5 km, (10.2 mi), 1433 m (4700 ft). Unless you arranged a shuttle, turn right and follow the highway southwest 1.2 km (0.75 mi) to your vehicle at the Kindersley Pass trailhead.

TRIP 35

Tumbling Pass

LOCATION	Kootenay National Park
SHUTTLE TRIP	24.6 km (15.2 mi) one way
ELEVATION CHANGE	770-m (2526-ft) gain 805-m (2640-ft) loss
KEY ELEVATIONS	Paint Pots trailhead 1440 m (4723 ft) Tumbling Pass 2210 m (7250 ft) Numa Creek trailhead 1405 m (4608 ft)
HIKING TIME	7 to 8 hours
DIFFICULTY	challenging
MAPS	page 499; Gem Trek *Kootenay National Park*; Mount Goodsir 82 N/1

OPINION

To promote peace, to advance social justice, to foster more soulful living, we need new ideas. But we won't find them by hunkering longer at the office, behind the newspaper, or in front of the TV. To change the world, we must join it. We must get outdoors, where we can see, hear, feel what's happening around us. The answer is to walk. It can shift your awareness to the here and now. It's the optimal pace for allowing your senses to appreciate your surroundings. And, by emulating the rhythm of your beating heart, it balances and centers you, inducing clarity and focus. Walking, anywhere, will open you to what really matters. And spending an entire day walking the trail through Tumbling Pass could be among the more profound walking experiences of your life.

An alluring goal, solitude, and an exhilarating sense of adventure will enhance your Tumbling Pass journey. The goal is to see the famous Rockwall (Trip 89). Solitude is likely while ascending the Tumbling Creek trail, which few people use to access or depart the Rockwall. And the adventure comes from sheer magnitude: big mileage and substantial elevation change in a single day.

Attempt this one-way dayhike only if (1) you're confident you have the strength, speed and determination to see it through and (2) physical accomplishment thrills you. Going part way is pointless. Even after witnessing Tumbling Pass, an extraordinary sight, if you must return the way you came, your efforts will not be adequately rewarded. Your goal here should be to cover a vast expanse of wilderness in a single day; to feel the nervous thrill of being way out there with only a daypack on your back; to revel in the freedom, the physicality, the perpetual motion of trekking from breakfast until dinner.

You'll hike a long way before you see anything but forest. Granted, it's luxuriant for the Rockies. The big spruce trees here are impressive. But it's unlikely to hold your interest all the way to the pass. And though the trail follows Tumbling Creek,

Tumbling Pass

rarely is the water visible or even audible. On the rare occasions when you can glimpse the bigger picture, it's not suitable for framing: just nondescript, forested slopes. Tumbling Falls is an interesting diversion but doesn't compare to Helmet Falls, farther north on the Rockwall trail. Tumbling Pass, the Rockwall, and Tumbling Glacier are beyond Tumbling Falls. But once you see them, you'll dismiss the travails en route.

The Rockwall is a sheer limestone cliff extending nearly unbroken for 35 km (22 mi) along the Great Divide. It rises some 700 m (2300 ft) above the trail at Tumbling Pass. You'll also see Tumbling Glacier up close. Because Tumbling Pass is usually visited by backpackers plying the Rockwall trail, dayhiking through such grandeur feels surreptitious. The affect of the scenery is magnified by the sense that you've snatched it, unnoticed, from the jaws of unlikelihood.

After proceeding through the pass, the trail plunges into the avalanche bowl of upper Numa Creek basin. It's as large as an open pit mine, but as wild and green as Borneo. Pause and absorb the unfettered fecundity of the scene before you descend, because it's eyes-on-the-trail steep all the way down. Also observe Numa Pass, southeast. Numa is another highlight of the Rockwall trail—which you can now see is topographically manic-depressive.

Hiking out beside Numa Creek is way more enjoyable than hiking in along Ochre and Tumbling creeks. Numa Creek is lovely, and the trail hugs it all the way to the bridged crossing after which you veer off to reach the highway.

FACT

By Vehicle

The Paint Pots trailhead parking lot is on the northwest side of Hwy 93. Reach it by driving 9.5 km (6 mi) southwest of the Banff-Kootenay boundary, or 84 km (52 mi) north of Kootenay Park's West Gate at Radium. Elevation: 1440 m (4723 ft). Begin hiking here.

The Numa Creek trailhead parking lot is 4.5 km (2.8 mi) south of the Paint Pots trailhead. It's on the southwest side of Hwy 93. Reach it by driving 14 km (8.7 mi) southwest of the Banff-Kootenay boundary, or 79.5 km (49.4 mi) north of Kootenay Park's West Gate at Radium. Elevation: 1405 m (4608 ft). Leave a vehicle here, where the one-way shuttle trip ends.

On Foot

Start by the sign at the lower end of the huge parking lot. The trail initially descends to the **Vermilion River**. Cross the bridge to the west bank and bear left (southwest) where a trail to Marble Canyon forks right. In another 10 minutes, walk past the large **paint pots** (ochre beds) and enter forest. At the 1.4-km (0.9-mi) junction, continue left (west). Right leads 3.5 km (2.2 mi) to Marble Canyon.

The ascent is gentle through the densely forested valley. About 35 minutes from the trailhead, pass through cow parsnip in a broad avalanche slope allowing a view left (south) to Ochre Creek. At 3.9 km (2.4 mi)—about 45 minutes for fast hikers—reach a junction. Go left (southwest) for Tumbling Pass. The Ochre Creek trail to Helmet Creek and Falls continues straight (northwest).

In a few minutes, cross a bridge spanning **Ochre Creek** and reach **Tumbling/ Ochre Junction campground** at 4.4 km (2.7 mi), near the confluence of Tumbling and Ochre creeks. Open gravel bars here are a good place to sit and appreciate the beauty of the area. Stay left through the campground. The trail then ascends steeply above **Tumbling Creek**, switchbacks once, then heads south, ascending gradually above the creek.

Following Tumbling Creek upstream, the trail curves southwest, ascends to about 1707 m (5600 ft), then levels. Soon glimpse rock and snow above treeline. The trail parallels the raging, silt-darkened creek for a few minutes, passes the site of an old bridge, then reaches a new, strong, aluminum bridge at 6.7 km (4.2 mi). Cross to the creek's south bank. Proceed southwest through avalanche slopes where berry bushes and willows flourish. Tall grass threatens to swallow the narrow trail.

Pass 25-m (80-ft) **Tumbling Falls** at 10 km (6.2 mi). Reach a junction at 10.9 km (6.7 mi), 1880 m (6166 ft). **Tumbling Creek campground** is just west of the creek; beyond it the Rockwall trail continues northwest, cresting Wolverine Pass in 3.1 km (1.9 mi). Stay east of the creek and go left (south) for Tumbling Pass—2.3 km (1.4 mi) distant.

The trail narrows and steepens. There are no switchbacks, and the surface is slippery even when dry. A creeklet flows beside the moraine near the pass. This is a good place to refill water containers.

At treeline you can see the Rockwall looming ahead, extending north beyond Rockwall Pass. Southeast is 3200-m (10,496-ft) Mt. Foster—a distinctly high, pyramidal peak. Crest **Tumbling Pass** at 13.2 km (8.2 mi), 2210 m (7250 ft). Tumbling Glacier dominates the scene west of the pass. The mountain rising directly south above the glacier is unnamed. The peak northwest is Mt. Gray.

Alpine red paintbrush

Elephant's head

The trail continues southeast through the pass. About 20 minutes beyond, begin an intimidating 715-m (2345-ft) descent into **Numa Creek basin**. Cross a snow-fed creeklet with sheer cliffs above you and an avalanche bowl below. Soon cross another runoff stream. The Rockwall trail's steep ascent route to Numa Pass is visible southeast, across the lush basin. Soon plunge into luxuriant, head-high foliage.

At 18 km (11.2 mi)—about 45 minutes from Tumbling Pass for fast hikers—intersect the **Numa Creek trail**. Here, at 1510 m (4953 ft), you've completed the drastic descent; the rest is gradual. The Rockwall trail continues right (south), passing Numa Creek campground in 0.4 km (0.25 mi), then climbing south-southeast over Numa Pass to reach Floe Lake (Trip 48) in 10.2 km (6.3 mi). Turn left (northeast) to complete the one-way shuttle trip out to Hwy 93, which is now just 6.6 km (4.1 mi) distant.

Heading for the highway, soon cross a bridge over a tributary. The trail then follows **Numa Creek** downstream, usually within view of the water, often beside it. Looking back, you'll see the Rockwall soaring above 3050 m (10,000 ft). Near 20 km (12.4 mi) fork right (east), still following Numa Creek. At 22.3 km (13.8 mi) cross a sturdy aluminum-and-plank bridge to the creek's south bank. Leaving the creek now, the trail climbs moderately on a frustrating, seemingly pointless detour. It heads southeast, paralleling the **Vermilion River** until reaching a bridge spanning the canyon. Just north of the bridge, reach the **Numa Creek trailhead**, on Hwy 93, at 24.6 km (15.2 mi).

TRIP 36

Bald Hills

LOCATION	Jasper National Park
ROUND TRIP	12.6 km (7.8 mi)
ELEVATION GAIN	610 m (2000 ft)
KEY ELEVATIONS	trailhead 1690 m (5543 ft) summit 2320 m (7610 ft)
HIKING TIME	4 hours
DIFFICULTY	easy
MAPS	page 504; Gem Trek *Jasper & Maligne Lake*; Athabasca Falls 83 C/12

OPINION

Baldness is greatly admired among certain factions. Neo-Nazis. Parents of newborns. Fans of Shrek. And hikers—because a bald summit makes an excellent grandstand. The Bald Hills in particular offer a panoramic reward way out of proportion to the trifling effort required to ascend them. You'll see razorback ridges, silver and gray, above the immense turquoise majesty of Maligne Lake. Many of the peaks look like cresting tsunami waves in a petrified sea. One monster mountain is swirled, forming a pipeline. Come see for yourself.

This destination, more than any other, screams "Jasper!" It's even better than Opal Hills (Trip 57), because here your eyes can gobble all of Maligne Lake and the Queen Elizabeth Ranges. Gleaming white glaciers southeast are a foil for the desolate rock faces and deep green forests that complete the scene. Northwest are the expansive alpine meadowlands sliced by the Skyline trail. You can also peer southwest into Evelyn Creek valley and wonder how many bears are roaming that lonely refuge.

The name Bald Hills refers only to the absence of trees. The hills aren't totally bald, just buzzcut. They're adorned with heather and, in July and August, dappled with wildflowers. Look for dark-purple gentian, yellow stonecrop, lavender bellflowers, and fuchsia moss-campion.

A dusty, tiresome road leads you up the hills. On a clear summer day, it's hot as a tin roof. You can abandon the road, however, about 45 minutes up, where a cutoff trail branches left. The trail is steeper, but more pleasant and less busy. It ascends open forest and heathery slopes. Definitely take the trail down, departing near the hitching posts.

It's a short hike to the top of the first baldy. From there you can wander all day. The Bald Hills are actually a ridge, 7 km (4.3 mi) long, hikeable as far south as the main Maligne Range. For a full day up here, be a camel: carry at least 2 liters (quarts) of water per person. There's none in them thar hills.

Maligne Lake and Queen Elizabeth Ranges, from Bald Hills

FACT

By Vehicle

From Jasper townsite, drive 5 km (3 mi) east on Hwy 16 to Maligne Lake Road. Follow it 44.3 km (27.5 mi) to Maligne Lake. Continue past the lodge to the parking lot at road's end, elevation 1690 m (5543 ft). The trailhead is at the signed, gated, dirt road across from the lot.

On Foot

Set out on the broad fire road, heading generally west. Within 10 minutes, proceed straight on the road, passing a signed trail left (south) to Moose Lake and Maligne Pass (Trip 93). At 2.5 km (1.6 mi), 1918 m (6290 ft), the optional **cutoff trail** branches steeply left. You'll reach the Bald Hills in 35 to 50 minutes via the trail; 45 to 60 minutes via the longer, more gradual road.

If you take the trail, at 4 km (2.6 mi) you'll intersect the road. Turn right. In 70 m (77 yd), reach the former site of the **Bald Hills fire lookout**, on a bare dirt promontory, at 2170 m (7117 ft). There are hitching posts here for the tourist-laden horse trains.

If you stay on the road and pass the optional cutoff trail, you'll quickly reach a signed junction at 3.2 km (2 mi). Right drops to Evelyn Creek and intersects the Skyline trail. Bear left, soon attaining views northeast to the rust-coloured Opal Hills, and north to where the Jacques Lake trail (Trip 123) threads between the Colin and Queen Elizabeth ranges. The road soon levels, looping south then east. About 1½ hours from the trailhead, at 5.2 km (3.2 mi), reach the lookout site described above. Follow the road another 70 m (77 yd) to descend left via the cutoff trail.

To escape mounted tourists and attain a 360° vista, hike higher. A 20-minute ascent south-southwest gaining 130 m (425 ft) in 1 km (0.6 mi) will grant you the **summit** of the next bald hill. Elevation: 2320 m (7610 ft). From the big stoneman cairn, continue right (southwest) to see Evelyn Creek valley and the Maligne Range (west).

Lupine in subalpine meadow

FACT

By Vehicle

From Hwy 5, follow the Waterton Park entrance road south-southwest 5.6 km (3.5 mi). Turn right (northwest) onto Red Rock Parkway, just north of Blakiston Creek bridge. Follow it 15 km (9.3 mi) to where the road ends in the Red Rock Canyon parking area, at 1495 m (4905 ft).

On Foot

Cross the bridge spanning Red Rock Canyon. This is the Snowshoe trail, an old road. Watch for the namesake white-footed rabbits. You're penetrating Bauerman Valley, heading northwest through an open forest of lodgepole pine, spruce, aspen and birch, roughly following **Bauerman Creek** upstream. Anderson Peak dominates left (south).

The road-trail undulates but is mostly level. Within 30 minutes, reach a stream (dry by late summer) in an alluvial fan, where boulders provide rest-break seating. One hour from the trailhead, at 4.3 km (2.7 mi), reach a signed **junction**. The Snowshoe trail continues left. Goat Lake is right (northwest), 2.5 km (1.6 mi) distant.

The trail immediately begins climbing in earnest. Soon enter the subalpine zone and enjoy a steadily improving vista southwest over the forested Bauerman Valley. At the base of the headwall are the Twin Lakes (Trip 100), hidden from view. Your trail slices upward across steep, rocky slopes to the lip of the hanging valley that cradles Goat Lake. Reach the lake's outlet stream where it drools over the lip. **Goat Lake** is a few minutes farther, at 6.8 km (4.3 mi), 2020 m (6625 ft). Near the east shore is a campground with log benches and tables. The pit toilet is just past the bear pole.

If you're aiming for Avion Ridge, take the faint trail leading northwest from the campground. It soon curves left to a tiny creek and a pile of colourful rocks. Cross to the rockpile and head straight through krummholz. The narrow trail enters a meadow where yellow glacier lilies thrive in June. Ahead, you can see where the Avion Ridge route begins: above the cascade, on the crest of the cirque. Re-enter forest before ascending subalpine slopes again. Attain the **ridge** at 2271 m (7450 ft), a very steep 1.6 km (1 mi) from Goat Lake.

Airy traverse to Goat Lake

TRIP 39

Cory and Edith Passes

LOCATION	northwest of Banff townsite
ROUND TRIP	11 km (6.8 mi) to Cory Pass
CIRCUIT	12.9 km (8 mi) around Mt. Edith
ELEVATION GAIN	900 m (2952 ft) to Cory Pass 1000 m (3280 ft) on circuit
KEY ELEVATIONS	trailhead 1460 m (4789 ft) Cory Pass 2360 m (7741 ft) Edith Pass 1950 m (6396 ft)
HIKING TIME	4½ to 6 hours for circuit
DIFFICULTY	challenging
MAPS	page 524; Gem Trek *Banff Up-Close*

OPINION

The optimal speed at which to appreciate Banff National Park is between 3.2 and 4.8 kph (2 and 3 mph).

How do I know this? I recently consulted the Walk the Earth Institute. Membership in this highly exclusive think tank is limited to me and Kathy. Both of us are self-appointed experts on everything to do with foot travel, and our methods are rigourously scientific: if we agree, it must be so.

At the Institute's last convention (yesterday's hike), we were speculating about the speed at which most tourists stroll the sidewalks of Banff Avenue: 1.6 kph (1 mph) or less, we decided.

Optimal hiking pace was the Institute's next topic of discussion. We then asked ourselves, "In the unlikely event these tourists are capable of maintaining minimum speed requirements, and assuming they really want to see Banff Park, where should they be walking?" "Cory Pass," Kathy said. I agreed. So it was unanimous and therefore indisputable.

Starting just a few minutes' drive from Banff Avenue, the Cory Pass hike is an athletic endeavour. Some might call it "punishing." An 885-m (2903-ft) ascent in just 4.5 km (2.8 mi) places shocking demands on lethargic muscles. But the exhilarating scenery more than compensates for the effort required.

Well before reaching Cory Pass, the airy trail (acrophobes beware) traverses the steep west face of Mount Edith. Lift your eyes from the abyss below your feet, and you'll see Mount Cory looming just across the canyon. Behind you, the Sundance Range fills the southern horizon.

Rock pinnacles give Cory Pass a feral atmosphere. Just beyond the pass, the fang-like 500-m (1640-ft) face of Mt. Louis looms like a monster in a child's nightmare. The first person to climb it was Conrad Kain, sort of the Captain Cook of the Canadian Rockies.

Trail to Cory Pass

From Cory, keen, strong hikers drop into the aptly named Gargoyle Valley. They round the talusy north side of Mt. Edith, then return via forested Edith Pass. The circuit adds variety and allows a more gradual, comfortable descent.

Though this is strictly a hike, requires no scrambling and poses no dangerous exposure, the terrain is rugged, the trail steep. It's not for the inexperienced or unfit.

Turn around at Cory Pass, and you'll endure a toe-jamming, knee-pounding descent. Proceed into Gargoyle Valley only if you're secure on loose rock and will remain confident where the way forward briefly requires vigilance.

You're a capable hiker? You'll enjoy the challenges of the Cory-Edith circuit because they make it a spicy journey. Just give the snowpack on the far side of Cory Pass time to melt; wait til mid-July. Snow usually bars easy passage to Cory until late June. Whenever you go, expect thirsty work on dry terrain. Pack at least two litres of water per person.

Also be prepared to endure highway noise from the Trans-Canada while hiking the trail's lower reaches. The sound of passing vehicles is even louder than it should be, because the majority far exceed the park's 90 kph (56 mph) speed limit.

"Much too fast," Kathy said. I agreed. There you have it: another certifiable fact, brought to you by the Walk The Earth Institute.

FACT

By Vehicle

From where Bow Valley Parkway (Highway 1A) departs the Trans-Canada Highway, just west of Banff townsite, drive the Parkway north 0.5 km (0.3 mi). Then turn right onto the access road for the Fireside Picnic Area. Continue 1 km (0.6 mi) to road's end. The trailhead is near the bridge over the creek, at 1460 m (4789 ft).

On Foot

Cross the bridge and pass the picnic area. Head east, initially on an old road. In 200 m (656 ft) follow a trail left (marked by a hiker sign). It leads through forest lightened by aspen and broken by meadows. Reach a junction at 1 km (0.6 mi). The trail to Edith Pass continues straight. If you complete the circuit, you'll return that way from Edith. Go left (north) for Cory Pass.

The Cory Pass trail climbs skyward, generally northwest, up the south-facing slope. Crest the forested south ridge of Mt. Edith at 1900 m (6232 ft), having hiked just over 2 km (1.2 mi). Rewarding views begin. Mt. Bourgeau is southwest. The Sundance Range is south. Mt. Rundle is southeast. The trail bends north-northwest and the ascent eases. Ahead is 2553-m (8374-ft) Mt. Edith. Northwest is 2801-m (9187-ft) Mt. Cory. Between them is Cory Pass.

The trail follows the ridgeline, continuing at a moderate grade with one steep section. At 2045 m (6708 ft), it drops 14 m (46 ft) into an awkward declivity, then ascends gradually across the barren southwest slope of **Mt. Edith**. The long, airy traverse is on a very narrow trail crossing several avalanche chutes that are precarious even when snowfree. Snow is still present? Stop. Assess the danger. Lacking an ice axe and self-arrest skills, be willing to turn back rather than risk a serious fall. Traverse the canyon headwall to reach the narrow defile of **Cory Pass** at 5.5 km (3.4 mi), 2360 m (7741 ft). Directly north, across Gargoyle Valley, is 2682-m (8797-ft) Mt. Louis.

To continue the Cory-Edith circuit, descend the precipitous north side of the pass. The trail curves right (northeast), dropping rapidly across steep talus through short **Gargoyle Valley**. Rounding the north side of Mt. Edith, stay high, just beneath the cliffs. You'll see gargoyle pinnacles through here. Closely follow the cairns through bulky rubble.

Mt. Louis, from Cory Pass

Near 2000 m (6560 ft), the trail works its way right (southeast). Maintain your elevation while crossing a boulder field for ten minutes. Then watch for a yellow-orange hiker sign on a tree; that's where the trail enters forest.

Ascend then descend yet again before reaching 1950-m (6396-ft) Edith Pass at 9 km (5.6 mi). Mt. Edith is now right (west), Mt. Norquay left (east). Trails depart both sides of **Edith Pass**. Don't turn left (north), or you'll drop to the Forty Mile Creek trail. Go right (south), and descend—steeply at first, then moderately—through forest.

Reach a junction 2.9 km (1.8 mi) from Edith Pass. You're now on familiar ground. Right leads north to Cory Pass. Straight leads 1 km (0.6 mi) generally south-southwest back to the trailhead.

TRIP 40

Rock Isle, Grizzly and Larix Lakes

LOCATION	Banff National Park
CIRCUIT	7.9 km (4.9 mi) to 11.8 km (7.3 mi)
ELEVATION GAIN	180 m (590 ft) to 300 m (984 ft)
KEY ELEVATIONS	trailhead 2195 m (7200 ft) Grizzly Lake 2225 m (7300 ft)
HIKING TIME	3 to 4 hours
DIFFICULTY	easy
MAPS	page 493; Gem Trek *Banff & Mt. Assiniboine*; Banff 82 O/4

OPINION

Meadow cultists throng these lakes. Rock Isle averages 60 visitors on a sunny, summer day, and has hosted 130. That explains the assiduously maintained trail and the huge viewing platform that softens human impact. It also justifies the criticism that this trip is too crowded and tame to be rated *Premier*.

But ease and convenience, combined with the vast, incredible beauty of nearby Sunshine Meadows, make it a very rewarding walk for anyone unable to climb high or trek far. This is their opportunity to ingest the distilled essence of the Canadian Rockies —the opiate for which some of us continually venture deep into the lonely wilds.

The lakes themselves are lovely, but it's the meadowy, mountainous expanse fanning out in all directions that will rapidly fill your camera's memory card. On a clear day, you'll see Mt. Assiniboine thrusting its horn skyward. In fall, stands of larch trees add brilliant gold to the alpine palette, especially around Grizzly and Larix lakes.

Our route description **begins in Sunshine Village, at 2195 m (7200 ft).** To get there, you must hike the restricted-use access road or ride the White Mountain Adventures shuttle bus, both of which depart the Sunshine Ski Area gondola station.

The road ascends 520 m (1706 ft) in 6.5 km (4 mi). Walking it is a bore and a chore. We know. We've done it. You'll see nothing but unremarkable trees for 1½ hours. And you'll have to plod back down as well. Ride the shuttle. The time and effort you'll save is well worth the cost.

FACT

Before Your Trip

Visit whitemountainadventures.com to learn more about the White Mountain Adventures shuttle bus from the Sunshine parking lot to Sunshine Village. Check current prices and make reservations by calling (403) 760-4403 October through June 14, (403) 762-7889 June 15 through September, or (800) 408-0005.

Rock Isle Lake

By Vehicle and Bus

Follow directions for Citadel Pass (Trip 3) to reach Sunshine Village.

On Foot

From Sunshine Village ski lodge, at 2195 m (7200 ft), walk south past the left (east) side of the saloon. Go uphill 200 m (220 yd) to the Parks Canada cabin. Fifteen metres past it, turn left (east-southeast) onto the well-groomed gravel path. It ascends gently. Go right (south) at the first junction, at 2290 m (7510 ft), and continue the easy ascent.

In another 5-7 minutes, reach the next junction at 1.2 km (0.7 mi). This is the **summit of the Great Divide**, at 2300 m (7544 ft). The narrower path left (southeast) leads to Citadel Pass. Go right (west) on the wider path for Rock Isle, Grizzly and Larix lakes.

Reach **Rock Isle Lake overlook** at 1.6 km (1 mi). Mt. Assiniboine is visible southeast, beyond Quartz Hill. About 200 m (220 yd) past the overlook, the **Twin Cairns trail** bears right. Stay left for Grizzly and Larix lakes. Descend to Rock Isle Lake's outlet stream. Grizzly and Larix lakes are visible below. Larix, to the south, is the largest of the three. The botanical name for the alpine larch trees you see here is also *Larix*.

Continuing, the trail descends. Reach a **fork** at 2.7 km (1.7 mi). Go either way and loop back to this point. Keeping right, you'll drop to cross **Grizzly Lake's inlet stream** at 2225 m (7300 ft). A little farther is a view of Simpson River valley. The trail then curves back and ascends, rounding the shore of **Larix Lake** and rejoining the trail where you previously dropped to Grizzly Lake. Bear right to the familiar junction at 6.1 km (3.8 mi). Here, right leads back to Sunshine Village for a total of 7.9 km (4.9 mi).

Or, from the 6.1-km (3.8-mi) junction, go left (west) on the **Twin Cairns trail** for a longer return to Sunshine Village. Total mileage this way will be 11.8 km (7.3 mi). Go right at the next junction to ascend 120 m (395 ft) in 0.6 km (0.4 mi) to superb 2420-m (7938-ft) **Standish Viewpoint**. Descend back to the junction. Go right (northwest) for 2.3 km (1.4 mi) through meadows and subalpine forest, descending to another junction. Go right to reach Sunshine Village in 1.7 km (1.1 mi).

TRIP 41

Twin Lakes / Gibbon Pass

LOCATION	Banff National Park
ROUND TRIP	16.4 km (10.2 mi) to Lower Twin Lake, plus 5.4 km (3.3 mi) to pass
ELEVATION GAIN	1065 m (3493 ft) for Lower Twin Lake plus 240 m (787 ft) to pass 1305 m (4280 ft) total
KEY ELEVATIONS	trailhead 1695 m (5560 ft) Lower Twin Lake 2060 m (6757 ft) pass 2300 m (7545 ft)
HIKING TIME	5½ to 7 hours for lake, 6½ to 8 for pass
DIFFICULTY	moderate backpack challenging dayhike to pass
MAPS	page 506; Gem Trek *Banff & Assiniboine*; Mount Goodsir 82 N/1, Banff 82 O/4

OPINION

Greed is maligned. It's not always sinful. In the mountains, greed can be a virtue. Desire to see more, hike farther, climb higher, wring a little more adventure from the day—these are virtues. So if you hike to Twin Lakes, don't be satisfied at Upper Twin. Be greedy. Go a bit farther, to Lower Twin. The lake is bigger and the setting grander. And don't stop there unless you have to. Be greedier yet. Push on to Gibbon Pass. It's considerably higher, but only slightly farther. And if it's mid- to late-September, you'll witness a profusion of golden larches as sensational as anywhere in the range.

Actually, larch season is *the* time to hike here. The awesome larch display, which climaxes on the ascent from Lower Twin to Gibbon Pass, is what earns this trip a *Worthwhile* rating. Earlier in summer, any experienced, discerning hiker not seeking to rationalize the energy expended, would agree that the Twins and even Gibbon Pass are less impressive than many destinations in Banff Park, for example Eiffel Lake (Trip 28) or Lake Annette (Trip 6).

So September's the season. And backpacking's the reason. While a dayhike to Gibbon Pass is enjoyable once the larches turn, a one-way trek through it is more so. Then the onus isn't on the pass to make you swoon, which it won't. It'll be an exciting prelude to the highlights beyond: Whistling Pass and Healy Pass (Trip 79).

Another option, for short-range backpackers, is the campground at Upper Twin Lake. A late start, a turtle's pace, a comet tail of kids—none will keep you from arriving here at a reasonable hour. Next morning, you can admire the Twins' jade water lapping at the walls of Storm Mountain. And you can do it during optimal lighting, before the sun sinks behind the mountain (about 1 p.m. in fall). Then, lightly laden, you can scoot up to Gibbon Pass before breaking camp and heading home.

So, what will you find at Gibbon Pass, other than larches? A meadowy expanse dappled with stunted trees, between nameless mountains. The views are good, not great. Mt. Assiniboine is visible south, Mt. Hector north; both are distant. For a soul-rousing vantage, scramble higher, east of the pass. You'll spy Shadow Lake below, and massive, glacier-crowned Mt. Ball nearby.

Whether you're dayhiking or backpacking, the trail's initial 125-m (410-ft) descent to Vista Lake is irksome. Like starting in reverse. Equally grating is the whine and whoosh of vehicles on the highway, which you'll hear for the first hour. Your compensation? The trail is merciful, liberally granting views. Never does it test your patience in a dispiriting forest. From Vista Lake, you'll ascend through a grove burned long ago, now regaining its former beauty yet still open enough to let you admire nearby peaks.

There are two ways to ascend to Twin Lakes. The access described here is superior. The other—Altrude Creek—is joyless. A *Double Don't Do*. It plows 13 km (8 mi) through viewless forest. Upon finally emerging in the subalpine zone, the last stretch to Lower Twin Lake is a Slurpee. Spare yourself the scenic deprivation of this toilsome slog.

FACT

By Vehicle

Drive Highway 93 southwest 8.4 km (5.3 mi) from Castle Junction, or northeast 2 km (1.2 mi) from the Banff-Kootenay boundary at Vermilion Pass. Be aware, slow down, and use your turn signal; exiting here is potentially dangerous. From either approach, turn into the paved Vista Lake viewpoint, on the southeast side of the highway, at 1695 m (5560 ft).

On Foot

The trail starts on the northeast side of the viewpoint, behind the kiosk. Vista Lake is visible below. Descend the wide trail. Within 20 minutes, reach the northeast shore of **Vista Lake**, at 1.4 km (0.9 mi), 1570 m (5150 ft). It's an odd name for a lake at the bottom of a viewless fold.

Cross the bridged outlet stream and begin a persistently steep ascent southeast. In the next ten minutes, more bridges aid your progress.

After hiking about 50 minutes, reach a vantage at 1799 m (5900 ft). Boom Creek valley (Trip 65) is right (northwest) across the highway. Left (west-northwest) is 3001-m (9847-ft) Chimney Peak, at the head of an unnamed drainage. Enter a skeleton forest regenerating from a 1968 fire.

An hour from the trailhead, highway vehicle noise remains audible. The impressive southwest face of Castle Mtn is northeast. Encounter larches at 2023 m (6635 ft), then enter a forest of primarily fir. Soon pass a pond in a marshy, treed bowl. The grade eases shortly before reaching jade **Arnica Lake** at 5 km (3.1 mi), 2155 m (7070 ft), about 1½ hours from the trailhead. It's cupped in a cirque on the north side of Storm Mtn. Subalpine forest encircles the lake except where talus tumbles to the southwest shore.

Half an hour beyond Arnica, and 95 m (300 ft) higher, the trail heads south-southeast through a broad, grassy corridor bound by larches. Gibbon Pass is visible ahead. Ascend to a 2285-m (7495-ft) **saddle** on a northeast-jutting ridge of Storm Mtn.

Lower Twin Lake, beneath Storm Mountain

Then drop to **Upper Twin Lake**, at 7.2 km (4.5 mi), 2090 m (6855 ft), 2½ hours from the trailhead.

Cross the outlet stream at the lake's southeast end. The trail bisects the **campground**, then drops in 15 minutes to a **junction**. Left is the Altrude Creek trail. It descends northeast 8 km (5 mi) to a trailhead just off the highway near Castle Junction. Proceed straight, cross the footbridge over the outlet stream, and in 200 m (220 yd) arrive at the north end of **Lower Twin Lake**, at 8.2 km (5.1 mi), 2060 m (6757 ft).

Before resuming to the pass—and especially if you're *not* resuming to the pass—take a 20-minute detour along the water's edge to fully appreciate the lake. The bootbeaten path on the east shore is rough, possibly sloppy, but easy

Arnica Lake

and fun. A long cascade graces the cliffy west shore. If proceeding to the pass, you have a choice: return to the main trail, or forge on past the lake's south end.

The main trail leads southeast from the outlet-stream footbridge, ascending moderately through an increasingly larch-dominated subalpine forest, to reach **Gibbon Pass** at 10.9 km (6.8 mi), 2300 m (7545 ft).

The pass, however, is directly south-southeast of Lower Twin Lake's south end. The intervening terrain and vegetation allow trouble-free cross-country travel. So, you can just keep hiking south on the bootbeaten path along the east shore. The path fades uphill, south of the lake, but it remains evident a long way. Just keep the forest edge to your left, the rockslide to your right.

You'll know you've reached the pass when you've surmounted most of the trees. Atop the north end of the pass, beside the trail, is a cairn bearing a metal plaque. It states the elevation and assures you that, yes, this really is Gibbon Pass. Having arrived here via the cross-country route from Lower Twin Lake, you can quicken your return by opting for the main trail.

You've reached Gibbon Pass with time to spare? Try scrambling (no hands required) up the gentle, scree-covered peak east-northeast. Game trails are visible traversing it. From the summit, you'll see Shadow Lake south-southeast.

Backpacking over Gibbon Pass to Shadow Lake, Whistling Pass, and/or Healy Pass? Follow the directions in Trip 79.

Gibbon Pass

TRIP 42
Taylor Lake

LOCATION	Banff National Park
ROUND TRIP	12.6 km (7.8 mi) to lake 17 km (10.5 mi) to Panorama Meadow
ELEVATION GAIN	595 m (1952 ft) to lake 730 m (2395 ft) to meadow
KEY ELEVATIONS	trailhead 1470 m (4822 ft) lake 2065 m (6773 ft) upper meadow 2235 m (7331 ft)
HIKING TIME	4 to 6 hours
DIFFICULTY	easy
MAPS	page 505; Gem Trek *Lake Louise & Yoho*; Lake Louise 82 N/8

OPINION

A hanging-valley lake gripped by brash cliffs is the revelatory sight that rewards those who persist here. But the trail (much of it an old road) is a long, steep, dispiriting bore. The grim forest—spruce and lodegpole pine—denies views and quashes enthusiasm like a heartless prison guard. Yet the lake's popularity and small viewing area ensure you'll be mingling with a crowd, or disgruntled.

Despite Taylor Lake's laudable beauty, anyone whose time is limited should hike elsewhere. Choose a trip that rewards more quickly and generously. Nearby Saddleback and Fairview Mtn (Trip 29) or Mt. Saint Piran (Trip 26), for example. Those trails lead to summits with stupefying views of Lake Louise. But if you prefer lakeshores to mountaintops, maybe Taylor's a good choice.

Fit hikers who dispatch the grunt work efficiently will arrive at the lake within 1½ hours. After resting and appreciating the scene, you can choose from a couple, easy, worthwhile side trips. To the south is O'Brien Lake, smaller than Taylor but equally wonderful. Be prepared for a soggy approach. An even better option is Panorama Meadow, a lush basin to the north beneath the cliffs of Panorama Ridge. It's stuffed with wildflowers and framed by alpine larch.

Lake Louise

Taylor Lake

If you're looking for a hike between the towns of Banff and Lake Louise, Boom Lake (Trip 65) might pique your curiosity along with Taylor Lake. Taylor's more rewarding, even though the lake is a third the size, and the trail is slightly longer and way steeper. Taylor's cirque is truly impressive. And the trail's end viewpoint here, unlike at Boom Lake, allows you to fully appreciate the setting.

FACT

By Vehicle

Drive the Trans-Canada Hwy northwest 8 km (5 mi) from Castle Junction, or southeast 17 km (10.5 mi) from Lake Louise village. Turn west into Taylor Creek picnic area. The trail starts at the end of the parking lot, just across the bridge. Elevation: 1470 m (4822 ft).

On Foot

At the south-southeast corner of the parking lot, cross the bridge over Taylor Creek. You'll be hiking generally west all the way to Taylor Lake. The trail ascends gently, then moderately. The creek helps mask highway noise. At 1 km (0.6 mi), 1540 m (5050 ft), about 15 minutes from the trailhead, cross another bridge over Taylor Creek, this time to the northwest bank. Near 2 km (1.2 mi) the grade steepens. At 5.8 km (3.6 mi) cross a bridge to the creek's south bank.

At 6.1 km (3.8 mi), just before arriving at Taylor Lake, reach a signed junction. Left (southeast) leads to O'Brien Lake. Proceed straight (west) 200 m (220 yd) through soggy subalpine meadow to reach **Taylor Lake** at 2065 m (6773 ft).

There's a small, two-tentsite campground above the northeast shore. It has four tables. This camp is unusually close to the lake. Be vigilant to prevent polluting the water.

The 800-m (2625-ft) north face of Mt. Bell soars dramatically from the lake's south shore. Taylor Pass is west, above the far shore; it's the cleft between Panorama Ridge and the northwest arm of Mt. Bell.

PANORAMA MEADOW

Pick up the trail behind and to the right of the campground. Follow it northwest. After a moderate, 0.5-km (0.3-mi) ascent, you're in open forest of larch and fir. A creeklet drains the meadow. Reach fairly level ground in 20 minutes, at 2200 m (7216 ft). The trail fades, but continuing is easy.

The southeast curving flank of Panorama Ridge is nearby left (west). An aerial view of the Bow Valley is east. A faint route ascends gently along the creek's left side. Within five minutes, reach a fir flagged with yellow tape; hop the creek here. Head northwest deeper into the basin. Several giant alpine larch deserve close inspection. Their bark is especially beautiful. Reach a shallow pond at 2235 m (7331 ft).

A vague, dreary route—for hard-headed, unimaginative explorers only—continues north of the meadow. It plows through forest, curves around Panorama Ridge, then becomes more distinct before intersecting the Consolation Lakes trail near Moraine Lake. Total distance: 10 km (6.2 mi) from Taylor Lake.

O'BRIEN LAKE

At the signed junction 200 m (220 yd) east of Taylor Lake, follow the O'Brien Lake trail southeast. Rockhop Taylor Creek. The trail descends to skirt the east-jutting cliffs of Mt. Bell, then regains that elevation. About 1.4 km (0.9 mi) from the junction, turn right (southwest) on a spur to reach O'Brien Lake within 0.4 km (0.2 mi). The spur fades in wet meadows before the lake; follow the left (southeast) bank of the outlet creek upstream (southwest). O'Brien Lake is at 2140 m (7019 ft), in a cirque formed by the east wall of Mt. Bell.

The trail from Taylor Lake continues beyond where you turned onto the O'Brien Lake spur. It heads generally southeast to intersect the Boom Lake trail in 6.6 km (4.1 mi). It's forested, sketchy, rough, not recommended.

The bark of an ancient, alpine larch

TRIP 43
Consolation Lakes

LOCATION	Banff National Park
ROUND TRIP	6 km (3.8 mi)
ELEVATION GAIN	60 m (197 ft)
KEY ELEVATIONS	trailhead 1885 m (6183 ft) lower lake 1945 m (6380 ft)
HIKING TIME	2 hours
DIFFICULTY	easy
MAPS	page 505; Gem Trek *Lake Louise & Yoho*; Lake Louise 82 N/8

OPINION

Tour buses disgorge crowds all day at Moraine Lake. But just beyond the mind-rattling cacophony is a quiet, lovely enclave that might ease your distress. Gazing at these aptly named lakes, it's easy to imagine you're deep in the wilderness.

The shimmering Consolation Lakes lie beneath hulking cliffs impressive as any in the mountain parks. If the lower lake is too crowded to console you as promised, continue to the quieter upper one. The rough trail beyond the first lake demands more of you, like proper boots, but ensures casual strollers are left behind. Even as you depart the lakes, your return to civilization will be eased by the absorbing sight of Mt. Temple.

Keep this walk in mind for a rainy day. Should the tops of the cirque walls be shrouded in mist, you'll be denied a bit of scenic impact, but go anyway. There's still plenty to see. Better that than sit out a drizzle.

FACT

By Vehicle

From Lake Louise village, drive uphill, southwest, on Lake Louise Drive. Turn left on Moraine Lake Road and follow it 12.5 km (7.8 mi) to the huge parking lot at road's end. Elevation: 1885 m (6183 ft).

Before your trip

Read page 37 about possible hiking restrictions due to bears.

On Foot

From the southeast end of the parking lot (nearest Moraine Lake), cross bridged Moraine Creek. Proceed over the large rockslide that naturally dams Moraine Lake. The rockpile trail forks right. Continue straight and ascend into forest. At 1.6 km (1 mi), bear right. Left heads north to round Panorama Ridge en route to Taylor Lake. About 15 minutes beyond that junction, pass through a boggy meadow.

Lower Consolation Lake

At 3 km (1.9 mi), 1945 m (6380 ft), reach the north end of **Lower Consolation Lake**. Panorama Ridge is the swooping mountain to your left (east). Mt. Bell is southeast. Two-peaked Bident Mtn and four-peaked Mt. Quadra (both over 3000 m / 10,000 ft) are ahead, at the south end of the valley. The east face of Mt. Babel is on the right (west) side of the upper lake.

Want to visit Upper Consolation Lake? It's about 30 minutes farther. From the north end of the lower lake, where you arrived, turn left (east) and ford the outlet stream: Babel Creek. Past the far bank, head right (southeast) on a crude, wet path at the forest edge. You're paralleling the lower lake's east shore. Continue over the rockslide dividing the two lakes.

It's possible to proceed around the south end of the upper lake. By scrambling north over boulders along the west shores of both lakes, you can return to where you first arrived at the lower lake. Only experienced mountaineers should explore the higher reaches of the valley's south end.

TRIP 44

Boulder Pass

LOCATION	Banff National Park
ROUND TRIP	17 km (10.5 mi)
ELEVATION GAIN	645 m (2116 ft)
KEY ELEVATIONS	trailhead 1700 m (5575 ft), pass 2345 m (7692 ft)
HIKING TIME	6 to 8 hours
DIFFICULTY	easy
MAPS	page 517; Gem Trek *Lake Louise & Yoho*; Lake Louise 82 N/8, Hector Lake 82 N/9

OPINION

Towns lacking distinction trumpet themselves as the gateway to someplace famous. It's a ruse to lure visitors, and one the marmots of Boulder Pass might try if they launched a tourism campaign. Truth is, the pass should be only a landmark on an exciting, overnight exploration to points beyond, like Skoki Valley and Red Deer Lakes. But lacking time for that, sampling the area on a dayhike to this mere gateway is worthwhile.

En route you'll cross meadows ringed by mountains. Just over the pass is Ptarmigan Lake. Visible beyond are Deception Pass, Fossil Mtn, and gray, scree-dominated, Slate Range peaks. It's a bleak but spaciously intriguing scene. Look back, in the direction you came, and you'll see the triumphant giants—Mt. Temple, Mt. Victoria and several of the Wenkchemna Peaks—across Bow Valley, 15 to 18 km (9 to 11 mi) distant.

Moderate-paced dayhikers who hop to it by 9 a.m. should have time for a side-trip to Hidden or Redoubt lakes. Go to tiny Hidden Lake for flower fireworks in the surrounding meadows; Redoubt Lake to admire a sheer mountain rocketing out of the 1.2-km (0.7-mi) long lake.

A big black mark against this hike is the broad brown swath you'll endure for 8 km (5 mi) of the round-trip distance. The road departing the trailhead doesn't taper to trail until you're behind Lake Louise ski area. Even then, it's wide and often muddy, because it's popular.

Cycling the road as far as Temple Lodge (part of the ski area) makes the trip way more enjoyable. It also gives you a couple extra hours to visit Hidden and Redoubt lakes. Hike hard after cranking up the road and maybe you'll have time to scramble onto Heather Ridge, from the northeast shore of Redoubt Lake.

Ptarmigan Lake, from Boulder Pass

FACT

By Vehicle

Turn north off the Trans-Canada Hwy at the signs for Lake Louise Ski Area. Follow Whitehorn Road, passing Bow Valley Parkway (Hwy 1A) on the right. At 2 km (1.2 mi) turn right onto gravel Fish Creek Road. Continue 1.1 km (0.7 mi) to the Fish Creek trailhead parking area, at 1700 m (5575 ft).

On Foot

Hike or bike 3.8 km (2.4 mi) up the dirt, forest-enclosed Temple fire road. In about 15 minutes from the trailhead, stay straight on the main road at the junction. Near the end of the road, pass Temple Lodge. At road's end, go uphill to your right, across a ski slope, to the hiking and horse trail that re-enters forest. The trail heads north, ascending more gradually than the fire road did. At about 6.5 km (4 mi) emerge in **subalpine meadows**. From here on, you're in open country with views. Boulder Pass is northeast. The highest peaks in the Slate Range are north-northwest; from left to right, they are Mt. Richardson, Pika Peak and Ptarmigan Peak. The trail crosses to the west side of Corral Creek.

Halfway Hut, an historic log structure, is to the right, at 7.1 km (4.4 mi). The hut served skiers making tracks for Skoki Lodge in the 1890s. Redoubt Mountain is right (southeast). At 7.3 km (4.5 mi) a left (northwest) spur leads to a **campground** in 100 m (110 yd), then ascends 85 m (280 ft) through meadows and open, larch forest to reach **Hidden Lake** at 1.3 km (0.8 mi). Hidden Lake is set in alpine tundra beneath Mt. Richardson, and Pika and Ptarmigan peaks.

Passing Hidden Lake cirque, en route to Skoki Valley

The next section through meadows gets muddy when wet, due to horse traffic. The trail steepens, ascending northeast to reach **Boulder Pass** at 8.5 km (5.3 mi), 2345 m (7692 ft), above the southwest shore of long Ptarmigan Lake. Redoubt Mountain (2902 m / 9518 ft) is directly south. Mt. Temple is in full view 15 km (9.3 mi) southwest. The trail to Deception Pass and Skoki Valley (Trip 82) continues around the north side of Ptarmigan Lake.

Redoubt Lake is 0.9 km (0.6 mi)—about 30 minutes—from Boulder Pass. The route gains only 60 m (197 ft). It starts at a sign just east of the pass. Go right (east-southeast) through the boulders south of Ptarmigan Lake. You can hike around Redoubt Lake by following a rough track south (down the west side), then returning north (up the east side) on the highest of several ledges. From the north end of Redoubt Lake, near where you arrived, a trail leads north 1.1 km (0.7 mi), around the northeast end of Ptarmigan Lake to intersect the trail to Deception Pass and Skoki Valley.

TRIP 45

Bow Glacier Falls

LOCATION	Banff National Park
ROUND TRIP	9 km (5.6 mi)
ELEVATION GAIN	148 m (485 ft)
KEY ELEVATIONS	trailhead 1940 m (6365 ft) base of falls 2090 m (6850 ft)
HIKING TIME	2½ to 4 hours
DIFFICULTY	easy
MAPS	page 494; Gem Trek *Bow Lake & Saskatchewan Crossing*

OPINION

Witness the tumultuous birth of a great river. Investigate the chaos left in the wake of a retreating glacier. Walk the shore of a lake so colourful it looks like paint. All in a few leisurely hours.

Bow Glacier Falls crashes down a 152-m (500-ft) cliff at the foot of Bow Glacier. This is the thrillingly wild headwaters of the Bow River, which soon composes itself and flows placidly south to Banff, then winds lazily out of the mountains, into the prairie, through Calgary.

You'll reach the falls by hiking along brilliant turquoise Bow Lake, across austere glacial outwash flats, and next to an incisive gorge. Most of the way is nearly level, beneath soaring Crowfoot Mtn. Early on, you'll glimpse Bow Glacier mounted on the western horizon.

FACT

By Vehicle

Follow directions for Bow Hut (Trip 31) to reach the trailhead parking area near Num-ti-jah Lodge.

On Foot

The level trail gradually curves southwest around the northwest shore of **Bow Lake**. South (left) is 3050-m (10,004-ft) Crowfoot Mtn. Reach the lake's west end in 20 minutes. Proceed south across gravel flats. The trail beside the inlet stream is cairned. If the water's too high,

Bow Lake and Crowfoot Glacier

follow the parallel, alternate trail 30-60 m to the west, undulating over terminal moraines (now forest-and-brush-covered lumps).

Reach a **gorge** at 3.3 km (2 mi). A reinforced trail steeply ascends the north edge. At 1997 m (6550 ft), about 45 minutes from the trailhead, arrive at a **limestone boulder** bridging the gorge. That's the way to Bow Hut (Trip 31). For Bow Glacier Falls, don't cross. Bear right and continue ascending. After a brief, precarious stretch, top out on the crest of a **terminal moraine** at 3.7 km (2.3 mi). Your destination, the waterfall, is visible crashing down the basin headwall southwest. The view left (south) reveals the up-canyon route toward Bow Hut.

Follow the trail right, descend into the basin, then proceed across 0.8 km (0.5 mi) of rubble to reach the base of **Bow Glacier Falls** at 4.5 km (2.8 mi), 2090 m (6850 ft). Total hiking time: about 1½ hours. Bow Glacier meltwater feeds the falls. It pools up in a lake—hidden from view, just above the cliff. The view northeast, across the Parkway, includes Cirque Peak (Trip 8) on the right.

Bow Glacier Falls

TRIP 46
Bow Lookout

LOCATION	Banff National Park
ROUND TRIP	6 km (3.7 mi)
ELEVATION GAIN	235 m (770 ft)
KEY ELEVATIONS	trailhead 2080 m (6822 ft) lookout 2315 m (7593 ft)
HIKING TIME	1½ to 2 hours
DIFFICULTY	easy
MAPS	page 494; Gem Trek *Bow Lake & Saskatchewan Crossing*

OPINION

A yipping coyote can be heard farther than you'll walk here. But it's enough to stretch your legs, breathe deeply of mountain air, and escape the crowd at Peyto Lake viewpoint. The destination is a fire lookout site high on the southwest side of Bow Pass. The lookout is gone, the commanding vista remains.

The first ten minutes of the trip are on a paved path, possibly tourist congested. Then you'll likely be alone on an old dirt road. It traverses open slopes with eye-exercising views. Nearby rugged cliffs on the north ridge of Mt. Jimmy Simpson lend a mountain-climbing atmosphere to this short, easy excursion.

Awaiting you at the lookout site is a fine view of peaks lining the Icefields Parkway and a new perspective of Bow Lake. You can even see the upper reaches of Crowfoot Glacier.

FACT

By Vehicle

Drive the Icefields Parkway south 16.5 km (10.2 mi) from Waterfowl Lakes campground, or north 4.7 km (2.9 mi) from the Num-Ti-Jah Lodge / Bow Glacier turnoff on the north side of Bow Lake. At Bow Summit, turn southwest and follow the paved access road 0.5 km (0.3 mi) to the Peyto Lake viewpoint main parking lot, at 2080 m (6822 ft).

On Foot

Start by the interpretative signs at the northwest end of the parking lot. Walk the signed, paved path 0.6 km (0.4 mi) to the **viewing platform** overlooking Peyto Lake. Stop here to see the lake and Peyto Glacier.

From the platform, return to the paved path and turn right. Pass the dirt path descending right to Peyto Lake (Trip 9). Stay straight (west-northwest) and ascend the steep paved path.

Bow Lake and Crowfoot Glacier

A minute farther, at the **3-way junction**, follow the paved, middle path. (Sharp left connects to the upper parking lot. Right is an interpretive loop.) At the next fork, a paved nature trail signed "Explore" curves right. Proceed straight (south-southeast) on the gently ascending, dirt road. This used to be the fire lookout access road. The slopes above and below the road are home to graceful-yet-tough alpine fir. In summer, you'll also see a plethora of wildflowers here, including white-flowered valerian and the ubiquitous Indian paintbrush (deep red).

The road makes long switchbacks: first south-southeast, then north-northwest. At 2190 m (7183 ft), about 20 minutes from the parking lot, reach a **viewpoint** in a clearing. Caldron Peak (west-northwest) rises steeply above Peyto Lake's west shore. Caldron Lake (Trip 9) is hidden from view, but Dragon Glacier is visible west-southwest, high above the lake's west shore. Meltwater cascading off the glacier feeds the lake. A cascade is also visible below the lake, spilling down sheer cliffs into Peyto basin.

Continuing to the lookout, take the far left trail to shortcut the switchbacking road and rejoin it above. Or simply stay on the road, which is less steep. The road progresses generally southeast.

At 2240 m (7347 ft) the road crosses a stream that, in early summer, drains the shaded, snowy basin above. At 2.5 km (1.6 mi) the road dips into a **trough,** crosses another stream, then resumes a moderate southward ascent. Near the stream you're likely to see yellow-flowered, long-stemmed ragwort, and long, red-stemmed saxifrage

Globeflower

with tiny white flowers. Look carefully for a few plum-coloured lousewort, or even mountain sorrel with red, papery sepals.

Reach the **lookout site** at 3 km (1.9 mi), 2315 m (7593 ft), about 50 minutes from the parking lot. The slopes here are rife with mountain heather (tiny flowers, white or pink) and white mountain avens.

Cirque Peak (Trip 8) is east-southeast. Dolomite Peak is southeast. Farther southeast is glacier-draped Mt. Hector. Crowfoot mountain and glacier are south of Bow Lake. Mistaya Valley is north of Bow Pass. North-northeast of the pass is the smooth face of 3174-m (10,411-ft) Observation Peak. Just north of it is castellated Silverhorn Mtn.

Crowfoot pass and mountain (Trip 7), south of Bow Lake.

TRIP 47

Saskatchewan Glacier

LOCATION	Banff National Park, south of Sunwapta Pass
ROUND TRIP	13.6 km (8.4 mi)
ELEVATION GAIN	340 m (1115 ft)
KEY ELEVATIONS	trailhead 1645 m (5396 ft) forested hill 1760 m (5770 ft) chasm 1713 m (5620 ft) glacier tongue 1890 m (6200 ft)
HIKING TIME	5 to 6 hours
DIFFICULTY	moderate due only to rocky terrain
MAPS	page 496; Gem Trek *Columbia Icefield*

OPINION

Hikers communing with nature are often assisted by paths built by miners or loggers pillaging nature. But even more incongruous is hiking into a glacial valley so freshly scoured it seems you're witnessing creation, while underfoot is a road built by men sharpening their powers of destruction: U.S. mountain troops training on Saskatchewan Glacier during World War II.

The glacier is huge yet only hints at the vastness of the Columbia Icefield from which it flows. This is the longest—about 5 km (3.1 mi)—of the icefield's six principal tongues. It has retreated dramatically since the soldiers were here, yet the valley feels as intensely wild as it did 12,000 years ago when it was rubbed raw by a sheet of ice deep enough to bury a skyscraper. The receding glacier left behind the rocky, river-riddled chaos you see here today.

Just below the glacier tongue is a broad, shallow, meltwater lake. Down-valley are the ever shifting powder-blue headwaters of the North Saskatchewan River. Towering above are Mounts Athabasca and Andromeda.

Though you'll gain little elevation here, you'll soon reach the glacial outwash flats and begin negotiating trackless, rocky rubble. Where the rocks are small and stable, you can stride. Much of the way, however, the rocks are unstable or large, which makes for tedious hiking. Awareness and balance are necessary to maintain speed. That, and the ever-increasing distance to the ice, ensure you of solitude.

If you prefer a well-maintained trail and are undeterred by a crowd, zip up to Parker Ridge (Trip 11) for an aerial view of Saskatchewan Glacier.

FACT

By Vehicle

If you're heading northwest on the Icefields Parkway, drive 6 km (3.7 mi) past Cirrus Mtn campground and turn left (southeast) onto an obscure, unpaved road

Looking east, from North Saskatchewan River glacial outwash flats

dropping below the highway. It's just before the Parkway's Big Bend switchback.

If you're heading southeast on the Icefields Parkway, drive 11.7 km (7.2 mi) past the Banff-Jasper boundary at Sunwapta Pass. (Ignore the pullout at the gravel flats, in the middle of the Big Bend switchback; that's not the trailhead.) Turn right (southeast) onto an obscure, unpaved road dropping below the highway.

From either approach, park just before the bridge spanning the North Saskatchewan River, at 1645 m (5396 ft).

On Foot

Cross the bridge. Immediately after, ignore a trail forking right. Just beyond, turn right onto a second trail. Follow it southwest, paralleling the river and highway. In about 300 m (328 yd), intersect the WW II road. Turn right and continue southwest. Soon cross gravel flats. At 1.2 km (0.75 mi) ascend into forest on the road.

About 25 minutes from the trailhead, crest a **forested hill** at 1760 m (5770 ft). Ahead, the road descends gradually. Behind, the hill blocks highway noise. Near 2.7 km (1.7 mi), emerge onto open, **glacial outwash flats**. The braided North Saskatchewan River has largely obliterated the rest of the road. Parker Ridge (Trip 11) is the valley's green, north wall. The Saskatchewan Glacier is visible ahead (west), about 5 km (3.1 mi) distant.

Ignore the remnant road proceeding west. Bear right (north), cross-country. At 2.8 km (1.7 mi), 1713 m (5620 ft) reach a deep, narrow **chasm** funneling the **North Saskatchewan River** into a torrent. The constriction is strewn with heaps of deadfall.

For years, enough tree trunks have spanned the chasm to grant hikers passage to the north bank. Before crossing, carefully assess the risk. If the trees have shifted, perhaps they no longer create a natural bridge. If they've weakened, they might not support your weight. Falling here would be fatal. If you question your safety, turn back. Instead hike upstream (west) above the river's south bank.

If you cross the chasm, go left (west / upstream) above the river's **north bank**. Pick up a bootbeaten path. It closely follows the river's **northernmost channel**. In about 15 minutes, however, your progress will slow on the sharp, vegetated slope. You'll see the barren, flat, valley floor is more attractive hiking terrain. Turn left (south) and rockhop or ford the river channel. It's usually narrow and shallow, with negligible current.

Proceed up-valley (generally west) across trackless, rocky rubble until reaching the **tongue of the Saskatchewan Glacier** at about 6.8 km (4.2 mi), 1890 m (6200 ft). Your precise route will depend on what you perceive to be the easiest way forward, which will depend on the shifting course of the meltwater. To actually touch the ice, another ford (broader, deeper, swifter) might be necessary. Do not proceed onto the ice without the requisite equipment and training.

Floe Lake, from just below Numa Pass (Trip 48)

TRIP 48

Floe Lake / Numa Pass

LOCATION	Kootenay National Park
SHUTTLE TRIP	27.5 km (17 mi) in Floe Creek, out Numa Creek
ELEVATION GAIN	1000 m (3280 ft)
KEY ELEVATIONS	trailhead 1348 m (4420 ft) lake 2040 m (6690 ft), pass 2355 m (7724 ft) Numa Creek camp 1510 m (4953 ft)
HIKING TIME	7 to 10 hours
DIFFICULTY	challenging
MAPS	page 499; Gem Trek *Kootenay National Park;* Mount Goodsir 82 N/1

OPINION

After a spate of gloomy weather, the unveiling of our sacred star is dazzling. A hiker's first glimpse of Floe Lake has a similar effect, especially now that the approach through Floe Creek valley was laid waste by fire during the summer of 2003, when much of northern Kootenay Park was ablaze.

Surmount the final steep switchbacks, which seem to lengthen like a slinky, and you'll be greeted by soaring cliffs rising abruptly from the azure water. Ice floes plastered to the rock are mirrored in the lake, hence the name. Alpine larches—some of them unusually big—are profuse between Floe Lake and Numa Pass. In late September they turn electric gold, as if plugged in. The pass affords a revelatory view of the Rockies in general and the awesome Rockwall in particular. From the pass, the trail plunges into lush Numa Creek basin, where the final leg of this long, one-way dayhike dances along the bank of thundering Numa Creek. (*Numa* means *thunder* in the Cree language.)

The fire-affected approach, however, might make you question the trip's merit. Previous editions of this book suggested Floe Lake/Numa Pass be an out-and-back dayhike and rated it *Outstanding*. That's when the Floe Creek drainage harboured the Rockies' best imitation of a rainforest. The trail ascended through thigh-thwacking foliage in a dense, mature woodland of girthy trees. What remains is a 10.5-km (6.5-mi) stretch of spindly, charred snags. Though the area is recovering robustly and is now far from dismal, it's reasonable that most people would still prefer not to undertake a round trip when a one-way shuttle trip is viable: up to Floe Lake, over Numa Pass, and out Numa Creek. The fire stopped before the Floe Lake campground, where all the trees survived. Beyond, the hike retains its original magnificence. Just be prepared for a big, challenging day in the mountains. Both the distance and the elevation gain are significant. And determination rather than inspiration must now fuel your initial upward effort, though the absence of trees does grant hikers more enticing views of their high-country goal. If you're strong—mentally as well as physically—stride on.

Floe Lake and Numa Pass, however, are best appreciated as the first of many thrilling sights while backpacking the Rockwall (Trip 89). If you camp at the lake on your first night out, force yourself to get up early so you can photograph the cliffs flawlessly reflected in the calm water. For a shorter, one- or two-night outing, skip the fire-affected Floe Creek approach, enter via Numa Creek, pitch your tent at Numa Creek campground, then dayhike the 14.2-km (8.8-mi) round trip to Numa Pass. High in the flower-dappled alpine tundra, you'll enjoy an aerial perspective of Floe Lake and the Rockwall towering 1000 m (3280 ft) above it.

As shuttle trips go, this one's easy to arrange, because the distance between the Floe Lake and Numa Creek trailheads is just 8.5 km (5.3 mi). Hitchhiking should also pose no difficulty, but do it in the morning before you set out on foot. Knowing your vehicle awaits you at trail's end is reassuring. Having to hitch in the evening is more difficult and less safe.

FACT

By Vehicle

The Floe Lake / Hawk Creek trailhead parking lot is on the southwest side of Hwy 93. Reach it by driving 22.5 km (14 mi) south of the Banff-Kootenay boundary, or 71 km (44 mi) north of Kootenay Park's West Gate at Radium. Elevation: 1348 m (4420 ft). Begin hiking here.

The Numa Creek trailhead parking lot is 8.5 km (5.3 mi) northwest of the Floe Lake/Hawk Creek trailhead. It's on the southwest side of Hwy 93. Reach it by driving 14 km (8.7 mi) southwest of the Banff-Kootenay boundary, or 79.5 km (49.4 mi) north of Kootenay Park's West Gate at Radium. Elevation: 1405 m (4608 ft). Leave a vehicle here, where the one-way shuttle trip ends.

On Foot

After descending south to a bridge over **Vermilion River**, the trail turns right (northwest). At 1.7 km (1.1 mi) cross a bridge to the north bank of **Floe Creek**. The trail then turns southwest—your general direction of travel nearly all the way to the lake. The initially gradual ascent soon steepens, gaining 152 m (500 ft).

The trail contours for about 1 km (0.6 mi). The Ball Range is visible behind you (northeast) across the Vermilion River Valley. At 1534 m (5030 ft), about 1¼ hours from the trailhead, cross a broad avalanche slope rife with fuchsia fireweed in July. The Rockwall's southeast end is visible ahead (southwest).

About 20 minutes farther, at 6 km (3.7 mi), 1585 m (5200 ft), ascend switchbacks. The trail then levels. At 8.4 km (5.2 mi), begin a 2-km (1.2-mi) section of steep switchbacks heading northwest. Enter **Floe Lake campground**, just above the east shore, at 10.7 km (6.6 mi), 2040 m (6690 ft).

Just before the warden cabin near Floe Lake's northeast shore, the Rockwall trail (Trip 89) ascends northwest. It's another 2.7 km (1.7 mi) from the lake to 2355-m (7724-ft) **Numa Pass**—the Rockwall trail's highest point. That's a gain of 315 m (1033 ft), most of which you'll endure in the final kilometre. On top, you can see Floe Lake (south), sharply pyramidal 3200-m (10,496-ft) Foster Peak (southwest), Numa Mtn (northeast), and Tumbling Pass (northwest, beyond the Numa Creek drainage).

From Numa Pass, the trail plummets 745 m (2445 ft) in 5.5 km (3.4 mi) generally north-northwest into lush Numa Creek basin. Just below the pass, tight switchbacks ease your descent, but then the trail steepens before moderating near 1770 m (5800 ft). You'll hike through verdant meadows and avalanche swaths and cross numerous small tributary streams. Reach **Numa Creek campground** at 20.5 km (12.7 mi), 1510 m (4953 ft). Bear right. Five minutes downstream intersect the **Numa Creek trail** at 20.9 km (13 mi). The Rockwall trail continues left (west), reaching Tumbling Pass campground in 7.5 km (4.7 mi). Go right (northeast) to complete the one-way shuttle trip out to Hwy 93.

Heading for the highway, cross a bridged tributary. The trail then follows **Numa Creek** downstream, usually within view of the water, often beside it. Near 23 km (14.3 mi) fork right (east), still following Numa Creek. At 25.3 km (15.7 mi) cross a sturdy aluminum-and-plank bridge to the creek's south bank. Leaving the creek now, the trail climbs moderately on a frustrating, seemingly pointless detour. It heads southeast, paralleling the **Vermilion River** until reaching a bridge spanning the canyon. Just north of the bridge, reach the **Numa Creek trailhead**, on Hwy 93, at 27.5 km (17 mi).

Stanley Glacier (Trip 49)

TRIP 49

Stanley Glacier

LOCATION	Kootenay National Park
ROUND TRIP	11.2 km (6.9 mi)
ELEVATION GAIN	484 m (1587 ft)
KEY ELEVATIONS	trailhead 1595 m (5232 ft)
	highpoint 2060 m (6756 ft)
HIKING TIME	3 to 3½ hours
DIFFICULTY	easy
MAPS	page 499; Gem Trek *Kootenay National Park*

OPINION

Hiking to Stanley Glacier is a life-and-death venture.

The journey begins in a forest that, not once but twice in recent years, was devastated by wildfire: 1968 and 2003. The trail climbs slopes punctuated with charred trees. Though vanquished, many still stand defiantly erect.

A Lazarus-like rebirth followed both blazes. No longer overshadowed, the ground cover has been awash in sunlight and is flourishing. Each summer, the lush greenery is dappled with wildflowers, most notably fireweed (fuchsia) and heart-leaved arnica (yellow).

Your destination—the farthest reaches of the glaciated basin, where the ancient, frozen tongue still licks the surrounding rubble—is also a striking contrast between the living and the inanimate. You'll stand precisely where the ice and rock give way to grass and trees. It's like witnessing birth while being serenaded by a soothing symphony of streams and cascades.

Between the trailhead and glacier, you'll hike through a narrow, hanging valley whose southwest wall is a soaring, vertical cliff. Water constantly plummets off it in dramatic, diaphanous plumes, then trickles into a scree slope bursting with lavender penstemon.

Elsewhere, these unlikely rock gardens would be a surprising sight. Here, after you've witnessed the pervasive mortality of the forest below, they're a marvel. Death, after all, is what makes life important.

FACT

By Vehicle

Hwy 93 runs generally north-south, linking Hwy 1 (at Castle Junction, between Banff townsite and Lake Louise Village) with Hwy 95 (at Radium). Drive Hwy 93 southwest 3.2 km (2 mi) from the Banff-Kootenay parks boundary at Vermilion Pass, or northeast 3.8 km (2.4 mi) from Marble Canyon. Trailhead parking is on the southeast side of the highway, at 1595 m (5232 ft).

On Foot

Descend to 1585 m (5200 ft), cross the **Vermilion River** bridge, then begin switchbacking up through the burn. In summer, fuchsia fireweed brightens the slopes. Castle Mtn is visible left (north-northeast).

Your general direction will remain southeast to the toe of Stanley Glacier. In ten minutes, approach **Stanley Creek**. It helps mask the sound of vehicle traffic on the highway, but you must hike about 30 minutes before escaping civilization entirely. By then the ascent eases near the **mouth of the glaciated basin**.

At 2.4 km (1.5 mi) cross a bridge to the northeast bank of **Stanley Creek**. The capricious nature of wildfire is evident here: the forest is an odd mixture of green, thriving trees and their dead-standing brethren who were incinerated. Paralleling Stanley Creek upstream, the trail continues probing the **basin**. The glacier is visible ahead. The basin's right (southwest) wall—an outlier of 3154-m (10,345-ft) Stanley Peak—is a sheer, towering cliff.

Above most of the trees, about an hour from the trailhead, reach a **sign** among rocks. It's at 4.8 km (3 mi), 1950 m (6396 ft), across from a long, slender waterfall on the right (southwest) wall. The sign states "Trail ends, not maintained beyond this point." Ignore it. But before continuing, pause here and survey the basin.

About 0.8 km (0.5 mi) directly ahead, like an altar in a cathedral, is a bench atop an escarpment cleaved by a cascade: the incipient Stanley Creek. The bench top is level, meadowy, lightly treed. It's the optimal vantage for admiring the glacier, which is just above and beyond. So your goal is to surmount that bench and, despite what the sign suggests, an easy-to-follow bootbeaten route allows you to do so.

From near the sign, cairned routes continue on both sides of the basin, so you can loop over the bench. Left begins on chunky boulders and ascends east-southeast. Right leads south-southeast and is almost entirely visible from near the sign. Go that way. Follow the cairns, dip into the **rocky gully**, then ascend on scree.

About 15 minutes from the sign, reach a **cave** at the base of the right (southwest) **wall**. Continue traversing talus and hopping streamlets. Wildflowers (Indian paintbrush, Lyall's saxifrage, fleabane, arnica, sawwort) thrive here and beyond. Soon reach the level **bench** at 5.6 km (3.5 mi), 2060 m (6756 ft). The route momentarily vanishes in this small, subalpine meadow.

It's possible to work your way up the talus to the tongue of **Stanley Glacier** but doing so will not earn you a revelatory perspective. Though the glaciated headwall is the commanding sight, the view also extends down-valley (northwest), across Hwy 93 to 2845-m (9332-ft) Mt. Whymper.

Loop back to the "end of maintained trail" sign by proceeding left (east) across the bench. Hop the braided stream, ascend briefly, then look for the cairned route. It resumes among stunted trees atop the small **knob** adjacent to the bench. From the knob, the route plunges generally northwest, down the talus-strewn northeast wall of the basin, back through chunky boulders to the sign.

Upon reaching the **sign**, you're on familiar ground. Retrace your steps by following the trail back to Hwy 93.

Penstemon

TRIP 50
Ottertail Fire Road to Goodsir Pass

LOCATION	Yoho National Park
ROUND TRIP	29 km (18 mi) by bike plus 21.4 km (13.3 mi) on foot
ELEVATION GAIN	335 m (1100 ft) by bike plus 775 m (2542 ft) on foot
KEY ELEVATIONS	trailhead 1195 m (3920 ft) stop cycling/begin hiking 1480 m (4855 ft) pass 2210 m (7250 ft)
TRAVEL TIME	9 hours
DIFFICULTY	moderate
MAPS	page 504; Gem Trek *Lake Louise & Yoho*, Gem Trek *Kootenay National Park*

OPINION

Goodsir Pass is too far from any trailhead to be a reasonable dayhike destination. But if you're a serious outdoor athlete, you can get there in a single day with the help of your iron steed. You'll find the pass extraordinary, the accomplishment exhilarating.

The pass—among the most spectacular in the Canadian Rockies—is a vast, rock-strewn, flower-dappled, alpine meadow beneath soaring Sharp Mtn, Sentry Peak, and Mt. Goodsir. The twin-towered Goodsir is the highest mountain in Yoho Park. This is as close as you'll get to it on a trail. It rises an astonishing 1950 m (6400 ft) from the creekbed below its northeast face.

If Goodsir Pass were easier to reach, it would be too popular for its own good, because the Goodsir Towers rival the Ramparts (Trips 94-98) or a chunk of the Ten Peaks (Trip 5) for visual impact. But access is sufficiently inconvenient to discourage the multitudes. So it's possible you'll be here alone, which will greatly enhance the experience.

The first 14.5 km (9 mi) are on a fire road. It makes for lousy hiking but fun biking. The grade is gentle, gaining only 360 m (1180 ft), and views are frequent. Then the trail and the hard work begin. You'll hike 10.7 km (6.6 mi) and gain 770 m (2525 ft), almost entirely in forest, before entering Goodsir Pass. Allow yourself a couple hours at the pass, so you can wander farther into it and appreciate the magnificent scenery. With even more time and energy, you could roam the open slopes north of the pass.

Ascending the fire road, you'll see the peaks of the Ottertail Range, across the Ottertail River valley. Visible are 3319-m (10,886-ft) Mt. Vaux, 3133-m (10,276-ft) Mt. Ennis, and 2911-m (9810-ft) Allan Peak. Get a good look on the way up, because on the way down gravity will pull you into a screaming descent.

Goodsir Towers

FACT

By Vehicle

Drive the Trans-Canada Hwy through Yoho Park 8.4 km (5.2 mi) southwest of Field to the Ottertail fire road parking area on the left (south) side of the highway, at 1195 m (3920 ft). This is 150 m (165 yd) northeast of the Ottertail River bridge.

By Bike

Follow the fire road gently ascending the Ottertail River valley. Your general direction of travel will be southeast all the way to McArthur Creek. There's little elevation gain the first 3.2 km (2 mi). The road then climbs moderately to about the 5-km (3-mi) point. After that, you can coast downhill for 1 km (0.6 mi). Cross **Float Creek bridge** at 6.2 km (3.8 mi). A short, switchbacking ascent is followed by a level stretch. Near 10 km (6 mi), the road ascends, pulling farther away from the river.

At 14.5 km (9 mi), 1480 m (4855 ft), reach a **junction** beyond which bicycles are prohibited. Left (north) ascends to McArthur Pass (Trip 114). Park your bike in the trees and proceed for Goodsir Pass.

On Foot

Bear right (southeast) at the junction and immediately cross McArthur Creek bridge. Pass a **campground** at 14.8 km (9.2 mi) and, a few minutes farther, McArthur Creek warden cabin. At 15.5 km (9.6 mi) cross the **Ottertail River bridge**. Just beyond is a junction. Straight leads directly to the pass. Left is a 2-km (1.2-mi) detour to **Ottertail Falls**. After the falls viewpoint, the spur trail rejoins the main trail to the pass. If you're on a daytrip, it makes sense to leave the falls until you return from the pass. See if you have time and energy for it then.

Ignoring the falls for now and continuing directly to the pass, you'll reach the southern spur trail to the falls in about 10 minutes. Proceed straight, ascending steeply. The trail drops then regains the lost elevation to enter the pass.

Just before the pass, attain a view across the valley to the 3562-m (11,683-ft) South Tower and 3525-m (11,562-ft) North Tower of Mt. Goodsir. On their southeast side, Sentry Peak continues the rugged chain.

Reach the northwest end of 2210-m (7250-ft) **Goodsir Pass** at 25.2 km (15.6 mi). Sharp Mtn rises south of the pass.

Hamilton Lake (Trip 51)

TRIP 51

Hamilton Lake / Emerald Col

LOCATION	Yoho National Park, near Emerald Lake
ROUND TRIP	11 km (6.8 mi) to lake, plus 3.2 km (2 mi) to col
ELEVATION GAIN	838 m (2749 ft) to lake, plus 250 m (820 ft) to col
KEY ELEVATIONS	trailhead 1312 m (4303 ft), lake 2150 m (7052 ft) col 2400 m (7872 ft)
HIKING TIME	4 hours for lake, plus 2 hours for col
DIFFICULTY	moderate to lake or col
MAPS	page 508; Gem Trek *Lake Louise & Yoho*

OPINION

What oxygen is for your body, solitude is for your soul. But solitude alone does not make a hike worthwhile. You want oxygen *and* food; solitude *and* beauty.

Hamilton Lake—viewed from trail's end on its south shore—is not beautiful compared to many Canadian Rockies' backcountry lakes. The trail to Hamilton is less popular than others radiating from Emerald Lake, therefore more solitudinous, but it lacks the elements of beauty—visual allure, aural atmosphere, singularity—that help make being alone a transcendent experience.

So don't stop at Hamilton's south shore. The dotted line on the map ends there, but that's merely a suggestion. Keep hiking beyond trail's end. Few hikers visit the lake, but virtually none proceed beyond. Solitude is thus a near certainty. And the lake basin does harbour abundant beauty.

From atop the knoll above the northwest shore, turn and look back: south, across the lake. *Now* you can appreciate how high the lake is perched on the wall of the Kicking Horse Valley. Several of Yoho Park's ice-armoured peaks are visible on the horizon.

Just north of the lake, the rock underfoot is fascinating. Stones of such warm complexion and striking shapes make you wish you could haul them home in your pack. Because this is barren, alpine terrain, you can meander, head down, admiring whatever cobbles catch your eye.

Exploring farther, you'll find the slope of the basin is ideal: steep enough that rapidly improving scenery coaxes you upward, yet not so steep that it's taxing. The topography is ideal, too: varied enough to be intriguing, yet not so varied that it limits your freedom to roam.

All this blithe wandering culminates at Emerald Col, where you can gaze in peace at massive Michael Peak. Mike's the one that Emerald Lake visitors—colliding like bumper cars—ogle from the shore near Emerald Lake Lodge.

You'll need endurance and tenacity to propel yourself to this superior, aerial vantage. The trail to the lake is more demanding than the stats indicate. Not only must you climb 838 m (2749 ft), you must do it in 5.5 km (3.4 mi). Wffew. And the ascent is largely through viewless forest. Ugh.

Michael Peak, from Emerald Col

But that's the bulk of the task. If you can reach the lake, and you're mentally comfortable forging cross-country, above treeline, you should have no difficulty continuing to the col, which is only 1.6 km (1 mi) farther and 250 m (820 ft) higher.

FACT

By Vehicle

From the Yoho Park Visitor Centre, in Field, B.C., drive the Trans-Canada Hwy southwest 1.6 km (1 mi). Turn right (west) onto Emerald Lake Road. Continue 8 km (5 mi) to the road's end parking lot. The trailhead sign is near the parking lot entrance, on the left (west) side, at 1312 m (4303 ft).

On Foot

In two minutes, reach a signed junction. Left (south) is the Emerald River trail. Proceed straight (west-southwest), ascending at a moderate grade through forest.

In about 15 minutes, pass the **Hamilton Falls** viewpoints (left). The trail then steepens, heading generally northwest. Near 4 km (2.5 mi), overlook Emerald Lake (right / east). Beyond the lake is Wapta Mtn, traversed by the Wapta Highline (Trip 52).

Reach the south shore of **Hamilton Lake** at 5.5 km (3.4 mi), 2150 m (7052 ft). The basin walls rise to 3040-m (9971-ft) Mt. Carnarvon (left / north-northwest), 2555-m (8380-ft) Emerald Peak (right / northeast), and an unnamed block between them.

Hop the outlet stream, round the left (west) shore, and follow a bootbeaten path cresting the **knoll** above the northwest shore. From here, the Ottertail Range is visible south, beyond the lake, across the Kicking Horse Valley.

Continue north, up the talus, until you can easily traverse right (east) into 2400-m (7872-ft) **Emerald Col**. It's at 7.1 km (4.4 mi), between the unnamed block and Emerald Peak. Total elevation gain: 1088 m (3569 ft). Choose your perch, marvel at 2696-m (8843-ft) Michael Peak (northwest, across Emerald Basin), and luxuriate in the solitude.

TRIP 52
Emerald Triangle

LOCATION	Yoho National Park
LOOP	19.7 km (12.2 mi)
ELEVATION GAIN	868 m (2847 ft)
KEY ELEVATIONS	trailhead 1312 m (4303 ft) Burgess Pass 2180 m (7150 ft) Yoho Pass 1826 m (5990 ft)
HIKING TIME	6½ to 8 hours
DIFFICULTY	moderate
MAPS	page 508; Gem Trek *Lake Louise & Yoho*

OPINION

Pupil-dilating views will keep your synapses firing on the Wapta Highline section of this triangular loop. The visual stimuli include the glacier-laden ramparts of the President Range, the towering faces of Mt. Burgess and Wapta Mtn, lofty perspectives of the entire Emerald Lake basin and the Kicking Horse Valley, and Mt. Stephen looming above the town of Field.

Despite its moderate length, however, the loop is taxing. The initial ascent is long, steep, and nearly viewless. You'll need strength and discipline to prevail. And the descent is a sustained, ankle-eating plunge. Keep your eyes on the trail. Smell something burning? It's your brake pads.

The Wapta Highline vistas, and a well-deserved sense of accomplishment at trail's end, make the triangle a worthwhile trip. But you'll be out of the trees on the Highline for only 35 minutes, unless you stop there, which you certainly should. The scenic section of trail along Emerald Lake's west shore is usually crowded. And the famous Burgess Shale Beds, above the Wapta Highline, are open to the public only by pre-arranged guided tour. If you have time for only one hike in Yoho Park, the Iceline (Trip 13) or the Lake O'Hara region (Trips 14-19) are more rewarding choices.

A minor attraction of the Wapta Highline is the flora on the initial ascent. Here, in the shade of Mt. Burgess, a cool, moist micro-climate conspires with the low elevation to create a lusher forest than is common in the Canadian Rockies. Instead of the usual knot of scrawny, graceless lodgepole pines and Engelmann spruce, you'll be greeted by elegance and immensity: ferns, Devil's club, western hemlock, and western red cedar, which are more typical of B.C.'s interior ranges. Yoho Park's largest cedar forest resides on this southeast shore of Emerald Lake.

Also of interest—geologic as well as arboreal—is the alluvial fan dominating the northern half of Emerald Lake basin. The trail crosses this gravelly, watery plain for nearly 2 km (1.2 mi). Composed of debris flowing from Emerald Basin (Trip 51), the fan is slowly filling Emerald Lake. The lodgepole pines scattered across the fan look puny and feeble but are actually rather heroic. Some are 150 years old. Their dwarfish girth and height are due to the brutally harsh growing conditions created by poor soil, ever-changing watercourses, and fierce winds. Hiking this section of trail, you'll cross numerous boardwalks. Some might appear unnecessary—bridging shallow, dry, rocky gullies. Others might end midstream. It's because there are dozens of rivulets here, and they fluctuate constantly. During peak runoff in August, a trail crew repositions the portable boardwalks. But the water refuses to cooperate and stay put. Expect to do a little rockhopping to keep your boots dry.

Because the Emerald Triangle is a loop, you can hike it in either direction. Clockwise—Yoho Pass first, then Burgess Pass—allows a more gradual ascent. The route description below, however, directs you counterclockwise: up to Burgess Pass, then down from Yoho Pass. Our reasoning? The ascent, though more abrupt, is in verdant forest, so on a hot day it's much cooler. You'll dispatch the ascent immediately, rather than enduring it longer. You'll hike the Wapta Highline northward, with the most impressive scenery in front of you, rather than at your back. And, on the descent, you'll be looking down at Emerald Lake.

FACT

Before your trip

The Wapta Highline, a section of trail on the Emerald Triangle, passes beneath the Burgess Shale Beds, a UNESCO World Heritage Site. More than 140 species of fossils approximately 530 million years old have been unearthed here. Though visible from the trail, the site is closed to the public. If a guided tour interests you, call 1-800-343-3006, or (250) 343-6006. They begin taking reservations in February. You should reserve months in advance.

By Vehicle

From the Yoho Park Visitor Centre, in Field, B.C., drive the Trans-Canada Hwy southwest 1.6 km (1 mi). Turn right (west) onto Emerald Lake Road, then continue 8.5 km (5.3 mi) to the road's end parking lot, at 1312 m (4303 ft).

On Foot

At the north end of the parking lot, go right (east) over the bridge spanning Emerald Lake's outlet stream. Follow the paved road behind **Emerald Lake Lodge** (left) and above a creek (right). Go right (southeast) onto the brick walkway. Pass the fire pit. Continue among the cabins. About seven minutes from the parking lot, the brick walkway ends in a small cul-de-sac, at 1329 m (4360 ft). Proceed straight (southeast) into the forest on the signed **Emerald Lake circuit** trail.

At 0.6 km (0.4 mi), bear left. Right (west) returns to the parking lot. A few minutes farther, bear left again. Go northeast, over the bridge. The next junction, about eight minutes farther, is easily missed; stay alert. Watch for a sign up-slope, in the brush, possibly obscured by cedar branches. Here, at 1.5 km (0.9 mi), go right (northeast) for Burgess Pass. Left is the Emerald Lake circuit, which continues generally north along the west shore.

The trail climbs through a lush forest of western red cedars, Douglas firs, and Devil's club. Stay on the main path, ignoring any spurs. The ascent eases in about 45 minutes. The sheer north face of Mt. Burgess is briefly visible right (south). The stature of the forest is diminishing. Black, hanging moss is profuse.

Michael Peak, from Wapta Highline

At 1864 m (6115 ft), the trail curves right (south) along a **ridge**. Strong hikers will be here about 1⅓ hours after leaving the lakeshore. The Wapta Highline is visible left (east), in the alpine zone, above and beyond a gorge. About 30 minutes farther, at 2035 m (6675 ft), beneath Mt. Burgess, attain a view right (west) into Yoho Park's western reaches. The south end of Emerald Lake is visible west-northwest. Soon descend to a bridged creeklet. Cross another shortly beyond. The ascent resumes.

At 2150 m (7050 ft), about 30 minutes from the creeklets, begin the final push southeast to Burgess Pass. North-northeast, just across the gorge, is the airy Wapta Highline, which you'll soon be hiking. North-northwest is the great massif known as The Vice President, topped by Emerald Glacier.

Where a spur tempts you to continue straight across a rough, steep slope, bear right and immediately enter **Burgess Pass** at 7.5 km (4.7 mi), 2180 m (7150 ft). The clearing in this small gap is rife with heather and wildflowers. Mt. Burgess is right (west-southwest). Wapta Mtn is left (northeast). Strong hikers will arrive here in 2¼ hours, others within 3 hours. From the signed junction in the pass, go left (east). Right (south) plunges 8.2 km (5.1 mi) through forest to a trailhead just off the Trans-Canada Hwy.

A minute past the junction, Field and the Trans-Canada are visible right (south), far below. After rounding the corner, the Goodsir Towers (Trip 50) are visible back right (south-southeast). Glacier-bearing Mt. Stephen is nearby southeast. After descending slightly from the pass, the trail levels and is again in trees. Pass a sign announcing that the **Burgess Shale**, just ahead, is closed to public visitation. Curve north on the rocky slope and proceed onto the section of trail known as the **Wapta**

Highline (labeled Burgess Highline on the Gem Trek map.) The President Range is visible northwest. Emerald Lake's east end is west-northwest. The trail leads generally north across alpine slopes that, in summer, are brightened by dollops of wildflowers, primarily magenta herb-willow.

After another Burgess Shale restriction sign, pass a trail descending left (west). Continue contouring on the main trail north-northwest. Walk through krummholz (stunted trees), then descend. Watch your step. After ten minutes in forest, continue across a rockslide for seven minutes. Then the descent begins in earnest. At 1870 m (6130 ft), traverse beneath a rock wall on the face of Wapta Mtn. A couple long cascades are visible northwest, fed by Emerald Glacier atop The Vice President. The descent resumes in forest.

At 13.6 km (8.4 mi), 1826 m (5990 ft), reach a Y-junction in forested **Yoho Pass**. Straight (northeast) reaches Yoho Lake in 0.7 km (0.4 mi) and the Whiskey Jack Youth Hostel, on the Yoho Valley Road, in 4 km (2.5 mi). Go left (west) for Emerald Lake, 4.3 km (2.7 mi) distant.

The trail is steep, rocky, rooty, allowing no opportunity to relax unless you stop completely. About 30 minutes below the pass, at 1524 m (5000 ft), the trail skirts the lower cascade that you saw from the rock-wall traverse. Beyond, the descent is even rougher, requiring total concentration.

One hour from Yoho Pass, cross a **bridged creek**—the first reliable water source on the entire hike—at 1340 m (4400 ft). The descent is complete and the hiking now much easier. You've arrived at the north end of the alluvial fan that dominates the northern half of Emerald Lake basin. The trail crosses this gravelly, watery plain for nearly 2 km (1.2 mi). Scatterings of stunted lodgepole and hardy white spruce are impressive survivors in this inhospitable terrain.

Proceed south-southwest, crossing numerous streamlets on a series of small bridges. At 17.9 km (11.1 mi), 1316 m (4315 ft), reach a signed junction just before **Emerald Lake**. Left (south) rounds the east shore, arriving at the parking lot in 3.5 km (2.2 mi). Go right (southwest) to round the west shore and arrive at the parking lot in 1.8 km (1.1 mi).

Where the signed Emerald Basin trail forks right (north), bear left. Bear left again (south-southwest) where a horse trail forks right (southwest). Continue along the shoreline trail to reach the parking lot at 19.7 km (12.2 mi).

Paget Lookout (Trip 53)

TRIP 53

Paget Lookout and Peak

LOCATION	Yoho National Park
ROUND TRIP	7.4 km (4.6 mi)
ELEVATION GAIN	520 m (1705 ft) to lookout plus 430 m (1410 ft) to summit
KEY ELEVATIONS	trailhead 1615 m (5297 ft) lookout 2135 m (7002 ft), summit 2565 m (8415 ft)
HIKING TIME	4 hours
DIFFICULTY	easy
MAPS	page 500; Gem Trek *Lake Louise & Yoho;* Lake Louise 82 N/8

OPINION

Fire lookouts were built throughout the Canadian Rockies in response to devastating forest fires in 1936 and 1940. The lookout sites, chosen for their unrestricted views, were invaluable until the late 1970s, when more advanced means of fire-detection made lookouts obsolete. The views, however, remain vast, so lookouts like the one on Paget Peak are worthwhile hiking goals.

The stiff climb to Paget Lookout requires determination, of course, and the final 0.8 km (0.5 mi) are rudely steep, but the panorama more than compensates. You'll see the Kicking Horse Valley, peaks over 3050 m (10,000 ft), and the mountains ringing Lake O'Hara. You're a scrambler? Don't turn around at the lookout. A 20-minute burst of energy will propel you onward to the summit of Paget Peak, for an even grander vista.

FACT

By Vehicle

Follow directions for Sherbrooke Lake / Niles Meadow (Trip 12) to Wapta Lake Picnic Area, at 1615 m (5297 ft).

On Foot

Follow the directions in Trip 12 to the **signed junction** at 1.4 km (0.9 mi), 1771 m (5810 ft). Left (north-northwest) leads to Sherbrooke Lake. Go right (north-northeast) for Paget lookout and peak.

The trail steepens. Continue through forest, then onto subalpine talus slopes. Reach **Paget Lookout** at 3.7 km (2.3 mi), 2135 m (7002 ft). Directly west is 2695-m (8840-ft) Mt. Ogden. Across the highway, 3199-m (10,493-ft) Mt. Stephen is southwest, Vanguard Peak is south, and between them is 3073-m (10,079-ft) Cathedral Mtn. The big drainage south is Cataract Brook Valley, descending from Lake O'Hara (Trips 14 – 19).

Given a little scrambling experience, or the desire to gain some, you should have no trouble romping up the talus and summiting 2565-m (8415-ft) **Paget Peak**. Here, the view expands to include desolate but impressive mountains. See image on page 10.

TRIP 54

Geraldine Lakes

LOCATION	Jasper National Park, near Athabasca Falls
ROUND TRIP	10.5 km (6.5 mi) to second lake 13 km (8.1 mi) to fourth lake
ELEVATION GAIN	407 m (1335 ft) to second lake plus 90 m (295 ft) to fourth lake
KEY ELEVATIONS	trailhead 1480 m (4854 ft) second lake 1887 m (6190 ft) fourth lake 1976 m (6480 ft)
HIKING TIME	5 hours to 2 days
DIFFICULTY	moderate to 2nd, challenging to 4th
MAPS	page 523; Gem Trek *Jasper & Maligne Lake;* Athabasca Falls 83 C/12

OPINION

When people describe what they enjoy about hiking, they extoll the scenic rewards. And that's enough. Witnessing the raw beauty of our unique planet justifies a journey by foot. But if you keep listening, most will say they hike to experience solitude and tranquility. Probe further and they'll explain how being alone on the trail or mountaintop is comforting, healing, because it restores a measure of balance and sanity to their lives.

Yet there's an even deeper reason most of us hope to be alone beyond the trailhead. It's rarely stated because few are conscious of it, but it's true nonetheless: Other people remind us of ourselves, which is precisely what we're out there to lose.

We leave civilization and enter the wilderness to forget ourselves. To meld with something bigger than ourselves. We do it for the same reason we close our eyes when we pray: to feel we're alone with The Source. That's why Jasper National Park is immensely appealing to hikers. Less than 5% of park visitors venture onto the 1207 km (750 mi) of trails lacing the 10,878 sq km (4,200 sq mi) of backcountry.

One of Jasper's more secluded dayhikes leads to the Geraldine Lakes, where you'll hike beside streams, past cascades and waterfalls, up a glacier-gouged stairway.

The first of the four Geraldines is pleasant, but forest-ringed, unremarkable, often less than serene. It's a quick, easy hike, suitable for waddlers and toddlers. The second lake is a more worthy goal, a genuine hike requiring strength and tenacity. You'll negotiate a cantankerous trail, roots, rocks, and a steep, wickedly slick ascent. The scenic climax? A plummeting cataract and a tremendous ridgetop vantage. A little over a kilometre long, the second lake is the biggest of the Geraldines. It's bounded on the east by a rockslide where, if you keep hiking, you'll enjoy continuous views of the lake and nearby mountain walls.

The third and fourth lakes are ethereal sights: pools of deep teal liquid detained in emerald meadows beneath 3360-m (11,024-ft) Mt. Fryatt. But to see these upper

Fourth Geraldine Lake

lakes you'll have to be tough as a yak. There's no trail beyond the second lake. The route is discernible thanks to the hardy few who've persisted before you. It requires you to crash through dense brush and krummholz (stunted trees). And it's worth it.

Solitude is likely at the third lake; a near certainty at the fourth. The surrounding alplands are wondrously wild, inviting further exploration. With the courage of Lassie, and a couple extra days, you could enjoy an adventurous cross-country backpack trip here. Powerful hikers who blast out of the trailhead by 9 a.m. will find the fourth lake a reasonable dayhike destination. Most people will turn around, satisfied, atop the ridge where the second lake is initially visible.

FACT

By Vehicle

Where Hwy 93-A departs the Icefields Parkway (Hwy 93) at Athabasca Falls (31 km / 19.2 mi south of Jasper townsite), drive 93-A northwest 1.1 km (0.7 mi). Turn left (southwest) onto the narrow, rough, unpaved Geraldine Fire Road. Continue 5.5 km (3.4 mi) to the trailhead parking lot at 1480 m (4854 ft).

On Foot

After a short, mild ascent west, the trail curves left (south) and descends. This will remain your general direction of travel all the way to the fourth lake.

Within 20 minutes, reach the forest-shrouded **first lake** at 2 km (1.2 mi), 1607 m (5270 ft). Follow the rough, muddy, rooty path along the west shore for about 15 minutes to the lake's south shore at 2.7 km (1.7 mi).

An hour from the trailhead, approach a 90-m (295-ft) **cascade** and start ascending. Enjoy glimpses of the tumbling water on the way up, because krummholz soon blocks it from view.

The trail climbs over roots and rocks beside the cascade to reach a boulder field. Cairns indicate the way forward. An avalanche slope, draping off a jagged peak, is visible east of the stream. Craggy peaks rise to the west.

Proceed above and left of **shallow tarns**, into a scraggly forest harbouring a confusion of routes. Do not turn west. Continue south, following a path through more rocks.

Begin a steep, 150-m (492-ft) climb left of an impressive **waterfall**. The route is scratched into a rib of dirt and loose rock. Before ascending, be sure you'll be able to safely descend this dicey stretch.

At 5 km (3 mi), crest a **ridge** above the waterfall and attain a broad view. Mt. Fryatt looms southeast. A few minutes farther, the second lake is visible.

Moderate-paced hikers arrive at the north shore of the **second lake** about 2¼ hours after leaving the trailhead. Continue to the far (south) shore by crossing several boulder fields along the east shore.

At 6.2 km (3.8 mi), 1887 m (6190 ft), reach a bridge spanning the second lake's inlet stream. West, just across the bridge, is a small **campground**.

Up for the challenging route to the third and fourth lakes? Don't cross the bridge to the campground. Stay on the east bank. Follow the sketchy, sporadically cairned, bootbeaten path south.

Negotiate a rockslide. After about three cairns, stay right on a narrow, faint track through stunted trees and brush. Wade into thigh-thwacking krummholz for 10 to 15 minutes, then enjoy a respite while crossing more boulders.

Soon depart the creek and march back into krummholz. Visible ahead is an unusually big cairn—a **stoneman**. From there, aim for the lower waterfall at the head of the valley. Beat your way for another five minutes through willow and alder until you're again near the left bank of the creek, where the path resumes in the trees.

Glacier lily

Arrive at the **third lake**—smallest of the four, fringed with meadows and krummholz—after 45 minutes of determined hiking from the bridge at the south end of the second lake. To continue, sniff out the path around the right (west) shore of the third lake.

The ramparts of Mt. Fryatt are now more striking. Cross the fourth lake's shallow outlet stream (perhaps on a logjam), scramble up a short, steep rise, and the **fourth lake** is yours. Elevation: 1976 m (6480 ft). Visible south is 3105-m (10,188-ft) Mt. Lapensee. Hiking from outlet to outlet between the upper lakes takes about 25 minutes.

It's possible to continue exploring south to a verdurous pass 270 m (885 ft) above and one hour beyond the fourth lake. From there, you can peer down at two lakes that feed Divergence Creek.

TRIP 55

Angel Glacier / Cavell Meadows

LOCATION	Jasper National Park
CIRCUIT	6.1 km (3.8 mi) to 7.9 km (4.9 mi)
ELEVATION GAIN	420 m (1378 ft) to 558 m (1831 ft)
KEY ELEVATIONS	trailhead 1730 m (5676 ft) highpoint 2288 m (7507 ft)
HIKING TIME	2 to 3 hours
DIFFICULTY	easy
MAPS	page 502; Gem Trek *Jasper National Park*

OPINION

Angel Glacier leaps off the vertical north face of Mount Edith Cavell. It's an astounding sight from the natural grandstand of Cavell Meadows. It's also one that few Jasper visitors miss, so you'll join leather-sheathed bikers, motorhome muffins, and eager kids towing parents on this easy excursion. Wear a smile. And post a sentry before you stop to pee.

Snarly weather discourages most people, yet often enhances a close-up view like this one by creating atmosphere. The crowd won't be here then; maybe you should be. The flower-rich heather meadows are impressive rain or shine. Angel Glacier, whose tongue hangs down a 300-m (985-ft) cliff, can be more alluring wreathed in clouds.

Serious hikers seeking a wilderness experience should invest the couple hours they'd spend here on a more adventurous trip, like Geraldine Lakes (Trip 54) or Verdant Pass (Trip 21). If you're intent on visiting Cavell Meadows, come early (before 8 a.m.) or late (a couple hours prior to dusk).

Angel Glacier, Cavell Meadows, and 3363-m (11,033-ft) Mt. Edith Cavell were named in honour of a British nurse who helped hundreds of allied soldiers escape German-occupied Belgium during WWI. Her subsequent execution garnered sympathetic media coverage worldwide. So Angel Glacier is a reminder: angels are real, and the world needs more of them.

FACT

Before your trip

Ask the Jasper Info Centre about current conditions at Cavell Meadows. To safeguard sensitive subalpine and alpine vegetation, hiking might be restricted here until mid-July, when the meadows are snowfree. But even if the extended trail is closed, a 1.8-km (1.1-mi) loop—partly paved, known as the Path of the Glacier trail—remains open and affords views of Angel Glacier.

Remind everyone in your group to stay on the trail. Be especially vigilant about this with children. Explain why, so they understand: meadows are quickly, easily trampled, and the short growing season near and above treeline prevents recovery, thus the damage is permanent.

More than 45,000 people visit Cavell Meadows each summer. Many wander off trail, either thoughtlessly shortcutting or inanely attempting to keep their footwear out of the mud. So, in 2003, the Friends of Jasper, Parks Canada, and local residents worked to restore and protect the meadows. They rerouted sections of trail, improved drainage, erected signs displaying maps, and blocked or rehabilitated 50 ad hoc paths. With the official trail now obvious, and the temptation to hike off-trail reduced, the meadows are recovering. Visit www.friendsofjasper.com/projects/cavell.htm to see before-and-after photos of Cavell Meadows and read trail updates.

By Vehicle

From the junction of Hwy 16 and the Icefields Parkway (Hwy 93), at the southwest edge of Jasper townsite, drive the Parkway south 7.2 km (4.5 mi). Turn right (west) onto Hwy 93A. At 9.7 km (6 mi), stay left on Hwy 93A where Marmot Basin Road forks right. At 12.5 km (7.8 mi) turn right onto Mount Edith Cavell Road. (The parking lot here is for trailers and large RVs, which the narrow, winding road ahead does not accommodate.) Pass the youth hostel (left) at 17.4 km (10.8 mi). Just beyond, pass the Astoria River / Tonquin Valley trailhead parking lot (right). At 27 km (16.7 mi) enter the Angel Glacier / Cavell Meadows trailhead parking lot at road's end. Elevation: 1730 m (5676 ft).

On Foot

Start on the left (east) arm of the paved **Path of the Glacier trail**. It departs the southwest corner of the parking lot. Initially follow either the steps or the gently ascending path. They rejoin just uphill.

Pavement ends within ten minutes. Proceed on the dirt-and-gravel trail. Reach a **junction** at 0.5 km (0.3 mi). The Path of the Glacier trail goes right (southeast), returning to the parking lot to complete a 1.8-km (1.1-mi) loop. Turn left (north-northeast) onto the Cavell Meadows trail.

Switchback up over a lateral moraine. At 1.4 km (0.9 mi), about 20 minutes above the junction, attain the first full view of **Angel Glacier**. The pond below the glacier's toe is also visible. The trail then climbs steeply through subalpine forest, granting occasional glimpses of the glacier.

Reach the next **junction** at 2 km (1.2 mi). You'll return here on the Cavell Meadows circuit. Go right (southeast) for the easiest ascent. Soon enter the **meadows**. In July you'll likely see yellow glacier-lilies, golden marsh marigolds, and white globeflowers.

The ascent continues. Mt. Edith Cavell and Angel Glacier are prominently visible. From this higher vantage, the wings look less angelic because it's now apparent the right one is shorter and bulkier.

At 2.8 km (1.7 mi), 2065 m (6775 ft), reach a **fork** at the south end of the meadow circuit. Right (east-southeast), a cairned spur leads one minute to a viewpoint. Turn left to ascend north and continue the circuit.

Reach a **junction** at 3 km (1.9 mi), 2150 m (7054 ft). Left descends north, offering the shortest possible meadow circuit. To continue the full circuit, ascend right.

Angel Glacier

At 3.4 km (2.1 mi), 2200 m (7218 ft), reach another junction. Left (west) is the return leg of the circuit. Right (northeast) is a spur leading to the east end of the circuit: a **climactic viewpoint** at 3.9 km (2.4 mi), 2288 m (7507 ft).

After admiring the vista, descend to the previous junction. Bear right (west) and begin the return leg of the circuit. Soon bear right again at the next junction.

At 5.1 km (3.2 mi) reach the junction where you began the circuit. You're now on familiar ground. Bear right and descend back to the moraine.

Rejoin the **Path of the Glacier trail** at 6.6 km (4.1 mi). Go right (northwest) to arrive at the trailhead in ten minutes. Or, lengthen your hike (reaching the trailhead in 25 minutes) by going left (southeast).

Taking the longer option, you'll skirt the **pond** below the glacier's toe in 0.5 km (0.3 mi) then descend northwest to arrive at the parking lot, where your total distance will be 7.9 km (4.9 mi).

TRIP 56

Indian Ridge

LOCATION	Jasper National Park
ROUND TRIP	7 to 10 km (4.3 to 6.2 mi)
ELEVATION GAIN	585 m (1920 ft) to bump four
KEY ELEVATIONS	upper gondola terminal 2265 m (7430 ft) Whistlers summit 2466 m (8088 ft) bump four 2685 m (8810 ft)
HIKING TIME	5½ hours
DIFFICULTY	challenging
MAPS	page 507; Gem Trek *Best of Jasper*; Jasper 83 D/16

OPINION

In Jasper townsite, face southwest and look skyward. See the lackluster mountain strung with cables and towers? Well, they don't hoist that gondola up there for nothing. The summit panorama will give your eyeballs a wonderful workout. You can survey all the lakes surrounding the townsite, and a huge chunk of Jasper Park.

But don't hike to the top (Trip 73). Let the gondola whisk you up. You'll gain 965 m (3165 ft) in minutes—an ascent that would take a hardened hiker 2 ½ sweat-drenched hours. With the time and energy you save, you can spurt past the tourists, ogle the scenery from The Whistlers summit, then dash on, roaming alpine basins and ridges all day. Though many of the 200,000 people a year who ride the gondola also hike the easy, 1.3-km (0.8-mi) path to the summit, almost none seize the opportunity to explore beyond. You're likely to have the outback to yourself.

Know before you go. Few people are capable of completing the Indian Ridge circuit. You might, however, make it part way up, and even that's an excellent adventure. From The Whistlers summit, scope out Indian Ridge (southwest). If you're a strong hiker, with some scrambling under your boots, go for it. Negotiate the east arm of the ridge first, curve northwest along the crest, continue out the west arm, then return east through the basin. But if what you see makes you hesitant, limit your foray to the basin. The east arm of the ridge, initially a series of talused bumps, poses a rugged challenge. There's no trail; only a faint route. And ascending the final bump requires a wickedly steep traverse, or an exposed spider-walk. A misstep on either could be tragic. So be prepared to turn back, content with your accomplishment.

On bump #4 of Indian Ridge

FACT

By Vehicle

From the junction of Hwy 16 and the Icefields Parkway, at the southwest edge of Jasper townsite, drive the Parkway south 1.8 km (1.1 mi). Turn right (west) onto Whistlers Road. Follow it 4 km (2.5 mi) to the large, paved parking lot at the gondola base. Elevation: 1305 m (4280 ft). Ride the gondola up to 2265 m (7430 ft). It operates seven days a week. Confirm current schedules and prices with the Jasper Tramway: phone (780) 852-3093, fax (780) 852-5779.

On Foot

From the upper gondola terminal, climb the boardwalk stairs. On your right, pass The Whistlers trail (Trip 73) that descends to the base of the mountain. Proceed straight on the wide, trampled, dirt path. It leads you southwest up the ridge. Gain 225 m (738 ft) in 1.3 km (0.8 mi) to **The Whistlers summit**, marked with a large, stoneman cairn. Elevation: 2470 m (8102 ft). Panorama: 360°.

On a clear day, you'll see all of the following and more. Indian Ridge is nearby southwest, separated from you by a green tundra saddle. Marmot Mtn is directly south. Terminal Mtn is just west of south. Manx Peak, shouldering a snowfield, is southwest. In the distance, just north of west, you can identify snowcapped Mt. Robson. The jagged rampart of Mt. Bridgeland is west, in front of Robson. Pyramid Mtn is north. The Colin Range is northeast. And the Maligne Range, where the Skyline trail (Trip 81) soars, is east.

A path continues beyond The Whistlers summit. It descends, curving northwest. To proceed to Indian Ridge, walk about half way out, then drop left (southwest) into the **saddle**. Bottom-out at 2305 m (7560 ft). Pick up the bootbeaten route, which is now visible, ascending several talused bumps on the east arm of Indian Ridge.

Traverse the northwest side of **bump #1**. Proceed south (left) steeply up **bump #2**, reaching 2535 m (8310 ft). Don't follow the game path right. A fainter route continues to the third, more difficult bump. Go southeast of the top of **bump #3**. Then scramble straight up (southwest) on **bump #4** at 2685 m (8810 ft). You're now about 1½ hours from the stoneman on The Whistlers summit.

The going is much more difficult ahead. Only experienced scramblers or climbers should proceed. To reach the base of **bump #5**, cross a short ridge that feels exposed—it's only 1 m/yd wide. From here, either climb right or traverse left to attain the 2715-m (8900-ft) crest of **Indian Ridge**. Both routes are dangerous. If you need directions, you're in over your head. Turn back now.

Prefer rambling to scrambling? From the saddle below The Whistlers summit, descend 120 m (400 ft) west into the verdant basin. From there, ascend northwest to the small saddle on the west arm of Indian Ridge. For a better view, turn left (southwest) and continue ascending Indian Ridge as far as you feel comfortable. Check your watch, so you don't miss the last gondola down.

Interested in a one-way trip? Cross-country trekkers armed with a map can depart the saddle below The Whistlers summit and, heading generally south, skirt Indian Ridge, drop into the Whistlers Creek drainage, climb to Marmot Pass, drop to Portal Creek, intersect the trail, then turn left (northeast) and hike out to Marmot Basin Road. Pre-arrange a shuttle, or rely on your lucky thumb. The trip is doable in a long day.

Alpine wallflower

TRIP 57
Opal Hills

LOCATION	Jasper National Park
CIRCUIT	8.2 km (5.1 mi)
ELEVATION GAIN	460 m (1500 ft)
KEY ELEVATIONS	trailhead 1700 m (5576 ft), highpoint 2160 m (7085 ft)
HIKING TIME	3 to 4 hours
DIFFICULTY	moderate
MAPS	page 504; Gem Trek *Jasper & Maligne Lake*

OPINION

If these hills are alive with music, you'll hear it all, from the swooning melodrama of an orchestral movie score, to the intimate honesty of a solo aboriginal shaman playing an eagle-bone whistle. Because hiking up the Opal Hills, you'll see it all, from vast, turquoise, mountain-squeezed Maligne Lake, to diminutive wildflowers clinging to life in the rock and tundra.

Come on up. Nestle in the lee of a slope. Luxuriate in the greenery and tranquility. Gaze at the distant Rocky Mountain horizon. Maybe soak up some sun. Or go hunting; in the dales between the hills lurk rare, indigo-coloured, waxy king gentian.

To get there, however, you must lay siege to these steep hills. The ascent lacks switchbacks, so it's slippery when wet. But it's short enough that most hikers won't complain. Just don't go on a rainy day, when the trail is laundry-chute slick, and you'll be deprived of the rapturous view over Maligne Lake.

Gentian

FACT

By Vehicle

From Jasper townsite, drive 5 km (3 mi) east on Hwy 16 to the Maligne Lake Road. Follow it 44.3 km (27.5 mi) to Maligne Lake. Turn left into the main parking area, just before the lodge. Stay left to reach the third and highest lot, at 1700 m (5576 ft).

Alpine bladderpod

On Foot

Departing the north side of the third and highest parking lot, the trail heads east-northeast. In 200 m (220 yd) stay left where the Maligne Lakeshore trail forks right. Begin a steep ascent northeast through lodgepole pine forest. At the 1.6-km (1-mi) junction, where the Opal Hills loop begins, bear right and continue northeast, moderately uphill. The trail gradually curves northwest. At 2.6 km (1.6 mi) reach alpine meadows. At 3.2 km (2 mi), attain the loop **highpoint**: 2160 m (7085 ft). Ascend one of the grassy hills for a view southeast over Maligne Lake to glacier-dappled Mts. Charlton and Unwin. The Bald Hills (Trip 36) are visible southwest across the valley.

Maligne Lake and Mounts Unwin and Charlton, from Opal Hills

From the highpoint, proceed through gentle meadowland between low hills. The trail gradually curves southeast. At 4.7 km (2.9 mi) the trail leaves the meadows and hills and descends into forest. At 6.6 km (4.1 mi) arrive back at the loop junction. Go right (southwest) to return to the trailhead and complete the 8.2-km (5.1-mi) circuit.

TRIP 58

Sulphur Skyline

LOCATION	Jasper National Park
ROUND TRIP	8 km (5 mi)
ELEVATION GAIN	636 m (2086 ft) to summit
KEY ELEVATIONS	trailhead 1380 m (4524 ft), summit 2016 m (6612 ft)
HIKING TIME	3 hours
DIFFICULTY	moderate due only to steepness
MAPS	page 509; Gem Trek *Jasper & Maligne Lake*

OPINION

Jasper Park dispenses scenery with the generosity of a banker. The rewards are here—just farther from the pavement. Backpackers rave about the park's long trails. Dayhikers, not so much. But here's a happy exception. Steep but not far, the Sulphur Skyline trail quickly leads to a gratifying summit panorama. You can peer deep into remote valleys and appreciate nearby sharp-edged peaks.

A wilderness experience, however, this decidedly is not. The trail is nearly road-width the entire way. It's tennis-shoe smooth, too, until near the rocky summit. Numerous benches en route add to the city-park atmosphere. You half expect an ice-cream vendor to appear. And forget solitude. The hike begins at the popular Miette Hot Springs. A steady stream of people waddle up here before or after their soak, though many turn back—bested by the unrelenting steep grade—well below the summit.

The easterly location of this little mountain, and its exposure to the sun, make it a viable early-season destination. But the trail can be mercilessly hot on a sunny day. Pack full water bottles. Fall is the optimal time to hike here, but remember: the approach road usually closes in mid-October.

FACT

By Vehicle

From the junction of Hwy 16 and the Icefields Parkway, at the southwest edge of Jasper townsite, drive Hwy 16 northeast 44.3 km (27.5 mi). Or, from Jasper Park's East Gate, drive Hwy 16 southwest 7 km (4.3 mi). From either approach, turn southeast onto Miette Hot Springs Road. Continue 17 km (10.5 mi) to the road's end parking lot, at 1370 m (4490 ft).

On Foot

From the parking lot, walk up to the hot springs pool building. The entrance and passenger-dropoff loop are on the building's south side. The trail—initially a paved path—departs the east side of this loop, between the trailhead sign (left) and an info kiosk (right). Elevation: 1380 m (4524 ft). The trailhead sign states: Sulphur Ridge 5 km, Mystery Lake 12 km. Follow the path east and begin a gradual ascent.

Within five minutes, a paved path forks left (north-northeast) to a water tank. Proceed straight (east) on the main trail. It's unpaved from here on, but remains broad and smooth. A minute farther, ignore the horse trail branching left to a bridged stream crossing. Proceed straight (east), uphill

The trail soon steepens, curving southeast. Cross a stream in a culvert and pass a bench blocking a defunct path. This is the first of more than a dozen benches en route to the summit. The eastward ascent steepens. Soon, Sulphur Skyline ridge is visible right (southeast). About 30 minutes from the trailhead, pass the third bench. It affords an unobstructed view south, across a forested basin, to the Skyline.

Within 40 minutes reach a junction in **Shuey Pass** at 2.2 km (1.4 m), 1638 m (5374 ft). Left (northeast) descends to the Fiddle River then continues to Mystery Lake, a disappointing destination at the end of a miserable, thrash-bash-and-splash route. Go right (east) to resume the Skyline ascent. Stay on the main trail, ignoring occasional spurs. These narrow, bootbeaten shortcuts deface the mountain and are way too steep to be helpful. Soon attain views northeast, beyond the Yellowhead Hwy.

After hiking about an hour and gaining 440 m (1443 ft), get a glimpse into the valley southeast. Just ten minutes farther, the trail levels at 1896 m (6220 ft) on a **broad shoulder** beneath the summit. There's a big, prominent, white boulder here. Numerous benches invite you to appreciate the grand panorama (southeast, north, and west).

Beyond the shoulder, the trail steepens dramatically. Expect insecure footing on loose rock. Swift hikers will stride onto the flat, spacious, 2016-m (6612-ft) **summit** within 1½ hours of leaving the trailhead. Total distance: 4 km (2.5 mi). The 360° view is captivating. Utopia Mtn is close-by southwest. The Miette Range runs northwest. Across from it is sawtoothed Ashlar Ridge. You can also see a long way up the Fiddle River valley (southeast). It's possible to continue hiking west, out Skyline Ridge, but it's lower than the summit, so the view is inferior. A speedy, nonstop descent to the parking lot takes about 40 minutes.

Alpine forget-me-nots

Fiddle River valley, from Sulphur Skyline summit

TRIP 59

Vimy Peak

LOCATION	Waterton Lakes National Park
ROUND TRIP	25.6 km (16 mi)
ELEVATION GAIN	1095 m (3592 ft)
KEY ELEVATIONS	trailhead 1285 m (4215 ft), summit 2380 m (7805 ft)
HIKING TIME	9 to 10 hours
DIFFICULTY	challenging
MAPS	Gem Trek *Waterton Lakes National Park*

OPINION

Like a moat-protected castle, Vimy Peak poses substantial obstacles to would-be assailants. Before you storm this bastille, a few discouraging warnings:

(1) The Waterton Lakes bar quick access, so the approach is tediously long. (2) The trail plows through prime grizzly habitat in a park known for its heavy concentration of bears. Dense bush limits visibility, increasing the likelihood of an encounter. To complete such a long trip in a single day, you must brave that bear habitat when you set out in the morning and again when you return in the evening—the times when bears are most active. (3) The trail is flat for miles, so the ascent is dauntingly steep, much of it on a rough, unmaintained route. (4) To safely complete the trip before nightfall, and to be assured of the views that are the chief goal of any summit bid, you need a clear summer day, when the exposed upper slopes can be excruciatingly hot. (5) Vimy is not surrounded by peaks, but is bordered by prairie, so even if you endure this crusade, the scenic reward pales compared to other Rocky Mountain summits.

Granted, Vimy Peak is hard to ignore. Its proud, isolated, almost swaggering stance, directly above the lakeshore, goads anyone with gumption to climb it. And because so few people do (for the sensible reasons listed above), solitude is almost guaranteed. Plus, the view from the top is worth a few snapshots. The jagged peaks of Waterton Park are visible west. You get a UFO pilot's perspective of the Waterton Lakes (west and north), and Crypt Lake basin (south). And beyond Crypt, across the international border, you can see the highest peak in the Peace Park: 3190-m (10,466-ft) Mt. Cleveland. With binoculars you can even spy on the citizens of Lethbridge, 120 km (74 mi) east.

Still, Vimy isn't worth the effort and risk, unless you've hiked everything else Waterton has to offer. For further dissuasion, read about Carthew Summit (Trip 23) and Lineham Ridge (Trip 2). That should at least knock Vimy off your short list.

Vimy Peak, above Waterton town

FACT

By Vehicle

From the park entrance-junction, drive Hwy 5 southeast 0.9 km (0.6 mi) to the intersection with Chief Mtn Hwy 6. Turn right (southeast) and continue 0.5 km (0.3 mi) to a gated access road on the right. Park in the pullout on the north side of the highway, at 1285 m (4215 ft).

On Foot

Cross the highway and head southwest on the gated road, known as the Wishbone trail. The first 2.6 km (1.6 mi) to the Y Camp are an easy stroll through mixed deciduous forest with lots of aspen and birch. The Stoney Creek flats allow an open view of Vimy Peak directly ahead. The trail fades into grass in places, but markers above the plain should keep you on track. Soon after crossing **Sofa Creek** at 5.5 km (3.4 mi) re-enter forest. You're on flat ground until **Vimy junction** at 7 km (4.3 mi), where you turn left (east).

The Wishbone trail continues straight (southwest), grazes the shore of Middle Waterton Lake, and at 12 km (7.4 mi) passes the peninsula jutting north into Bosporus strait. The trail then bends south to reach Crypt Landing and trailhead (Trip 22) at 14 km (8.7 mi).

Heading left at Vimy junction, climb steeply up a drainage on the eastern shoulder of Vimy Peak, passing beneath the limestone outcrop called Lion's Head. The trail switchbacks along a subalpine creek and ends in a small basin at 11.8 km (7.3 mi), 2085 m (6840 ft). From there, a faint route zigzags northwest 1 km (0.6 mi) to the 2380-m (7805-ft) **summit.**

TRIP 60

Blakiston Creek Valley

LOCATION	Waterton Lakes NP, Red Rock Parkway
ROUND TRIP	2 km (1.2 mi) to Blakiston Falls 4 km (2.5 mi) or more for Blakiston Creek 28 km (17.4 mi) to Lone Lake
ELEVATION GAIN	negligible to Blakiston Falls 55 m (180 ft) or more for Blakiston Creek 501 m (1643 ft) to Lone Lake
KEY ELEVATIONS	trailhead 1495 m (4905 ft) Tamarack junction 1920 m (6298 ft) Lone Lake 1996 m (6547 ft)
HIKING TIME	40 minutes for Blakiston Falls 1½ hours or more for Blakiston Creek 6 to 7 hours for Lone Lake
DIFFICULTY	easy for Blakiston falls and creek moderate for Lone Lake
MAPS	page 515; Gem Trek *Waterton Lakes National Park*

OPINION

You want to see the Rockies, not the Tree-ies. So the tame, forested, Blakiston Creek Valley will probably disappoint. Avalanche swaths grant glimpses of the nearby summits, but these are not impressive peaks.

It's raining? Persistent, low cloud cloaks the mountains? You're exhausted from yesterday's epic hike? That's when Blakiston becomes a brighter prospect. Nosing around Red Rock Canyon, then sauntering to Blakiston Falls and along the creek, can be a satisfying if unadventurous outing. The trail hugs the bank, allowing you to admire the mauve, argillite creekbed.

Studying a map, you might notice the Blakiston and Bauerman valley trails form "A loop! A loop!" Curb your excitement. The loop is 25 km (15.5 mi) long yet only a short stretch near Twin Lakes is notably scenic. You're better off hiking in via Bauerman Creek (the Snowshoe trail), perhaps detouring to Twin Lakes, then completing a thrilling circuit over Avion Ridge (Trip 100).

You're determined to dayhike Blakiston Valley? Aim for Lone Lake, 3.9 km (2.4 mi) beyond Tamarack junction. The trail steepens markedly about 1 km (0.6 mi) shy of Tamarack junction, but if you punch through you'll find the grade eases in meadowy clearings between the junction and the lake.

Curious about the trail beyond Lone Lake? It's a *Worthwhile*, one-way, one-night backpack trip, if you can arrange a shuttle or you're willing to hitchhike back to your vehicle. The initial leg—starting at Red Rock Canyon, ending at the pleasant Lone Lake campground—is easy. Then comes payday: into Blakiston Creek's headwater basin, over Lineham Ridge (Trip 2), and down past the Rowe Lakes to Akamina Parkway. Total distance: 31.7 km (19.7 mi).

FACT

By Vehicle

From Waterton Park entrance, near the junction of Hwys 5 and 6, drive 5.6 km (3.5 mi) southwest into the park. Turn right (northwest) onto Red Rock Parkway, just northeast of Blakiston Creek bridge. Follow it 15 km (9.3 mi) to where the road ends in the Red Rock Canyon parking lot, at 1495 m (4905 ft).

On Foot

Begin by crossing the bridge over Red Rock Creek, then immediately turn left (south). In a couple minutes cross the bridge over Bauerman Creek. Pass **Blakiston Falls** near 1 km (0.6 mi) and begin a mild ascent southwest into Blakiston Creek Valley.

The trail follows **Blakiston Creek** upstream along the north bank. The mauve argillite creekbed is frequently visible. Cottonwoods are prevalent. Occasionally glimpse the valley walls: 2509-m (8230-ft) Lost Mtn (right / north) and 2685-m (8807-ft) Mt. Hawkins (left / south). Other then a few, brief ascents, the grade remains gentle.

Cross a broad, dry drainage at about 40 minutes. Pass a double cascade at about one hour. At 5.3 km (3.3 mi), about 1½ hours from the trailhead, pass the confluence of Blakiston and Lone creeks. Left (south) is the broad mouth of upper Blakiston Creek Valley. The trail continues generally west, along the north bank of **Lone Creek**.

At two hours, 8.5 km (5.3 mi), 1720 m (5642 ft), cross a footbridge spanning a creeklet. Begin a switchbacking ascent to intersect the **Tamarack trail** at 10.1 km (6.3 mi), 1920 m (6298 ft). At a moderate pace, expect to arrive here in 2 ¼ hours.

From Tamarack junction, right (north-northwest) climbs over forested 2070-m (6790-ft) Bauerman Divide, drops to Twin Lakes at 2.8 km (1.7 mi), 1950 m (6396 ft), and ultimately affords a loop (via the Snowshoe trail) back to Red Rock Canyon trailhead.

For Lone Lake—a mere 45 minutes distant—go left (south) at Tamarack junction. In 50 m/yd, ignore a right (west) spur. It ascends 170 m (558 ft) in 1 km (0.6 mi) to end at South Kootenay Pass, on the Alberta / B.C. boundary. Continue contouring south on the Tamarack trail.

After a level ten minutes, drop into a meadow at 1890 m (6199 ft). The trail then begins a gradual ascent curving left (southeast) into forest. Pass a warden cabin at 2030 m (6658 ft). Reach the **Lone Lake campground** at 2015 m (6609 ft), 3.9 km (2.4 mi) from Tamarack junction. **Lone Lake** is immediately below (south), at 1996 m (6547 ft). Total distance from Red Rock Canyon: 14 km (8.7 mi).

Beyond Lone Lake, the Tamarack trail ascends south over an arm of Festubert Mtn, probes the upper reaches of Blakiston Creek Valley, surmounts Lineham Ridge (Trip 2), then descends past Rowe Lakes to intersect Akamina Parkway.

Blakiston Creek

TRIP 61

Mt. Rundle

LOCATION	Banff National Park
ROUND TRIP	10.8 km (6.7 mi) to cliff band on first peak 15 km (9.3 mi) to summit
ELEVATION GAIN	993 m (3255 ft) to cliff band 1579 m (5179 ft) to summit
KEY ELEVATIONS	trailhead 1370 m (4495 ft) cliff band 2363 m (7750 ft) summit 2949 m (9673 ft)
HIKING TIME	5 hours to cliff band 8 or 9 hours to summit
DIFFICULTY	very challenging to summit
MAPS	page 526; Gem Trek *Banff & Mt. Assiniboine*; Banff 82 O/4

OPINION

Looking like a wall between worlds, Mt. Rundle is a dramatic sight. You can appreciate it best from the Trans-Canada Hwy viewpoint above Vermilion Lakes, west of Banff townsite. Whether crowned by a rainbow, capped by clouds, or sharply outlined by brilliant blue, Mt. Rundle's ridgecrest slicing the sky is one image every Banff visitor takes home. Which is why many hikers—some strong, others naive—are powerfully drawn to Rundle when they learn a trail ascends part way up the mountain's west slope.

Leave the summit to mountaineers. Where the trail ends at 5.3 km (3.3 mi), an ordeal ensues—half slog, half scramble. It requires persistence and caution. The route is relentlessly steep, climbing 949 m (3113 ft). That's in addition to the 630 m (2066 ft) you initially gain via trail. Add it up. If you've never vanquished that much elevation in a day, this is no place to try it for the first time. Don't be misled by the seemingly short distance. Scree will slow your pace. There's a narrow, airy section that many find gripping. Toiling for hours above treeline, you'll be exposed to whatever the sky throws at you. Once the snow melts, the route is desert dry.

Even the lower stretch, via trail, deserves two thumbs down. It's a crushing bore. Totally in trees. Your impatience compounds on stretches where you can see far ahead and you realize no surprises await you on this treadmill. You're granted only a few porthole views across Spray River Valley to forested Sulphur Mtn. And the first hour of the trudge is distressingly loud. The construction fracas, the beep-beep-beep of tourist buses in reverse, and the ceaseless hum of traffic suggest money madness has supplanted mountain madness in Banff.

Near trail's end beneath Mt. Rundle's first summit

Hikers will be happier choosing almost any other trail in the area. Cory Pass (Trip 39), for example, is equally convenient and far more exciting. Scramblers too are better off elsewhere. Though Rundle's summit panorama includes Mt. Assiniboine, there are easier off-trail adventures that will reward you with more thrilling scenery. Try Cirque Peak, above Helen Lake (Trip 8).

For this trip to be worthwhile, you must be resolutely determined to accomplish one of two goals: (1) summit the main peak, or (2) attain the glorious, narrow perch beneath the first peak, where a cliff band blocks non-climbers' upward progress. Ascending part way, then bagging out, is a waste of time. We've seen people, miserable and exhausted, turn back below treeline, having earned zilch for their effort.

We've also seen others who were packless (and apparently brainless), carrying nothing more than a water bottle, wearing nothing more than flimsy shoes and a cotton tank-top, setting out for the summit. Bring at least two liters (quarts) of water per person for the round trip to the base of the first peak. Bring more on your summit bid. Read *Prepare for Your Hike* for further equipment suggestions.

FACT

By Vehicle

In downtown Banff, drive Banff Avenue south. Cross the Bow River bridge, turn left, and follow signs for Banff Springs Hotel. At 0.8 km (0.5 mi) from the bridge, turn left toward Banff Springs Golf course and Bow Falls. Then bear right. At 1.3 km (0.8 mi), pass the parking area for Bow Falls on your left. Proceed across the Spray River bridge, stay left, and in another 200 m (220 yd) park in one of the dirt pullouts on either side of the road, next to the golf course. The elevation here is 1370 m (4495 ft).

On Foot

Walk the road east from where you parked. Go to the end of the wood fence. Round the first golf course green, then go right. Staying close to the green, proceed onto a wide horse trail. In five minutes reach a signed junction. Go left onto a broad path signed for Mount Rundle and the Spray Loop. At 1.3 km (0.8 mi), about 15 minutes from your car, the Rundle trail forks left from the Spray River fire road. The moderately steep trail ascends generally southeast through forest. Hit switchbacks after crossing a little gorge.

About 1 hour up, near 1830 m (6000 ft), reach the first viewpoint. Sulphur Mtn is west and southwest, with the Upper Hot Springs at its base. Northwest, across the Trans-Canada, are Mts. Louis and Cory in the Sawback Range. The Palliser Range is north.

About 80 m (260 ft) higher, at 3.7 km (2.3 mi), you can see south up Spray Valley to Goat Peak, which divides Goat Creek from the Spray River. Banff townsite is partly visible. About 1½ hours up, at 4.4 km (2.7 mi), 2000 m (6560 ft), the **trail forks**. Left climbs steeply toward Mt. Rundle's first peak. Right ascends more gradually to a huge gully, which you cross en route to the summit of Mt. Rundle.

Turning left toward the **first peak**, the trail continues through forest but rapidly deteriorates, becoming incredibly steep and rooty. The angle is an awkward 45°, making the route slippery even when dry, and precarious when wet. Near 2195 m

(7200 ft), reach a sign NOTICE / AVIS. MOUNTAIN EXPERIENCE RECOMMENDED FOR ROUTE AHEAD. The forest soon opens up, allowing views of the Sundance Range southwest, above and beyond Sulphur Mtn.

A 35-minute, 305-m (1000-ft) ascent toward the first peak will bring you to a minor junction near treeline. The cairned route right stays in trees, then contours across talus toward a huge gully. Don't go that way expecting to connect with the route up the main summit. Stay left at this minor junction. In 5 minutes, the route angles right and follows the base of a **cliff band**. Here, at 2363 m (7750 ft), hikers can enjoy an excellent view. Lacking the necessary skill and equipment, you'll be unable to climb higher on the first peak.

Back at the 2000-m (6560-ft) fork, if you turn right toward the **summit of Mt. Rundle**, you'll reach a huge gully in 0.8 km (0.5 mi). At this point, you've hiked 5.2 km (3.1 mi) from your car. Looking up the gully, you can see the summit, but do not attempt to ascend that way. A sign warns the inexperienced not to proceed. The route continues directly across the gully. Scan the far side for an arrow on a tree; it points straight up the forested slope. Follow that arrow. Watch for blue and white paint blazes thereafter. The wickedly steep route eventually breaks out of the trees, allowing you to set your sights on the 2949-m (9673-ft) summit—another 1 hour distant.

Approaching the false summit (right), en route to the 2998-m (9836-ft) true summit (left) of Cascade Mountain (Trip 63)

TRIP 62

Sulphur Mountain via Gondola Trail

LOCATION	Banff National Park
ONE WAY	5.6 km (3.5 mi)
ELEVATION GAIN	660 m (2165 ft)
KEY ELEVATIONS	trailhead 1600 m (5250 ft)
	upper gondola terminal 2260 m (7413 ft)
HIKING TIME	1 to 2 hours
DIFFICULTY	moderate due only to elevation gain
MAPS	page 526; Gem Trek *Banff Up-Close*

OPINION

Several thousand people a day ride the gondola up Sulphur Mtn. The biggest one-day turnout was 5,500. If you want to experience Mardi Gras on a pinhead, get in line. But why hike there?

The view of surrounding mountains and the townsite below is excellent. Check it out on any postcard rack on Banff Avenue. And the ascent is manageable for most—easy if you're buffed—thanks to moderately-graded switchbacks. But the trail climbs beneath the gondola line—so closely that, at times, you can exchange words with passengers. Save for the summit and a viewpoint halfway up, you'll see little but trees. All you'll hear is the ruckus of raging tourism in what should be a national sanctuary for wild animals, not retail shops.

The bustling atmosphere at the upper gondola terminal is an exasperating reprise of downtown Banff. The shopping herds ride up here between gawking at knick-knacks and purchasing geegaws. It's a traumatic end to a hike. And there's little room to escape. The ridgecrest trail south of the terminal is less than a kilometre long.

Too much humanity. Too much monotony. They add up to an obvious conclusion: pick another trail. Hiking in Banff National Park can be so much more than this. Don't squander your time stomping up Sulphur Mtn via the gondola trail.

If you must see the postcard view from the summit, pay to be whisked up and down. Then invest your time and energy on a more adventurous hike. Though locals who ascend Sulphur Mtn on foot can descend the gondola for half the price of a one-way ticket, a round-trip scamper on a wilder peak is way more fulfilling. Fit keeners should ascend nearby Mt. Bourgeau (Trip 4) or, farther north, Bow Peak (Trip 7).

If you're staying in the town of Banff, and you want a quick workout, Tunnel Mtn (Trip 125) is the most convenient option. But hoofing it up Sulphur might be worthwhile too, if the goal is simply exercise. To be sure of a knee-saving ride down, check the gondola's hours of operation by calling 762-2523. Set out early, beat the first gondola of the day, and you can savour the scenery in solitude, like meteorologist Norman Sanson did. He hiked up here more than a thousand times, long before the gondola was built.

Sulphur Mountain gondola. Mt. Rundle beyond.

FACT

By Vehicle

In downtown Banff, drive Banff Avenue south. Cross the Bow River bridge and turn left onto Spray Avenue. In 100 m (110 yd), bear right on Mountain Avenue, signed for the hot springs. Follow it 3.3 km (2 mi) to the Upper Hot Springs parking lot. The trailhead is near the northwest corner, at a gated service road. Elevation: 1600 m (5250 ft).

On Foot

Start hiking up the service road, which turns right. After 100 m (110 yd) switchback left. Don't stay on the service road. At 2.3 km (1.4 mi) a left spur leads to a small waterfall. Proceed up the main trail. The next switchback brings you to the old resthouse. The remainder of the ascent is steeper. Reach the Sulphur Mtn **upper gondola terminal** at 5.6 km (3.5 mi), 2260 m (7413 ft).

For an improved view, cross the gondola platform and follow the boardwalk northwest 0.5 km (0.3 mi) along the ridgecrest to 2270-m (7446-ft) **Sanson Peak**. The stone building here is an historic meteorological station.

South of the gondola terminal, a trail leads 0.8 km (0.5 mi) through subalpine forest to another vantage. The view is only slightly different, but the setting is more tranquil and natural.

TRIP 63

Cascade Amphitheatre

LOCATION	Banff National Park
ROUND TRIP	14.8 km (9.2 mi)
ELEVATION GAIN	685 m (2247 ft)
KEY ELEVATIONS	trailhead 1700 m (5575 ft) amphitheatre mouth 2125 m (6972 ft)
HIKING TIME	5 hours
DIFFICULTY	moderate
MAPS	page 524; Gem Trek *Banff & Mt. Assiniboine;* Banff 82 O/4

OPINION

Hoodwinked into a bogus venture called *snipe hunting*, naive greenhorns undertake a futile search. Much like hikers seeking mountain grandeur where it doesn't exist: on the trail to Cascade Amphitheatre.

The trip starts with an obligatory tour of Mt. Norquay ski area. After plodding around and under all those contraptions, you'll suffer spruce and lodgepole forest as ugly as it gets in the Rockies. The trail is viewless most of the way. Focus on conversation, because you'll find little else to enjoy. And the amphitheatre is disappointing, with no lake and only a small subalpine meadow. You see less of Cascade Mountain here than is visible from Banff townsite or the Minnewanka Road. The wildflower display can be winsome but doesn't justify the hike.

Approaching the col below the summit of Cascade Mountain

Proximity to the townsite is no excuse for hiking here, unless you're continuing to the summit of Cascade Mountain (see page 225). Now that's an outstanding trip, but long and steep. Even if you can dance like Pan on vertiginous terrain—boulders, talus, ledges—you're in for a nine-hour day. Trail ends at the amphitheatre. Beyond is a route that experienced explorers consider obvious and enjoy following. The summit panorama is spectacular.

If you insist on seeing Cascade Amphitheatre, do so in late June, when yellow glacier lilies at the edges of receding snow brighten the cirque, and lingering ice lends a decorative touch to the gray limestone walls. Aiming for the summit? Wait until August, when the route should be safely snow-free. Each pair of would-be summiteers should pack at least five liters of water. The mountain is as dry as a law-abiding town during Prohibition.

FACT

By Vehicle

From Banff townsite's west interchange on the Trans-Canada Hwy, ascend the switchbacking Mt. Norquay Road north 5.8 km (3.6 mi) to the far end of the ski-area parking lot. The trail, initially a road, leads between the ski lodge buildings, at 1700 m (5575 ft).

On Foot

Walk the dirt road north. Pass the Cascade chairlift. About eight minutes from the ski lodge, signed trail begins right of (behind and below) the Spirit chairlift. Follow it north. Do not go right over the bridge onto the Stoney Squaw bridal path.

About 15 minutes from the parking lot, at 1655 m (5430 ft), continue the gradual descent right of the Mystic chairlift. Drop deeper into forest. Reach a junction at 2.4 km (1.5 mi). Left (west) is the Forty Mile Creek trail heading upstream toward Mystic Lake (Trip 109). Go right (northeast) and descend. A minute farther, at 1570 m (5150 ft), cross a bridge over **Forty Mile Creek**. You've lost 130 m (426 ft) since leaving the trailhead. Begin a moderate ascent north.

About an hour from the trailhead, reach a junction at 3.8 km (2.4 mi), 1725 m (5658 ft). Left leads north to Elk Lake (Trip 108). Go right (northeast) for Cascade Amphitheatre. Begin a steep, switchbacking ascent generally east through scraggly forest. About 30 minutes farther, enter the mouth of **Cascade Amphitheatre** at 6.4 km (4 mi), 2125 m (6970 ft). If you're not ascending the mountain, amble about 1 km farther.

Ambitious hikers are just beginning the day's adventure. The route to Cascade Mtn starts just outside the amphitheatre mouth. At the meadow's edge, turn around and walk back 155 paces. Turn left onto a path that might still be crudely blocked by logs.

This well-trod spur ascends south-southeast through forest onto the **ridge** forming Cascade Amphitheatre's southwest wall. Soon attain a view behind you, up-valley, northwest to Mt. Brewster and Elk Pass.

Break out of the subalpine zone and proceed on chunky talus. The slope is strewn with cairns left by idiots. Ignore them. Just keep ascending: left, near the amphitheatre edge.

This broad, rocky slope gradually narrows to a **crest** above. Pick up a boot-beaten path on the right side of the crest. Follow it. From here on, the cairns are helpful. Keep oriented by occasionally looking ahead and noting where the path climbs the mountain.

At 2546 m (8350 ft), about an hour after leaving the amphitheater mouth, come to a seemingly vertical drop. Look closer. It's possible to carefully step down this **steep pitch** to easier terrain 30 m (98 ft) below. Beyond, the route is visible continuing up the crest then traversing right. Follow the **traverse**. Above it is a false summit—a deceptive energy waster.

After rounding a **shoulder**, the route turns north-northeast. The true summit is now in view. Cross a **saddle**, then knock off the final, steep approach to attain the apex of 2997-m (9833-ft) **Cascade Mtn** at 10.5 km (6.5 mi). The panorama reveals much of southern Banff Park. South, below you, is Banff townsite. Northeast you can see about 9 km (5.6 mi) up Lake Minnewanka.

TRIP 64

Rockbound Lake

LOCATION	Banff National Park, near Castle Junction
ROUND TRIP	16.8 km (10.4 mi)
ELEVATION GAIN	770 m (2526 ft)
KEY ELEVATIONS	trailhead 1450 m (4756 ft) Tower Lake 2120 m (6954 ft) Rockbound Lake 2210 m (7249 ft)
HIKING TIME	4½ to 5½ hours
DIFFICULTY	moderate
MAPS	page 520; Gem Trek *Banff Egypt Lake*

OPINION

Just as fishermen driving riverside roads glance at the water wondering where a stealthy presentation might land a lunker, hikers driving mountain roads scan for breaches through which they can climb high, explore deep, see far. You're sure to notice one such opportunity while motoring north from Banff townsite toward Lake Louise. It's the hanging valley wedged between Castle Mtn and Helena Ridge.

What an intriguing sight. And once you learn the valley harbours two lakes with tantalizing names—Tower Lake, Rockbound Lake—the intrigue is difficult to resist. But resist you should, because the trail is acutely boring. It makes the moderate distance and ascent seem excruciatingly long and steep.

Most of the way, the trail is a former road, so it's never engaging. Though it climbs steadily, it remains below treeline. The forest—primarily lodgepole pine, whose trunks are tall, skinny, featureless—is dense. It denies views yet is itself unsightly. Toiling upward among these monotonous trees, it's easy to imagine they're the spawn of an ill-conceived cloning experiment gone berserk.

Castle Mtn, which forms the outer wall (Trans-Canada side) of the hanging valley, is magnificent, especially when admired from afar. So it's natural to assume you'll be marvelling at it en route to Rockbound Lake. But you won't. And after dispatching this tedious trail, you'll be on the other side of the mountain, squinting up at it, your perspective foreshortened and disappointing.

Tower Lake is small, as are the nearby subalpine meadows: scenic crumbs tossed to visually-starved hikers. The ambitious larches vigourously growing atop chunky boulders deserve applause, but they don't justify hoofing this far. Upon arrival at Tower Lake, your desire to continue will likely have been quashed. Too little distraction from constant labour. Nothing in view motivating you to persist.

You will find Rockbound Lake impressive should you endure. The soaring, limestone cliffs that distinguish it are arresting. And from the rocky shore, wfffewww, finally, you begin to see what initially lured you here: the heart of this great, hanging valley. But it's an insufficient climax, especially considering the dispiriting trudge back to the trailhead.

Rockbound Lake

FACT

By Vehicle

From the intersection of Hwys 1 and 93, drive 1 km (0.6 mi) northeast, over the Bow River, to Castle Village. Turn right (east) onto Bow Valley Parkway (Hwy 1A). In 200 m (220 yd) turn left (north) into the trailhead parking area, at 1450 m (4756 ft), next to the warden's residence.

On Foot

The trail, a former road, initially heads northeast. Reach a fork at 0.3 km (0.2 mi). Bear left, curving north, for Rockbound Lake. Right proceeds northeast 0.6 km (0.4 mi) to double-tiered Silverton Falls plunging into a chasm.

Continuing to Rockbound, the road/trail ascends steeply via switchbacks. It finally curves left (northwest) into a **hanging valley** at 1883 m (6176 ft), about 70 minutes from the trailhead. You're still in forest. After a level ten minutes, hop a streamlet big enough to refill water bottles.

Resume ascending. Ignore a cairned, blazed fork veering left (south-southwest). Proceed northwest into the **subalpine zone**, where the road/trail narrows. Silverton Creek is in the gorge below. Above are Castle Mtn (left / south) and Helena Ridge (right / north). Pass beneath sheer cliffs. Enter meadows scattered with larch and studded with boulders.

At 7.7 km (4.8 mi), 2120 m (6954 ft), the trail skirts the right (east) shore of **Tower Lake**. Hop the outlet stream on the north shore. Begin a short, sharp ascent to a 2220-m (7282-ft) **shoulder** where your destination is visible ahead (north), just beyond an open forest comprising larch, spruce and fir.

A brief descent ends on the south shore of **Rockbound Lake** at 8.4 km (5.2 m), 2210 m (7249 ft), about 2½ hours from the trailhead. Spacious, limestone slabs invite you to lounge near the water's edge.

TRIP 65

Boom Lake

LOCATION	Banff National Park
ROUND TRIP	10.2 km (6.4 mi)
ELEVATION GAIN	175 m (575 ft)
HIKING TIME	3 hours
DIFFICULTY	easy
MAPS	page 505; Gem Trek *Banff & Mt. Assiniboine*

OPINION

Walking to Boom Lake illustrates the elasticity of time. Though fast hikers can zip there in an hour, the 60 minutes seem like 90 on this broad, treadmill-tedious cat-track. Walled in by trees the entire way, you're granted only prison views of Boom Mtn. Boom Creek is never visible or even audible. A few ancient Engelmann spruce and alpine fir are exceptionally large, but insufficient to keep you from mumbling the mantra of the impatient traveler: "When are we gonna get there?"

The trail does eventually spit you out at the lake, in an uncomfortable jumble of boulders where you'll find little room to escape other hiking parties. From this dump-off point, your view of the lake is still partially obscured. In search of solitude and a better vantage point, try wandering west along Boom Lake's north shore.

Despite these disappointments, Boom Lake is beautiful. A 600-m (1970-ft) cliff soars above the southern shore. Snowfields festoon the slopes rising from the west end.

Fledgling or elderly hikers might appreciate the Boom Lake trail because it's broad and gentle. Also keep it in mind for a quasi-shoulder-season training tromp. We've listed it as a summer trip to warn away part of the crowd that flocks here then. But Boom Lake can be snow-free in June and October. Even under 15 cm (6 in) of snow, the trail is pleasantly hikeable because it gains little elevation.

FACT

By Vehicle

From where it departs the Trans-Canada Hwy at Castle Junction, drive Hwy 93 southwest 7.2 km (4.5 mi) to the Boom Creek Picnic Area. It's on the north side of the highway, at 1720 m (5640 ft).

On Foot

Enter the picnic area, cross the bridge over Boom Creek, and follow the wide path gently ascending through forest. In ½ hour, reach a junction. Right leads to O'Brien and Taylor lakes. Stay left. Occasionally glimpse Boom Mtn left (south) across the valley. In 1 to 1½ hours, arrive at Boom Lake. Elevation: 1895 m (6215 ft). The wall of 2760-m (9055-ft) Boom Mtn is south and west. 3174-m (10,410-ft) Mt. Quadra is northwest.

TRIP 66

Lake Agnes

LOCATION	Banff National Park
ROUND TRIP	7 km (4.3 mi) to lake 9.6 km (6 mi) to Big Beehive
ELEVATION GAIN	390 m (1280 ft) to lake 540 m (1770 ft) to Big Beehive
KEY ELEVATIONS	trailhead 1730 m (5675 ft) lake 2120 m (6955 ft) Big Beehive 2270 m (7446 ft)
HIKING TIME	3 to 4 hours
DIFFICULTY	easy
MAPS	page 497; Gem Trek *Lake Louise & Yoho*; Lake Louise 82 N/8

OPINION

On a sunny, summer day, typically 15,000 tourists mill about the paved path along the shore of Lake Louise, in front of the famous Chateau. Of those, 1,000 extend their promenade to the teahouse at Lake Agnes.

Aren't these teahouse-bound lemmings missing the point? Don't they have an abundance of beverage-dispensing machines and enterprises where they live? Isn't it the *absence* of civilization that distinguishes Banff National Park from their urban homes and attracted them to vacation here?

If you're capable of walking to the teahouse, you'll find more fulfillment on other trails, where you might experience at least an inkling of the wildness intrinsic to the beauty of the Canadian Rockies.

Compared to nearby alternatives, the Lake Agnes cirque isn't even that compelling a sight. En route, you'll see the Bow Valley, but other equally accessible vantages are superior. Upon arrival at the teahouse, herds of incessantly chattering people will likely spoil what little visual delight the scenery offers. Only in spring and late fall does the stampede subside.

Saddleback (Trip 29) and Larch Valley (Trip 5), both near Lake Louise, are much more climactic goals than Lake Agnes yet require only slightly more effort. They too, however, are popular.

To make the Lake Agnes stroll worthwhile, stop there only for a peek, then continue on a genuine hike. You have several options. (1) Ascend to Mt. St. Piran (Trip 26), perhaps with a quick side trip to the Little Beehive. (2) Nip up to the Big Beehive, for a between-your-toes perspective of Lake Louise, then drop to the Highline trail and proceed out to the Plain of Six Glaciers (Trip 118). (3) From Big Beehive saddle, ascend the Devil's Thumb (Trip 27).

Fit, determined striders who start early can partake of all these options in a rewarding but challenging, 23-km (14.3-mi) day. Atop Piran or the Thumb, you'll see few other hikers, if any. The Six Glaciers trail is crowned with yet another anachronistic teahouse, so expect a throng, but the peaky, icy panorama here is a vast improvement on the skimpy view at Lake Agnes.

It's raining? Then Lake Agnes might be a worthwhile destination, despite gaining more elevation than other trips recommended for dismal weather. The trail is in trees all the way to the lake, so lightning is no concern. And you can warm yourself at the teahouse.

FACT

By Vehicle

From Lake Louise village, go south-southwest on Lake Louise Drive. Continue uphill 5.3 km (3.3 mi) to the actual *Lake* Louise. About 200 m (220 yd) before the road ends at Chateau Lake Louise, turn left into the bi-level parking lot, at 1730 m (5675 ft).

Before your trip

Read page 37 about possible hiking restrictions due to bears.

On Foot

From the west end of the lower parking lot, walk the paved path west to **Lake Louise**, at 1731 m (5678 ft). Bear right. Follow the path around the end of the lake. Pass the **Chateau**. On the northeast shore is a trail sign (starting point for distances below). Go right (northwest), away from the lake. Proceed into the **forest** on a well-maintained trail.

A break in the trees soon grants a view south, across the lake, to 2744-m (9000-ft) Fairview Mtn. At 2.4 km (1.5 mi) bear left (west) where a horse trail goes right to Lake Louise village. A few minutes farther, at 2.6 km (1.6 mi), 2025 m (6642 ft), reach a junction at **Mirror Lake**. Turn left and, in 100 m (110 yd), turn right for the direct ascent to Lake Agnes. (Right at the Mirror Lake junction also leads to Lake Agnes, but it's slightly farther that way.)

Reach the **Lake Agnes teahouse** at 3.1 km (1.9 mi), 2120 m (6955 ft), above the northeast shore. The Big Beehive rises above the southeast shore. Mounts Niblock (west) and Whyte (west-southwest) create the cirque.

LITTLE BEEHIVE

Behind the **Lake Agnes teahouse**, turn right on the trail to the Little Beehive. Ascend northeast. In 200 m (220 yd) pass a trail descending right. At 0.5 km (0.3 mi), pass the left spur ascending north-northwest to Mt. Saint Piran (Trip 26). Continue straight. Reach the **Little Beehive** at 0.7 km (0.4 mi), 2210 m (7250 ft).

The view extends northwest, up the Bow Valley, and southeast, down-valley, to the mountains around Banff townsite. The Slate Range, with 3086-m (10,122-ft) Mt. Richardson the highest peak, is northeast across the highway.

After departing the Little Beehive, you have the option of not returning via Lake Agnes. Instead, about two-thirds of the way back to the lake, you can descend left. Then, shortly beyond, turn left again. Soon reach Mirror Lake, where you're on familiar ground. From there, return the way you came.

Lake Agnes teahouse, looking northeast to Whitehorn Mtn (Louise ski area)

BIG BEEHIVE

From the **Lake Agnes teahouse**, follow the trail southwest along the lake's north shore. Curve around the west shore. Ascend switchbacks southeast to a 4-way junction atop the ridge, at 1.3 km (0.8 mi). This is **Big Beehive saddle**. Straight (south) descends to the Highline trail and accesses the Plain of Six Glaciers (Trip 118). Right (southwest) is the unsigned route to Devil's Thumb (Trip 27). Go left (east-northeast) along the ridgecrest five minutes to the gazebo atop **Big Beehive**, at 4.8 km (3 mi), 2270 m (7446 ft). You're now 150 m (492 ft) above Lake Agnes, and 540 m (1771 ft) above Lake Louise. Both are visible below.

HIGHLINE

From **Mirror Lake**, the Highline trail leads 3.1 km (1.9 mi) southwest to intersect the **Plain of Six Glaciers trail** (Trip 118). Atop cliffs, above the southwest end of Lake Louise, the Highline affords views of the Chateau, at the lake's northeast end. At the Highline / Plain of Six Glaciers trail junction, turn right (southwest) to proceed up-valley toward the glaciers, or left (northeast) to return to the Chateau via the northwest shore of Lake Louise.

TRIP 67

Cirque and Chephren Lakes

LOCATION	Banff National Park
ROUND TRIP	7.4 km (4.6 mi) to Chephren 8.8 km (5.5 mi) to Cirque 13.2 km (8.2 mi) to both
ELEVATION GAIN	80 m (262 ft) to Chephren 60 m (197 ft) more to Cirque
KEY ELEVATIONS	trailhead 1675 m (5495 ft) Cirque Lake 1800 m (5900 ft)
HIKING TIME	2 hours for either, 3½ to 4 hours for both
DIFFICULTY	easy
MAPS	page 508; Gem Trek *Bow Lake & Saskatchewan Crossing*

OPINION

Arriving at Cirque or Chephren lakes, hikers don't whoop for joy. They utter a disheartened "Oh" or "Hmm" thinking of the tedious, rooty, muddy trail they tromped to get there and must endure on the return.

Don't be lured by the false promise of the lakes' august names. The Continental Divide peaks above the lakes are a more stirring sight from the Icefields Parkway. Standing on either lakeshore, you actually see less of the mountains. Both trails end at limited, awkward vantage points. At neither is it easy to distance yourself from other people, and you're unlikely to be alone. The huge campground adjacent to the trailhead spews unwitting hikers daily.

In other mountain ranges, the Cirque and Chephren lake settings would be considered outstanding. But the Canadian Rockies are awash with more impressive lakes. Many are visible from your car, such as Hector, Bow and Maligne. Others, such as Louise, Moraine and Peyto, require only a couple-minute walk. Not that easy access is paramount. But if you're here to hike, why choose a trail less rewarding than a bus tour?

Even if you're settled in at Waterfowl campground, don't light out for Cirque or Chephren just because they're convenient. Superior options are not far away. Consider Bow Hut (Trip 31) or Bow Glacier Falls (Trip 45).

Chephren Lake

FACT

By Vehicle

Drive the Icefields Parkway north 19 km (11.8 mi) from Bow Summit, or south 19 km (11.8 mi) from Saskatchewan River Crossing. Turn west onto the Waterfowl Lakes campground access road. Drive in 75 m (80 yd). Do not enter the campground. Continue left 350 m (0.2 mi) to a parking area on the left, at 1675 m (5495 ft). The trail sign is on the right.

On Foot

Follow the wide gravel path along the edge of forest on the south side of the campground. Cross the bridge spanning the **Mistaya River**, then ascend generally southwest through forest. At 1.5 km (0.9 mi) arrive at a junction. Cirque Lake is left. The larger Chephren Lake is right.

Heading for Chephren, at 2 km (1.2 mi), 1738 m (5700 ft), pass a meadow allowing you to see Howse Peak southwest. Reach the north shore at 3.7 km (2.3 mi), 1720 m (5642 ft). The lake is almost 3 km (2 mi) long. Glacier-cloaked, 3290-m (10,793-ft) Howse Peak is south. Pyramidal, 3266-m (10,715-ft) Mt. Chephren is west.

Heading for Cirque, a rougher, steeper trail ascends from the 1.5-km (0.9-mi) junction. Reach the north shore at 4.4 km (2.7 mi), 1800 m (5900 ft). The lake is backed by the sheer cliffs of (from right to left) Midway, Stairway and Aries peaks on the Continental Divide.

TRIP 68

Sarbach Lookout

LOCATION	Banff National Park
ROUND TRIP	10.6 km (6.6 mi)
ELEVATION GAIN	570 m (1870 ft)
KEY ELEVATIONS	trailhead 1520 m (4986 ft) lookout 2055 m (6740 ft)
HIKING TIME	4 hours
DIFFICULTY	moderate
MAPS	page 509; Gem Trek *Bow Lake & Saskatchewan Crossing*

OPINION

An *Encyclopedia of Rationalizations* could be handy. On a lousy hike, you could look up *lousy hike* and find encouragement: *Experiencing the bad helps you appreciate the good*. But most people need more encouragement than that to trudge up to Sarbach Lookout. It's a really lousy hike.

The trail is persistently steep yet never escapes the trees. The forest is uninspiring. It grudgingly allows only an occasional peek at the surrounding mountains. And the destination is so inconsequential you could pass it without knowing, if the trail continued. Where the fire lookout used to stand, trees deny you a perfect panorama. Though on the way up you'll see the confluence of three mighty rivers—Mistaya, Howse, and North Saskatchewan—it's nothing to shout about. Or hike this hard for.

Faint footpaths, meandering uphill from the lookout site, tantalize with possibilities. But they soon halt, leaving their promise unfulfilled. Broader views are beyond most hikers' reach. Scrambling up these precipitous slopes of loose rock is difficult; down climbing more so.

There *is* one worthwhile sight on this trip: Mistaya Canyon. It's only a 12-minute walk from the trailhead. When driving past on the Icefields Parkway, stop to see the Mistaya River surge through this deep, narrow, sensuously eroded gorge.

FACT

By Vehicle

From the Waterfowl campground entrance, drive the Icefields Parkway north 14.2 km (8.8 mi). Or, from Saskatchewan River Crossing, where Hwy 11 joins the Parkway, drive south 5.3 km (3.3 mi). Park at the Mistaya Canyon pullout, on the west side of the highway, at 1520 m (4986 ft).

On Foot

Walk the dirt road descending 35 m (115 ft) in 0.5 km (0.3 mi) to the bridge spanning Mistaya Canyon. Across the bridge, turn right onto a signed trail and

Mt. Murchison, from Sarbach Lookout

begin the ascent. In a couple minutes, the trail divides at the top of a bluff. Straight (northwest) leads to Glacier Lake and Howse Pass. Sharp left (southwest) climbs southwest to Sarbach Lookout.

About 40 minutes from the trailhead, near 1555 m (5100 ft), the trail pulls away from the canyon and provides a view of the forested slope you must ascend. The highway noise, no longer masked by the river's roar, is now constantly audible. The climb is relentless and entirely in trees, mostly alpine fir and lodgepole pine. The only relief are glimpses of tantalizing peaks northwest.

Near 2 km (1.2 mi), ignore an old route descending left. Your trail steeply switchbacks up a forested ridge. About 1½ hours from the trailhead, near 1982 m (6500 ft), attain a **grand view** northwest up the Icefields Parkway. Continuing up the trail, encounter thick, muscular whitebark pines and flower-filled grassy patches. Soon reach trail's end and the flat **lookout site**, at 5.3 km (3.3 mi), 2055 m (6740 ft). The rock-lined paths are the handiwork of the lookout attendants. Remnants of trails fan out from here but quickly vanish. To the south, Mt. Sarbach continues rising out of sight. Directly east, across the highway, is 3333-m (10,932-ft) Mt. Murchison. Plunging off this leviathan mountain is a double waterfall 250 m (820 ft) high.

TRIP 69

Hawk Creek / Ball Pass

LOCATION	Kootenay National Park northwest of Vermilion Crossing
ROUND TRIP	19.4 km (12 mi)
ELEVATION GAIN	862 m (2827 ft)
KEY ELEVATIONS	trailhead 1348 m (4420 ft), pass 2210 m (7249 ft)
HIKING TIME	4½ to 5 hours
DIFFICULTY	moderate
MAPS	page 499; Gem Trek *Kootenay National Park*

OPINION

Sometimes we think the Earth is talking to us.

We won't elaborate on the long conversations we've had with the Earth, because it's hard to go hiking in a padded cell. But we will tell you what she said last time we hiked to Ball Pass: "Welcome back."

We'd largely avoided Kootenay National Park after it was ravaged by wildfire in 2003. About 12.5% of the park burned. Hwy 93, which runs the length of the park through the Vermilion Valley, still gives the impression you're touring one of the lower rings of hell.

But on the Hawk Creek trail to Ball Pass, we were reminded you really can't see much from behind a windshield. Within minutes of the trailhead, we were hiking through vegetation so lush and brilliantly coloured, we frequently stopped and admired it.

The next-generation pine forest is thriving. The young trees are thick as weeds in a vacant lot. And they're not just green, they're blazing green. Among them are thigh-high fireweed and various shrubs, all of which, in late summer, turn scarlet, burgundy, crimson… every imaginable shade of red.

So maybe the Earth was actually saying, "Merry Christmas."

Whatever the message, it was cheerful and averted our attention from the fire-blackened trees. We noticed them little more than we would a subtle, elegant frame on a beautiful work of art.

What's very apparent, however, is the greatly expanded view. Instead of a visually impenetrable wall of lodgepole pines (tall, skinny trunks, token greenery way up top, sort of a Rocky Mountain palm tree), now you see the peaks girding Hawk Creek Canyon, which makes the ascent much more inspiring.

Within an hour, you'll exit the burn zone and hike beneath sheer cliffs. Above, the trail enters green forest, asks that you endure only one, brief, sharp ascent, then follows a series of meadows to the pass and an arresting sight: glacier-hatted Mt. Ball.

When you stop staring at all that ice, you'll realize you can also see Shadow Lake in the valley far below. And that's when the beauty of Ball Pass becomes obvious. The south side, by which you approached, rises at a compassionate grade.

Yet the north side is sheer, so everything between you and the Massive Range is visible.

You might be here alone, too. On our last trip, we saw little evidence of human visitation. No boot prints. No trekking-pole dimples. Much of the trail has become mossy and grassy during the lonely years since the fire.

Perhaps you'll find the silent atmosphere conducive to hearing what the Earth has to say. We certainly did.

So why is Ball Pass rated *Don't Do*? Because when reprinting this book for 2009, it wasn't physically possible to restructure the contents, so we couldn't move the trip to a higher category. The best we could do was leave it in place but offer this new, updated *Opinion*. In the next completely revised edition of this book, you'll find Ball Pass rated *Worthwhile*.

Ball Glacier

FACT

By Vehicle

Hwy 93 runs generally north-south, linking Hwy 1 (at Castle Junction, between Banff townsite and Lake Louise Village) with Hwy 95 (at Radium). Drive Hwy 93 south 22.5 km (14 mi) from the Banff-Kootenay parks boundary at Vermilion Pass. Turn right into the Floe Lake / Hawk Creek trailhead parking lot. It's on the southwest side of the highway, at 1348 m (4420 ft).

On Foot

Return to the highway and cross to the northeast side. Look for a signed, gravel path. Follow it northwest, paralleling the highway 0.3 km (0.2 mi) to **Hawk Creek**. Cross the creek on a culvert. The trail curves right, rises into the forest, then levels, heading generally northeast.

You're following the creek upstream, above its northwest bank. Within ten minutes the trail begins a gentle, rolling ascent. After hiking about 45 minutes, cross a footlog over a boisterous **tributary** at 4.2 km (2.6 mi), 1690 m (5543 ft). A large, flat boulder and a nearby bench insist you take a rest break here.

About an hour from the trailhead, surmount the upper reaches of the burn zone near 1795 m (5888 ft). Heading east, the trail crosses rockslides beneath stark, south-

Hawk Creek Canyon

facing cliffs on the lower reaches of Isabelle Peak. Behind you (west-southwest), beyond the highway, is the famous Kootenay Park massif called "The Rockwall."

Soon reach a stand of **mature forest**, then cross more rocky terrain beneath cliffs at 1930 m (6330 ft). After seeing a cascade in the gorge on your right, re-enter forest. The trail is briefly creekside before ascending steeply north. Having hiked less than two hours, you're now approaching the pass.

The ascent eases in ten minutes at 2100 m (6888 ft). A left (northeast) spur stops in a **small meadow** cleaved by a creeklet. Detour here for your first glimpse of Mt. Ball. Then bear right (southeast) on the main trail to curve around the meadow and proceed north.

The trail soon skirts a **long meadow**, then rises through increasingly open forest. Rockhop a couple more streams, gain a little more elevation, cross one more meadow, and suddenly arrive at a tumult of rock at the crest of 2210-m (7249-ft) **Ball Pass**. Total distance: 9.7 km (6 mi). Hiking time: about 2½ hours.

The pass is squeezed between 2938-m (9637-ft) Isabelle Peak (left / west) and a huge-but-nameless 2800-m (9184-ft) mountain (right / east-southeast). Ahead (north-northwest) is 3311-m (10,860-ft) Mt. Ball, bearing an impressive glacier. North-northeast in the valley beyond is Shadow Lake.

Both **shoulders of Ball Pass** allow easy, intriguing, cross-country ascents to superior viewpoints, but most hikers will be gratified with a rocky perch immediately above where the trail plunges north into forest.

When you're ready to head home, it's possible to return to the trailhead in 2 hours.

TRIP 70

Hunter Lookout

LOCATION	Yoho National Park
ROUND TRIP	7 km (4.4 mi) to lower lookout site 13 km (8 mi) to upper
ELEVATION GAIN	425 m (1394 ft) to lower lookout site 825 m (2705 ft) to upper
KEY ELEVATIONS	trailhead 1125 m (3690 ft) upper lookout site 1950 m (6396 ft)
HIKING TIME	2 to 3 hours for lower lookout site 4 to 5 hours for upper
DIFFICULTY	easy to moderate
MAP	McMurdo 82 N/2

OPINION

Mt. Hunter is aptly named. You have to hunt for something worth looking at up here. Is this really Yoho? Stronghold of brazen peaks and ethereal alplands? Hard to believe. Here on the southwest edge of the park, the mountains rapidly diminish from G.I. Joe's chiseled face to Fred Flintsone's jelly belly.

Further discouragement: (1) The Trans-Canada clutches the ridge like a vise, so highway noise is a torment. You'll hear it while climbing the south slope, then be assaulted again from the east side when you gain the ridge. (2) The forest is grim, crowded with anorexic trees skinny as broomsticks. It's a hill of quills. Maybe that's how Porcupine Peak, just north of Hunter, got its name. (3) Communications apparatus wrecks the view at the lower lookout site.

No single reason justifies hiking here. You need several. You must be seeking exercise only, not a scenic reward. You must be curious about the Kicking Horse and Beaverfoot valleys, which are the dominant sights. You must already be in the area. And it must be shoulder season, when trails deeper in the range are snowbound. In summer, hiking anywhere else in the parks is preferable. Most *Don't Do* trips are way better than this one.

Strong hikers can bag the lower lookout site in an hour or less. Others might take twice as long. Continuing to the upper lookout site almost makes the trip worthwhile, but not quite.

FACT

By Vehicle

Drive the Trans-Canada Hwy east 5 km (3 mi) from Yoho Park's West Gate, or southwest 25 km (15.5 mi) from Field. Just west of the Chancellor Peak Campground turnoff, near where the highway curves radically, turn south onto the Wapta Falls dirt access road. Park in the lot just off the highway, at 1125 m (3690 ft).

On Foot

The signed trail starts on the north side of the highway. Be careful walking across. In a few minutes, cross the railroad tracks. After gaining 140 m (460 ft) in 15 to 25 minutes, attain minor views. Highway noise is still audible. Crest Mt. Hunter's southeast ridge in 25 to 40 minutes. The highway and railroad tracks mar the scenery. The lower lookout site is soon visible ahead (northwest) on a forested promontory. It appears close, but the trail wraps around behind it. Ascend steeply through scraggly trees. At a signed junction, go left 200 m (220 yd) to reach the **lower lookout site** at 3.5 km (2.2 mi), 1550 m (5085 ft). There's a cabin here, open to the public.

Visible west is a clearcut just outside the park boundary. Southwest is the Beaverfoot Range. Southeast is the Beaverfoot River valley. Northeast, across the highway, is 3320-m (10,891-ft) Mt. Vaux. East is 3281-m (10,761-ft) Chancellor Peak. Between them is the canyon of the Hoodoos (Trip 134). North is the Kicking Horse River valley and the President Range. Northeast are the peaks above Field.

The **upper lookout site** is northwest about 1¼ hours beyond the lower one. You can get there by turning right at the junction just below the lower lookout site. Or, if you visit the lower one first, a shortcut trail west of the cabin ascends the ridgecrest to rejoin the main trail in a few minutes. Reach the upper lookout site at 6.5 km (4 mi), 1950 m (6396 ft).

Emerald Lake and the President Range, from lakeshore trail (Trip 71)

TRIP 71

Emerald Basin

LOCATION	Yoho National Park
ROUND TRIP	9.2 km (5.7 mi)
ELEVATION GAIN	248 m (813 ft)
KEY ELEVATIONS	trailhead 1312 m (4303 ft) basin 1560 m (5117 ft)
HIKING TIME	3 to 3½ hours
DIFFICULTY	easy
MAPS	page 508; Gem Trek *Lake Louise & Yoho*

OPINION

Most outdoor shops have a short, stone-studded ramp for boot testing. It gives you an inkling of how a pair of boots might actually feel on a hike. The Emerald Basin trail is like one of those ramps. It gives you an inkling of how it can feel to hike in the Canadian Rockies. But only an inkling. The first half of the trip is crowded, preventing you from experiencing any sense of wilderness. And the destination is anticlimactic, failing to elicit a lasting emotional high.

The trailhead is at Emerald Lake—Yoho's version of Lake Louise: staggeringly beautiful and, as a result, insufferably crowded in summer. The paved access road all but plunges into the lake. A famous lodge hogs the most scenic stretch of shoreline. Cars and buses jostle for limited parking space before disgorging swarms of lumbering tourists. So, if you're bound for Emerald Basin, you'll probably start by fleeing the most impressive sight on the entire trip.

Soon, before you've outdistanced the strollers trickling around the lakeshore path, you'll turn away from the lake and begin ascending into forest. The trail is steep enough to deter crowds. Finally, peace. But at trail's end, you'll discover your effort has earned you little more.

Emerald Basin is scooped from the cliffs of the President Range. The setting seems to call for a lake, but there is none; just a couple cascades and a stream. Jewelry without a jewel can be unaffecting. And here, the jewelry itself is tiny, just a constricted cul-de-sac with impressively steep, rocky sides. Swivel your head and you've seen it all. It's certainly wild, though. The chaotic array of debris on the basin floor is from avalanches roaring down the cliffs in winter.

Despite Emerald Basin's relatively low elevation, wait until early July to hike here. The final approach is on a shaded east-facing slope that retains snow. And the aforementioned avalanches inundate the basin floor with heaps of snow that linger into summer.

After visiting the basin and returning to Emerald Lake, if you have more time and energy, continue around the lake—either all the way, or part way then up toward Yoho Pass. The rugged but exciting trail to the pass ascends beneath the massive south face of Michael Peak. Turn around at the cascade, before the trail enters thick forest. On your way back to the trailhead, if it's early evening and the crowds are gone, relax on one of the lakeshore benches; you might spy a beaver.

FACT

By Vehicle

From the Yoho Park Visitor Centre, in Field, B.C., drive the Trans-Canada Hwy southwest 1.6 km (1 mi). Turn right (west) onto Emerald Lake Road, then continue 8.5 km (5.3 mi) to the road's end parking lot, at 1312 m (4303 ft).

On Foot

The trail departs the north end of the parking lot. Don't cross the bridge spanning the outlet stream and leading to the lodge. Follow the trail north-northwest, around the southwest shore of **Emerald Lake**. Continue northeast, then north, along the lake's west shore.

At the lake's northwest corner, pass a horse trail (left / southwest), curve right, and reach a signed junction near a bench, at 1.6 km (1 mi). Right follows the lake's north shore. Turn left (north), across open gravel, away from the lake.

Reach another signed junction at 2 km (1.2 mi), on the gravelly, alluvial fan. Proceed straight. The next junction is shortly beyond, at 2.2 km (1.4 mi). Right (northeast) leads to Yoho Pass. Go left (northwest) for Emerald Basin.

The trail steepens, becoming rooty and rocky. Ascend 150 m (460 ft) through a lush forest of western hemlock and red cedar. In the gorge below you is the stream that drains the basin. Where the grade eases, at 2.8 km (1.7 mi), Michael Peak is visible northeast.

At 3.8 km (2.4 mi) the trail crosses an avalanche swath and drops to the stream. A rocky path continues, reaching the heart of **Emerald Basin** at 4.6 km (2.9 mi), 1560 m (5117 ft). A rough, bootbeaten path probes another 1 km (0.6 mi) to the head of the basin and a pair of cascades.

A 3138-m (10,293-ft) peak called The President presides above the basin's upper, northern reaches. You'll see a bit of Emerald Glacier tumbling through President Pass. Mt. Carnarvon and Emerald Peak form the basin's west and southwest walls.

TRIP 72

Yoho Valley

LOCATION	Yoho National Park
ROUND TRIP	9.4 km (5.8 mi) to Laughing Falls 17 km (10.5 mi) to Twin Falls
ELEVATION GAIN	90 m (295 ft) to Laughing Falls 290 m (950 ft) to Twin Falls
KEY ELEVATIONS	trailhead 1510 m (4955 ft) Twin Falls 1806 m (5925 ft)
HIKING TIME	4 to 5 hours
DIFFICULTY	easy
MAPS	page 497; Gem Trek *Lake Louise & Yoho*

OPINION

Too many people plod the Yoho Valley trail to Twin Falls and back. It's understandable. Awesome Takakkaw Falls, visible from the road, seems to presage further marvels up-valley. And the hiking is sleepwalk easy, much of it on a broad, smooth path, flat as a prairie highway. But it's submerged in forest, a scenic zero if you're here to admire mountains. A few minor falls are the only diversions until reaching the 80-m (260-ft) twin-plumed dynamo.

Though robust hikers can smoke the trail at 6.5 kph (4 mph), that energy is squandered. Just above is the dazzling Iceline (Trip 13). It's much steeper, but exploding horizons draw you onward, so it seems easier than lumbering along the valley bottom, staring at tree trunks.

Twin Falls is a spectacle. See it on your way down from the Whaleback (Trip 90). Then, hiking the Yoho Valley trail one way, as the final leg of an alpine journey, makes sense. After the exposure and glare of the harsh landscape above, cruising the cool, softly lit, verdant forest can be a welcome relief. One reason to stay on the valley trail, up and back, is rain. When visibility is nil at higher elevations, a walk in the woods to a waterfall is attractive. You'll reach the first two cascades in less than 3 km (1.9 mi).

What's great about the Yoho Valley trail is Takakkaw Falls campground—within ten minutes of the trailhead. The Park supplies pushcarts, so you don't have to backpack to experience a night on the trail. That small buffer from the road assures you of more tranquility than is possible at other front-country campgrounds.

Want to meet the backcountry a bit more on its own terms? Perhaps with children or grandparents? Backpack to Laughing Falls campground. It's an easy walk up-valley from Takakkaw. And it's beautifully situated between the Yoho and Little Yoho rivers, where you'll be serenaded by stereophonic water music. It's beyond pushcart range, but the distance is short enough that willing, hardy hikers can play Sherpa for loved ones unable to lug their own overnight gear.

Laughing Falls

FACT

By Vehicle

Follow the directions for the Iceline (Trip 13) to the Takakkaw Falls parking lot at 13.5 km (8.4 mi). Bear right and curve around to the far end, where you might find space in the smaller lot at the Yoho Valley trailhead. Elevation: 1510 m (4955 ft).

On Foot

From the north end of the parking lot, follow the gated path. Your general direction of travel nearly all the way to Twin Falls will be north-northwest. Ignore the sign overestimating the distance to the campground; it's actually just 0.3 km (0.2 mi). In one minute, bear left (northwest) on the road. Within five minutes, reach **Takakkaw Falls campground**. Proceed through it. Just past the outhouse, bear left (west). One minute farther, turn right (north-northwest) and pass the **trailhead kiosk** at 0.5 km (0.3 mi).

Heading up-valley, cross a couple footbridges over streamlets on the rocky alluvial plain, then enter beautiful forest. The trail is wide and smooth. About twelve minutes from the campground, graze the west bank of the **Yoho River**. At 2.7 km (1.7 mi), 1545 m (5065 ft), about 20 minutes from the campground, reach a junction. Angel's Staircase cascade is right (east). Point Lace Falls is left (northwest) 150 m (165 yd). After these very short excursions, resume hiking north-northwest on the main trail. It narrows, becoming rocky and rooty. After a steep, seven-minute ascent, it levels at 1605 m (5265 ft).

At 3.2 km (2 mi), a left spur leads 200 m (220 yd) northwest to shallow Duchesnay Lake. Look for grass-of-Parnassus (white, green-veined flowers) and cinquefoil (yellow flowers) near this junction. Up-valley on the main trail, thundering water is audible. Soon, a short descent leads to a bridged crossing of the swift **Little Yoho River**. On the far bank is **Laughing Falls campground**, at 4.7 km (2.9 mi), 1600 m (5250 ft), near the confluence of the Yoho and Little Yoho rivers.

Arrive at a junction 100 m (110 yd) past the campground. Left ascends generally west, following the Little Yoho River upstream, past the Whaleback, into Little Yoho Valley. For Twin Falls, go right (north-northwest).

At 6.8 km (4.2 mi), the Yoho Glacier trail forks right (northwest). Go left (west) and pass **Twin Falls campground** in 200 m (220 yd). At 8.4 km (5.2 mi), 1806 m (5925 ft), reach signed Twin Falls junction. The Twin Falls Chalet is visible left. The base of the falls, where the twin torrents complete their 80-m (263-ft) dive off a sheer limestone cliff, is also nearby (south). You'll find picnic tables there. Right is a steep ascent—generally north, then curving south—reaching the **top of Twin Falls** in another 2.7 km (1.7 mi).

TRIP 73

The Whistlers

LOCATION	Jasper National Park
ROUND TRIP	19.4 km (12 mi)
ELEVATION GAIN	1216 m (3990 ft)
KEY ELEVATIONS	trailhead 1250 m (4100 ft) upper gondola terminal 2265 m (7430 ft) Whistlers summit 2466 m (8088 ft)
HIKING TIME	6 hours
DIFFICULTY	challenging
MAPS	page 507; Gem Trek *Best of Jasper*; Jasper 83 D/16

OPINION

Climb like a yak for three hours. Endure an ascent as severe as any in the range. See little but trees. Only to reach a gondola terminal where gawking tourists are constantly disgorged? That's not hiking. That's masochism. About 10,800 strides worth. It's also no way to save money. You'd burn up more dollars worth of energy bars than the cost of the gondola to get up there. And who knows how much worth of knee cartilage on the way down.

There's a tremendous panorama to be enjoyed from The Whistlers. And hiking beyond the upper gondola terminal, where you can explore alpine bowls and scramble over Indian Ridge (Trip 56), is definitely worthwhile. Plenty challenging, too. So don't punish yourself getting up there. Enjoy the gondola ride, blast past the tourists, then roam at will above treeline for an entire, sublime day.

Marmots are also known as whistlers.

FACT

By Vehicle

From the junction of Hwy 16 and the Icefields Parkway, at the southwest edge of Jasper townsite, drive the Parkway south 1.8 km (1.1 mi). Turn right (west) onto Whistlers Road. Follow it 2.7 km (1.7 mi), then turn left onto a gravel road—about 200 m (220 yd) before the youth hostel. Drive 0.3 km (0.2 mi) to the trailhead parking area at 1250 m (4100 ft).

Read Trip 56 if you'd rather ride the gondola and start hiking with views like this.

On Foot

Ascend through dense brush and a deciduous forest of aspen, alder and birch. Near 4 km (2.5 mi), pass beneath the gondola line. The forest becomes more open. Meadows punctuate the spruce and alpine fir. The trail turns south and climbs a rocky gully. It then switchbacks and steepens. Reach the **upper gondola terminal** at 8.5 km (5.3 mi), 2265 m (7430 ft). From the upper gondola terminal, follow the trampled, dirt trail 1.2 km (0.75 mi) southwest up the ridge to **The Whistlers summit** at 2466 m (8088 ft).

TRIP 74

Saturday Night Lake

LOCATION	Jasper National Park
LOOP	25.3 km (15.7 mi)
ELEVATION GAIN	770 m (2525 ft)
KEY ELEVATIONS	trailhead 1085 m (3560 ft), highpoint 1625 m (5330 ft)
HIKING TIME	7 to 9 hours
DIFFICULTY	moderate
MAPS	page 522; Gem Trek *Best of Jasper*, Gem Trek *Jasper and Maligne Lake*

OPINION

Quantity, not quality, is what you get here: up to a dozen lakes on a single trip, but none particularly striking. Longer than most shoulder-season options, this low-elevation trail might keep you entertained while you tune up your mountain muscles.

Forget it during summer, unless it's a rainy day. Your small pleasures will be noting the subtle differences distinguishing each lake, and appreciating the wildflowers. Look for yellow arnica, calypso orchids, Indian paintbrush, wild roses, red-orange western wood lilies, and possibly red columbine.

Although you won't emerge above treeline, you'll get a workout while the trail undulates through the foothills of the Victoria Cross Ranges. Mountain views are minimal, except near Cabin Lake. Hike there, but no farther, to quickly sample the area. You can reach Cabin Lake on a 5.2-km (3.2 mi) round trip by setting out in the opposite direction than suggested for the full, 25.3-km (15.7-mi), clockwise loop. Both trips are described below.

Black bears frequent the lakes, so stay alert, constantly scan ahead, and make noise to warn them of your presence. Read our *Bears* section for further suggestions. Also be wary of mountain bikers who might not be watching for hikers.

FACT

Before your trip

Want to captain a rowboat on Cabin Lake? Curries Guided Fishing keeps one locked on the southeast shore. Call them at (780) 852-5650, then pick up the key at Source for Sports, 416 Patricia Street, Jasper. Better yet, rent a boat on Beaver Lake (Trip 123) beneath soaring cliffs.

By Vehicle

In Jasper townsite, follow the main road—Connaught Drive—to Pine Avenue. It's the first left after entering the townsite from the southwest, off the Icefields Parkway (Hwy 93). Stay on Pine five blocks, until it turns into Pyramid Lake Road at a wide intersection with Miette. Turn left. In one block, Pyramid

Cabin Lake

becomes Cabin Creek Road. Bear right. Proceed 0.6 km (0.4 mi) to the bearproof garbage bins. Turn right here and ascend a gravel spur. Just 50 m/yd up this spur is the trailhead parking area, at 1085 m (3560 ft).

On Foot

Depart the left (south) side of the **parking lot**, by the kiosk. The trail immediately drops to cross a bridged stream. Proceed south-southwest, behind the houses.

After heading generally west for 2.2 km (1.4 mi), the trail rounds the north shore of **Marjorie Lake**. At 2.6 km (1.6 mi), a right spur leads 0.5 km (0.3 mi) northwest to green **Hibernia Lake**.

At 3.6 km (2.2 mi) on the main trail, ignore a left (southeast) fork. Stay straight on the main trail. Your general direction of travel will be northwest until the far end of the loop.

At 4 km (2.5 mi), 1161 m (3808 ft), the trail parallels the northeast shore of **Caledonia Lake**. Look for western wood lilies and wild roses here in June. Beyond, ascend steeply to a beaver marsh.

At 9.2 km (5.7 mi), a left spur leads 0.4 km (0.25 mi) west-northwest to **Minnow Lake and campground**. The main trail bears right, ascends forested ridges and crosses a bridge. At 12.2 km (7.6 mi), a right spur leads 50 m (55 yd) to **High Lakes campground** and continues 175 m (190 yd) to one of the tiny lakes.

At 12.8 km (7.9 mi) on the main trail, reach a large, mossy cascade. Having attained the loop's 1625-m (5330-ft) **highpoint**, begin a long, forested descent generally southeast, back to Jasper townsite. At 18 km (11.2 mi), a left spur ascends northeast, reaching **Saturday Night Lake and campground** in 0.4 km (0.25 mi).

The main trail, still descending southeast, passes huge beaver ponds before reaching the north shore of **Cabin Lake** at 21.4 km (13.3 mi). Mt. Hardisty and Mt. Kerkeslin are soon visible southeast.

Reach a junction near the east end of Cabin Lake, at 22.3 km (13.8 mi). Left leads generally north, past Mina Lake. Proceed straight. Reach another junction at 22.5 km (14 mi). Left is a road signed #3 leading generally east. It does not return to the trailhead; ignore it. Turn right (south) and cross the **Cabin Lake dam**. You're now on an old, double-track road. Follow it down through forest to where it ends at **Cabin Creek**. Cross the footbridge and hike over a rise, generally southeast, to reach the **parking lot** at 25.3 km (15.7 mi).

CABIN LAKE

On the upper (north) side of the **parking lot**, follow the trail ascending steeply north. It immediately turns left. Follow it generally northwest. After gaining 73 m (240 ft), the ascent eases. Attain a view south-southwest to The Whistlers and south-east into the broad, forested Athabasca River Valley.

The trail climbs at a moderate grade to 1185 m (3887 ft), where a logged **clearing** affords a view. Visible east-southeast are Mt Tekarra and Amber Mtn, both near the Skyline (Trip 81). Southeast are Mounts Hardisty and Kerkeslin.

Descend slightly to a footbridge over **Cabin Creek**. Proceed on the old, double-track road. After a brief, gradual ascent, reach a fork at 1220 m (4000 ft). Go left (west). Two minutes farther, at 2.6 km (1.6 mi), reach the southeast shore of **Cabin Lake**. Pyramid Mtn is visible north-northwest. Other peaks of the Victoria Cross Range are northwest.

Daisies

Mt. Robson and Robson Glacier, from trail to Snowbird Pass (Trip 84)

Backpack Trips

TRIPS 75 – 78

Mt. Assiniboine Region

LOCATION	Banff National Park / Mt. Assiniboine Prov. Park
DISTANCE	55 km (34 mi) circuit 56.4 km (35 mi) shuttle trip
ELEVATION GAIN	622 m (2040 ft) for circuit 482 m (1580 ft) for shuttle trip
HIKING TIME	3 to 6 days
KEY ELEVATIONS	Sunshine Village trailhead 2195 m (7200 ft) Citadel Pass 2360 m (7740 ft) Lake Magog 2190 m (7183 ft) Nub Peak 2748 m (9013 ft) Wonder Pass 2395 m (7856 ft) Bryant Creek trailhead 1770 m (5806 ft)
DIFFICULTY	moderate
MAPS	pages 510-11; Gem Trek *Banff & Mt. Assiniboine*; Mount Assiniboine 82 J/13

OPINION

St. Peter's is not Rome. Disneyworld is not Florida. Mt. Assiniboine is not Mt. Assiniboine Provincial Park. Landmarks often deceive. Overshadowed by a dominating mountain, the scenery in this enchanting park is more marvelously varied than you might think. That's why it's premier backpacking country. Your enjoyment isn't limited to seeing the namesake peak. It's only one of many powerful sights.

Ravishing Lakes Park would be an equally apt name. Seven of them are clustered beneath a classic Northern Rockies massif. And the massif comprises a dozen eminent peaks. Though Mt. Assiniboine is one of them, even if its top were lopped off, the remaining scene would still be Sierra Club calendar material. Meadows are another salient feature of the park. You'll hike through vast expanses of green alpine carpet here.

The high-voltage scenery, however, is concentrated near the southeast corner of the roughly triangular-shaped park. Naturally, that's where most of the trails lead and where a trail network has developed. So despite competition for your attention, you'll see the famous mountain—assuming the visibility's good. And Mt. Assiniboine's icon status is justified. A pyramidal, grand poohba's hat, it resembles Switzerland's Matterhorn. But it's only the Canadian Rockies' seventh highest peak—3618 m (11,867 ft)—a statistic that belies how frequently and far away The Boine is visible and recognizable.

Most backpackers visiting the park share the same initial destination: Lake Magog, in the basin north of The Boine. Strong hikers can tag Magog on a weekend—one long day in, one long day out. Too fast. Give yourself at least a third day

Mt. Assiniboine and Lake Magog

for a sidetrip. Ignore the nearby ridges and lakes and you'll leave with a limited impression of this magnificent park.

SIDETRIPS FROM LAKE MAGOG

Nub Peak affords the supreme vantage of the Mt. Assiniboine region. From the summit of this modest mountain, you can see Elizabeth, Wedgwood, Cerulean, Sunburst, Magog, Gog and Og lakes, as well as The Boine and its attendant peaks. Mounts Ball, Temple and Hector are even visible way northwest. Ascending Nub Peak, however, requires you to negotiate a short but narrow ridge. Accomplished hikers would agree: it's not quite a scramble, and there's no real exposure, so the ridge poses no obstacle whatsoever. Yet timid or inexperienced hikers might be unnerved. Try it. See how you feel. If you're capable, summiting Nub Peak is de rigueur. It will be the climax of your Mt. Assiniboine journey.

If you can't surmount Nub Peak, go as high as possible. Part way up, just before the narrow ridge, is a bump called the Nublet. The panorama here is incomplete, but you'll still see most of the Mt. Assiniboine region from a stupendous aerial perspective. And if the steep route to the Nublet is more than you can muster, just below it is a saddle on Nub Ridge. Anyone who hikes to Lake Magog can certainly manage the moderate ascent on good trail to this saddle, where the view is sufficiently grand to warrant lingering for hours and absorbing at a cellular level.

The shortest, easiest sidetrip is to Sunburst and Cerulean lakes. Starting at Lake Magog campground, you'll quickly pass both lakes en route to Nub Peak. Starting at Mt. Assiniboine Lodge, you can loop past them after descending Nub Peak. Following the trail around Cerulean's northwest shore is a lovely walk, but continuing from there down to Wedgwood Lake, up to Ferro Pass, then looping back via Mitchell Meadow, Sunburst Valley and Elizabeth Lake is more tedious than rewarding. You might enjoy the solitude, but you'll pay for it labouring down and up through forest. And you'll see little that isn't better appreciated from high on Nub Peak. Windy Ridge and Wonder Pass are much more enjoyable sidetrips than Ferro Pass. The optimal view of Elizabeth Lake is from the narrow ridge above the Nublet. If you insist on visiting Elizabeth's shore, do so by descending from the junction just north of Cerulean Lake.

Windy Ridge and Wonder Pass are equally attractive. Windy Ridge is among the highest trail-accessible points in the mountain parks. Others are North Molar Pass (Trip 88) and Fairview Mtn (Trip 29). En route to Windy Ridge, the views begin early—in Og Meadows. You'll also have the option of nipping into Og Pass. The wildflower display can be heavenly on the final ascent. And the ridgecrest vista is superb. It reveals the Goodsir Towers in Yoho Park, and Kootenay's Rockwall, as well as the Boine massif. Wonder Pass is aptly named. A less strenuous sidetrip than Windy Ridge, it quickly lofts you into wondrous alpine scenery. Proceed through the pass, down the other side, then up to Wonder Pass viewpoint to overlook Marvel Lake (also aptly named) and to gaze at numerous glacier-mantled peaks. Only day-hike to Wonder Pass, of course, if it's not how you're entering or exiting the Mt. Assiniboine Region. Even if you enter or exit via Citadel Pass, however, Windy Ridge offers a sufficiently different perspective that it's a worthwhile sidetrip.

Cerulean Lake and The Marshall, from the Nublet

APPROACHES TO LAKE MAGOG

Choose between two approaches to Lake Magog: 29 km (18 mi) starting at Sunshine Village and hiking over Citadel Pass, or 27.5 km (17 mi) starting at Mt. Shark trailhead and hiking along Bryant Creek, then over Assiniboine Pass or Wonder Pass. The distances are too similar to be distinguishing criteria. Your choice will depend on how much time you have, and how willing you are to arrange a shuttle.

You can spare yourself the expense of the bus up to Sunshine Village by driving to Mt. Shark trailhead. On a round trip starting here, hike over Assiniboine Pass first. It's the easiest, quickest access to Lake Magog, it climaxes with an arresting view of The Boine, and it poses a less taxing ascent than does Wonder Pass. Upon departing Magog, create a circuit by hiking over Wonder Pass (much easier in this direction) then down past Marvel Lake. The disadvantage to this plan is having to hike the Bryant Creek trail (a monotonous exercise in scenery deprivation) not just once, but twice. While the circuit adds scenic variety, you'd see much more by hiking one way, starting at Sunshine Village and ending at Mt. Shark trailhead. (Arrange the shuttle with friends, or book with White Mountain Adventures—listed below, under *By Bus*.) The ideal Mt. Assiniboine Park tour, however, is feasible only if you have sufficient time: hike in *and* out via Citadel Pass, and devote two or three days to sidetrips from your Lake Magog basecamp; one of those, of course, being to Wonder Pass.

Hiking from Sunshine Village over Citadel Pass is the optimal start to this world-class trek. As described in Trip 3, you'll begin above treeline and spend the first several hours striding through sky-high alplands that unleash a brilliant wildflower display in summer. Trudging through forest from Mt. Shark trailhead is purgatorial by comparison. Strong hikers who depart Sunshine early can make it all the way to Lake Magog. An early start should enable most hikers to march 20.6 km (12.8 mi) to Og Lake campground on day one. A late start might necessitate spending the first night at Porcupine campground, at 13.3 km (8.3 mi). Only if you start lake *and* hike slowly should you spend the first night at Howard Douglas Lake campground, at 5.7 km (3.5 mi).

Reaching Porcupine campground entails detouring off the main trail. It's a steep descent on a rough spur. The campground is secluded, tranquil, deep in forest, apparently unmaintained. From Porcupine, you have the choice of ascending directly back to the main trail, or staying low and following a minor trail until it rejoins the main trail in Golden Valley. The minor trail is a bit more demanding overall but spares you the all-at-once ascent. Traveling in the opposite direction (exiting Lake Magog via Citadel Pass), you'll make more progress by continuing to Porcupine rather than stopping at Og Lake campground. If the Lake Magog area was hectic during your visit, you might appreciate the serenity of Porcupine. Upon departing Porcupine and heading for Citadel Pass, however, the sharp ascent to the main trail is unavoidable.

Besides Simpson River (Trip 112), rated *Don't Do*, the only other way to access Lake Magog is via Marvel Pass. Perched at the head of three valleys, surrounded by glorious mountains, Marvel Pass is indeed marvelous. There are two ways to get there. The Aurora Creek trail is highly scenic, but it's outside Banff Park and starts at a remote trailhead off the Kootenay-Palliser Forest Service road, so it's not in this book. The other way to reach Marvel Pass is via the Owl Lake trail (Trip 107), branching off the Bryant Creek trail. It's an inefficient, roundabout way to get to Lake Magog. And, until cresting Marvel Pass, it affords no views that warrant the extra time and effort. Consider it a *Don't Do*.

Finally, a request. Please respect the reverie of fellow Magogites. The campground is huge and frequently populous. Never yell—day or night. Be rock quiet after 10 p.m. Anyone who hikes this far is entitled to tranquility. If your loud, obnoxious behaviour disturbs others here, you deserve whatever retribution they choose to inflict.

RECOMMENDED ITINERARIES

Five Days

A journey of less than five days will force you to make difficult choices and skip significant sights. For example, "Should I go to Wonder Pass, or Nub Peak?" Allow yourself five days and you can see both, plus a lot more. Start by catching the shuttle bus up to Sunshine Village, then backpack over Citadel Pass and camp at Og Lake. On day two, backpack to Lake Magog, pitch your tent, then dayhike past Sunburst and Cerulean lakes to Nub Peak. On day three, dayhike past Gog Lake, over Wonder Pass, to Wonder Pass viewpoint. On day four,

From Citadel Pass, en route to Golden Valley

dayhike through Og Meadows to Windy Ridge. On day five, depart Lake Magog early and backpack all the way to Sunshine Village. Arrive by 5 p.m. to catch the last shuttle bus down to the parking lot. Or, if you can't cover that distance in a single day, instead of dayhiking to Windy Ridge on day four, backpack to Og Lake or Porcupine campgrounds, then backpack out to Sunshine Village on day five.

Four Days

Start by catching the shuttle bus up to Sunshine Village, then backpack over Citadel Pass and camp at Og Lake. On day two, backpack to Lake Magog, pitch your tent, then dayhike past Sunburst and Cerulean lakes to Nub Peak. On day three, break camp, backpack to the Naiset cabins. Leave your food in the bear-proof food storage and your pack in a cabin, then dayhike past Gog Lake, over Wonder Pass, to Wonder Pass viewpoint. Upon returning to the cabins, reclaim your food and gear, then backpack to Og Lake and camp there. On day four, depart Og Lake early and backpack to Sunshine Village. Arrive by 5 p.m. to catch the last shuttle bus down to the parking lot.

Three Days

You won't see it all in three days, but you can see a lot—if you're strong and motivated. You'll need to arrange a shuttle, either with friends or White Mountain Adventures. Start by catching the first shuttle bus up to Sunshine Village, then backpack over Citadel Pass—all the way to Lake Magog if possible, or at least to Og Lake. Reaching Magog in a single day is problematic in September. But you should have ample time in July, when the sun doesn't set until 10 p.m. Moderate-paced hikers can reach Magog by 8 p.m. Consider cooking dinner en route, perhaps at Og Lake. On day two, whether or not you have to finish backpacking to Lake Magog, dayhike past Sunburst and Cerulean lakes to Nub Peak. On day three, depart Lake Magog early, backpack over Wonder Pass, down past Marvel Lake, and out Bryant Creek to the Mt. Shark trailhead. Just how early you must leave Magog depends on your shuttle arrangement. It's possible to cover that distance in 7½ hours. Most hikers will take 9 hours.

FACT

Cycling is no longer permitted on the Bryant Creek trail. You can still ride the short distance from Mt. Shark trailhead to Trail Centre, but it's not worth the trouble.

During September and October, hunting is permitted in Mt. Assiniboine Park, outside the core area. That's west of Cerulean Lake, and between Og Lake and Citadel Pass. Stay on the trail, be aware, and be bright.

Before your trip

Pack a reliable stove and plenty of fuel. Open fires are prohibited in the Lake Magog area.

If you intend to stay at Howard Douglas Lake campground (northwest of Citadel Pass), any of the campgrounds along Bryant Creek, or in the Bryant Creek shelter, make reservations with the Banff Info Centre.

Camping reservations are unnecessary in Mt. Assiniboine Park, but there is a fee at Og Lake and Lake Magog campgrounds. Bring cash to pay the warden. Porcupine campground (just south of Citadel Pass) is little used and apparently unmaintained. In the unlikely event that a warden shows up at Porcupine and asks you to pay, have cash available, but before handing it over ask him to point out precisely what it is you're paying for—other than his fee-collection service. Mitchell Meadow campground, between Cerulean Lake and Ferro Pass, is unmaintained and free of charge.

To stay in the Naiset cabins, near Lake Magog, make reservations with Mt. Assiniboine Lodge (see contact info below). Hike without a tent only if you're certain you have a reservation. You'll still need a mattress, sleeping bag, stove and fuel. The cabins are frequently booked full, and each accommodates four people, so expect to get chummy with new acquaintances.

To stay at Mt. Assiniboine Lodge (www.assiniboinelodge.com), check current prices and make reservations by writing to info@assiniboinelodge.com, or phoning (403) 678-2883.

Mt. Assiniboine and Lake Magog

By Vehicle

Sunshine Ski Area Parking Lot

Drive the Trans-Canada Hwy east 21 km (13 mi) from Castle Junction, or west 9 km (5.6 mi) from Banff townsite. Turn south onto the signed Sunshine Village road. Proceed 8.3 km (5.1 mi) to the parking lot at the gondola station. The gondola does not operate in summer.

Mt. Shark trailhead

Drive the Trans-Canada Hwy to Canmore, just southeast of Banff Park's East Gate. Through downtown, follow signs directing you to the Nordic Centre and Spray Lakes. From the Nordic Centre, the trailhead is more than 40 km (24.8 mi) distant, mostly via good, gravel road. Passing the Nordic Centre, proceed onto unpaved Smith-Dorrien/Spray Trail (Hwy 742). Ascend through Whiteman's Gap. Drive south into Kananaskis Country. Pass the south end of Spray Lakes reservoir. Turn right (west) onto Watridge logging road, signed for Mt. Engadine Lodge. Continue 5.3 km (3.3 mi) to Mt. Shark trailhead, at 1770 m (5805 ft).

Break-ins have become common here. Hide valuables, so they're not visible to thieves peering into your vehicle. Better yet, leave nothing of value. To be completely safe, use the White Mountain Adventures shuttle bus, described below.

By Bus

From the parking lot at the Sunshine gondola station, a restricted-use access road ascends 6.5 km (4 mi) to Sunshine Village, at 2200 m (7215 ft). You can hike the road, or ride the White Mountain Adventures shuttle bus. Call 1-800-408-0005 (403-760-4403) for current schedules, prices and reservations. Buses operate the third week of June through September 30. Service is offered every hour, on the hour. If requested by backpackers, a bus departs as early as 8 a.m. Shuttles return every hour on the ¼ hour until 12:15 pm and every hour on the ½ hour from 2:30 pm until 5:30 pm (4:30 pm after Sept. 6th). White Mountain also offers shuttle service to Sunshine Village from Banff townsite and Canmore.

Want to backpack one-way without shuttling your own vehicles? White Mountain will pick you up at 4 p.m. (mountain daylight savings time, on the day you specify in advance), in the Mt. Shark trailhead, after you exit via Bryant Creek. Service usually starts the third week of June. The bus will take you back to Canmore. Want to enter via Bryant Creek? Inquire about dropoff times at Mt. Shark.

On Foot

TRIP 75 – SUNSHINE VILLAGE TO LAKE MAGOG CAMPGROUND VIA CITADEL PASS

ONE WAY	29 km (18 mi)
ELEVATION CHANGE	520-m (1706-ft) gain; 605-m (1985-ft) loss
KEY ELEVATIONS	Citadel Pass 2360 m (7740 ft) Valley of the Rocks 2045 m (6708 ft) Og Lake campground 2060 m (6757 ft) Lake Magog campground 2190 m (7183 ft)
HIKING TIME	9 to 12 hours
DIFFICULTY	moderate

Follow the directions in Trip 3 from Sunshine Village to **Citadel Pass**, at 9.3 km (5.8 mi), 2360 m (7740 ft). Just below the pass, shortly after entering Mt. Assiniboine Provincial Park, fill your water bottles at the tarns. Water will then likely be scarce until Og Lake, unless you drop to Porcupine campground.

From Citadel Pass, the trail descends southeast, initially at a gentle grade. Beyond the tarns in the alpine meadows, enter forest of larch and alpine fir. About five minutes farther, the switchbacking descent steepens dramatically, but it eases again within 15 minutes.

The forest is lush, the trees beautiful, the undergrowth bushy; you're obviously in British Columbia now. About 45 minutes down, two structures are visible south-southwest in Police Meadows, across the forested **upper Simpson River Valley**. A cascade plummets into the valley from a basin high above on Simpson Ridge. You can even hear the Simpson River, far below. Reach a junction at 12.7 km (7.9 mi), 2065 m (6773 ft). Right descends southwest, plunging 205 m (672 ft) in 0.6 km (0.4 mi) to **Porcupine campground**. If you stay there, it's unnecessary to ascend back to this junction. A lower trail runs southeast from the campground. It rejoins the main, upper trail in Golden Valley, en route to Og Lake, about 2 km (1.2 mi) from Porcupine.

Go left (south-southeast) at the 12.7-km (7.9-mi) junction to continue on the main, upper trail. A gently descending traverse ensues, across the brushy slope of

Golden Mtn. The luxuriant upper Simpson River Valley is below you, west and southwest. Beside the trail, watch for lavender penstemon, Indian paintbrush, pink wild roses, white yarrow, pale yellow locoweed, and grass-of-Parnassus.

Reach the next junction at 15.1 km (9.4 mi), 2015 m (6610 ft), in **Golden Valley**. If you're desperate for water, there might be a shallow pond right (west) 30.5 m (100 ft) below the trail. Reaching it entails negotiating a small rockslide. Proceed straight (southeast) for Og Lake, 5.5 km (3.4 mi) distant. Right (west) ascends briefly, descends steeply, then undulates north-northwest to Porcupine campground, 2 km (1.2 mi) distant. That's the lower trail mentioned earlier.

Heading for Og Lake, soon enter **Valley of the Rocks**. The trail wiggles generally southeast for a couple kilometres through rolling, open forest studded with a chaotic array of sharp boulders and rock clumps. Elevation: 2045 m (6708 ft). Dull, gray talus slopes are visible left (east).

After hiking about three hours from Citadel Pass, attain a view of **Og Lake** below (south) and Mt. Assiniboine beyond. Descend to reach the **campground**, above the west shore, at 20.6 km (12.8 mi), 2060 m (6757 ft). Wardens (rangers) rarely patrol here, so there's an iron ranger (hollow metal post) for depositing camping fees. It's a disappointing campground: treeless and sloping. There's bear-proof food storage and a toilet here, but little else. No tables. Not even level tentsites. The Park did manage, however, to build a substantial but unnecessary info kiosk. At least the view is excellent. Mt. Assiniboine and (left of it) Mt. Magog are south. Cave Mtn is southeast. Windy Ridge on Og Mtn is northeast. The ridgeline linking Cave and Og is the boundary separating B.C. from Alberta, and Assiniboine Provincial Park from Banff National Park.

Departing Og Lake, the trail ascends gradually through willow bushes and meadows. Your general direction will remain south all the way to Lake Magog. The view ahead to Mt. Assiniboine grows increasingly impressive.

You'll soon encounter numerous junctions. All are clearly signed. Our detailed written directions should be unnecessary. Simply follow the signs. It's easier and more enjoyable than stopping to read every few minutes. And it will help you better understand the network of trails in the heart of Mt. Assiniboine Park, so you can start dayhikes more efficiently.

Reach a signed **junction** at 24.6 km (15.3 mi), 2120 m (6950 ft). Proceed straight (south) for Lake Magog. Og Pass and Windy Ridge (described below as a dayhike from Magog) are left (north-northeast).

After pretty subalpine forest, continue south through a small, rocky gap. Two minutes farther, reach a signed **junction**. Go left (southeast) for Lake Magog campground.

After a gentle ascent, intersect the **Assiniboine Pass trail** at 27 km (16.7 mi), 2165 m (7100 ft). Sharp left leads northeast to Assiniboine Pass in 2 km (1.2 mi). Turn right (southwest) for Lake Magog campground.

At the next **junction**, proceed straight (south-southwest) for Lake Magog campground, 1.6 km (1 mi) distant. Left (southeast) leads to Mt. Assiniboine Lodge in 0.5 km (0.3 mi), the Naiset cabins in 1 km (0.6 mi), and Wonder Pass in 3.5 km (2.2 mi).

Pass a panoramic view of Lake Magog and Mt. Assiniboine, then reach another **junction**. Straight (west) leads to Lake Magog campground, 1 km (0.6 mi) distant.

Right (northwest) reaches Sunburst Lake in 1.5 km (0.9 mi), Elizabeth Lake in 3.5 km (2.2 mi), and Nub Peak in 4.5 km (2.8 mi).

At the next **junction**, proceed straight (southwest) for Lake Magog campground. Left leads southeast to the lodge and cabins.

Finally, having hiked 29 km (18 mi) from Sunshine Village, enter **Lake Magog campground**, at 2190 m (7183 ft).

TRIP 76a – LAKE MAGOG CAMPGROUND TO NUB PEAK VIA SUNBURST AND CERULEAN LAKES

ROUND TRIP	11.4 km (7.1 mi)
ELEVATION GAIN	558 m (1830 ft)
HIKING TIME	5½ hours
DIFFICULTY	moderate

Begin near the #2 tentsite, at the northeast corner of Lake Magog campground. Elevation: 2190 m (7183 ft). Follow the trail north, paralleling the stream.

Near tentsites 25 and 26, and the bear-proof food storage, go right (north) and cross the stream. At the signed fork, proceed straight (west). About ten minutes from the #2 tentsite, reach **Sunburst Lake**, at 2230 m (7314 ft), beneath the cliffs of the Sunburst Peaks. Directly north is Nub Ridge and the Nublet. North-northwest is rounded Nub Peak. They're connected by a rough ridge.

Continue northwest, bearing left where a trail joins from the right (east). Soon reach the northeast shore of **Cerulean Lake**, at 1.9 km (1.2 mi). Mt. Watson (flat summit) is visible southwest. The Marshall is south-southwest, behind the ridge of Wedgwood Peak, which is south beyond Sunburst Peaks. The trail forks here at Cerulean Lake. Left rounds the lake's north and west shores, en route to Wedgwood Lake and Mitchell River. Go straight (north) for Elizabeth Lake and the Nub.

A moderate ascent leads to a signed **junction** at 2280 m (7478 ft). Straight (north-northwest) is briefly level before dropping steeply to Elizabeth Lake then continuing to Ferro Pass via Sunburst Valley. (The lake is not visible from the junction and is only partially visible on the descent.) Turn sharply right (east) for the Nub. A few minutes above, attain an improved view of Cerulean Lake and The Marshall.

At 3.6 km (2.2 mi), 2392 m (7846 ft), reach a junction in the saddle on **Nub Ridge**. A sign points back in the direction of Elizabeth Lake. Sharp left ascends north to the Nublet. Right (southeast), just five minutes farther, is a knoll affording a panoramic view. A trail continues down the far side of the knoll, reaching Mt. Assiniboine Lodge in about 3 km (1.9 mi). In summer, yellow cinquefoil, moss campion, and alpine forget-me-nots brighten the knoll. The view is, of course, dominated by the Mt. Assiniboine massif. Most of the park's core area is visible as well, including Lake Magog and the lakes you recently hiked past: Sunburst and Cerulean.

From the junction in the saddle on Nub Ridge, it's a vigourous 15-minute ascent north to an even better view atop **the Nublet**, at 4.1 km (2.5 mi), 2535 m (8315 ft). For the ultimate vantage, proceed north-northwest to Nub Peak.

Expect a mild sense of exposure along the narrow ridge high above Elizabeth Lake. At 2625 m (8610 ft), attain a broad slope where walking requires less care. Just

Overlooking Nestor Creek basin, from Nub Peak

keep aiming for the highpoint north-northwest. The view comprises Og Pass (northeast), Assiniboine Pass (east), and the forested approach to Ferro Pass (west). Wedgwood Lake (southwest) is increasingly visible as you ascend.

About 1¼ hours after departing the Nublet, top out on **Nub Peak** at 5.7 km (3.5 mi), 2748 m (9013 ft). The view is awesome. Og Lake is north-northeast, Valley of the Rocks north, even the traverse above upper Simpson River valley is visible north-northwest. Ball Peak is distant northwest. Below you, southwest, are Nestor Creek and Mitchell Meadow. Also below you, northwest, are two small lakes in an otherwise hidden subalpine basin. Distant southeast, beyond Wonder Pass, are several big peaks in Kananaskis Country. South-southeast, slightly beyond and left of Mt. Assiniboine, is Eon Mtn.

TRIP 76b – ASSINIBOINE LODGE TO NUB PEAK

ROUND TRIP	10 km (6.2 mi)
ELEVATION GAIN	568 m (1863 ft)
HIKING TIME	3 to 4 hours
DIFFICULTY	moderate

Begin at Mt. Assiniboine Lodge, above the northeast shore of Lake Magog. Elevation: 2180 m (7150 ft). Go right (northwest) on the trail in front of the lodge. Quickly reach a junction; go left (west). The trail forks at another junction; go right.

Then reach a three-way junction; go left (west). You're now on the Nub Ridge trail ascending generally west.

Reach a junction where left leads to Sunburst and Cerulean lakes. Go right and ascend northwest. After hiking about 3 km (1.9 mi) from the lodge, reach a junction in the saddle on **Nub Ridge**, at 2392 m (7846 ft). Here you have a choice: (1) follow the trail descending left (west) to Cerulean or Elizabeth lakes, or (2) ascend north another 2 km (1.2 mi) to Nub Peak.

(1) Go left (west) at the saddle. Descend to a junction where right drops north to **Elizabeth Lake**, left drops southeast to **Cerulean Lake**. At the junction on Cerulean Lake's northeast shore, go left toward **Sunburst Lake**. Soon reach another junction. Go left again to intersect the Nub Ridge trail beneath Nub Ridge. You're now on familiar ground and can retrace your steps back to the lodge.

(2) Go north from the saddle and ascend 15 minutes to the **Nublet**, at 2535 m (8315 ft). From there, continue 1¼ hours up the ridgecrest north-northwest to the 2748-m (9013-ft) summit of **Nub Peak**. For more detailed directions, read the *Lake Magog Campground to Nub Peak via Sunburst and Cerulean Lakes* description, starting at the fifth paragraph.

TRIP 77 – LAKE MAGOG CAMPGROUND TO MT. SHARK TRAILHEAD VIA WONDER PASS AND BRYANT CREEK

ONE WAY	27.5 km (17 mi)
ELEVATION GAIN	230 m (754 ft)
HIKING TIME	8 to 10 hours
DIFFICULTY	easy

Begin near the #2 tentsite, at the northeast corner of Lake Magog campground. Elevation: 2190 m (7183 ft). Immediately cross the bridge over the stream. Stay on the trail leading northeast around Lake Magog's north shore. Bear right at all junctions. Follow signs for the Naiset cabins.

In 20 minutes, at 1.4 km (0.9 mi), pass the left spur to **Mt. Assiniboine Lodge**. Cross a bridge over Magog Creek. On boardwalk, pass between the **Naiset cabins** (right) and the **park headquarters** cabin (left) at 1.9 km (1.2 mi). The trail leads southeast, following Gog Creek upstream, ascending gently across meadows and through open, larch-strewn forest.

At 2.4 km (1.5 mi), cross a bridge to Gog Creek's east bank. The trail continues upstream (southeast). Pass the northeast corner of **Gog Lake** at 2.8 km (1.7 mi). The trail gradually steepens. Larch prevail on the grassy slopes. Re-cross the creek. Switchbacks aid your ascent. At 3.7 km (2.3 mi), 2290 m (7511 ft), overlook a waterfall in a bedrock punchbowl. Slender pinnacles called The Towers are prominent right (south) on a rugged ridge. Crest 2395-m (7856-ft) **Wonder Pass** 4.3 km (2.7 mi) from Lake Magog campground.

Crossing the pass, the trail enters Banff Park and descends south. Near the last rise, before the larches, reach a fork at 5 km (3.1 mi). A cairned left spur leads southeast 0.6 km (0.4 mi) to **Wonder Pass viewpoint**, on an open slope. Don't stop at the plateau with a partial view. Skirt that small rise, then drop to a more open vantage. Aye Mtn is southwest. Mt. Gloria is south-southwest, and Eon Mtn is beyond it.

Mt. Gloria, Eon and Aye mtns, above Lake Gloria, from Wonder Pass trail

Below, Lake Gloria is southwest, long Marvel Lake is southeast, and tiny Lake Terrapin is between them. Marvel Peak is southeast, above Marvel Lake.

From the 5-km (3.1-mi) fork, follow the main trail south. Begin a long, steep, switchbacking descent. The view improves below. Reach a junction at 7.4 km (4.6 mi). Right continues plunging south, crosses the inlet stream near Marvel Lake's southwest shore, then climbs south to Marvel Pass (Trip 107). Go left on the main trail. Descending more gradually now, it leads northeast through forest and across rocky avalanche paths above the northwest shore of **Marvel Lake**.

At 12 km (7.5 mi) a spur forks right (south) to Marvel Lake's northeast end. Stay on the main trail, heading generally northeast. Cross Bryant Creek bridge at 13 km (8 mi), then cross meadows. At 13.3 km (8.2 mi), 1845 m (6052 ft), intersect the **Bryant Creek trail** near a warden cabin. Turn right and follow the broad, smooth, mostly-level trail generally southeast. Pass the Bryant Creek shelter, a right fork leading southwest back to Marvel Lake, and a right fork leading southwest past Owl Lake to Marvel Pass. Pass a warden cabin near the southwest tip of **Spray Lakes Reservoir**. The trail forks. Left leads northeast along the reservoir's northwest shore. Go right (south) and quickly reach another junction. Right (south) is the Palliser Pass trail. Go left, heading generally east-southeast past Watridge Lake, then generally east-northeast to **Mt. Shark trailhead**, at 1770 m (5806 ft). Total distance from Lake Magog campground: 27.5 km (17 mi).

Trip 78 – LAKE MAGOG CAMPGROUND TO OG PASS AND WINDY RIDGE

ROUND TRIP	20.4 km (12.6 mi)
ELEVATION GAIN	585 m (1919 ft)
HIKING TIME	6 to 7 hours
DIFFICULTY	moderate

Begin near the #2 tentsite, at the northeast corner of Lake Magog campground. Elevation: 2190 m (7183 ft). Immediately cross the bridge over the stream. Follow the trail northeast.

Reach a junction. Right leads to Mt. Assiniboine Lodge and the Naiset cabins. Proceed straight (northeast).

Reach the next junction at 1 km (0.6 mi). Left (northwest) leads to Sunburst Lake. Proceed straight (east). Pass a panoramic view of Lake Magog and Mt. Assiniboine.

Reach another junction at 1.6 km (1 mi). Right (southeast) leads to the lodge and cabins. Proceed straight (north-northeast).

At 2 km (1.2 mi), 2165 m (7100 ft), reach another junction. Right leads northeast to Assiniboine Pass, 2 km (1.2 mi) distant. Go left. The trail gently descends northwest to another signed junction. Proceed straight (north) through a small, rocky gap.

At 4.4 km (2.7 mi), 2120 m (6950 ft), reach another signed junction. Straight (north) is the way to Og Lake, Valley of the Rocks, Citadel Pass, and Sunshine Village. Turn right (north-northeast) for Og Pass and Windy Ridge. The trail crosses **Og Meadows**.

Shortly beyond, bear left where the Assiniboine Pass horse trail forks right. Soon begin ascending north into forest.

At 8 km (5 mi) reach a junction. Go left (north) for Windy Ridge. Right leads northeast, cresting 2309-m (7574-ft) **Og Pass** in 0.3 km (0.2 mi), then descending southeast to intersect the Allenby Pass trail.

Ascend among larches, cross a prolific alpine flower garden with a panoramic view, and continue up a steep talus slope. Crest **Windy Ridge**, a saddle on Og Mtn, at 10.2 km (6.3 mi), 2635 m (8643 ft). On the east side, 427 m (1400 ft) directly below, is a blue tarn in a hanging valley. You can also see northeast down forested Brewster Valley. Look for Halfway Cabin on the edge of a meadow.

LAKE MAGOG CAMPGROUND TO SUNSHINE VILLAGE VIA PORCUPINE CAMPGROUND

ONE WAY	29.3 km (18.2 mi)
ELEVATION GAIN	830 m (2722 ft)
HIKING TIME	9 to 12 hours
DIFFICULTY	moderate

Leave Lake Magog campground as if heading for Og Pass and Windy Ridge (described above). Reach a signed junction at 4.4 km (2.7 mi), 2120 m (6950 ft). Right (north-northeast) leads to Og Pass and Windy Ridge. Proceed straight (north) to reach **Og Lake campground** at 8.4 km (5.2 mi), 2060 m (6757 ft).

Before departing Og Lake, fill your water bottles. Between here and the tarns just below the south side of Citadel Pass, water is scarce. The only reliable water source is Porcupine campground.

From Og Lake, follow the trail ascending north. Soon enter **Valley of the Rocks**. The trail wiggles generally northwest for a couple kilometres through rolling, open forest studded with a chaotic array of sharp boulders and rock clumps. Elevation: 2045 m (6708 ft).

Reach a **junction** at 13.9 km (8.6 mi), 2015 m (6610 ft), in **Golden Valley**. If you're desperate for water, there might be a shallow pond left (west) 30.5 m (100 ft) below the trail. Reaching it entails negotiating a small rockslide. Straight (north) is the higher, main trail that bypasses Porcupine campground and heads directly to Citadel Pass, saving a little distance and some elevation loss/gain. Turn left (west) for the lower trail to Porcupine.

Briefly ascend past the pond, descend steeply 37 m (120 ft) on a rough slope, then contour north-northwest. The trail is narrow but distinct. It drops a bit more before leveling in shrubby vegetation.

Soon the trail resumes undulating. Gain and lose 24 m (80 ft). Almost an hour from the pond, reach a **junction** at 15.5 km (9.6 mi). Left leads generally southwest into upper Simpson River Valley, arriving at Police Meadows shelter in 2.5 km (1.5 mi). Go right (north-northwest) for Porcupine. About five minutes farther, pass a left spur leading to the dodgy-looking but functional bear-proof food storage. One minute farther, enter **Porcupine campground**, at 16 km (9.9 mi), 1860 m (6100 ft). Immediately after passing the first tentsite (right), hop over a creeklet. The trail curves left to reach the other tentsites—among tall trees, beside a small meadow. There's a ramshackle outhouse here, but little else. The campground is rough, apparently unmaintained.

Leaving Porcupine campground, follow the trail past the outhouse, around the meadow, northeast into forest. It ascends moderately for the first ten minutes, severely for the next ten, then varies. The trail is just a route—a narrow, overgrown, eroded scratch in the dirt—but it serves its purpose. About 35 minutes from Porcupine, having gained 205 m (672 ft) in 0.6 km (0.4 mi), intersect the main, **upper trail** at 16.6 km (10.3 mi), near 2065 m (6773 ft). Right (south-south-east) leads back through Golden Valley and Valley of the Rocks, past Og Lake to Lake Magog. Go left and continue ascending steeply north to crest 2360-m (7740-ft) **Citadel Pass** at 20 km (12.4 mi). From there, the trail leads generally northwest, past Howard Douglas Lake, to reach **Sunshine Village** at 29.3 km (18.2 mi), 2195 m (7200 ft).

Porcupine

TRIP 79

Gibbon, Whistling & Healy Passes

LOCATION	Banff National Park
SHUTTLE TRIP	40.4 km (25 mi)
ELEVATION GAIN	1730 m (5670 ft)
KEY ELEVATIONS	trailhead 1695 m (5560 ft) Gibbon Pass 2300 m (7545 ft) Shadow Lake 1852 m (6075 ft) Whistling Pass 2290 m (7511 ft) Egypt Lake camp 1995 m (6545 ft) Healy Pass 2330 m (7642 ft) Sunshine parking lot 1675 m (5495 ft)
HIKING TIME	2 to 3 days
DIFFICULTY	moderate
MAPS	page 506; Gem Trek *Banff and Mt. Assiniboine*; Banff 82 0/4

OPINION

Naming this backpack trip after the passes it traverses is arbitrary. It could also be called "Twin, Shadow and Egypt Lakes." Knowing that, you can begin to fathom the scope and splendor of the journey. This is classic Banff National Park: big mountains, beautiful lakes, alpine passes, larch forest, spacious meadows, myriad wildflowers, even a glimpse of a glacier. Two or three days here just might sate a scenery glutton.

The passes received marquee billing, so let's begin with the lakes. Upper Twin is pretty. Lower Twin is impressive. Trip 41 describes the Twin Lakes, along with larch-fringed Gibbon Pass, in detail. Shadow Lake is gorgeous. Much bigger than the Twins, it looms beneath glacier-stuccoed Mt. Ball. You can visit Shadow Lake, as well as Whistling Pass and Egypt Lake, in an epic, one-day bike-and-hike (Trip 25). Of all these significant sights, however, only Egypt Lake is famous.

Long ago, a surveyor noted the name *Pharaoh Peaks* and recognized an opportunity for a refreshing, exotic theme. He named the nearby lakes Egypt, Scarab and Mummy. It's been a successful advertising campaign. This and Skoki Valley are the busiest backpacking destinations in Banff Park. But here, the product falls short of the image. Small, shrouded by forest, Egypt Lake's inflated popularity is due to its intriguing aura, proximity to Banff, and convenient campground and hut—not to its beauty. And certainly not to its tranquility. The area is often crowded. So don't fixate on Egypt Lake as a destination. Buzzing past it on this backpack trip should quell your curiosity.

Ascending to Whistling Pass. Mt. Ball upper left.

Indeed, you'll see Egypt Lake, and it's companion, Scarab Lake, from the two optimal perspectives: Whistling Pass and Healy Pass. These aerial vantages reveal not just the lakes, but the mountains ringing them. As a result, detouring to the lakeshores will likely seem unnecessary and would certainly be anticlimactic. Mummy Lake, however, will remain hidden from view. So, if you overnight at Egypt Lake campground, consider dashing to Mummy. It's above treeline and therefore more visually striking than its neighbours.

These two passes bookending Egypt Lake—Whistling and Healy—are the scenic climaxes of the trip. Whistling Pass is a sort of feral Japanese garden—both delicate and raw. After hiking past (and perhaps relaxing beside) marvelous Haiduk Lake, you can peer back down on it from Whistling Pass. Haiduk eclipses Egypt in every respect, yet remains little known and lightly visited. The Whistling Pass view even extends back to Mt. Ball and through Gibbon Pass. The name *Whistling Pass* refers to the resident marmots, also known as *whistlers*, or *whistle pigs*.

Whistling Pass is short, pinched between mountains. Healy Pass is different—a broad, open highland. In season, the sweeping Healy meadows detonate a dazzling floral display. And the Healy Pass perspective of Mt. Assiniboine makes that Matterhorn-look-alike appear invitingly close. From Healy, you'll not only see Egypt and Scarab lakes, but also the Pharaoh Peaks cupping tiny Pharaoh and Black Rock lakes. So your survey of the over-hyped Egypt Lake basin will be complete.

About that hut at Egypt Lake campground. It's just a cheerless shelter that sleeps 16. Even if you score a reservation, you might regret spending the night in such cramped, noisy quarters—unless you're of sufficient stature to make inconsiderate loudmouths quake with fear when you glare at them.

If swift and determined, you can bound over all three passes in two long days. Pitch your tent at Ball Pass Junction campground. If three days better suits your pace, there are campgrounds at Upper Twin Lake, Shadow Lake, Egypt Lake, plus a tiny one on Healy Creek. Upper Twin is usually tranquil and might be ideal if you start late the first day. Shadow Lake and Ball Pass Junction are also peaceful. You're an average hiker intending to start reasonably early? Stop at Shadow. Egypt Lake is the logical choice for a second night out, but it's usually jumpin'. If you don't mind company and/or you want scoot up to Mummy Lake, stay here. Healy Creek is useful only as a last resort, because it's just 7.2 km (4.5 mi) from trail's end at the Sunshine ski-area parking lot. In late fall, after an arid summer, Healy Creek might be dry; inquire before reserving a site.

This being a one-way shuttle trip, you'll obviously need two vehicles or the gumption to hitchhike. Both options have drawbacks, but remember: this trip's worth it.

One final suggestion. Don't just give yourself a couple days. Give yourself at least a week. Let the trip described here be merely the first half of an even greater trek. From Healy Creek, continue over Simpson Pass to Sunshine Village. From there, follow directions in Trip 75. Hike over Citadel Pass to Mt. Assiniboine, then exit via Wonder Pass and Bryant Creek. Now, that's an adventure you'll talk about the rest of your life.

Mt. Ball, from Haiduk Lake

FACT

Before your trip

Considering the shuttle trip but lack a second vehicle? Hitchhiking is possible but will likely be difficult. It will probably require three separate rides. Try it the morning you start the hike, rather than the evening you finish.

To stay in the Egypt Lake hut, check current prices and make reservations with the Banff Info Centre.

By Vehicle

Follow directions for Trip 41 to reach the Vista Lake trailhead on Hwy 93, where you'll begin hiking. Follow directions for Trip 3 to leave a vehicle at the Sunshine parking lot, where you'll finish hiking.

On Foot

Follow directions for Trip 41 to **Gibbon Pass**, at 2300 m (7545 ft). From the Vista Lake trailhead on Hwy 93, it's 10.9 km (6.8 mi) generally south- southeast. Proceed through the pass. At its southeast end, where the trail begins descending, icy Mt. Ball is visible right (south-southwest) beyond the slope of an unnamed peak.

After losing 445 m (1460 ft) in about 40 minutes, reach a signed T-junction at 14 km (8.7 mi). It's just 12 m/yd behind **Shadow Lake Lodge**. The cabins are ahead (south). Left (east) passes Shadow Lake campground within 1 km (0.6 mi), then follows Redearth Creek downstream (northeast) to Hwy 1. Go right (west, then southwest).

Soon cross a bridged creeklet and quickly arrive at a signed junction. The right (west) spur ascends briefly, rolls through forest along Shadow Lake's north shore, and eventually fades near the lake's southwest end, about 2 km (1.2 mi) distant. Proceed left (southwest) on the main trail.

In a few minutes, come to a large bridge over the outlet stream at the northeast end of **Shadow Lake**. Elevation: 1852 m (6075 ft). You've now hiked 15 km (9.3 mi) from the Vista Lake trailhead on Hwy 93. Proceed over the bridge. Follow the trail southwest, away from the lake.

About 20 minutes from the bridge, attain a view right (west-northwest) into the cirque (created by Storm Mtn on the north, Mt. Ball on the south) above Shadow Lake. A little farther, cross to the west bank of a bridged creek and continue upstream. Heading generally south, the narrow, rocky, rooty trail skirts a scruffy willow meadow.

About an hour from Shadow Lake, enter tight forest rife with sphagnum moss. Five minutes farther, reach **Ball Pass Junction campground**, at 19.3 km (12 mi). First, on the right, is a path to the cooking area and bear-proof food storage. Two minutes farther, immediately after a bridged creeklet, a right (south) spur accesses the six tent sites.

Immediately before that bridged creeklet, the trail forks. Right (southwest) ascends to 2202-m (7224-ft) Ball Pass in 2.7 km (1.7 mi). Due to the 2003 fire that ravaged Kootenay Park, this is now the best way to reach the pass. The other access, Hawk Creek canyon (Trip 69), was badly burned. The Ball Pass view, which includes the glacier atop Mt. Ball, remains unchanged, so the ascent is worthwhile.

Continuing to Whistling Pass from the bridged creeklet at Ball Pass Junction campground, follow the main trail left (east-southeast) into forest. After a 15-minute ascent, the trail levels at 1966 m (6450 ft). Five minutes farther, attain a view up-valley (southeast) to Whistling Pass. The cliffs of Haiduk Peak are right (west and southwest). Larch are increasingly prevalent. About an hour after leaving the campground, enter a long, flat, grassy meadow. Ten minutes farther reach **Haiduk Lake** at 21.8 km (13.5 mi), 2070 m (6790 ft).

The trail follows the east shore of the lake. Hop two inlet streams at the lake's southeast end, then begin an aggressive ascent into forest. After gaining 91 m (300 ft) in the next 15 minutes, you're again near a stream among larches. Step over two more streamlets prior to attaining 2290-m (7511-ft) **Whistling Pass,** at 24.7 km (15.3 mi). Haiduk Lake is visible below.

The trail descends generally southeast, into an alpine basin of primarily rock and grass, then switchbacks steeply down into forest. At 26.5 km (16.4 mi), 2180 m (7150 ft), reach a signed junction among larch and big fir. Right (south-southwest) leads to Scarab (0.8 km / 0.5 mi) and Mummy (1.5 km / 0.9 mi) lakes. Go left (northeast) for Egypt Lake and Healy Pass. After a short ascent, descend steeply again. About 40 minutes after departing Whistling Pass, having lost 280 m (918 ft), cross a marshy clearing.

Several minutes farther, arrive at a signed junction. Right (south) rapidly drops to Egypt Lake. Proceed straight, soon reaching **Egypt Lake campground** at 28 km (17.4 mi), 1995 m (6545 ft). The tent sites offer a modicum of privacy. They're on the edge of a meadow, backed by alpine fir, with a partial view of mountain cliffs. The Egypt Lake shelter is a minute farther. Shortly beyond that is the bridge over **Pharaoh Creek**.

Between the shelter and the creek, the trail forks. Left follows Pharaoh Creek downstream (generally north-northeast) to its confluence with Redearth Creek (Trip 25). For Healy Pass, bear right, cross the Pharaoh Creek bridge, then turn left (east). Right (south) crosses Redearth Pass in 2.4 km (1.5 mi), where a spur leads southwest 1.2 km (0.75 mi) to Natalko Lake.

Bound for Healy Pass, you'll see a warden cabin on the left, a few minutes from the Pharaoh Creek bridge. A long, moderately steep ascent ensues. About 30 minutes up, at 2150 m (7052 ft), larches appear. Ten minutes farther, attain a panoramic vantage. Egypt and Scarab lakes are west, across Pharaoh Creek valley. (Scarab is in the cirque above Egypt.) Haiduk Peak is west, above Whistling Pass. The Pharaoh Peaks are northwest, cupping the smaller Pharaoh and Black Rock lakes.

The trail levels in **Healy Pass** at 31.2 km (19.3 mi), 2330 m (7642 ft). The peaks visible from here are described in the last paragraph of Trip 24.

It's 9.2 km (5.7 mi) from Healy Pass, down Healy Creek, to the Sunshine parking lot. The elevation loss is 655 m (2148 ft). Departing the pass, the trail initially leads southeast. Reach junctions at 1.5 km (0.9 mi) and 3.4 km (2.1 mi) from the pass. Bear left at both; right at either accesses Simpson Pass and Eohippus Lake. At 3.8 km (2.4 mi) from the pass, reach a small campground beside Healy Creek. Upon arrival at the **Sunshine parking lot**, you'll have hiked 40.4 km (25 mi) from the Vista Lake trailhead on Hwy 93.

Lupine

TRIP 80
Pipestone Pass / Devon Lakes

LOCATION	Banff National Park
ROUND TRIP	60 km (37.2 mi)
ELEVATION GAIN	1768 m (5800 ft)
KEY ELEVATIONS	trailhead 1830 m (6000 ft) North Molar Pass 2590 m (8500 ft) Fish Lakes 2225 m (7300 ft) Pipestone Pass 2460 m (8070 ft) Clearwater Pass 2340 m (7660 ft) Upper Devon Lake 2315 m (7590 ft)
HIKING TIME	3 to 5 days
DIFFICULTY	moderate
MAPS	page 514; Hector Lake 82 N/9

OPINION

High-elevation hiking is soul expanding in a way that a walk in the woods just isn't, no matter how beautiful the forest. In the upper-subalpine and alpine zones—where trees are few and unobtrusive, the views vast and constant—we're released from physical and mental confinement. Our awareness swells with the spaciousness.

These moments of high-country rapture are rare and fleeting. That's why the trek over North Molar Pass, beyond Fish Lakes, through Pipestone Pass, up to Clearwater Pass, and down to Devon Lakes, is *Premier*. Fully 28 km (17.5 mi) of it is high elevation.

Striding that far through such a scenic, wild vastness might open you in surprising ways, for example to the concept that you and the earth are not separate. That light and eye, oxygen and lung, ground and foot, are, as Asian philosophers articulate it, *not two*. Or, as the Gaia Hypothesis suggests, that all of Earth's billions of life forms, you included, are a single, conscious, living being.

Can a backpack trip really have such a psilocybin effect? Find out. Follow the directions in Trip 88 to Fish Lakes campground. Upper Fish Lake, between a fortress-like wall and spacious alplands, is a lovely setting for an evening and morning in the mountains. Across the Pipestone River Valley, 3333-m (10,932-ft) Cataract Peak and its brawny brethren seem to barricade the eastern front. The sense of isolation here is delicious. Civilization, it seems, is a long way off, doesn't need you, nor you it. Yet you're about to leave it even farther behind. The next leg of the journey is a long, relatively gentle yet continually exhilarating high-country traverse. Pipestone Pass is starkly alluring, almost frighteningly feral, and a superb vantage. Lonelier yet are the rolling alplands of Clearwater Pass. And Devon Lakes are on the edge of the back-of-beyond.

Upper Fish Lake. Cataract Peak beyond.

Between Fish Lakes and Pipestone Pass, a highline trail has developed that's easier, more direct, and more scenic than the Pipestone River Valley trail. Only the valley trail, however, is indicated on the Hector Lake 82 N/9 topo map. Yet it's critical—for efficiency and enjoyment—that you hike the highline. This sensible, genial path contours northwest, along the upper valley's southwest side. It's evident the entire way and poses no difficulties other than a few mucky sections.

Recommended itinerary? Four days is rational and comfortable, allowing you to spend nights one and three at Fish Lakes, night two at Devon.

It's taxing, rushed, but feasible to see it all in three days. Here's the challenge: 14.8 km (9.2 mi) to Fish Lakes on day one; 16.6 km (10.3 mi) over Pipestone Pass to Devon Lakes on day two; and 31.4 km (19.5 mi) all the way back out on day three. We've done it but don't recommend it. If, upon departing Devon, you want to hike farther than Fish Lakes (or must hike farther because you couldn't reserve a site at Fish Lakes campground), pitch your tent at Mosquito Creek campground on night three.

Because Fish Lakes campground is popular, often booked full, either reserve well in advance, or stay loose about your start date. Random camping is permitted in the remote Devon Lakes area, but you must (1) pitch your tent at least 70 m (76 yd) from any water source, (2) be bear aware (read *Bears,* page 34), and (3) leave no trace of your stay (read *Wilderness Ethics*, page 22).

FACT

Before your trip

No established campground at Devon Lakes means no convenient bear-proof food storage. Complicating matters, the alpine environment here lacks trees tall enough to hang food out of bears' reach. And bears do frequent the area. The optimal solution is to pack your food in a bear-proof canister or bag. Visit www.ursack.com to learn about a lightweight but still reasonably safe solution. Your food is packed in a normal, nylon stuff sack? As far as possible from your camp, either hang it off a tall escarpment, or bury it in a talus slope, then hope you're lucky.

By Vehicle

Follow the directions for North Molar Pass / Fish Lakes (Trip 88), to the Mosquito Creek trailhead, at 1830 m (6000 ft).

On Foot

Follow the directions in Trip 88 to **Fish Lakes campground**, midway along the upper lake's forested northwest shore, at 14.8 km (9.2 mi), 2225 m (7300 ft).

From the campground, proceed east-northeast on the main trail. Be alert. In 0.3 km (0.2 mi), arrive at a **signed fork**. Right soon plunges into the Pipestone River Valley. Turn left (northeast) and begin a brief descent. Pass between a meadow (left) and the **warden cabin** (right). Just below the cabin, rockhop a creek at 2140 m (7019 ft).

The trail then ascends into forest, switchbacking generally north. About 15 minutes above the creek, cross a **small meadow** at 2280 m (7478 ft). Descending north-northwest, reach the marshy, southeast end of **Moose Lake** at 2185 m (7167 ft), about 15 minutes below the small meadow. You've now hiked 18.5 km (11.3 mi) from Mosquito Creek trailhead.

Moose Lake, en route to Pipestone Pass

Rockhop the lake's **outlet stream**. Go left (north). The trail is faint in this perpetually soggy area, but it soon becomes distinct again. Stay on the principal path to avoid creating new scars. Continue around the lake's northeast shore. Proceed northwest. This will remain your general direction of travel nearly all the way to Pipestone Pass.

The trail rises through a few trees, crosses moist meadows, and requires you to rockhop a cascading stream. Pass right (west of) and above **Iceberg Lake** at 21 km (13 mi), 2280 m (7478 ft). The valley trail, climbing from the Pipestone River, is visible below.

Having reached drier, alpine terrain, the trail rises along the spine of a gentle ridge. Left (southwest) below you is a creek gully. Right (northeast) below you is the headwater drainage of the Pipestone River. Ahead (northwest) is a prominent **knoll**. On the knoll's left (southwest) side is 2425-m (7950-ft) Pipestone Pass. Right (northeast) of the knoll is the V-shaped gap you'll be hiking through.

Nearing the knoll, curve right (north) across red-hued scree on its southeast slope. The trail is sketchy here. Fix it in your mind, in case inclement weather on your return impairs visibility. In the **gap**, ascend right 20 m/yd to intersect the main **Pipestone River Valley trail** at 24 km (14.9 mi), 2460 m (8070 ft). You're now 1 km (0.6 mi) northeast of Pipestone Pass.

Devon Mtn is nearby, north. The view extends northwest, beyond the Siffleur River Valley's alpine upper reaches, nearly 19 km (12 mi) into its forested mid-section. Visible west-northwest of the knoll, are small lakes on a vast, gently-rolling alpine shelf that invites exploration.

Approaching Pipestone Pass

From the gap, the trail briefly ascends northeast before descending northwest. But if the gap is snow-free, descend directly northwest, down the draw, and rejoin the trail below. Either way, having exited the gap, follow the trail northwest. It descends moderately, then gently, along the west slope of **Devon Mtn**.

Reach a junction at 27 km (16.7 mi), 2256 m (7400 ft). Straight (northwest) continues descending the **Siffleur River Valley** (Trip 111). Turn right and follow the rough trail, ascending little terraces, 1 km (0.6 mi) northeast into the rolling, willow-and-heather meadows of 2340-m (7660-ft) **Clearwater Pass**. Biology trivia hounds might be interested to know this is the northern limit of subalpine larch in Alberta.

Proceed northeast through the pass. The braided trail bends east at 28.3 km (17.5 mi). Shallow **Upper Devon Lake** is visible ahead. Pass the lake's northwest shore at 28.6 km (17.7 mi), 2315 m (7590 ft). You're now north of Devon Mtn, which rises above the lake's south shore.

Carry on northeast, above the 0.7-km (0.4-mi) long lake's north shore. Near 30 km (18.6 mi), 2317 m (7600 ft), where the trail begins descending generally east into the forested **Clearwater River Valley**, abandon it. Turn right, rockhop the upper lake's outlet stream, and hike south-southeast. In about 1 km (0.6 mi), reach the larger of the two **Lower Devon Lakes**, at 2285 m (7490 ft), tucked below the northeast slope of Devon Mtn.

Between North Molar Pass and Fish Lakes

TRIP 81

The Skyline

LOCATION	Jasper National Park
SHUTTLE TRIP	44.5 km (27.6 mi) one way
ELEVATION CHANGE	1205-m (3952-ft) gain, 1735-m (5690-ft) loss
KEY ELEVATIONS	trailhead 1690 m (5543 ft) Big Shovel Pass 2320 m (7610 ft) Amber Mtn 2530 m (8300 ft)
HIKING TIME	2 to 3 days
DIFFICULTY	moderate
MAPS	page 513; Gem Trek *Jasper & Maligne Lake;* Athabasca Falls 83 C/12, Medicine Lake 83 C/13

OPINION

The human flair for getting up on our hind legs and not face-planting while we walk distinguishes us from other animals. Revel in that ability on the Skyline.

True to its name, the Skyline allows you to stride above treeline for days. Starting at Maligne Lake, you'll gain surprisingly little elevation for such a long hike. You'll have to gear down only once, midway, when you climb the Notch. The Skyline's topographical profile resembles the spine of a brontosaurus. It's way easier than the Rockwall (Trip 89), which is stegosaurus terrain.

You'll see peaks near and far, some ferocious, others meek. The limestone canines of the Queen Elizabeth Ranges are visible from the trail as it plies meadows spangled with flowers. The name Skyline refers to the section northwest of the Notch, where you walk a 4.5-km (2.8-mi) mountain crest with body-slam scenery in all directions. Southwest is 3368-m (11,047-ft) Mt. Edith Cavell, the biggest incisor in the northern two-thirds of Jasper Park. West are toothy peaks rising above Tonquin Valley (Trips 94-98). Northwest, 80 km (50 mi) distant, is Mt. Robson (Trips 82-84).

Fast trekkers can buzz this trip in two days and still have time to wallow in all the flowers: multi-hued Indian paintbrush, lavender lupine, bright yellow cinque-foil, and fluffy, white pulsatilla, to name a few. On the less hospitable dirt-and-rock passes, look for tenacious bluebells. Allow at least an extra day if you want to roam the green ridges west of the trail between Little and Big Shovel passes.

The final 8 km (5 mi) are on an old, viewless road descending Signal Mountain. It seems like a never-ending plunge, but you gotta pay if you wanna play. You'd be crazy to begin your hike straining up this end. Starting at Maligne Lake knocks 530 m (1738 ft) off your total elevation gain. If you have just one vehicle, leave it at the trailhead near the Maligne Canyon parking lot, then hitchhike to the lake. It shouldn't be difficult. When you finish the hike, having your vehicle waiting for you is a relief.

Over the Notch and onto the definitive Skyline ridge-walk, Mt. Edith Cavell in the distance

If you're traveling to Jasper from far afield, reserve campsites on the Skyline several months ahead—or risk missing this world-famous hike. Schedule your trip after late July, to ensure the Notch (a steep, narrow pass) will be sufficiently snow-free to allow safe passage. Curator campground, about half way, is the logical choice for your one night out on a two-day trip. But the viewless, trampled-dirt sites at Curator are dismal. Tekarra Lake campground, two-thirds of the way along, is more pleasant.

Don't get caught up here in a storm. This is an alpine route—high and exposed. You'll be vulnerable to lightning. Snowstorms are possible even in summer. Check the weather forecast at the Jasper Info Centre before heading out. Pack foul-weather gear, regardless.

FACT

By Vehicle

From the junction with Connaught Drive at the north end of Jasper townsite, drive Hwy 16 northeast 1.8 km (1.1 mi). Turn right (east) onto Maligne Lake Road. It's signed for Jasper Park Lodge. Set your odometre to 0 here, then cross the Athabasca River bridge. At 0.2 km (0.1 mi) go left for Maligne Lake. At 5.4 km (3.3 mi) turn right into the Signal Mountain trailhead parking area. This is the Skyline trail's northwest terminus, where we recommend ending the hike. If arranging a shuttle, leave one vehicle here. Otherwise, park here and hitchhike. If the Signal Mountain parking area is full, drive 0.8 km (0.5 mi) farther and park in the Maligne Canyon parking lot. This is where you should start hitchhiking anyway, just past where tourists resume driving to Maligne Lake.

To reach the southeast terminus of the Skyline trail—where we recommend starting the hike—drive or hitchhike the remaining 40 km (25 mi) to Maligne Lake. Continue past the lodge to the parking lot nearly at road's end. It's just above the lake's northwest shore, at 1690 m (5543 ft).

On Foot

The signed trailhead is just above the parking lot's southwest end, on the forest edge, 40 m/yd before the Bald Hills fire road. Head initially northwest, ascending at a gentle grade through lodgepole pine forest. Within half an hour, pass **Lorraine Lake** (left / southwest) at 2 km (1.2 mi), 1760 m (5770 ft), and **Mona Lake** (right / north-northeast) at 2.2 km (1.4 mi). The trail curves around Mona's southwest shore, high above it.

At 5.2 km (3.2 mi), 1817 m (5960 ft), reach a junction. Left (south-southeast) intersects the Bald Hills trail (Trip 36) in 2.2 km (1.4 mi). Bear right, immediately cross a bridge to the west bank of **Evelyn Creek**. The **campground** here has two tables and bear-proof food storage. Atop the next switchback, pass four tentsites. The ascent continues, tempered by more switchbacks. Heading west into the Maligne Range, the trail affords only glimpses through thinning forest until 2050 m (6724 ft), where the first vista (southwest to southeast) reveals rounded mountains with talus-slope sides.

A stream is audible in the forested valley below, just before reaching **Little Shovel campground** at 8.5 km (5.3 mi), 2140 m (7020 ft). It's in the trees and has a couple tables and bear-proof food storage. Five minute farther, the trail gently ascends into alplands. The road-trail on the Bald Hills is visible east-southeast, beyond the first ridge. The sharply-peaked Queen Elizabeth Range is east.

In alpine meadow, about 30 minutes beyond Little Shovel campground, the trail curves northwest and grants a revelatory view of the open terrain ahead. Crest **Little Shovel Pass** at 10.2 km (6.3 mi), 2240 m (7347 ft). The left side is mostly scree, the right largely heather and krummholz. From the pass, descend into the **Snowbowl**—a vast, alpine basin where wildflower meadows spread to the horizon.

The trail is rough where it drops into a gorge carved by a swift creek. Rockhop the creek at 2085 m (6840 ft). Five minutes beyond is **Snowbowl campground,** at 12.2 km (7.6 mi), 2090 m (6855 ft). It has a couple tables and bear-proof food storage. Scattered alpine fir on the grassy slopes makes this an inviting site. The peak rising above Little Shovel Pass is visible southeast. Only a sliver of the Queen Elizabeth Range is visible right (northeast).

Carry on northwest. Gentle ridges of the Maligne Range (left / west) invite off-trail exploration. In ten minutes, cross the bridged south fork of diminutive **Jeffrey Creek**. Cross the bridged north fork 1.4 km (0.9 mi) farther. A gentle ascent crests **Big Shovel Pass** at 17.8 km (11 mi), 2320 m (7610 ft). An equally gentle descent leads 200 m (220 yd) to a junction. Right (east-northeast) ascends to Watchtower Col, then plunges into Watchtower Basin (Trip 103). Sans pack, dashing to the col is a quick, easy, scenically worthwhile detour. (See page 288 for details.) Bear left (northwest) on the main trail to continue hiking the Skyline.

Vast meadows on the Skyline

Descend barren slopes beneath Curator Mountain (left / southwest). Reach a **junction** at 19.8 km (12.3 mi), 2200 m (7216 ft). Go right (north-northeast) for the Skyline. Left (west) descends 120 m (395 ft) to reach **Curator campground** in 0.8 km (0.5 mi). It has a couple tables and bear-proof food storage. Rated *Don't Do,* the trail beyond Curator descends through forest 10.6 km (6.6 mi) to Wabasso Lake, then continues another 3.2 km (2 mi) to the Icefields Parkway, for a total elevation loss of 1100 m (3610 ft).

After the 19.8-km (12.3-mi) junction, the Skyline trail curves northwest, around the northeast shore of turquoise **Curator Lake**. It then steepens, approaching **the Notch**—a narrow, 2510-m (8233-ft) col. Its southeast side can remain snow-covered until mid-August. Be prepared to kick-step footholds on the final ascent.

Atop the Notch, the view extends southwest across the Athabasca River to Mt. Edith Cavell, and northwest to Mt. Robson. A brief, off-trail scramble—145 m (475 ft) up the steep-but-easy slope north of the Notch to a minor summit—significantly broadens the panorama.

Back on the trail, resume hiking northwest from the Notch, onto the definitive Skyline. The journey climaxes for the next 4.5 km (2.8 mi), along the barren summit ridge of **Amber Mtn**. Ups and downs are slight. 360° views are constant. Cruising elevation: 2480 m (8135 ft). Highpoint: 2530 m (8300 ft).

About 1 km (0.6 mi) northwest of the Amber Mtn summit, the trail begins switchbacking down the northeast slope, into the basin cupping **Centre Lake**. At 28.2 km (17.5 km), 2180 m (7150 ft), reach the lake's outlet stream on the basin floor.

Rockhop to the northeast bank. The slope to your right (east) rises to Centre Mtn. Just down-valley (northwest) is 2694-m (8836-ft) Mt. Tekarra.

Follow the trail generally north, into the subalpine zone. For about 2.5 km (1.6 mi), enjoy easy walking among scattered fir trees. Pass right (east) of **Tekarra Lake** (unnamed on the topo), at 2090 m (6855 ft). About 0.6 km (0.4 mi) farther, reach **Tekarra campground** at 30.5 km (18.9 mi), 2055 m (6740 ft). Situated in open forest, near the creek, next to subalpine meadows, it has a couple tables and bear-proof food storage.

Just north of the campground, rockhop to the creek's west bank, and follow the trail northwest. After a brief, gentle ascent, begin an hour-long contour between 2120 m (6954 ft) and 2160 m (7085 ft): generally north-northwest beneath **Tekarra Mtn**, curving west then west-northwest onto the flowery slope of **Signal Mtn**. The angular peaks of the Colin Range are visible north, across Maligne River Valley.

Intersect the Signal Mountain fire road at 36 km (22.3 mi), 2150 m (7052 ft). The Athabasca River Valley is west, far below. A left spur leads south-southwest 0.8 km (0.5 mi) to the site of the former Signal Mtn fire lookout. Bear right, pass **Signal campground** in 100 m (110 yd), and follow the road generally north-northwest. You've begun the final leg of the trip: a viewless, 8.5-km (5.3-mi) descent through forest. Make noise frequently to avoid surprising a bear at close range. The road eventually curves east-northeast, then northwest to reach **Maligne Lake Road** at 44.5 km (27.6 mi), 1160 m (3805 ft).

WATCHTOWER BASIN

From the junction in Big Shovel Pass, at 18 km (11.2 mi), 2320 m (7610 ft), ascend the narrow path right (east-northeast) 0.4 km (0.25 mi) to 2380-m (7806-ft) **Watchtower Col**. The new view here is north into Watchtower Basin (Trip 102). For a much-improved perspective west-northwest of the Notch and Curator Lake, continue ascending left (northwest) from the col, up the **ridgecrest**, to 2420 m (7935 ft).

Want to explore Watchtower Basin? Before dropping into it, note the location of the highest lakelet, on the basin's left (west) wall. Make that your goal. Then follow the trail down: west across scree, curving north through heather. From the col, you'll lose 365 m (1197 ft) in 3 km (1.9 mi) to reach **Watchtower campground** at 2015 m (6610 ft).

Monkeyflower

TRIP 82 – 84

Mt. Robson Region

LOCATION	Mt. Robson Provincial Park
ROUND TRIP	42 km (26 mi) to Berg Lake campground
ELEVATION GAIN	786 m (2578 ft) to Berg Lake campground
KEY ELEVATIONS	trailhead 855 m (2804 ft) Berg Lake 1646 m (5400 ft) Snowbird Pass 2410 m (7905 ft) Hargreaves Glacier 2150 m (7050 ft)
HIKING TIME	2 to 5 days
DIFFICULTY	moderate
MAPS	page 512; Mt. Robson Park; Mt. Robson 83 E/3

OPINION

TRIP 82 – BERG LAKE

It's the stick that stirs the drink: so high it creates its own weather. It's the loftiest peak in the Canadian Rockies, towering 528 m (1732 ft) above its nearest challenger. And it looms more than 3000 m (9840 ft) above the trailhead, which is in one of the lowest valleys in the entire range. It's 3954-m (12,970-ft) Mt. Robson, a preposterously vertical, staggeringly atmospheric summit. If not veiled by swirling mist or shrouded by sodden clouds, its gleaming white, glacier-laden immensity is a jaw-dropping spectacle from Hwy 16.

Yet it's the scenery west and north of this Rocky Mountain icon that inspires many hikers to return religiously. It's nonstop extraordinary. The lush rainforest along the Robson River could be in Costa Rica. The Valley of a Thousand Falls (if it's raining, count 'em) is suggestive of New Zealand's verdant vales. The gravelly glacial flats in the upper Robson Valley feel like the Yukon. The Mist, Berg, and Robson glaciers gnawing at the flanks of the mountain might make you wonder, "Who needs Alaska?" Extending the hike to Snowbird Pass, and watching the Reef Icefield give birth to the Coleman Glacier, is an experience reminiscent of Patagonia. And the Hargreaves Glacier / Toboggan Falls / Mumm Basin sidetrip is such an improvement on the already picture-perfect view of Mt. Robson from the shore of Berg Lake, it could inspire even an American to sing *Oh Canada*. (That's our national anthem, in case you didn't know.)

As a result, the trail to Berg Lake is the most heavily traveled in the Canadian Rockies. Yet the powerful scenery instills a sense of reverence in most hikers, which can help make the company tolerable. Because this trip is widely known, think of it as a time for stimulating encounters. We've met a hyena specialist from Berkeley, California; a couple from Valemount, B.C. with an infant and a hiking three-year-old; Jasper railroad engineers; and keen trekkers from Amsterdam, Frankfurt, and

Auckland. We've sparked friendships here with people we've since hiked with many times. A commodious, enclosed cooking shelter at Berg Lake campground no doubt enhances the conviviality. So does a paltry mosquito population. Due to the abundant ice and thus frigid water, Berg Lake isn't plagued with infestations that force you to abandon conversation and flee to your tent.

It's warmer and wetter in Robson Park than in Jasper or Banff, so Berg Lake can be accessible by mid-June, up to a month earlier than most backpack trips in the range. Before mid-July, however, expect the Snowbird Pass trail to be snowbound.

It's possible to flash the one-way trip to Berg Lake in six or seven hours. After mid-July, include a day in your itinerary for the demanding excursion from Berg Lake to Snowbird Pass. Too vigourous? Devote that extra day to the Hargreaves-Mumm sidetrip; though easier, the vistas are comparably striking. So, if you're a strong strider, plan three days for the round trip, preferably four. Amblers, requiring two days to reach Berg Lake and two days to hike out, will want at least five days for the round trip. Care to extend your journey into lonelier country? Allow two more days and forge on to Moose Pass (Trip 105).

TRIP 83 – HARGREAVES GLACIER / TOBOGGAN FALLS / MUMM BASIN

Ascend to a glacier. Touch the pristine ice. Where the ice has receded, admire its patient handiwork: beautifully polished, pumpkin-coloured limestone. Lift your eyes to an astounding perspective of Mt. Robson's icy north face. Then traverse rock and meadow, past a charming cascade, to a flowery basin affording oh-my-gosh views of Berg Lake below and the majestic mount beyond. You'll retrace not a step on this exhilarating sidetrip. It's a loopster's delight.

You can hike a shorter loop, if you prefer, by not continuing into Mumm Basin and instead descending the Toboggan Falls trail that bisects the longer loop. Even if you're hiking the full loop, however, detour at least 200 m (220 yd) along the falls. Sit down. Lean close. Peer at the sensuously convoluted rock and dancing water. It's easy to imagine the tiny riffles are huge torrents roaring through colossal chasms.

Your motivation to continue the grand loop is twofold: ever changing but consistently pupil-dilating views, and the resplendent alpine wildflower display that graces Mumm Basin every summer. But the way is often steep, a few sections are rough, and, to stay on course, you must occasionally be attentive for cairns. Take pleasure in the multifarious surfaces your boots will touch along the way: dirt, gravel, scree, heather, boulders, and glacier-grated bedrock.

TRIP 84 – SNOWBIRD PASS

Berg Glacier is impressive, but it's only about a third the size of astounding Robson Glacier. The trail to Snowbird Pass climbs immediately above the yawning crevasses of this frozen river. Gaze into the crystalline-blue ice. It has a flame-like power to enthrall, to penetrate deep recesses of consciousness, perhaps rousing cellular memories of ancient times when life was a quest for fire. But prodigious Mt. Robson is breathing over your shoulder, commanding your attention back to the here and now. Your ice-trance will be short lived.

Berg Glacier and Berg Lake

Before this exciting trail was built, only climbers and the pluckiest of hikers appreciated Mt. Robson's awesome northeast face. Thinking of their more rigorous achievements might help you muster the energy to continue to Snowbird Pass. Go at least part way, to see the ice. Go farther, and you'll discover a surprisingly fecund meadow in this unlikely, barren setting. Go all the way, and you'll attain a climactic view of the Coleman Glacier oozing off the Reef Icefield. This is how the world must have looked eons ago.

FACT

Before your trip

Obtain a backcountry camping permit (per-person fee) at the Visitor Centre on Hwy 16. Though about 20% of the tentsites are reservable up to three months in advance, an abundance of campgrounds makes reservations unnecessary. Four of the six campgrounds on the Berg Lake Trail (Kinney Lake, Whitehorn, Berg Lake, and Robson Pass) have cooking shelters with wood stoves. Firewood is provided. To ensure you have a site at a particular campground, call Discover Camping at 1-800-689-9025.

By Vehicle

From Jasper townsite, drive west 84 km (52 mi) on Yellowhead Hwy 16. From Tete Jaune Cache junction, drive east 16 km (10 mi). Stop at the Mt. Robson Visitor Centre on the north side of the highway. Then, from the nearby gas station / store, follow the access road north 2 km (1.2 mi) to the trailhead parking lot, at 855 m (2804 ft).

Don't have a vehicle? Greyhound buses make daily runs east and west on Hwy 16. Ask the driver to stop at the Robson viewpoint, near the Visitor Centre.

On Foot

TRIP 82 – BERG LAKE

Departing the trailhead's northwest corner, immediately cross a bridge spanning the **Robson River**. The trail, initially a former road, is well constructed and maintained its entire distance. On the northwest bank, it follows the river upstream, generally north-northeast, through moist, luxuriant forest of cedar and mountain hemlock. Wildflowers brighten the path's edge. The river is audible and occasionally visible.

At 4.3 km (2.7 mi), cross a bridge over the **Kinney Lake** outlet. Continue north around the east shore. The former road ends; trail resumes. It undulates through forest around the northeast shore. At 7 km (4.3 mi), 985 m (3230 ft), reach **Kinney Lake campground.** There's an open-air shelter here. Just past the camp is a bike rack. Cycling is prohibited beyond.

The trail continues generally northwest, past the north end of the lake, onto open gravel flats. At 8.5 km (5.3 mi), cross a bridge to the Robson River's west bank. Proceed onto a broad alluvial plain. At 9 km (5.6 mi) begin the steep ascent of **Whitehorn Hill**.

At 11 km (6.8 mi), 1120 m (3475 ft), reach a suspension bridge over the Robson River. On the west bank, about 150 m (165 yd) left (north), is a ranger station. Cross to the east bank and arrive at **Whitehorn campground**. It has a spacious, open-air

Emperor Falls

cooking shelter. The trail continues generally north, into **Valley of a Thousand Falls**, and remains level.

At 11.8 km (7.3 mi) cross another suspension bridge, back to the river's west bank. Heading north, begin a stiff ascent. The trail gains 450 m (1476 ft) in the next 3.5 km (2 mi) along the rugged Robson River gorge. Pass White Falls, Falls of the Pool, and 60-m (197-ft) **Emperor Falls**. At 15.4 km (9.5 mi), take the short spur to pay homage to the mighty Emperor.

Near **Emperor Falls campground,** at 16 km (9.9 mi), 1630 m (5346 ft), the trail levels. It heads northeast, then curves east. Enter rocky terrain in the upper Robson River Valley. The cliffs of Mt. Robson now dominate the scene. Mist Glacier is soon visible right (east).

Reach **Marmot campground** at 18.8 km (11.7 mi), 1645 m (5396 ft). At 19.1 km (11.8 mi), the Hargreaves Glacier / Mumm Basin trail forks left, ascending generally north-northwest. (Skip below for directions.) Bear right on the main trail, heading generally northeast, paralleling the northwest shore of **Berg Lake**. Across the lake, Berg Glacier is soon visible. It creeps down Mt. Robson to the southeast shore, where it occasionally calves RV-sized icebergs into the powder-blue water. From the lake, Mount Robson rises 2316 m (7596 ft).

Hargreaves shelter at Berg Lake

Reach **Berg Lake campground** at 21 km (13 mi), 1646 m (5400 ft). The Hargreaves Shelter, a cozy cabin built by a horse outfitter in the 1920s, serves backpackers who want to cook indoors. It has a woodstove and food-storage bins. Just 100 m (110 yd) past the campground, immediately after the Toboggan Creek bridge, the trail to Toboggan Falls forks left and ascends generally northwest. (Skip below for directions.) If you want more privacy than is possible at Berg Lake, and you're willing to forego quick access to the shelter, continue up the main trail, past the lake's northeast end, to **Rearguard campground**, at 22 km (13.6 mi).

Beyond Rearguard, the trail leads generally east-northeast onto a gravel flat. Reach a junction at 22.4 km (13.9 mi). Right leads east to Snowbird Pass. (Skip ahead two pages for directions.) Straight passes a ranger station in 100 m (110 yd) then continues generally northeast, reaching **Robson Pass campground** at 23 km (14.3 mi). Only at this campground are open fires permitted. This is also where the Mumm Basin trail intersects the main trail.

Continuing northeast, the main trail crosses **Robson Pass** and the Robson-Jasper parks boundary at 23.5 km (14.6 mi), 1652 m (5420 ft). Reach **Adolphus Lake** at 24.3 km (15.1 mi). Proceed northeast, paralleling the northwest shore, to reach **Adolphus Lake campground** at 25.7 km (15.9 mi).

TRIP 83 – HARGREAVES GLACIER / TOBOGGAN FALLS / MUMM BASIN

ROUND TRIP	6-km (3.7-mi) short loop, 12-km (7.5-mi) full loop
ELEVATION GAIN	300 m (984 ft) on short loop, 505 m (1656 ft) on full loop
HIKING TIME	2½ to 4 hours for short loop, 5 to 7 hours for full loop
DIFFICULTY	moderate

TOBOGGAN FALLS

If you're hiking either the short or long loop, skip below; you'll pass Toboggan Falls en route. But if you want to see the falls on a quick, one- or two-hour dash from **Berg Lake campground**, here's how. It's an easy, rewarding, 2-km (1.2-mi) round trip.

Follow the main trail 100 m (110 yd) northeast of the campground. Immediately after the **Toboggan Creek bridge**, the trail to the falls forks left and begins a steep ascent, generally northwest, above the creek's northeast bank. At 0.4 km (0.25 mi) you'll see the falls sliding over smooth limestone slabs, into a small gorge.

There are more falls above. The trail briefly detours into forest, then returns creekside. The elevation gain grants improved views of Berg Lake and Mt. Robson. After gaining 190 m (623 ft) from the campground, reach a **bench** at 1 km (0.6 mi). The upper falls, as well as Mt. Robson's north face, are visible here.

At 1.2 km (0.7 mi), intersect the loop trail at a **four-way junction**. Left leads southwest to Hargreaves Glacier. Right leads northeast to Mumm Basin. Straight climbs steeply northwest through a recent burn. It gains another 245 m (804 ft), affords panoramic views, and ends at a cave. Total distance from the campground: 2.4 km (1.5 mi).

HARGREAVES GLACIER / MUMM BASIN LOOP

From **Berg Lake campground**, hike southwest on the main trail paralleling the lake's northwest shore. Arrive at a **junction** in 1.9 km (1.2 mi). Turn right (north). Ascend a steep, rough trail along a dry streambed. Cairns indicate the way.

Mt. Robson at twilight, from near Adolphus Lake

After gaining 300 m (984 ft), reach the **lateral moraine of Hargreaves Glacier** at 3.4 km (2.1 mi), 1945 m (6380 ft). Atop the moraine, you can survey the basin, glacier, and marginal lake. About 200 years ago, the glacier reached to where you now stand. Berg Glacier and Mt. Robson are visible southeast.

Proceed northeast to treeline. Adolphus Lake, beyond Robson Pass, is visible northeast. Descend steeply through subalpine meadows. Cross **Toboggan Creek** and reach a **four-way junction** at 4.7 km (2.9 mi). Left climbs steeply northwest, through a burn, to a cave. Right (southeast) is Toboggan Falls and Berg Lake campground. Straight (northeast) is Mumm Basin.

Hiking the short loop? Turn right (southeast) at the four-way junction. Descend past **Toboggan Falls**. Intersect the main **Berg Lake trail** at 5.9 km (3.7 mi). Turn right, cross the Toboggan Creek bridge, and enter **Berg Lake campground** at 6 km (3.7 mi).

Hiking the full loop? Proceed straight (northeast) at the four-way junction. The trail ascends steeply among whitebark pine to treeline, then crosses open scree slopes. Where the track is faint, watch for cairns. Cross a creek gorge and reach **Mumm Basin summit** at 6.9 km (4.3 mi), 2150 m (7052 ft)—the highest point on the loop. The view of Berg Lake and Mt. Robson is superb.

Descend into **Mumm Basin**. Traverse heather meadows and rock slabs. At 7.9 km (4.9 mi) reach another vantage, atop a cairned knob. The mountainous panorama extends east-northeast, past Adolphus Lake, into Jasper Park.

The trail then descends northeast. It briefly swings into Alberta and Jasper Park before curving south-southwest along the edge of a cliff and dropping into Robson Pass. About 100 m (110 yd) beyond **Robson Pass campground**, intersect the main **Berg Lake trail** at 9.9 km (6.1 mi). Turn right and hike generally southwest to reach **Berg Lake campground** at 12 km (7.5 mi).

TRIP 84 – SNOWBIRD PASS

ROUND TRIP	21.2 km (13.2 mi)
ELEVATION GAIN	758 m (2486 ft)
HIKING TIME	6½ to 8 hours
DIFFICULTY	moderate

From **Berg Lake campground**, follow the main trail northeast. In 100 m (110 yd), immediately after the Toboggan Creek bridge, the trail to Toboggan Falls forks left and ascends generally northwest. Proceed on the main trail. Pass **Rearguard campground** at 1 km (0.6 mi).

Beyond Rearguard, the trail leads generally east-northeast onto a gravel flat. Reach a **junction** at 1.4 km (0.9 mi), 1652 m (5420 ft). Straight passes a ranger station in 100 m (110 yd) then continues generally northeast to Robson Pass campground. For Snowbird Pass, go right (southeast) and hike along the meltwater stream toward the toe of Robson Glacier.

At 2.2 km (1.3 mi), bear right (southeast) where a cutoff trail to Robson Pass forks left (northwest). Ahead, the marginal lake at the glacier's toe is where the Robson River begins. Lynx Mtn is visible southeast, between Tatei Ridge (left / east-northeast) and Rearguard Mtn (right / south).

The trail ascends the lateral moraine of **Robson Glacier**, enabling you to overlook the ice for the next 3 km (2 mi). Visible south is 3426-m / (11,237-ft) Resplendent Mtn. The terrain is rocky, the undulating trail occasionally steep. Beneath the rocks, the core of the moraine is ice. Be cautious: the rocks cave in where the ice has melted.

At 7.4 km (4.6 mi), the trail turns away from the glacier and begins a switchbacking climb past a cascade. A steep, eastward ascent follows the left (north) side of a stream. The grade eases in an **alpine meadow** frequented by hoary marmots. Visible southwest, at the head of Robson Glacier, is the rounded, ice-covered summit of The Dome. That's one of the two standard climbing routes to the top of Mt. Robson.

A couple bootbeaten paths have developed in the meadow, but the tread is obscure. Aim for the low point on the ridge ahead (east). The superior route bends left and stays north of the stream. Finally, follow cairns up a steep boulder-and-scree field to crest **Snowbird Pass** at 10.6 km (6.5 mi), 2410 m (7905 ft). Below you (east and southeast) is the Reef Icefield. Left (north) is its offspring, the Coleman Glacier. Right (south) is Chushina Ridge, an extension of Lynx Mtn.

En route to Snowbird Pass

Robson Glacier

TRIP 85

Egypt Lake

LOCATION	Banff National Park
ROUND TRIP	24.8 km (15.4 mi) to Egypt Lake campground
ELEVATION GAIN	990 m (3247 ft)
KEY ELEVATIONS	trailhead 1675 m (5495 ft) Healy Pass 2330 m (7642 ft) Egypt Lake campground 1995 m (6545 ft)
HIKING TIME	2 to 3 days
DIFFICULTY	moderate
MAPS	page 506; Gem Trek *Banff & Mt. Assiniboine*; Banff 82 O/4

OPINION

The amount of time most of us are able to immerse ourselves in nature is but a sliver of our lives. Yet those few weekends, those fleeting holidays, powerfully influence how we assess the quality of our existence. So whenever we lace up our hiking boots, we should aim them where we're sure to be greeted by an alpenhorn blast of spectacular scenery. Egypt Lake is such a place.

"Egypt Lake" is actually just a handle for the area. It's a logical one, because the lake is central, and there's a backcountry campground and hut nearby. But you won't be blown back when you see Egypt. Sure, it's impressive. But the nearby lakes—Scarab, Mummy, and Natalko—the surrounding passes—Healy, Whistling, and Sphinx—and the attendant mountains—the Pharaoh Peaks, Haiduk Peak, and The Monarch—are what make this a stunning destination for backpackers.

Of the three primary approaches to Egypt Lake, the optimal one begins at the Vista Lake trailhead, on Hwy 93. It entails a one-way journey over Gibbon, Whistling and Healy passes (Trip 79). The next best option—the shortest possible round trip—begins at the Sunshine ski-area parking lot, enters via Healy Pass (Trip 24) and exits the same way. The third option—a dreary slog through the forested valleys of Redearth and Pharaoh creeks—should be a consideration only if you're cycling the initial road section (Trip 25).

This trip description assumes you've read Trip 24 and intend to follow those directions to Healy Pass. From Healy, you'll descend 335 m (1099 ft) to Egypt Lake campground—which means you'll face a significant ascent upon departing. Once you've pitched your tent or dumped your gear in the hut (described below), you have options.

Whistling Pass should be your top-priority excursion. From the campground, you'll ascend 305 m (1000 ft) in 3.7 km (2.3 mi) to the pass squeezed between Haiduk Peak and the Pharaoh Peaks. There you can peer down on Haiduk Lake and the exquisite Whistling Valley. The glacier-stuccoed summit of 3306-m (10,847-ft)

Southeast side of Whistling Pass, Scarab Lake lower center, Sphinx Pass upper center

Mt. Ball is visible beyond. Listen and watch for the namesake whistlers (marmots). Whistling Pass also affords an aerial view of Scarab Lake.

From Whistling Pass, it's a 233-m (764-ft) descent in less than 2 km (1.2 mi) to Haiduk Lake—very rewarding if you'll have time to relax on the meadowy northeast shore before returning. But a more pressing opportunity beckons: detouring from the Whistling Pass trail to Scarab and Mummy lakes. Scarab is subalpine, Mummy is alpine, but they're equally marvelous. (A "scarab" is a beetle sacred to the ancient Egyptians.) When exploring the Egypt Lake area, make Scarab and Mummy your second priority after Whistling Pass. Allow about three hours for the round trip.

You insist on a thorough inspection of the entire Egypt Lake area? Good. From Mummy Lake, scramble east into Sphinx Pass, descend south-southeast to the meadowy shore of Natalko Lake, then return north to Egypt Lake via Redearth Pass. It's an easy-yet-exciting, half-day loop from the campground. The name "Natalko" refers to the National Talc Company, which mined near the lake in the 1920s. Some maps label it "Talc Lake."

Pharaoh and Black Rock lakes are another possible sidetrip. Their setting is bleak but impressive: tucked beneath the dark Pharaoh Peaks. Their appearance is softened by surrounding stands of larch. Allow about 1½ hours for the round trip. The third member of this group, Sphinx Lake, is merely a pond accessed by a seldom-trod, sketchy to nonexistent route. Forget it.

Mummy Lake

Sphinx Pass

The Monarch Ramparts, an alpine ridge extending southeast from Healy Pass, offers Egypt Lake visitors another premier excursion, but the logical time to do it is after surmounting Healy Pass on the way out. Read the end of Trip 24 for details.

Now, about that hut at Egypt Lake campground. It's just a small, cheerless shelter that sleeps 16. A night in such crowded, noisy quarters could qualify as torture. We recommend the tranquility of the campground's reasonably-spaced tentsites.

FACT

Before your trip

To ride the White Mountain Adventures shuttle bus from the Sunshine parking lot to Sunshine Village, check current prices and make reservations by calling (403) 760-4403.

If you want to stay in the Egypt Lake hut, check current prices and make reservations with the Banff Info Centre.

By Vehicle

Follow the directions for Healy Pass (Trip 24).

On Foot

Follow the directions in Trip 24 to **Healy Pass**, at 2330 m (7642 ft). From the pass, the trail descends northwest—gradually at first, then more intently. Soon after passing a right (north) spur to a warden cabin, reach a junction near the bridge over **Pharaoh Creek**, 3 km (1.9 mi) from and 335 m (1099 ft) below Healy Pass. Left (south) leads upstream to Redearth Pass. Proceed across the Pharaoh Creek bridge. Shortly beyond and above, arrive at **Egypt Lake hut and campground**. The tentsites are right and left (north and south) of the hut. The elevation here is 1995 m (6545 ft).

PHARAOH AND BLACK ROCK LAKES

From Egypt Lake hut, follow the trail north. Bear left (north) where right drops to the Pharaoh Creek bridge. At 0.5 km (0.3 mi) reach another fork. Straight (north) follows Pharaoh Creek downstream to its confluence with Redearth Creek (Trip 25). Turn left (west). Cross a small meadow and begin a stiff climb. Reach the east shore of **Pharaoh Lake** at 1.3 km (0.8 mi), 2129 m (6983 ft).

Rockhop Pharaoh Lake's outlet stream. Follow a rooty trail north-northwest through larch forest. The ascent is moderate. Reach the east shore of **Black Rock Lake** at 2.4 km (1.5 mi), 2209 m (7245 ft), having gained 214 m (702 ft) from Egypt Lake hut.

EGYPT, SCARAB AND MUMMY LAKES

From Egypt Lake hut, follow the trail south-southwest. At 0.5 km (0.3 mi) fork left (south) for a quick detour to **Egypt Lake**. The long cascade plunging to the southwest shore originates in Scarab Lake. Return to the main trail. Turn left and switchback steeply up through forest on the south end of the Pharaoh Peaks.

A brief descent leads to a junction at 1.9 km (1.2 mi). Right ascends to Whistling Pass. Go left (south), descend through a meadow, and quickly arrive at the rocky east shore of **Scarab Lake**. A great wall crowds the west and south shores. Short spur trails allow you to overlook Egypt Lake (left / east). The main trail continues south to the outlet stream. Ford or rockhop it if no footlog is in place. On the south bank, detour downstream one minute to where you can peer over the lip of the cascade you previously saw from Egypt Lake.

Resume south on the main trail. It ascends over a ridge, drops past a pond, then climbs right (southwest) to a 2270-m (7446-ft) ridge above the east shore of **Mummy Lake**. You've hiked 1.4 km (0.9 mi) from the junction above Scarab Lake, for a total of 3.3 km (2 mi) from Egypt Lake hut.

NATALKO LAKE

Depart Mummy Lake as if returning to Scarab, but lose as little elevation as possible. As soon as the boulders to your right (east) look accommodating, abandon the trail and begin the easy scramble to Sphinx Pass. The pass is between The Sphinx (the peaklet immediately south of Egypt Lake) and the ridge separating Mummy and Natalko lakes. Ascend east-northeast on talus (perhaps snow-covered), then southeast into 2320-m (7610-ft) **Sphinx Pass**.

From the pass, descend cross-country, south-southeast—staying in the draw, out of the trees on either side—to the meadowy northeast shore of **Natalko Lake** at 2180 m (7150 ft). You've now hiked 1.4 km (0.9 mi) from Mummy Lake, for a total of 4.7 km (2.9 mi) from Egypt Lake hut. On the lake's east shore, a trail leads left (east) above the outlet stream's north bank. It soon veers left, away from the stream, and descends north. Where it passes unusually big larch trees, it's evident the trail was once a mining road. Below a switchback, cross East Verdant Creek to intersect the Redearth Creek trail on the northeast bank at 2040 m (6691 ft). This is 1.9 km (1.2 mi) from Natalko Lake. Turn left and follow the trail generally north 2.3 km (1.4 mi) to the bridge over Pharaoh Creek. You're now on familiar ground. **Egypt Lake hut** is just above (left / southwest). Total loop distance: 8.9 km (5.5 mi).

WHISTLING PASS

From Egypt Lake hut, follow the trail south-southwest. Pass Egypt Lake (left / south). Continue to the 1.9-km (1.2-mi) junction above Scarab Lake. Bear right and ascend. The trail curves right (northwest) into subalpine rock gardens. Top out in 2300-m (7544-ft) **Whistling Pass** at 3.7 km (2.3 mi), having climbed 305 m (1000 ft) from Egypt Lake hut. Haiduk Lake, at 2067 m (6780 ft), is visible below (northwest). The trail descends 233 m (764 ft) in less than 2 km (1.2 mi) to the shore and continues through Whistling Valley.

TRIP 86

Skoki Valley / Merlin Lake

LOCATION	Banff National Park
ROUND TRIP	31.4 km (19.5 mi) to Merlin Meadows campground
ELEVATION GAIN	1110 m (3640 ft)
KEY ELEVATIONS	trailhead 1700 m (5575 ft) Deception Pass 2485 m (8151 ft) Merlin Meadows 2130 m (6986 ft) Merlin Lake 2240 m (7347 ft)
HIKING TIME	2 to 3 days
DIFFICULTY	easy
MAPS	page 517; Gem Trek *Lake Louise & Yoho*; Lake Louise 82 N/8, Hector Lake 82 N/9

OPINION

Look for the exits. Plan your escape route. Make it a habit in any crowded place, like the West Edmonton Mall, the Metropolitan Opera House, or Lake Louise. Here, you'll want to bolt east, as far as possible from all the tourists milling about the Chateau and the village. A sensible destination is Skoki Valley.

Backpacking to Skoki, you'll cruise through expansive meadows and desolately beautiful alpine country. In fall, after the sun has beaten the greenery into submission, the long approach to Deception Pass looks almost lunar. Some of the Slate Range mountains add to the bleak atmosphere, appearing more crumbled than solid. But this is also a land of lakes. Merlin Lake, for example, is sublime. It's wedged between the aptly named Merlin Castle and the Wall of Jericho. In fine weather, lingering on the grass-carpeted slope above the shore and admiring the lake's reflections of glacier-encrusted Mt. Richardson might be the zenith of your trip.

Solitude is elusive at Skoki. Widely known, it siphons off many of the hikers visiting Lake Louise. There's also the Skoki Lodge, popular with trekkers and skiers who prefer wood walls to nylon. But you don't have to hang out near the lodge. There are several backcountry campgrounds in the area; Merlin Meadows and Baker Lake are best. A variety of sidetrips helps disperse people from the main thoroughfares. Baker Lake (Trip 87) deserves a visit, even if you're not camping there. On your hike in, veer off to Packer's Pass to overlook the Skoki Lakes: Zigadenus and Myosotis. Scramble up Skoki Mountain to survey most of the area's scenic highlights.

The worthwhile detours to Hidden and Redoubt lakes are outlined in the Boulder Pass (Trip 44) description. If you have an extra day, hike the Trip 87 circuit: from Merlin Meadows (or the lodge), northwest through Jones Pass to the Red Deer Lakes, returning south through Cotton Grass Pass to the shores of resplendent Baker Lake. You'll walk pastoral valleys lined with unexciting peaks that nevertheless contribute to the overall beauty.

Ptarmigan Lake, en route to Deception Pass

The initial 8.5 km (5.3 mi) of the Skoki approach are the same as for Boulder Pass. The first 4 km (2.5 mi) are pure trudgery, on a dusty fire road through claustrophobic forest. It's energy-sapping. Cycling to road's end makes sense if you're dayhiking, but carrying a fully loaded backpack on a bike can make for a wobbly, exhausting ride. Most backpackers will just have to march up the road. Even though it's a road, do make noise to warn the resident grizzlies you're passing through.

You'll also endure ugly, braided trail much of the way. If it's raining, expect mud. Skoki's fame is to blame. Prevent further scars by staying on the dominant trail wherever there's a choice, especially near Deception Pass. The pass, by the way, was named for the trip ascending out of Skoki Valley. You're not the only one for whom the trail seems to lengthen.

FACT

Before your trip

Make reservations months in advance if you want to stay at Skoki Lodge. Call (403) 256-8473 in Calgary, or (800) 258-7669, ext 3.

By Vehicle

See Boulder Pass (Trip 44) for directions to Fish Creek trailhead, at 1700 m (5575 ft), near Lake Louise ski area.

On Foot

See Boulder Pass (Trip 44) for directions to **Boulder Pass**, at 8.5 km (5.3 mi), 2345 m (7692 ft). It's above the southwest shore of long Ptarmigan Lake. From the pass, keep left for Skoki Valley. The trail rises above the north side of Ptarmigan Lake.

At 9.1 km (5.6 mi) a route forks left, gaining 70 m (230 ft) in 1.2 km (0.7 mi) to **Packer's Pass**. Experienced hikers might opt for this longer route instead of the main trail over Deception Pass. It rejoins with the main trail in 3 km (1.9 mi). You'd get a closer view of the cirque and the lakes it contains. The 2470-m (8102-ft) pass is north of Ptarmigan Lake and overlooks Zigadenus Lake. A bit farther north and east, Myosotis Lake is visible. Together they're called the Skoki Lakes. A short cliff below the lower lake prevents this route from being used much. It's best to attempt it on the way out of Skoki, so you'll know before investing too much effort whether you can proceed.

Where the Packer's Pass route forks left, the **main trail** to Skoki Valley continues straight (northeast) above Ptarmigan Lake. At 10.5 km (6.5 mi) reach a **junction**. Right (east) leads to Baker Lake in 1.5 km (0.9 mi). Turn left and begin the short, steep climb northeast to Deception Pass.

Top out on **Deception Pass** at 11 km (6.8 mi), 2470 m (8102 ft). Fossil Mtn is right (northeast). Skoki Valley is north. Ptarmigan Lake and Boulder Pass are southwest; beyond them are the peaks above Lake Louise. Proceeding through the pass, the Skoki Lakes come into view left (northwest).

Descend the north side of Deception Pass to re-enter forest in Skoki Valley. At 13.4 km (8.3 mi), the Packer's Pass route rejoins on the left. At 14.1 km (8.7 mi) reach a **junction**. Right (west) leads through Jones Pass (Trip 87). Continue straight to reach **Skoki Lodge** at 14.6 km (9.1 km), 2165 m (7100 ft).

Unless you have reservations at the lodge, follow the trail past it, northwest. For sidetrips on another day, note the spur trail left (southwest) over the bridged creek to Merlin Lake and the one right (northwest) ascending Skoki Mtn. Reach **Merlin Meadows campground**, just inside forest, at 15.7 km (9.7 mi), 2130 m (6986 ft).

MERLIN LAKE

There are three approaches to Merlin Lake. The most enjoyable begins at the bridge in front of Skoki Lodge. You'll gain 200 m (656 ft) on the 5.8-km (3.6-mi) round trip.

Cross the bridge. Reach a fork at 0.3 km (0.2 mi). Left (southeast) leads to Skoki Lakes. For Merlin Lake, go right (west) and begin ascending. Traverse a **boulder field** beneath the Wall of Jericho. The section of trail with carefully-placed stones was constructed by Lawrence Grassi, mountaineer and master trail builder. He did it in 1945, while working at Skoki Lodge.

Where the trail fades, a cairned route continues. At 1.8 km (1.1 mi), drop toward tiny **Castilleja Lake**. See the cliffband southwest? The Merlin Lake cirque is above it. Ascend steep scree. Follow cairns west. Ascend a gully of loose scree to penetrate the limestone **headwall**. From the cliff top, descend west to reach the northeast shore of **Merlin Lake** at 2.9 km (1.8 mi), 2240 m (7347 ft).

The direct route (5-km / 3.1-mi round trip) from Merlin Meadows campground to Merlin Lake is marshy. It angles southwest across the meadow to intersect the

Merlin Lake

cairned route (described above) southwest of Castilleja Lake. Don't take the horse trail. Immediately northwest of Merlin Meadows campground, it forks left to cross Skoki Creek.

SKOKI MTN

The route up this conical mountain's west side is straightforward. March over scree for 2.2 km (1.4 mi), gaining 531 m (1742 ft) in about 1½ hours, and you'll attain the 2696-m (8843-ft) summit. The 360° view will help you decide where to invest your time in the area.

Start between the two Skoki Lodge outhouses and head generally northeast. Where the bootbeaten path climbs above treeline, continue on a sketchy route through scree. The panorama, starting in the north and continuing clockwise, includes Little Pipestone Creek and Cyclone Mtn (north), the Red Deer Lakes and Pipestone Mtn (northeast), Oyster Peak (east), Fossil Mtn and Deception Pass (south), Packer's Pass (south-southwest), the Skoki Lakes, Ptarmigan Peak, Pika Peak, and Mt. Richardson (southwest), and the Merlin Valley (west-southwest). Mounts Douglas and St. Bride are the bigger peaks farther east.

TRIP 87

Red Deer & Baker Lakes

LOCATION	Banff National Park
LOOP	15 km (9.3 mi) starting in Skoki Valley
ELEVATION GAIN	355 m (1165 ft)
KEY ELEVATIONS	Jones Pass 2250 m (7380 ft) Red Deer Lakes 2090 m (6855 ft) Cotton Grass Pass 2190 m (7183 ft) Baker Lake 2210 m (7250 ft)
HIKING TIME	1½ days
DIFFICULTY	moderate
MAPS	page 517; Gem Trek *Lake Louise & Yoho*; Lake Louise 82 N/8, Hector Lake 82 N/9

OPINION

On the difficulty spectrum—stroll, jaunt, walk, ramble, hike, trek, expedition, pilgrimage—looping around Fossil Mtn is somewhere on the left. But the scenery en route and the sense of wilderness you'll attain would befit those on the right. So, prior to setting out for Skoki Valley (Trip 86), arrange to include this short but rewarding extension in your plans.

From near Skoki Lodge, you'll hike through Jones Pass, visit the Red Deer Lakes, proceed through Cotton Grass Pass to Baker Lake, then rejoin the trail you originally hiked to Skoki. On this open-sided loop (horseshoe-shaped, to be precise) you'll circumambulate Fossil Mtn, the summit of which is hiker accessible via a route veering east-northeast atop Deception Pass.

Jones Pass is forested, notable only because it's the easiest, quickest passage to Red Deer Lakes. The option—rounding the north side of Skoki Mtn—is a miserable trail: muddy, brushy, braided, confusing, energy-sapping. Even if you camp at Merlin Meadows, backtrack to Skoki Lodge and hike through Jones Pass.

The Red Deer Lakes are shallow, marshy. The main lake, though pretty, serves primarily to entice hikers into this broad, lonely, little-visited valley where they'll appreciate, if only briefly, the pervasive wilderness atmosphere more than they will any one spectacle. The main lake's west shore is treed; grassy meadows and willow flats border the east and southeast shores. The slopes of the surrounding mountains are forested.

Cotton Grass Pass, on a sunny, summer day, is dreamy. The trail rises out of dense forest into a scattering of trees, then enters sweeping, picturesque meadows. Oyster Mtn, walling off the east side of the 2-km (1.2-mi) long pass, is not a remarkable peak, but it does have a long, hikeable, ridgecrest affording vast views. The summit route follows Oyster Creek past Oyster Lake, which is tucked into a cirque beneath its namesake mountain.

Red Deer Lake

After exiting Cotton Grass Pass, a short, lenient ascent ends at Baker Lake—the trip's scenic climax. A trail encircles the grassy shore of this impressively big alpine lake. The Baker Lake campground, perched above the northeast shore, is excellent. A couple tentsites have lake views. A sidetrip to nearby smaller lakes is appealing. Plan to sleep here, instead of at Red Deer Lakes campground, which is small, far from its namesake lakes, in forest, beside a small stream.

Reasonably-fit backpackers can dispatch the 17.5 km (10.1 mi) from Fish Creek trailhead to Red Deer Lakes campground in a day. The optimal plan, however, is to stop at Merlin Meadows campground first. On day two, enjoy an excursion to Merlin Lake (Trip 86), maybe summit Skoki Mtn as well, and stay at Merlin Meadows again. On day three, hike through Jones Pass to Red Deer Lakes campground. Eat lunch there. Use the bear-proof food storage to cache your gear while you enjoy an exploratory sidetrip to the main Red Deer Lake. Then hoist packs, hike through Cotton Grass Pass, and camp at Baker Lake your last night.

FACT

By Vehicle

See Boulder Pass (Trip 44) for directions to Fish Creek trailhead, at 1700 m (5575 ft), near Lake Louise ski area.

On Foot

Follow the directions to **Boulder Pass** (Trip 44). Then follow the directions to **Skoki Valley** (Trip 86). At the 14.1-km (8.7-mi) junction, where left (northwest) reaches Skoki Lodge in just 0.5 km (0.3 mi), turn right (east) for Jones Pass. (If staying at Merlin Meadows campground, shortly past the lodge, read Trip 44 about sidetrips to Merlin Lake and Skoki Mtn.)

The trail leads generally northeast through forested **Jones Pass**. Gaining little elevation, it tops out at 2250 m (7380 ft). The pass separates Skoki Mtn (north) from Fossil Mtn (south). Emerging from the pass, reach a fork at 1.6 km (1 mi). Right (east) curves southeast over the shoulder of Fossil Mtn, into Cotton Grass Pass. Bear left (northeast). About 15 minutes farther, reach another junction, at 2.7 km (1.7 mi). Bear left (northeast) again. Right leads south into Cotton Grass Pass; that's the way you'll go after leaving Red Deer Lakes.

The trail ahead tends to be muddy. Some of the spruce and fir in this forest are 250 years old. At 3.2 km (2 mi), a route forks left (west-northwest) through willow flats to the main Red Deer Lake. Proceed straight (north) to reach **Red Deer Lakes campground**, on the right, at 3.4 km (2.1 mi), 2090 m (6855 ft).

Departing Red Deer Lakes campground for a sidetrip to the main Red Deer Lake? Hike north. Cross a bridge over a headwater tributary of the Red Deer River. Reach a T-junction at 0.5 km (0.3 mi). This is the **Red Deer River trail**. Right leads northeast, passing the Cyclone warden cabin in 200 m (200 yd). Go left (west).

The trail curves west-northwest to a junction at 1.2 km (0.75 mi), near the northeast shore of the **main Red Deer Lake**. Left (south) is a 1.4-km (0.9-mi) route that skirts the lake's east shore, then curves east-southeast to intersect the Jones Pass trail just south of Red Deer Lakes campground. Straight (west-northwest) reaches another junction at 1.6 km (1 mi), where left (southwest) is a muddy trail—not recommended—to Merlin Meadows.

Departing **Red Deer Lakes campground**, heading for Baker Lake? Hike south. (The following distances are cumulative, resuming from 3.4 km / 2.1 mi. They do not include the sidetrip to the main Red Deer Lake.) At 3.6 km (2.2 mi) proceed straight (south) where a route forks right (west-northwest). At 4.1 km (2.5 mi), go left (south) toward Cotton Grass Pass. The trail follows Oyster Creek upstream, well away from the west bank. The forest soon gives way to open meadowland.

Reach a junction at 5.6 km (3.5 mi). Right leads northwest to Jones Pass. Proceed straight (south-southeast). The ascent is gentle. Oyster Peak is left (east). Fossil Mtn is right (southwest). Cross grassy, willowy meadows. Reach the trail's highpoint in **Cotton Grass Pass** at 2190 m (7183 ft) before gradually descending.

At 7.3 km (4.5 mi), a faint route leads east, following Oyster Creek to Oyster Lake (hidden in a cirque), then north to the summit of Oyster Peak. (Wow, that's a lot of oysters.) Proceed straight (south) on the main trail. After it gradually curves right (southwest), reach a junction at 8.4 km (5.2 mi). Left (south) begins descending the Baker Creek drainage to Wildflower Creek (Trip 101). Go right (southwest) and ascend 65 m (213 ft).

Reach the northeast corner of **Baker Lake** at 9.1 km (5.6 mi), beneath the south slope of Fossil Mtn. A left spur leads south 50 m/yd to **Baker Lake campground**, at 2210 m (7250 ft). The tentsites are among clumps of stunted fir and spruce, just above the outlet stream. Rock ribs at the water's edge are a

Baker Lake

comfortable place to appreciate the scenery. The campground is ideally situated for the prevailing wind to keep mosquitoes grounded. Skip below for details about a short sidetrip southeast of Baker Lake.

Departing the campground, follow the trail west, along the lake's north shore. You're still in the alpine zone, so views are superb. At 10.2 km (6.3 mi), where a left (south) fork rounds the lake's west shore, proceed straight (west) and begin ascending. At 11.7 km (7.3 mi), 2350 m (7710 ft), intersect the trail over **Deception Pass**. Having completed a loop around Fossil Mtn, you're now on familiar ground. Right ascends northeast, over the pass. Go left (southwest), contour above **Ptarmigan Lake**, and retrace your steps past **Lake Louise Ski Area**, back to **Fish Creek trailhead**. Your total distance—including the sidetrip to the main Red Deer Lake, excluding a foray to Merlin Meadows—is 39.5 km (24.5 mi).

LITTLE BAKER, TILTED, & BRACHIOPOD LAKES

Starting at Baker Lake campground, you can see all three of these small lakes on a 4.8-km (3-mi) circuit. They're southeast of Baker, beneath the northeast face of Brachiopod Mtn. En route, you'll get a good view back north-northwest to Fossil Mtn, which rises sharply from Baker's north shore. Brachiopod Lake, however, is merely a pond. In late summer, don't hike the 0.6-km (0.4-mi) round-trip extension to see it, because you won't. It will probably have dried up by then.

From the campground, descend south, cross the Baker Lake outlet stream, and follow the trail curving right (southwest) around the east and southeast shores, through open larch forest. (Ignore the left fork descending east along the outlet stream into the Baker Creek drainage.)

At 0.7 km (0.4 mi), fork sharply left (east). Reach a junction at 1.5 km (0.9 mi), just north of Little Baker Lake. You'll return here after looping past the small lakes. For now, go left (east-southeast) and reach the north end of **Tilted Lake** at 1.8 km (1.1 mi).

Curve right (southwest). Reach a fork at 2.2 km (1.4 mi). Left leads south 0.3 km (0.2 mi) to **Brachiopod Lake**. The loop continues right (west) from this junction. It curves north, rounding the west shore of **Little Baker Lake**. At 2.7 km (1.7 mi), reach the junction where you began the loop.

After returning to the south shore of Baker Lake, you can continue retracing your steps (right / northeast) to arrive at the campground within 15 minutes, or go left (west-northwest) and hike all the way around the lake to complete a 6.5-km (4-mi) tour (including Brachiopod).

Sunrise, upper Fish Lake (Trip 88)

TRIP 88

North Molar Pass / Fish Lakes

LOCATION	Banff National Park
ROUND TRIP	23 km (14.3 mi) to North Molar Pass 29.6 km (18.4 mi) to Fish Lakes
ELEVATION GAIN	762 m (2500 ft) to pass, 1128 m (3700 ft) for lakes
KEY ELEVATIONS	trailhead 1830 m (6000 ft) pass 2590 m (8500 ft) lakes 2225 m (7300 ft)
HIKING TIME	8 hours for pass, 2 days for lakes
DIFFICULTY	moderate
MAPS	page 514; Hector Lake 82 N/9

OPINION

Give a Banff Avenue postcard rack a twirl. That's what you won't see here: individually awesome features. The Canadian Rockies have grander mountains, bigger lakes, more glaciers elsewhere. Yet this trip is exceptional because the scenery is consistently outstanding. You'll have no reason to seek solace in your Rainforest Crunch chocolate bar.

The treed ascent is gentle and, after 2 km (1.2 mi), often near Mosquito Creek. (Don't be deterred by the name. Insectile vampires are not especially abundant here.) Though the trail is initially rooty, and remains muddy and braided much of the way—a condition aggravated by horsepackers—it quickly lofts you into sprawling subalpine meadows. About one-and-a-half hours from the trailhead, the allure of vast, open, park-like slopes will help dispel your annoyance at the slop underfoot.

Upper Fish Lake, between a fortress-like wall and spacious alplands, is a lovely setting for an evening and morning in the mountains. Across the Pipestone River Valley, 3333-m (10,932-ft) Cataract Peak and its brawny brethren seem to barricade the eastern front. The sense of isolation here is delicious. Civilization, it seems, is a long way off, doesn't need you, nor you it.

The Fish Lake campground, however, is proof that too little of what the Park collects in fees is going to backcountry maintenance. The tent sites here are uncomfortably, unnecessarily close together. Many are not level. All are on muddy hardpan that you'll need kryptonite tent stakes to pierce. Worse, the campground is *on* the trail. Bears use trails, especially at night. We were reminded of that during our last stay here, when a grizzly snuffled and snorted around our tent. So, be vigilant about keeping a clean, odour-free camp. Then, upon your return, if you agree with this assessment, contact Banff Park and say so. Ask for increased investment in backcountry trail and campground maintenance. Specifically, request they (1) build gravel tent pads at Fish Lake campground, (2) ban horses from Mosquito

Creek and North Molar Pass, and (3) repair and re-vegetate this area's braided, eroded, entrenched trails.

Camping at Fish Lakes allows you time—either after you arrive, or the next morning—to explore north and southeast of the lakes, and overlook the upper Pipestone River Valley. Roadrunners (beep! beep!) can reach Fish Lakes on a dayhike. But descending the far side of North Molar Pass and having to regain that elevation loss, all in a single day, isn't worth it. Either devote a couple days to backpacking here, or dayhike only as far as the pass. The lakes aren't visible from there, but scrambling up the ridge remedies that. Ideally, Fish Lakes should be merely your first stop on an even longer trek over Pipestone and Clearwater passes to Devon Lakes (Trip 80).

Because Fish Lakes campground is popular, often booked full, either reserve a tentsite well in advance, or stay loose about your start date. As for when to hike here, you can expect to encounter snow snuggled into the east side of the pass through July. North Molar is one of Banff Park's highest trail-accessible passes. Another is Badger Pass (Trip 101).

FACT

By Vehicle

From the junction of Trans-Canada Hwy 1 and the Icefields Parkway (Hwy 93), drive the Parkway northwest 24 km (14.9 mi). Or, from Crowfoot Glacier viewpoint, drive the Parkway southeast 9 km (5.6 mi). From either approach, turn west into the entrance for Mosquito Creek campground and youth hostel. Park in the gravel lot on the left, immediately below the Parkway. The trailhead is on the Parkway's east side, just north of Mosquito Creek bridge, at 1830 m (6000 ft).

On Foot

Just past the trailhead kiosk, begin a brief climb north above **Mosquito Creek**. The trail gradually returns creekside and continues upstream (north). All the crossings of Mosquito and its tributaries are bridged. The ascent is gentle, the tread rooty and rocky. Proceed through open, coniferous forest, often on the creek's level, broad, boulder-strewn bank.

Reach **Mosquito Creek campground** at 5.5 km (3.4 mi), 2015 m (6610 ft). Just past the campground, cross to the creek's south bank. The trail gradually curves east, remaining creekside for another 1 km (0.6 mi). The ascent is moderate. Cross back to the north bank at 6.7 km (4.2 mi), now curving southeast.

Reach a **junction** at 7.3 km (4.5 mi), 2195 m (7200 ft). Right (southeast) leads to Molar Pass (Trip 30) in 3 km (1.9 mi). For North Molar Pass, bear left and ascend generally northeast into alpine meadows.

Heading east, pass **Mosquito Lake** (unlabeled on the topo map) at 9 km (5.6 mi), 2310 m (7577 ft). The trail steepens at 10.5 km (6.5 mi) and begins curving southeast. Cross the rocky gap of **North Molar Pass** at 11.5 km (7.1 mi), 2590 m (8500 ft). If you're not proceeding to Fish Lakes, scramble up the east side of the pass to survey the lakes and upper Pipestone River Valley.

Backpacking to the lakes? Push on through the pass and begin a steep southward descent, unless the snow is frightfully deep. Under light snow cover, the route

West of North Molar Pass

should remain apparent, perhaps indicated by the bootprints of hikers preceding you. It quickly descends 365 m (1200 ft) across open terrain.

Leveling out below the pass, the braided, trenched trail curves southeast, along the southwest bank of the **brook** draining this **upper basin**. Prevent the creation of new ruts by picking one and staying in it. With no trees to impede the view, you can fully appreciate the impressive scenery. Molar Mtn looms ahead (south-southeast). After a bridged stream crossing above a small canyon, the final descent is generally east. Upper Fish Lake is visible below, until you drop past treeline.

Reach **Fish Lake campground**, midway along the upper lake's forested northwest shore, at 14.8 km (9.2 mi), 2225 m (7300 ft). The trail continues northeast, passing a warden cabin at 15 km (9.3 mi), and descending into Pipestone River Valley. Directly east of the upper lake is the much smaller **Lower Fish Lake**, encircled by alpine larch, at 15.7 km (9.7 mi).

If you're not proceeding to Pipestone Pass, consider these short forays: (1) Rockhop Upper Fish Lake's outlet stream, then hike east 0.8 km (0.5 mi) to visit tiny Lower Fish Lake. (2) From Lower Fish Lake, hike southeast then south, contouring at about 2195 m (7200 ft), to reach a larger, unnamed lake in 2 km (1.2 mi). (3) Hike north of the campground, hop the creek, then ascend northeast about 1 km (0.6 mi) to where upper Pipestone River Valley is in full view.

TRIP 89

The Rockwall

LOCATION	Kootenay National Park
SHUTTLE TRIP	55 km (34 mi) one way
ELEVATION CHANGE	2260-m (7416-ft) gain, 2225-m (7298-ft) loss
KEY ELEVATIONS	Floe Lake trailhead 1348 m (4420 ft) Numa Pass 2380 m (7800 ft) Tumbling Pass 2210 m (7250 ft) Rockwall Pass 2241 m (7350 ft)
HIKING TIME	3 to 5 days
DIFFICULTY	challenging
MAPS	page 499; Gem Trek *Kootenay National Park;* Mount Goodsir 82 N/1

OPINION

The need for mystery is greater than the need for any answer. And the Rockwall trail is sufficiently long, arduous and stirring that it just might induce you to ponder a few of life's enduring mysteries. It's also sufficiently varied that you'll at least muse upon the most elementary and popular mystery of all: "What's next?"

Thigh-throbbing ascents to climactic vistas are followed by long knee-crunching swoops into forest. The trail slams up against a stone monolith, glides through meadows, dips under glaciers, and whips past lakes and waterfalls. Though affected by the summer 2003 fires, its appeal is only slightly diminished.

Despite the trail's serrated profile, you'll frequently be hiking above or near treeline, beside the sheer limestone cliffs of the 35-km (22-mi) Rockwall on the Great Divide. This solid eastern face of the Vermilion Range is broken only once along its length—at tight Wolverine Pass. The Rockwall is a fantastic sight, more than compensating for the strenuous effort necessary to admire it.

Driving through Kootenay Park, south of Marble Canyon, glimpses of pulse-quickening summits are few and fleeting—unlike in Banff, Jasper and Yoho parks. Only a couple tantalizing peaks are visible from Hwy 93. They're far up the forested valleys to the west. They're part of the Rockwall. To enter this sequestered realm of mountain majesty, you must commit to one of those long approaches.

By starting at the Floe Lake trailhead and hiking the Rockwall trail northwest, you'll dispatch the stiffer climbs on the first half of the trek. At a race pace you can finish in three days: one afternoon, two full days, and one morning. Floe Lake, beneath 1000-m (3330-ft) cliffs, is a gorgeous setting for your first night. On the second night, stay at Tumbling Creek campground. Shoot for Helmet Falls campground your last night. The waterfall plunges 350 m (1148 ft), making it one of

The Rockwall and Floe Lake

Canada's four highest. (See image on inside back cover.) If you need more time to complete the trip, spend your second night at Numa Creek campground, below the steep ascent to Tumbling Pass.

If you exit via Helmet and Ochre creeks, you'll complete a 55-km (34-mi) one-way trip. Some backpackers extend this to a four- to six-day trek by proceeding north over Goodsir Pass (Trip 50) into Yoho Park, then up McArthur Creek to Lake O'Hara, for a total of 67 km (41.5 mi). We don't recommend it. The most efficient way to visit Goodsir Pass is on a half-day hike from Helmet Falls campground. And Lake O'Hara (Trips 14-19) offers enough *Premier* hiking to deserve a pilgrimage exclusively to that region. The descent from Goodsir Pass to the Ottertail River is largely through viewless forest. To reach Lake O'Hara from there, you must hike the McArthur Creek trail (Trip 114), rated *Don't Do*.

Try to allow enough time on your Rockwall journey to include the half-day hike from Helmet Falls to vast, lonely, lovely Goodsir Pass, where you'll see the twin-horned Goodsir Towers. This 8-km (5-mi) round-trip excursion requires you to ascend and descend 450 m (1475 ft). Proceed northwest through the pass for a direct view of the Goodsirs, which rise 1950 m (6400 ft) from Goodsir Creek. Don't have time for the entire Rockwall? Consider Trips 35 and 48—shorter hikes that feature some of the trail's highlights.

What happened to the Rockwall trail during the summer 2003 fires? Only the Floe Lake approach was burned, the rest was untouched. On September 8, a severely hot blaze raced up the valley and stopped at the final switchbacks below Floe Lake. All the trees around the campground and lake were untouched. The magnificent meadows and larches between Floe Lake and Numa Pass remain.

Previously, the Floe Creek drainage harboured the Rockies' best imitation of a rainforest. The trail plowed through thigh-thwacking foliage in a dense, mature woodland of girthy trees. What remains are spindly, charred snags. It's a 10.5-km (6.5-mi) stretch—a small percentage of the trip's overall length—but if you prefer to avoid it, you can. The other Rockwall approaches—Numa Creek, Tumbling Creek, Ochre and Helmet creeks, and Goodsir Pass—were unscorched, so you have numerous entry and exit options.

One evasive tactic is to enter via Numa Creek. Within 30 minutes, the trail is creekside. It remains within view of the water, and is often beside it, all the way to the Rockwall trail junction. Camp at Numa Creek campground the first and second nights. Spend the second day hiking to Numa Pass—a 15-km (9.3-mi) round trip culminating with a panoramic vista that includes an aerial perspective of Floe Lake. Camp at Helmet Falls campground the third night. Spend half a day visiting Goodsir Pass the next day, then camp at Helmet Creek or Helmet/Ochre Junction campground the fourth night. Exit on day five.

FACT

Before your trip

Want to extend this hike to Lake O'Hara? Read Trip 14, then make the required reservations. Also read *Before your trip* on page 413, about McArthur Creek valley.

By Vehicle

The Floe Lake / Hawk Creek trailhead parking lot is on the southwest side of

The Rockwall

Hwy 93. Reach it by driving 22.5 km (14 mi) south of the Banff-Kootenay boundary, or 71 km (44 mi) north of Kootenay Park's West Gate at Radium. Elevation: 1348 m (4420 ft).

The Paint Pots trailhead parking lot is 13 km (8 mi) northwest of the Floe Lake/Hawk Creek trailhead. It's on the northwest side of Hwy 93. Reach it by driving 9.5 km (6 mi) southwest of the Banff-Kootenay boundary, or 84 km (52 mi) north of Kootenay Park's West Gate at Radium. Elevation: 1440 m (4723 ft). If arranging a shuttle, leave one car there.

The Numa Creek trailhead parking lot is 4.5 km (2.8 mi) south of the Paint Pots trailhead. It's on the southwest side of Hwy 93. Reach it by driving 14 km (8.7 mi) southwest of the Banff-Kootenay boundary, or 79.5 km (49.4 mi) north of Kootenay Park's West Gate at Radium. Elevation: 1405 m (4608 ft).

On Foot

To begin hiking at the Floe Lake trailhead, read the *On Foot* section for Trip 48. Follow the directions to **Floe Lake**, at 10.7 km (6.6 mi), 2040 m (6690 ft). Continue to **Numa Pass**, at 13.4 km (8.3 mi), 2355 m (7724 ft)—the Rockwall trail's highest point. From there, the trail drops 830 m (2722 ft) down the north side of the pass into lush Numa Creek basin. Reach Numa Creek campground at 20.5 km (12.7 mi). The Rockwall trail intersects the Numa Creek trail just beyond, at 20.9 km (13 mi). Turn left (west) to continue hiking the Rockwall trail. Right immediately crosses a tributary, then follows Numa Creek downstream 6.6 km (4.1 mi) to Hwy 93.

To begin hiking at the Numa Creek trailhead, cross the bridge over the Vermilion River gorge. The trail curves northwest, ascends briefly, then descends. At 2.3 km (1.4 mi), cross the sturdy, aluminum-and-plank bridge spanning Numa Creek. On the north bank, follow the trail upstream: initially west for about 15 minutes, then curving southwest, which will remain your general direction of travel until intersecting the Rockwall trail. At 4.6 km (2.9 mi) bear left; stay on the trail paralleling the creek. Soon, you'll see the Rockwall ahead, soaring to 3200 m (10,500 ft). At 6.6 km (4.1 mi), 1510 m (4953 ft), cross to the south bank of a bridged tributary and intersect the Rockwall trail. Right (west) enters Numa basin and within 1 km (0.6 mi) begins a steep ascent to Tumbling Pass. Left (south) reaches Numa Creek campground in 0.4 km (0.25 mi). From there, it continues southeast, climbing 845 m (2772 ft) in 7.5 km (4.7 mi) to crest **Numa Pass** at 2355 m (7724 ft).

To resume hiking the Rockwall trail from its junction with the Numa Creek trail, proceed west into Numa basin. The grade steepens. Switchbacks aid your progress on the 740-m (2427-ft) ascent. After turning northwest, surmount 2250-m (7380-ft) **Tumbling Pass** amid larch trees at 25.7 km (15.9 mi), 2210 m (7250 ft). Tumbling Glacier is left (west) on Mt. Gray. Foster Peak is southeast, above Numa Pass.

If you accessed the Rockwall trail via Numa Creek, even after a round trip detour to Numa Pass, you'll have hiked only slightly farther than the distances stated here, which are based on starting at Floe Lake trailhead. Simply add 0.7 km (0.4 mi). Your total distance to Tumbling Pass, for example, would be 26.4 km (16.4 mi).

At Tumbling Pass, the trail crosses larch-scattered, **subalpine meadows**, then parallels a terminal moraine. In just over a kilometre, begin a rapid descent north. At 28 km (17.4 mi), 1890 m (6200 ft), reach a junction near Tumbling Creek. Right (northeast), initially staying on the creek's right (east) bank, is the Tumbling Creek trail. It descends the valley to reach Hwy 93 in 10.9 km (6.8 mi). Turn left (west), cross the bridge over the creek, then follow the trail left (upstream) 0.3 km (0.2 mi) to **Tumbling Creek campground**. Proceed through the campground to where the Rockwall trail begins a switchbacking ascent northwest initially among fir trees, later among larches.

At 30.8 km (19.1 mi) reach the southeast side of meadowy **Wolverine Plateau**. About five minutes farther, a trail forks left (west) through 2210-m (7250-ft) Wolverine Pass—a narrow cleft between Mts. Gray (left/south) and Drysdale (right/north). Just 120 m (130 yd) into the pass, you'll cross the provincial and park boundaries and attain a view west to B.C.'s Purcell Range. Go right (north) of the small berm to glimpse the Bugaboos.

Continuing north on the Rockwall trail, a gentle ascent leads to 2241-m (7350-ft) **Rockwall Pass** at 31.5 km (19.5 mi). You're in a vast meadow beside the Rockwall. This limestone bulwark—4 km (2.5 mi) long, rising 670 m (2200 ft) above you, linking 2932-m (9620-ft) Mt. Drysdale and 2878-m (9440-ft) Limestone Peak—is unique in the Canadian Rockies.

About ten minutes farther, begin descending. Pass a glacial pond. About 220 m (720 ft) below the pass, cross a bridged stream. The trail then follows a lateral moraine down to a meadow, ascends briefly, crosses another small bridge, and resumes descending. It bottoms-out in a drainage, then climbs 220 m (722 ft) through an extensive, larch-lined meadow to crest a 2170-m (7118-ft) shoulder of **Limestone Peak**.

Tumbling Glacier (left), Mt. Gray (right), from near Wolverine Pass

A long, steep descent ensues. One minute farther, where the trail angles west, the top of 350-m (1148-ft) Helmet Falls is visible. You might also hear it crashing into the broad amphitheatre created by Sharp Mtn (northwest), Helmet Mtn (west-southwest), and Limestone Peak (southeast).

On the valley floor, cross bridged Helmet Creek and arrive at a signed junction. Left (southwest) leads 0.5 km (0.3 mi) to the falls. Go right (north-northeast) to reach **Helmet Falls campground** on an alluvial flat at 39.8 km (24.7 mi). A warden cabin is just past the campground. A bit farther, reach a junction at 40.4 km (25 mi), 1765 m (5790 ft). To reach the Paint Pots trailhead on Hwy 93, bear right (east) and descend along the north bank of Helmet Creek. To visit Goodsir Pass or extend your trek into Yoho Park, ascend left (north); skip below for further directions.

Descending Helmet Creek valley, cross a bridge at 42.7 km (26.5 mi) to the creek's south bank. Cross a bridged fork of Helmet Creek at 48.2 km (30 mi). A few minutes farther, cross bridged Ochre Creek and reach a junction with the **Ochre Creek trail** at 48.8 km (30.3 mi). Helmet/Ochre Junction campground is here. Left (north) ascends to Ottertail Pass. Go right (southeast).

At 51.1 km (31.7 mi) stay left (east) where the Tumbling Creek trail (Trip 35) forks right (west), crosses Ochre Creek and passes **Ochre Creek campground**. At 53.6 km (33.2 mi) turn right (south) where a trail to Marble Canyon bears left (east). Your trail then exits the forest and passes the large paint pots (ochre beds). At a fork where straight (northeast) leads to Marble Canyon, turn right and immediately cross the Vermilion River suspension bridge. In a couple minutes, arrive at the **Paint Pots trailhead** parking lot on Hwy 93, having completed a 55-km (34.1-mi) journey.

Heading for Goodsir Pass or Yoho Park? At the 40.4-km (25-mi) junction on the north side of Helmet Creek, fork left (north). The trail gains 445 m (1460 ft) in 4 km (2.5 mi) to enter meadowy, larch-fringed **Goodsir Pass** at 2210 m (7250 ft). From the southeast end of the pass, a moderate cross-country ascent will reward you with a commanding view atop the ridge on the northeast side of the pass. Transcend treeline about 15 minutes up.

South-southwest of the pass is 3049-m (10,000-ft) Sharp Mtn. Southwest, behind Sharp, is 3267-m (10,716-ft) Sentry Peak. West are the twin towers of Mt. Goodsir. The south tower is 3562 m (11,683 ft), the north tower is 3525 m (11,562 ft). Northwest of the pass, the trail enters Yoho Park at 48 km (29.8 mi). About 2 km (1.2 mi) through the pass, where you start descending, attain a better view across Goodsir Creek valley to the northeast face of the Goodsir Towers.

From the Kootenay-Yoho boundary, the trail descends steadily through dense forest to **Goodsir Creek**. Near 53.5 km (33.2 mi), stay left (northwest) where a trail detours right (northeast) to Ottertail Falls. Stay left again in ten minutes, just before the Ottertail River bridge. Near 54.5 km (33.8 mi) pass the McArthur Creek warden cabin, from which the Goodsir Towers are visible. McArthur Creek campground is just beyond. Cross the **McArthur Creek bridge** and reach a junction at 55 km (34.1 mi), 1460 m (4790 ft). Bearing left, the Ottertail River fire road (Trip 50) leads northwest 16.2 km (10 mi) to the **Trans-Canada Hwy**. Right leads north to McArthur Pass and Lake O'Hara; for directions read Trip 114.

Wolverine Plateau, Rockwall trail

TRIP 90

Little Yoho Valley / Kiwetinok Pass / Whaleback / Waterfall Valley

LOCATION	Yoho National Park
CIRCUIT	28.8 km (17.9 mi), with sidetrips 37.8 km (23.4 mi)
ELEVATION GAIN	circuit 1050 m (3444 ft) with sidetrips 1648 m (5405 ft)
KEY ELEVATIONS	trailhead 1675 m (5495 ft) Little Yoho Valley 2075 m (6805 ft) Whaleback 2210 m (7250 ft) Kiwetinok Pass 2460 m (8070 ft)
HIKING TIME	10 hours or overnight
DIFFICULTY	moderate
MAPS	page 497; Gem Trek *Lake Louise & Yoho*

OPINION

Yoho is a Cree exclamation of astonishment, roughly equivalent to *Wow!* The first leg of this journey—the Iceline (Trip 13)—reveals why the Park's name is apt. And the wonders don't stop there.

The crowd doesn't stop there either. Each of the trails linked to create this trip are popular dayhikes, so you won't enjoy the solitude that's usually a reward of backpacking. The benefit of a trip comprising various trails, however, is flexibility: you decide the total distance.

From the Iceline, you'll drop into Little Yoho Valley. There's a campground here, as well as Stanley Mitchell hut. The lovely meadow at the head of the valley allows unobstructed views of the surrounding mountains, including the glacier-encrusted President Range.

Above Little Yoho, on the rocky slopes of Mt. Kerr, the earth is magnificently garbled. Here, Kiwetinok lake and pass are your goals on a short but climactic side-trip. The trail briefly fades to a cairned route where an unbridged creek crossing requires you to rockhop or ford. It then reappears and conveys you efficiently into the alpine zone. You'll pierce a miniature canyon, admire the lake's stark setting, crest the pass, and gaze across the Kiwetinok and Amiskwi river valleys, beyond the Columbia River Valley, to peaks in Canada's Glacier National Park.

Exiting Little Yoho, continue over the 2210-m (7250-ft) Whaleback, where you can survey the stupendous topography walling in Yoho Valley. The highlights are Yoho Glacier, Glacier Des Poilus, and Waputik Icefield. You can also gaze northwest into Waterfall Valley—an enticing sidetrip. Next stop: 80-m (262-ft) Twin Falls. Perch on the precipice for an exhilarating, perhaps scary reminder of how tenuous life is. Careful. A few hikers have fallen to their deaths.

Don't get suckered into the slightly shorter approach to Little Yoho Valley via Yoho Valley, unless it's a rainy day. The trail is swallowed in forest. Opt for the vastly more scenic Iceline. You'll have to climb 125 m (410 ft) higher, but you'll be transported to heady emotional heights.

The logical first-night refuge is Little Yoho Valley, at the campground or hut. That's only 10.4 km (6.4 mi) via the Iceline, so after arriving you should have time to explore Kiwetinok Pass. Next day, complete the trip by traversing the Whaleback, side-tripping into Waterfall Valley, descending to the base of Twin Falls, then hiking all the way out Yoho Valley, for a total of about 20.5 km (12.7 mi). The only ascent on day two would be an easy 305 m (1000 ft) over the Whaleback.

To slow the trip down to three days, spend the second night creekside, in beautiful forest, at Twin Falls campground. The distance between Little Yoho and Twin Falls campgrounds is only 10.3 km (6.4 mi), so en route you'll have time to explore Waterfall Valley. Laughing Falls campground, shortly down-valley from Twin Falls campground, is another attractive, creekside option.

Eliminating Little Yoho Valley and Kiwetinok Pass whittles the trip down to a long dayhike. It's more important to attain the stupendous Whaleback vantage than to see Little Yoho or Kiwetinok. Consider a one-day, 27-km (16.7-mi) loop: the Iceline, a short up-and-back detour to the Iceline highpoint, the descent past Lake Celeste, the Whaleback traverse, Twin Falls, and a gently-graded return via Yoho Valley.

FACT

By Vehicle

Follow the directions for the Iceline (Trip 13) to the Takakkaw Falls parking lot. From the south end of the parking lot, walk the trail back to the Yoho Pass trailhead, in front of the youth hostel. Elevation: 1520 m (4985 ft).

Before your trip

To stay in the Whiskey Jack Youth Hostel, at the trailhead, make reservations with Lake Louise International Hostel. To stay in the Stanley Mitchell hut, in Little Yoho Valley, make reservations with the Alpine Club of Canada. The contact information for both is listed under *Information Sources* in the back of this book. To stay in the Twin Falls Chalet, call (403) 228-7079.

On Foot

From the northwest side of the parking lot, in front of the **Whiskey Jack Youth Hostel**, ascend the **Yoho Pass trail** into forest. It curves southwest, then south. Keep right at the 1-km (0.6-mi) and 1.3-km (0.8-mi) forks. At 2.5 km (1.6 mi) turn right again, onto the **Iceline trail**. Left leads south to Yoho Lake and Pass.

The Iceline ascends northwest, soon emerging from trees. Traverse rocky slopes with Emerald Glacier left (west) above you. Hop across a couple streams. The trail undulates over moraine, ascending steadily to a junction at 5.7 km (3.5 mi), 2190 m (7183 ft). Right (north) descends past Lake Celeste. Go that way if dayhiking over the Whaleback; skip to the third full paragraph on page 323. If backpacking, stay left and proceed northwest to the 2210-m (7250-ft) **highpoint** on a moraine, at

Twin Falls Creek roaring to its 80-m (262-ft) drop

6.4 km (4 mi). Having climbed 690 m (2265 ft) from the trailhead, you're now in a rocky amphitheatre beneath Emerald Glacier. The 3066-m (10,059-ft) Vice President is nearby southwest. North-northwest, across Little Yoho Valley, are Whaleback Mtn (right) and Isolated Peak (left).

From the 6.4-km (4-mi) highpoint, descend to a blue **tarn** chilled by ice slabs. The trail heads generally northwest. Enter meadows and subalpine forest near 8.5 km (5.3 mi). The north side of the President Range is visible south.

Reach a junction in **Little Yoho Valley**, at 10.5 km (6.5 mi), 2075 m (6805 ft), just south of the **Little Yoho River**. The **Stanley Mitchell hut**, across the river, is visible here. For Kiwetinok Pass, go left (west-southwest), upstream, on the south bank; skip to page 325 for directions. Right (northeast) quickly reaches a bridge to the north bank. Just shy of the hut is a junction. Go left (west) 200 m (220 yd) to enter **Little Yoho campground**. Right (east) is the Little Yoho River trail descending into Yoho Valley.

Down-valley, at 14 km (8.7 mi), the right fork ascends past Lake Celeste. Stay straight. Only 100 m (110 yd) farther, at 1905 m (6250 ft), turn left and begin a steep ascent of the Whaleback. Straight continues descending to intersect the Yoho Valley trail.

The trail climbs north, gaining 305 m (1000 ft) in only 2.1 km (1.3 mi) via tight switchbacks. Crest the **Whaleback** at 16.2 km (10 mi), 2210 m (7250 ft). Visible south are The President and The Vice President. West, above Kiwetinok Pass, are Mounts Kerr and Pollinger. Northwest are Waterfall Valley and Glacier Des Poilus. North are Yoho Peak and Yoho Glacier. Northeast are Mt. Balfour and Trolltinder Mtn. East is Waputik Icefield. Southeast is Mt. Niles.

Proceeding north-northeast, a moderate descent of the Whaleback leads to a bridge over **Twin Falls Creek** at 17.5 km (10.9 mi), 1980 m (6495 ft), just above **Twin Falls**. A mere 100 m (110 yd) north-northeast of the bridge, a cairned spur forks left (northwest) probing **Waterfall Valley**; skip below for directions.

From the top of Twin Falls, the main trail ascends north about 15 minutes through open forest, along the edge of an escarpment. Attain views east to 3272-m (10,732-ft) Mt. Balfour, and south into Yoho Valley. At 2035 m (6670 ft), begin descending short, steep switchbacks. Reach signed **Twin Falls junction**, on the valley floor, at 20.3 km (12.6 mi), 1806 m (5925 ft). The Twin Falls Chalet is visible ahead. Ignore the unscenic Marpole Connector trail beyond the chalet. The base of the falls, where the twin torrents complete their 80-m (263-ft) dive off a sheer limestone cliff, is also nearby (south). You'll find picnic tables there. Turn left (northeast) to continue hiking down-valley.

The trees in this forest are stately. A few are so big, three adults with arms outstretched couldn't encircle their trunks. Pass a narrow chasm where Twin Falls Creek, having regained momentum below the falls pool, roars deeper into the valley. Reach **Twin Falls campground** at 21.7 km (13.5 mi). A fork gives you the option to skirt left of it. Level tent pads and the roar of the nearby creek are conducive to a restful night here. There are several tables on the rocky beach.

At the east end of the campground, cross a bridged creek. Then intersect the **Yoho Valley trail** at 21.9 km (13.6 mi), 1686 m (5530 ft). Left (north-northwest) leads 2.3 km (1.4 mi) to a view of Yoho Glacier. Turn right to continue hiking down-valley. Your general direction of travel will be southeast all the way to the trailhead. The grade remains gentle.

At 1620 m (5315 ft), cross a substantial bridge to the west bank of the **Yoho River**. Five minutes farther, reach a junction at 24 km (14.9 mi), 1607 m (5270 ft). Right (west-southwest) leads 2.2 km (1.4 mi) to the Whaleback trail that you previously ascended from Little Yoho Valley. Proceed straight (downstream). In a couple minutes, pass **Laughing Falls campground**. Beyond, pass spurs forking to Duchesnay Lake, Point Lace Falls, and Angel's Staircase. Stay on the main trail. Shortly after passing through **Takakkaw Falls campground**, enter the **Takakkaw Falls parking lot** at 28.8 km (17.9 mi).

WATERFALL VALLEY

Two minutes north-northeast of the **bridge spanning Twin Falls Creek**, immediately after crossing a dry streambed at 1982 m (6500 ft), look left for a cairned spur. Follow it northwest into open forest, departing the main trail.

Within five minutes, pass a voluminous **cascade** crashing over rock ledges. Continue following the path generally northwest. At 2200 m (7216 ft), about 35 minutes from the main trail, attain a view northwest into the moraine-and-ice choked expanse of **Waterfall Valley**. It's bound by Isolated Peak (nearby, west-southwest), Mt. Des Poilus (northwest), and Yoho Peak (nearby, north). Behind you (southeast) is Mt. Niles (Trip 12), which towers above Takakkaw Falls. Distant south-southeast, past Hwy 1, are the Cathedral Crags. The path then descends briefly.

About 40 minutes from the main trail, cross a **brook** at 2 km (1.2 mi), 2180 m (7155 ft). A path continues west onto tan bedrock but soon vanishes. Curiosity is now your guide. One option is to proceed 50 m (65 yd) beyond the last pond, then ascend a moraine north-northwest to a **promontory**. After exploring, retrace your steps to the main trail at Twin Falls.

KIWETINOK PASS

From the 10.5-km (6.5-mi) junction at 2075 m (6805 ft), just south of the **Little Yoho River**, go left (west-southwest). Upstream, ascend above a deep gorge. Exiting forest, approach the broad, rocky creekbed. It's tempting to hike south on the east bank toward visible ice, but resist. Look for cairns indicating where the trail resumes on the west bank, then find an easy place to rockhop or ford.

On the west bank, ascend generally west. Except for a short, steep pitch, the trail climbs moderately above treeline. At 2454 m (8050 ft) reach the south shore of **Kiwetinok Lake**. It abuts the east edge of the pass. A snow-capped slope rises sharply from the west shore. Midway along the shore, past the cornice, ascend left. Quickly crest the ridge—just above and south of 2460-m (8070-ft) **Kiwetinok Pass**.

Kiwetinok Lake

TRIP 91

Tangle Pass / Beauty Lakes

LOCATION	Jasper National Park
ROUND TRIP	9 km (5.6 mi) for pass, 16 km (10 mi) for lakes
ELEVATION GAIN	680 m (2230 ft) for pass, 1175 m (3855 ft) for lakes
KEY ELEVATIONS	trailhead 1860 m (6100 ft), pass 2540 m (8330 ft) Beauty Creek 2235 m (7330 ft) lakes 2425 m (7955 ft)
HIKING TIME	5 to 6 hours for pass, overnight for lakes
DIFFICULTY	challenging
MAPS	page 501; Gem Trek *Columbia Icefield;* Sunwapta Peak 83 C/6

OPINION

Bashing your way through Borneo, or slogging across the North Pole, a GPS unit would be invaluable. But most hikers need GPS like they need a brick in their pack. GPS can even be a disadvantage. Rely on it too much, and you'll succumb to Gadget Pea-brain Syndrome: failure to acquire the invaluable skill of reading the land. You could even end up a Gadget Pampered Sissy. Or worse, a Gadget Plagued Stooge.

So, contrary to the hype spewed with breathless enthusiasm by outdoor magazines, you don't need a GPS unit to hike cross-country over Tangle Pass to the Beauty Lakes. Though most of the journey is off-trail, all you need is a topo map, compass, and a little routefinding experience, or the desire to gain some. You'll discover a lonely, lovely, alpine basin dotted with lakes. You'll likely gain a confidence-building sense of achievement. And perhaps you'll learn that finding your own way through the mountains is more rewarding than being pulled along by an electronic ring through your nose.

Tangle Pass and *Beauty Lakes* are not labeled on maps. The names are unofficial but logical. Tangle Pass is north-northeast of Tangle Creek's north fork, and southeast of Tangle Ridge. The creek and ridge *are* labeled on maps. The Beauty Lakes are north of Beauty Creek valley's upper reaches. Beauty Creek is also labeled on maps. In its lower reaches, it flows through a beautiful canyon (Trip 135) just before reaching the Icefields Parkway (Hwy 93) and contributing to the headwaters of Sunwapta River. The Beauty Lakes, however, would be horrendously difficult to reach via Beauty Creek canyon, hence the much easier route described here.

The lakes are a mere 7.5 km (4.7 mi) from the Parkway, yet there's alchemy in this journey. A high-elevation trailhead, rapidly changing scenery—from shadowy forest to alpine desolation—and utter tranquility conspire to elicit the feeling of having trekked several days. Tangle Pass, attainable within two-and-a-half hours, affords a grand view. You'll see glacier-laden Mt. Athabasca, meadowy Wilcox Pass

Fording Beauty Creek en route to Beauty Lakes

(Trip 20), Upper Beauty Creek valley (see page 533), and the Beauty Lakes basin. The valley and basin have the enigmatic appearance of having never been visited prior to your triumphant arrival.

Upon entering the basin, pitch your tent (1) at least 70 m/yd away from any water source, and (2) where it will have minimal impact on the fragile vegetation. Leave no trace of your stay. While exploring the basin, you'll find the topo map motivational, because it reveals intriguing options for wandering surprisingly far. It also divulges that Jonas Pass (Trip 92) is just over the basin headwall.

Despite the short round-trip distance, only fleet, experienced, determined hikers who start before 9 a.m. in mid summer should attempt to visit the lakes on a dayhike. Even if you meet all those requirements, you'll have only about an hour to probe the basin. The trail-less terrain makes this a more challenging, time-consuming venture than the statistics insinuate. If backpacking, however, even an afternoon start should give you ample time to reach the basin before nightfall.

Dayhiking? Turn around after enjoying lunch at Tangle Pass. But instead of retracing every step, consider hiking out to the Parkway via Wilcox Pass. Don't have two vehicles to arrange a shuttle? It's only a short hitchhike from the Wilcox Pass trailhead to the Tangle Falls parking lot.

FACT

Before your trip

Read *Before your trip* for Pipestone Pass / Devon Lakes (Trip 80). It describes how to safely store food in an alpine environment, like the Beauty Lakes, where there is no official campground.

By Vehicle

From the Icefield Centre, drive the Icefields Parkway (Hwy 93) northwest 7.2 km (4.5 mi). Turn left (west) into the Tangle Falls parking lot, at 1860 m (6100 ft). There are pit toilets here. The trail departs the opposite (northeast) side of the Parkway, right (southeast) of the falls, where a sign states: Wilcox Pass 7.5 km, Wilcox campground 12 km.

On Foot

The trail initially ascends southeast, paralleling the highway. It then veers left into the forest and ascends north. Within ten minutes, it levels at 4415 m (6550 ft) and affords views of the glacier-draped peaks west and southwest beyond the highway. Proceed north-northeast.

Within 20 minutes of the trailhead, glimpse Tangle Ridge through the trees. It's northeast, beyond the Tangle Creek drainage. A few minutes farther, **Tangle Creek** is visible below you. At about 30 minutes, the trail grazes the creek and follows it upstream (east-northeast). Tangle Pass is now visible. It's the obvious U-shaped gap between smooth scree slopes on the right (southeast) end of Tangle Ridge.

If you notice cairns on the far bank of Tangle Creek, ignore them. Don't ford the creek here. Stay on the trail. About 45 minutes along, at 2090 m (6850 ft), cross a **bridged tributary**. The trail then curves southeast. The north end of Wilcox Pass is now visible ahead. About 55 minutes along, the trail approaches a **low rock wall**. At the wall's right (south) end, which is about head high, the trail does a hairpin turn to lead you north-northeast atop the wall.

The trail then curves right (east), en route to Wilcox Pass. **Abandon the trail here**. Ascend north-northeast into the forest. Maintain that direction, but follow the path of least resistance. Don't descend into the minor drainage to your left. Stay right of it and keep ascending.

At 2230 m (7310 ft), about 1¼ hours from the trailhead, surpass the trees and proceed across a level, brushy **bench**. Your goal, Tangle Pass, is in full view north-northeast. See the creek drainage descending from it? You'll follow it to the pass.

Meanwhile, cross the bench—about a five-minute task. A short, sharp descent then leads to **Tangle Creek**. Rockhop to the far bank, angle right, and proceed generally north toward the pass. The ascent is gradual now but the ground cover remains dense. Bash onward.

We prefer to initially stay left (west) of the creek flowing from the pass, then cross to the right (east) side about a third of the way up. However you proceed, the grade soon steepens. The terrain is rockier above, and barren on top.

At 4.5 km (2.8 mi), 2552 m (8370 ft)—about 2¼ hours from the trailhead—enter **Tangle Pass**, a broad alpine saddle unnamed on maps. Tangle Ridge (named on maps) is left (west-northwest). On your return trip, consider ascending the ridge for a greatly expanded view.

Proceed through the pass to overlook the upper reaches of Beauty Creek valley and peer into Beauty Lakes basin (north-northeast). The red-hued mountain left of the basin is unnamed. Northwest of it is sharp, anvil-shaped, 3316-m (10,875-ft) Sunwapta Peak.

Most dayhikers turn around at the pass. Backpackers should pause here to survey the next leg of their journey: descending into the valley, then ascending to the lakes basin.

Start the descent into Beauty Creek valley on a **scree slope** 25 m/yd left (north) of where a stream plummets through a snow-choked defile. The slope is steep, but the soft scree provides secure footing.

Below the scree slope, work your way down through rocky terrain. Stop above the **cliff band** and traverse right (east) until a break in the solid rock allows you to step onto another **scree slope** and resume descending.

About 30 minutes from the pass, stride onto the treeless valley floor at 2287 m (7500 ft). A few minutes farther, reach **Beauty Creek** at 6.5 km (4 mi), 2235 m (7330 ft). Expect a calf-deep ford, though it might be shallow enough to rockhop.

On the far bank, hike generally north across the **alplands** toward Beauty Lakes basin. You'll step over two streams. After the second one, which drains the basin, angle north-northeast. The ascent steepens yet again.

About 40 minutes from Beauty Creek, pass a pond and arrive at the first of the **Beauty Lakes**—a long, slender one, tucked against the basin wall. Stay about 10 m (33 ft) above the lake and continue north across tussocky grass.

Pass a tarn and surmount a rib at 7.5 km (4.7 mi), 2430 m (7970 ft)—about 50 minutes from Beauty Creek—to reach the **largest lake**. You'll find flat patches of gravel that make ideal leave-no-trace tent sites.

The most secure way to cache your food in this alpine environment is to use a bear canister. If all you have is a stuff sack and a rope, suspend your food from the rock arch above the largest lake's outlet stream.

The view south-southwest is gratifying. From here, the Tangle Pass route looks impossibly steep. Beyond it is the Columbia Icefield.

Tangle Ridge and the lower Beauty Lake

TRIP 92

Jonas Pass / Poboktan Pass / Brazeau Lake

LOCATION	Jasper National Park
DISTANCE	79.3-km (49.2-mi) circuit including Brazeau Lake 74-km (46-mi) round trip to Poboktan Pass 54.2-km (33.6-mi) shuttle trip over Jonas Pass, out Poboktan Creek
ELEVATION GAIN	1830 m (6002 ft) on circuit 2050 m (6725 ft) on round trip 1250 m (4100 ft) on shuttle trip
ELEVATION LOSS	2000 m (6560 ft) on circuit 2050 m (6725 ft) on round trip 1378 m (4520 ft) on shuttle trip
KEY ELEVATIONS	trailhead 1860 m (6100 ft) Nigel Pass 2195 m (7200 ft) Jonas Pass 2320 m (7610 ft) Jonas Shoulder 2470 m (8100 ft) Poboktan Pass 2300 m (7545 ft) Brazeau River Valley 1720 m (5640 ft)
HIKING TIME	3 to 5 days
DIFFICULTY	moderate
MAPS	page 516; Gem Trek *Columbia Icefield* (for south half); Sunwapta Peak 83 C/6 (for north half), Columbia Icefield 83 C/3

OPINION

Time spent playing in the mountains will not be subtracted from your life. It might even lengthen it. Find out, on this marvelous multi-day adventure.

Begin with an easy, scenic ascent to Nigel Pass (Trip 33), where the panorama is striking in its sharp-edged austerity. The perception of mountains as cold, hard and unforgiving is irrefutable here. Later, the opposite appears true, as you're gently welcomed into the soft, green alplands of Jonas Pass. This is the climax of the trip. Lined by glaciated peaks, the pass is actually a long, high valley. Walking its 11-km (7-mi) length on a fine day is bliss. From there it's up to Jonas Shoulder, where you'll attain a stirring view: way down the meadowy valley to serpentine Jonas Creek; beyond to glacier-frosted mountains—mostly unnamed, seemingly unsullied as a result; and above Poboktan Creek to intriguing slopes that all-but-audibly invite exploration. Watch for hoary marmots and mountain caribou; Jonas and Poboktan passes are prime habitat for both.

Upper Brazeau River valley

Before committing to the entire circuit, be as aware of its drawbacks as you are of its highlights. After an exciting plunge from Poboktan Pass into John-John Creek canyon, you'll endure 14.5 km (9 mi)—past Brazeau Lake, well into the Brazeau River Valley—mostly in lodgepole-pine dominated forest. Lodgepoles are roughly the mountain equivalent of a palm tree—skinny trunks, green only up top—so when they line the trail, all you see is dark, flaky bark. A lodgepole forest is a grim sight, regardless what those spin-doctoring biologists tell you. The darned trees even impair your appreciation of 5-km (3-mi) long Brazeau Lake. It's one of the ten largest in the Canadian Rockies backcountry, but the perimetre is heavily forested, and the trail touches the shore only once: at the campground. The glacier beyond the lake's northwest end? It's briefly visible, though so distant it looks like a mere snowflake.

Next, you'll enter the Brazeau River Valley and suffer yet more forest, more nondescript mountains. The tranquil, riverbank setting of Wolverine South campground makes up for its lack of scenery. Up-valley, the ensuing 6.5 km (4 mi) to Four Point campground are beautifully pastoral. Then it's back into trees for 3.3 km (2 mi) to Boulder Creek campground before re-entering the alpine zone on the approach to Nigel Pass. There. You've imagined the worst. You should probably hike the entire circuit anyway. It's a grand journey into vast, solitudinous wilderness. The sense of accomplishment more than compensates for the bouts of monotony.

Strong trekkers who start early on day one can scorch the circuit in three days, spending the first night at Jonas Cutoff, the second at Wolverine. Most hikers will take five days, camping at Four Point, Jonas Cutoff, Brazeau Lake, and Wolverine. Assuming the weather's good when you begin, hike the circuit clockwise so you reach Jonas Pass ASAP, before a storm can mar your enjoyment of the trip's raison d'etre.

If you decline the circuit in favour of a round trip to Poboktan Pass, you'll save little or no time, but you will spare yourself almost all the forest-bound tedium, plus you'll enjoy Jonas Pass twice. Stay at Four Point the first night, Jonas Cutoff the second and third nights (so you can roam the Poboktan Pass environs on day three), then return to Four Point or Boulder Creek for the fourth night.

Whatever your itinerary, it must allow for the awkward fact that camping is verboten the entire length of Jonas Pass. For most hikers, that means camping at Four Point the first night out, even though it's just 14 km (8.7 mi) from the trailhead. You can turn that into an advantage, however, by starting early, stashing your backpack near the Brazeau River crossing beneath Nigel Pass, then exploring upper Brazeau canyon (Trip 10). It's a superb sidetrip revealing a bizarre juxtaposition of elements, colours, textures and angles.

Departing Four Point on the second morning, most hikers will face a 19-km (11.8-mi) day—through Jonas Pass, over Jonas Shoulder—to Jonas Cutoff campground. But much of that distance is relatively level. Only the initial ascent into the pass and the final vault onto the shoulder are steep. An early start from Four Point will avail you the opportunity to linger in the meadows of Jonas Pass and perhaps ramble up a tussocky hill for a peek into one of the small cirques along the southwest wall.

The one-way shuttle trip over Jonas Pass and out Poboktan Creek? Huh uh. Don't. We've presented here as an option only to be democratic. It's an unscenic 21-km (13-mi) trudge from Jonas Cutoff to the Icefields Parkway (Hwy 93). The

Upper Brazeau River Valley

valley-bottom trail plows through bogs churned to slop by horsepackers. A couple waterfalls are the only diversion from dreary forest.

Sunshine, always desirable for hiking, is critical on trips like this one and the Skyline (Trip 81), where the trail sings along above treeline. You're exposed to the weather's full force. Leaden clouds obliterate the scenery. Keep that in mind and stay flexible when planning. Rain is forecast for a few days? Try hiking the circuit counterclockwise—*if* it's likely to clear by the time you reach Poboktan Pass. Here's another weather-related consideration: the trail over Jonas Shoulder is the second highest in Jasper Park, and the north slope can be snowbound until August.

So, what if Jonas Cutoff campground is booked full when you want to be here? You can still see Jonas Pass. On day one, hike over Nigel Pass and camp at Four Point. On day two, hike through Jonas Pass, up to Jonas Shoulder, then back to Four Point—a 15.8-km (9.8-mi) round trip, without the burden of a full pack. After spending the second night at Four Point, return to the trailhead via Nigel Pass on day three. That excludes Poboktan Pass, but it's still an outstanding journey.

FACT

By Vehicle

Drive the Icefields Parkway (Hwy 93) south 8.5 km (5.3 mi) from the Banff-Jasper boundary at Sunwapta Pass, or north 37 km (23 mi) from Saskatchewan River Crossing. The Nigel Pass trailhead parking area is on a dirt access road, below the northeast side of the Parkway, at 1860 m (6100 ft). Southbound drivers: beware of the awkward, dangerous, sharp-left turn off the Parkway, onto the access road.

If arranging a shuttle for the one-way trip, leave a vehicle at the Poboktan Creek trailhead. It's also on the Parkway, 44.3 km (27.5 mi) northwest of the Nigel Pass trailhead, immediately south of Sunwapta Warden Station, at 1540 m (5050 ft).

On Foot

Follow directions for Trip 33 to 2195-m (7200-ft) **Nigel Pass** at 7.2 km (4.5 mi). You're now astride the Banff-Jasper parks boundary. Bearing a full backpack, strong hikers will be here in about three hours. The White Goat Wilderness is east, beyond the next ridgecrest. The Brazeau River Valley is north-northwest. Directly west is 3213 m (10,539-ft) Nigel Peak. South, across the Parkway, beyond Parker Ridge, is 3344-m (10,968-ft) Mt. Saskatchewan and various glaciers.

The trail nips over Nigel Pass and quickly drops to reach the south fork of the **Brazeau River** at 7.5 km (4.7 mi), 2180 m (7150 ft). It's unbridged but broad and shallow—easy to ford or rockhop. On the northeast bank, the main trail—indicated by a yellow blaze on a tree—ascends left (north). The sketchy path to Cataract Pass (Trip 10) heads right, upstream. Read that trip description before dashing into upper Brazeau canyon.

Continuing toward Jonas Pass, the trail ascends to 2220 m (7275 ft) in just five minutes and affords a glimpse southeast into upper Brazeau canyon. A few minutes farther, begin descending the barren, rocky slope. About 0.8 km (0.5 mi) from Nigel Pass, attain a **viewpoint** overlooking the Brazeau River Valley and a cascade plummeting through a gorge at the north end of Nigel Pass. The slopes rising to Jonas Pass are also visible, north-northeast. Below this viewpoint, the descent briefly but dramatically steepens before easing into the Brazeau River Valley.

Heading north, the trail contours just above the grassy river flats. After crossing a bridge over the **Brazeau River**, turn right (north-northeast) and continue downstream above the west bank. In a few minutes, reach **Boulder Creek campground** at 10.7 km (6.6 mi), 2024 m (6640 ft). It has a table, an outhouse, and bear-proof food storage.

For about the next eight minutes, the trail jounces across lumpy ground amid boulders and spruce trees. Cross to the north bank of bridged **Boulder Creek** and reach a fork. Go right (east). A gentle descent ensues through forest. About 15 minutes from Boulder Creek, the trail levels in willow-filled meadows.

At 13.9 km (8.6 mi), 1927 m (6320 ft), reach **Four Point campground**. The nearby Brazeau River is obscured by trees but the riffles are audible. You'll find a couple tables here, in addition to an outhouse and bearproof food storage. About 100 m (110 yd) past the campground is **Jonas Pass junction**. Proceeding through Jonas Pass? Go left (north). The next campground in that direction is Jonas Cutoff, 19 km (11.8 mi) distant. Straight (northeast) proceeds through the Brazeau River Valley; that's the way you'll return if hiking the circuit clockwise.

Bound for Jonas Pass, begin a moderate ascent among scruffy Engelmann spruce and heather-and-juniper understory. After gaining 150 m (492 ft) in about 1.6 km (1 mi), the ascent eases. When Four Point Creek is audible, the trail grants you a ten-minute level respite before the next moderate ascent, which

Jonas Pass

lasts another ten minutes. The spruce are noticeably bigger at this elevation. The trail levels then dips into the subalpine zone at 2120 m (6950 ft). Hop across a tributary stream. About 20 minutes farther, hop another tributary, then emerge above treeline at 18.4 km (11.4 mi). You've entered the southeast end of **Jonas Pass**—a 9-km (5.6-mi) alpine valley. The trail proceeds northwest into a vast meadowland. The southwest wall of the pass harbours glacial cirques that release meltwater, which creates the numerous small feeder streams through here. Soon cross to the northeast bank of Four Point Creek. Top-up your water bottles. If the tarns ahead are dry, the next readily available water might be at Jonas Cutoff.

Crest the **summit of Jonas Pass** (marked by a boulder-top cairn) at 23.8 km (14.8 mi), 2320 m (7610 ft). Above the benches lining the southwest wall of the pass are cirques secreting small glaciers. Descending the northwest side of the pass, the trail follows **Jonas Creek** downstream (northwest). Within 45 minutes of the summit, the trail vaulting over Jonas Shoulder—a long, grassy ridge—is visible ahead. Descend about 140 m (460 ft) toward a rockslide. Pass left of it at 27 km (16.7 mi). Then begin a 290-m (950-ft) switchbacking ascent of the shoulder.

A third of the way up, two lakes are visible west across Jonas Creek valley. Scan the slopes on both sides of the trail; you're in caribou country. The trail contours ten minutes, then resumes ascending. It passes through patches of heather scattered among dirt and scree. Looking back over Jonas Pass, small, dirty glaciers are visible in four cirques. These are rock glaciers, composed largely of rock debris with just enough ice lubricating the mass so it creeps downhill.

The trail grants a couple-minute respite before the final moderate ascent. Enter a tiny gap atop **Jonas shoulder** at 29.6 km (18.4 mi), 2470 m (8100 ft). The shoulder divides Jonas and Poboktan drainages. It's a panoramic perch. South-southeast is Jonas Pass. Southwest is 3360-m (11,020-ft) Sunwapta Peak and several unnamed mountains. West-northwest is Jonas Creek valley. North-northwest is Poboktan Creek valley. North is 3323-m (10,900-ft) Poboktan Mtn. Northeast, just over the next rise, are the slopes above Poboktan Pass.

Departing Jonas Shoulder, the trail descends three long switchbacks across scree, then heads generally north. It crosses and stays east of a tributary gully. A 355-m (1165-ft) descent ensues. Follow the cairned main trail, avoiding bootbeaten paths. Gradually curve north-northwest. After entering forest, a left (west) spur leads to **Jonas Cutoff campground** at 33 km (20.5 mi), 2135 m (7003 ft). It has a table, an outhouse, and bear-proof food storage.

About 200 m (220 yd) past the campground, the main trail reaches a T-junction on the south bank of **Poboktan Creek**. The elevation here is 2115 m (6937 ft). Left descends Poboktan Creek valley to the Icefields Parkway (Hwy 93); skip below for details. Go right, cross a bridge to the creek's northeast bank, and begin a gradual 185-m (607-ft) ascent generally southeast through meadows to Poboktan Pass. *Poboktan*, by the way, is a Stoney Indian word meaning *owl*.

Crest 2300-m (7545-ft) **Poboktan Pass** at 36 km (22 mi). Easy, extensive roaming is possible north. Continue east-southeast through the gentle pass. Flat Ridge, a huge mesa, dominates the southeast horizon. At the far end of the pass, the slope above is steep, yet the trail is level. About 15 minutes farther, begin a rough, sharp descent through forest into **John-John Creek valley**. You'll see big spruce in this wetter drainage. John-John Creek's upper basin (right / south) invites experienced routefinders to explore.

Turning northeast, the trail heads downstream above the creek's northwest bank. At 2050 m (6720 ft), it's within 10 m (33 ft) of the water. Austere, rugged cliffs of Le Grand Brazeau are left (northwest) above the trail.

At 40.3 km (25 mi), 2020 m (6626 ft), reach **John-John Creek Campground**. It's in open forest, within earshot of the creek. You'll find a couple tables here, in addition to an outhouse and bear-proof food storage. Just beyond the campground is a sign stating distances, and shortly past that is a footbridge spanning the creek. Don't cross it. Stay on the creek's left (northwest) bank. Follow the trail downstream, generally northeast.

About a kilometre (0.6 mi) from the campground, cross a clear, narrow tributary stream. At 44.5 km (27.6 mi), 1835 m (6020 ft), cross a bridge to John-John Creek's east bank. A swatch of Brazeau Lake is visible east. Though it appears close, be patient. The trail takes a circuitous route through heavy timber. It entails ups and downs that seem unnecessary and are therefore frustrating.

Near 1900 m (6232 ft) the ascent finally relents on a small plateau. Descend to 1805 m (5920 ft) and cross a wide bridge to the northwest bank of the **North Fork Brazeau River** at 48.2 km (30 mi). Here, immediately southeast of Brazeau Lake's outlet, is a signed **junction**. Left (initially west-southwest) reaches the lakeshore campground in

Caribou near Jonas Shoulder

0.5 km (0.3 mi). Right (north-northeast) continues the circuit, passing the Brazeau River campground in 2 km (1.2 mi).

Brazeau Lake campground is just above the shore, at 1810 m (5937 ft). The tentsites are too close together, many are unlevel, all are in the forest, none have lake views. The tables in the communal eating area, however, are closer to the water. The bear-proof food storage is the campground's centerpiece. There's an outhouse, of course. For a view up the lake, walk 100 m (110 yd) along the shore, around a point. The lake is fed by the icefield on 3470-m (11382-ft) Mt. Brazeau, to the north.

To resume the circuit, return to the junction beside the bridge and proceed north-northeast. The trail follows the North Fork Brazeau River downstream, staying high above the north bank. Reach a T-junction at 50.3 km (31.2 mi), 1720 m (5640 ft). Straight (east) continues along the river's north bank, then curves northeast, following the Brazeau River downstream along Jasper Park's south boundary, passing Arete campground in 10 km (6.2 mi). To complete the circuit, turn right (south) and cross the second bridge spanning the North Fork Brazeau. In another 50 m/yd arrive at small **Brazeau River campground**. It has a table, an outhouse, and bear-proof food storage.

Beyond the campground, ascend at a moderate grade through pine forest for 15 to 20 minutes, then descend. Pass above a narrow chasm. Five minutes farther, at 53.6 km (33.2 mi), 1790 m (6180 ft), cross a bridge to the east bank of the **Brazeau River**. The trail continues upstream, generally south.

Near 1840 m (6035 ft), cross a large willow field. Valley views open up here and continue for much of the rest of the journey. Marble Mtn dominates the west side of the valley. Reach **Wolverine campground** at 59.3 km (36.8 mi), 1855 m (6084 ft). It's pleasantly small, offering only a few tentsites in a stand of trees just above the riverbank. You'll find a couple tables here, in addition to an outhouse and bear-proof food storage.

Proceeding up-valley, the trail often plies meadows and swaths of low willows, so views are frequent. At 61.2 km (37.9 mi), about 30 minutes from Wolverine, cross a bridge to the Brazeau River's west bank. The trail continues upstream, generally south-southwest. About 40 minutes farther, pass a signed left spur leading east-southeast 200 m (220 yd) to Cline horse camp. Fifteen minutes beyond that, cross a bridge over boisterous **Four Point Creek** and pass Four Point **warden cabin**. A few minutes farther, at 64.8 km (40.2 mi), reach **Jonas Pass junction,** where you began the circuit. You're now on familiar ground.

Bear left. Pass **Four Point campground**. Cross Boulder Creek, then pass **Boulder Creek campground** at 68.3 km (42.3 mi). Cross a bridge to the Brazeau River's east bank. At 71.8 km (44.5 km), ford the upper Brazeau River below **Nigel Pass**. Scurry over the pass, then hike the final 7.2 km (4.5 mi) back to the **trailhead**. Upon arrival at the Icefields Parkway (Hwy 93), your total distance will be 79.3 km (49.2 mi).

POBOKTAN CREEK

From **Jonas Cutoff campground**, at 33 km (20.5 mi), 2135 m (7003 ft), follow the trail northwest about 200 m (220 yd) to a T-junction on the south bank of **Poboktan Creek**. The elevation here is 2115 m (6937 ft). Right crosses a bridge to the creek's northeast bank and ascends generally southeast to Poboktan Pass. Go left (initially west) to descend Poboktan Creek valley 21 km (13 mi) to the Icefields Parkway (Hwy 93).

The trail curves northwest and follows Poboktan Creek downstream. Reach **Waterfall campground** at 42.3 km (26.2 mi). Reach **Poboktan Creek campground** at 47 km (29.1 mi). Cross bridged **Poligne Creek** at 48.2 km (30 mi). Just beyond is a junction. Right (north) leads to Maligne Pass (Trip 93). Proceed straight, initially west, then generally west-southwest.

Immediately after crossing a bridge to Poboktan Creek's south bank, arrive at the **trailhead** on the Icefields parkway (Hwy 93). Elevation: 1540 m (5050 ft). It's just across the river from Sunwapta Warden Station. Having completed the one-way shuttle trip, your total hiking distance is 54.2-km (33.6-mi).

Columbine

TRIP 93

Maligne Pass

LOCATION	Jasper National Park
ROUND TRIP	30.4 km (18.8 mi)
ELEVATION GAIN	691 m (2265 ft)
KEY ELEVATIONS	trailhead 1540 m (5050 ft) campground 2037 m (6680 ft) pass 2230 m (7315 ft)
HIKING TIME	9 hours or overnight
DIFFICULTY	moderate dayhike, easy backpack
MAPS	page 517; Gem Trek *Jasper and Maligne Lake*; Sunwapta Peak 83 C/6, Southesk Lake 83 C/11

OPINION

The peaks ringing it are unexceptional, yet Maligne Pass is deeply moving to a sensitive soul. It must be the copious, luxuriant, poly-hued greens speaking to you of fertility, rejuvenation, vitality. Bounteous meadows and a half dozen small lakes summon you to wander, to explore the possibilities—emotional as well as geographical. This compulsion is, in itself, renewing. It avails you of hidden reserves of energy and desire. You don't have to die to be reborn.

You'll bound over hilly meadows, spy a lake here, a tarn there, and yet more soft ridges to surmount beyond. In July's full bloom, the vast carpets of heather are magnificent, sporting their own tiny, yellow and pink blossoms and harbouring a rainbow of brilliant wildflowers. Here, beneath Endless Chain Ridge, you'll savour a wee taste of the Scottish Highlands.

Fleet, resolute striders can dayhike to the pass. Do it in July, when you'll have maximal daylight. Allow eleven hours: nine for hiking, two for lounging at the pass. Due to the distance, however, a dayhike here is strictly out and back, with no time to meander the width of the pass. So consider a one-night backpack trip. Avalanche campground, at the south edge of the pass environs, is a superior site. It occupies a clearing in lightly-treed subalpine forest. The views are pleasing. And nearby Poligne Creek provides constant water music. For backpackers, Avalanche is only four hours from the trailhead, so they can start late, then spend the next day leisurely crisscrossing the pass before departing.

Despite its length, the trail to Maligne Pass is neither taxing nor boring. The ascent is usually gentle and never exceeds moderate. You'll be following Poboktan and Poligne creeks, which are often visible and frequently audible. The trail crosses Poligne Creek repeatedly, but barring a recent, destructive torrent, bridges will keep your feet dry. Though you'll hike 11 km (6.8 mi) to surmount the forest, from there on you'll enjoy constant views, and you'll relish the alpine heather meadows for a full 2 km (1.2 mi).

Given a winter of normal to heavy snowfall, it will be mid-July before the pass melts out. Photographers and wildflower lovers should wait until late July, despite the mosquitoes. By September, the first paragraph of this description will no longer be accurate, but you will witness a brilliant flash of yellow and crimson before the flora is again dormant. To be among those who prefer this time of year, you'll need a warm sleeping bag.

You don't want to hike to Maligne Pass during or just after heavy rain. Much of the way is naturally wet, especially the area immediately past Avalanche campground. And horses have been churning the mud since the two adventurous Marys—Schaffer and Adams—were guided through Maligne Pass in 1908. The trip is still popular with horse packers. As a result, hiking here can be a slopfest. Hope for a dry spell.

Completion freaks might want to tromp the entire trail. From Maligne Pass, it descends the forested Maligne River valley, generally north-northwest, 33 km (20 mi) to the north end of Maligne Lake. Mud, muskeg and limited views are valid reasons not to proceed. So is Jasper's abundance of superior backpacking options. Tonquin Valley (Trips 94-98), the Skyline (Trip 81), and the Jonas Pass loop (Trip 92) are all nearby.

FACT

By Vehicle

From Columbia Icefield Centre, drive the Icefields Parkway (Hwy 93) north 31.5 km (19.5 mi). Or, from the junction of Hwys 93 and 16, on the southwest side of Jasper townsite, drive Hwy 93 southeast 71.7 km (44.5 mi). From either approach, turn east into the trailhead parking area. It's immediately south of the Sunwapta Warden Station and the Poboktan Creek bridge. Elevation: 1540 m (5050 ft).

On Foot

Start at the kiosk and bearproof garbage can on the left (north) side of the parking area, halfway up from the highway. Descend northeast toward Poboktan Creek. In two minutes, cross a hefty bridge to a **T-junction** on the creek's north bank. Go right (northeast) for Maligne Pass. Left leads to the warden station.

Within 15 minutes begin a gradual ascent. The trail is broad and generally smooth—not rooty enough to be troublesome. You're heading west-northwest.

About 30 minutes along, after gaining 116 m (380 ft), open forest allows views south and west to snowfields among the peaks. The river, though way below, is audible. Enough light penetrates the forest to nurture grassy groundcover.

Soon cross a **creeklet**. Hop three more in the next 15 minutes. The trail then levels. Watch for wildflowers: elephant's head, paintbrush, cinquefoil, purple milk-vetch, and the elusive wintergreen (white petals, pale-lime centre, with orchid-like complexity).

About an hour from the trailhead, cross a footlog over a creeklet. Just beyond, the trail again grazes the north bank of Poboktan Creek. A rugged cleft in the mountains is visible downstream. Proceeding up-valley, the trail ascends gently.

Within 1½ hours, swift hikers will reach a **junction** at 6.2-km (3.8-mi), 1755 m (5756 ft), on the west bank of roaring **Poligne Creek**, just upstream from its **confluence** with Poboktan Creek. Turn left (north-northwest) to reach Avalanche camp-

Maligne Pass

ground in 5 km (3.1 mi), and Maligne Pass in 9 km (5.6 mi). The trail proceeding straight (east), across the bridge, passes a campground in 1 km (0.6 mi). It then curves southeast, following Poboktan Creek upstream toward Poboktan and Jonas passes. A more scenic way to reach those premier alplands, however, is the loop described in Trip 92.

The trail follows Poligne Creek upstream through a tight forest of scrawny spruce and pine. Though rootier and rockier than the Poboktan Creek trail, it poses no difficulties. You're now skirting the southeast extremity of Endless Chain Ridge, proving what a specious name that is. In three minutes, cross the first of eight bridges (12 to 18 minutes apart) leading back and forth across the creek. After the first bridge, a sharp ascent ensues but soon moderates. After the second bridge, the creek remains audible because the trail is always beside or near it. Scree slopes rise above to the east.

About 40 minutes above the confluence junction, cross the fourth bridge. The trail becomes rootier and muddier. Watch for yellow-beaked lousewort among the heather. At this elevation (1875 m / 6150 ft), the spruce trees are noticeably larger.

One hour above the confluence junction, the sixth bridge leads to Poligne Creek's north bank. The trail fades here, and the muck thickens. Seven minutes beyond that bridge is a beautiful **cascade**. It's left of the trail, at 1995 m (6545 ft). And seven minutes past the cascade is the seventh bridge. After crossing it, go left

Flowering heather

(downstream) 70 m/yd to enter **Avalanche campground**. The trail to Maligne Pass forks right.

The campground is at 11.2 km (6.9 mi), 2037 m (6680 ft), in the subalpine zone, on a bank above boisterous Poligne Creek. There are four tentsites, two tables, a couple fire pits, and bear-proof food storage. The toilet—a green, plastic throne—is uphill behind the sites.

Proceeding up-valley (northwest), Maligne Pass is visible ahead. Endless Chain Ridge is left (west-northwest). The ascent to the pass is gentle but steady. Purple fleabane is profuse in these wet meadows. Broad swaths have been churned to a quagmire by horse packers. The trail all but disappears in the sodden greenery, among low, patchy willow. Be attentive. The eighth footbridge leads to Poligne Creek's north bank. The worst of the slop, requiring the most careful routefinding, is 200 m (220 yd) farther. The trail soon ascends onto firmer, rockier ground.

About 40 minutes from the campground, reach 2133 m (6995 ft) on the northeast slope of Maligne Pass. In July, this vast **heather meadow** is dappled with pink and yellow wildflowers. (Heather, by the way, has stiff, short, narrow, dark-green, almost needle-like leaves.) The trail is skinny and deeply trenched here.

Fast hikers will stride through long, wide **Maligne Pass** about four hours after leaving the trailhead. The highpoint is at 15 km (9.3 mi), 2230 m (7315 ft), before the trail passes above the east shore of a small, unnamed lake. If you backpacked to Avalanche campground, wander the meadows northwest and southwest of the lake.

Maligne Pass

It's a pleasure that dayhikers won't have time to pursue. Replica Peak rises right (east) of the trail. North, beyond the pass, peeking above a green slope, is Mt. Mary Vaux. North-northwest, down the upper Maligne River valley, are snowcapped Mt. Unwin (left) and Mt. Charlton (right). The trail continues northwest from the pass, reaching Mary Vaux campground at 19.2 km (11.9 mi). It ends at 48 km (29.8 mi), near Maligne Lake.

If possible, dayhikers should proceed to the far end of the pass. From there, angle right (north), cross-country. Ascend 120 m (394 ft) to the crest of a **shoulder**, where you can see a 1-km (0.6-mi) long lake southwest that wasn't visible from the pass. Below, north-northeast, you'll spy the basin below Mt. Mary Vaux. Northeast is the ridge separating upper Maligne River valley from Coronet Creek valley.

At a brisk pace, dayhikers can expect to reach Avalanche campground an hour after leaving the north end of Maligne Pass. It takes another hour to descend to the confluence junction. From there, the trailhead is 1½ hours distant. In total, allow at least four hours for the return trip.

TRIPS 94 – 98

Tonquin Valley / Amethyst Lakes / The Ramparts

LOCATION	Jasper National Park
SHUTTLE TRIP	43 km (26.7 mi) in Maccarib Pass, to Surprise Point, out Astoria River
CIRCUIT	35 km (21.7 mi) in and out Astoria River, to Surprise Point
ELEVATION GAIN	905 m (2970 ft) for shuttle trip 460 m (1510 ft) for circuit
KEY ELEVATIONS	Portal Creek trailhead 1480 m (4855 ft) Maccarib Pass 2180 m (7150 ft) Tonquin Hill 2396 m (7860 ft) Amethyst Lakes 1985 m (6510 ft) Oldhorn Mtn traverse 2100 m (6888 ft) Astoria River trailhead 1730 m (5680 ft)
HIKING TIME	2 to 5 days
DIFFICULTY	moderate
MAPS	page 519; Gem Trek *Jasper National Park;* Amethyst Lakes 83 D/9

OPINION

Peaks as high as Roy Orbison falsettos. Lakes as blue as a Billie Holiday tune. Meadows that stretch out like a tribal chant. Tonquin Valley is a harmonious blend of all that's best about the Canadian Rockies.

As a result, it attracts an annual surge of hikers and horse packers who churn the trails to mud. A couple lodges, a whopper of a hut, and several campgrounds diminish the sense of wilderness. Gluttonous proboscises are sure to annoy in summer. If not mosquitoes, it'll be black flies buggin' you. Bears also frequent the area; ask the Jasper Park Info Centre about recent sightings, posted warnings, or trail closures.

At the heart of Tonquin Valley are the Amethyst Lakes. Rocketing from their western shores, and extending 14 km (8.7 mi) along the Continental Divide, is a 1000-metre (3280-foot) wall aptly called the Ramparts. Names of the individual peaks are equally evocative: Turret, Bastion, Drawbridge, Redoubt, Dungeon, Paragon, Parapet. Not only is the valley girded by this tumultuous topography, it's broad, with enough meadowy viewpoints to allow frequent gazing—an ineffable joy on a clear day. Possible explorations are numerous, for example to Tonquin Hill (Trip 95), or Eremite Valley (Trip 97).

The Ramparts and Moat Lake

For an efficient, in-and-out-the-same-way backpack trip, hike the Astoria River trail (Trip 98). This is the Tonquin expressway, a wide, smooth, mostly level path allowing you to motor at full throttle. But it plows through viewless, unremarkable forest until ascending past Switchback campground, near 13 km (8.1 mi). For a more rewarding experience, hike the Portal Creek trail over Maccarib Pass (Trip 94). It grants views up Portal Creek valley within 1½ hours. Penetrating the pass, you'll enjoy a leisurely tour of meadows and streams for 7 km (4.3 mi).

It's only a couple kilometres farther to Amethyst Lakes via Maccarib Pass than via Astoria River. The Maccarib approach has only two disadvantages: (1) It's steeper, requiring you to gain 245 m (805 ft) more, but that's offset by the resplendent scenery. (2) It crosses meadows that all but advertise *Smorgasbord for Bears*. An encounter is more likely here than on the forested Astoria River trail, but hiking in a group (four is good, six is better) can help ensure your safety.

The quandary over which way to enter Tonquin Valley is easily settled by arranging a shuttle between trailheads, or resigning yourself to hitchhiking. You can then complete a one-way trip: entering on one trail, exiting the other. Crunched for time? It's possible to hike the shuttle trip in just two days. But to attain a sense of fulfillment, allow at least three. Leaving this nirvanic valley immediately after arriving is painful.

A three-day trip will allow strong hikers to squeeze in one of the two sidetrips mentioned above: (1) Tonquin Hill (Trip 95) at the north end of Tonquin Valley, or

(2) Eremite Valley (Trip 97) at the south end of Tonquin Valley. Decide which you want to attempt, then plan your trek accordingly.

Tonquin Hill is beyond the ken of neophytes. The route, both sketchy and steep, involves bushwhacking and routefinding, demands strength and tenacity. But the summit of Tonquin Hill affords an awesome panorama of the entire Tonquin Valley: a Valkyrian landscape of dragontooth peaks above a palette of amethyst and emerald. A slice of the seldom-seen Bennington Glacier is even visible. Bring a map to help you identify all the peaks. Moat Lake, en route to Tonquin Hill, is beautifully situated, but reaching it means negotiating the horse-tromped environs of Tonquin Valley Lodge, and appreciating it necessitates bashing along the lake's trackless north shore. Don't bother, unless continuing up Tonquin Hill.

The most popular Tonquin Valley sidetrip is south of Chrome Lake, into narrow Eremite Valley. In its upper reaches, past Arrowhead Lake, you can marvel at the chaos left behind by retreating glaciers. More moving and memorable than anything you'll see in Eremite, however, is the singular view from atop the natural grandstand of Tonquin Hill. Yet the hill is rarely summited, while Eremite—because it's an easier hike, conveniently near Wates-Gibson hut—is frequently visited.

The hut is huge, accommodating up to 40 snoring, flatulent hikers. It's in the forest, near tiny, unremarkable Outpost Lake. Don't let the attraction of a roof overhead, or the allure of travelling tent-less, curtail your appreciation of Tonquin Valley. Brave the elements instead. Camp at Surprise Point (Trip 96), on the southeast corner of lower Amethyst Lake, where the view of the Ramparts is astonishing. Compared to the hut, Surprise is only 0.9 km (0.6 mi) farther from Eremite. Need further dissuasion from making the hut your base? Maccarib campground, above the north end of Tonquin Valley, is immensely appealing, with a distant yet still arousing view of the Ramparts.

If you enter Tonquin Valley on the Astoria River trail, because you're staying at either the hut or Surprise Point, go via Chrome Lake. Upon reaching Astoria River junction, 8 km (5 mi) up Astoria River valley, turn left. Cross the bridge to the south bank, and hike the Chrome Lake trail, initially southwest. It continues following the Astoria River upstream, high above its south bank, through pleasant, moist forest. It's narrower, less traveled, more intimate than the road-like main trail. And it will save you time and energy.

The main trail—climbing from Astoria River junction onto the slopes of Oldhorn Mtn, accessing Switchback and Clitheroe campgrounds—is a longer, circuitous way to reach the hut, but it affords a grand vista of Amethyst Lakes and the Ramparts. It's the most direct route to Amethyst campground, on the upper lake's east shore. And it's certainly the trail to use if scurrying through Tonquin Valley on a two-day blitz.

You're entering *and* exiting Tonquin Valley via the Astoria River trail? On the way in, you're hiking the Chrome Lake trail to either the hut or Surprise Point? Then, on the way out, complete a circuit by hiking from Surprise Point to Clitheroe campground, and following the main trail past Switchback campground, back to Astoria River. Your journey will be more varied and scenic.

Nearing Maccarib Pass. Mt. Edith Cavell in background.

OPTIMAL ITINERARIES

Three Days

Hike up Portal Creek, cross Maccarib Pass, and spend the first night at Maccarib campground. On day two, start early and hightail up Tonquin Hill, then continue to Surprise Point campground. Or, go directly to Surprise Point campground and, after pitching your tent, probe Eremite Valley. On day three, hike out Astoria River.

Four Days

Hike up Portal Creek, cross Maccarib Pass, and spend the first night at Maccarib campground. On day two, ascend Tonquin Hill, then return for a second night at Maccarib. On day three, continue to Surprise Point campground. On day four, start early, probe Eremite Valley (perhaps leaving backpacks at the hut), then hike out Astoria River.

FACT

Before your trip

Several encounters between hikers and bears have occurred in or near Tonquin Valley. They've ranged form frightening to fatal. The northern approach via Maccarib Pass crosses meadows much beloved by bears, unlike the more forested, southern approach via Astoria River valley. Check with the Jasper Park Info Centre before setting out on the Portal Creek trail. If it's closed, acknowledge that this is the bears' home and you are an unwanted visitor. Hike elsewhere.

Mosquitoes are insignificant compared to bears, but you'll definitely encounter them here during summer. Thousands of them. Can't come in September, after the infestation subsides? Then prepare for battle. Long pants and a long-sleeve shirt (both made of lightweight, quick-drying synthetics) will be essential. You'll also want a hat, a bug-proof head net, and thin, lightweight gloves (perhaps made of polypropylene). And bring repellent, of course.

Accommodations

If you want to stay in the Wates-Gibson hut, check the current price and make reservations with the Alpine Club of Canada. The contact numbers are listed under *Information Sources* in the back of this book.

There are two lodges in Tonquin Valley. Tonquin Valley Lodge (www.tonquin-valley.com) is at the north end of Amethyst Lakes. Check the current price and make reservations by writing to Box 550, Jasper, AB T0E 1E0, or phoning (780) 852-3909. Tonquin-Amethyst Lake Lodge (www.tonquinadventures.com) faces the Amethyst Lakes narrows. Check the current price and make reservations by writing to P.O. Box 1795, Jasper, AB T0E 1E0, or phoning (780) 852-1188.

By Vehicle

From the junction of Hwy 16 and the Icefields Parkway (Hwy 93), at the south-west edge of Jasper townsite, drive the Parkway south 7.2 km (4.5 mi). Turn right (west) onto Hwy 93A. Set your trip odometre to 0.

For the Astoria River trailhead, follow Hwy 93A south 5.3 km (3.3 mi) and turn right onto Mount Edith Cavell Road. At 17.5 km (10.9 mi), just past the youth hostel, turn right into the Astoria River trailhead parking area. Elevation: 1730 m (5680 ft).

To reach the Portal Creek trailhead, drive Hwy 93A south 2.5 km (1.6 mi). Turn right onto Marmot Basin Road. At 9.1 km (5.6 mi) turn left into the Portal Creek trailhead parking area. Elevation: 1480 m (4855 ft).

On Foot

TRIP 94 – TONQUIN VALLEY VIA MACCARIB PASS

ONE WAY	18.3 km (11.3 mi) to Maccarib campground
ELEVATION GAIN	730 m (2395 ft)
HIKING TIME	5 to 6 hours
DIFFICULTY	moderate

The trail departs the south end of the Portal Creek trailhead parking area. Follow it south. Within five minutes, at 0.5 km (0.3 mi), cross a large, sturdy bridge spanning **Portal Creek**. On the northwest bank, turn left (right is the horse trail) and begin a gentle descent west-southwest through dense forest. Note the impressively girthy spruce trees.

At 4 km (2.5 mi), 1774 m (5820 ft), cross a bridge to the southwest bank of **Circus Creek**. The trail curves west-northwest, then south-southwest, entering The Portal—a narrow, rocky canyon. Fifteen minutes farther, valley views open up. Cross rockslides below Peveril Peak. The trail contours between short, gentle ascents.

The Ramparts, from Surprise Point

At 1950 m (6396 ft), about two hours from the trailhead, the up-valley view extends to the green slopes below the pass. The spiky tips of the Ramparts are visible above a distant ridge. After a gradual descent, cross a low bridge in a marshy area. In open forest, the trail follows Portal Creek upstream, generally southwest.

Reach **Portal Creek campground**, in willow flats, on the right (north) side of the trail, at 9 km (5.6 mi), 2010 m (6593 ft). The distance to Maccarib campground is less than the sign's stated 12 km (7.5 mi). Soon cross a bridge over Portal Creek. A gradual ascent ensues, generally southwest.

Enter grassy, subalpine meadows among alpine fir and Engelmann spruce. In summer, wildflowers here include elephant's heads, grass-of-Parnassus, purple fleabane, and yellow daisies. Cross another bridge over Portal Creek and begin a moderate ascent.

At 10 km (6.2 mi) the trail steepens at the base of Maccarib Pass. Ascend west, across alpine terrain. Left (south) is 2986-m (9797-ft) Oldhorn Mtn. Crest **Maccarib Pass,** between smooth, gray talus slopes, at 12.4 km (7.7 mi), 2180 m (7150 ft). *Maccarib* is a native word for caribou.

Soon rockhop across Maccarib Creek, which flows west-northwest into the north end of Tonquin Valley. Expect mud here. Follow the creek downstream through extensive meadows. The north end of the Ramparts is visible ahead. Drawbridge Peak is west-southwest. Bastion Peak is west. North of Drawbridge is Tonquin Hill (Trip 95). Moat Pass is between Bastion and the hill.

The Maccarib Creek drainage is lush, marshy, buggy. At 2045 m (6708 ft), cross several bridges over the slow, limpid creek. Reach **Maccarib campground** at 18.3 km (11.3 mi), 2020 m (6625 ft). It's on the right, above the creek's north bank, atop a knoll, among scattered trees. Before arriving, you'll see the bear-proof food-storage poles. The half-dozen tent sites are fairly level, tucked among bushes. The green, plastic, open-air latrine affords a superb view of the Ramparts, across the north end of Tonquin Valley.

TRIP 95 – TONQUIN HILL

ROUND TRIP	12 km (7.4 mi) from Maccarib campground
ELEVATION GAIN	576 m (1890 ft)
HIKING TIME	5 to 6 hours
DIFFICULTY	moderate

On the main trail below **Maccarib campground**, cross a bridge to the south bank of **Maccarib Creek**. Proceed through open spruce forest, generally southwest. Amethyst Lakes, beneath the Ramparts, are visible within ten minutes. Tonquin Hill is the small, solitary mountain west-northwest across Tonquin Valley.

Reach a **junction** at 0.9 km (0.6 mi), 1990 m (6527 ft). The main trail continues straight (south), along the east shore of Amethyst Lakes. Turn right (west) for Moat Lake and Tonquin Hill.

Follow the stony, braided, rutted, horse-tromped trail into dense forest. Reach a fork at 1.5 km (0.9 mi). Turn left (south-southwest) on a path signed for Tonquin Valley Lodge. At the next fork, go straight (south-southeast), where right (west) leads to Moat Lake. (It's easier via the lodge.) A few minutes farther, pass a corral and enter the grounds of **Tonquin Valley Lodge** at 1.8 km (1.1 mi).

Behind the central cabin is a wood-cutting hut. From there, follow a road-like path right (west-northwest). (If in doubt, ask one of the lodge staff to point you toward Moat Lake.) Within ten minutes, proceed west into brushy meadows. Yellow blazes indicate the way. Nearby left are Drawbridge Peak (south-southwest) and Bastion Peak (west-southwest).

At 2.8 km (1.7 mi), 1920 m (6298 ft), rockhop **Moat Creek**—actually a brook. Tonquin Hill is northwest, but follow the bootbeaten path west. Fix this spot in your mind. As described below, the shortest way to return from Tonquin Hill is to hike cross-country through the tussocky meadows, back to this crossing of Moat Creek.

Rockhop another branch of the creek. Moat Lake is visible ahead. Elephant's heads (mauve and fuchsia) are rife in this moist, heather meadow. Reach the east shore of **Moat Lake** at 3.6 km (2.2 mi). Curve around to the north side of the 1.3-km (0.8-mi) long lake. Follow the willowy, bouldery shoreline west-northwest, initially on a bootbeaten track. It soon disappears. Bash on regardless, if your goal is the top of Tonquin Hill. Pass the lake's west end in about 30 minutes.

Angle north-northwest toward the forest edge. Two minutes beyond the lake, pass a **pond** on the left, at 5 km (3.1 mi). The forest edge is now 25 paces to your right. Three minutes farther, reach a national park sign and a yellow blaze indicating the **Alberta-B.C. boundary**.

Maccarib Creek

Visible left, about 15 paces away, is an old, **primitive campsite**. In the middle of the valley, about 50 m/yd left (south-southwest) of the campsite, is a thigh-high, pyramidal, boundary marker.

Turn right (north-northeast) away from the campsite. Walk uphill among the trees. In one minute, about 70 m (77 yd) from the campsite, reach the timbers of a defunct **corral**. Turn right (east) and walk through it. Continue about 25 paces beyond the east side of the corral. Look left for two **blazed fir trees**, about 9 m (30 ft) tall. Walk between them and pick up a bootbeaten path. A rough, strenuous ascent ensues. The route is sketchy to nonexistent. But the summit is attainable in just one hour. Press onward.

Turn left (north) up a meadowy swath through the forest. The faint path leads right, back among the trees. The path becomes clearer north-northeast. About fifteen minutes from the corral, hop over a **stream**. A blazed route ascends north-northeast. The Ramparts are increasingly visible. Also attain views west, through Moat Pass, into B.C.

About ten minutes below the summit ridge, the route disappears in a boulder slide. Pick your own way upward. Reach the 2396-m (7862-ft) summit of **Tonquin Hill** at 6.8 km (4.2 mi). Despite the hill's relatively modest height, its isolated stance grants you a 360° panorama.

Southeast are Tonquin Valley and Amethyst Lakes. Beyond is Mt. Edith Cavell. South, behind the Ramparts, is the Bennington Glacier, ringed by massive mountains.

Northwest, below you, is Vista Pass. North-northeast is Meadow Creek valley, which used to be the primary Tonquin Valley access. East-southeast is Maccarib Pass.

You can, of course, retrace your steps down Tonquin Hill and along Moat Lake. But there's a better way: southeast along the spine of the summit ridge. You'll enjoy the views longer. You'll also save time and energy, because the ridge route is more direct, eliminating the Moat Lake shoreline bushwhack. Be prepared for a steep descent off the hill's forested southeast end. And be aware that the whole way is trackless, until you cross Moat Creek and reach familiar ground. But it's no more difficult than the route by which you ascended Tonquin Hill. Ready? Here goes.

Hike southeast along the **Tonquin Hill summit ridge**. Stay on the stony crest. About 45 minutes from the summit, having descended 265 m (870 ft), cross left through a band of krummholz and reach a meadow. You've another 213 m (700 ft) to lose before reaching level ground. Head southwest into the trees. The descent steepens sharply, but the tight forest has mossy groundcover that affords stable footing. Continue down-slope, working your way generally southeast. You should exit the forest and reach **flat meadow** a short distance northeast of Moat Lake's east shore.

Rather than go back to the lake, which is now out of the way, proceed cross-country, generally east-southeast, through the meadow. Your immediate goal is the **Moat Creek** crossing, at 1920 m (6298 ft). Reach it, and you're again on familiar ground. Pick up the blazed path leading generally east, out of the meadow, over the rise, back to **Tonquin Valley Lodge**.

From the lodge, retrace your steps (about 30 minutes) to the junction above the northeast corner of Amethyst Lakes. Or, to avoid re-hiking the braided, rutted, lodge trail, return to the junction by following the lakeshore, if it's not too soggy.

Intersect the **main Tonquin Valley trail** at the junction. Go left (northeast) to reach Maccarib campground within 20 minutes. Go right (south), along the east shore of Amethyst Lakes, for Amethyst, Clitheroe, Surprise Point, or Switchback campgrounds, or Wates-Gibson hut.

TRIP 96 – AMETHYST LAKES TO CHROME LAKE VIA SURPRISE POINT

ONE WAY	10.5 km (6.5 mi)
ELEVATION CHANGE	100-m (328-ft) gain, 435-m (1427-ft) loss
HIKING TIME	2½ to 3½ hours
DIFFICULTY	easy

Entering Tonquin Valley via Maccarib Pass, you'll reach **Maccarib campground** at 18.3 km (11.3 mi). Resuming from there, the following directions are cumulative.

On the main trail below Maccarib campground, cross a bridge to the south bank of **Maccarib Creek**. Proceed through open spruce forest, generally southwest. Amethyst Lakes, beneath the Ramparts, are visible within ten minutes. Tonquin Hill is the small, solitary mountain west-northwest across Tonquin Valley.

Reach a **junction** at 19.2 km (11.9 mi), 1990 m (6527 ft). Right (west) leads to Moat Lake and Tonquin Hill. Continue straight (south) on the main trail, following the east shore of upper Amethyst Lake.

Near Chrome Lake, Bennington (left) and Parapet (right) peaks

Reach **Amethyst campground** at 21.6 km (13.4 mi), 1985 m (6510 ft), on the left (east) side of the trail, among scattered trees. (Horses from the nearby lodge graze in this vicinity. The tinkle of their bells keeps some campers awake at night. You might need earplugs.)

About fifteen minutes south of the campground, where a right fork leads to **Olson's Tonquin Valley Lodge** (visible ahead), curve left (east) on the main trail. About five minutes farther, the trail veers left and crosses a **long bridge** over a bog. A moderate ascent ensues. (If bound for Surprise Point, which is at lake level, this ascent is frustrating because it seems pointless, but there's no alternative.)

Above, follow a hiker sign left, onto a narrow trail to a bridged creek crossing, then rejoin the main trail. A few minutes farther, reach a **junction** at 24.8 km (15.4 mi), 2085 m (6840 ft). The main trail ascends left (north-northeast), leads generally southeast to Switchback campground in 3.8 km (2.4 mi), then descends to reach Astoria River junction in 8.8 km (5.5 mi). Read Trip 98a for further directions. Descend right (east-southeast) for Clitheroe or Surprise Point campgrounds, Wates-Gibson hut, or Eremite Valley.

Just 100 m (110 yd) from the junction, enter **Clitheroe campground**, in thick forest. Beyond, the trail continues descending into Amethyst Lakes basin. Pass a **warden cabin** at 25.8 km (16 mi). One minute below it, reach a fork. Bear left (southwest).

Soon pass the southeast corner of lower Amethyst Lake. Cross the bridged outlet stream, which feeds Astoria River. About 300 m (328 yd) farther, fork right to reach **Surprise Point campground** at 26.9 km (16.7 mi), 1985 m (6510 ft). Total distance from Maccarib campground: 8.6 km (5.3 mi).

The six tentsites here are level and spaced well apart. Two tables are at the south end of camp, away from the tentsites. Get water (be sure to filter or purify it) from the lakelet on the west edge of camp. A couple-minutes north of camp is a lakeshore view of nearby 3129-m (10,266-ft) Dungeon Peak (west) and 3077-m (10,096-ft) Redoubt Peak (northwest).

For Wates-Gibson hut, Eremite Valley, or the Chrome Lake trail to Astoria River valley, depart the south end of Surprise Point campground, near the tables. Follow the rough, rooty, narrow trail south-southeast. In 30 minutes, the view south reveals peaks and glaciers at the head of Eremite Valley.

Reach a **T-junction** at 28.5 km (17.7 mi), 1845 m (6052 ft). More glacier-stuccoed peaks are visible west. Left leads generally east, passing **Chrome Lake** in 200 m (220 yd) and reaching Astoria River junction in 6.4 km (4 mi). Read Trip 98a for further directions. Turn right (west-southwest) for Eremite Valley and Wates-Gibson hut. Read Trip 97 for directions. (It's a clear day? First deviate to Chrome Lake to see the Eremite Valley mountains reflected in it.)

TRIP 97 – EREMITE VALLEY / WATES-GIBSON HUT

ROUND TRIP	8.6 km (5.3 mi)
ELEVATION GAIN	240 m (787 ft)
HIKING TIME	3 to 4 hours
DIFFICULTY	moderate

From the T-junction just northwest of **Chrome Lake**, go west-southwest: left if coming from the Astoria River valley, right if coming from Surprise Point. The trail forks in just 0.3 km (0.2 mi).

Turn right (west) at the 0.3-km (0.2-mi) fork to cross Penstock Creek, ascend a steep knoll, and reach **Wates-Gibson hut** at 1.1 km (0.7 mi). It's above the north shore of tiny, forest-ringed **Outpost Lake**.

Turn left (south) at the 0.3-km (0.2-mi) fork for Eremite Valley. Visible west is 3090-m (10,135-ft) Bennington Peak. Cross **Penstock Creek** on a natural bridge. At 1 km (0.6 mi) cross unbridged **Eremite Creek**. (This can be challenging on hot days when meltwater is high. Expect the creek to be even higher when you return in the afternoon.)

After the ford, ignore the left (east) spur to Chrome Lake's south shore. Follow the faint track south, on the west side of the bedrock ridge separating Eremite Creek from Chrome Lake. Traverse **willow flats** for 1 km (0.6 mi). Pass the former Alpine Club campground at 2.3 km (1.4 mi). Ascend steeply into subalpine forest.

Where the route dips into a small draw, follow the left (east) arm. Continue ascending on rockslide debris and through krummholz. At 4.1 km (2.5 mi) pass silt-laden **Arrowhead Lake**. At 4.3 km (2.7 mi) the route vanishes in a meadow crossed by meltwater streams. Rockhop the streams, then scamper south onto the moraines. Elevation: 2020 m (6526 ft). The peaks, glaciers and tarns at the head of **Eremite Valley** are in full view.

Thunderbolt Peak forms the valley's east wall. From left to right (south-southeast to southwest) are Angle Peak, Alcove Mtn, and Eremite Mtn. Eremite Glacier is on the valley's west wall. Behind it is 3118-m (10,230-ft) Mt. Erebus.

An eremite, by the way, is a hermit, or religious recluse. It's an apt name for the freshly-scoured desolation that surrounds you.

TRIP 98a – TONQUIN VALLEY TO ASTORIA RIVER TRAILHEAD

If you start your Tonquin Valley shuttle trip by hiking over Maccarib Pass, you'll complete it by hiking out Astoria River valley. But there are two ways to reach this final leg of the journey. The decision point is the junction immediately above Clitheroe campground. Here are your options: (1) Ascend left (north-northeast), traverse southeast across the slopes of Oldhorn Mtn to Switchback campground, then descend to Astoria River junction. (2) Descend right (east-southeast) for Clitheroe or Surprise Point campgrounds, Wates-Gibson hut, or Eremite Valley (Trip 97), then follow the Chrome Lake trail east to Astoria River junction.

(1) Clitheroe Campground to Astoria River Trailhead

After following the directions in Trip 96 through paragraph six, you've reached the junction at 24.8 km (15.4 mi), 2085 m (6840 ft). Right (east-southeast) enters **Clitheroe campground** in 100 m (110 yd), then descends into Amethyst Lakes basin. Go left (north-northeast).

The trail rises, drops, then contours near 2100 m (6888 ft) through subalpine meadows. You're heading generally southeast, traversing the slopes of **Oldhorn Mtn**. The impressive view extends across the southern Tonquin Valley to 3129-m (10,266-ft) Dungeon Peak (west) and 3090-m (10,135-ft) Parapet Peak (southwest) at the south end of the Ramparts.

At 28.6 km (17.7 mi), a spur descends right 200 m (220 yd) to **Switchback campground**, at 2100 m (6888 ft). The main trail continues generally southeast. In another 1 km (0.6 mi), it begins a switchbacking plunge into forest.

Where the descent eases, the trail curves northeast and glides to **Astoria River junction,** at 33.6 km (20.8 mi), 1713 m (5620 ft). Right (south), across the bridge, is the Chrome Lake trail. Bear left (northeast). Follow the Astoria River downstream, initially above the north bank. The Astoria River trailhead is 8 km (5 mi) distant. The broad, smooth trail plows through forest. Though monotonous, it allows easy striding.

Reach **Astoria campground** at 34.8 km (21.6 mi), on a knoll above the river. At 36.4 km (22.6 mi), cross a bridge to the Astoria River's south bank, near the mouth of Verdant Creek valley (south). Leave the river behind and begin a long, gradual ascent northeast.

In the next ten minutes, cross bridged Verdant Creek and, at 37.1 km (23 mi), proceed straight where the trail to Verdant Pass (Trip 21) forks right (south). After crossing the broad bridge over the **Cavell Lake** outlet stream, ascend the final 15 m (50 ft) to reach the **Astoria River trailhead** at 41.6 km (25.8 mi), 1730 m (5680 ft).

(2) Chrome Lake to Astoria River Trailhead

After following all the directions in Trip 96, and having just come from Surprise point, reach a **T-junction** at 28.5 km (17.7 mi), 1845 m (6052 ft), immediately northwest of Chrome Lake. Turn left (east). (If coming from Eremite Valley or Wates-Gibson hut, turn right.)

Heading east, pass the north shore of **Chrome Lake** in 200 m (220 yd). Round the lake's north-northeast corner, curve right (south), and cross the bridged outlet stream at 1832 m (6010 ft). Thrash through a brushy, soggy area, then resume eastward. The narrow trail follows the Astoria River downstream, high above its south bank, through pleasant, moist forest. It's a refreshing change from the road-width, horse highway in Tonquin Valley.

Nearly 1½ hours from Chrome Lake, rockhop **Campus Creek** at 1738 m (5700 ft). Shortly beyond, cross two more bridged creeklets, rockhop another stream, then descend to the bridge spanning **Astoria River**. Cross it at 35 km (21.7 mi), 1713 m (5620 ft), and reach **Astoria River junction** on the north bank. Left (southwest) traverses Oldhorn Mtn and returns to Tonquin Valley, accessing Switchback and Clitheroe campgrounds en route. Go right, through a gate, and continue following the Astoria River downstream, generally northeast. The Astoria River trailhead is 8 km (5 mi) distant. The broad, smooth trail plows through forest. Though monotonous, it allows easy striding.

Reach **Astoria campground** at 36.2 km (22.4 mi), on a knoll above the river. At 37.7 km (23.4 mi), cross a bridge to the Astoria River's south bank, near the mouth of Verdant Creek valley (south). Leave the river behind and begin a long, gradual ascent northeast.

In the next ten minutes, cross bridged Verdant Creek and, at 38.5 km (23.9 mi), proceed straight where the trail to Verdant Pass (Trip 21) forks right (south). After crossing the broad bridge over the **Cavell Lake** outlet stream, ascend the final 15 m (50 ft) to reach the **Astoria River trailhead** at 43 km (26.7 mi), 1730 m (5680 ft).

TRIP 98b – ASTORIA RIVER TRAILHEAD TO TONQUIN VALLEY

If you start at the Astoria River trailhead, you must choose one of two ways to enter Tonquin Valley. The decision point is Astoria River junction, 8 km (5 mi) up Astoria River valley. Here are your options: (1) Stay on the main trail and traverse Oldhorn Mtn, accessing Switchback and Clitheroe campgrounds en route. It's the most direct route to Amethyst campground, on the upper lake's east shore. (2) Turn left (south), cross the bridge to the Astoria River's south bank, and hike the Chrome Lake trail. It continues following the Astoria River upstream, high above its south bank, through pleasant, moist forest. It's narrower, less traveled, more intimate than the road-like main trail. It's the direct route to Wates-Gibson hut. It also saves time and energy if your goal is Surprise Point campground.

(1) Astoria River Trailhead to Astoria River Junction to Tonquin Valley

The trail departs the north end of the **Astoria River trailhead** parking area. Descend 15 m (50 ft) on an old, dirt road. Cross the bridge spanning the **Cavell Lake** outlet stream. Curve right and ascend, ignoring the left spur to a horse corral. You're now on the broad Astoria River trail, gradually descending southwest through forest, along the northwest slope of Mt. Edith Cavell.

At 4.5 km (2.8 mi) proceed straight on the main trail where the unsigned trail to Verdant Pass (Trip 21) forks left (south). Five minutes farther, cross the bridge spanning **Verdant Creek**. The trail continues gently descending to a bridged crossing of **Astoria River**, at 5.2 km (3.2 mi). Head upstream, now on the river's north bank. **Astoria campground** is at 6.8 km (4.2 mi).

At 8 km (5 mi), 1713 m (5620 ft), reach **Astoria River junction**. Left (south), across the bridge, is the Chrome Lake trail. (Skip below for directions.) Bear right, stay on the north bank, and follow the main trail generally southwest.

In 1 km (0.6 mi), begin a steep, switchbacking ascent northwest onto the slopes of **Old Horn Mtn**. Gain 300 m (984 ft) in the next 3 km (1.9 mi). Top out at 2100 m (6888 ft) in subalpine meadows near treeline. The Ramparts and Amethyst Lakes are visible northwest. Chrome Lake is southwest. At 13 km (8.1 mi), a spur descends left 200 m (220 yd) to **Switchback campground**.

Continuing generally northwest, reach a junction at 16.8 km (10.4 mi). Descend left (east-southeast), as described in Trip 96, for Clitheroe or Surprise Point campgrounds, Wates-Gibson hut, or Eremite Valley. **Clitheroe campground** is just 100 m (110 yd) from the junction, in thick forest. Proceed straight (northwest) to reach Amethyst campground, on upper Amethyst Lake's east shore, at 20 km (12.4 mi).

(2) Astoria River Junction to Tonquin Valley via Chrome Lake Trail

After hiking 8 km (5 mi) from Astoria River trailhead, reach **Astoria River junction**, at 1713 m (5620 ft). Turn left (south), cross the bridge to the Astoria River's south bank, and proceed southwest on the Chrome Lake trail. It continues following the Astoria River upstream (west), high above its south bank, through forest.

Rockhop a stream, cross two bridged creeklets, then rockhop Campus Creek. At 14.2 km (8.8 mi), 1832 m (6010 ft), reach the north-northeast corner of **Chrome Lake**. Cross the bridged outlet stream, round the lake's north shore, and reach a junction at 14.4 km (8.9 mi), 1845 m (6052 ft). Right leads 1.7 km (1.1 mi) generally north to **Surprise Point campground**, on the southeast corner of lower Amethyst Lake. Left leads 0.3 km (0.2 mi) to a fork, where right leads 1.1 km (0.7 mi) to **Wates-Gibson hut**, and left leads south into **Eremite Valley** (Trip 97).

Prelude to winter

TRIP 99

Heart of the South Boundary

LOCATION	Jasper National Park
ROUND TRIP	14 km (8.7 mi) to Rocky Pass 56.6 km (35.1 mi) to Cairn Pass
ELEVATION GAIN	160 m (525 ft) to Rocky Pass 1037 m (3400 ft) to Cairn Pass
KEY ELEVATIONS	trailhead 1830 m (6002 ft) Rocky Pass 1960 m (6430 ft) Medicine Tent River 1713 m (5620 ft) Cairn Pass 2255 m (7396 ft)
HIKING TIME	4 to 5 hours for Rocky Pass 3 days for Cairn Pass
DIFFICULTY	moderate
MAPS	page 518; Mountain Park 83 C/14, Southesk Lake 83 C/11

OPINION

Hikers are temporary monks, withdrawing from society to commune with the divine. The more solitude, the deeper the communion. So we set out from the trail-head hoping to see few people en route and perhaps be alone at our destination. But that's increasingly improbable, unless we deny ourselves the most stirring scenery, or undertake offbeat adventures like this one to Cairn Pass.

The South Boundary Trail is a solitudinous journey indeed. Its daunting, 166-km (103-mi) length, and its forested, valley-bottom route have discouraged all but the most hardy and monkish backpackers. And now even they will likely be dissuaded, because the Rocky River Valley fire devastated the trail's northern reaches during the summer of 2003.

Luckily, Cairn Pass, the scenic climax at the heart of the South Boundary Trail, was untouched by the blaze. And studious scrutiny of a map reveals the pass is accessible via an alternative, shortcut trail starting outside the national park. It's an intriguing invitation to weekend monks seeking earthly beauty as well as ethereal seclusion.

The journey begins with a long drive to the trailhead. If you're coming from Jasper Park, your heart might collapse a little. Instead of mountains, you'll see foot-hills. Instead of wilderness, you'll see the industrial eyesores of coal-mining country. Instead of hikers, you'll see equestrians and ATVers. Then the pavement vanishes. But the road remains smooth until near the end, where its sudden deterioration might elicit raised eyebrows and nervous glances among occupants of low-clearance cars. Just slow down and carry on. The rough stretch is short, and the hike is worth it.

Rocky Pass

Immediately before the road's final descent to the trailhead, it crests Cardinal Divide. The reason you came is now evident. You might even feel a rush of anticipation. The divide is a broad alpine ridge that affords an exciting view of the Rockies walling off the western horizon and, in summer, spawns a gaudy wildflower display. If your timing is fortunate, you'll see the blues of Jacob's Ladder and alpine forget-me-nots; the yellows of arnica, mountain buttercups, and brook ragwort; the pinks of wandering daisies; the purples of monkshood and larkspur; and the reds of Indian paintbrush. Scientists speculate that, during the last Ice Age, the divide was a nunatak—an earth island in a sea of glaciers, thus a haven for plants and animals. That could explain the presence of species that are rare in Alberta (the wooly lousewort, for example) or isolated from their main populations. Trails depart both sides of the divide, bidding you to saunter through the alpine zone for a few hours, either before or after your Cairn Pass backpack trip.

From the trailhead (where you can free camp, by the way), you must endure one final obstacle—a half-hour walk on a seismic-line road—before your enthusiasm can soar. But it will. Soon. As you penetrate the Canadian Rockies' eastern defenses by way of a little-known and therefore surprisingly beautiful alpine breach called Rocky Pass. Ahead, you'll see peaks and glaciers in the main range. It's easy to imagine yourself a mythic hero who, having approached the fortress walls with a pure heart, has been granted permission to pursue your quest in the wilderness kingdom beyond. Because Rocky Pass is just two hours from the trailhead, it's an easy, worthwhile destination for a dayhike, should you lack time to backpack to Cairn Pass. Enduring the long drive to and from the trailhead for such a short hike, however, is questionable.

The trail careens out of Rocky Pass into the forested Medicine Tent River valley, where it intersects the venerable South Boundary Trail. It's soon evident that few hikers pass this way. Occasionally the trail is faint, the way forward momentarily unclear. The campgrounds are tiny, hardly noticeable. Bear diggings and scat might well outnumber fresh bootprints. Yes, it's likely to be just you and the bears. Make noise while hiking and keep a fastidiously clean camp.

After a mere couple hours of southward progress on the South Boundary Trail, you'll enter the meadowy Medicine Tent Lakes basin. The overused adjective *pristine* actually applies here. Views of the basin improve during the final, gradual climb to the sumptuous green expanse of Cairn Pass. Arrive early enough to relax, eat lunch, then wander for several hours. Ascend the north-northeast slope, then proceed through the pass before turning back. You can lose yourself in such vastness, which can be both fearsome and comforting.

Cardinal Divide should be reachable and hikeable in early May. Waves of resplendent wildflowers continue blossoming on the divide through July. Rocky Pass can be snowfree in early June, but en route you'll likely squish through mushy meadows and face three calf-deep fords of the Cardinal River. By fall, the meadows are dry, and the river crossings are reduced to rockhops. Wait until at least mid-July to backpack to Cairn Pass. Below the far side of Rocky Pass is a very short section of extremely narrow trail on a precariously steep slope. A patina of ice, or even snow, would make it obviously dangerous, forcing wary hikers to turn back—unharmed but perhaps scarred by frustration.

Punchbowl Cascade, below Rocky Pass

FACT

Before your trip

If you're coming from Jasper townsite, wait to fill your vehicle with gas until reaching Hinton, where it's usually less expensive.

By Vehicle

From the southwest edge of **Jasper townsite**, at the junction of Hwy 16 and the Icefields Parkway (Hwy 93), drive Hwy 16 northeast 51.3 km (31.8 mi) to Jasper Park's East Gate. Continue east another 22 km (13.6 mi) to Hwy 40S on the right (southeast). It's signed for Cardinal Divide and Cadomin.

Or, from **Edmonton**, drive Hwy 16 east about 283 km (176 mi) to **Hinton**. Then, from Hinton's west edge, near the Canadian Tire and Walmart stores, drive Hwy 16 west another 1.5 km (0.9 mi) to Hwy 40S on the left (southeast). It's signed for Cardinal Divide and Cadomin.

From either approach, turn south onto paved Hwy 40S, which is also signed Ridge Road 254. The trailhead is about an hour distant. Set your trip odometre to 0, then follow the distance log below.

0 km (0 mi)
Departing Hwy 16, heading south on **Hwy 40S**.

22.7 km (14.1 mi)
Cross a bridge over Gregg River.

23 km (14.3 mi)
Sphinx Mtn is visible south.

37.7 km (23.4 mi)
Cross another bridge over Gregg River, then pass the **Gregg River Mine** (right). The pavement narrows and deteriorates near Luscar.

40 km (24.8 mi)
Pavement ends, but the road remains broad and smooth. Pass more coal plants.

47 km (29.1 mi)
Cross a bridge over Luscar Creek. A sign here promises groceries and a B&B ahead.

47.6 km (29.5 mi)
Reach a **T-junction**. Go right (south-southwest) to Cadomin. Hwy 40S (left) leads 38 km (23.6 mi) northeast to Robb.

49.4 km (30.6 mi)
Pass a public telephone, cross railroad tracks, and enter the hamlet of **Cadomin**. Pavement briefly resumes. There's a gas station, café and motel here.

50.9 km (31.6 mi)
Exiting Cadomin, pavement ends.

52.5 km (32.6 mi)
Pass **Whitehorse Wildland Provincial Park** (right). Though unpaved, the road is still well maintained. (The park has toilets, tables, and a short trail.)

55.8 km (34.6 mi)
Pass **Whitehorse Creek Recreation Area** (right), at 1600 m (5250 ft). The road veers southeast, then ascends. (There's a camping fee at Whitehorse. A couple sites have tables and tent pads off the access road. A few others are near the creek. The hitching posts are 0.7 km (0.4 mi) back, near the end of the access road. The Whitehorse Creek trail leads to Fiddle Pass.)

58 km (36 mi)
The road descends.

Approaching Cairn Pass, from near Medicine Tent Lakes

58.2 km (36.1 mi)
Cross a bridge over Prospect Creek, where it's possible to free camp.

63.1 km (39.1 mi)
Cross a bridge over Thornton Creek. The road bends south.

64.6 km (40.1 mi)
Pass Mtn Park Cemetrey (left).

65.1 km (40.4 mi)
Pass **Mtn Park Staging Area** (left). Beyond, the road ascends steeply. (The staging area has tables and a spacious parking lot.)

66.8 km (41.4 mi)
Pass a sign for **Wildhorse Provincial Park**. The road deteriorates.

70.1 km (43.5 mi)
Crest **Cardinal Divide,** at 1981 m (6498 ft). Descend east-southeast on the rough, rocky road. (Cardinal Divide separates two major river systems: the Athabasca and North Saskatchewan. The Athabasca River flows north to the Arctic Ocean. The North Saskatchewan winds across the prairie provinces to Hudson's Bay. The eastern edge of the Rockies, known here as the Nikanassin Range, spans the western horizon. Due west are Climax and Blackface mountains. Southwest is Mt. Cardinal, which forms the west wall of Rocky Pass. Trails depart both sides of the divide—southwest and northeast—inviting you to ramble through the alpine zone.)

71.7 km (44.5 mi)
Turn right and follow a spur 100 m (110 yd) to the **Rocky Pass trailhead**. Elevation: 1830 m (6002 ft).

On Foot

Begin hiking on the seismic-line road. It's left of a green Cardinal Access sign. Follow the level road generally southwest. After hiking 1.7 km (1.1 mi) in about 25 minutes, pass a clearing. About 40 m/yd beyond the clearing, look for a trail departing the left side of the road. It's between two boulders, one with a cairn on top. Leave the road and follow the trail southwest through scrawny trees.

About ten minutes from the road, pass a brushy meadow. Proceed among willows, through cow-tromped grass, for about five minutes. Rocky Pass is visible ahead. Pass a pond (left). About ten minutes farther, left of another pond, the trail forks. Right (west-northwest) rejoins the road. Go left (southeast).

One minute from the fork, pass the remains of a cabin. Two minutes farther, at 3.5 km (2.2 mi), pass an outfitter's camp. Just 200 m (220 yd) beyond the camp arrive at the edge of a steep slope. You're now overlooking the **Cardinal River**, about an hour from the trailhead. Rocky Pass is visible southwest.

Switchbacks ease the sharp descent to the river (actually a creek). At 1850 m (6068 ft), cross to the south bank. Expect a calf-deep ford in spring or summer, an easy rockhop in fall. Turn right (west) and follow the trail upstream through open forest. In ten minutes, rockhop to the river's west bank. Three minutes farther, cross to the southwest bank. Here, the trail plows into forest, rapidly deteriorates, and abruptly tilts skyward. Clamber upward through a rocky, eroded defile, or opt for the rooty, sketchy dirt track left of it.

Though aggressive, the ascent is short. It soon relents in a small grassy, willowy clearing, at 1890 m (6200 ft)—about 1½ hours from the trailhead for most backpackers. The trail curves right (west) on the edge of the clearing. The ascent is now moderate, the trail agreeable. Soon reach the open hillside northeast of and above Rocky Pass. The Cardinal Divide is visible behind you (northeast).

For the next 20 minutes, follow the trail southwest across grassy, shrubby slopes to cross **Rocky Pass** at 7 km (4.3 mi), 1960 m (6430 ft). (It's labeled *Cardinal Pass* on the government topo.) Just beyond a large tarn is a sign informing you that you're entering Jasper National Park. Dayhikers with sufficient time and energy should continue another 30 minutes to fully enjoy the pass and overlook Medicine Tent River valley.

The trail descends briefly, ascends to 1990 m (6527 ft) above the left (east) side of a canyon, then plunges south through forest. Reach a **bedrock punchbowl** where a cascade funnels through a chasm, at 10 km (6.2 mi), 1814 m (5950 ft). After hopping the creeklet, encounter a precariously steep slope where the trail is extremely narrow. Step mindfully. In a couple minutes, the trail is again broad and safe, but the sharp descent continues. Lose 91 m (300 ft) before the trail is comfortably smooth and the descent gentle. Proceed through rooty, marshy, pine-and-spruce forest. About 30 minutes from the punchbowl, at 11.3 km (7 mi), 1713 m (5620 ft), intersect the **South Boundary Trail**. The junction is about 10 m/yd above the Medicine Tent River.

Right (northwest) leads to **Medicine Tent campground** in 100 m (110 yd). It's small, beneath big trees, on the river's edge. Of the few tentsites, only one is level. From the campground, the South Boundary Trail continues northwest, soon following the Rocky River, eventually turning southwest toward Jacques Lake (Trip 123) and Maligne Lake Road.

Turn left (southeast) to follow the South Boundary Trail to Cairn Pass. About 30 minutes along, cross a bridged tributary stream. Here the trail is indistinct. Turn sharply left. Follow the wet, stony strip between grass and willows. Enter forest near river's edge. Look for a blazed tree along the bank. The next blaze is 80 m (87 yd) upriver. Enter forest again. 15 minutes farther, follow cairns across a wide, rocky drainage. Back in forest, pass through a stock fence. In another three minutes, reach a **warden cabin** on the edge of a large clearing, at 15.2 km (9.4 mi), 1780 m (5840 ft).

From the warden cabin, the South Boundary Trail continues generally southeast to Cairn Pass. It follows the Medicine Tent River much of the way, though the river is almost never in sight. The trail, mostly in forest, grants views where it crosses rocky drainages and a creeklet. The ascent is gentle to moderate.

An hour from the warden cabin, at 20.3 km (12.6 mi), 1940 m (6360 ft), reach **La Grace campground**. The river flows through tight willows just below it. The camp is small. None of the few tentsites is level. (Bears sometimes use trails at night, so don't be tempted to pitch your tent on this or any other trail.)

Shortly beyond the camp, attain the first significant view up-valley. Ascend five minutes through a rough boulder field. At 24.7 km (15.3 mi), 2073 m (6800 ft), about one hour past La Grace, reach the first **Medicine Tent Lake**. The trail skirts the lake basin, then ascends willowy slopes. At 28.3 km (17.5 mi), about two hours from La Grace, crest 2255-m (7396-ft) **Cairn Pass**, also known as Southesk Pass.

Immediately southwest of the pass is Southesk Cairn (mountain). Ruby Mtn is north, Thistle Mtn is northeast, and Mount Southesk is 6 km (3.7 mi) south. The trail continues southeast, dropping from the alpine zone into Cairn River valley. **Cairn Pass campground** is in trees, 2 km (1.2 mi) beyond the pass. To survey the pass environs, follow the trail southeast to where it begins descending, or ramble north-northeast up gentle, inviting slopes.

Cairn Pass

TRIP 100

Avion Ridge / Twin Lakes

LOCATION	Waterton Lakes National Park
CIRCUIT	24 km (14.9 mi), plus 6.4 km (4 mi) round trip to Twin Lakes
ELEVATION GAIN	945 m (3100 ft), plus 230 m (754 ft) for Twin Lakes
KEY ELEVATIONS	trailhead 1495 m (4905 ft) Twin Lakes 1950 m (6400 ft) Avion Ridge 2440 m (8003 ft) Goat Lake 2020 m (6625 ft)
HIKING TIME	2 to 3 days
DIFFICULTY	challenging
MAPS	page 515; Gem Trek *Waterton Lakes National Park*

OPINION

Commercial jets fly too high. Hang gliding is too risky. Friends with pilot licenses are too rare. Bungee jumping is too fleeting. Most of us wingless humans who yearn for the joy of sustained, low-level flight have only one recourse: find a high, narrow, airy ridge and start hiking. Avion Ridge will do quite nicely. Given a sunny, summer day, a smile will splurge across your face for the hour or so that you soar along the crest.

It seems the name Avion could have originated from the Latin avian, referring to birds. But it didn't. The ridge is named after a town in France where Canadians fought in 1917. And you too might face a battle of Avion—with Waterton's infamous winds. Pack your windproof shell even if the sky is blue. Also remember to fill waterbottles at Snowshoe Campground, before you ascend the dry-as-dust ridge. The next available water on the loop is in Goat Lake basin.

To avoid crossing dangerous snowfields, don't attempt Avion Ridge until mid-July. Ask at the park information centre about current conditions. If you're acrophobic, don't attempt Avion Ridge period. Though never seriously steep, the ridge route is alarmingly narrow (30 cm / 12 in) in places, on loose scree, next to adios-amigos drop offs.

Hike the loop clockwise: to Snowshoe campground then over the ridge and down past Goat Lake. It's an easier, more gradual ascent this way. Your momentum and anticipation will build to a satisfying climax. Attaining the ridge via Goat Lake is too gruelling—an assault, instead of a seduction.

Though the initial 8.2 km (5.1 mi) to Snowshoe campground are on an old fire road, the hiking is agreeable. Aspen lighten the forest. Wildflowers soften the roadside. Views are frequent. Two creek-crossings allow enjoyable rest stops.

Avion Ridge

The sidetrip to Twin Lakes is a worthwhile addition to the Avion Ridge circuit. It's a not-too-taxing tour of delightful subalpine environs. The Twin Lakes campground is lovely, in an open larch forest, with private sites. Go slightly farther, to the saddle beyond Lower Twin Lake, for a big view south. Don't bother nipping up to Sage Pass unless you want to stare at lumpy mountains and ugly clearcuts.

Actually, most of the highpoints visible from Avion ridge offer little inspiration. You'll see lots of round profiles and scree slopes—the topographical equivalent of fat bellies and lifeless faces. Avion itself is rather blunt, which is why it's walkable. But the panorama it allows you to behold is grand in its vastness. And the airborne sensation it provides is glorious.

Near the end of Avion Ridge, before dropping into Goat Lake basin, the route traverses fantastic rock escarpments splotched with orange, rust, olive, lime, and white lichen. It's the most vivid and varied lichen-palette we've seen.

Avion also presents an opportunity for athletic accomplishment. Though most hikers should make this a two- or three-day backpack trip, the super fit can dayhike it. In July, start by 8 a.m. in August, get cracking earlier. It's even possible to include Twin Lakes in the one-day blitz. If you do, you'll deserve a Rip van Winkle sleep afterward.

Going overnight? Snowshoe campground is worn out, cramped, viewless, dismal. If you have to stay there, spend the afternoon at Twin Lakes. Camping at Twin Lakes is the most attractive option, well worth the short detour. Goat Lake campground, near the end of our suggested loop, is acceptable. Descending into the Goat basin from Avion Ridge is a thrill; camping near the tiny lake is not, but you'll find it practical if you're out two nights.

In shoulder season, consider backpacking to Twin Lakes via the Snowshoe trail. Cycling is another possibility on this old fire road. The terrain is gentle, so pedaling is easy. Ride to Snowshoe campground (bikes are prohibited beyond), then hike 4.8 km (3 mi) to the 2065-m (6775-ft) saddle above Blue Grouse Basin. On this bike/hike combination, you'll ascend 225 m (740 ft) on your steed, 345 m (1130 ft) on foot. Traveling swiftly on a bike, it's critical to make warning calls to prevent surprising a bear.

FACT

By Vehicle

From Hwy 5, drive the Waterton Park entrance road 5.6 km (3.5 mi) southwest into the park. Turn right (northwest) onto Red Rock Parkway, just north of Blakiston Creek bridge. Follow it 15 km (9.3 mi) to where the road ends in the Red Rock Canyon parking area, at 1495 m (4905 ft).

On Foot

Though the route atop Avion Ridge is not indicated on most topo maps, it's a well-worn path, easy to follow with these directions. Before setting out, look northwest from the trailhead. You can see the ridge. Counting right to left, it's the third bump on the horizon.

Begin by crossing the bridge spanning Red Rock Canyon. This is the Snowshoe trail, an old road. Watch for the namesake white-footed rabbits. You're penetrating **Bauerman Valley**, heading northwest, roughly following Bauerman Creek upstream. Anderson Peak dominates left (south).

At 4.6 km (2.9 mi), after one hour of mostly level walking, reach a signed **fork**. Right ascends 2.4 km (1.5 mi) to Goat Lake and 4 km (2.5 mi) to Avion Ridge. Following our recommended clockwise loop, you'll descend the ridge that way. So proceed left, gaining elevation gradually. The road-trail is treelined, but there are views.

Another 45 minutes of striding will bring you **to Snowshoe campground** at 8.5 km (5.3 mi), 1720 m (5642 ft). From here it's 17.9 km (11.1 mi), including a 720-m (2362-ft) climb, back to the trailhead via Avion Ridge. If you're only equipped for a dayhike, think carefully before embarking on the long ascent to the ridge. Be certain you'll have sufficient daylight, energy, water and food to pull it off.

Snowshoe campground is where the Twin Lakes trail departs the Avion Ridge loop. **To visit the lakes**, go left (southwest) and cross the bridge. Climb 70 m (230 ft) aided by a couple switchbacks. The trail levels out as you hike 10-15 minutes through meadows. Then enter thick timber, ascending the north side of the valley. At 11.6 km (7.2 mi), ignore the spur trail veering right (northwest). It gains 180 m (590 ft) in 1.5 km (0.9 mi) to reach insignificant 2165-m (7100-ft) **Sage Pass**.

Continue straight on the main trail. It curves left (southwest), and in 100 m (110 yd) grazes the shore of upper **Twin Lake** at 1950 m (6400 ft). Twin Lakes campground has tables, benches and a lake view for pleasant lounging. Lower Twin Lake is visible a few minutes past the campground, left (east) of and well below the trail.

To continue the Avion Ridge circuit, from Snowshoe campground follow the signed trail northwest. Fast hikers will attain the highpoint in about 2 hours. Reach

Rock atop Avion Ridge

a junction in 0.8 km (0.5 mi). Left leads to tiny **Lost Lake** in 1.1 km (0.7 mi), but it's visible from above. Proceed straight. The trail continues angling northwest, away from your intended destination, but does so to grant you a gentler line of ascent. Within one hour of Snowshoe, reach 1985-m (6511-ft) **Castle River Divide,** at 11.6 km (7.2 mi) from the trailhead. The Avion Ridge route forks right (east-northeast). The crest is now only 3 km (1.9 mi) farther, but the ascent is aggressive.

The forest soon thins, providing views over your right shoulder (southwest) to Lost Lake and the massive wall running north-south along Castle Divide. Yellow signs along the Avion Ridge route indicate the Waterton Park boundary. The icy-shouldered peaks way south and west are across the U.S. border, in Glacier National Park. The trail's highpoint is just below the 2440-m (8003-ft) **crest of Avion Ridge**. The route traverses the south slope, heads east, then descends left (north) behind the first hump. Soon cross to the west side of the ridge. The route is now quite narrow, with a steep drop to your left.

Eventually contour around to a 2311-m (7580-ft) **saddle** beneath Newman Peak. This is your **exit-point from the ridge** and might still be signed as such. Northwest is the Castle River drainage. Southeast is the Goat Lake basin, into which you now descend. The faint route drops abruptly right (east). Goat Lake looks close. It's only 1.9 km (1.2 mi) distant, but takes longer to reach than you might think, because the going is rough.

Watch for cairns. Stay left (north) of the headwall stream. By a little cascade over a short rock band, go right around a small, treed bench to find the easiest way down to a better trail. About 45 minutes below the saddle, cross a creekbed and, a few minutes farther, arrive at **Goat Lake**. Elevation: 2015 m (6610 ft). The trail passes between the lake (right) and the campground (left). You've hiked 19.4 km (12 mi) from the trailhead.

To complete the Avion Ridge loop, descend left of the Goat Lake outlet stream. The trail is initially steep and narrow, but well defined. Intersect the **Snowshoe trail** 2.4 km (1.5 mi) from Goat Lake. You're now on familiar ground, at 1570 m (5665 ft). Turn left (southeast) for the 4.6-km (2.9-mi) mostly level road-walk back to the trailhead at Red Rock Canyon.

TRIP 101

Pulsatilla & Badger Passes

LOCATION	Banff National Park, northeast of Castle Junction
ROUND TRIP	44.4 km (27.5 mi) to Badger campground plus 7.8 km (4.8 mi) to Pulsatilla Pass plus 10 km (6.2 mi) to Badger Pass 62.2 km (38.6 mi) total
ELEVATION GAIN	711 m (2332 ft) to Badger campground plus 319 m (1046 ft) to Pulsatilla Pass plus 519 m (1702 ft) to Badger Pass 1549 m (5081 ft) total
KEY ELEVATIONS	trailhead 1430 m (4690 ft) Luellen Lake 1975 m (6478 ft) Badger campground 2050 m (6724 ft) Pulsatilla Pass 2345 m (7692 ft) Badger Pass 2545 m (8348 ft)
HIKING TIME	4 days
DIFFICULTY	moderate
MAPS	page 520; Gem Trek *Banff & Mt. Assiniboine*

OPINION

New Zealanders don't call it *hiking*. They call it *tramping,* which suggests labourious slogging rather than buoyant striding. Yet it makes sense in New Zealand, where many trails (Kiwis call them *tracks*) tunnel long distances through jungly bush. In the Canadian Rockies, only occasionally do hikers feel like trampers. But one of those places is Johnston Creek Valley, through which you must trundle your bundle if you want to see Pulsatilla and Badger passes.

Pulsatilla Pass is a splendidly scenic, sequestered vantage. The view is huge: up Wildflower Valley, down Johnston Creek Valley. The Sawback Range is on one side, the massif comprising Pulsatilla Mountain on the other. Crowning the panorama is Pulsatilla Lake, in an alpine basin. This is the *big wild* that most Banff Park visitors hope to experience but don't because they're psychologically tethered to pavement.

Badger is one of Banff Park's highest trail-accessible passes. Long-lingering snow conspires with remoteness to discourage visitors. You're as likely to see a bear here as you are to meet another hiker, because the trail breaching the pass drops into prime grizzly habitat: Cascade River Valley and Flint's Park. This lonely, feral atmosphere sharpens the beauty of the Badger Pass wildflower meadows but might also keep you on edge.

So, one trip, two desirable destinations. Plus the journey begins in Johnston Creek Canyon, which ranks among Banff Park's renowned sights. Nevertheless,

The catwalks in Johnston Canyon are 1.6 km (1 mile) long.

Inkpots and Mt. Ishbel, Johnston Creek Valley

Upper Johnston Falls

weighing the pros and cons of backpacking here, the balance tips only slightly to the positive. That's because nearly 28 km (17.4 mi) of the round trip between the canyon and the passes is tedious tramping in Johnston Creek Valley. The trail is rooty, horse-pummelled, deep in forest. Views are limited. You'll glimpse mountains but see nothing exhilarating.

If you're compelled to hike here, allow four days. Start by aiming for Luellen Lake campground. On day two, continue up-valley to Badger campground, then visit Pulsatilla Pass that afternoon. Devote your third day to exploring Badger Pass. On day four, cruise from Badger campground down-valley to the trailhead.

Just don't select this trip as your first or only extended foray into backcountry Banff. Superior options? Gibbon, Whistling & Healy Passes (Trip 80) and Pipestone Pass / Devon Lakes (Trip 81) are more consistently scenic and lack glaring deterrents on the order of Johnston Creek Valley.

In previous editions of this book, we described a one-way trek: from Johnston Creek Canyon, up Johnston Creek Valley, over Pulsatilla Pass, into Wildflower Creek canyon, through upper Baker Creek Valley, past Baker and Ptarmigan lakes, over Boulder Pass, and out to Fish Creek trailhead via Lake Louise Ski Area. Beyond Pulsatilla Lake, the trail has largely vanished due to repeated washouts and decades of no maintenance. Except between Baker Lake and the ski area (Trips 86 and 87), it was never an easy or scenic journey. Linking Pulsatilla and Baker lakes is now a challenging, wearisome bushwhack—a preposterous undertaking for the average hiker. Forget it.

What about continuing just part way beyond Pulsatilla Lake, then exiting to Hwy 1A via lower Baker Creek Valley? Forget that, too. Long ago we were among the last to attempt what was, even then, a barely decipherable, exasperating route. Thrashing through the knee-deep bogs was to relive prehistory, as if following in the flipper-steps of the first amphibians to crawl onto land. Banff Park now warns hikers away from this valley. It's a Special Protection Area for the resident grizzlies. Judging by all the scat we saw, they love it there.

FACT

By Vehicle

Drive Highway 1A (Bow Valley Parkway) to Johnston Canyon. It's 6.5 km (4 mi) southeast of Castle Village (across the Bow River from Castle Junction), or 17.5 km (10.9 mi) northwest of the Trans-Canada junction near Banff townsite. Parking is on the northeast side of the highway, across the creek from the resort, at 1430 m (4690 ft).

On Foot

Cross the highway bridge over Johnston Creek to the resort side, turn right, and follow the path upstream (generally north) above the west bank.

Ascending the narrow canyon, you'll cross steel catwalks attached to rock walls. Reach the **lower falls** at 1.1 km (0.7 mi); the 30-m (100-ft) **upper falls** at 2.7 km (1.7 mi).

Beyond the falls, the trail climbs to merge with an old road from Moose Meadows at 3.2 km (2 mi), 1602 m (5255 ft). Stay right at this junction. A moderate ascent through forest tops out at 1736 m (5695 ft). While descending north-northeast, attain glimpses into upper Johnston Canyon. The grade steepens into Johnston Creek Valley, where the view expands.

Luellen Lake

At 5.9 km (3.7 mi), 1645 m (5395 ft), about 1½ hours from the trailhead, arrive at the **Inkpots**—small, round, aquamarine pools fed by mineral springs. Trivia Alert: The Inkpots maintain a constant temperature of 4° C (39.2° F). What you see at the bottom of the pools is quicksand.

The pools are just above Johnston Creek. Surrounding them is a meadow full of willows and dwarf birch. Several benches invite you to rest and appreciate the journey's first significant vista. The dominant sight is southeast: 2908-m (9538-ft) Mt. Ishbel.

Proceed left (northwest) of the Inkpots to continue up-valley. In two minutes, cross a large, wood bridge over **Johnston Creek**. On the east bank, the trail turns left (north).

Hop over braided meltwater streams. After a short, steep ascent, the trail levels in forest again. Reach **Larry's Camp** at 7.9 km (4.9 mi), 1677 m (5500 ft). Immediately beyond, the trail drops to an unnamed tributary of Johnston Creek. Go right (east) upstream, cross the creek on a bridge, and arrive at a signed junction on the tributary's north bank.

Right (northeast) follows the tributary upstream to Mystic Pass (Trip 109). Proceed straight (northwest) on the Johnston Creek Valley trail. This will remain your general direction of travel all the way to Badger campground.

The valley forest is interspersed with meadows. Reach the next junction at 16.4 km (10.2 mi). Left leads 200 m (220 yd) to a small campground beside Johnston Creek. The creek is bridged here. A spur continues west, ascending 76 m (250 ft) in about 1 km

Upper Johnston Creek Valley

(0.6 mi) to **Luellen Lake campground**, near the east shore at 1975 m (6478 ft). Helena Ridge rises above the south shore of the 2-km (1.2-mi) long, forest-ringed lake.

Resuming up-valley (northwest), cross a bridge to the west side of Johnston Creek. With the trees thinning, the Sawback Range is visible right (east). Another bridge soon returns you to the east bank. In the willow-choked upper valley, the lengthy, east face of 3035-m (9955-ft) Pulsatilla Mtn is visible left (west).

Rockhop Badger Creek to reach a junction at 21.7 km (13.5 mi), 2026 m (6645 ft). Right leads northeast to Badger Pass. Just ahead, at 22.2 km (13.8 mi), 2050 m (6724 ft), is **Badger campground**. It's on a treed knoll with views north-northwest toward Pulsatilla Pass and northwest to nearby Pulsatilla Mtn.

Continuing north-northwest to Pulsatilla Pass from Badger campground, the trail crosses the now trickling Johnston Creek. Before the final ascent, an alpine cirque (right / north) invites exploration. If you decline, bear left (north-northwest) toward the obvious low gap. Crest **Pulsatilla Pass** at 25.6 km (15.9 mi), 2345 m (7692 ft). North-northwest, in the alpine basin below, is Pulsatilla Lake. Mt. Avens is left (west) above the pass.

The trail descending to **Pulsatilla Lake** is evident. It skirts the east shore at 27.1 km (16.8 mi), 2210 m (7249 ft). Without dropping over the lip of the basin, you can gaze north-northwest, down Wildflower Creek Valley, toward the bear haven of Baker Creek Valley.

For **Badger Pass**, return to the junction near Badger Creek, immediately south of Badger campground. Follow the trail forking left (northeast). It ascends moderately but steadily through stream-fed wildflower meadows. Top out in 5 km (3 mi), at 2545 m (8348 ft). From the east end of the pass, the trail plunges south, then follows the Cascade River downstream (east) into Flint's Park.

TRIP 102

Watchtower Basin

LOCATION	Jasper National Park
ROUND TRIP	25.6 km (16 mi) to headwall saddle
ELEVATION GAIN	1000 m (3280 ft)
KEY ELEVATIONS	trailhead 1380 m (4525 ft) basin 2015 m (6610 ft) headwall saddle 2380 m (7805 ft)
HIKING TIME	9 hours or overnight
DIFFICULTY	challenging
MAPS	page 513; Gem Trek *Jasper & Maligne Lake;* Medicine Lake 83 C/13

OPINION

The wealthy pay big bucks for mud baths at posh spas. You can take one for free here. And you will if you slip—a likelihood on this sodden, quaggy trail. But with the agility to pirouette over all the muck, or the indifference to bull your way through, a weekend backpack trip to Watchtower Basin can be gratifying.

The sprawling basin is subalpine in its lower reaches, alpine above. In between, the trail becomes reasonably dry and remains so the rest of the way. The campground, just above a gentle creek, is sufficiently treed to feel sheltered, exposed enough to allow views. From there on, your eyes as well as your feet have plenty of room to roam.

The upper tundra bowl would be easy to hike if it didn't constantly tempt you to loll. Not because of the meadows, which are only moderately floral. Or the mountains, which are more Pillsbury Dough Boy than The Hulk. But simply because of the sheer, sweeping, open expanse. This is, after all, an approach to the decidedly alpine Skyline (Trip 81). That's why it's imperative you keep going through the basin and ascend the gentle, scree-slope headwall. You'll see the Skyline trail just below you, and more significant, you'll snatch one of the views that have earned it worldwide fame. The peaky panorama includes Mt. Geikie, highest in the Tonquin Valley area.

If you're Roadrunner quick and Wile E. Coyote tough, you can dayhike into Watchtower Basin. Start early and you can even nip up to the headwall saddle. The basin is too far and the trail too muddy, however, to entice many dayhikers, which adds another reason to backpack: tranquility.

Definitely don't dayhike here unless you're sure you can reach the upper basin. The lower basin, with all that standing water, fosters a mosquito breeding frenzy. Until you're past the campground, rest stops can be miserable without donning full coverage. Most hikers would agree, at its buggy worst this is Willpower Basin.

FACT

By Vehicle

From the junction with Connaught Drive at the north end of Jasper townsite, drive Hwy 16 northeast 1.8 km (1.1 mi). Turn right (east) onto Maligne Lake Road. It's signed for Jasper Park Lodge. Set your odometre to 0.

Immediately cross the Athabasca River bridge. In 200 m (220 yd), go left for Maligne Lake. At 18.2 km (11.3 mi) turn right (southwest) into Watchtower Basin trailhead parking lot, at 1380 m (4525 ft).

On Foot

Descend to the Maligne River, cross the bridge, then climb steeply southwest into a forest of lodgepole pine, Engelmann spruce, and alpine fir. The trail soon veers left (southeast). The ascent eases but continues, traversing the lower, northern slopes of The Watchtower. The mountain seems to be weeping. Muddy stretches are frequent, some laid with puncheon (log boardwalk).

At 5.5 km (3.4 mi) curve south, into the forested Watchtower drainage. The trail sidles up to **Watchtower Creek**, then enters the lower reaches of the basin. The ascent is now gentle. Follow the trail south-southwest, on the west side of the creek, through bushy meadows and open forest. Expect very muddy, boggy conditions, especially in early summer. Views extend all the way to the basin headwall.

At 9.6 km (6 mi) a cairn indicates where to turn left (east) and ford the creek. On the east bank, turn right (south). Follow the creek upstream where the trail is indistinct. At 9.8 km (6.1 mi) the left fork leads to **Watchtower campground**, on a bench above the creek, at 2015 m (6610 ft). If you camp here, consider a short, cross-country sidetrip west—gaining 160 m (525 ft) in about 1 km (0.6 mi)—to a small lake beneath The Watchtower.

Proceeding south from the campground, gain drier ground as you enter the **upper basin**. The trail eventually fades, but the open, alpine slopes are easy to navigate. Aim for the saddle on the headwall ridge. Two poles—spaced far apart—will help guide you. Basically stay to the east side of the basin until you pick up the trail worn into the talus slope. You can see this trail from a distance; it angles up the headwall.

Crest the **headwall** at 12.8 km (7.9 mi), 2380 m (7805 ft). Curator Mtn is nearby, southwest. The Notch is northwest. The Skyline trail is visible below. Your trail descends south about 0.4 km (0.25 mi) to intersect the Skyline at 2320-m (7610-ft) Shovel Pass. Read Trip 81 if you're proceeding through The Notch to hike the airy ridge beyond.

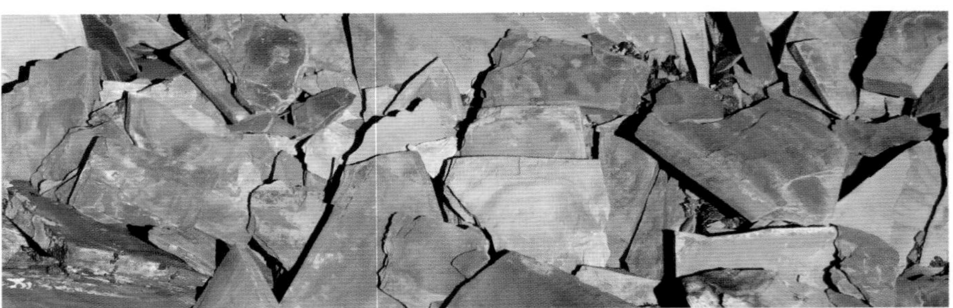

Slate

Watchtower Basin

TRIP 103
Elysium Pass

LOCATION	Jasper National Park
ROUND TRIP	27 km (16.7 mi) to overlook 29 km (18 mi) to pass
ELEVATION CHANGE	1110-m (3641-ft) gain to overlook 230-m (754-ft) loss from overlook to pass
KEY ELEVATIONS	trailhead 1100 m (3608 ft) overlook 2210 m (7249 ft) pass 2025 m (6642 ft)
HIKING TIME	9 hours for overlook 10 hours or overnight for pass
DIFFICULTY	moderate
MAPS	page 522; Gem Trek *Jasper and Maligne Lake*; Jasper 83 D/16

OPINION

Vigorous exertion sends a message to your cells. It shouts, "Gird your cellular loins for challenges ahead!" And your cells respond by snapping to attention, keeping you young, fit and able. Sloth sends the opposite electro-chemical message. It mumbles, "I'm layin' you off. We're shuttin' the plant down." Elysium Pass is a vigorous hike indeed. Want to alert your cells to expect a long, invigorating, ripsnorting life? Here you go.

The challenge of Elysium is as much mental as physical. The elevation gain and distance are substantial, but it's the tedium that will sap you. Even a swift hiker, carrying only a daypack, will plod at least three-and-a-half hours before seeing anything but grim forest. That's, gulp, seven hours round trip; perhaps eight for the average hiker, nine for others.

After three-and-a-half hours, speedy dayhikers will break into the subalpine zone and begin flanking Emigrants Mtn. Wildflowers and panoramic vistas will reward them for the next hour, until reaching the Elysium Pass overlook—a viewpoint so awesome it's on the cover of this book. Glacier-dolloped Monarch Mtn lends a regal flourish to the scene. The wild vastness both intimidates and beckons. From the overlook, it's a long, steep drop to Elysium Pass and the campground just below it. Having to regain that lost elevation will deter most dayhikers from continuing beyond the overlook.

Backpacking makes more sense. After descending from the overlook, pitch your tent at the primitive, unmaintained Elysium Pass campground. From there, you can light out on any of several scenically spectacular excursions into the surrounding alplands. Chief among them, an easy scramble to the summit of nearby

Monarch Mtn, from Elysium Pass overlook

Elysium Mtn. The longer your stay at Elysium Pass, the more you'll amortize the trudgery of the approach. A couple days will make the effort to get there unquestionably worthwhile.

Before setting out for Elysium Pass, especially if you're dayhiking, be fully cognizant of the trip's downside. For the first hour-and-a-half, you'll hear cars whizzing along the highway and perhaps a train or two as well. In summer, you'll encounter clouds of mosquitoes. The trail crosses boggy terrain where thick forest deters wind from grounding the buggers. (Elysium Pass overlook, however, is blessedly dry, open and breezy.) Stretches of trail tend to be faint and muddy. Horse travel is permitted to Elysium Pass, which only makes trail conditions worse. After penetrating the subalpine zone on the south face of Emigrants Mtn, you'll be in prime grizzly habitat.

But don't let that long warning list stop you. According to Greek myth, Elysium is where virtuous souls dwell in the afterlife. It's a place of bliss, of complete happiness. Seeking to probe the heart of Canadian Rocky Mountain majesty, you'll find Elysium Pass is aptly named.

FACT

By Vehicle

From the junction of Hwys 93 and 16, on the southwest side of Jasper townsite, drive Hwy 16 west 11 km (6.8 mi), just past the Meadow Creek bridge. Turn north into the trailhead parking area, at 1100 m (3608 ft).

On Foot

Follow the service road northwest, past the gate and kiosk. Cross the culvert. Immediately beyond, a sign points right to a trail ascending to the railroad tracks. Step over the tracks, then follow the trail down to a hefty bridge spanning the Miette River. On the far bank, the trail—signed 3e—curves left (northwest).

After hiking about 15 minutes, the trail zigs, ascending moderately to a rounded ridge. It levels briefly here. The highway noise temporarily abates behind a bluff. Heading north now, the trail descends to cross bridged **Minaga Creek** at 2.3 km (1.4 mi), 1306 m (4285 ft), about 30 minutes from the trailhead. Look for orange-and-yellow columbine just before the bridge. From the creek's northeast bank, the trail leads north, then northwest. In ten minutes, reach a junction at 2.7 km (1.7 mi), 1270 m (4166 ft).

Right (north-northeast) leads to **Dorothy, Christine, and Virl lakes**. Leave them for the return trip. Then, if the daylight or your curiosity haven't waned, hike 0.8 km (0.5 mi) to a junction where Virl Lake is a couple hundred metres right. Dorothy Lake is left (northeast) 0.5 km (0.3 mi), followed by Christine Lake nearby northwest. All the lakes are, of course, cloaked in forest.

From the 2.7-km (1.7-mi) junction, proceed left (northwest) for Elysium Pass. Soon attain a view of forested slopes south and west. Leaving the stately Douglas firs behind, ascend through a forest of lodgepole pine and Engelmann spruce. The trail soon contours high above Minaga Creek.

The train and highway traffic remain audible 1¼ hours from the trailhead. Drop to a footbridge over a creeklet at 6 km (3.7 mi), 1480 m (4855 ft). The trail then curves north-northeast, through a willowy swath, up to a ridge. A bit farther, about two hours from the trailhead, reach a **bog**—the first significant break in the forest. Elephant's head (deep magenta) flourishes here. So do mosquitoes. The trail fades but should be discernible. Follow it right (north) across the bog, back into forest. Ten minutes beyond, cross a bridge over a muckhole. Then ascend gradually through drier forest.

At 1707 m (5600 ft), about 2¼ hours from the trailhead, begin a switchbacking ascent. The trail steepens. With increased elevation, the forest opens, breeze is more prevalent, and bugs diminish. At 1945 m (6380 ft), the wildflower show commences. Watch for lupine (purple), Sitka valerian (white to pinkish), and columbine (yellow to orange). Soon enter rock gardens. Expect muddy stretches of trail.

Enter the **subalpine zone** at 2018 m (6620 ft), at the top of a boulder slide. Strong striders will be here 3½ hours after leaving the trailhead. From south to west, the horizon is now visible. Directly south is Meadow Creek, draining the north end of Tonquin Valley (Trip 94). Frontier Peak and Mt. Fitzwilliam (Trip 104) are southwest. Just two minutes farther, Rampart Peak appears west-northwest. The hiking is finally enjoyable. Views are panoramic. And the trees are beautiful: big spruce (square needles), and full-skirted, subalpine fir (flat needles, resin blisters on bark).

Ahead (right / north-northwest) is Emigrants Mtn. The trail continues along its fractured south side, eventually curving around its west shoulder. Cross another boulder slide at 9 km (5.6 mi). There's a shallow creeklet here. Lupine clusters grace the slopes. Also look for pale yellow-green western lousewort with tiny hooked beaks, and lavender aster with 25-30 slender petals. Hop over four more creeklets in the next 15 minutes. Turn southeast to see the confluence of the Miette and Athabasca rivers. East of the Athabasca River Valley is Mt. Tekarra. Right of it is the long ridgeline of Amber Mtn, where the Skyline (Trip 81) lives up to its name.

Willow-herb and paintbrush

Traversing the south side of Emigrants Mtn, the trail is briefly a sodden, bootbeaten route. But it's soon distinct again. At 2203 m (7225 ft), Moose Lake is visible southwest, beside Hwy 16. Ahead (west-northwest) are the gentle slopes of Elysium Mtn.

At 13.5 km (8.4 mi), 2210 m (7249 ft), on the shoulder of Emigrants Mtn, attain the Elysium Pass **overlook**. This is the highpoint of the trip. Strong hikers will arrive here in 4½ hours. There's a spacious open area (dirt and heather) where dayhikers can relax and savour the view before galloping back to the trailhead.

Elysium Pass is visible below (northwest). Ice-capped Monarch Mtn rises just beyond Elysium Mtn. The Elysium Pass campground—just shy of and slightly below the pass—is visible west-northwest, left of a forested knoll. If you're spending the night there, you'll probably want to scramble up Elysium Mtn. Plan your ascent route while sitting at the overlook, where you can study the entire mountain. The red-orange Victoria Cross Range (north-northeast) is reminiscent of southwest Colorado. Adventurous hikers will yearn to wander cross-country, beyond Elysium Pass, into the sprawling alplands at the base of those distant peaks.

Continuing beyond the overlook? The trail descends sharply. In about 15 minutes, rockhop a creek at 14.3 km (8.8 mi). Follow it downstream (left / southwest) to the unmaintained **campground**, at 1980 m (6494 ft). It's in the first stand of trees, in the middle of the meadowy drainage, 230 m (754 ft) below the overlook.

From the creek crossing, go right (north) through alpine meadow to crest 2025-m (6642-ft) **Elysium Pass**, at 14.5 km (9 mi).

EXCURSIONS FROM ELYSIUM PASS CAMPGROUND

(1) Hike north-northeast about 15 minutes. Curve right (east) into the rift on the north side of Emigrants Mtn. It harbours a tarn.

(2) Hike southwest for several minutes, then turn west and work your way up the south end of Elysium Mtn. The summit overlooks Elysium Pass and affords a fine view of Monarch Mtn.

(3) Try heading north-northwest along the grassy, lightly treed slopes west of Elysium Pass. Contour across the east side of Elysium Mtn to a viewpoint beneath Monarch Mtn.

(4) Having hiked across the south slope of Emigrants Mtn, and perhaps having surveyed it from elsewhere in the Elysium Pass environs, choose a route and scramble to the summit of this mountain with the oddly unpunctuated name. Maybe you'll find the long-lost apostrophe.

TRIP 104

Fitzwilliam Basin

LOCATION	Mt. Robson Provincial Park
ROUND TRIP	27 km (16.7 mi)
ELEVATION GAIN	951 m (3120 ft)
KEY ELEVATIONS	trailhead 1113 m (3650 ft), basin 2035 m (6675 ft)
HIKING TIME	9 hours to 3 days
DIFFICULTY	challenging
MAPS	page 515; Jasper D/16

OPINION

Powerful scenery is high-octane fuel. You fill up with your eyes, then your heart pumps it to your muscles. The longer between inspirational sights, the less you have in your tank. On this trip, you could run out of gas.

Not until you scale the fortress of Fitzwilliam Basin will it be obvious why you came. It's a long boring hike through cheerless forest—to a point just less than halfway. Then it's a long, rough, slog-splash-bash-scramble into the basin. Lifting your eyes from the trail is fruitless for the first three hours around the base of Mt. Fitzwilliam. So what makes Fitz worthwhile?

It's an impressive, alpine basin. The campground is just above the shore of a crystal-clear lake cupped by desolate Frontier Peak, Mt. Clairvaux, and Kataka Mtn. A rugged pass and two other nearby lakes invite exploration. And solitude is a strong possibility. On a sunny, August weekend, we saw only one tent in the basin. Compare that with the mob scene at Berg Lake (Trip 82) and Fitz looks attractive.

In the Sierra, Fitz might be a premier destination. For the Canadian Rockies, it's not outstanding. Peaks, meadows, lakes, streams—all the elements of mountain splendor are here. But they're dispensed with an eyedropper instead of a fire hose. And the basin walls are mostly talus, which is less striking than sheer cliffs or solid ice.

Fitz appeals more to rockhounds than meadow muffins. The boulder fields and moraines are a spectacle. The final 2 km (1.2 mi) are a chaotic jumble of stones—all sizes, colours and compositions. It's challenging to hike through, but interesting to examine. If you've trekked in Utah's Canyonlands, you'll feel you've been here before. Potentially hot weather could spark deja vu as well.

If you must limit yourself to one backpack trip, the Skyline (Trip 81) or Berg Lake are far superior choices. Though even rougher than Fitz, the journey past the fourth Geraldine Lake (Trip 54) is prettier and probably lonelier. If you're toned and taut, try dayhiking into Fitz Basin. It *can* be done.

Should you backpack here, don't add to your troubles by detouring to Miette Hill on the Great Divide, as the BC Parks signboard suggests. The hill is above the highway, well outside the basin, and requires a 210-m (690-ft) ascent. Devote your

Fitzwilliam Basin

playtime to the basin lakes, and the pass between Frontier Peak and Mt. Clairvaux. Bring a topo map to navigate your way to the pass; the rugged route is unsigned.

FACT

By Vehicle

If you're driving east through Mt. Robson Park on Yellowhead Hwy 16, go 3 km (2 mi) past the Lucerne campground on Yellowhead Lake. If you're driving west from Jasper Park on Yellowhead Hwy 16, go 7 km (4.5 mi) past the Alberta-B.C. boundary at Yellowhead Pass.

From either approach, turn north into the Yellowhead Lake boat launch and picnic area. Park here, at 1113 m (3650 ft). You'll see a BC Parks signboard with a map of the Fitzwilliam Basin trail. The stated distances vary slightly from ours. We believe ours are more accurate.

On Foot

From the parking lot, cross to the south side of the highway and look for a trail sign. Walk the trail 40 m south, then turn right (southwest) onto the overgrown road—a pipeline right-of-way. Proceed 0.7 km (0.4 mi) to a hiker sign on your left, where the trail departs the road. There's a self-registration board here. Switchback up through scrawny trees. The highway and a creek are initially audible. You'll glimpse Yellowhead Lake and tiny Whitney Lake, but little else until Rockingham Creek campground.

Within 45 minutes (for fast hikers) the grade eases. After a curve and a short descent, the trail steepens and continues southeast. The trail levels, allowing you to cruise the last 15 minutes to the campground.

Reach **Rockingham Creek campground** at 6.3 km (3.9 mi), 1605 m (5265 ft). Fast dayhikers will be here in 1½ hours, backpackers in about 2½ hours. Wood-chip tent sites are crammed together near the creek. Mt. Fitzwilliam confronts you southeast. Cross the creek on a sturdy bridge. A narrow, rooty, often muddy trail resumes east. You're now hiking parallel to and above Fitzwilliam Creek, which is on your left (north). The trail works its way around the base of Mt. Fitzwilliam, which is on your right (south).

About 45 minutes beyond Rockingham, after gaining 160 m (525 ft), the trail breaks out of forest into **meadow**. Lavender fleabane, yellow asters, and elephant's heads brighten the subalpine greenery. Cross the bottom edge of a **rockslide** near 10.3 km (6.4 mi). The trail peters out in this rough terrain as the route bends due south. This is a good place to rest, because the rocks harbour fewer mosquitoes than the moist meadow. A few minutes farther, a prominent headwall comes into view. That's your objective; above and beyond it is the basin.

The following directions sound complex, but should be clear en route. Basically, you want to **approach the headwall**, turn left (southeast) along its base, then ascend around its east end.

Heading due south toward the headwall, look for **cairns** guiding you along the right (west) side of a small lake, a slow stream, and a boggy area. Cross the next **rockslide** where it's level. Aim for a hiker sign on a post next to a large salmon-coloured boulder, 40 m/yd from the forest edge. Facing the headwall, you're now near the base of a steep, rocky chute that the old route ascended. Don't go that way. Instead, wind southeast along the stream, at the forest edge. There are big, beautiful spruce here. A few yellow arrows on trees mark the route. Cross the stream a couple times.

Proceed about 0.5 km (0.3 mi) in and beside a creekbed (possibly dry), at the bottom of a **small canyon**, along the base of the headwall. Ahead is the Fitzwilliam Basin outlet stream cascading down a small gorge. Cross the stream at the bottom of the cascade. Aim for a cairn on the moraine to your left. Then turn right and ascend the rock gully on the creek's left (east) side.

You're now about 2½ hours of determined hiking beyond Rockingham Creek. Looking northwest, across the highway, you can see a vast, intriguing expanse of wilderness in Jasper Park. Head south, over sharp rocks and boulders. The basin is only 15 minutes farther. Angle right to reach the lakeshore, near the outlet stream. Total distance: 13.5 km (8.4 mi). Elevation: 2035 m (6675 ft). Hiking time: 4 hours for swift dayhikers, 6 hours for backpackers. The **Fitzwilliam Basin campground** is sheltered by krummholz, on a grassy knoll, just above the shore and the stream.

For a short, couple-hour excursion, roam west from the campground and visit the other two lakes in the basin. You'll gain only 30 m (100 ft) in about 15 minutes to the first lake. Proceed west beyond it. In the next 1.3 km (0.8 mi), drop slightly and gain 60 m (200 ft) to reach the second, higher lake.

Backpackers with an extra day in the basin, and a topo map in hand, can go around the west side of the main lake, then scramble southeast, gaining 520 m (1705 ft) to the pass between Mt. Clairvaux and Frontier Peak. Allow 5 to 7 hours for this round trip from the campground.

TRIP 105
Moose Pass

LOCATION	Mt. Robson Prov. Park / Jasper National Park
ROUND TRIP	78 km (48.3 mi)
ELEVATION GAIN	1230 m (4034 ft)
KEY ELEVATIONS	trailhead 855 m (2804 ft) Robson Pass 1652 m (5420 ft) Moose Pass 2025 m (6642 ft)
HIKING TIME	6 days or more
DIFFICULTY	challenging due to remote destination and unmaintained trail
MAPS	page 527; Mt. Robson 83 E/3; BC Parks brochure

OPINION

Influences on the North American psyche include one that is foreign to most Europeans and Asians: space. We inhabit enormous countries comprising vast quantities of undeveloped land. Since our nations' inception, space was perceived as a prized commodity, certainly by westward-bound settlers, but also by eastern urbanites. Even the poor were enriched by the wealth of possibility and opportunity that so much untouched territory represented. If nothing else, it gave them hope. Today, with the alarming scarcity of wild land finally penetrating our collective awareness, the affect on our psyche is changing. We now look to the land as we would a wise elder whose passing could be imminent. The time to commune with it is now. While there are still places like Moose Pass: easily accessible merely by walking, little changed since natives first witnessed it, and so beautiful that its full impact on you is unfathomable.

Though Moose Pass is lonely, this hike is an extension of the most popular backpack trip in the Canadian Rockies: Mt. Robson / Berg Lake (Trip 83). Be prepared for a social experience, until you cross Robson Pass. From there on, you might well be alone, because Moose Pass is also an offshoot of the Canadian Rockies' longest and most solitudinous backpack trip: the North Boundary Trail. Actually, venturing to Moose Pass would be a good first foray into remote country for hikers accustomed to the security of the beaten path but eager to extend their range of exploration. No routefinding is required here. You'll follow a trail the entire way, though at times it's obscure.

Fording a channel of the Smoky River en route to Calumet Valley

Nor will you face any serious obstacles. If you can slog through boot-sucking mud, you can make it. Plus, you'll have the security of knowing that Moose Pass is a mere 15.5 km (9.6 mi) from the radio-equipped Robson Pass ranger cabin.

In addition to achieving a sense of isolation, come here to appreciate the extensive Moose Pass meadows. The annual carpet of wildflowers, usually peaking between mid-July and early August, is lavish. And be sure to read about Hargreaves Glacier / Mumm Basin (Trip 84) and Snowbird Pass (Trip 85). Both are Premier sidetrips that no Berg-Lake-bound hiker should miss, and therefore any Moose-Pass-bound hiker should seriously consider. To see the best of the entire Berg Lake / Moose Pass area requires seven to nine days. You can lighten the necessary load by leaving a couple days' food at the Hargreaves shelter (Berg Lake) while you hike to Moose Pass.

FACT

Before your trip

Read Trips 83, 84, and 85 to gain an understanding of the first two-thirds of this journey. • Stop at the Mt. Robson Park Visitor Centre, on Hwy 16. You'll need a backcountry permit to camp en route to Robson Pass. Though about 20% of the tentsites are reservable in advance, an abundance of campgrounds makes reservations unnecessary. • Call or visit the Jasper Park Info Centre. You'll need a backcountry permit to stay at Adolphus or Calumet campgrounds. • Understand that beyond Yates Torrent, you're in prime grizzly habitat. Be prepared. Stay alert. Avoid an encounter by diligently following all the recommended precautions. Read our *Bears* section (page 34).

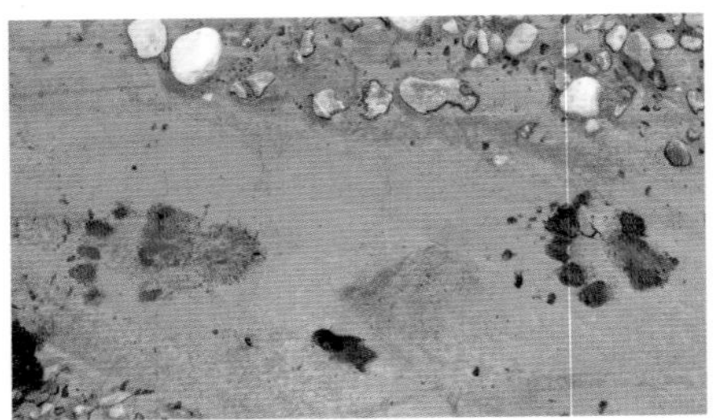

Bear print beside Calumet Creek

By Vehicle

From Jasper townsite, drive west 84 km (52 mi) on Yellowhead Hwy 16. From Tete Jaune Cache junction, drive east 16 km (10 mi). Stop at the Mt. Robson Visitor Centre on the north side of the highway. Then, from the nearby gas station / store, follow the access road north 2 km (1.2 mi) to the Berg Lake trailhead parking lot, at 855 m (2804 ft).

Don't have a vehicle? Greyhound buses make daily runs east and west on Hwy 16. Ask the driver to stop at the Robson viewpoint, near the Visitor Centre.

On Foot

Follow directions in Trip 83 to **Berg Lake**. Proceed northeast, crossing **Robson Pass** and the Robson-Jasper parks boundary at 23.5 km (14.6 mi), 1652 m (5420 ft). Reach **Adolphus Lake** at 24.3 km (15.1 mi). Carry on northeast through forest. Reach **Adolphus campground**—left (west) of the trail, well beyond the lake—at 26.1 km (16.2 mi).

From Adolphus campground, the trail resumes north. Soon pass a right (east) spur accessing a warden cabin (visible) and horse camp. You're following the incipient Smoky River downstream, staying far above the left (west) bank.

Calumet Peak above Moose Pass

Reach **Moose Pass junction** at 29 km (18 mi), 1615 m (5297 ft). Left is the North Boundary Trail, which continues following the Smoky River downstream (northwest). For Moose Pass, fork right and descend north. A couple minutes below, cross a log spanning the first channel of the **Smoky River**.

Immediately ahead (east) is a **river flat** strewn with boulders and deadfall, occasionally rearranged by floods. This is the confluence of the Yates Torrent (meltwater from Coleman Glacier) and the Smoky River. Do not attempt to ford the torrent; it's deep, swift, perilous. Proceed about 20 minutes southeast, up the torrent, where it funnels through a slot canyon spanned by a bridge.

How you'll reach the bridge depends on the condition of the river flat when you arrive and what you perceive to be the easiest way forward. You'll likely detour briefly upstream (right / south), ford perhaps two more small channels of the Smoky River, then work along the forest margin to pick up the trail (narrow but distinct) ascending upstream (southeast) above the torrent.

The old bridge spanning Yates Torrent

Cross **Yates Torrent bridge** at 29.5 km (18.3 mi). On the far bank, the trail ascends north, but only to 1646 m (5400 ft). A right fork leads east toward Coleman Glacier; ignore it. Descend left (northwest) back to the **river flat**, opposite of where you first reached it. Here the trail turns right (north-northeast), away from the torrent, and re-enters forest. Rarely traveled, never maintained, it's a narrow, overgrown, rocky, rooty, muddy route but remains serviceable. Curving right (northeast), it climbs to 1798 m (5900 ft).

Meadowy clearings welcome you to **Calumet Valley** at 33 km (20.5 mi), 1759 m (5770 ft). The valley floor—broad, level, grassy, flowery, and very boggy—grants an unobstructed view of your objective: Moose Pass, directly ahead (east-northeast). Continuing up-valley (east), the trail remains evident, south of Calumet Creek. It fades in the sodden terrain, however, after an easy ford of a placid tributary.

You'll notice the north bank affords unimpeded travel on a dry, gravel bed. You'll also notice that fording to the north bank is possible here, because the creek is broad, braided, shallow. But if you cross now, you'll be forced to re-cross upstream where the creek is a treacherous cataract. Keep slogging along the south bank.

Where forest borders the creekbed, continue hiking upstream, staying close to the creek. Reach **Calumet campground**, above the creek's south bank, at 35.5 km (22 mi), 1798 m (5900 ft). It's officially a horse camp, but there is no hikers-only option. Basecamp here and dayhike to the pass.

Beyond the campground, the trail is once again distinct. Ascending northeast, bending right (east), it surmounts treeline and enters vast meadows. Glacier-laden Calumet Peak is visible left (north). Behind you (west-southwest), beyond the Smoky River, is the Mural Glacier surrounded by (left to right) Mumm Peak, Mt. Phillips, and Gendarme Mtn. At 39 km (24.2 mi), crest 2025-m (6642-ft) **Moose Pass** and cross the Jasper-Robson parks boundary.

After admiring the view and exulting in your accomplishment, make the most of this opportunity by piercing the pass. Hike generally southeast about 3.5 km (2.2 mi) to reach a pair of small lakes and survey upper **Moose River Valley.** A rugged route, entailing numerous fords, continues descending southeast to Hwy 16—about 44 km (27.3 mi) distant. It's for hardened explorers only.

Looking toward Moose Pass, from Calumet Valley

TRIP 106
Tamarack Trail

LOCATION	Waterton Lakes National Park
SHUTTLE TRIP	36.4 km (22.6 mi)
ELEVATION GAIN	1440 m (4723 ft)
KEY ELEVATIONS	trailhead 1495 m (4905 ft) Twin Lakes 1950 m (6400 ft) Bauerman Divide 2070 m (6790 ft) Lineham Ridge 2560 m (8397 ft)
HIKING TIME	2 to 3 days
DIFFICULTY	moderate
MAPS	page 527; Gem Trek *Waterton Lakes National Park*

OPINION

Most of Waterton's premier scenery is within range of strong dayhikers. Few will see the middle of the Tamarack trail unless they trundle their home on their back, but there's nothing remarkable about it, so why bother?

The ends of the Tamarack trail are Red Rock Canyon in the north, Akamina Parkway in the south. And that's where the highlights are. The Tamarack's northern leg is the Snowshoe trail, which serves as part of the Avion Ridge circuit (Trip 100). The Tamarack's southern leg is the Rowe Lakes trail to Lineham Ridge (Trip 2). Avion is usually backpacked, but is also dayhikeable. Lineham is definitely a dayhike. Both are rated *Premier*. So break the Tamarack into two shorter, superior trips. Save time. Forego the burden of a full pack. And avoid the uneasiness of backcountry camping in a park known for its high concentration of bears.

All you'll miss is about a day of marching through forest. Oh, alright, you'll miss a few meadows too. But you'll lay eyes on perhaps the prettiest—Blue Grouse Basin—if you reach the saddle above Twin Lakes while sampling the north end of the Tamarack. That saddle also enables you to survey a lot of the Tamarack's midsection. You'll see why it's one of those *tell-me-your-life-story* hikes.

Backpacking is great, where the effort is warranted. Check out the excellent options just over the border, in U.S. Glacier National Park, or farther north in the Canadian Rockies.

FACT

By Vehicle

Read Trip 100 for directions to Red Rock Canyon, the Tamarack trail's north terminus, where the *On Foot* description begins. Read Trip 2 for directions to Rowe Lakes trailhead, the south terminus. Tamarack Shuttle Service drives to both ends of the trail. Call (403) 859-2378 for current schedules and prices. Or ask at the sports shop in Tamarack Village Square, Waterton townsite.

Lower Twin Lake. Bauerman Valley beyond.

On Foot

Follow the directions in Trip 100 to **Upper Twin Lake campground** at 11.7 km (7.3 mi), 1950 m (6400 ft). It has tables, benches, and a lake view. Lounging here is pleasant. Lower Twin Lake is visible a few minutes past the campground, left (east) of and well below the trail.

From Lower Twin viewpoint, the trail traverses southeast across the headwall, soon vaulting over 2070-m (6790-ft) **Bauerman Divide**. The meadows of **Blue Grouse Basin** are visible below, to the south. Farther south is Festubert Mtn (see image on page 48). The peaks left of it, in order, are Lone (forested), Hawkins (crescent-shaped), and Blakiston (southeast). Blakiston Creek valley (Trip 60) is beneath the northern slopes of those mountains. From the saddle, it's 5.7 km (3.5 mi) south to the campground at Lone Lake.

Descend into the basin. Beyond it, reach the **junction with Blakiston Creek trail** at 14.7 km (9.1 mi), 1915 m (6280 ft). Bear right (south). In another 100 m (110 yd) a right fork ascends southwest 1 km (0.6 mi) to South Kootenay Pass. Proceed straight (south) through mostly-level forest and meadows.

The trail curves southeast to reach **Lone Lake campground** at 18.7 km (11.6 mi), 2015 m (6610 ft). Beyond, ascend steeply south to Festubert Saddle at 2220 m (7282 ft).

Descend steeply southeast toward Blakiston Creek's south fork, near 2000 m (6560 ft). Then rev your engine for a long, steep, switchbacking climb. Crest **Lineham Ridge** at 27.8 km (17.2 mi), 2560 m (8397 ft). North, below you, are the Lineham Lakes. Southeast, across Rowe Basin, are the Rowe Lakes.

Follow the trail on a swooping descent of the Rowe Basin headwall's mauve talus slopes. Reach a **junction** in the verdant basin at 31.2 km (19.3 mi). Right climbs 1.2 km (0.9 mi) to Upper Rowe Lake. Bear left and descend generally east, staying above Rowe Creek's north side. Reach **Akamina Parkway** at 36.4 km (22.6 mi).

TRIP 107

Owl Lake / Marvel Pass / Marvel Lake

LOCATION	Banff National Park, Mt. Assiniboine Prov. Park
CIRCUIT	46 km (28.5 mi)
ELEVATION GAIN	730 m (2394 ft)
KEY ELEVATIONS	trailhead 1770 m (5806 ft) Owl Lake 1940 m (6363 ft) Marvel Pass 2190 m (7183 ft)
HIKING TIME	2 to 3 days
DIFFICULTY	challenging
MAPS	page 511; Gem Trek *Banff & Mt. Assiniboine;* Mount Assiniboine 82 J/13

OPINION

Marvel Pass is perched at the head of three valleys and surrounded by captivating mountains, including several peaks in the awesome Mt. Assiniboine massif. The pass is even crowned with a lovely, larch-framed lake. But traversing this subalpine gap poses difficulties that would frustrate and possibly alarm the average hiker. Plus, it's just far enough out-of-the-way that most hikers visiting the Mt. Assiniboine region (Trips 75-78) will find it requires more time than they can allot, or demands they cut short their stay at Lake Magog.

So, why not just hike a circuit through Marvel Pass without visiting Magog? Perhaps, but only if you've already thoroughly explored the Mt. Assiniboine region. Coming so close, without actually grabbing that brass ring, is unthinkable. Also, the Marvel Pass circuit has only one scenic highlight: the pass itself. The rest of the hike—and it's a long one—is largely in forest.

The aforementioned difficulties include deadfall, brush, bogs and fords. Southwest of Owl Lake, the unmaintained trail deteriorates substantially. Nor is it always reassuringly obvious south of Marvel Lake. Then there's the distance. Hiking 46 km (28.5 mi) for the privilege of bobbing into the subalpine zone just once? That's a poor effort/reward ratio for the Canadian Rockies.

If entering or exiting the Mt. Assiniboine region via Wonder Pass, you'll peer into Marvel Pass from afar. It's a tantalizing sight. Savour the mystery of it. In search of the solitude rarely found on the trails spider-webbing out from Lake Magog, experienced trekkers with plenty of time will no doubt enjoy cracking that mystery. Bring a map and compass. Camp on the B.C. side of Marvel Pass (south of Aurora Lake's north shore), where there are no restrictions other than the moral obligation to Leave No Trace. Finally, before departing the pass, be sure to ascend about 15 minutes onto the shoulder of Marvel Peak, where the view is panoramic. You'll see Aurora and Marvel creek canyons, Mt. Gloria, Mt. Assiniboine, Lake Gloria, Wonder Pass, and Marvel Lake.

FACT

By Vehicle

Follow the directions in Trip 77 to the Mt. Shark trailhead, at 1770 m (5805 ft).

On Foot

Set out as if bound for the Mt. Assiniboine region. Follow the main trail (broad, mostly level, through forest) generally west-southwest. Approaching **Watridge Lake**, bear right (northwest) at 3.7 km (2.3 mi).

Cross the Spray River bridge and reach a junction at 6 km (3.7 mi), 1710 m (5610 ft). Left (south) leads to Palliser Pass. Go right (north-northwest). Pass the southwest tip of **Spray Lakes Reservoir** to reach a junction near a warden cabin at 6.7 km (4.2 mi). Right leads generally northeast along the reservoir. Go left (northwest) paralleling the northeast bank of Bryant Creek, which is hidden from view.

Pass **Big Springs campground** at 9.5 km (5.9 mi). Reach a junction at 12 km (7.4 mi), 1770 m (5806 ft). Straight continues northwest up Bryant Creek Valley to enter the Mt. Assiniboine region via Assiniboine Pass. Go left (southwest) for Owl Lake and Marvel Pass.

Descend to cross a bridge over **Bryant Creek** at 12.3 km (7.6 mi). The bridge is 200 m (220 yd) upstream from the horse ford. Beyond the bridge, the trail gradually ascends southwest into Owl Lake basin, where it crosses meadows distinguished by low ridges of chaotic rock.

Reach a junction near the north shore of **Owl Lake** at 15.5 km (9.6 mi), 1940 m (6363 ft). A left spur descends to the water's edge in 100 m (110 yd). Bear right on the main trail. It curves south and parallels the lake's west shore. Visible ahead are Mt. Byng (south-southeast) and Aurora Mtn (south-southwest). Pass the south end of the lake at 17 km (10.5 mi).

Heading for Marvel Pass, the trail follows Owl Creek upstream. Staying above the west bank, it curves south-southwest into a meadow. Near the far end of the meadow, follow a cairned route rising onto the slope of Marvel Peak. Ascend southwest, gradually curving west. Cross lush avalanche swaths. This is prime grizzly-bear habitat. To avoid surprising a mountain monarch, announce your presence by making lots of noise.

The trail levels as it rounds the north shore of small **Aurora Lake** and passes the remains of a cabin. Shortly beyond, enter **Marvel Pass** at 20.2 km (12.5 mi), 2190 m (7183 ft), on the Alberta-B.C. boundary. The scenery is grand. Aurora Mtn is south-southeast, Mt. Alcantara south-southwest, Aurora Creek valley southwest, Eon Mtn west, and Mt. Gloria northwest.

For even better views, depart the lake's west shore on a short, easy, cross-country ascent. Go left, generally north, to a thinly forested saddle on a **shoulder of Marvel Peak**. You'll glimpse Mt. Assiniboine northwest, behind Mt. Gloria. Keep rounding the grassy, subalpine slope. Angle upward to 2260 m (7413 ft). More of the Boine is soon visible. Wonder Pass is north.

Marvel Pass and Aurora Lake

From Aurora Lake, head northwest to begin the 390-m (1280-ft) descent to Marvel Lake. Aim for the long, thin **lakelets** indicated on the topo map and visible from the shoulder of Marvel Peak. Below the lakelets, proceed north down the drainage, through meadows and open forest. Follow the switchbacking trail that drops steeply into Marvel Lake basin.

Ford the stream channels that drain Lake Terrapin and feed Marvel Lake. Pass the southwest end of **Marvel Lake** at 1800 m (5904 ft), then ascend steeply north to a junction at 25.8 km (16 mi), 1975 m (6478 ft). Turn right (east-northeast) to continue looping back to Bryant Creek; skip below for directions. Left (west-northwest) begins switchbacking north. It climbs 420 m (1378 ft) in 3.1 km (1.9 mi) to Wonder Pass, then descends northwest to Lake Magog, beneath Mt. Assiniboine (Trip 77).

If looping back to Bryant Creek, before doing so, consider stashing your pack at this junction and dashing up to **Wonder Pass viewpoint**. Start by ascending the Wonder Pass trail. Gain 345 m (1132 ft) in 2.4 km (1.5 mi), then turn right (southeast) onto a cairned spur. Proceed 0.6 km (0.4 mi), gaining another 60 m (197 ft), to an open slope. Don't stop at the plateau with a partial view. Skirt that small rise, then drop to a more open vantage. Aye Mtn is southwest. Mt. Gloria is south-southwest, and Eon Mtn is beyond it. Below, Lake Gloria is southwest, long Marvel Lake is southeast, and tiny Lake Terrapin is between them. Marvel Peak is southeast, above Marvel Lake.

From the junction above the southwest end of Marvel Lake, continue looping back to Bryant Creek by following the trail east-northeast. It soon leads generally northeast, paralleling Marvel Lake, high above its northwest shore. A gradual descent ensues, through forest and across rocky avalanche paths. Reach a junction at 30.3 km (18.8 mi). Right leads south to Marvel Lake's northeast shore. Proceed straight, heading generally northeast.

Cross a bridge over **Bryant Creek**. A few minutes farther, reach a T-junction at 31.8 km (19.7 mi). Left (northwest) quickly passes **McBride's campground** and a warden cabin, then continues up Bryant Creek Valley to enter the Mt. Assiniboine region via Assiniboine Pass. Go right, following the broad, nearly-level trail generally southeast through forest. Pass the **Bryant Creek shelter** at 32.4 km (20.1 mi).

Reach a junction at 32.9 km (20.4 mi), 1770 m (5806 ft). Right (southwest) is the trail you previously followed to Owl Lake. You're now on familiar ground. Proceed straight, generally southeast, retracing your steps past Spray Lakes Reservoir to reach the **Mt. Shark trailhead** at 46 km (28.5 mi), 1770 m (5805 ft).

Elk Lake and Mt. Brewster (Trip 108)

TRIP 108

Elk Lake

LOCATION	Banff National Park
ROUND TRIP	27 km (16.7 mi)
ELEVATION GAIN	830 m (2722 ft)
KEY ELEVATIONS	trailhead 1700 m (5575 ft) highpoint 2174 m (7130 ft), lake 2120 m (6954 ft)
HIKING TIME	9 hours to 2 days
DIFFICULTY	easy
MAPS	page 524; Gem Trek *Banff & Mt. Assiniboine;* Lake Minnewanka 82 O/6

OPINION

The solitude you're likely to experience on this trip is nice. Striding along the comfortable trail is nice. The lake setting is nice. Dining out is nice. Playing cards is nice. Being friendly is nice. But nice is only nice. It's nothing you can tether your soul to. A nice life can be shallow, mundane, trivial. If you seek powerful experiences, you have to go beyond nice. Someplace other than Elk Lake.

Often, "nice and easy" trails are boring. Choose one for a backpack trip and you're betting solely on the destination. That gamble pays off at the end of the trudge to Mt. Assiniboine (Trip 77), or Tonquin Valley via Astoria River (Trip 98). But not Elk Lake. Here, occasional avalanches ravaging the cliffs above the lake are the only stirring sight, and you've no guarantee of those.

The trail to Elk Lake is lined with the scrawny trees of a disenchanted forest. It's a scene fit for a nightmare. After a couple hours, you'll hike through so-called meadows, but only for about 30 minutes. And they're shrubby, willowy; not the pastoral grass-and-heather alpine meadows that make Healy Pass, Helen Lake, or Jonas Pass so appealing. Once you reach Elk Lake, you can't even pitch your tent there. The campground is well outside Mt. Brewster's embrace of the tiny lake.

Jet, and you can scorch the distance to Elk Lake in under four hours. If you've never been there, it might be a worthwhile destination for a one-day training hike or run, when mileage is what matters. Don't be tempted by this approach to a longer backpack trip into the Cascade River Valley. The valley trail is a fire road. Horse packers frequently travel Elk and Dormer passes. Stony Creek to Flint's Park is prime grizzly habitat. And the scenery would not justify your effort.

FACT

By Vehicle

From Banff townsite's west interchange on the Trans-Canada Hwy, ascend the switchbacking Mt. Norquay Road north 5.8 km (3.6 mi) to the far end of the ski-area parking lot. The trail, initially a road, leads between the ski lodge buildings, at 1700 m (5575 ft).

On Foot

Walk the dirt road north. Pass the Cascade chairlift. About eight minutes from the ski lodge, signed trail begins right of (behind and below) the Spirit chairlift. Follow it north. Do not go right over the bridge onto the Stoney Squaw bridal path.

About 15 minutes from the parking lot, at 1655 m (5430 ft), continue the gradual descent right of the Mystic chairlift. Drop deeper into forest. Reach a junction at 2.7 km (1.7 mi). Left (west) is the Forty Mile Creek trail heading upstream toward Mystic Lake (Trip 109). Go right (northeast) and descend. A minute farther, at 1570 m (5150 ft), cross a bridge over **Forty Mile Creek**. You've lost 130 m (426 ft) since leaving the trailhead. Begin a moderate ascent north.

About an hour from the trailhead, reach a junction at 4.1 km (2.5 mi), 1725 m (5658 ft). Right (northwest) leads to Cascade Amphitheatre (Trip 63). Go left for Elk Lake, continuing the gentle ascent north through forest.

Near 9 km (5.6 mi) reach **subalpine meadows** comprising low willows, stunted evergreens and shrubby birch. Immediately east is the shoulder of Cascade Mtn. Like a spilled box of matches, prostrate trees litter the open ridge. Elk Lake cirque is identifiable northwest. The Vermilion Range is west, running north-south. You can even see southeast into the Spray River valley and southern Banff Park.

Continue on the wide, muddy, horse-trodden trail. At 11.5 km (7.1 mi), 2055 m (6740 ft), a signed left spur enters **Elk Lake Summit campground**—in trees, beside a tiny stream. 100 m (110 yd) up the main trail is a 3-way junction. Sharp left returns to the campground. The middle fork (also left) leads 2 km (1.2 mi) to Elk Lake. Right proceeds through 2060-m (6757-ft) Elk Pass, reaching Stony Creek and Cascade Fire Road in 10 km (6.2 mi).

The lake trail climbs 125 m (410 ft) up a forested ridge. On the crest, you can look south down the valley you hiked from Mt. Norquay. Descending the other side of the ridge, the lake is on your right, but it's obscured by trees. To see it, you must drop nearly to the shore—about 45 minutes from the 3-way junction.

Elk Lake, really a large tarn, is at 14 km (8.7 mi). Elevation: 2120 m (6954 ft). Mt. Brewster wraps around the lake's south, west and north sides. Yellow cinquefoil and white marsh marigold dot the meadows in July. Look for pink and beet-coloured elephant's heads in seeps.

Cinquefoil

TRIP 109

Mystic Pass and Lake

LOCATION	Banff National Park
ROUND TRIP	28.2 km (17.5 mi) to pass, 36 km (22.3 mi) to lake
ELEVATION GAIN	855 m (2804 ft) to pass 1190 m (3903 ft) to lake
KEY ELEVATIONS	trailhead 1425 m (4674 ft) pass 2280 m (7478 ft), lake 2040 m (6690 ft)
HIKING TIME	5 to 7 hours for pass, 6½ to 8½ for lake
DIFFICULTY	moderate
MAPS	page 520; Gem Trek *Banff & Mt. Assiniboine*; Castle Mtn 82 O/5

OPINION

You can read *The National Enquirer*, or *The New Yorker*. You can listen to Yanni, or Miles Davis. You can eat a Twinkie, or an organic apple. Quality is readily available. Given that life is brutishly hard and wretchedly short, why settle for inferior alternatives? Compared to many Canadian Rockies backpack trips, Mystic Pass and Lake is mediocre. The alpine pass is engagingly scenic, and the lake adorns an impressive cirque, but that's it. The rest of the journey, fully 98% of it, is unremarkable. Those two, brief, noteworthy sights don't warrant labouring under a full pack for two days mostly in forest and spending a night at the substandard campground in Mystic Valley. Superior choices abound. Gibbon, Whistling & Healy Passes (Trip 79), North Molar, Pipestone & Clearwater passes (Trip 80), and Maligne Pass (Trip 93) are but a few.

An almost-but-not-quite-justifiable reason to come here is that you're already in the vicinity. During mid-summer, when the sun doesn't set until 10 p.m., fleet, motivated backpackers plying Johnston Creek Valley (Trip 101) can see Mystic Lake and Pass on a sidetrip the first afternoon. Depart the trailhead early. Pitch your tent at Larry's Camp. If you hustle, you can nip over the pass to the lake and be back before dark.

Some people succumb to the allure of the name *Mystic*. Others irrationally insist on not straying far from Banff townsite. Should you backpack to Mystic Pass and Lake, whatever the reason, limit your trip to two days—one in, one out. Be aware that you have a choice of trailheads: Johnston Canyon, or Moose Meadow. Both approaches merge within an hour but are distinctly different. The chasms and cascades in Johnston Canyon (Trip 129) are compelling, but the paved path and incessant crowd are Disneyesque, and trundling a full pack among gaggles of waddling gawkers is a frustrating exercise in diplomatic restraint. Better to dash into Johnston Canyon another time—very early or late in the day, or during shoulder season—carrying only a waist pack. Your Mystic quest, though perhaps ill-conceived, should begin at Moose Meadow. You'll initially be hiking an abandoned, overgrown road through viewless forest, but you'll enjoy blessed solitude and tranquility, and you'll shorten the total round trip by 1 km (0.6 mi). Endeavour to reach Mystic Pass early, so you can savour it as long as possible before plunging 295 m (968 ft) down the other side into forest. While you're up there, drop your pack and ascend the ridgecrest northeast of the pass for a superior view.

Presumably you'll spend the night at Mystic Valley campground. Ugh. Not only is it a full 1 km (0.6 mi) from the lake, it's in an awkward setting and has no views to speak of. Plus the tentsites lack privacy and several are lumpy. The alternative, Larry's Camp, is little better. But it's *en route* to the pass, rather than beyond it, thus offering a potential advantage. If you pitch your tent there early, you can continue unburdened to the pass, perhaps even to the lake if you're swift.

Below Mystic Lake and Mystic Valley campground, the trail descends into forested Forty-Mile Creek Valley, which you can plod nearly back to Banff townsite, exiting at Mount Norquay ski area. "Ah, a one-way trip!" you're thinking. Whoa. Huh uh. Don't forego the small pleasure of seeing Mystic Pass a second time, on the way out.

FACT

By Vehicle

Follow the directions for Trip 101.

On Foot

Starting at Johnston Canyon

Cross the bridge over Johnston Creek to the resort side, turn right, and follow the path upstream above the west bank. You'll be hiking generally north through Johnston Canyon.

Pass the lower falls at 1.1 km (0.7 mi). Reach the 30-m (100-ft) upper falls at 2.7 km (1.7 mi). Beyond the falls, the trail ascends. **Intersect the Moose Meadow road** at 3.2 km (2 mi), 1602 m (5255 ft). Ascend right (west).

For further directions, skip below to the third paragraph under *Starting at Moose Meadow*. That approach, however, is slightly shorter. For example, the Moose Meadow road intersects the Johnston Canyon trail at 2.7 km (1.6 mi). So, from here on, you'll have hiked 0.5 km (0.3 mi) farther than the stated distances.

Starting at Moose Meadow

An old, overgrown road departs the north-northwest end of the parking lot and initially proceeds in that direction. After curving, begin a moderate ascent within ten minutes. About 15 minutes from the parking lot, reach a fork at 1492 m (4895 ft). A double-track road ascends left (east). Continue straight (southeast) on the wider road. Five minutes farther, the road forks again. Go left (east-northeast). In early summer, look for bunchberry (white, with four petals) on the forest floor.

About 25 minutes from the parking lot, follow the road north. It descends slightly here. Shortly beyond, merge left (northeast) onto a more distinct road. About 40 minutes from the parking lot, curve right (east) on the road, ignoring a hiker sign (pointing left) on a tree.

Mystic Pass

Five minutes farther, **intersect the Johnston Canyon trail** at 2.7 km (1.6 mi), 1602 m (5255 ft). Ascend left (west). Right (northeast) descends into Johnston Canyon in 200 m (220 yd) and reaches Hwy 1A in 3.2 km (2 mi).

The old road ascends at a moderate grade to 1736 m (5695 ft). It then descends, soon granting glimpses into upper Johnston Canyon. The descent steepens into Johnston Creek Valley, where views open. Southeast is 2850-m (9348-ft) Mt. Ishbel.

After hiking about 1½ hours, arrive at the **Inkpots**—small, round pools of aquamarine water, formed by mineral springs. Here, at 5.9 km (3.7 mi), 1645 m (5395 ft), just above Johnston Creek, several benches invite you to rest and appreciate the journey's first significant vista. The meadow surrounding the Inkpots is full of willows and dwarf birch.

The trail passes left (northwest) of the Inkpots, continuing up-valley (north-northeast). In two minutes, cross a large, wood bridge over **Johnston Creek**. On the east bank, the trail turns left (north).

Hop over braided meltwater streams. After a short, steep ascent, the trail levels in forest again. Reach **Larry's Camp** at 7.9 km (4.9 mi), 1677 m (5500 ft). It has seven tentsites, a fire pit, and bear-proof food storage. Immediately beyond, the trail drops to an unnamed tributary of Johnston Creek. Go right (east) upstream, cross the creek on a bridge, and arrive at a signed junction on the north bank.

Mystic Lake

The trail up Johnston Creek Valley to Pulsatilla Pass (Trip 101) continues straight (northwest). For Mystic Pass, go right (northeast), following the creek upstream. In ten minutes, cross a bridge to the east bank. You're in deep forest now. About 15 minutes of moderate ascent is followed by a ten-minute level respite.

At 1838 m (6030 ft), about 30 minutes above the junction, cross a creek on awkward logs and continue ascending northeast. Soon reach a grassy clearing beside a dry, rocky drainage. Past the next stand of trees is a broad **rockslide**. Ignore the 1.2-m (4-ft) cairn above. The trail stays low, curving around the base of the slide. Elevation: 1927 m (6320 ft).

Beyond the slide, enter forest whose aspect is softened by long-skirted spruce. Hop over a creeklet at 2055 m (6740 ft). An aggressive ascent ensues, but it's shorter than it appears. Within 15 to 20 minutes, the grade eases above a cascade, beside a creeklet, at 2172 m (7126 ft). Big cliffs are visible across the valley. Castle Mtn is west. Five minutes farther, the trail curves east-southeast, approaching Mystic Pass.

Opportunity alert: a sidetrip from here will enable you to more fully appreciate the pass environs. Drop your pack where the trail levels at the northwest end of the pass, just before entering a narrow cleft with scree on both sides. Look left (northeast). See the game path climbing diagonally across the talus slope? Scuttle up there and tag onto it. The path is steep but affords adequate footing. Follow it north to a 2500-m (8200-ft) dip on the ridgecrest. Immediately below the other side is a small lake. Far below is Forty-Mile Creek Valley extending north-northwest and south-southeast. The Vermilion Range forms the valley's east wall.

Back on the main trail, heading south-southeast, crest **Mystic Pass** at 14.1 km (8.7 mi), 2280 m (7478 ft). On the southeast side of the pass, the trail drops gently through subalpine meadows scattered with larches and, in summer, brightened by wildflowers. About 20 minutes below the pass, at 2168 m (7110 ft), the descent steepens. About 35 minutes below the pass, rockhop a stream flowing from a cascade far above.

The descent through fir and spruce forest continues to a long bridge spanning a creek and bog. About an hour below the pass, reach a **T-junction**, at 17.5 km (10.9 mi), 1995 m (6545 ft).

Right (west) at the T-junction ascends slightly, ending at Mystic Lake in 0.5 km (0.3 mi). (It takes only ten minutes to get there, but because the lake is more photogenic before noon, consider waiting until the next morning.) Shortly beyond the junction, the trail forks. Go right (west), down near the creek. Cross a log spanning a pool to reach the northeast shore of **Mystic Lake**, at 2040 m (6690 ft).

Left (east) at the T-junction descends to **Mystic Valley campground** in 0.5 km (0.3 mi). Elevation: 1945 m (6380 ft). Total distance from Moose Meadow parking lot: 18 km (11.2 mi). Total distance from Johnston Canyon trailhead: 18.5 km (11.5 mi). The campground has a small clearing, but is mostly in trees, on a rib between two creeks. Visible north are spiky, serrated cliffs above bushy avalanche swaths. The tentsites are jammed together. Some are not level. (You paid a hefty user fee to stay here. If you're dissatisfied, communicate that to Parks Canada.) Northwest of the tentsites, the trail descends to a bridged creek. The cooking area, table, fire pit and bear-proof food storage are just beyond the bridge.

From Mystic Valley campground, the trail descends northeast into Forty-Mile Creek Valley, reaching a junction in 3 km (1.9 mi). Left leads 0.8 km (0.5 mi) north-northeast to Mystic Junction campground and the Forty-Mile Creek trail, at 1846 m (6055 ft). Right leads generally east 0.5 km (0.3 mi) to the Forty-Mile Creek trail.

Plumed aven

TRIP 110

Pipestone River

LOCATION	Banff National Park
ONE WAY	37 km (23 mi) to Pipestone Pass
ELEVATION GAIN	905 m (2970 ft)
KEY ELEVATIONS	trailhead 1555 m (5100 ft), pass 2460 m (8070 ft)
HIKING TIME	2 days
DIFFICULTY	challenging due to river fords
MAPS	Gem Trek *Banff & Mt. Assiniboine*, Gem Trek *Bow Lake & Saskatchewan Crossing*; Lake Louise 82 N/8, Hector Lake 82 N/9

OPINION

Did the Budweiser Clydesdales puree this trail, or what? Enough pack trains, and that's the result: a pitted, sucky quagmire. You'll see more mud than mountains hiking the lower Pipestone River Valley. Several fords will also curtail your enjoyment and possibly your life. You'll need a wetsuit, mask, snorkel, and total disregard for your own safety. Don't expect the potentially treacherous river to subside until late summer.

Trying to enjoy this trail could rank with the major challenges of your hiking career. Upper Pipestone River Valley—where the forest is broken by meadows, and you can see surrounding peaks—is pleasant trekking country. But it's not worth the toil, monotony and danger of approaching via the lower valley. Pipestone Pass is starkly alluring, almost frighteningly wild, and a superb vantage, but there's a faster, more scenic access: North Molar Pass and Fish Lakes (Trip 88).

The Pipestone River is also one of two backdoor entrances to Skoki Valley (Trip 86). The other is Johnston and Baker creek valleys (Trip 101). But neither has an advantage, other than solitude, over the quick, direct trail starting near Lake Louise ski area.

You're still reading? Maybe a more philosophical line of reasoning will convince you not to hike the Pipestone River trail. Consider this. The world can't afford to lose hikers to drownings or boredom. We need you alive and motivated, working to preserve wilderness—including the areas where hiking is less than ideal.

FACT

By Vehicle

Drive the Trans-Canada Hwy northwest 0.8 km (0.5 mi) from the Lake Louise overpass. Turn right (north) onto Slate Avenue. Follow it uphill about 200 m (220 yd), keeping left, then turning right. The trailhead parking lot is 100 m (110 yd) farther, at 1555 m (5100 ft).

On Foot

Your general direction of travel all the way into upper Pipestone Valley is north, where the trail curves northwest to Pipestone Pass.

Begin by ascending north through forest. Within 1 km (0.6 mi), pass a spur trail forking right to Mud Lake. Descend to the Pipestone River at 3 km (1.9 mi). Head upstream on the river's west side. Pass a former campground at 6.6 km (4.1 mi). Cycling is prohibited beyond.

At 15 km (9.3 mi) is a potentially **hazardous ford** of the river. The trail continues upstream, now on the river's east side. At 18 km (11.2 mi) ford Little Pipestone Creek. At 19 km (11.8 mi), 1815 m (5955 ft), reach **Little Pipestone warden cabin** and a junction. Right (east) follows Little Pipestone Creek upstream to Red Deer Lakes and provides access to Skoki Valley (Trip 86). Bear left, ford to the west side of Pipestone River and immediately reach another junction. Left ascends Molar Creek valley northwest to cross Molar Pass (Trip 30). Go right to continue north, through forest broken by meadows, up the west side of Pipestone River.

Reach **Singing Meadows campground** at 28 km (17.4 mi), where you must ford to the river's east side. Reach a junction at 29 km (18 mi), 1980 m (6494 ft). Left fords the river to its west side and ascends to Fish Lakes and North Molar Pass (Trip 88). Proceed straight (northwest). The trail gradually steepens through upper Pipestone Valley. Cross a gap above **Pipestone Pass** at 37 km (23 mi), 2460 m (8070 ft).

From Pipestone Pass, the trail descends northwest. In 3 km (2 mi), an indistinct path forks right, leading 1 km (0.6 mi) northeast into the rocky alpland of Clearwater Pass; Upper Devon Lake is 1.6 km (1 mi) farther.

Size 11 boot = big bear

TRIP 111

Siffleur River / Dolomite Creek

LOCATION	Banff National Park
SHUTTLE TRIP	69.2 km (43 mi) from Clearwater Pass to Dolomite Pass
ELEVATION CHANGE	456-m (1496-ft) loss, 595-m (1952-ft) gain
KEY ELEVATIONS	trailhead 1830 m (6000 ft), Siffleur-Dolomite creek junction 1800 m (5904 ft) Dolomite Pass 2395 m (7856 ft)
HIKING TIME	4 to 5 days
DIFFICULTY	challenging
MAPS	page 514; Gem Trek *Bow Lake & Saskatchewan Crossing*; Hector Lake 82 N/9, Siffleur River 82 N/16

OPINION

Only Chris Townsend types should consider this back-of-beyond trek. He's the stoic who hiked the length of the Canadian Rockies, much of it trailless. Though there's a trail here, you'll need his cold-forged will to complete the 74-km (46-mi) circuit over North Molar and Pipestone passes (Trip 80), down the Siffleur River valley, up Dolomite Creek, over Dolomite Pass, and out via Helen Lake (Trip 8). We're talking lonely, unbridged, bug infested, gumboed wilderness.

There are scenic climaxes. Pipestone Pass, for example, is a thrilling alpine vantage, but you can dayhike there from a basecamp at Fish Lakes. Overall, the scenery doesn't justify this journey's epic difficulty. The solitude might, if that's all you're seeking.

The challenge intrigues you? Bring the maps; they're essential. Be prepared for several treacherous fords, perhaps thigh deep, best negotiated in autumn when water levels are lowest.

FACT

By Vehicle

For directions to Mosquito Creek trailhead, read Trip 30. Helen Lake trailhead (Trip 8) is 9.2 km (5.7 mi) farther northwest on the Icefields Parkway. If arranging a shuttle, leave one car there. Otherwise hitchhike.

On Foot

Read Trip 80 for directions over North Molar and Pipestone passes to the junction at 27 km (16.7 mi), 2256 m (7400 ft). Take a sidetrip 1 km (0.6 mi) northeast, following an indistinct path into the rocky alpland of Clearwater Pass. Upper Devon Lake is just beyond the pass.

Siffleur Valley, from Pipestone Pass

Continuing northwest on the main trail from the 27-km (16.7-mi) junction, descend gradually into the densely forested Siffleur River valley. Reach a **campground** at 36.2 km (22.4 mi). At 39.5 km (24.5 mi) **ford the Siffleur River** to its west bank. Brave a more dangerous **ford of Dolomite Creek** at 43.5 km (27 mi), 1800 m (5904 ft), and reach a **junction** above the west bank. Right (north) toils 29.5 km (18.3 mi) to the David Thompson Hwy 11. Left (south) labours 25.6 km (15.9 mi) up Dolomite Creek valley, over Dolomite Pass, through the Helen Lake meadows, to the Icefields Parkway.

Heading south on the Dolomite Creek trail, within 3.5 km (2.2 mi) you'll reach a campground near the southwest end of **Isabella Lake**. Continuing up-valley, the sketchy route crosses muddy flats and multiple stream channels. Beyond, you'll face two **deep fords** of the creek, and possibly more mud. During the final approach to Dolomite Pass, ascend steeply beside a waterfall. The trail fades in the alpine zone. Keep heading southeast, on the west side of the creek. When the route curves southwest, the pass is visible ahead. Crest 2395-m (7856-ft) **Dolomite Pass** at 60.2 km (37.3 mi).

Continue southwest to the north end of Lake Katherine. Then head west-northwest to a 2500-m (8200-ft) **ridge above Helen Lake**. Descend to reach Helen Lake at 63.2 km (39.2 mi), 2372 m (7780 ft). From here, follow the well-defined trail (generally south, then northwest) 6 km (3.7 mi) out to Hwy 93.

Willow-herb

TRIP 112

Simpson River / Surprise Creek

LOCATION	Kootenay and Mt. Assiniboine parks
ONE WAY	23 km (14.3 mi) to Ferro Pass 32.2 km (20 mi) to Lake Magog
ELEVATION GAIN	1325 m (4345 ft) to Lake Magog
KEY ELEVATIONS	trailhead 1250 m (4100 ft), Ferro Pass 2270 (7445 ft)
HIKING TIME	1½ to 2 days
DIFFICULTY	moderate
MAPS	page 510; Gem Trek *Banff & Mt. Assiniboine*, Gem Trek *Kootenay National Park*; Mount Assiniboine 82 J/13

OPINION

Of the three ways to approach or depart Mt. Assiniboine, this one is for self-flagellants. Forest engulfed, it doesn't come up for air until after Rock Lake, assuring you of a full day's trudgery: more than 18 km (11 mi). If you're a master of walking meditation (calm acceptance, no judgment), maybe your mind will survive without exploding shards of tedium, exasperation and claustrophobia. If you're demonically driven, maybe your legs will hold up without morphing into motivation-sapped rubber appendages. If you're like most of us, point your boots in another direction.

There are more attractive alternatives for a one-way trek through the Mt. Assiniboine area: the 29-km (18-mi) route from Sunshine Village (Trip 75), or the 27.5-km (17-mi) route via Bryant Creek and Assiniboine Pass (Trip 77). Entering via Bryant Creek is scenic after an easy 13 km (8 mi). Entering from Sunshine Village is beautiful and exciting the whole way but for a couple-kilometre stretch. Also, shuttling between those two trailheads is shorter than if you start or finish a one-way trip at the Simpson River trailhead. Still you'll need a non-hiking buddy or spouse willing to serve as your shuttle slave.

Ferro Pass, which the Surprise Creek trail eventually crosses, is worth a visit. The view comprises remote Wedgewood Lake backed by gigantic, glacier-slathered peaks. Go. But do it from the other side. Basecamped at Lake Magog, you can dayhike to Ferro Pass.

The directions below start at the west end of Simpson Creek and continue east to Ferro Pass. If you insist on hiking the Simpson River and Surprise Creek trails, do it on a one-way trip departing Lake Magog. Heading east to west, the elevation gain is less than 33% of what it is heading west to east. A final warning for the naively optimistic: stay away from the zombie tromp up the northeastern stretch of the Simpson River trail, beyond the Surprise Creek junction.

FACT

By Vehicle

Drive Hwy 93 through Kootenay Park to the Simpson River/Mt. Shanks Fire Lookout parking area, on the east side of the highway, beside the Vermilion River bridge. It's 36.5 km (22.6 mi) south of the Banff-Kootenay boundary, or 57 km (35.3 mi) north of Kootenay Park's West Gate at Radium. Elevation: 1250 m (4100 ft).

On Foot

Cross the Vermilion River bridge and follow the access road 200 m (220 yd) to a junction. Go right, passing a gravel pit and corrals. At 1 km (0.6 mi) the trail is along the north side of the Simpson River. You're heading generally west, up-valley, ascending moderately.

At 8.8 km (5.5 mi) leave Kootenay Park and enter Assiniboine Provincial Park. At 11 km (6.8 mi) reach a **junction** at 1400 m (4595 ft). The Simpson River hikers' trail continues straight (north) on the west side of the river. For the Surprise Creek trail to Ferro Pass and Lake Magog, turn right (east) and cross a suspension bridge over Simpson River. There's a campground and a hikers' shelter in 100 m (110 yd). The trail travels on the north side of Surprise Creek, ascending steeply through more forest.

At 14.5 km (9 mi) the trail curves south. At 18.4 km (11.4 mi), just before small, forested **Rock Lake,** a spur trail branches right. It heads downhill to the lake and a campground on its north shore. The main trail proceeds left (south), above the lake to Ferro Pass.

Soon attain views: northeast to the cliffs of Simpson Ridge, south to Indian Peak. The moderate ascent continues until 2270-m (7445-ft) **Ferro Pass** at 23 km (14.3 mi). Wedgwood Lake is visible southeast. It's backed by Mt. Watson (south), The Marshall (slightly southeast), and Wedgwood Peak (farther southeast). Mt. Assiniboine looms beyond Wedgwood Peak.

The trail drops 275 m (900 ft) from Ferro Pass to Mitchell Meadow campground at 1995 m (6545 ft). It then climbs 305 m (1000 ft) before entering Sunburst Valley. Reach **Lake Magog Campground** at 32.2 km (20 mi). Read Trip 75 for details.

Wild chives

TRIP 113
Prospectors Valley

LOCATION	Kootenay National Park, starting at Marble Canyon
ROUND TRIP	30 km (18.6 mi) to Kaufmann Lake
ELEVATION GAIN	568 m (1863 ft) to Kaufmann Lake
KEY ELEVATIONS	trailhead 1490 m (4887 ft) Kaufmann Lake 2058 m (6750)
HIKING TIME	6½ to 9½ hours
DIFFICULTY	easy backpack challenging dayhike due only to distance
MAPS	page 499; Gem Trek *Kootenay National Park*

OPINION

Ho-Masubi lives here? Maybe. He's the Japanese fire god,* which would explain the blazes that keep occurring in Prospectors Valley.

Although destructive by nature, Ho-Masubi tries to help. He provides light, warmth, and heat for cooking or manufacturing. But if people neglect him, he loses it, as he has here repeatedly.

The valley was incinerated during the summer of 2003, when much of northern Kootenay Park was ablaze. What remains are spindly, charred snags and blackened earth—from the trailhead at Marble Canyon, up Tokumm Creek, past Kaufmann Lake, all the way to the valley's upper reaches beneath Wenkchemna Pass.

Fay Hut, constructed on the north wall of the valley in 1927, was destroyed in the '03 fire. The Alpine Club of Canada, with generous volunteer help, built a beautiful, new Fay Hut in 2005. To their horror, it again burned to the ground in 2009.

Perhaps Ho-Masubi felt Prospectors Valley wasn't getting enough appreciation. But the truth is, even before the forest was laid waste, hiking up Tokumm Creek failed to excite. It was merely pleasant.

The valley-bottom trail's best attribute is that it hugs the creek much of the way, allowing you to appreciate the aluminum-like sparkle of the clear water. Another attraction is that it's mostly level, steepening only for the short, final pitch to Kaufmann Lake. It also has the advantage of early availability. You can enjoy snow-free hiking here perhaps by mid-June.

As for the lake, it's tucked below the south side of the Wenkchemna Peaks. As the snow flies, it's only 6 km (3.7 mi) from famous Moraine Lake, which is just north of the peaks. But the Kaufmann Lake setting never warranted comparison, and now its visage has been smudged by the inferno.

Previously, the lakeside campground made backpacking here worthwhile, but the park service has yet to reopen Prospectors Valley to camping. So how about a

Prospectors Valley

30-km (18.6-mi) round-trip dayhike up a scorched valley to a charred lakeshore? Uh, no thanks.

At the mouth of Prospectors Valley, however, is a startling sight: Marble Canyon, created by Tokumm Creek pounding through a fault in the bedrock for 10,000 years. The 30-minute walk is too short to qualify as a hike, but the canyon trail is captivating. Several bridges span the abyss, allowing you to peer down into it. Just don't forget to look up and bow to Ho-Masubi.

*Shinto was once the imperial religion of Japan and is still the common name for the nation's non-Buddhist ethnic religious practices. It coalesced from local mythologies around 712. The essence of Shinto is the worship of kami (spirits). Most kami are local—the souls of particular places—but some are universal, such as Ho-Masubi.

FACT

By Vehicle

The Prospectors Valley / Marble Canyon trailhead is on the northwest side of Hwy 93. Reach it by driving 16.8 km (10.4 mi) southwest from the junction with the Trans-Canada (Hwy 1), or 2.5 km (1.5 mi) northeast of the Paint Pots trailhead. The trail departs the north end of the main parking lot, at 1490 m (4887 ft).

On Foot

A few steps beyond the parking lot, arrive at a signed fork. Left contours to Marble Canyon. Go right for Prospectors Valley.

Stay on the broad, main trail. Ignore any spurs. You'll be hiking generally northwest, ascending at a gentle grade, all the way past the Fay Hut junction, until shortly before Kaufmann Lake. About ten minutes from the trailhead, highway noise is no longer audible, and creek music fills the valley.

Ahead are numerous Tokumm Creek **tributaries**. Those that could be difficult to cross are bridged. Near the eighth crossing, a cascade is visible on the valley's left (southwest) wall. About 40 minutes along, a gradual descent leads to a bridge spanning a sizeable tributary at 1555 m (5100 ft).

At 3.2 km (2 mi) the trail is in a **meadow** beside Tokumm Creek. It continues northwest, upstream, ascending gradually, on or near the creek's northeast bank. Distant peaks are visible up-valley.

After hiking just less than an hour, cross an **avalanche swath**. Fifteen minutes farther, cross a meadow at 1604 m (5260 ft). The 180° view includes cascades on the both valley walls. Cross a boisterous stream, two creeklets, then a swift, steeply tumbling creek. At 1636 m (5367 ft), about 1¾ hours along, the trail grazes the bank of Tokumm Creek, which flows more forcefully here.

About 30 minutes farther, near 8.5 km (5.3 mi), reach the bridged crossing of a major tributary. The trail then returns to the bank of Tokumm Creek. Shortly beyond, at a bend in the creek, **rock slabs** invite you to lounge.

Next, cross a bridge over the largest tributary—fed by meltwater from the Wenkchemna Icefield. On the tributary's northwest bank, reach a **junction** at 10.5 km (6.5 mi), 1677 m (5500 ft). Bear left and continue west-northwest for Kaufmann Lake. Right (north) ascends 434 m (1425 ft) in 2.4 km (1.5 mi) to the former site of the Fay Hut at 2111 m (6925 ft), 12.9 km (8 mi) from the trailhead.

Marble Canyon, mid-April

The Prospectors Valley trail remains close to Tokumm Creek but from here on has not been maintained since the '03 fire. Sections are obscure. Deadfall is profuse. Cross Kaufmann Lake's braided **outlet stream** at 13.3 km (8.2 mi). Several minutes farther, the trail veers right and steepens significantly.

Heading generally north, ascend 243 m (797 ft) in 1.5 km (0.9 mi) via switchbacks to reach a moist meadow on the south shore of **Kaufmann Lake** at 15 km (9.3 mi), 2060 m (6757 ft). The cirque above the north shore comprises 3424-m (11,231-ft) Deltaform Mtn, 3245-m (10,644-ft) Mt. Tuzo, and 3310-m (10,857-ft) Mt. Allen.

TRIP 114

McArthur Pass via McArthur Creek

LOCATION	Yoho National Park
ONE WAY	10.3 km (6.4 mi)
ELEVATION GAIN	730 m (2395 ft)
KEY ELEVATIONS	confluence junction 1480 m (4855 ft) pass 2210 m (7250 ft)
HIKING TIME	3½ hours
DIFFICULTY	moderate
MAPS	page 498; Gem Trek *Lake Louise & Yoho*

OPINION

Maps suggest there's a convenient way to extend the Rockwall (Trip 89) to Lake O'Hara (Trip 14). But the link, via McArthur Creek, leads only to regret.

Unmaintained for years, thus inundated with deadfall and avalanche debris, the trail has indecipherable sections where routefinding is necessary. Plus, the McArthur Creek valley is prime bear habitat. That's why Yoho Park authorities have let the wilderness reclaim the trail: to give the resident grizzlies a haven from ever-encroaching humanity. And while you might see a bruin here, you'll see little else to compensate your effort. The scenery is lackluster.

Flanking McArthur Creek valley are Goodsir and McArthur passes. Both are scenic prizes worth attaining. But both have easier, more enjoyable approaches. Hike to Goodsir Pass via Helmet Falls (Trip 89), or bike-and-hike to it via the Ottertail fire road (Trip 50). Swing through McArthur Pass while dayhiking from Lake O'Hara to Lake McArthur (Trip 17). Except on the return leg of that bike-and-hike trip, there's no compelling reason to descend north of Goodsir Pass. Nor is there any reward for descending southwest of McArthur Pass to the Ottertail River. You'd just have to get your tired mule up and trudge out of the deep, forested valley.

You're a connect-the-dots-at-all-costs fanatic? Intent on extending your Rockwall hike into Lake O'Hara? Please read one last deterrent: it's a selfish endeavour and potentially desecrating. Bears, a glorious manifestation of wilderness, are at risk of extinction. To deliberately hike in a bear refuge despite many other more attractive options, is to invite a bear encounter. Bears provoked to attack, even if doing so out of inexorable natural instinct—protecting their young, for example, or guarding a food cache—will likely be destroyed by Park authorities. So hiking McArthur Creek valley endangers not just you, but the bears. For their sake, don't do it.

You still insist? Be on full alert for bears. Constantly scan ahead. Make noise frequently to warn bears of your presence. Read our *Bears* section for further suggestions. And while crossing McArthur Pass, make the short detour to ink-pot blue, cliff-ringed Lake McArthur.

FACT

Before your trip

Ask the Yoho Visitor Centre about the status of McArthur Creek valley, where hiking is severely restricted to preserve grizzly-bear habitat. The area is closed September 16 through August 14, with access granted to just two parties per week—by permit only—August 15 through September 15. One of the weekly openings is reservable up to three months in advance, the other only 24 hours in advance. Reservations are also required to stay in the Lake O'Hara region, as described in Trip 14.

By Vehicle

Neither end of the McArthur Creek trail is vehicle accessible. It's simply a connecting route. Reach it by hiking from Lake O'Hara (Trip 14), by hiking over Goodsir Pass from Helmet Falls and the Rockwall (Trip 89), or by hiking or biking up the Ottertail fire road (Trip 50).

On Foot

Read the Ottertail fire road (Trip 50) or the Rockwall (Trip 89) for directions to the three-way junction near the **confluence** of the Ottertail River and McArthur Creek. The McArthur Creek trail begins here, at 1480 m (4855 ft), just north of the McArthur Creek bridge. If you started hiking the Rockwall trail at the Floe Lake trailhead, you're total mileage to this point is 53.4 km (33 mi).

Follow the McArthur creek trail generally north. It ascends gradually along the creek's west bank. During the 730-m (2395-ft) climb to McArthur Pass, be especially wary of bears while crossing avalanche paths.

After the initial 1.8 km (1.1 mi), the trail contours for nearly 2.5 km (1.6 mi), then begins a gradual ascent. At 6 km (3.7 mi) cross a bridged tributary and curve gradually northeast. The trail steepens near 1800 m (5900 ft). Reach a junction in 2210-m (7250-ft) **McArthur Pass** at 10.3 km (6.4 mi).

Straight continues north-northeast into the Lake O'Hara region (Trip 15 - 19). Turn right and ascend south, then southeast on the Lower McArthur trail. It gains 65 m (213 ft) in 0.9 km (0.5 mi) to arrive at Lake McArthur—a stupendous sight. At the lake, the trail turns left (northeast), briefly follows the northwest shore, but soon curves left (northwest) where it's known as the McArthur Cutoff. Stay on it.

At the next junction, 1 km (0.6 mi) from Lake McArthur, turn right and proceed into the Lake O'Hara region. From the highpoint on the cutoff trail, you'll descend 300 m (984 ft) to **Lake O'Hara**. If you started hiking the Rockwall trail at the Floe Lake trailhead, your total distance to Lake O'Hara—including the 2-km (1.3-mi) sidetrip to Lake McArthur—will be 69 km (43 mi).

TRIP 115

Fryatt Valley

LOCATION	Jasper National Park
ROUND TRIP	44 km (27.3 mi)
ELEVATION GAIN	810 m (2657 ft)
KEY ELEVATIONS	trailhead 1220 m (4002 ft) Upper Fryatt Valley 2000 m (6560 ft)
HIKING TIME	3-day backpack, or 1-day bike/hike
DIFFICULTY	challenging
MAPS	page 523; Gem Trek *Jasper & Maligne Lake;* Athabasca Falls 83 C/12

OPINION

A drudgery reduction device is what you need here. A mountain bike. The trip begins on a fire road and burrows through forest half the way. Then you'll need an entertaining companion on the order of Eddie Izzard to ease the monotony of hiking the next stretch. Finally, you'll need willpower to prevail on a soul-crushing ascent. What could justify all that?

Climbers say the upper Fryatt Valley does. It's a wee, hanging valley, only a kilometre long, but as fetching as any in the Canadian Rockies. It harbours a glacier-fed lakelet amid flowery subalpine meadows, and is wreathed by fantastic alps: Mts. Christie, Lowell, Xerxes, Parnassus, Belanger, Fryatt, and Brussels Peak. But numerous climbing routes rocket out of the upper Fryatt; of course climbers love it. Hikers are less enthusiastic. Despite the beauty of this hidden vale, they see it as a tiny, one-look wonder. One quick look around and there's little for a hiker to do but wonder if all the effort was really worth it.

If you're considering hiking here, be very clear about what the journey entails. The first noteworthy view is 16 km (10 mi) from the trailhead. The scenic jackpot, in the vaunted upper valley, is 6 km (3.7 mi) farther. Assaulting the headwall, you'll climb a merciless 200 m (656 ft) in 0.8 km (0.5 mi). If those statistics don't mean much to you now, they will. Also, camping is verboten in the upper valley. There is a comfortable Alpine Club hut there, open to the public, but it's small, requires reservations, and is likely to be booked full. It's best to drop your backpack and pitch your tent at Headwall campground, then daytrip into the upper valley. Sunset draws the blinds on the scenery anyway, and the headwall ascent is much easier bearing only a daypack. Of course, like all national park backcountry campgrounds, those in the lower valley require reservations and fees. Book early. Despite its many drawbacks, Fryatt Valley is popular.

Fryatt Valley

Put off by the ordeal, yet still curious about the famous Fryatt? Knock it off in a one-day epic. Possessing Olympian endurance, you can bike to Lower Fryatt campground, dash in and out of the upper valley on foot, then ride an endorphin high while you pedal back to the trailhead.

FACT

Before your trip

If you want to stay in the Fryatt Hut (also called the Vallance Hut), check the current price and make reservations with the Alpine Club of Canada. The contact numbers are listed under *Information Sources* in the back of this book.

If you need to rent a bike, call Vicious Cycle in Jasper: (780) 852-1111. They usually let you pick the bike up at the end of the day before your rental, so you can get an early start the next morning.

By Vehicle

Where Hwy 93A departs the Icefields Parkway (Hwy 93) at Athabasca Falls (31 km / 19.2 mi south of Jasper townsite), drive 93A northwest 1.1 km (0.7 mi). Turn left (southwest) on the narrow, rough, dirt Geraldine Fire Road. Continue 2 km (1.2 mi) to the trailhead parking area, at 1220 m (4002 ft).

On Foot

Note: The times stated below assume that you're cycling to Lower Fryatt campground, then hiking.

Begin by heading southeast on the old fire road—mostly level and smooth—through forest. You're roughly paralleling the Athabasca River and the Icefields Parkway. Both are left (east) of the road and initially out of sight. Ten minutes along, cross a creek channel (usually dry), on a two-plank bridge. Go right (southwest). In 30 m/yd a skinny log spans the creek. Decline its precarious invitation and continue another 45 m/yd upstream where you'll find a comfortable, three-plank bridge. Resume on the fire road.

At 7.2 km (4.5 mi), you're beside the Athabasca River. The Parkway is visible, just 100 m (110 yd) distant. Most hikers wish the cable car that crossed the river here was still in use. The benefit of this inconvenience is that it keeps Fryatt Valley from being rampaged.

About five minutes farther, the path ascends to a 1277-m (4190-ft) vantage before leveling again. Southwest is your goal: the mouth of Fryatt Valley. South-southeast is 3102-m (10,178-ft) Mt. Christie. After undulating atop an eroded slope, the path is riddled with baby heads (large stones embedded in dirt). A rough, rooty section then ensues.

Reach **Lower Fryatt campground** at 11.6 km (7.2 mi), 1287 m (4220 ft), about 1¾ hours from the trailhead. It has tables, a fire pit, and bear-proof food storage. Cycling is prohibited beyond, so stash your bikes and cycling gear and begin hiking. Cross to the south bank of bridged Fryatt Creek and follow the trail up-valley (southwest). You're still in forest and will remain so until 16 km (9.9 mi).

In 15 minutes, soon after the 8-mile blaze, the trail steepens, ascending above Fryatt Creek. Berry bushes are profuse. At 1585 m (5200 ft), about an hour from the campground, enjoy a pleasant, stretch of creekside trail. The undergrowth is lusher, and bigger firs enhance the forest.

At 16 km (9.9 mi) cross a long bridge to the creek's west bank. The headwall cascade draining upper Fryatt Valley is visible south-southwest. Proceed up-valley. Cross several streamlets.

Reach **Brussels campground** at 17.7 km (11 mi), 1630 m (5346 ft). It's in open, stony flats. Mt. Christie (3102 m / 10,175 ft) and, just south of it, Brussels Peak (3160 m / 10,365 ft) create the left (southeast) wall of this lower valley. Mt. Fryatt (3360 m / 11,021 ft) forms the right (northwest) wall.

Continue southwest, on a bootbeaten path cairned over a rockslide. Soon see **Fryatt Lake**. Descend 30 m (98 ft) to reach its forested north shore at 18.7 km (11.6 mi), 1720 m (5642 ft). Swift hikers will arrive here two hours after departing Lower Fryatt camp. The trail, rooty and rocky, rounds the west shore.

From the south shore, at 19.5 km (12.1 mi), ascend through yet more forest to arrive at **Headwall campground**. Total distance from the trailhead: 21 km (13 mi). Elevation: 1780 m (5838 ft). The eight tent sites are crammed into the willowy hillside near the base of the headwall cascade. The campground has tables, a fire pit, and bear-proof food storage.

The headwall ascent looks nearly vertical. The trail, really just a route, gains 200 m (656 ft) within 0.8 km (0.5 mi). It's as difficult to surmount as it appears.

Fryatt Hut

Just reaching the base of the headwall, the route is narrow, rooty, rough. From there on, it's just a persistent gash in the dirt.

Half way up, a mudslide washed out a section of the route. Perhaps it's been improved; if not, cross to the right of the slide and ascend through a rocky gouge. From Headwall camp, it takes 28 to 35 minutes to attain the upper valley rim. From the rim, it takes about 20 minutes to get back down to Headwall camp.

Having surmounted the final obstacle, enter the hanging **upper valley** at 21.9 km (13.6 mi), 2000 m (6560 ft). Behind you (northeast), all of lower Fryatt Valley is visible. The Maligne Range rises beyond the Parkway.

The **Fryatt Hut** is 100 m (110 yd) past the upper valley rim. You're now in subalpine meadowland, surrounded by icy peaks. Mt. Belanger rises on the right (west-northwest) side of the valley. The two prominent peaks at the head of the valley are Mt. Xerxes (left), Mt. Parnassus (right). These are unofficial names adopted by the Alpine Club.

A trail continues southwest from the hut, deeper into the upper valley. It's sketchy in places, soggy in others. After climbing a moraine, drop to a small, opaque lake at 23.2 km (14.4 mi), 2040 m (6691 ft).

Giant Douglas firs enhance the initial walk to Celestine Lake.

Shoulder-Season Trips

TRIP 116

Lineham Creek Falls

LOCATION	Waterton Lakes National Park
ROUND TRIP	8.4 km (5.2 mi)
ELEVATION GAIN	375 m (1230 ft)
KEY ELEVATIONS	trailhead 1575 m (5166 ft), trail's end 1950 m (6396 ft)
HIKING TIME	2½ hours
DIFFICULTY	easy
MAPS	page 492; Gem Trek *Waterton Lakes National Park*

OPINION

Waterton is a compact park, so most trails are busy. This one's an exception, because it lacks a grand finale. It drops you unceremoniously in a rocky, subalpine basin. You can see the 100-metre waterfall from there, but it's half a kilometre away. Still, this hike is enjoyable, especially on a rainy day when climbing into the clouds seems pointless, or when snow prevents you from climbing anywhere. Just past the trailhead, you'll get a good look at Lineham and Cameron Creek valleys. When the trail dives into forest, it's a pleasing mixture of evergreens and aspen. The cliff band blocking hikers' progress beyond the basin is an impressive fortress wall. And the possibility of being here alone is a bonus.

Unless you're a black-belt rock climber, forget about assaulting the cliff band. It will defeat you. A climbing permit is necessary anyway; check at the park information centre for details. If you're intrigued by the Lineham Lakes, which are cupped in the upper basin and feed the waterfall tumbling into the lower basin, hike to Lineham Ridge (Trip 2) for a hawk's-eye view.

Scorpionweed

Lineham Lakes, above Lineham Falls

FACT

By Vehicle

From the junction just north of Waterton townsite, drive the Akamina Parkway 9.3 km (5.8 mi) to the signed pullout on the right, before the Lineham Creek bridge, at 1575 m (5166 ft).

On Foot

A moderately steep trail whisks you northwest, out of the forested Cameron Creek valley. With the aide of a single steep switchback, climb above Lineham Creek, on an open, south facing, subalpine slope with views galore. At 2 km (1.2 mi) re-enter forest as the ascent eases. A small sign in a meadow marks the end of maintained trail at 4.2 km (2.6 mi), 1950 m (6396 ft). **Lineham Falls**, plummeting down the cliff band, is visible about 0.5 km (0.3 mi) distant. To approach the falls, look for one of a couple routes scruffed out by climbers. When the route angles cliffward, point your boots at the falls.

TRIP 117

Aylmer Lookout and Pass

LOCATION	Banff National Park
ROUND TRIP	23.4 km (14.5 mi) to lookout 27 km (16.7 mi) to pass, 30.2 km (18.7 mi) for both
ELEVATION GAIN	570 m (1870 ft) to lookout 803 m (2634 ft) to pass, 942 m (3090 ft) for both
KEY ELEVATIONS	trailhead 1482 m (4860 ft) lookout 2052 m (6730 ft) ft), pass 2285 m (7495 ft)
HIKING TIME	7 to 8 hours for lookout, 10 to 11 for both
DIFFICULTY	moderate
MAPS	page 525; Gem Trek *Banff & Mt. Assiniboine*; Lake Minnewanka 82 O/6

OPINION

Ticks can live up to two years without a meal. Imagine the feast they're planning at Aylmer Lookout, where they patiently await your arrival. But don't let that stop you. They like this southwest-facing slope because it's sun exposed—dry and hot—which means it's also ideal for ambitious, scenery-seeking hikers in early summer. If you're dissatisfied plodding viewless, low-elevation trails until the snowpack melts, point your boots up here.

The lookout is on Mt. Aylmer's south ridge, where it commands a dazzling view of Lake Minnewanka—a long, winding, inland fiord—570 m (1870 ft) below. The panorama includes Mts. Inglismaldie and Girouard, across the lake, and the Bow Valley's southern reaches beneath the Mt. Rundle massif. Because the fire lookout building is long gone, the lookout is actually just a lookout *site*. But the view is as sweeping and stirring as ever. And bighorn sheep are just as prevalent now as they were when the lookout attendants set out salt blocks.

Aylmer Pass is farther, higher, and remains snowbound longer than the lookout. Yet the scenery is less dramatic. No lake view, no nearby imposing peaks. Just lots of rocks and tundra in a long, broad, alpine groove in the south end of the Palliser Range. The extra time and effort to reach the pass is worthwhile, however, simply to experience the sharp sense of wilderness that such desolate, high-elevation settings invariably elicit. Plus, the pass is usually hikeable by mid-June, when most passes in the Canadian Rockies have yet to shed their white winter coats. The possibility of cresting a genuine pass so early in the summer is an irresistible invitation to any strong, serious hiker.

No way you'll reach both the lookout and the pass? Choose the lookout. And not just because the trail to the lookout is shorter and less steep. The upper elevations here in Banff Park's southern reaches are bleak, devoid of glaciers,

Lake Minnewanka, from just above Aylmer Pass junction

Lake Minnewanka, from Aylmer Lookout

deprived of greenery. So what you see from the pass is a vast expanse of gray. But the culminating sight at the lookout is the strident blue of Lake Minnewanka splashed across that grayness.

Fleet hikers can reach the lookout or the pass and return in a long day. Robo hikers can tag both in a one-day epic. To more comfortably achieve either of those goals, ride a mountain bike as far as the 7.8-km (4.8-mi) junction on the Lake Minnewanka trail. Then stash your bike, lace up your boots, and strap on your jet pack. The ascent is eager, or merciless, depending on your fitness level. To slash the sweat factor, make this a backpack trip: pitch your tent at the junction campground, then dayhike to both the pass and the lookout. (The campground and the trail to Aylmer Pass are closed annually, July 15 to Sept. 30, due to bears in the area.) Camping on the shore of Banff Park's largest lake is a joy, especially in early summer. The distance and elevation gain to that point are insignificant, so carrying a full backpack is not onerous. The ascent comes later—from the junction to the lookout and pass—where you'd carry only a daypack or lumbar pack. So, this is an exceptionally easy overnighter.

Whatever your plan, before ascending from the junction, guzzle and refill. Your choice of refreshments: stream or lake. Both require filtering. The ensuing climb can be a sweltering ordeal even in June. The next reliable water source is an hour or more up the trail. And remember to check for ticks at rest stops and day's end. (See our Ticks section, page 32.)

FACT

By Vehicle

Read Trip 121 for directions to the large, paved parking lot at 1482 m (4860 ft), just above the west end of Lake Minnewanka.

On Foot

Read Lake Minnewanka (Trip 121) for directions to **Aylmer Pass junction**, at 7.8 km (4.8 mi), 1490 m (4887 ft). After refilling your water containers at the bridged creek immediately before the junction, turn left (north) to begin ascending to Aylmer lookout and pass. Straight (east-northeast) continues paralleling the lakeshore. Right (southeast) soon enters LM8 campground and ends at the lakeshore in 0.4 km (0.25 mi). Just before the shore, the cooking area and bearproof food storage are right (west). The campground also has platform tables, a fire pit, and firewood.

AYLMER LOOKOUT

From **Aylmer Pass junction**, the trail ascends generally north-northwest at a moderate grade. Aylmer Lookout is 3.9 km (2.4 mi) distant and 570 m (1870 ft) above you. Aylmer Creek, in the gorge below, is audible. Blue clematis is prolific here. It creeps like a vine onto tree trunks and low branches, brightening the forest.

About 30 minutes above the junction, the trail levels at 1838 m (6030 ft). At 10.1 km (6.3 mi), 1921 m (6300 ft), reach **Aylmer Lookout fork** in a tiny clearing. Fit hikers will arrive here about 40 minutes after leaving Aylmer Pass junction. Straight (north) continues to Aylmer Pass. Turn right (northeast) to reach the lookout—1.6 km (1 mi) farther—in another 35 minutes.

Lake Minnewanka, from just below Aylmer Lookout

The lookout trail ascends from the fork, but it soon levels. Ten minutes farther, it descends about 8 m (26 ft), then resumes climbing. About 30 minutes from the fork, it levels again, on an open slope. Lake Minnewanka is visible below.

After several switchbacks, reach the site of **Aylmer Lookout** at 11.7 km (7.3 mi), 2052 m (6730 ft). The lookout was dismantled in 1985. Only the cement footings remain.

Banff townsite and Tunnel Mtn are visible southwest. The north end of Mt. Rundle is south-southwest, above the Bow Valley. South, across the lake, are 2963-m (9719-ft) Mt. Inglismaldie and 2994-m (9820-ft) Mt. Girouard. A 10-km (6.2-mi) stretch of the lake is visible southeast before it bends out of sight.

AYLMER PASS

From **Aylmer Lookout fork**, at 10.1 km (6.3 mi), 1921 m (6300 ft), you'll gain 364 m (1194 ft) in 3.4 km (2.1 mi) to the summit of Aylmer Pass. The total ascent from Aylmer Pass junction, on the Lake Minnewanka trail, is 795 m (2608 ft) in 5.7 km (3.5 mi).

At the lookout fork, refill your water containers. About 3 m/yd north of the fork, a very steep path descends left (west) to Aylmer Creek. Be cautious.

Departing the lookout fork, proceed straight (north) for Aylmer Pass. The ascent remains earnest as you follow the trail up the forested canyon between Mt. Aylmer (right) and Mt. Astley (left).

Lake Minnewanka, from just above Aylmer Pass junction

About 30 minutes above the fork, enter the subalpine zone at 2010 m (6592 ft). The forest is now more open and the trees smaller. The ascent steepens. Cross several lush avalanche paths, including one with a big rockslide. In early summer, expect to see cascades and wildflowers. Globeflowers (creamy white, five petals, a central cluster of yellow stamens) are prominent. Also look for western spring-beauty (dainty, pink stripes, white petals).

Where the trail drops into an avalanche chute (possibly snow-filled in early summer), cross it then turn sharply left up the far side. A steep, tussocky, gravelly slope on the right indicates you're near the pass. About an hour above the lookout fork, enter the alpine zone at 2200 m (7216 ft). The trail dips left into a gully then rises over a rockslide.

Reach the south end of 1.2-km (0.75-mi) long **Aylmer Pass,** at 12.8 km (7.9 mi), 2265 m (7430 ft). In early summer, avoid snow by staying high on the talus-and-dryas-covered east slope. It might be convenient to abandon the trail by bearing right where it nips into a trough. Then proceed cross-country north-northeast until you can see down the north side of the pass. If the area appears to be snowfree, however, stay on the trail and rockhop to the west bank of Aylmer Creek. Then follow an intermittent path ascending gently over scree about 0.7 km (0.4 mi) to the **summit of Aylmer Pass**, at 13.5 km (8.4 mi), 2285 m (7495 ft).

Apparition Mtn is visible north. Walling off the east side of the pass is 3161-m (10,371-ft) Mt. Aylmer—a non-technical but exhausting scramble. South-southeast, above Lake Minnewanka's far shore, is 2963-m (9722-ft) Mt. Inglismaldie. The austere, gray, limestone peaks of the Palliser Range are north-northwest.

Atop Aylmer Pass, the trail exits Banff Park. It continues north, descending into Spectral Creek valley, in the **Ghost River Wilderness**, where no permit is required to camp. As far as Spectral Creek, the trail is reputed to be adequate. But from there, downstream to the Ghost River, you should expect to be bushwhacking—if you can first find a compelling reason to go.

Budgeting your time in hope of also visiting Aylmer Lookout? Swift hikers can descend from the summit of Aylmer Pass to Aylmer Lookout fork in about 40 minutes.

TRIP 118

Plain of Six Glaciers

LOCATION	Banff National Park, above Lake Louise
ROUND TRIP	11.2 km (6.9 mi) to teahouse 13.8 km (8.6 mi) to trail's end
ELEVATION GAIN	339 m (1112 ft) to teahouse 464 m (1522 ft) to trail's end
KEY ELEVATIONS	trailhead 1731 m (5678 ft) teahouse 2070 m (6790 ft) trail's end 2195 m (7200 ft)
HIKING TIME	3 hours for teahouse, 4 hours for trail's end 5 hours including optional return via Lake Agnes
DIFFICULTY	easy to teahouse and trail's end moderate for optional return
MAPS	page 497; Gem Trek *Lake Louise & Yoho*

OPINION

We once watched a seven-year-old boy and his nine-year-old sister sprint up the lateral moraine to the end of the trail in the rock-and-ice sanctuary beyond Lake Louise.

They peered at glaciers below and above. They gazed at the towering peaks encircling them. And they proved how remarkably easy it is to reach the most celebrated spectacle in the Canadian Rockies.

Few trails anywhere rival this one's reward-to-effort ratio. At the trailhead, you stare across turquoise Lake Louise to the icy bulk of Mt. Victoria, and already you're awestruck. En route, you're rarely deprived of a view, because glaciation has scoured the upper valley, preventing trees from colonizing it. Before reaching trail's end, you're scouring the recesses of your vocabulary for words to describe the overwhelming scenery and your emotional response to it.

Either that, or you just start speaking in tongues, like that boy did when he witnessed an avalanche plummet down the far cirque wall.

"Dad! Look! The mountain's comingnslkjl jadkn ilkj cudfh wetcs oyom, I'm not kidding, it's skj euie!"

Everyone within earshot understood him. We were all thinking the same thing but appreciated having such an eloquent spokesperson. "Amen, brother" added one of the nearby adults.

The fact that several of us had congregated, however, illustrates the one valid criticism of this hike: accessible + dazzling = popular.

The trail, initially a paved path, begins at a world-famous hotel and leads to a subalpine teahouse deep in the colossal amphitheatre. Crowds are inevitable. Especially when hot chocolate and fresh banana bread are involved.

So begin hiking early. Start by 8 a.m. if you want to photograph the icy crags in optimal lighting. Or sleep late, relax, punch in for the more tranquil evening shift. Set out at 5 p.m. during the long days of early summer, 4 p.m. during the shorter days of late summer. You'll still complete the trip before dark, and you won't feel Desi Arnaz is up ahead leading the conga line.

Experienced hikers, particularly locals, wince at the thought of dekeing through the tourists who constantly mob the shore of Lake Louise. But if you want to fill your mental gallery with as many of nature's masterpieces as possible, you'll hike here regardless. Just be sure to post a sentry before stopping to pee.

FACT

By Vehicle

Drive Hwy 1, 1A, or 93 to Lake Louise. From Lake Louise Village, drive uphill (southwest) on Lake Louise Drive. Continue to the actual *Lake* Louise. Near road's end, 200 m (656 ft) before the Chateau Lake Louise, turn left into the multilevel parking area.

On Foot

From the west end of the lower parking lot, walk the paved path west to **Lake Louise**, at 1731 m (5678 ft). Bear right. Follow the path around the end of the lake. Pass the **Chateau**. On the northeast shore is a trail sign (starting point for distances below). Proceed left on the paved, level, lakeshore path.

At 2 km (1.2 mi), reach the southwest end of the lake, near **Louise Creek**. Climbing routes garnish the purple-hued cliffs (right). From the Chateau, striders will arrive here in 20 minutes, strollers 35.

Proceed southwest through **willow flats** on a luxurious, raised trailbed. The creek becomes a cascade in a few minutes. At 2.4 km (1.5 mi) begin a gentle ascent. At 3.4 km (2.1 mi), 1850 m (6068 ft), stay straight (southwest) where the Highline shortcut ascends right to Lake Agnes (Trip 66). At 4.2 km (2.6 mi), 1975 m (6478 ft), stay straight again (southwest) where the Highline trail ascends right to Lake Agnes. Soon enter **glacial rubble**.

Ascending switchbacks near 5 km (3.1 mi), bear right, closer to the brush, on the main trail. Ignore the rougher spur (straight) probing the moraine. Directly ahead (southwest) is 3464-m (11,362-ft) Mt. Victoria. Left of it (south) is 3423-m (11,227-ft)

Plain of Six Glaciers teahouse

Plain of Six Glaciers

Mt. Lefroy. Between them is Abbot Pass and the Victoria Glacier. Lefroy Glacier and The Mitre are left of Mt. Lefroy. The Chateau and Lake Louise are visible northeast.

The trail levels at 5.6 km (3.5 mi), 2070 m (6790 ft), near a bridged creeklet. The **teahouse** is behind you, among the trees. There are also benches and outhouses here.

To resume hiking, cross the bridge. The trail leads another 1.3 km (0.8 mi) southwest along the crest of a **lateral moraine**, above the Victoria Glacier.

The **trail ends** at 6.9 km (4.3 mi), 2195 m (7200 ft), on a steep talus slope—an unaccommodating but magnificent viewpoint. You're now close to the cliffs of Victoria (right) and Lefroy (left). Abbot Pass—the cleft between them—is in full view. Abbot Pass Hut is visible atop the 2922-m (9584-ft) pass, just above the "Death Trap" couloir.

The hut was built in 1922. It commemorates Philip Abbot, who died on Mt. Lefroy in 1896. His was the first fatality in the recorded history of North American climbing.

It's possible to extend your return to the Chateau. The following circuit adds 4.1 km (2.5 mi) and a gain of 280 m (918 ft) to the Plain-of-Six-Glaciers round trip.

After descending to the **junction below the teahouse**, turn left onto the Highline trail and follow it northeast. Bear left at the next junction and continue northeast.

Reach another junction and go left again, ascending steeply northwest. Crest a ridge. Turn right (northeast) for an easy, 0.6-km (0.4-mi) round-trip detour along the ridge to the Big Beehive, then descend northwest to **Lake Agnes**.

The trail rounds the lake's southwest and northwest shores to reach the **Lake Agnes teahouse** perched above the northeast corner. From there, descend southeast to **Mirror Lake** and reach a junction: right leads south, back to the Highline; left curves around Mirror Lake's west shore. Go left.

Soon reach another junction: left leads north to the Little Beehive, right switchbacks down to the Chateau. Go right. Approaching **Lake Louise**, bear right and intersect the paved lakeshore path.

TRIP 119

Waterton Lakeshore

LOCATION	Waterton Lakes National Park
ONE WAY	12.8 km (7.9 mi)
ELEVATION GAIN	approximately 145 m (475 ft)
HIKING TIME	5 hours
DIFFICULTY	easy
MAPS	page 503; Gem Trek *Waterton Lakes National Park*

OPINION

cabin fever *n* (1918) : extreme irritability and restlessness from living in isolation or a confined indoor area for a prolonged time

If you're afflicted, here's the antidote: a long, gently graded, well-maintained trail usually snow-free April through October, on the west shore of Upper Waterton Lake. It's sure to provide relief. Just don't expect a miraculous cure. The scenery isn't what you might imagine of a trail linking the national parks of two nations. So hike here only in spring, when more radical therapy is unavailable to hikers.

The lakeshore trail offers three options: (1) Start in Waterton townsite and hike 12.8 km (7.9 mi) south to Goat Haunt, then ride the tour boat back. (2) Ride the tour boat to Goat Haunt, then hike north to Waterton townsite—without worrying about the boat schedule. (3) Hike south from the townsite as far as you like, then walk back, figuring the tour-boat fare you saved paid for this book.

We recommend the third option. It's not only free, it gives you flexibility. Besides, you'll miss little by not hiking the whole way. After the scenic overlook at 1.5 km (0.9 mi), the trail allows snippet views of the lake and mountains. South of the international border, it's totally in trees; if you didn't know the lake was nearby, you'd never guess it. If you're intent on seeing the two obelisks marking the international border, and leaving your bootprint in the U.S.A. at Boundary Bay, a round trip from the townsite is no farther than hiking one-way after paying for the boat.

The trip highlights are the aforementioned scenic overlook and the Bertha Bay beach. Other beaches are scattered along the trail. They're great for lounging, reading, and sunning. Bertha, and the bay just south of it, offer an unlimited supply of thin, flat, oval stones, perfect for skipping. Imagine: The First-Annual World Rock-Skipping Championship, at Bertha Bay, Alberta. "Ladies and Gentleman, collect your rocks!"

Campgrounds along the lakeshore trail make spring backpacking viable and attractive. Bertha Bay campground, only a short distance from Waterton townsite, is an ideal destination for novices trying out new gear, or families trying out new kids. It has four comfortably-spaced tentsites between Bertha Creek and the lakeshore, in an open forest of mostly cottonwoods. There's also a communal fire pit here.

Bertha Bay

It's true that you'll see more of the lake and surrounding mountains by riding the tour boat than by striding the lakeshore trail. Nevertheless, if you're a hiker, you'll prefer the trail. Ride the boat only to reach the Crypt Lake (Trip 22) trailhead, which is ridiculously difficult to access on foot.

Okay, so you've hiked the lakeshore trail and you're now at Boundary Bay. Studying the map, you notice a trail leading west, up Boundary Creek, to Summit Lake. Don't be tempted. This scenically-challenged trail is more appealing to grizzly bears than to people.

FACT

Before your trip

Visit the Waterton Park Visitor Info Centre to get a backcountry camping permit for Waterton River campground or Goat Haunt hikers' shelter in U.S. Glacier National Park. You're a Canadian or U.S. citizen? No worries. You can hike the Waterton Lakeshore trail across the border in either direction. Just make sure you report to the rangers at Goat Haunt. You're not a citizen of either country? You will not be permitted to hike across the border.

By Vehicle

To start hiking in Waterton townsite, drive Evergreen Avenue south along the west side of town. From where the road crosses the bridge at the base of Cameron

Falls, continue 0.5 km (0.3 mi) and turn right into the gravel parking lot signed for Bertha Lake. This is opposite the townsite campground. The trail starts in the upper left corner of the lot, at 1295 m (4248 ft).

To begin the trip by riding the tour boat to Goat Haunt, at the far (south) end of Upper Waterton Lake, park in the large paved lot by the boat landing in Waterton townsite.

By Boat

The tour boat departs Waterton townsite at 10 a.m. It stops at Goat Haunt from early June to mid-September. A 9 a.m. departure is scheduled July 1 through August 31. Cruising time is about two hours. If you're hiking south to Goat Haunt, the boat departs there at 2:25 p.m. and 5:25 p.m., with an additional 8:05 p.m. departure July 1 through August 31. Confirm current schedules and prices with the Waterton Inter-Nation Shoreline Cruise Company: (403) 859-2362.

On Foot

Starting at Bertha Lake trailhead, in Waterton townsite

Follow the trail up the hillside, then generally south. The open forest occasionally grants views of Upper Waterton Lake. In 20 to 30 minutes, at 1410 m (4625 ft), reach a **scenic overlook**. Vimy Peak is east, across the lake. Just beyond and slightly below the overlook, reach a junction at 1.5 km (0.9 mi). Right leads to Bertha Lake (Trip 37). Go left. After a substantial descent, cross a bridge over Bertha Creek and reach **Bertha Bay campground** at 2.4 km (1.5 mi).

Continuing south from Bertha Bay, ascend a section of trail blasted out of a cliff. A gradual, 15-minute descent leads to a tiny beach at the base of a boulder slide. Five minutes farther, negotiate the logs spanning an unbridged stream. Ascend, then drop back to the lakeshore.

Immediately before rockhopping the next stream, look left. Just beyond the fringe of brush and trees, you'll find a 150-metre (165-yd) long, south facing, pebbly beach that affords more solitude than the Bertha Bay beach. Mt. Boswell is visible east-southeast, across the lake. The distinctively sharp Citadel Peaks are south, beyond the shoulder of Campbell Mtn.

After hiking about an hour south of Bertha Bay, reach the **international border** and **Boundary Bay campground** at 5.8 km (3.6 mi). There's a small dock here, and a pair of commemorative obelisks. Dayhikers intending to turn around here should continue about five minutes farther south to the bridge over Boundary Creek, for a view upstream into a chasm.

The Boundary Creek trail forks right (west) just south of the bridge. Continue straight (south) on the lakeshore trail. It's 6.6 km (4.1 mi) farther to the Goat Haunt boat dock. Nearing the south end of Upper Waterton Lake, stay right where a spur trail forks left to **Waterton River campground**. The main trail pulls away from the lake. Intersect the Boulder Pass trail at 11.5 km (7.1 mi) and stay left. Cross a suspension bridge over Waterton River, then stay left again, passing the spur trail to Rainbow Falls. Continue 0.4 km (0.25 mi) past the **Goat Haunt Ranger station** to the boat dock on the east shore at 12.8 km (7.9 mi). Pitch your tent in the hikers' shelter, which has two concrete walls and a roof. Cook your meals at the boat-dock pavilion.

Trailside art, Waterton lakeshore

Starting at the Goat Haunt boat dock, at the south end of Upper Waterton Lake

Head southwest around the shore. Arrive at the ranger station in 0.4 km (0.25 mi). At 0.9 km (0.5 mi) stay right where a spur forks left to Rainbow Falls. (If you have time, the 0.8-km / 0.5-mi one-way detour to the falls is worth it.) Continue right (east) where the Boulder Pass trail departs left (west) at 1.3 km (0.8 mi). Soon a spur trail to Waterton River campground forks right. Bear left (north) through forest.

At 6.6 km (4.2 mi) intersect the Boundary Creek trail. Stay right. Reach the **international border** and Boundary Bay campground at 7 km (4.3 mi). **Bertha Bay** and campground are at 10.4 km (6.4 mi).

From Bertha Bay, ascend north to a junction at 11.3 km (7 mi). Bertha Lake (Trip 37) is left. Stay right and in a few minutes attain the trail's best viewpoint of Upper Waterton Lake. Vimy Peak (east) is across the lake.

At 12.8 km (7.9 mi) arrive abruptly at civilization, in the trailhead parking lot opposite Waterton townsite campground. Cut east through the campground to tag onto a lakeshore walkway, which you can follow north into town.

TRIP 120

Sulphur Mountain via Cosmic Ray Road

LOCATION	Banff National Park
ONE WAY	8.5 km (5.3 mi)
ELEVATION GAIN	880 m (2886 ft)
KEY ELEVATIONS	trailhead 1390 m (4560 ft) Sanson Peak 2270 m (7446 ft) upper gondola terminal 2260 m (7413 ft)
HIKING TIME	3 to 4 hours
DIFFICULTY	moderate due only to elevation gain
MAPS	page 526; Gem Trek *Banff Up-Close*

OPINION

Cap'n Crunch, an 80-something-year-old hiker, earned his nickname when his crackling knee joints got so loud they became audible to others on the trail. He was a walking reminder of how resilient our bodies can be to a rigourous mountain life, and also how delicately vulnerable. Knees are especially at risk during plunging, pounding descents. Mitigating that risk requires trekking poles. Unless you're on Sulphur Mountain, where you can ride the gondola down.

The ascent via Cosmic Ray Road is on a sunny southwest-facing slope, snow-free early and late in the year. Much of the way is also tree-free, so views are plentiful. And the summit panorama is vast. You'll look up the Bow River Valley all the way to Mt. Temple, near Lake Louise. You'll also see the town of Banff, far below.

A bit of Banff Avenue will also be waiting for you atop Sulphur Mtn. Upon reaching the summit-ridge boardwalk (!) expect to join a crowd of shuffling tourists. That's one reason why the other Sulphur Mtn approach, via the gondola trail (Trip 63), is rated *Don't Do*. But the other reasons (a shady, northeast-facing slope that retains snow and thus is not viable in shoulder season; a viewless ascent through forest; a gondola skimming overhead; and the audible hubbub of Banff townsite) don't apply to Cosmic Ray Road. Here, you'll likely be alone until summiting.

The hike begins on a paved path, which leads to the road, which ascends to the mountaintop boardwalk. It's far too civilized to be an authentic Canadian Rockies hiking experience, so don't come here during summer. Why plod up a road to join a flock of tourists, when you can be hiking a trail and communing with nature? But you'll appreciate this walk when most trails are buried in snow and deep in shade. In May, come here to train. In November, come here to extend the oh-so-short hiking season. An early fall snowstorm might leave up to 20 cm (8 in) on this side of Sulphur Mtn, but you can still tromp through it on the road without snowshoes. The extra effort will be worth it, because the peaks within view are more striking when snow-crusted.

Ascending Cosmic Ray Road in mid-November

The name *Cosmic Ray Road*, by the way, isn't a joke. The road was built in 1956 to facilitate cosmic ray research. Sulphur Mountain was one of eight such sites in Canada; one of 98 worldwide. Research here ceased in 1978. Cosmic rays are produced by solar explosions and are believed to cause the Northern Lights. Cosmic rays would obliterate life on earth were it not for our planet's protective atmosphere and magnetic field.

You can see Cosmic Ray Road from Trans-Canada Hwy 1. While driving eastbound toward Banff townsite, look right (east-southeast) shortly after passing the Sunshine exit.

FACT

Before your trip

Check the gondola's hours of operation by calling (403) 762-2523. You don't want to miss the last ride down, especially on a chilly fall evening. In the past, the gondola stopped running at 6 p.m. in May, and at 4:30 p.m. in November.

Hiking up Cosmic Ray Road, on the west face of the mountain, then riding the gondola down the east face, will necessitate two cars and a short shuttle, hence the two sets of *By Vehicle* directions below.

Hitchhiking is possible, but thumbing rides for short distances within a town tends to be difficult, because you don't engender the sympathy that you would on a highway. If you intend to hitch, chat up likely prospects at the upper gondola terminal. Or at least smile benevolently at everyone so they'll think kindly of you when they see you on the road.

By Vehicle

To leave a vehicle at the lower gondola terminal, where this trip ends, drive Banff Avenue south through downtown Banff. Cross the Bow River bridge and turn left onto Spray Avenue. In 100 m (110 yd), bear right on Mountain Avenue, signed for the hot springs. Follow it 3.3 km (2 mi) to the Sulphur Mtn gondola parking lot, at 1600 m (5250 ft).

To reach the trailhead, where you'll start hiking, drive back to the Bow River Bridge. But don't cross the bridge. Proceed straight on Cave Avenue and continue 1.1 km (0.7 mi) to the Cave and Basin parking lot. The trail departs the southwest corner, at 1390 m (4560 ft).

On Foot

Follow the paved path southwest to the Cave and Basin complex. The hot springs pool here is now closed. Go around the right (north) side of the stone building, as if heading to Sundance Canyon. Arrive at a signed junction in 15 minutes. The Marsh Loop forks right. Proceed straight (northwest) on pavement and curve west along the Bow River.

After hiking a level 2.7 km (1.6 mi) in about 30 minutes, reach a three-way junction. Right (west) is the Brewster Creek trail, which accesses the Healy Creek trail. Straight (south) leads to Sundance Canyon. For Sulphur Mtn, go left (southeast) and begin ascending the dirt road. Five minutes farther, pass a trail forking left (northeast) signed for Banff. Continue straight (south-southeast) up the road.

At 1550 m (5084 ft), about 45 minutes from the trailhead, the road turns sharply east-southeast. A long, steady ascent ensues. The Sundance Range is visible southwest. The Massive Range is west-northwest, towering above Hwy 1. Fifteen minutes farther, Mt. Louis is visible north-northwest through Cory Pass (Trip 40). About 1½ hours from the trailhead, the road is no longer tree-lined, so views are constant.

Reach the **summit ridge boardwalk** at 8 km (5 mi). Total hiking time: 2¾ hours at a moderate pace. A couple-minute detour left, up the stairs, will grant you the optimal view from 2270-m (7446-ft) **Sanson Peak**. The stone building here is an historic meteorological station. West-southwest is 2931-m (9615-ft) Mt. Bourgeau (Trip 4), at the south end of the Massive Range. East is 2949-m (9673-ft) Mt. Rundle (Trip 61). Even the icy summit of 3543-m (11,621-ft) Mt. Temple (Trip 5) is distinguishable way northwest.

Sanson Peak was named after meteorologist Norman Sanson, who hiked from Banff townsite to the top of Sulphur Mtn more than a thousand times between 1896 and 1931 In winter he trudged up in snowshoes. The gondola wasn't built until 1959.

Follow the boardwalk generally southeast to the **upper gondola terminal**, at 8.5 km (5.3 mi), 2260 m (7413 ft). Ideally, the gondola hasn't stopped for the evening and you can enjoy the ride down. Should you hike down, either by choice or necessity, the trail starts southeast of the terminal. Via moderately-graded switchbacks, it descends 660 m (2165 ft) in 5.6 km (3.5 mi) to the **lower gondola terminal**, at 1600 m (5250 ft).

If there's sufficient daylight, minimal snow atop Sulphur Mtn, and adequate time before the gondola stops, the trail departing the terminal's south side is worth hiking. It leads 0.8 km (0.5 mi) south-southeast, undulating through subalpine forest along the rocky ridge. You'll descend about 30 m (98 ft) and ascend about 60 m (197 ft) before gaining a new vantage atop steeply tilting limestone slabs. The view is only slightly different, but the setting is more tranquil and natural.

Banff townsite below Cascade Mountain, from Sulphur Mountain

TRIP 121

Lake Minnewanka

LOCATION	Banff National Park, northeast of Banff townsite
ROUND TRIP	15.6 km (9.7 mi) to Aylmer Pass junction and first lakeshore campground
ELEVATION GAIN	100 m (328 ft)
KEY ELEVATIONS	trailhead 1482 m (4860 ft), highpoint 1527 m (5009 ft)
HIKING TIME	3½ to 5 hours
DIFFICULTY	easy
MAPS	page 525; Gem Trek *Banff & Mt. Assiniboine*

OPINION

Here in the Rockies, keen local hikers ache most of the year. Not from hiking, but from the unfulfilled desire to hike. Snowdrifts that could bury an NBA team keep hiking season cruelly short. Only after mid-July can you expect rock, not ice, to be crunching beneath your boots on the high passes.

But there are a few special places where snow-free hiking is both possible and enjoyable in May. One of them is Lake Minnewanka, the 22-km (13.6-mi) long, fiord-like lake just northeast of Banff townsite.

Clinging to the lake's forested north shore is a trail where even a trifling effort rewards you with grand scenery. The enormous lake is often in view. So are the shriekingly steep cliffs of Mt. Inglismaldie, above the south shore. Yet the elevation gain is minimal for the first 7.8 km (4.8 mi), making this hike suitable for anyone.

Striding a mere 2.5 km (1.6 mi), or about 30 minutes, will earn you an immense panorama. Carry on and you'll soon have opportunities to scramble down to the rocky shore where you can appreciate the view in solitude, savour your bison sandwich and ginger snaps, and, if it's sunny, soak up your minimum daily requirement of Vitamin D.

It's cloudy? Rainy? Of all the Banff-area trails, this one's the most enjoyable in foul weather. Even when low-flying clouds are banging into the peaks, the lovely lake remains in view because it's below the trail.

Minnewanka, by the way, is a Stoney Indian name meaning *Water of the Spirits.* According to legend, the lake is haunted by fish-people. Aboriginal artifacts discovered here suggest human habitation 11,000 years ago.

The original, much smaller body of water was dammed to create today's reservoir. It's the only hydroelectric power source in a Canadian national park. Despite its vast surface area, the lake is only 97 m (318 ft) deep.

Energetic hikers will reach a lakeside campground in about two hours, at 7.8 km (4.8 mi). After a leisurely rest in this grassy, park-like setting, you can turn back or push on.

Clematis

Sunbathing in May at Lake Minnewanka

Stewart Canyon. More images of Lake Minnewanka begin on page 423.

Aylmer lookout is an hour and fifteen minutes farther, although just five minutes in that direction will greatly expand your view. It's a stiff, 562-m (1844-ft) climb to the fire-lookout site atop a bluff. Read Trip 117 for further directions.

FACT

By Vehicle

From the Banff Park entrance near Canmore, drive the Trans-Canada Hwy northwest toward Banff townsite. Take the first Banff townsite exit (right), also signed for Lake Minnewanka. At the first stop sign, turn right (north) onto the Lake Minnewanka Road. Left (south) passes under the Trans-Canada and continues into the townsite.

Or, from Banff townsite, drive Banff Avenue (the main street) north out of town. After it passes under the Trans-Canada Hwy, it becomes the Lake Minnewanka Road.

From either approach, starting near the Trans-Canada underpass, drive the Lake Minnewanka Road north 5.5 km (3.4 mi) to the large, paved parking lot at 1482 m (4860 ft), just above the lake's west end.

The Lake Minnewanka Road is blocked? No worries. The trailhead is accessible year-round, despite the November 15 through April 15 road closure. Immediately before the barricade, turn right. Follow signs for Two Jack Lake. Beyond the Two Jack Lake Picnic Area, the road reaches the shore of Lake Minnewanka. Proceed northwest across the dam, into the parking lot described above.

On Foot

Walk the paved service road generally east-northeast past the boat dock, picnic area, and three cooking shelters. Pavement ends and the signed trail begins at 0.6 km (0.4 mi). Proceed north on the wide, level, forest-enclosed path.

In about 20 minutes, at 1.5 km (0.9 mi), cross a bridge over **Stewart Canyon**. The Cascade River enters the lake via this fault in the limestone bedrock. Above the far (east) bank, turn left. Pass a left spur leading up-canyon (northwest). Bear right and begin ascending.

Soon curve right (south-southeast). Cascade Mountain is visible right (west-southwest) through a forest of lodgepole and limber pine, Douglas fir, birch, and aspen. Look for lavender clematis here. Ahead, the trees were scorched by a controlled burn during the summer of 2003, but you'll quickly exit the blackened area.

At 2.5 km (1.6 mi), 1527 m (5009 ft), reach a **highpoint** overlooking the lake. Mt. Rundle, across the Bow Valley, dominates the southern horizon. The trail now traverses rocky ground, curving northeast up the lake. A gentle descent ensues. For the next 20 minutes, the lake is constantly in sight. So is rugged Mt. Inglismaldie, above the south shore.

Continuing through open forest, the trail is mostly level, except for brief ups and downs. Cross a series of streambeds (usually dry). About two hours from the parking lot, cross a footlog spanning **Aylmer Creek**. Just beyond, in a grassy clearing, reach signed **Aylmer Pass junction** at 7.8 km (4.8 mi), 1490 m (4887 ft).

Straight (east-northeast) continues along the lakeshore, passes three campgrounds, and reaches the lake's east end at 23 km (14.3 mi). Left (north) climbs to Aylmer lookout and pass (Trip 117). Right (southeast) soon enters **LM8 campground** and ends at the lakeshore in 0.4 km (0.25 mi). The campground has platform tables, a fire pit, firewood, and bearproof food storage.

The campground and the trail to Aylmer Pass are closed annually, July 15 to Sept. 30, due to bears in the area.

TRIP 122

Glacier Lake

LOCATION	Banff National Park
ROUND TRIP	18 km (11.2 mi) to 27 km (16.7 mi)
ELEVATION GAIN	475 m (1558 ft)
KEY ELEVATIONS	trailhead 1450 m (4756 ft) highpoint 1680 m (5510 ft), lake 1435 m (4707 ft)
HIKING TIME	5 to 8 hours or overnight
DIFFICULTY	easy
MAPS	page 521; Gem Trek *Bow Lake & Sask. Crossing*

OPINION

Glacier Lake is big: 4.5 km (2.8 mi) long, 1 km (0.6 mi) wide. The water looks like turquoise paint, due to the rock flour (glacial dust) in suspension. The icy wall of Lyell Glacier on Division Mtn is just 7 km (4.3 mi) beyond the lake. The immense cliffs of Mt. Outram above the south shore are dramatic. Nevertheless, in mid-summer, when the Canadian Rockies' grandest scenery is most accessible, Glacier Lake isn't a sufficiently compelling spectacle to warrant the long, tedious, forested approach.

In shoulder season, however, when it's a gift simply to be walking in the mountains, Glacier Lake is a superior destination. Then, you might welcome striding the long approach. Spring is when it's most appealing. The snowpack melts quickly in this broad, sunny valley. The sights and sounds of new life lend an energizing aura to the otherwise dull forest. The relatively level trail gives winter-weak muscles a gentle re-introduction to the demands of hiking. You might even want to backpack here. Imagine waking up, alone, beside an impressive backcountry lake—in May. It could be an exhilarating way to inaugurate the season of adventure that lies ahead.

To gain an improved glacier-view, more fully appreciate the lake, and thus capitalize on your effort, hike the trail along the north shore. From the east end, where you arrive, it's an easy, mostly level, 9-km (5.6-mi) round trip to the west end. That boosts the trip's total mileage to 27 km (16.7 mi). Strong dayhikers will enjoy it. But only backpacking will grant you time to explore the river flats and moraines beyond the lake. Experienced routefinders can follow the braided Glacier River up-valley, toward Southeast Lyell Glacier.

The Glacier Lake environs are bear habitat. Black bear sightings are common. Be vigilant and make noise while hiking. Use the campground's bear-proof food storage if you stay overnight. Easily stolen food trains bears to think of people as meals on wheels. That endangers you, other hikers, and the bears, who will likely be shot by park wardens if they attack someone.

FACT

By Vehicle

From Saskatchewan River Crossing, where the David Thompson Hwy (11) intersects the Icefields Parkway (Hwy 93), drive the Parkway 1 km (0.6 mi) northwest. Turn left (southwest) into the trailhead parking area. Elevation: 1450 m (4756 ft).

On Foot

Head southwest on an old access road. Thin lodgepole pines, regrowth from a 1940 fire, allow views of surrounding mountains. Within ten minutes, a right (west) spur detours 10 m/yd to a viewpoint. A few of the major peaks are Mt. Murchison (southeast), Mt. Sarbach (south), Mt. Outram (southwest), Mt. Erasmus (west), and Mt. Wilson (north). All are over 3100 m (10,200 ft). Glacier Lake, not yet visible, is in the forested valley southwest, between Mt. Erasmus on the north and Mt. Outram on the south.

At 1.1 km (0.7 mi), 1412 m (4630 ft), cross a hefty bridge over the **North Saskatchewan River**. At 2.2 km (1.3 mi), enjoy the view left (south) over the braided Howse River to Mt. Sarbach. The trail eases down to the river's north bank. Gravel bars here provide a pleasant resting spot.

Continuing southwest, away from the river flats, the trail undulates through viewless forest. Cross four footbridges during the gentle ascent of a forested ridge. Reach a **highpoint** at 6.4 km (4 mi), 1680 m (5510 ft), then start a long gradual descent through yet more forest.

Just before arriving at Glacier Lake, a left fork leads southeast to intersect the Howse River trail. Bear right (west-southwest) on the main trail. At 9 km (5.6 mi), 1435 m (4707 ft), reach the northeast end of **Glacier Lake**. Fast hikers will be here in two hours. Southeast Lyell Glacier is visible west-southwest.

The trail continues along the north shore. The **campground** is at 9.2 km (5.7 mi). Reach bushy flats, where the Glacier River feeds the lake, at 13.5 km (8.4 mi). Within another 2 km (1.2 mi), the faint trail dwindles. Keen, experienced explorers can persist to the toe of Southeast Lyell Glacier, 20.5 km (12.7 mi) from the trailhead.

Wandering daisy

Glacier Lake

TRIP 123

Beaver, Summit and Jacques Lakes

LOCATION	Jasper National Park
ROUND TRIP	9.6 km (6 mi) to first Summit Lake 22.4 km (13.9 mi) to Jacques Lake
ELEVATION GAIN	77 m (253 ft) to first Summit Lake
KEY ELEVATIONS	trailhead 1450 m (4756 ft) first Summit Lake 1527 m (5010 ft) Jacques Lake 1495 m (4904 ft)
HIKING TIME	2½ to 3½ hours for first Summit Lake 5 to 7 hours for Jacques Lake
DIFFICULTY	easy
MAPS	page 509; Gem Trek *Jasper and Maligne Lake*

OPINION

The trail to Jacques Lake is about as level as this sentence. Likewise, the scenery fails to elicit emotional highs or lows. It's never thrilling. But it's not disappointing either. It simply offers enough views and variety to hold your interest. And it's as easy as any backpack trip in the Rockies. Strong striders can dayhike it.

You'll travel a long, narrow valley before reaching Jacques Lake deep in forest. En route you'll pass several lesser lakes—Beaver, the two Summit Lakes, and an unnamed fourth—and walk beside a creek. The trail is in trees much of the way, but you'll occasionally lift your eyes to the soaring sawtooth ridges of the Queen Elizabeth Ranges. What you're unlikely to see here is a crowd. This is a fine choice if you're seeking a quiet walk in the woods.

When the alplands are snow splattered in late fall, and you're wondering "what now?" Jacques could be the answer. The creek crossings beyond the second Summit Lake are insignificant then, and the entire valley is less muddy. Also keep this hike in mind for a rainy day. Even if clouds are banging into the peaks, you'll glimpse mountain walls. And the threat of a lightning strike in such a sheltered valley is minimal. Admittedly, the trail to Jacques is most enjoyable in summer, when the valley is idyllically green and warm breezes invite languorous lakeside lounging. But strong, adventurous hikers should be rocketing into the alpine zone then, fully relishing the Canadian Rockies' unique grandeur.

Though smaller, the Summit Lakes are as enjoyable as Jacques. Their pebble beaches are spacious. And the airy, cottonwood poplars ringing their shores are a

Beaver Lake and the Queen Elizabeth Ranges

welcome change from pines, especially in fall when the leaves are golden. On a sunny October afternoon, this is a good place to conceive the book you want to write, ponder names for your baby-to-be, list the qualities you want in a mate, or, if you're tired of thinking, watch the loons or Harlequin ducks play. The shallow Summit Lakes recede substantially by late summer. Curiously, no creek appears to connect them. An underground stream is the umbilical cord.

Beaver Lake is an ideal destination for parents eager to introduce toddlers to hiking. Adults can reach this first lake in 20 minutes. With an inquisitive little one meandering to check out leaves and rocks, it might take an hour or more. Since the trail is an old fire road to Beaver Lake, and beyond to the first Summit Lake, it's possible to push a stroller. If you want to test your child on a camping trip, backpack to the single tent site near Beaver Lake's south shore. Prior to leaving Jasper, rent one of the rowboats described below (see *Before your trip*), and you'll enjoy a wonderful outing.

Dayhikers should go at least as far as the first Summit Lake—about a three-hour round trip. The forest opens here. The meadow at the south shore affords views of the surrounding high country. In spring, you can expect a colourful wildflower display comprising yellow avens, lavendar bluebells, and pink Alberta rose.

The attraction of Jacques Lake is its wilderness atmosphere, not dramatic scenery. So if you feel like turning around at the first Summit Lake, do so without concern of missing a climactic destination. The view is more expansive at the first Summit Lake than it is at the second. It's still another hour through forest to

Jacques. And banish all thoughts of hiking from Jacques Lake over Merlin Pass to Hwy 16. It's a 30.2-km (18.7-mi) trudge almost entirely in trees. The pass itself is below timberline. The trail is sketchy and sloppy. Leave it to the mosquitoes and bears.

FACT

Before your trip

Want to captain a rowboat on Beaver Lake? Call Curries Guided Fishing: (780-852-5650). Visit them at Source for Sports, 406 Patricia Street, Jasper. The boats are locked on the lakeshore, so you'll have to get a key.

By Vehicle

From the junction with Connaught Drive at the north end of Jasper townsite, drive Hwy 16 northeast 1.8 km (1.1 mi). Turn right (east) onto Maligne Lake Road. It's signed for Jasper Park Lodge. Set your odometre to 0. Immediately cross the Athabasca River bridge. In 200 m (220 yd), go left for Maligne Lake. Continue to 27.5 km (17.1 mi) and turn left (north) into the Beaver Creek Picnic Area. It's across from the south end of Medicine Lake. Elevation: 1450 m (4756 ft).

On Foot

A gated fire road departs the northeast corner of the parking area. Follow it north. Cross the bridged creek. Soon pass a ranger cabin on the right. A few minutes farther, the road parallels the creek. It then ascends gently.

About seven minutes from the trailhead, the road levels, still heading generally north. The creek (about 21 m / 70 ft below the road) is audible. Within 20 minutes, having gained just 32 m (105 ft), reach the south end of **Beaver Lake** at 1.6 km (1 mi). There's a picnic table, fire pit and outhouse here, as well as the aforementioned rowboats.

The road continues north-northwest along the west shore for five minutes. It then pulls away from the water briefly before passing the lake's north end and heading northwest. An open willow patch unveils an impressive peak to the right (west).

Attain open views about an hour from the trailhead. The mountains behind you (southeast) are now visible, in addition to the sheer, gray, Queen Elizabeth Ranges nearby right (west) where a cascade cleaves a high gully. From here on, the road is narrower, more overgrown.

Reach a junction at 4.8 km (3 mi), 1527 m (5010 ft). The right fork, signed for the South Boundary Trail, continues past the Summit Lakes to Jacques Lake, but there's a quicker, more scenic option. Instead, proceed straight (slightly left) and soon arrive at the meadowy south end of the **first Summit Lake**. Visible up-valley (northwest) is 2820-m (9250-ft) Sirdar Mtn.

A faint path rounds the right (northeast) shore. This is the shortcut. When it fades at the north end of the first Summit Lake, simply continue northwest five minutes through forest to the smaller, narrower, second Summit Lake.

Prefer the official trail? From the meadowy south end of the first Summit Lake, retrace your steps to the junction. Follow the signed South Boundary Trail. It skirts the northeast side of the first Summit Lake, well back from the shore. Rough and narrow, it undulates through tight forest, crossing several streamlets (possibly dry

Summit Lake and the southeast end of the Colin Range

in fall). After descending from a small rise, reach the **second Summit Lake** at 6 km (3.7 mi). Fast hikers will arrive here about 20 minutes after leaving the junction.

Regardless which way you arrived at the second Summit Lake, if continuing to Jacques Lake, follow the South Boundary Trail northwest around the right (northeast) shore of the second Summit Lake.

At 7.4 km (4.6 mi) skirt left of yet another tiny lake, then face several minor stream crossings. The trail gradually bends northeast.

Reach a junction at 11 km (6.8 mi). Left (northwest) leads to Merlin Pass. Proceed straight to reach the south end of **Jacques Lake** at 11.2 km (7 mi), 1495 m (4904 ft). There's a campground 1 km (0.6 mi) farther, near the north end.

From Jacques Lake campground, the South Boundary Trail resumes northeast, enters the 2003 burn, then turns right (east-southeast) into **Rocky River Valley**. Upon reaching the Rocky River, the trail continues upstream, generally southeast. It exits the burn before the Rocky Pass junction. From there, it proceeds to Cairn (Southesk) Pass (Trip 99).

TRIP 124

Bear's Hump

LOCATION	Waterton Lakes National Park
ROUND TRIP	2.4 km (1.5 mi)
ELEVATION GAIN	238 m (780 ft)
HIKING TIME	45 minutes to 1½ hours
DIFFICULTY	easy
MAPS	page 503; Gem Trek *Waterton Lakes National Park*

OPINION

Resolute hikers, capable of trooping through the wilderness for days, tend to overlook the Bear's Hump, thinking it not worthy of their attention. Surely a short trail starting beside a visitor info centre is nothing but a token for sedentary tourists and tots with tiny attention spans, no? Nope, not this one. Though quick, easy and convenient, it leads to a sucker-punch panorama.

On the summit, you'll survey the entire length of Upper Waterton Lake, all 11 km (6.8 mi) of it, well into Montana's Glacier National Park. You'll also gain a greatly improved perspective of the surrounding mountains, as well as an aerial view of Waterton townsite.

The trail is superbly engineered. Switchbacks make what would otherwise be a steep ascent manageable for almost anyone who can walk around a city block. Just keep going at whatever pace is comfortable for you. Fit, fast trekkers will top out in 20 minutes, so the Bear's Hump can serve as pre-hike hors d'oeuvre, or post-hike dessert.

Waterton Park is known for being windy, so bring all the clothing you'll need to comfortably stay on top long enough to fully appreciate the magnificent scenery. If it's raining, the view will still be impressive, as long as the clouds aren't oppressively low. But if the wooden beams along the trail are wet, they'll be very slippery; don't step on them.

FACT

By Vehicle

From Hwy 5, turn onto the road entering Waterton Lakes National Park. Follow it southwest 8 km (5 mi), then turn right into the Visitor Info Centre parking lot, at 1300 m (4260 ft).

On Foot

The signed trail starts just above the parking lot, near the Visitor Info Centre. It's broad, smooth, well maintained all the way to the top. The switchbacking ascent leads generally southwest through open, mixed forest of spruce, pine, and birch. There are three benches along the way. Surmount the Bear's Hump at 1.2 km (0.7 mi), 1537 m (5040 ft). It's actually a bluff, composed of limestone and dolomite, on Mount

Bear's Hump is a low ridge (left) on Mt. Crandell.

Crandell's south ridge. You'll find two more benches here, in a broad, level patch of gravel surrounded by rock outcroppings.

Waterton townsite is visible below. The Prince of Wales Hotel is nearby west, on the promontory above the Bosporus, a narrow strait linking Middle and Upper Waterton lakes. The view extends south, down the length of Upper Waterton Lake, deep into the mountains. Cameron Creek, in the canyon southwest, is audible. Experienced scramblers can continue ascending the ridgecrest.

Prince of Wales Hotel

TRIP 125

Tunnel Mountain

LOCATION	Banff National Park
ROUND TRIP	4.8 km (3 mi)
ELEVATION GAIN	240 m (787 ft)
KEY ELEVATIONS	trailhead 1450 m (4756 ft), summit 1690 m (5543 ft)
HIKING TIME	1½ hours
DIFFICULTY	easy
MAPS	page 526; Gem Trek *Banff Up-Close*

OPINION

Purists look down their noses at Banff townsite as if it were a cancerous growth. It is too big, crowded and commercial, considering it's in a national park. But Banff still has charm. The setting is exquisite. Looking down your nose at it from the nearby summit of Tunnel Mtn is a fun, easy way to appreciate it.

The trailhead is less than a kilometre from the Banff Avenue tourist carnival. So you don't even need a car to escape the hubbub. No wonder the trail is so heavily used. Your best shot at solitude is, of course, evening or early morning.

You're not a hiker? Not a problem. Tunnel is more of a hill than a mountain, so the summit is an attainable goal for most people. Just don't try it in sandals or dress shoes. At least wear tennis shoes or runners. And though civilization is close, don't leave your brain behind. Carry water (there's none on the trail) and anything else you think you'll need.

You might wonder where the tunnel is. Well, the mountain got its name when Major A.B. Rogers, who originally routed the Canadian Pacific Railroad through Banff, inexplicably decided it should go directly beneath the mountain. But sanity prevailed. The tunnel was never blasted. The CPR simply laid their track on the north side of the valley. Nobody bothered changing the then meaningless name back to its native appellation: Sleeping Buffalo Mtn.

FACT

By Vehicle

From the intersection of Banff Avenue and Wolf Street (St. Paul's church is on the southeast corner), follow Wolf Street 0.5 km (0.3 mi) east to where it T's at the foot of Tunnel Mtn. Turn right on St. Julien Road, immediately bear left, and drive 0.4 km (0.25 mi) to the signed trailhead parking area on the left, at 1450 m (4756 ft).

To shorten the round-trip hike by 0.6 km (0.4 mi), keep driving through the Banff Centre. Turn left onto Tunnel Mtn Drive and proceed uphill. Park in the pull-out on your left, above the Banff Centre, at 2.5 km (1.5 mi). The Tunnel Mtn trail, which started below, crosses the road here.

Mt. Rundle beyond Tunnel Mountain

Banff Springs Hotel, from Tunnel Mountain trail

On Foot

From the lower trailhead, ascend the forested west slope of Tunnel Mtn. Cross Tunnel Mtn Drive at 0.3 (0.2 mi). The wide trail switchbacks up through open forest on the west side of the mountain. Near 2.2 km (1.3 mi) crest the ridge. Take a cautious look right (east) over the cliff. The Bow River is below. Mt. Rundle is southeast. Turn left (north) and resume the now gradual ascent.

At 2.4 km (1.5 mi), 1690 m (5543 ft), reach the summit: an open, rocky bluff. Looking west, you can see the Vermilion Lakes and the Massive Range. Banff townsite is 307 m (1007 ft) below. Cascade Mountain is directly north, Sulphur Mtn is south-southwest.

TRIP 126

Stoney Squaw

LOCATION	Banff National Park
ROUND TRIP	4.5 km (2.8 mi)
ELEVATION GAIN	184 m (604 ft)
KEY ELEVATIONS	trailhead 1700 m (5575 ft), summit 1884 m (6180 ft)
HIKING TIME	1½ hours
DIFFICULTY	easy
MAPS	page 524; Gem Trek *Banff Up-Close*

OPINION

Don't let crowded sidewalks be your lasting impression of Banff. Go hiking. You can do it, even if you have only a couple hours to spare. Even if you're a little too soft for a big adventure. This trail threads a monotonous forest, but it's short, easy, starts just minutes from Banff Avenue, and will earn you an aerial view of Banff townsite. Come here to meld with the scenery that makes this mountain town unique.

FACT

By Vehicle

From Banff townsite's west interchange on the Trans-Canada Hwy, ascend the switchbacking Mt. Norquay Road north 5.6 km (3.5 mi) to the ski area. The trail starts at the near (south) end of the lodge parking lot, in the right (southeast) corner. Elevation: 1700 m (5575 ft).

On Foot

From the kiosk, the trail ascends east into a dense forest of scrawny lodgepole pine. About 20 minutes up, at 1820 m (5971 ft), the trail fades in a small clearing on a rocky fin. Go east, descend 3 metres, and turn sharply left (north). The trail is again obvious.

Ten minutes farther, at 1850 m (6068 ft), overlook Banff townsite. Beyond it are Mt. Rundle (southeast), the Spray River Valley (south-southeast), Sulphur Mtn (south), and the Sundance Range (south-southwest).

Within 35 minutes, top-out on Stoney Squaw at 2.2 km (1.4 mi), 1884 m (6180 ft). The summit affords a view north-northeast to the south face of 2997-m (9830-ft) Cascade Mountain, and east across the Bow Valley to the Fairholme Range.

To loop back to the trailhead, angle left from where you faced Cascade Mountain. Descend northwest on bare rock through a natural passage between trees. The trail is soon distinct.

About 20 minutes below, intersect a grassy road at 4 km (2.5 mi), 1725 m (5658 ft). Go left (south) 30 paces, curve right (west-southwest), and descend toward the green roof visible below. Go left of the ski lodge at 4.3 km (2.7 mi), enter the parking lot, and proceed 200 metres south to the trailhead kiosk.

TRIP 127
Bow River

LOCATION	Banff townsite, Banff National Park
ROUND TRIP	3.4 km (2.1 mi) to 6.2 km (3.8 mi)
ELEVATION GAIN	45 m (148 ft) to 110 m (361 ft)
KEY ELEVATIONS	trailhead 1415 m (4641 ft), Bow River 1370 m (4494 ft) Tunnel Mountain campground 1435 m (4707 ft)
HIKING TIME	1 to 2 hours
DIFFICULTY	very easy
MAPS	Gem Trek *Banff Up-Close*

OPINION

Like flags representing the animal kingdom, street signs in Banff townsite feature names of local creatures. You'll see streets honouring gophers, wolves, lynx, bears, elk, moose, rabbits, cougars, deer, squirrels, martens, beavers, muskrats, otters, lynx, caribou, wolverines, buffalo.

This feral street-name theme reminds us to honour the animal elements of our soul. It subliminally suggests we break from buzzy Banff Avenue and, in four-legged-fashion, prowl the serene forests and meadows, gaze at the great upheavals of rock, and let our overly-complex human nature evanesce into the mountain air.

You can do it in as little as a couple hours, without driving to a distant trailhead. Begin at the edge of Banff townsite, on the Bow River trail. You'll quickly enter a surprisingly natural setting and enjoy scenery worthy of a backpack trip.

After a short descent to the river, you'll follow it downstream, staying close to the bank. The trail is so easy that to say you "hike" it is an exaggeration. This is really just a lovely walk. Hiking boots are not necessary. Walking shoes will suffice.

Hoodoos above the Bow River

You'll soon admire the east face of Tunnel Mountain (Trip 125). Most tourists see only the west slope, which rises gently from town. Here, Tunnel is craggy, sheer, less like a hill, more like a mountain.

The Bow River trail's dominating sight is the sharp, northwest prow of Mt. Rundle and its long, sheer, north face: very impressive. You'll witness it, plus many of the townsite's other guardian peaks, from a perspective lacking signs of civilization, thus giving you the impression you're deep in the wilderness.

The river itself, however, is the prime attraction here. If it's a hot summer day, you might courageously splash—oh, perhaps thigh deep—into the frigid water. Yes, there's a sandy beach beside a narrow, slow channel.

For most people, the riverside meadow about midway along the trail serves as destination and turn-around point. Bring a picnic lunch. Bring a foam pad to sit on. Bring a little imagination, a lot of patience, and summon your totem animal.

FACT

By Vehicle

From the corner of Banff Avenue and Buffalo Street, drive east (toward Tunnel Mountain) on Buffalo. Ignoring the streets to the left, proceed on Buffalo as it curves right (southeast) and ascends. Just before it veers left (north), turn right (south) into the Bow Falls viewpoint parking lot at 1.2 km (0.7 mi), 1415 m (4641 ft).

On Foot

From the far (south) end of the parking lot, enter forest and descend steps to a signed fork. Go left (northeast). Begin a short, sharp descent.

The trail soon levels among big Douglas firs. Fork right (east-northeast) to stay near the Bow River. Two minutes ahead, a right spur ends at a **quiet channel** of the river. One minute farther downstream is a **sandy beach** and deep pool at a slow bend in the channel—an ideal place to cool off and relax on a hot day.

A couple minutes beyond the sandy beach, the trail reaches the **main channel of the Bow River**. Elevation: 1370 m (4494 ft). From here on, the trail leads generally north-northeast all the way to Tunnel Mountain campground.

Left (north), Tunnel Mountain rises abruptly from the forest. Right (southeast), on the river's far bank, is the Banff Springs golf course and immediately beyond is the nearly vertical wall of Mt. Rundle.

Ascend a staircase where the trail rises over a riverside bluff. Attain a surprisingly panoramic view encompassing the Fairholme Range ahead (east and northeast), Sulphur Mountain right (south-southwest), and the Spray River Valley (between Mt. Rundle and Sulphur Mountain).

Shortly after descending to the river bank, enter a spacious **meadow** at 1.7 km (1.1 mi). In summer, lavender harebells are prolific in this football-field-sized expanse of grass between the river and the forest. You can now appreciate the sheer, east face of Tunnel Mountain and gaze north to Cascade Mountain. Most people turn around here, thus completing a 3.4-km (2.1-mi) round trip.

From the meadow, the trail pulls away from the river and begins a sustained ascent. Ignore the left (north) fork, which curves left (west) to access hotels near the junction of Tunnel Mountain Drive and Tunnel Mountain Road. Proceed straight (north-northeast).

Intersect **Tunnel Mountain Road** at 3.1 km (1.9 mi), 1435 m (4707 ft). Swift striders will arrive here 45 minutes after departing the Bow Falls viewpoint parking lot, but most people will take at least an hour.

Directly across the road is the Tunnel Mountain campground (village 2) entrance. The trail continues right (generally east), following the road 1.5 km (0.9 mi) to the hoodoos trailhead parking lot. From there, a 0.8-km (0.5-mi) round-trip trail grants an overview of the hoodoos.

TRIP 128

C-Level Cirque

LOCATION	Banff National Park
ROUND TRIP	8.4 km (5.2 mi)
ELEVATION GAIN	455 m (1495 ft)
KEY ELEVATIONS	trailhead 1465 m (4805 ft), cirque 1950 m (6396 ft)
HIKING TIME	2 to 3 hours, more for exploring
DIFFICULTY	easy
MAPS	page 525; Gem Trek *Banff Up-Close*

OPINION

The guttural chanting of Tibetan monks..."looohww, looohww, looohww..." would seem appropriate in this austere cirque. For the rest of us less elevated incarnates, it's a great place to holler something silly and listen to the echo bounce back. Or stand in humble silence, hoping this small but affecting mountainscape will nudge us closer to enlightenment.

It's a short hike requiring little effort. Even going part way, to the Lake Minnewanka vantage, is worthwhile. You can also see Mt. Rundle, Canmore, the Bow Valley, and the august peaks of the Fairholme Range. The cirque itself was long ago scooped by a glacier from the sheer east wall of Cascade Mtn.

En route you'll pass the remains (mine shafts, buildings, tailings) from an early 1900s anthracite coal operation. The name C Level refers to the highest elevation at which miners worked the mountain. They lived in the former town of Bankhead, population 1,000, near the present-day picnic area and trailhead.

Ignore the mining mess and instead study the calypso orchids, blue clematis, and violets that splash the forest with colour in June. Later, usually in early July, yellow glacier lilies chase the snow from the cirque basin.

Allow an extra half hour for a round trip along the cirque's right edge, to a higher viewpoint. Or, if you've never seen a marmot, pull up a rock slab and sit still; they're likely to cavort for you here.

FACT

By Vehicle

From Banff townsite's east interchange on the Trans-Canada Hwy 1, drive the Lake Minnewanka Road north 3.5 km (2.2 mi), then turn left into the Upper Bankhead Picnic Area. The trail departs the west side of the parking lot, at 1465 m (4805 ft).

Lake Minnewanka, from C-Level Cirque trail

On Foot

Ascend through dense forest. In about 15 minutes, reach a junction and go left. A minute later, at 1.3 km (0.8 mi), take the short spur trail right. Standing atop the mine tailings, you can see Lake Minnewanka (northeast), the Fairholme Range (southeast), and Mt. Rundle (south).

Back on the main trail, continue north. Soon, stay left where there's a fenced mine shaft on the right. You'll pass others. At 1830 m (6000 ft), about 45 minutes up, the trail is more engaging as it traverses southwest across a steep slope, through aspen, lodgepole pine, and big spruce trees.

After about 1 hour of hiking, enter the cirque at 4.2 km (2.6 mi), 1950 m (6396 ft). Looking east, above and beyond the south end of Lake Minnewanka, you can see Mts. Inglismaldie, Girouard and Peechee. Looking southeast over tiny Two Jack Lake, you can see the high ridges and peaks of Princess Margaret Mtn and the long, great wall of Mt. Charles Stewart. A small, but well-trod trail continues upward along the cirque's right edge, to a superior viewpoint on a knoll.

TRIP 129

Johnston Canyon / Inkpots

LOCATION	Banff National Park
ROUND TRIP	11.8 km (7.3 mi)
ELEVATION GAIN	215 m (705 ft)
KEY ELEVATIONS	trailhead 1430 m (4690 ft) Inkpots 1645 m (5395 ft)
HIKING TIME	2 to 4 hours
DIFFICULTY	easy
MAPS	page 520; Gem Trek *Banff & Mt. Assiniboine*

OPINION

Johnston Canyon is flooded every summer—with windshield tourists. But they're here because the chasms and cascades are fantastic. So avoid the crowd, but don't miss the canyon. Come in shoulder season. Try as early as May, as late as mid-November. If there's no snow, you can extend the canyon walk into a hike. Continue beyond the falls to the Inkpots, where cold springs bubble to the surface, and views of Johnston Creek valley open up.

Lower Johnston Falls

FACT

By Vehicle

Drive Hwy 1A (Bow Valley Parkway) to Johnston Canyon. It's 6.5 km (4 mi) southeast of Castle Village (across the Bow River from Castle Junction), or 17.5 km (10.9 mi) northwest of the Trans-Canada junction near Banff townsite. Parking is northeast of the highway, across the creek from the resort, at 1430 m (4690 ft).

On Foot

Cross the bridge over Johnston Creek, turn right, and follow the path upstream above the west bank. Ascending the narrow canyon, you'll cross steel catwalks attached to rock walls. Reach the lower falls at 1.1 km (0.7 mi). Pass two cascades at 1.8 km (1.1 mi). Paved path continues to the 30-m (100-ft) **upper falls** at 2.7 km (1.7 mi), 1550 m (5084 ft).

Beyond the falls, the trail climbs to merge at 3.2 km (2 mi) with an old access road from Moose Meadows. Stay right at this junction. Ascend steeply through forest on the old road. Descend to the **Inkpots** at 5.9 km (3.7 mi), 1645 m (5395 ft). (See photo on page 371.) The trail continues northwest up Johnston Creek valley (Trip 101)—a multi-day backpack trip.

TRIP 130

Castle Lookout

LOCATION	Banff National Park
ROUND TRIP	7.4 km (4.6 mi)
ELEVATION GAIN	520 m (1705 ft)
HIKING TIME	3 to 3½ hours
DIFFICULTY	easy
MAPS	Page 520; Gem Trek *Banff & Mt. Assiniboine*; Castle Mountain 82 O/5

OPINION

As mountain wildflowers go, the prairie crocus is huge. It's eager, too, bursting out of the earth long before other spring posies have awakened in the Canadian Rockies. Though ambitious, it's not conservative. It has flamboyant lavender petals surrounding a yellow pompon of anthers. Also known as a pasque flower, it grows on dry slopes pummeled by sunshine. A prairie crocus promises snow-free hiking. And by May you'll find these beautiful harbingers of spring lining the trail to Castle Lookout—one of Banff Park's earliest available hiking destinations.

Prairie crocus

The lookout, constructed in the 1940s and abandoned in the 70s, is now gone. But the panorama it afforded—up and down the Bow Valley, and through Vermilion Pass into Kootenay Park—is as splendid as ever, well worth the steep ascent. Views begin about half an hour from the trailhead. You'll see a western horizon crowded with peaks that are especially showy when the high-elevation snowpack remains deep. You'll also see Castle Mountain's towering, astonishingly complex ramparts at close range.

Ascending the castle's southwest flank, you'll begin on an uninspiring old road. It doesn't narrow to a trail until you're more than halfway up. Another drawback to this hike is that Hwy 1A, the Canadian National Railway, and the Trans-Canada Hwy all graze the castle premises, so dissonant metal and rubber compete with the sounds of nature, and the sight of these broad, arterial scars degrade the scenery. But when you're storming the bastille in mid-April, you'll be smiling nevertheless.

Western horizon from Castle Lookout trail. Mt. Temple is far right.

Castle Mountain, above lookout trail

FACT

By Vehicle

From Lake Louise village, drive Hwy 1A (Bow Valley Parkway) southeast 20 km (12.4 mi). From Castle Junction village, drive Hwy 1A northwest 5 km (3 mi). From either approach, turn north into the parking lot, at 1460 m (4790 ft).

On Foot

Follow the old road departing the north end of the parking lot, right of the info kiosk. Begin a steady, moderate ascent through a forest of pine and spruce. Overall, your general direction of travel will remain east. At 1645 m (5396 ft), about 15 minutes up, pass the remains of a **cabin**.

The road narrows to **trail** at 2 km (1.2 mi), 1748 m (5733 ft)—about 30 minutes up for strong striders. A couple minutes farther, attain the first view across the Bow Valley. Left (south-southwest) is Storm Mtn. The peaks of Kootenay National Park are southwest, beyond Vermilion Pass. The cirque cupping Taylor Lake (Trip 42) is west. The peak behind it rises above Consolation Lakes (Trip 43). Glacier-hatted Mt. Temple is west-northwest.

Traverse open slopes, then switchback upward among rock outcroppings. At 1915 m (6280 ft) cross a creeklet in a steep, narrow **gorge** beneath Castle Mountain's fantastic turrets. After hiking 3.7 km (2.3 mi) in about an hour, arrive at the 1980-m (6495-ft) perch where the **Castle Mountain Lookout** once stood. The remaining cement foundation now serves as a bench. The panorama extends east-southeast to Mt. Ishbel, in the Sawback Range, and southeast to the Sundance Range, near Banff townsite.

TRIP 131

Juniper Loop

LOCATION	Kootenay National Park
ROUND TRIP	7.2 km (4.5 mi)
ELEVATION GAIN	227 m (745 ft)
KEY ELEVATIONS	trailhead 945 m (3100 ft) highpoint 1100 m (3608 ft)
HIKING TIME	1½ to 2 hours
DIFFICULTY	easy
MAP	Gem Trek *Kootenay National Park*

OPINION

Convenience and wilderness are mutually exclusive. On the Juniper Loop, for example, you can buy an ice cream cone at a snack bar. But your constant companion on this trail is a busy highway. It's usually audible and frequently visible.

Even highway-shunning hikers, however, occasionally appreciate convenience. The Juniper Loop is snow-free much of the year, due to its location on the far western edge of the Rockies, barely inside Kootenay National Park. It's possible to hike here as early as May or as late as the end of November. The trail is within walking distance of the Redstreak campground and Radium hotels. The loop is long enough, with sufficient elevation gain, to meet most people's minimum daily exercise requirement. If you're a runner, you'll find the smooth path ideal for a vigorous workout with little risk of ankle injury.

This convenient little hike also offers scenic variety. You'll drop into an intimate canyon, cross lovely Sinclair Creek, ascend an open forest of Rocky Mountain juniper and Douglas fir, attain an impressive view across the Columbia Valley, and wind through cool nooks shaded by western red cedar.

Walk the loop clockwise, as described below. If it's a hot summer day (when you really should be deeper in the mountains enjoying a more adventurous trip), hike counterclockwise so you ascend the shadier, cooler, south side of the canyon.

FACT

By Vehicle

From Radium townsite, drive Hwy 93 northeast. Proceed only 100 m (110 yd) past Kootenay National Park's south entrance. From the Radium hot springs pools, drive Hwy 93 southwest 1 km (0.6 mi). From either approach, turn into the signed trailhead pullout on the north side of the highway, at 945 m (3100 ft). It's within view of the park entrance.

On Foot

Descend the steps from the trailhead pullout. Switchback down into Sinclair Creek canyon among cedars and Douglas firs. Cedars, unusual in this dry region, are sustained here by the moist canyon microclimate.

Within five minutes reach a fork at 898 m (2945 ft) beside **Sinclair Creek**. Right (southeast) is a short spur to the base of Sinclair Falls. The main trail is left (northwest).

Fathom this: salmon used to migrate up tiny Sinclair Creek. They annually travelled 800 km (500 mi) from the Columbia River, until the construction of Grand Coulee Dam forever quashed their heroic upstream ritual.

On the main trail, cross the bridged creek and begin a switchbacking ascent. In about 20 minutes, overlook the Sinclair Canyon narrows. A bit farther, at 975 m (3198 ft), gaze across the Columbia Valley to the Purcell Mountains.

About 15 minutes farther, a level respite allows you to appreciate the views. Your descent route above the far canyon wall is now visible. Soon turn sharply left and ascend to 1100 m (3608 ft).

Contour among Douglas firs for about four minutes. Attain a view of the red-orange cliffs of the Redwall Fault. Then begin a switchbacking descent. Near the bottom, follow the main trail left.

At 4 km (2.5 mi), 1040 m (3411 ft), about 50 minutes to an hour from the trailhead, intersect the paved Radium Hot Springs Lodge road. Follow it down, cross the highway, and proceed into to the **pool complex**.

The trail resumes at the southwest corner of the main pool building, just past the toilets, across a short cement bridge. A sign here states that the trailhead is now 3 km (1.9 mi) distant. Ascend into cedar forest.

Sinclair Canyon

In a few minutes, enter **Place of Silence Peace Park** in a nook shaded by cedars at 1065 m (3493 ft). Benches here invite you to sit and contemplate the wisdom of a commemorative plaque: "Keep peace within yourself, then you can bring peace to others." The trail contours beyond.

About 15 minutes from the hot springs, pass a small utility building in a level, grassy clearing. Stay right (west) on the main trail and descend. Two minutes farther, a left (southwest) spur accesses a viewpoint and continues into Redstreak campground. Bear right (northwest) on the main trail and descend a staircase.

Fast walkers will intersect the **highway** about 35 minutes after leaving the hot springs. Cross to the sidewalk on the north side and turn left to quickly arrive at the trailhead pullout.

TRIP 132

Dog Lake

LOCATION	Kootenay National Park
ROUND TRIP	6.9 km (4.3 mi)
ELEVATION GAIN	195 m (640 ft)
HIKING TIME	2 hours
DIFFICULTY	easy
MAP	Gem Trek *Kootenay National Park*

OPINION

Most eagles spend 90% of their lives in semi-starvation. Their ability to tolerate hunger enables them to survive as strict carnivores. You might spot one of these ascetic birds here in late fall, when they come to feast on landlocked Kokanee salmon spawning in the Kootenay River. Watch for them in treetops above the riverbank.

In early June, look down instead of up. Eight species of orchids flourish here: some on the island between the bridges spanning the river; others throughout the forest.

Another noteworthy feature of this trip is the ancient, giant Douglas firs. Such an abundance of huge trees is rare in the Rocky Mountain parks.

But the real attraction of this hike is the lack of snow for probably eight months a year. Scenically, the trip doesn't register on the applause-o-metre. The awesome Goodsir Towers are visible at one point, but they're far, far north. And the soft summits of the Mitchell Range rise just beyond the placid lake. But all else is as uninspiring as the name Dog Lake. Compared to Twin Lakes (Trip 41), or even Boom Lake (Trip 65), Dog is a mongrel. But when you're blithely booting along here, while most trails require mushing, comparisons are irrelevant.

Mitchell Range, above Dog Lake

FACT

By Vehicle

From Kootenay Park's south entrance, near Radium, drive Hwy 93 northeast 26.5 km (16.5 mi) to the signed trailhead access on the right.

From the Continental Divide at Vermilion Pass, drive Hwy 93 generally south about 67 km (41.6 mi) through Kootenay Park. Slow down at McLeod Meadows campground. Continue 0.5 km (0.3 mi) beyond it, to the signed trailhead access on the left.

From either approach, proceed 250 m (275 yd) to the parking lot. The trail starts left of the picnic shelter, at 1158 m (3870 ft).

You're staying at McLeod Meadows? Tag onto the Dog Lake trail at the back of the campground. Head to the G loop. Walk a few paces past the historic McLeod Meadows Theatre. Turn left (northeast) onto the trail entering the woods.

Calypso orchid

On Foot

From the picnic shelter, follow the trail north across a bridged creeklet, then northeast. In a few minutes, cross a road that passes through McLeod campground. Proceed over two bridges spanning the **Kootenay River**.

On the river's east bank, a steady-but-moderate ascent leads to a fire road at 0.9 km (0.5 mi). Cross the road and proceed on trail among lodgepole pine, white spruce, and a few big Douglas firs. In June, you can expect to see red-orange western wood lilies.

Crest the trail's 1290-m (4231-ft) highpoint at 2 km (1.2 mi), then descend. Reach the marshy north shore of **Dog Lake** at 2.6 km (1.6 mi), 1225 m (4018 ft). Approach quietly and you might spy a moose, a beaver, or a pair of Canadian geese.

Most hikers turn around here. But there's a junction near a bridged **creek** at the lake's north end. Right (east) across the bridge, accesses the north shore. Straight (north), initially paralleling the creek's west bank, leads north-northwest 1.2 km (0.7 mi) to another small marshy lake, where you can opt for a circuitous return and lengthen your hike by 1.7 km (1.1 mi).

Reach a junction just shy of the **second lake**. Right continues north around the lake's east shore. Left leads generally south onto the old fire road that you crossed earlier while hiking the trail to Dog Lake. Where it intersects the trail, in 2.2 km (1.4 mi), you're again on familiar ground. Turn right and retrace your steps across the Kootenay River bridges to the trailhead.

TRIP 133

Wapta Falls

LOCATION	Yoho National Park
ROUND TRIP	4.8 km (3 mi)
ELEVATION GAIN	45 m (150 ft)
HIKING TIME	1 to 2 hours
DIFFICULTY	easy
MAP	McMurdo 82 N/2

OPINION

Bow Falls near Banff townsite? Just a pretty cascade. The torrential cataract on the Kicking Horse River? Voluminous. Savage. Frightening. The setting has the appearance of raw wilderness, which dials up the emotional effect of watching the water pound over a 30-m (100-ft) escarpment.

The trail to Wapta Falls is short, virtually level. It's just long enough to be a good before- or after-dinner leg stretcher. In foul weather, combine this with the Emerald River (Trip 134) for an enjoyable half-day outdoors. Descend to the lower viewpoint to fully feel the water's awesome power.

FACT

By Vehicle

Drive the Trans-Canada Hwy east 5 km (3 mi) from Yoho Park's West Gate, or southwest 25 km (15.5 mi) from Field. Just west of Chancellor Peak campground, where the highway curves radically, turn south onto the Wapta Falls dirt access road. Follow it 1.8 km (1.1 mi) to the trailhead parking area at road's end. Elevation: 1125 m (3690 ft).

On Foot

Head south on an old road. Near 1 km (0.6 mi) it tapers to trail. Reach the upper viewpoint on the edge of a precipice. There's a chain-link fence and a huge sign here, at 2.4 km (1.5 mi). A trail drops right to the lower viewpoint. Descend one minute, then turn left at the hiker sign to arrive at the lower viewpoint in another minute. Returning north to the trailhead, you can see Mt. Hunter (Trip 70) northwest.

Wapta Falls

TRIP 134

Emerald River

LOCATION	Yoho National Park
SHUTTLE TRIP	8.2 km (5.1 mi) from Emerald Lake to Natural Bridge
ELEVATION CHANGE	170-m (558-ft) gain, 275-m (900-ft) loss
KEY ELEVATIONS	trailhead 1312 m (4303 ft) confluence 1172 m (3845 ft) Natural Bridge 1207 m (3960 ft)
HIKING TIME	2 to 3 hours
DIFFICULTY	easy
MAPS	page 508; Gem Trek *Lake Louise & Yoho*; Golden 82 N/8

OPINION

Disappointment. Intrigue. Happy ending. There you go. That's the short version of the Emerald River story. Now here's the long version.

The start disappoints because you'll enter an unremarkable forest, skirt a small clearcut, then march into more scruffy forest strewn with deadfall. You won't reach the Emerald River (technically a mere creek) for an hour.

That's where it gets intriguing. The trail shadows the river. You'll see inviting places to drop your pack and relax beside the water. By mid-May, you'll notice Calypso orchids—fantastic beacons of spring—blooming in hothouse profusion. The massive peaks of the Ottertail Range are soon visible ahead. Then the river plummets into a canyon.

The trail gives chase, quickly dropping you to a revelatory sight: the confluence of the Emerald, Kicking Horse and Amiskwi rivers. The names suggest beauty, wildness, and mystery—qualities that any sensitive soul will observe and revel in here.

When we first saw the aquamarine Kicking Horse flowing through a chaotic boulder garden, our reaction was "Wow, now *that's* a river." When we arrived at the gravel beach on the bank of the Amiskwi, our reaction was to stop, drop, sunbathe and snooze. Happy ending, indeed.

From the confluence, it's only a short distance to the Natural Bridge parking lot. So you could skip the plot, and go directly to the finale. But don't. Earn it. Build up to it. You'll appreciate it more as a climactic destination than you will as a road-side viewpoint.

Make this a one-way, mostly downhill hike by parking at the Natural Bridge, then driving your shuttle vehicle or hitchhiking to Emerald Lake. The lakeshore trail, by the way, is an inferior shoulder-season option because it's very short, and the eastern half of the loop usually remains snow packed and icy well into May.

FACT

By Vehicle

From the Yoho Park Visitor Centre, in Field, B.C., drive the Trans-Canada Hwy southwest 1.6 km (1 mi). Turn right (west) onto Emerald Lake Road. Just 2.4 km (1.5 mi) farther is the Natural Bridge parking lot. That's where you'll finish this one-way hike. The Emerald Lake Road ends at 8.5 km (5.3 mi). That's where you'll start hiking: near the parking lot entrance, on the left (west) side, at 1312 m (4303 ft).

On Foot

In two minutes, reach a signed junction. Straight (west-southwest) leads to Hamilton Lake. Turn left (south) onto the Emerald River trail. One minute farther, ignore an old road descending left (southeast). Bear right (south) on the trail.

Within 10 minutes, cross a **clearcut** intended to protect Emerald Lake Lodge from wildfires. There are other clearcuts behind the lodge and around the lake's south shore. They're ugly. But this forest, as you'll see, is laden with deadfall—potent fuel for an inferno. The trail re-enters forest near a bridged creeklet. A gentle ascent leads to the trail's 1367-m (4485-ft) **highpoint**. Proceed over a section of boardwalk—the first of many trail improvements made long ago. It's surprising how much effort was invested in this trail, which now sees little use. Today, even the most popular trails lack the care this one once received.

At 4 km (2.5 mi), 1232 m (4042 ft), about one hour from Emerald Lake, the trail finally sidles up to its namesake: the **Emerald River**. About ten minutes farther, attain views south to the massive peaks of the Ottertail Range. At 5.3 km (3.3 mi), 1212 m (3976 ft), pass a crude **bridge** spanning the river. The old road on the west bank ascends 1 km (0.6 mi) to the Emerald Lake Road. Bear right (south) on the trail.

About 30 minutes farther, where the river careens into a narrow **chasm**, the trail ascends. On the ridge above, you'll see as many trees down as up—the result of a windstorm years ago. A sharp descent ends at a junction with the **Kicking Horse Fire Road** at 6.9 km (4.3 mi), 1172 m (3845 ft). Immediately ahead is the **Kicking Horse River**. Mt. Stephens, which rises above Field, dominates the eastern horizon.

Emerald River and Mt. Burgess

Right (west-southwest), the fire road crosses a bridge over the **Amiskwi River** in 80 m/yd. Beyond is a former day-use area with a picnic table. Just past that is a trail leading northwest to Amiskwi Pass, deep in the wilds.

Left (east), the fire road immediately crosses a bridge over the Emerald River then ascends to reach the **Natural Bridge** parking lot at 8.2 km (5.1 mi), 1207 m (3960 ft).

TRIP 135

Beauty Creek

LOCATION	Jasper National Park
ROUND TRIP	3.6 km (2.2 mi)
ELEVATION GAIN	40 m (130 ft)
HIKING TIME	1 hour
DIFFICULTY	easy
MAPS	Gem Trek *Columbia Icefield*; Sunwapta Peak 83 C/6

OPINION

Children are delighted by items scaled down to toy size. And hikers, after being overawed by grand mountains, are charmed by the human-scale beauty of this intimate chasm. You'll discover a series of lovely cascades a short way upstream. Be careful—especially if it's raining—where the narrow trail climbs steeply beside the canyon wall.

FACT

By Vehicle

Drive the Icefields Parkway south 2 km (1.2 mi) from Beauty Creek Hostel, or north 15.5 km (9.6 mi) from the Icefield Centre. From either approach, watch the east side of the road for a tiny sign depicting a hiker. Pull off the pavement here, across from the braided gravel flats of the Sunwapta River.

On Foot

Head east across the berm to a patch of forest. Proceed through the trees, then up onto the old highway bed. Turn right (southeast) and go 0.6 km (0.4 mi) to Beauty Creek. Turn left (east) onto a trail that ascends upstream above the creek's north side. Climb steadily through forest, near the edge of the canyon. You'll pass several small waterfalls. Reach the last and biggest, **Stanley Falls**, at 1.6 km (1 mi). The trail soon disappears on a steep slope.

Monkeyflower

Beauty Creek falls

TRIP 136

Wabasso Lake

LOCATION	Jasper National Park
ROUND TRIP	6.4 km (4 mi)
ELEVATION GAIN	110 m (360 ft)
KEY ELEVATIONS	trailhead 1100 m (3608 ft) lake 1155 m (3788 ft)
HIKING TIME	1 to 1½ hours
DIFFICULTY	easy
MAPS	page 521; Gem Trek *Best of Jasper*; Summer Trails: Jasper National Park (free)

OPINION

Easy is flavourless. And hiking to Wabasso Lake is very easy. The distance is short. The elevation gain minimal. But the trail is mildly diverting, and the destination—a small lake, surrounded by trees, in the broad, forested Athabasca Valley—is a welcome sight. Given a choice, you'll enjoy a spicier day hiking almost anywhere else in Jasper Park. Opt for Cavell Meadows (Trip 55) or Bald Hills (Trip 36), if possible. But in early spring or late fall, when snow is an obstacle on higher-elevation trails, and you just want a convenient place to stride for an hour, or perhaps run, Wabasso Lake will do.

The path starts beside Hwy 93, so your initial goal is simply to escape the distressing whine and whoosh of vehicles. It soon undulates over gentle ridges. After passing a cascade and affording a ridgecrest view, it skirts a pair of marshy ponds to arrive at Wabasso Lake. The lake's origin as a beaver dam is evident. The toothy, voracious, gnawing machines are still felling trees around the shore. Though it's possible to proceed northwest from Wabasso Lake to reach Valley of Five Lakes (Trip 137), the trail has been pulverized to dust by mountain bikers, and there's nothing of interest en route. If you want to visit the five lakes, hike to them separately.

FACT

By Vehicle

From the junction of Hwy 16 and the Icefields Parkway (Hwy 93), at the southwest edge of Jasper townsite, drive the Parkway south 14.5 km (9 mi). Or, from the junction with Hwy 93 A (near Athabasca Falls), drive the Parkway north 15 km (9.3 mi). From either approach, turn east into the Wabasso Lake trailhead parking area, at 1100 m (3608 ft).

On Foot

The trail departs the east corner of the parking lot, near the kiosk. Heading south, it briefly parallels the highway, then bends left (north) and ascends 10 m

Stonecrop

(33 ft). The forest you're entering is primarily lodgepole pine, with a few aspen. Though the trail dips east, behind a bluff, highway noise remains audible.

About 15 minutes from the trailhead, reach a signed **junction**. Right (south) is a horse trail. Bear left (north-northeast) and descend. Soon reach a creek. Cross it on a bridge at 1.5 km (0.9 mi), then pass a small meadow.

Arrive at a **fork** about 30 minutes from the trailhead. These diverging trails rejoin. For now, go left (northwest) on the broader, smoother one. It ascends moderately. Straight (east) passes a small cascade; that's the return route.

A few minutes beyond the fork, crest an **open hill** at 2.5 km (1.6 mi). Mt. Kerkeslin's 2956-m (9697-ft) summit is visible south-southwest. The trail levels at 1075 m (3527 ft), then curves southeast and descends a bit.

About 15 minutes beyond the fork, arrive at the **junction** where the cascade trail rejoins on the right (south-southeast). Go that way on the return; it follows a rushing creek, crosses two bridges, then passes the cascade. For now, go left (north) on Trail 9.

After a flat area, pass a **pond** on the right, then another pond. At 2.4 km (1.5 mi), 1155 m (3788 ft), reach the marshy southeast shore of **Wabasso Lake**. Proceed around the southwest and north shores to fully appreciate the lake and see its tiny island. Reach a **junction** at 3.2 km (2 mi), near the lake's northeast shore. Turn around here.

Trail 9 continues left. Heading generally northwest, it intersects the Valley of Five Lakes trail (Trip 137) in 5.6 km (3.5 mi). Right leads generally east. It climbs the steep, forested, west slope of the Maligne Range to intersect the Skyline (Trip 81) in 11.4 km (7.1 mi), just above Curator campground. Horsepackers ply that trail, heading for Shovel Pass Lodge (just below Curator), but it's a dismal way for hikers to access the Skyline.

Handiwork of voracious Wabasso Lake beavers

TRIP 137

Valley of Five Lakes

LOCATION	Jasper National Park
CIRCUIT	4.3 km (2.7 mi)
ELEVATION GAIN	80 m (262 ft)
KEY ELEVATIONS	trailhead 1080 m (3542 ft) highpoint 1128 m (3700 ft)
HIKING TIME	1 to 1½ hours
DIFFICULTY	easy
MAPS	page 521; Gem Trek *Best of Jasper*; Summer Trails: Jasper National Park (free)

OPINION

Life force-feeds us too much monotony. So on those rare occasions when you have total freedom of choice, opt for challenge and exhilaration. If you go hiking, choose a trip that, at day's end, will inspire you to pound your fist in the air and say "I did it!" That's certainly not Valley of Five Lakes. Hike here only from May to early June, or mid-October through November, when snow is an obstacle on higher-elevation trails, and you just want a convenient place to stride for an hour, or perhaps run.

Not far from Jasper townsite is the highest praise this trip deserves, because it lacks other distinguishing qualities. Even the word "lake" is an exaggeration. Three of the five are just large ponds. And the trail—mostly in forest—has been pulverized to dust by mountain bikers. Actually, that's what it's best suited for: cycling, an activity that is a thrill unto itself, requiring no scenic stimuli. If you're cranking, instead of walking, consider lengthening the trip. The Valley of Five Lakes trail intersects bikeable trails leading southeast to Wabasso Lake, and north-northeast to Old Fort Point (just outside Jasper townsite).

En route to the lake, the trail dips to cross a creek. The clearing here affords visual relief on the otherwise treed approach. Shortly beyond, if you follow the circuit described below, you'll arrive at the largest and northernmost of the five lakes. Though pretty, it's unimpressive. The others are no different. But you don't come here expecting to be amazed. You come to avoid sloshing through snow and slipping on ice. To take joy in the quintessentially human act of walking the bare earth.

FACT

By Vehicle

From the junction of Hwy 16 and the Icefields Parkway (Hwy 93), at the southwest edge of Jasper townsite, drive the Parkway south 9 km (5.6 mi). Turn left (east) into the trailhead parking lot. It's just north of a winter gate, at 1080 m (3542 ft).

On Foot

The trail departs the northwest corner of the parking lot, near the outhouse and trash bins. It heads north, then curves east, into a forest of primarily lodgepole pine. About 12 minutes from the trailhead, descend to a boardwalk spanning **Wabasso Creek** in a marshy clearing. There are benches on both sides. Beyond, the trail proceeds north-northeast, ascending a sunny, lightly-treed slope.

Half way up the slope, at 1 km (0.6 mi), reach a four-way **junction**. Continue to the lakes by ascending straight ahead on trail 9a/9b. Right (southeast), trail 9 leads 6 km (3.7 mi) to Wabasso Lake. Left (north-northwest), trail 9 leads 7.8 km (4.8 mi) to Old Fort Point (near Jasper townsite).

Atop the slope is the biggest Douglas fir most people will see in Alberta. A few minutes farther—about 20 minutes from the trailhead—arrive at a **fork** in mixed forest of aspen and fir. Elevation: 1120 m (3670 ft). Go left (north) on trail 9b to see the largest lake first. Right (east-northeast) leads to the smaller lakes; that's the way you'll return on the circuit.

About ten minutes from the fork, the trail descends slightly and passes between the southeast end of the **first lake** (left) and the northwest shore of the much smaller **second lake** (right).

Just beyond the first two lakes, reach a **T-junction** at 1.8 km (1.1 mi). Left (northwest) intersects trail 9 in 2.1 km (1.3 mi), then proceeds to Old Fort Point. Turn right (southeast) to continue the five-lakes circuit.

The trail passes the northeast shores of **lakes two, three and four**. The trip's best lake-and-valley views are along this stretch. Mt. Edith Cavell is visible south, Antler Mtn east-southeast, and Mt. Hardisty southeast.

At 2.6 km (1.6 mi) round the southeast shore of the **fourth lake**. The **fifth lake** is left (southeast). You're now on trail 9a. Follow it generally west-southwest. At 3.3 km (2 mi) intersect trail 9b. This is the **fork** where you began the five-lakes circuit. You're now on familiar ground. Descend left to the boardwalk spanning **Wabasso Creek**. Return the way you came. Upon arrival at the **trailhead**, you'll have hiked 4.3 km (2.7 mi).

TRIP 138
Celestine Lake / Devona Lookout

LOCATION	Jasper National Park
ROUND TRIP	19.2 km (11.9 mi)
ELEVATION GAIN	330 m (1082 ft)
KEY ELEVATIONS	trailhead 1080 m (3542 ft) lake 1270 m (4170 ft), lookout 1410 m (4625 ft)
HIKING TIME	4½ to 6 hours
DIFFICULTY	easy
MAPS	page 521; Gem Trek *Jasper and Maligne Lake*

OPINION

By mid-summer, most hikers would scoff at the suggestion of walking an old road, mostly through forest, to attain a view of a valley pierced by a major highway. But in early spring, walking anywhere off pavement and not post-holing through ice-crusted snow can be a jubilant experience. That's when Celestine Lake and Devona Lookout beckon. Their invitation is also appealing in late autumn, when a sudden blizzard can turn an alpine hike into an ordeal.

Patricia and Celestine lakes are shrouded in forest, unadorned by cliffy backdrops. Devona Lookout grants a panoramic view of the Athabasca River Valley, including Roche Miette, but it's only a marginal improvement on what you'll see while driving to the trailhead. So don't come here outside shoulder season, when more rewarding, higher-elevation trails like Bald Hills (Trip 36) or Verdant Pass (Trip 21) are available. If you want to herd children on an easy backpack trip, Celestine Lake has a pleasant campground and, for that reason, could be a worthwhile destination even in summer.

Cycling here is an option. But on a bike, you'll quickly dispatch the short distance, thus defeating the purpose of spending time outdoors in shoulder season. This trip is better indulged on foot, either in May, June, or October. Though you'll be walking a road, you'll appreciate that it grants a broader, more scenic passage through this exceptionally pretty forest of primarily aspen and Douglas fir. The sun liberally penetrates the open canopy to nourish tall, emerald grass and a plethora of wildflowers: lavender camas lily, yellow shrubby cinquefoil, white daisies, Indian paintbrush, lavender harebells, pink clover. The large bunches of complex, red-orange wood lilies that flourish here are a rare treat in the Canadian Rockies.

Driving to the trailhead is even more exciting than the hike. That's half the reason to come. The 28-km (17.5-mi) Celestine Lake Road is mostly unpaved. It plies the west side of the broad Athabasca River Valley, through open, scenic, quiet, montane country. It feels remote, because it's a single lane, but it's separated only by Jasper Lake

Celestine Road, above Jasper Lake

from the whoosh and whine of RVs and transport trucks on the Yellowhead Hwy. The road affords grand views over this shallow, placid lake, especially while climbing up and around an airy ridge.

To prevent collisions, the narrow Celestine Road is limited to one-way travel. The direction of travel alternates for one-hour periods throughout the day. The schedule is posted on the road and listed below.

Snaring River campground is a good place to stay the night before or after your Devona Lookout hike. You'll also pass two, small tentsites on the Celestine Road. Their location is indicated in the *By Vehicle* directions below.

FACT

Before your trip

From downtown Jasper, allow at least 45 minutes to reach the traffic-regulated section of Celestine Road. Below are the hours designated for one-way travel. Confirm with the Jasper Info Centre, or simply wait to read the sign on the road.

Inbound (north) one-way travel
8 to 9 am, 11 to 12 noon, 2 to 3 pm, 5 to 6 pm, 8 to 9 pm

Outbound (south) one-way travel
9:30 to 10:30 am, 12:30 to 1:30 pm, 3:30 to 4:30 pm, 6:30 to 7:30 pm

Though narrow and winding, the Celestine Road is passable in a 2WD car. But don't try it in an RV or with a trailer. Slow down on blind curves. Use your horn for safety.

By Vehicle

From Jasper townsite, drive north on Hwy 16. Pass the turnoff for Jasper Park Lodge (at the large, metal bridge) and continue 7.6 km (4.7 mi). Turn left (west) onto the road signed for Snaring River campground. Set your trip odometre to 0.

100 m (110 yd)	Drive beneath railroad trestle. Bear right.
5.1 km (3.2 mi)	Snaring River campground (left), then bridge.
5.5 km (3.4 mi)	Overflow camping (right).
6.3 km (3.9 mi)	Road curves left. Unpaved beyond. Sign states one-way hours. (Road does not end at 19 km, as indicated.)
11.5 km (7.1 mi)	Moberly Homestead (right).
12.6 km (7.8 mi)	Warden house (left). Road leads generally northeast.
14 km (8.7 mi)	One-way travel begins here. Check the posted times. Cross a rough, wood bridge over Corral Creek. Road beyond has tighter curves, but remains well graded.
14.5 km (9 mi)	Pretty Creek campground (right). No fee. Room for a couple vehicles and tents.
15.5 km (9.6 mi)	Cross narrow, rough bridge.
15.7 km (9.7 mi)	Cross bridge over Vine Creek.
17.5 km (10.9 mi)	Road curves around point, high on slope.
26 km (16.1 mi)	Devona campground (left). No fee. Room for one vehicle and tent.
28 km (17.4 mi)	Trailhead parking. Road gated beyond. Elevation: 1080 m (3542 ft).

On Foot

The North Boundary Trail begins here. Beyond the Celestine junction, at 5.2 km (3.2 mi), the trail is almost entirely in forest. Cycling is permitted only as far as Snake Indian Falls, at 26.5 km (16.4 mi).

From the gate, the road descends to an iron bridge over Snake Indian River, at 0.5 km (0.3 mi). On the far bank, a sweeping curve ascends a steep slope. Atop the bench, abundant sunshine enables huge Douglas firs to attain impressive height and girth. Your general direction of travel is now northwest and will remain so to Celestine junction. The ascent is gradual the entire way.

For about 15 minutes, enjoy open views left (west) across the Snake Indian River valley to the De Smet Range, and ahead (northwest) into the heavily forested North Boundary country.

At 5.2 km (3.2 mi), 1245 m (4084 ft), reach a signed **junction** in a clearing. The North Boundary Trail proceeds straight (northwest). It's 180 km (112 mi) to Mt. Robson. Go right (north, then northeast) for Celestine Lake. The ascent is minimal. From a small rise, descend a bit. At 6.7 km (4.2 mi) a short spur forks left to the south-

En route to Celestine Lake, in May

east shore of 1.5-km (0.9-mi) long, forest-enclosed **Princess Lake**. There's no place to sit on the shore. The Beaver Bluffs rise behind it (north).

Back on the main road/trail, continue 100 m (110 yd) to a fork. Left descends north, quickly ending on the west shore of **Celestine Lake** at 7 km (4.2 mi), 1241 m (4072 ft). Straight ascends southeast to Devona Lookout.

Lacking large boulders to sit on, the water's edge at Celestine Lake is unaccommodating. But among the spruce trees, just above the shore, is a small **campground** with five tentsites. The tables provide a comfortable vantage. There's also an outhouse, fire pit, and bear-proof food storage.

From where the road/trail forks at Celestine Lake, straight leads southeast to Devona Lookout. It's narrow, overgrown, ascending moderately along a gentle, forested ridge. Attain views in about 2 km (1.2 mi), on the right (southwest) at 1363 m (4472 ft). Reach the former site of **Devona Lookout** at 9.6 km (6 mi), 1400 m (4592 ft). Proceed straight, downhill slightly, for better views.

Jasper Lake is south. East, across the Athabasca River Valley and Hwy 16, is 2315-m (7593-ft) Roche Miette. The Miette Range builds southeast beyond it. The Rocky River Valley, paralleling the south slope of the Miette Range, burned in the summer of 2003. The fire was intentionally started by the Park service as a "controlled burn." It consumed much of the valley, well up the South Boundary Trail.

PREPARE FOR YOUR HIKE

Hiking in the Canadian Rockies is an adventure. Adventure involves risk. But the rewards are worth it. Just be ready for more adventure than you expect. The weather here is constantly changing. Even on a warm, sunny day, pack for rain or snow. Injury is always a possibility. On a long dayhike, be equipped to spend the night out. If you respect the power of wilderness by being prepared, you'll decrease the risk, increase your comfort and enjoyment, and come away fulfilled, yearning for more.

You Carry What You Are

Even with all the right gear, you're ill-equipped without physical fitness. If the weather turns grim, the physical capability to escape the wilderness fast might keep you from being stuck in a life-threatening situation. If you're fit, and a companion gets injured, you can race for help. Besides, if you're not overweight or easily exhausted, you'll have more fun. You'll be able to hike farther, reach more spectacular scenery, and leave crowds behind. So if you're out of shape, work on it. Everything else you'll need is easier to acquire.

Travel Light

Weight is critical when backpacking. The lighter you travel, the easier and more pleasant the journey. Carrying too much can sour your opinion of an otherwise great trip. Some people are mules; they can shoulder everything they want. If you'd rather be a thoroughbred, reduce your load and get lighter gear. You might have to sacrifice a little luxury at the campsite in order to be more agile, fleet-footed and comfortable on the trail, but you'll be a happier hiker.

Lake Louise Visitor Centre

Weigh your pack when it's empty. Switching to a newer, lighter model might shave a couple pounds off your burden. A palatial dome tent is overkill. Check out the smaller, lighter, anthropomorphic designs. A down sleeping bag will weigh less, stuff smaller and last longer than a synthetic-filled bag that has the same temperature rating. You can also cut weight and volume with a shorter, inflatable sleeping-pad instead of a full-length one made of thick foam. Forget that heavy, bulky, fleece jacket. If you get really cold at camp, wear your raingear over other insulating layers. And on any trek less than four days, it's possible to pack only real food and leave all that clunky cooking equipment at home. Try it. Hot meals aren't necessary. Playing outdoor chef and dishwasher is a time-consuming ordeal. It also makes it harder to leave no trace of your

In the Canadian Rockies, frigid temperatures are possible even in summer.

visit, and it can attract bears. Select the right foods and you'll find they weigh no more than a stove, fuel, pots, and pre-packaged meals.

These reductions long ago revitalized our interest in backpacking. Now we revel in going light. Lighter equipment is more expensive because the materials are finer quality and the craftsmanship superior. But it's definitely worth it. Consult reputable outdoor stores for specific brands.

Unnecessary Stuff

We once encountered two men labouring up a trail, bound for a distant, back-country lake, pushing wheelbarrows piled with camping "necessities." They had a cooler, tackle box, hatchet, lawn chairs, even a radio. They also had sore hands, aching spines, and a new appreciation for backpacks and minimal loads.

Unless you're in terrific shape, have a high pain threshold, or don't mind creeping along at a slug's pace, think about everything you pack. Jettisoning preconceptions will lighten your burden.

You don't need the entire guidebook. Take notes, or photocopy the pages of your book. Carrying the whole thing is like lugging a rock in your pack. Even an iPod is questionable, and not just because of the added weight. Toting tunes into the outdoors will deny you the delight of birdsong, windsong, riversong. Wearing headphones blunts your awareness, increasing the likelihood of a bear encounter.

An extra pair of shoes? No way. Even sandals are heavy. For in-camp comfort, bring a pair of beach flip-flops. The cheap, $1.99 variety are almost weightless, and their treadless soles are easy on the environment.

Jeans are ridiculous. They're heavy, restrictive, and don't insulate. Cotton sweatpants are almost as bad. Anything 100% cotton is a mistake, as explained below.

Layer with Wool and Synthetics

Don't just wear a T-shirt and throw a heavy sweatshirt in your pack. Cotton kills. It quickly gets saturated with perspiration and takes way too long to dry. Wet clothing saps your body heat and could lead to hypothermia, a leading cause of death in the outdoors. Your mountain clothes should be made of synthetic or wool fabrics that wick sweat away from your skin, insulate when wet, and dry rapidly. Even your hiking shorts and underwear should be at least partly synthetic. Sports bras should be entirely synthetic.

There are now lots of alternatives to the soggy T-shirt. All outdoor clothing companies offer short-sleeve shirts in superior, synthetic versions. Unlike cotton T-shirts, sweat-soaked synthetics can dry during a rest break.

For warmth, several layers are more efficient than a single parka. Your body temperature varies constantly on the trail, in response to the weather and your activity level. With only one warm garment, it's either on or off, roast or freeze. Layers allow you to fine tune for optimal comfort.

In addition to a short-sleeve shirt, it's smart to pack two long-sleeve tops (zip-T's) of different fabric weights: one thin, one thick. Wear the thin one for cool-weather hiking. It'll be damp when you stop for a break, so change into the thick one. When you start again, put the thin one back on. The idea is to always keep your thick top dry in case you really need it to stay warm. Covered by a rain shell (jacket), these two tops can provide enough warmth on summer dayhikes. You can always wear your short-sleeve shirt like a vest over a long-sleeve top. For more warmth in camp, consider a down or lofty-synthetic sweater. But don't hike in down clothing; it'll get sweat soaked and cease to insulate.

Guard your gear. Salt from sweat attracts animals.

For your legs, bring a pair of tights or long underwear, both if you're going overnight. Choose insulating wool or synthetic tights that have a small percentage of lycra for stretchiness. These are warmer and more durable than the all-lycra or nylon/lycra tights runners wear. Tights are generally more efficient than pants. They stretch, conforming to your movement. They're lighter and insulate better. You can wear them for hours in a drizzle and not feel damp.

Anticipating hot weather? Mosquitoes? Exposure to intense sun? You'll want long pants and a long-sleeve shirt, both made of tightly-woven synthetics and as lightweight as possible. Make sure they fit loosely enough to be unrestrictive. The shirt, designed for vigourous activity, should have a stand-up collar and a button front. Most outdoor clothing manufacturers offer them.

Raingear

Pack a full set of raingear: shell and pants. The shell (jacket) should have a hood. Fabrics that are both waterproof and breathable are best, because they repel rain *and* vent perspiration vapor. Gore-tex is the fabric of choice, but there are alternatives—less expensive and nearly as effective.

Don't let a blue sky or a promising weather forecast tempt you to leave your raingear behind. It can be invaluable, even if you don't encounter rain. Worn over insulating layers, a shell and pants will shed wind, retain body heat, and keep you much warmer.

Coated-nylon raingear might appear to be a bargain, but it doesn't breathe, so it simulates a steam bath if worn while exercising. You'll end up as damp from sweat as you would from rain. You're better off with a poncho, if you can't afford technical raingear. On a blustery day, a poncho won't provide impervious protection from rain, but at least it will allow enough air circulation so you won't get sweat soaked.

Boots and Socks

Lightweight fabric boots with even a little ankle support are more stable and safer than runners. But all-leather or highly technical leather/fabric boots offer superior comfort and performance. For serious hiking, they're a necessity. Here are a few points to remember while shopping for boots.

If it's a rugged, quality boot, a light- or medium-weight pair should be adequate for most hiking conditions. Heavy boots will slow you down, just like an overweight pack. But you want boots with hard, protective toes, or you'll risk a broken or sprained digit.

Grippy outsoles prevent slipping and falling. Sufficient cushioning lessens the pain of a long day on the trail. Lateral support stops ankle injuries. And stiff shanks keep your feet from tiring. Stiffness is critical. Grip the toe of a boot in one hand, the heel in your other hand. If you can bend the boot easily, don't buy it.

Out of the box, boots should be waterproof or at least very water resistant, although you'll have to treat them often to retain their repellency. Boots with lots of seams allow water to seep in as they age. A full rand (wrap-around bumper) adds an extra measure of water protection.

The key consideration is comfort. Make sure your boots don't hurt. If you wait to find out until after a day of hiking, it's too late; you're stuck with them. So before handing over your cash, ask the retailer if, after wearing them in a shopping mall, you can exchange them if they don't feel right. A half-hour of mall walking is a helpful test.

4WD

Socks are important too. To keep your feet dry, warm and happy, wear wool, thick acrylic, or wool/acrylic-blend socks. Cotton socks retain sweat, cause blisters, and are especially bad if your boots aren't waterproof. It's usually best to wear two pairs of socks, with a thinner, synthetic pair next to your feet to wick away moisture and alleviate friction, minimizing the chance of blisters.

Gloves and Hats

Always bring gloves and a hat. You've probably heard it, and it's true: your body loses most of its heat through your head and extremities. Cover them if you get chilled. Carry thin, synthetic gloves to wear while hiking. Don't worry if they get wet, but keep a pair of thicker fleece gloves dry in your pack. A fleece hat, or at least a thick headband that covers your ears, adds a lot of warmth and weighs little. A hat with a long brim is essential to shade your eyes and protect your face from sun exposure.

Trekking Poles

Long, steep ascents and descents in the Canadian Rockies make trekking poles vital. Hiking with poles is easier, more enjoyable, and less punishing to your body. If you're constantly pounding the trails, they could add years to your mountain life.

Working on a previous guidebook, we once hiked for a month without poles. Both of us developed knee pain. The next summer we used Leki trekking poles every day for three months and our knees were never strained. We felt like four-legged animals. We were more sure-footed. Our speed and endurance increased.

Studies show that during a typical 8-hour hike you'll transfer more than 250 tons of pressure to a pair of trekking poles. When going downhill, poles significantly reduce stress to your knees, as well as your lower back, heel and forefoot. They alleviate knee strain when you're going uphill too, because you're climbing with your arms and shoulders, not just your legs. Poles also improve your posture. They keep you more upright, which gives you greater lung capacity and allows more efficient breathing.

The heavier your pack, the more you'll appreciate the support of trekking poles. You'll find them especially helpful for crossing unbridged streams, traversing steep slopes, and negotiating muddy, rooty, rough stretches of trail. Poles prevent ankle sprains—a common hiking injury. By making you more stable, they actually help you relax, boosting your sense of security and confidence.

Don't carry one of those big, heavy, gnarled, wooden staffs, unless you're going to a costume party dressed as Gandalf. They're more burden than benefit. If you can't afford trekking poles, make do with a pair of old ski poles. They're not as effective or comfortable as poles designed specifically for trekking, but they're better than hiking empty handed. If at all possible, invest in a pair of true trekking poles with positive-angle grips, a soft anti-shock system, and adjustable, telescoping, super-lock shafts. We strongly recommend Lekis.

When backpacking, protect your trekking poles by keeping them inside your tent at night. Otherwise, the grips and straps—salty from your perspiration—will attract critters, such as porcupines, who will quickly chew them to shreds.

First Aid

Someone in your hiking party should carry a first-aid kit. Pre-packaged kits look handy, but they're expensive, and some are inadequate. If you make your own, you'll be more familiar with the contents. Include an anti-bacterial ointment; pain pills with ibuprofen, and a few with codeine for agonizing injuries; regular bandages; several sizes of butterfly bandages; a couple bandages big enough to hold a serious laceration together; rolls of sterile gauze and absorbent pads to staunch bleeding; adhesive tape; tiny fold-up scissors or a small knife; and a compact first-aid manual. Whether your kit is store bought or homemade, check the expiration dates on your medications every year and replace them as needed.

Instead of the old elastic bandages for wrapping sprains, we now carry neoprene ankle and knee bands. They slip on instantly, require no special wrapping technique, keep the injured joint warmer, and stay in place better.

Bandanas

A bandana will be the most versatile item in your pack. You can use it to blow your nose, mop your brow, or improvise a beanie. It makes a colourful headband that will keep sweat or hair out of your eyes. It serves as a bandage or sling in a medical emergency. Worn as a neckerchief, it prevents a sunburned neck. If you soak it in water, then drape it around your neck, it will help keep you from overheating. Worn Lawrence-of-Arabia style under a hat, it shades both sides of your face, as well as your neck, while deterring mosquitoes. For an air-conditioning effect, soak it in water then don it á la Lawrence. When shooing away mosquitoes, flicking a bandana with your wrist is less tiresome than flailing your arms. Carry at least two bandanas when dayhiking, more when backpacking.

Small and Essential

Take matches in a plastic bag, so they'll stay dry. It's wise to carry a lighter, too. A fire starter, such as Optimus Firelighter or Coghlan FireSticks, might help you start a fire in an emergency when everything is wet. Buy the short ones (finger size), not the barbecue wands.

Pack an emergency survival bag on dayhikes. One fits into the palm of your hand and could help you survive a cold night without a sleeping bag or tent. The ultralight, metallic fabric reflects your body heat back at you. Survival bags, which you crawl into, are more efficient than survival blankets.

Also bring several plastic bags in various sizes. Use the small ones for packing out garbage. A couple large trash bags could be used to improvise a shelter.

A headlamp is often helpful and can be necessary for safety. You'll need one to stay on the trail if a crisis forces you to hike at night. Monitor the life of your batteries.

Most people find mosquito repellent indispensable. If you anticipate an infestation, bring a mesh head-net.

For those dreaded blisters, pack Moleskin or Spenco jell. Cut it with the knife or scissors you should have in your first-aid kit.

Wear sunglasses for protection against glare and wind. A few hours in the elements can strain your eyes and even cause a headache. People who don't wear sunglasses are more prone to cataracts later in life. Also bring sunscreen and a hat with a brim. High-altitude sun can fry you fast.

And don't forget to pack lots of thought-provoking questions to ask your companions. Hiking stimulates meaningful conversation.

Keep It All Dry

Most daypacks and backpacks are not waterproof, or even very water resistant. To protect your gear from rain, organize it in ultralight, waterproof bags made by Sea To Summit. For extra assurance, use a waterproof pack cover. Rain is a constant likelihood, so always start hiking with your gear in bags. That's much easier than suddenly having to wrestle with it on the trail, in a storm.

Water

Drink water frequently. Keeping your body hydrated is essential. If you're thirsty, you're probably not performing at optimal efficiency. But be aware of giardia lamblia, a waterborne parasitic cyst that causes severe gastrointestinal distress. It's transported through animal and human feces, so never defecate or urinate near water. To be safe, assume giardia is present in all surface water in the Canadian Rockies. Don't drink any water unless it's directly from a source you're certain is pure, like meltwater dripping off glacial ice, or until you've boiled, disinfected or filtered it.

Boiling water is a time-consuming hassle, especially along the trail, before reaching your campsite. Boiling also requires you to carry a stove and extra fuel, making it the heaviest method of ensuring safe water.

Killing giardia by disinfecting it with iodine tablets can be tricky. The colder the water, the longer you must wait. Iodine also makes the water smell and taste awful, unless you use neutralizing pills. And iodine has no effect whatsoever on cryptosporidium, an increasingly common cyst that causes physical symptoms identical to giardiasis.

Carrying a small, lightweight filter is a reasonable solution. Some filters weigh just 240 grams (8 ounces). To strain out giardia cysts, your filter must have an absolute pore size of 4 microns or less. Straining out cryptosporidium cysts requires an absolute pore size of 2 microns or less.

After relying on water filters for many years, we've switched to Pristine water purification droplets. The Pristine system comprises two 30 ml bottles with a total combined weight of only 80 grams (2.8 ounces). It purifies up to 120 litres (30 gallons) of water. The active ingredient is chlorine dioxide, which has been used for more than 50 years in hundreds of water treatment plants throughout North America and Europe. You'll find Pristine at most outdoor stores. Using it is simple: mix two solutions, wait five minutes, then add it to your water. You can drink 15 minutes later knowing you won't contract giardia. Treating for cryptosporidium requires a higher dosage and/or longer wait.

Body Fuel

When planning meals, keep energy and nutrition foremost in mind. During a six-hour hike, you'll burn 1800 to 3000 calories, depending on terrain, pace, body size, and pack weight. You'll be stronger, and therefore safer and happier, if you fill up on high-octane body fuel.

A white-flour bun with a thick slab of meat or cheese on it is low-octane fuel. Too much protein or fat will make you feel sluggish and drag you down. And you won't get very far up the trail snacking on candy bars. Refined sugars give you a brief spurt that quickly fizzles.

For sustained exercise, like hiking, you need protein and fat to function normally and give you that satisfying full feeling. The speed of your metabolism determines how much protein and fat you should eat. Both are hard to digest. Your body takes three or four hours to assimilate them, compared to one or two hours for carbohydrates. That's why a carb-heavy diet is optimal for hiking. It ensures your blood supply keeps hustling oxygen to your legs, instead of being diverted to your stomach. Most people, however, can sustain athletic effort longer if their carb-heavy diet includes a little protein. So eat a small portion of protein in the morning, a smaller portion at lunch, and a moderate portion at dinner to aid muscle repair.

For athletic performance, the American and Canadian Dietetic Association recommends that 60 to 65% of your total energy come from carbs, less than 25% from fat, and 15% from protein. They also say refined carbs and sugars should account for no more than 10% of your total carb calories.

Toiling muscles crave the glycogen your body manufactures from complex carbs. Yet your body has limited carb storage capacity. So your carb intake should be constant. That means loading your pack with plant foods made of whole-grain flour, rice, corn, oats, legumes, nuts, seeds, fruit and vegetables.

Dining Out

Natural- or health-food stores are reliable sources of hiking food. They even stock energy bars, which are superior to candy bars because they contain more carbs and less fat. Whether dayhiking or backpacking, always bring extra energy bars for emergencies. We rely on Power Bars. They energize us faster and sustain us longer than any other brand we've tried.

On dayhikes, carry fresh or dried fruit; whole-grain pita bread filled with tabouli, hummus, avocado, cucumbers and sprouts; whole-grain cookies made with natural sweeteners (brown-rice syrup, organic cane-sugar, fruit juice, raw honey); whole-grain crackers; or a bag of organic tortilla chips (corn or mixed-grain) prepared in expeller-pressed safflower or canola oil. Our favourite trail food? Roasted almonds and dried apricots. For more substance, take marinated tofu that's been pressed, baked, and vacuum-packed. It's protein rich, delicious, and lasts about three days. Omnivores have other excellent protein options: hard-boiled eggs, wild-salmon jerky, free-range bison jerky, and tuna with mayonnaise in a vacuum-packed, tear-open bag. Don't rely solely on cheese for protein; beyond small amounts, it's unhealthy.

For a backpacking breakfast, spread butter, maple syrup and cinnamon on whole-grain bread, or in pita pockets. Or why not whole-grain cookies in the

Berg Lake (Trip 82)

morning? They're like cereal, only more convenient. The backpacking lunch menu is the same as for dayhiking. For dinner, try bean salad, rice with stir-fried veggies, or pasta with steamed veggies and dressing, all cooked at home and sealed in plastic. Bean burritos made ahead of time, then eaten cold on the trail, are great too. Fresh veggies that travel well include carrots and bell peppers.

For a one- or two- night trip, don't adhere blindly to tradition. Carry a stove only if cooking significantly increases your enjoyment. Real meals are heavier than pre-packaged, but they make up for it by eliminating the weight of cooking equipment and the bother of cooking and cleaning. Plus they're tastier, more filling, cheaper, and better for you. Fresh food tends to be too heavy, bulky and perishable for trips longer than three days. Then it makes sense to pack a stove and dehydrated food. Fast-and-easy options are soup mixes, lentils, and quick-cooking pasta or brown rice.

The best tasting, most nutritious pre-packaged meals we've found are made by Mary Jane's Farm: www.backcountryfood.org. They're dehydrated, so they retain more nutritional value than freeze-dried food. Mary Jane's wide range of delicious soups, pan breads, and dinners (pasta- or grain-based) have kept us from yearning for grocery stores and restaurants, even after a week on the trail. For breakfast, we recommend Mary Jane's *Outrageous Outback Oatmeal*. For dinner, each of us eats a soup as well as a main course. While visiting her website, read Mary Jane's life story. It's both interesting and inspiring. She was one of the first female wilderness rangers in the U.S. She later homesteaded, became an organic farmer, then created her organic backpacking food company.

INFORMATION SOURCES

Alpine Club of Canada

P.O. Box 8040, Indian Flats Rd.
Canmore, AB T1W 2T8
phone (403) 678-3200
fax (403) 678-3224
website www.alpineclubofcanada.ca
e-mail info@alpineclubofcanada.ca

Fees vary for each section of the country. For hut use, you must also pay an annual facilities fee. Then you pay for each night you stay in a hut. Non-members must pay about $10 more per night. Check the ACC website for current prices.

Banff Information Centre

Box 900, Banff, AB T0L 0C0
phone (403) 760-1305 for automated trail conditions and bear warnings, or (403) 762-1550 for general info and backcountry reservations
fax (403) 762-3380
website www.pc.gc.ca/banff
e-mail banff.vrc@pc.gc.ca
open daily 8 am to 8 pm July and August; 8 am to 5 pm Sept. through June

Canadian Parks Service

Suite 1550, 635 8th Ave. SW, Calgary, AB T2P 3M3
phone 1-888-773-8888, or (403) 292-4401 in Calgary
e-mail information@pc.gc.ca
open weekdays 8 am to 4 pm

Hostelling International

205 Catherine Street, Suite 400 Ottawa, ON K2P 1C3
phone (613) 237-7884
fax (613) 237-7868
website www.hihostels.ca
e-mail info@hihostels.ca

Icefield Information Centre

phone (780) 852-6288
open daily 9 am to 5 pm May through Oct. 15; 9 am to 6 pm in summer
If your backpack trip starts near the Columbia Icefield, ask the Jasper office to forward your backcountry permit to this centre.

Jasper Information Centre

Box 10, Jasper, AB T0E 1E0
phone (780) 852-6176 for general info,
or (780) 852-6177 for backcountry reservations
fax (780) 852-6152 **website** www.pc.gc.ca/jasper
e-mail jnp@pc.gc.ca
open daily 9 am to 5 pm mid-May through mid-June, and mid-Sept. through early Oct.; 8:30 am to 7 pm mid-June through mid-Sept.; weekdays 9 am to 4 pm in winter.

Kootenay Information Centre

Box 220, Radium Hot Springs, B.C. V0A 1M0
phone (250) 347-9615 for general info,
or (250) 347-9505 for backcountry reservations
fax (250) 347-9980 **website** www.pc.gc.ca/kootenay
e-mail kootenay.info@pc.gc.ca
open daily 9 am to 5 pm mid-May through June, and Sept. through mid-Oct.; 9 am to 7 pm July and August

Lake Louise Alpine Centre

Village Rd., P.O. Box 115, Lake Louise, AB T0L 1E0
phone (403) 522-2200 **fax** (403) 522-2253
e-mail lakelouise@hihostels.ca

Lake Louise Visitor Centre

Box 213, Lake Louise, AB T0L 1E0
phone (403) 522-3833 for general info,
or (403) 522-1264 in summer for backcountry reservations
website www.parkscanada.gc.ca/banff
open daily 9 am to 5 pm late May through June; 9 am to 7 pm July through early Sept.; 9 am to 5 pm mid-Sept. through winter.

Mt. Assiniboine Provincial Park

website www.bcparks.ca
phone (403) 678-2883 for Naiset Cabin reservations

Mt. Robson Provincial Park

Box 579, Valemount, B.C. V0E 2Z0
phone (250) 566-4325
fax (250) 566-9777
website www.bcparks.ca
open daily 8 am to 8 pm in summer

Chipmunk

Waterton Lakes National Park Visitor Centre

PO Box 50, Waterton Park, AB T0K 2M0
phone (403) 859-5133
fax (403) 859-2650
website www.pc.gc.ca/waterton
e-mail waterton.info@pc.gc.ca
open daily 9 am to 5 pm mid-May through mid-June; 9 am to 7 pm mid-June through mid-Sept.; 9 am to 5 pm mid-Sept. through mid-Oct.

Weather

Banff (403) 762-2088
Jasper (780) 852-3185

Yoho National Park Visitor Centre

Box 99, Field, B.C. V0A 1G0
phone (250) 343-6783 for general info, or (250) 343-6433 for Lake O'Hara bus & camping reservations
fax (250) 343-6012
website www.parkscanada.gc.ca/yoho
e-mail yoho.info@pc.gc.ca
open daily 9 am to 5 pm mid-May through June, and Sept.; 9 am to 7 pm July and August; 9 am to 4 pm September through mid-May.

Helena Ridge, above and beyond Rockbound Lake

Trip Maps

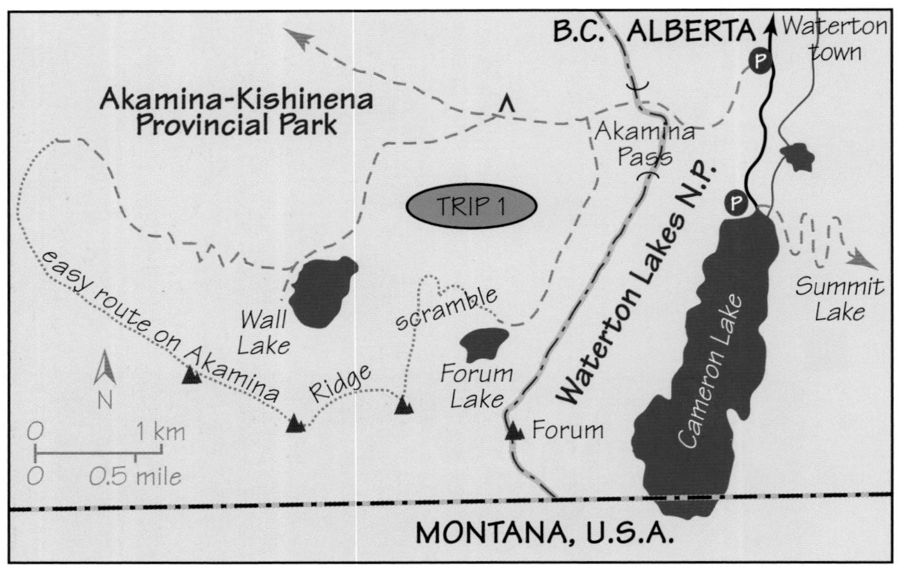
B.C.
ALBERTA
Waterton town
Akamina-Kishinena Provincial Park
Akamina Pass
TRIP 1
Waterton Lakes N.P.
Summit Lake
easy route on Akamina Ridge
scramble
Wall Lake
Forum Lake
Cameron Lake
Forum
N
0 1 km
0 0.5 mile
MONTANA, U.S.A.

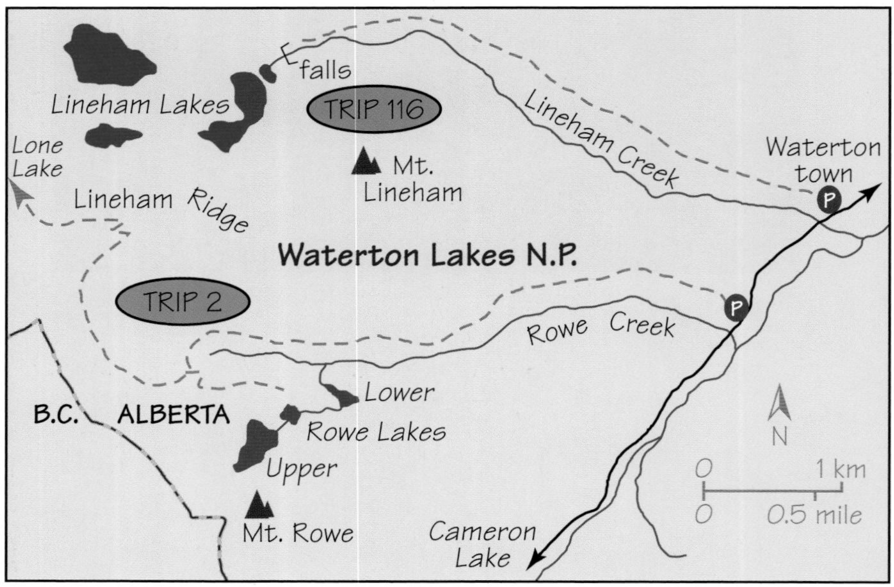
falls
Lineham Lakes
TRIP 116
Lineham Creek
Waterton town
Lone Lake
Mt. Lineham
Lineham Ridge
Waterton Lakes N.P.
TRIP 2
Rowe Creek
Lower
Rowe Lakes
Upper
B.C.
ALBERTA
Mt. Rowe
Cameron Lake
N
0 1 km
0 0.5 mile

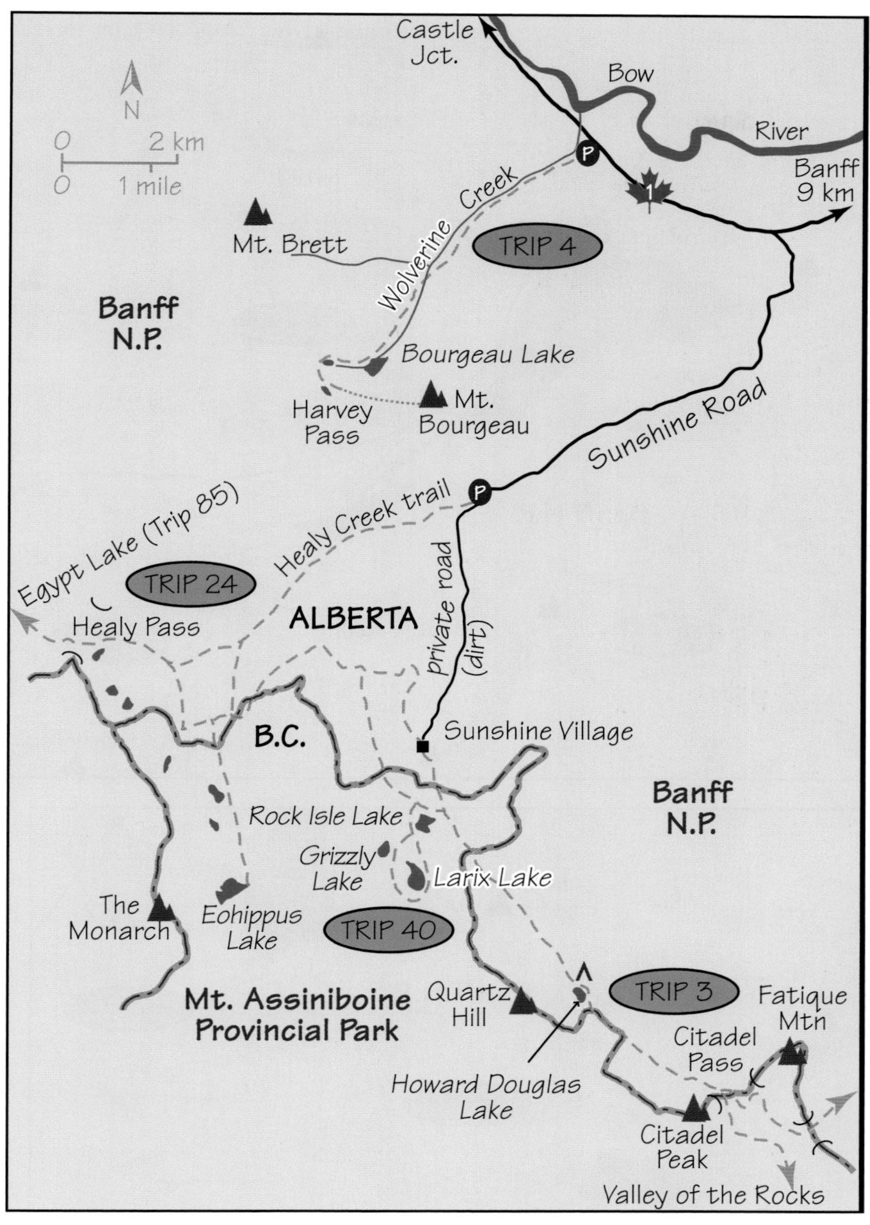
Castle Jct.
Bow
River
Banff 9 km
N
0 2 km
0 1 mile
1
Wolverine Creek
Mt. Brett
TRIP 4
Banff N.P.
Bourgeau Lake
Harvey Pass
Mt. Bourgeau
Sunshine Road
Healy Creek trail
Egypt Lake (Trip 85)
TRIP 24
Healy Pass
ALBERTA
private road (dirt)
B.C.
Sunshine Village
Banff N.P.
Rock Isle Lake
Grizzly Lake
Larix Lake
The Monarch
Eohippus Lake
TRIP 40
Mt. Assiniboine Provincial Park
Quartz Hill
TRIP 3
Fatique Mtn
Citadel Pass
Howard Douglas Lake
Citadel Peak
Valley of the Rocks

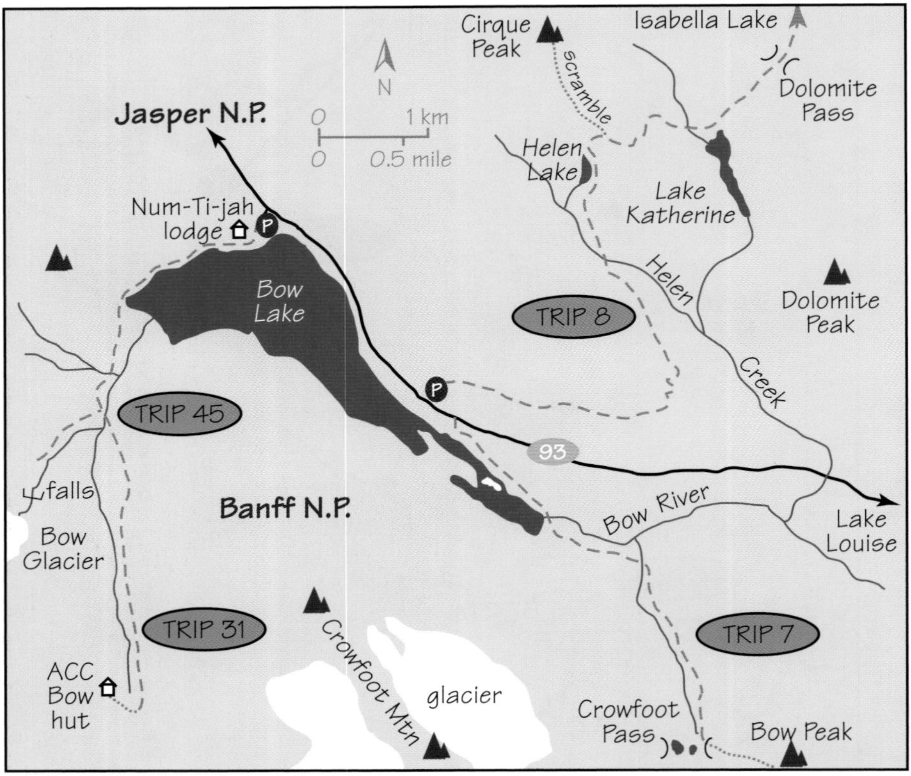

Cirque Peak
Isabella Lake
N
Dolomite Pass
Jasper N.P.
0 1 km
0 0.5 mile
scramble
Helen Lake
Lake Katherine
Num-Ti-jah lodge
P
Helen
Dolomite Peak
Bow Lake
TRIP 8
Creek
P
TRIP 45
93
falls
Banff N.P.
Bow River
Lake Louise
Bow Glacier
TRIP 31
TRIP 7
ACC Bow hut
Crowfoot Mtn
glacier
Crowfoot Pass
Bow Peak

Jasper
93
BOW PASS
Caldron Peak
Peyto Lake
P
Lake Louise
Banff N.P.
TRIP 46
Mistaya Mtn
N
TRIP 9
Caldron Lake
0 1 km
0 0.5 mile
route
Mt. Jimmy Simpson
Peyto Peak

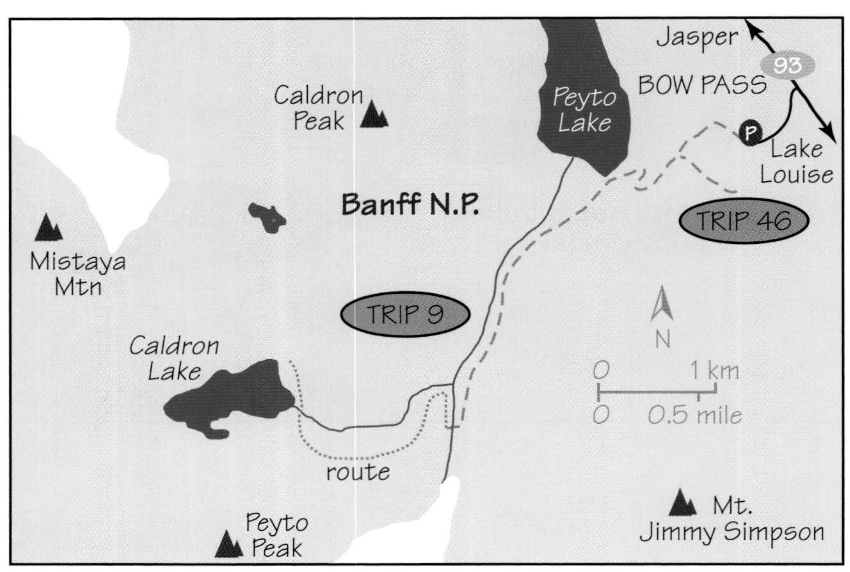

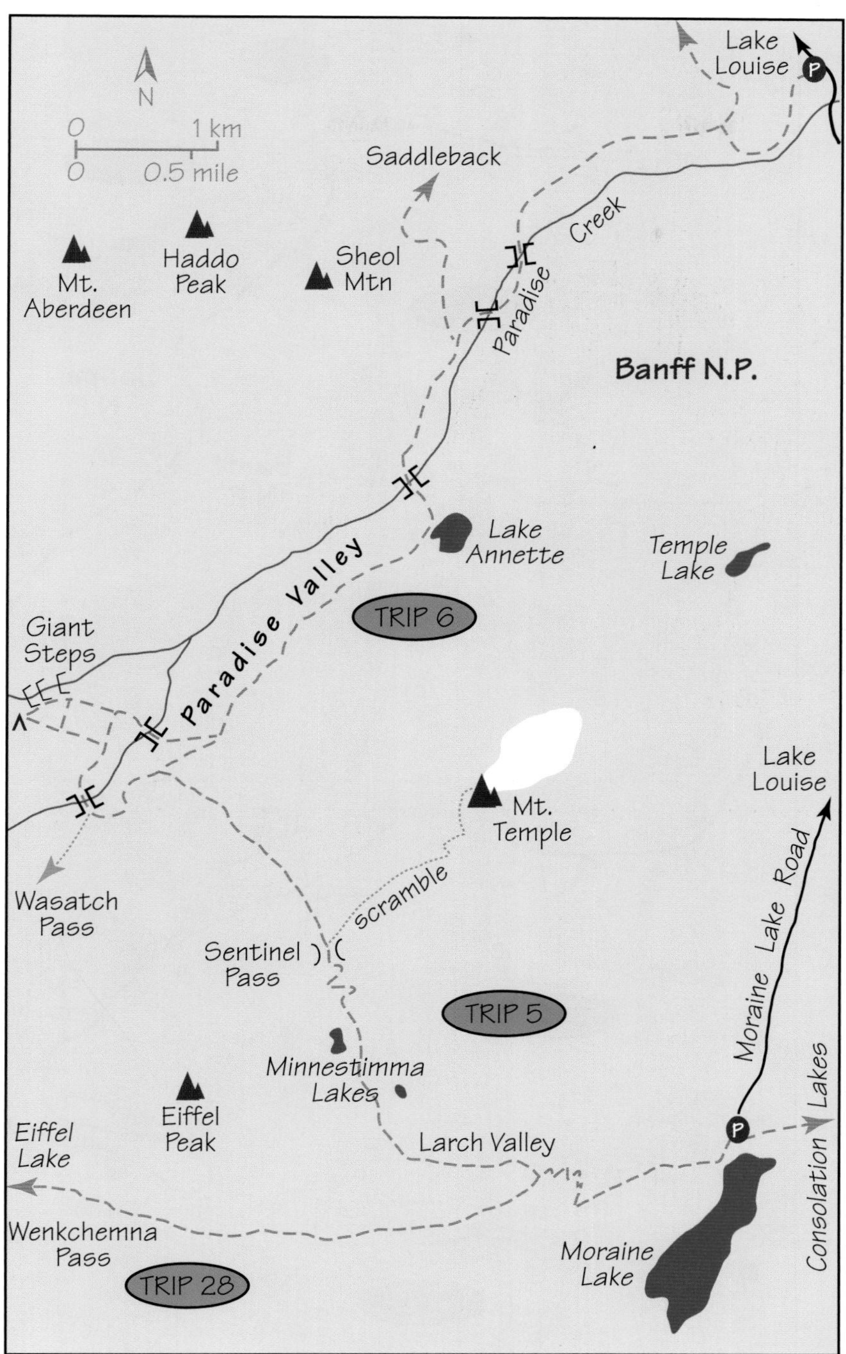
N
0
1 km
0
0.5 mile
Lake
Louise
Saddleback
Mt.
Aberdeen
Haddo
Peak
Sheol
Mtn
Paradise
Creek
Banff N.P.
Lake
Annette
Temple
Lake
Paradise Valley
TRIP 6
Giant
Steps
Lake
Louise
Mt.
Temple
Moraine Lake Road
Wasatch
Pass
scramble
Sentinel
Pass
TRIP 5
Minnestimma
Lakes
Eiffel
Peak
Consolation Lakes
Eiffel
Lake
Larch Valley
Wenkchemna
Pass
Moraine
Lake
TRIP 28

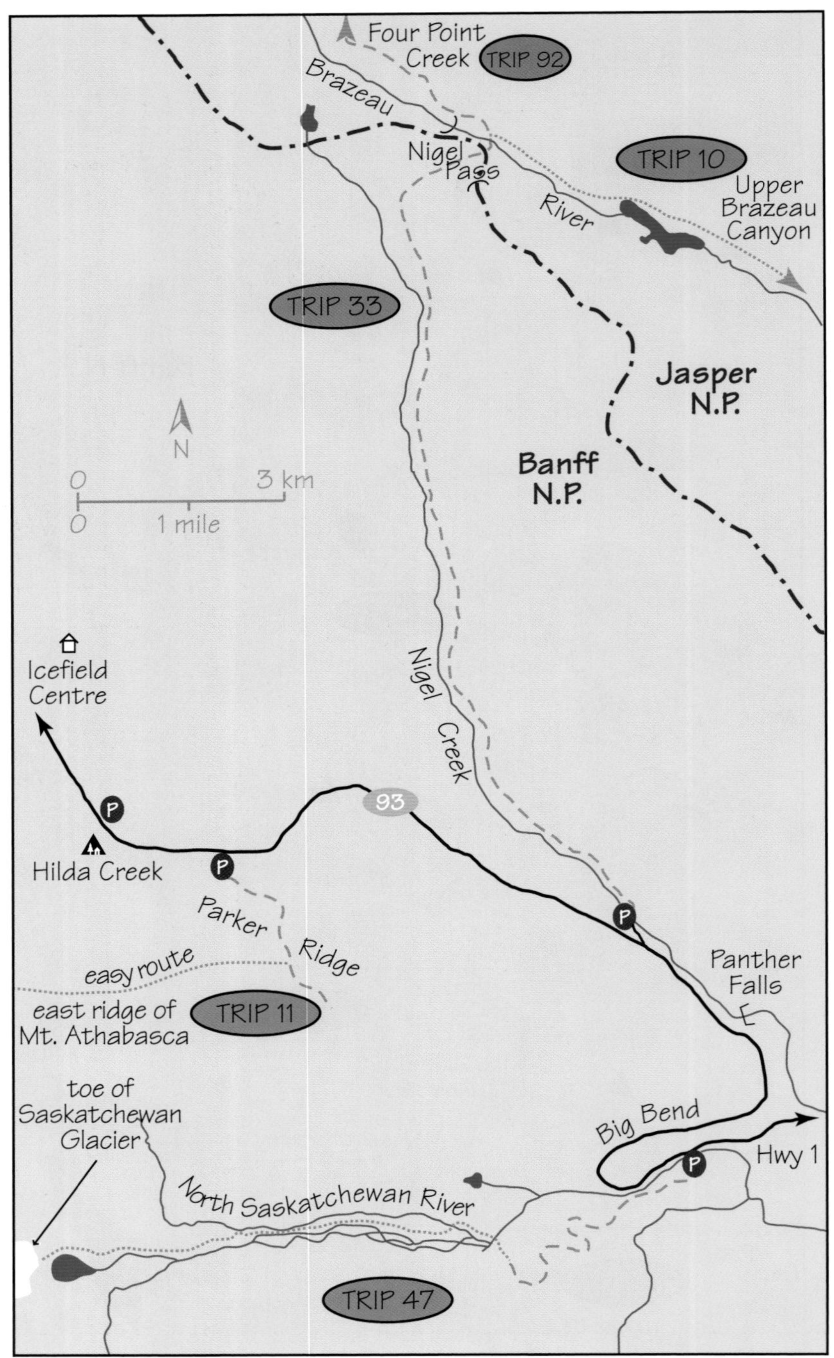
Four Point Creek
TRIP 92
Brazeau
Nigel Pass
TRIP 10
Upper Brazeau Canyon
River
TRIP 33
Jasper N.P.
Banff N.P.
N
0
3 km
0
1 mile
Nigel Creek
Icefield Centre
93
Hilda Creek
Parker Ridge
Panther Falls
easy route
east ridge of Mt. Athabasca
TRIP 11
toe of Saskatchewan Glacier
Big Bend
Hwy 1
North Saskatchewan River
TRIP 47

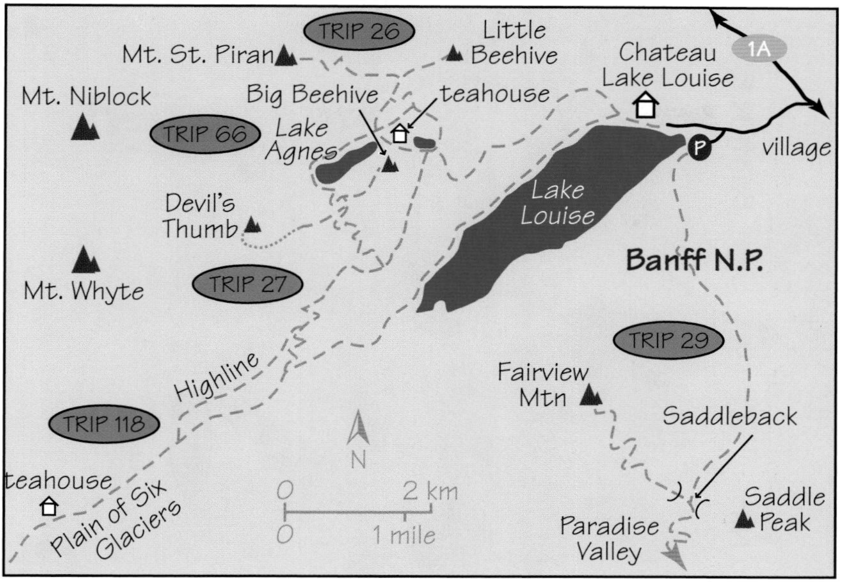

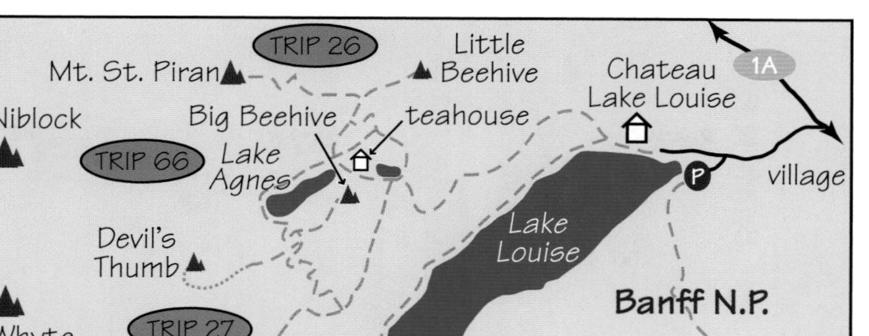
TRIP 26
Mt. St. Piran
Little
Beehive
Chateau
Lake Louise
1A
Mt. Niblock
Big Beehive
teahouse
TRIP 66
Lake
Agnes
village
Lake
Louise
Devil's
Thumb
Banff N.P.
Mt. Whyte
TRIP 27
TRIP 29
Highline
Fairview
Mtn
TRIP 118
Saddleback
N
teahouse
0
2 km
0
1 mile
Saddle
Peak
Plain of Six
Glaciers
Paradise
Valley

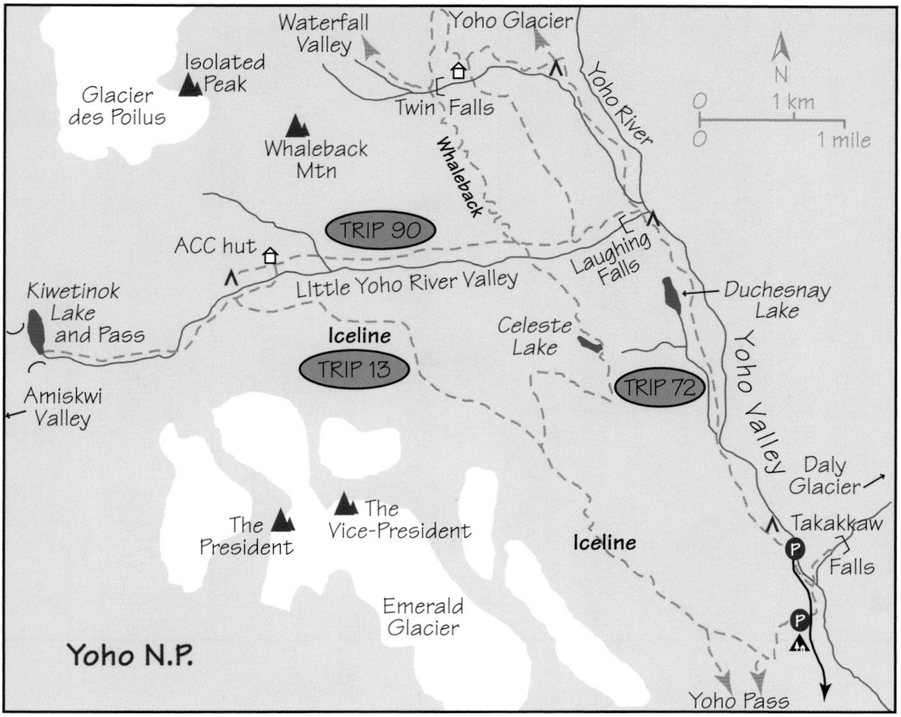

Waterfall
Valley
Yoho Glacier
Isolated
Peak
Glacier
des Poilus
Twin Falls
Yoho River
N
0
1 km
0
1 mile
Whaleback
Mtn
Whaleback
TRIP 90
ACC hut
Laughing
Falls
Little Yoho River Valley
Kiwetinok
Lake
and Pass
Duchesnay
Lake
Iceline
Celeste
Lake
TRIP 13
TRIP 72
Yoho
Valley
Amiskwi
Valley
Daly
Glacier
The
President
The
Vice-President
Takakkaw
Falls
Iceline
Emerald
Glacier
Yoho N.P.
Yoho Pass

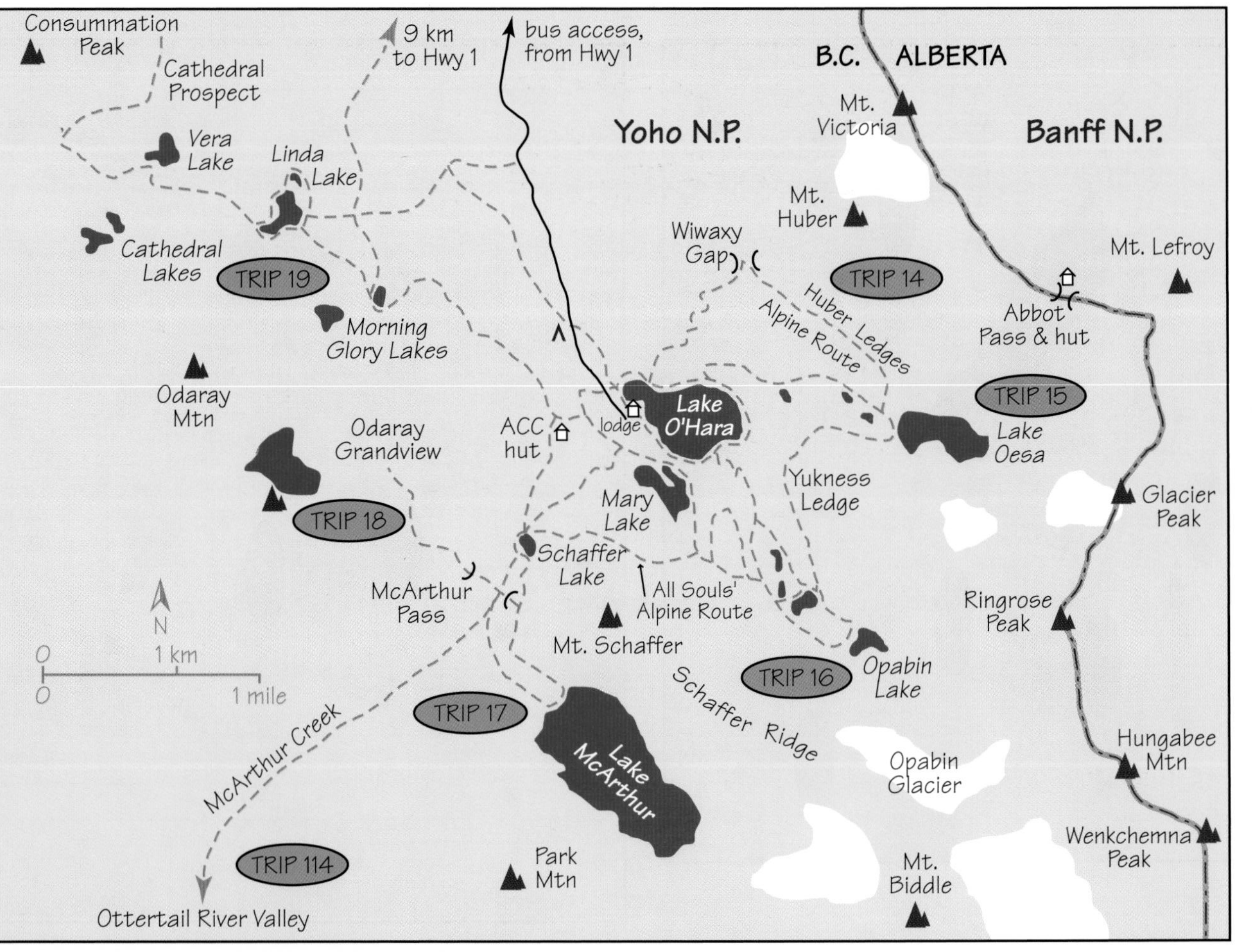
Consummation Peak
9 km
to Hwy 1
bus access,
from Hwy 1
B.C.
ALBERTA
Cathedral Prospect
Mt. Victoria
Yoho N.P.
Banff N.P.
Vera Lake
Linda Lake
Mt. Huber
Wiwaxy Gap
Mt. Lefroy
Cathedral Lakes
TRIP 19
TRIP 14
Huber Ledges
Alpine Route
Abbot
Pass & hut
Morning
Glory Lakes
Odaray Mtn
TRIP 15
Lake O'Hara
lodge
ACC hut
Odaray Grandview
Lake Oesa
Yukness Ledge
Glacier Peak
Mary Lake
TRIP 18
Schaffer Lake
All Souls'
Alpine Route
McArthur Pass
Ringrose Peak
N
Mt. Schaffer
0
1 km
0
1 mile
TRIP 16
Opabin Lake
Schaffer Ridge
TRIP 17
McArthur Creek
Lake McArthur
Opabin Glacier
Hungabee Mtn
Wenkchemna Peak
TRIP 114
Park Mtn
Mt. Biddle
Ottertail River Valley

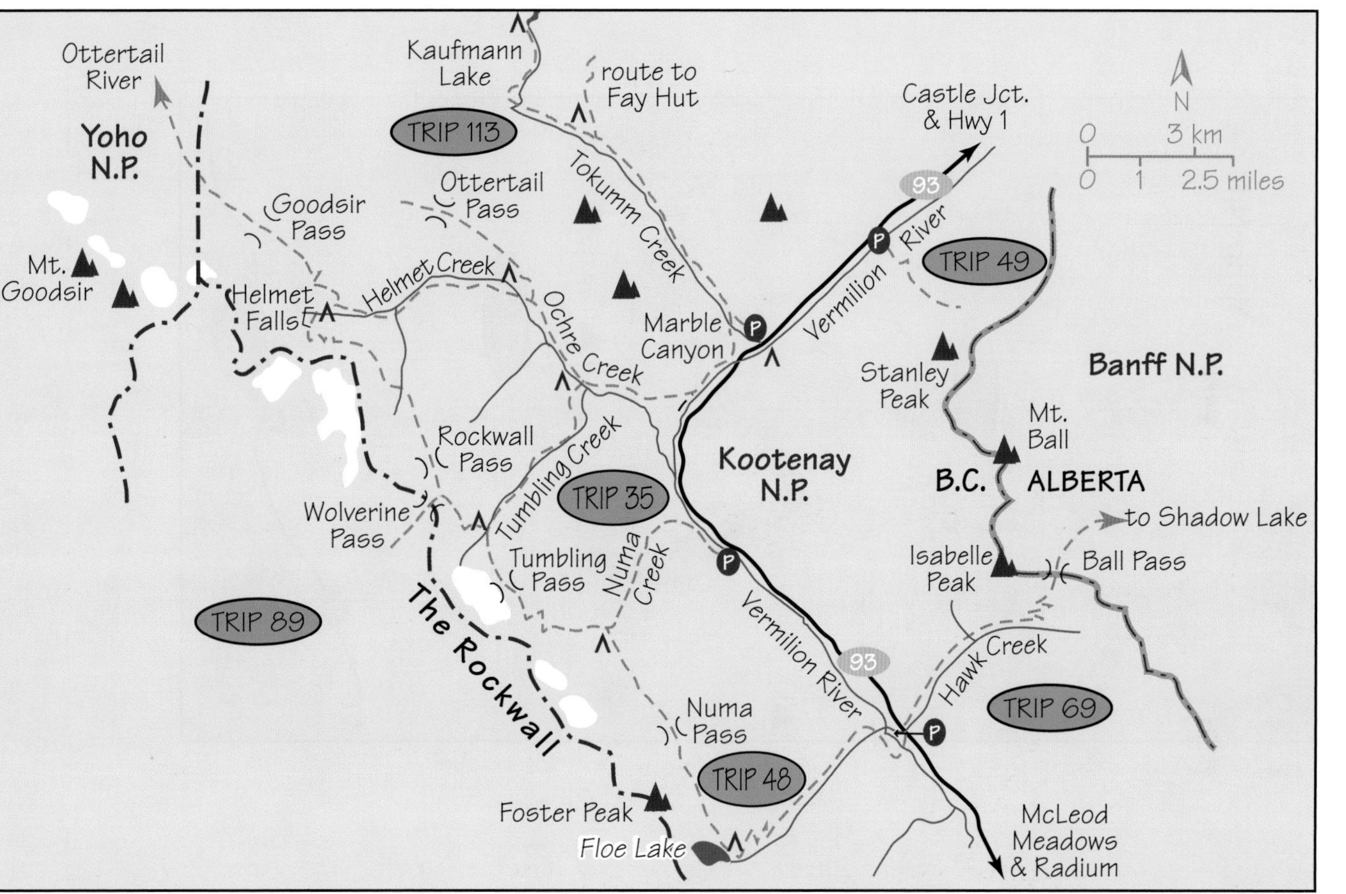
Ottertail River
Kaufmann Lake
route to Fay Hut
Castle Jct. & Hwy 1
N
0 3 km
0 1 2.5 miles
Yoho N.P.
TRIP 113
93
Ottertail Pass
Goodsir Pass
Tokumm Creek
River
TRIP 49
Mt. Goodsir
Helmet Creek
Helmet Falls
Vermilion
Ochre Creek
Marble Canyon
Stanley Peak
Banff N.P.
Mt. Ball
Rockwall Pass
Tumbling Creek
Kootenay N.P.
B.C.
ALBERTA
TRIP 35
Wolverine Pass
to Shadow Lake
Tumbling Pass
Numa Creek
Isabelle Peak
Ball Pass
TRIP 89
The Rockwall
Vermilion River
Hawk Creek
Numa Pass
TRIP 69
TRIP 48
Foster Peak
Floe Lake
McLeod Meadows & Radium

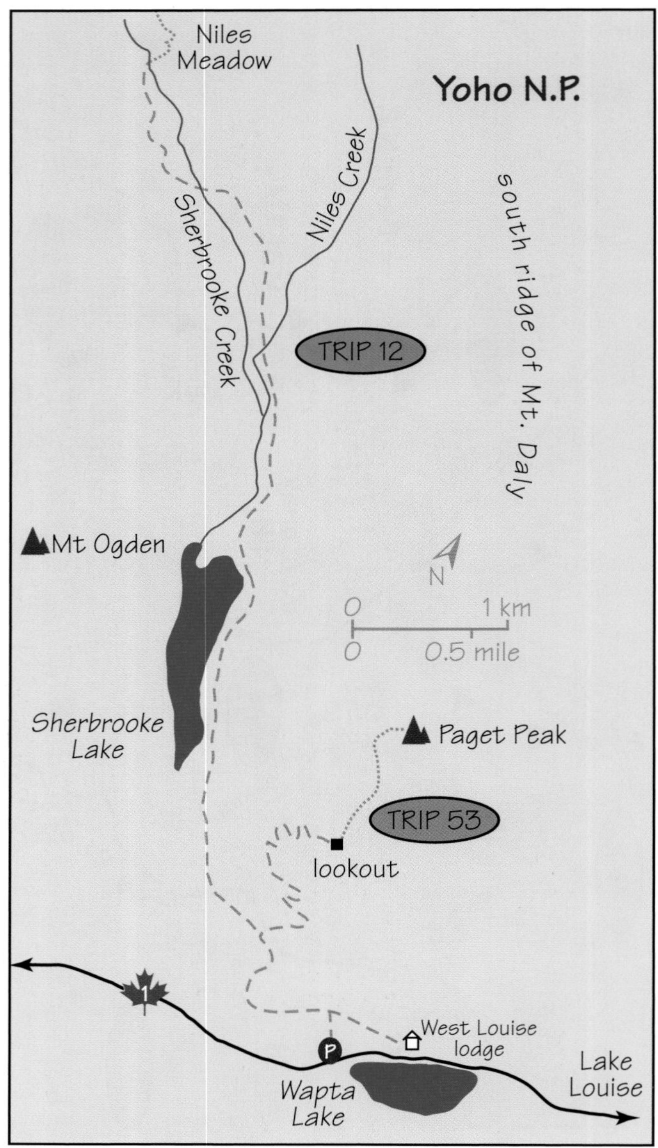
Niles Meadow
Yoho N.P.
Niles Creek
Sherbrooke Creek
south ridge of Mt. Daly
TRIP 12
Mt Ogden
N
0
1 km
0
0.5 mile
Sherbrooke Lake
Paget Peak
TRIP 53
lookout
1
West Louise lodge
P
Wapta Lake
Lake Louise

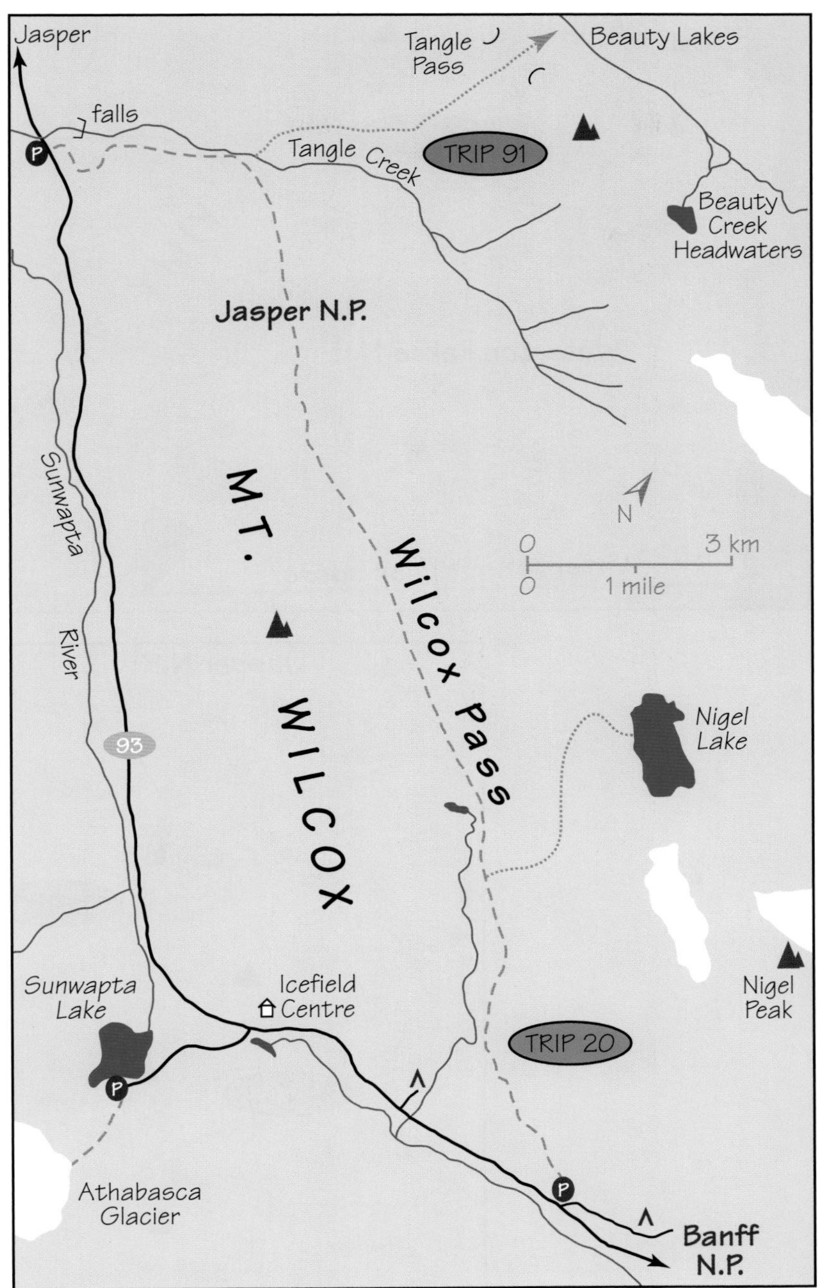
Jasper
Tangle Pass
Beauty Lakes
falls
Tangle Creek
TRIP 91
Beauty Creek Headwaters
Jasper N.P.
Sunwapta River
MT. WILCOX
Wilcox Pass
N
0 3 km
0 1 mile
93
Nigel Lake
Sunwapta Lake
Icefield Centre
Nigel Peak
TRIP 20
Athabasca Glacier
Banff N.P.

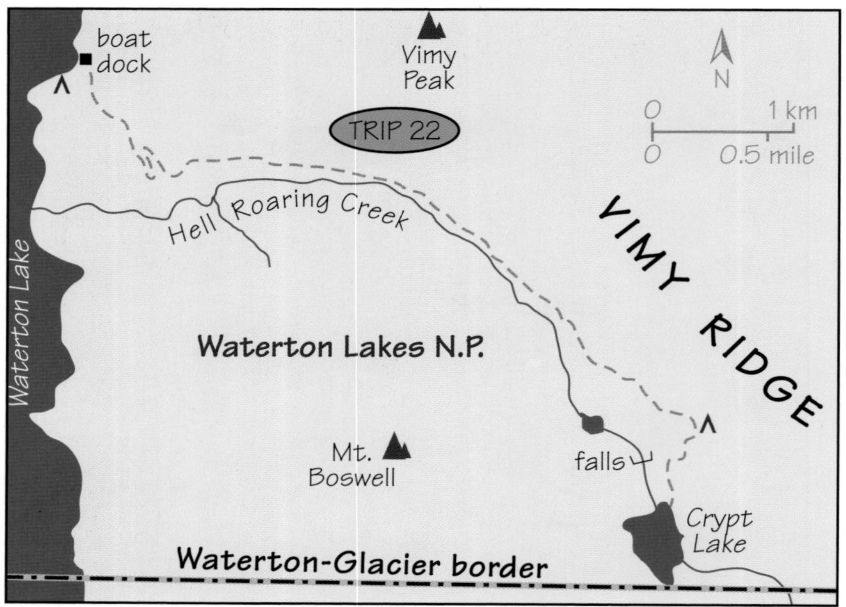
boat
dock
Vimy
Peak
TRIP 22
N
0
1 km
0
0.5 mile
Hell Roaring Creek
VIMY RIDGE
Waterton Lake
Waterton Lakes N.P.
Mt.
Boswell
falls
Crypt
Lake
Waterton-Glacier border

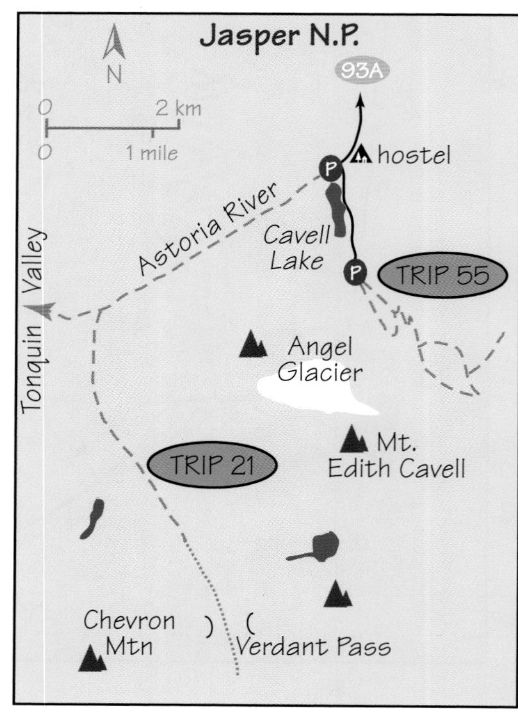
Jasper N.P.
N
93A
0
2 km
0
1 mile
hostel
Astoria River
Cavell
Lake
TRIP 55
Tonquin Valley
Angel
Glacier
Mt.
Edith Cavell
TRIP 21
Chevron
Mtn
Verdant Pass

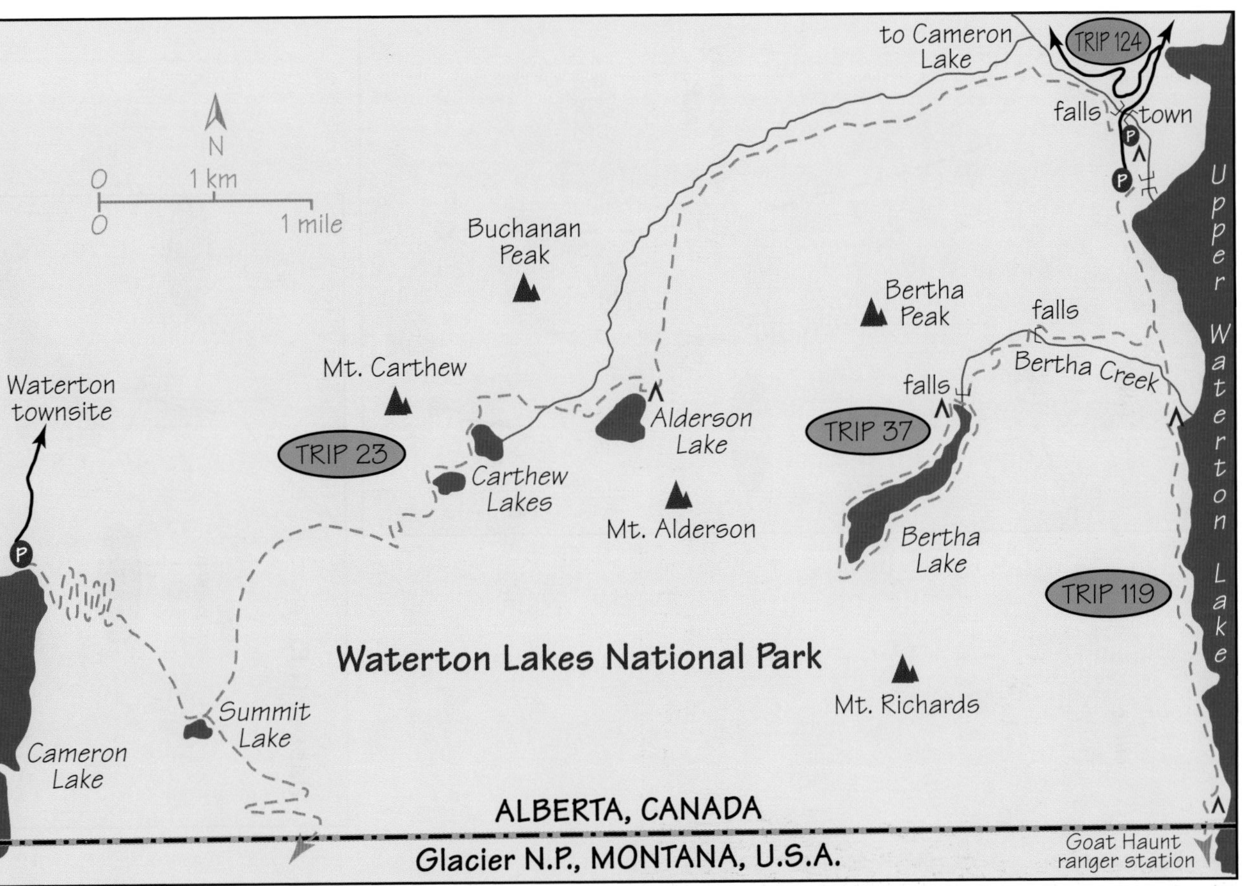
to Cameron Lake
TRIP 124
falls
town
N
0
1 km
0
1 mile
Buchanan Peak
Bertha Peak
falls
Bertha Creek
falls
Upper Waterton Lake
Mt. Carthew
Waterton townsite
Alderson Lake
TRIP 37
TRIP 23
Carthew Lakes
Mt. Alderson
Bertha Lake
TRIP 119
Waterton Lakes National Park
Mt. Richards
Summit Lake
Cameron Lake
ALBERTA, CANADA
Glacier N.P., MONTANA, U.S.A.
Goat Haunt ranger station

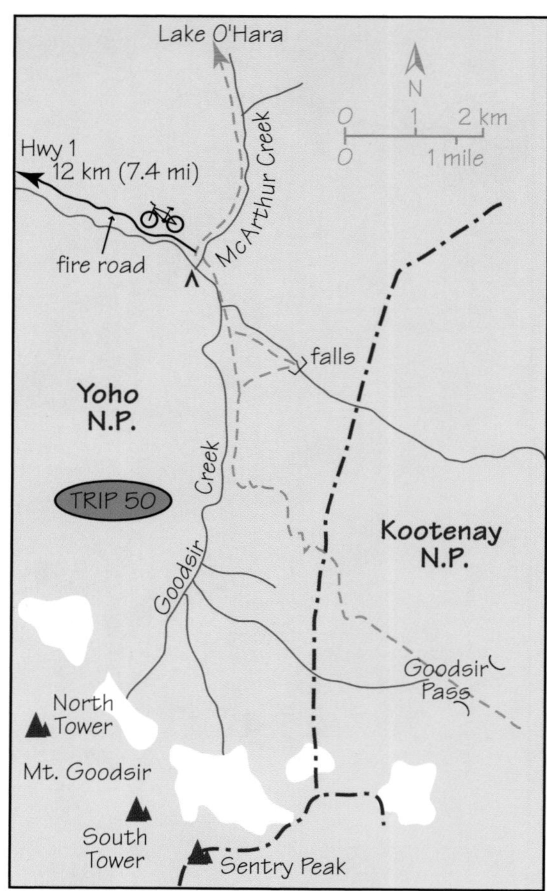
Lake O'Hara
N
0 1 2 km
0 1 mile
Hwy 1
12 km (7.4 mi)
McArthur Creek
fire road
falls
Yoho
N.P.
TRIP 50
Goodsir Creek
Kootenay
N.P.
Goodsir
Pass
North
Tower
Mt. Goodsir
South
Tower
Sentry Peak

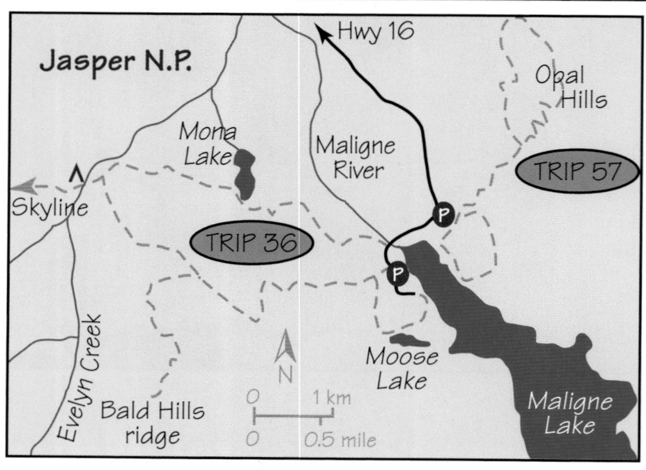
Hwy 16
Jasper N.P.
Opal
Hills
Mona
Lake
Maligne
River
TRIP 57
Skyline
TRIP 36
Evelyn Creek
N
0 1 km
0 0.5 mile
Moose
Lake
Maligne
Lake
Bald Hills
ridge

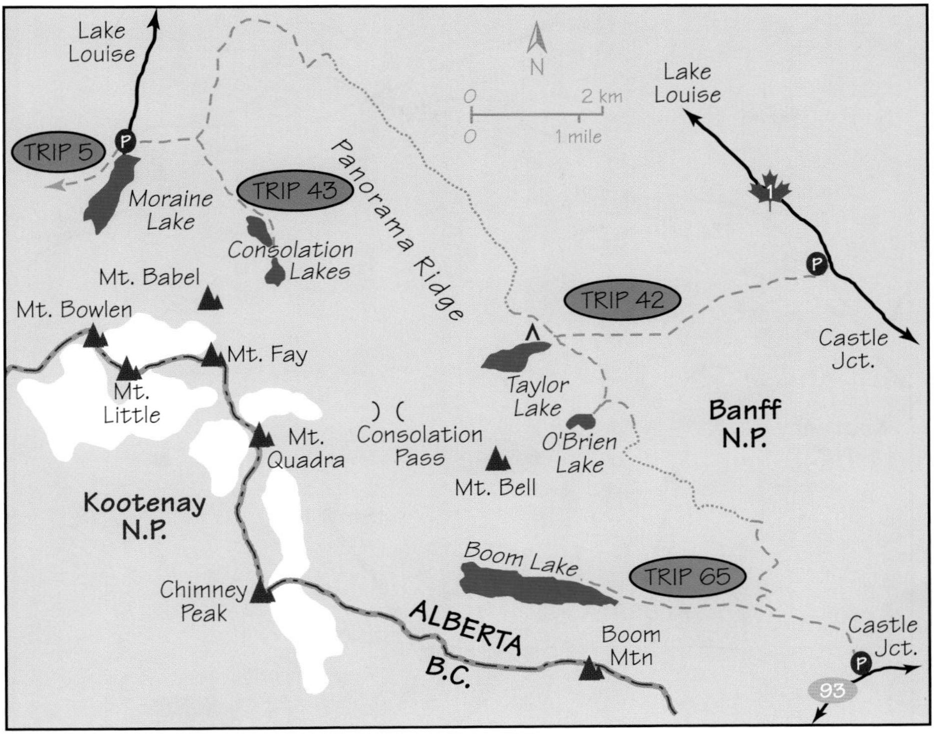

Lake Louise
TRIP 5
Moraine Lake
TRIP 43
Consolation Lakes
Panorama Ridge
N
0 2 km
0 1 mile
Lake Louise
1
TRIP 42
Castle Jct.
Mt. Babel
Mt. Bowlen
Mt. Fay
Mt. Little
Taylor Lake
O'Brien Lake
Consolation Pass
Mt. Quadra
Mt. Bell
Banff N.P.
Kootenay N.P.
Boom Lake
TRIP 65
Chimney Peak
ALBERTA
B.C.
Boom Mtn
Castle Jct.
93

Nixon Pass
TRIP 34
Kindersley-Sinclair Col
Sinclair Creek
Kindersley Pass
Lookout Point
N
0 2 km
0 1 mile
93
Kootenay N.P.
Radium

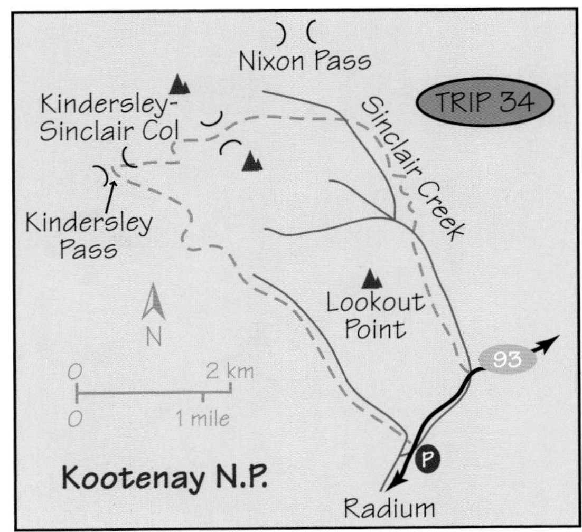

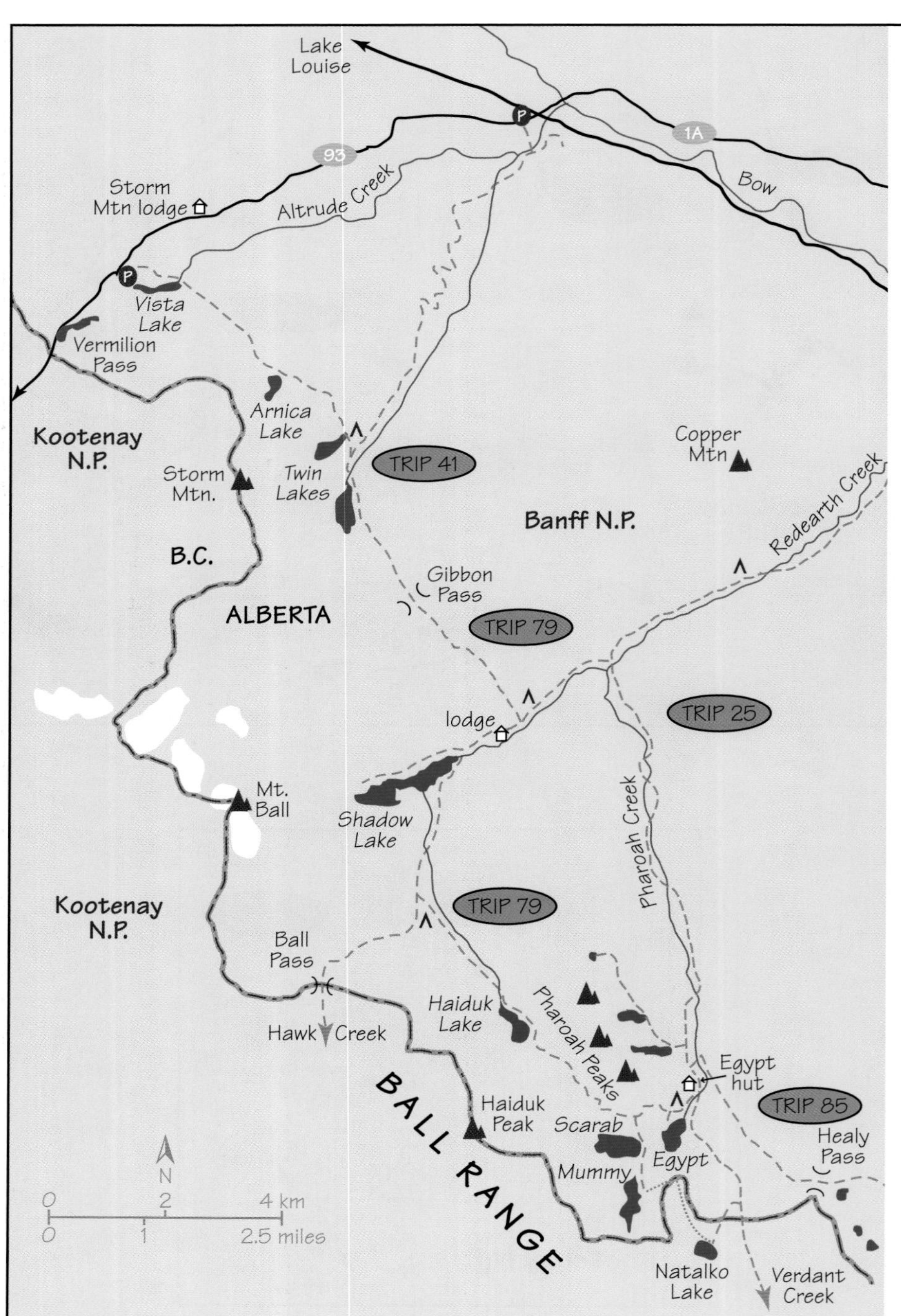
Lake Louise
93
1A
Bow
Storm Mtn lodge
Altrude Creek
Vista Lake
Vermilion Pass
Arnica Lake
Kootenay N.P.
Storm Mtn.
Twin Lakes
TRIP 41
Copper Mtn
Banff N.P.
Redearth Creek
B.C.
ALBERTA
Gibbon Pass
TRIP 79
lodge
TRIP 25
Mt. Ball
Shadow Lake
Pharoah Creek
Kootenay N.P.
TRIP 79
Ball Pass
Hawk Creek
Haiduk Lake
Pharoah Peaks
Egypt hut
BALL RANGE
Haiduk Peak
Scarab
TRIP 85
Healy Pass
Egypt
Mummy
N
0 2 4 km
0 1 2.5 miles
Natalko Lake
Verdant Creek

River
1
Banff
town
20 km (12.4 mi)
MASSIVE RANGE
TRIP 24
Sunshine
Meadows

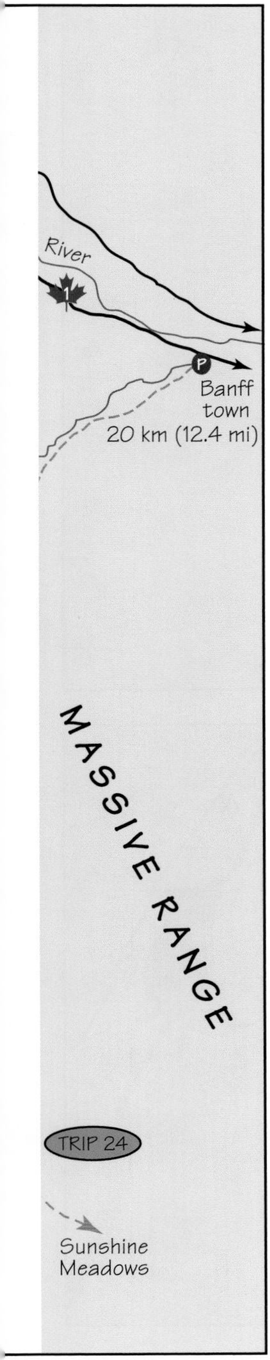

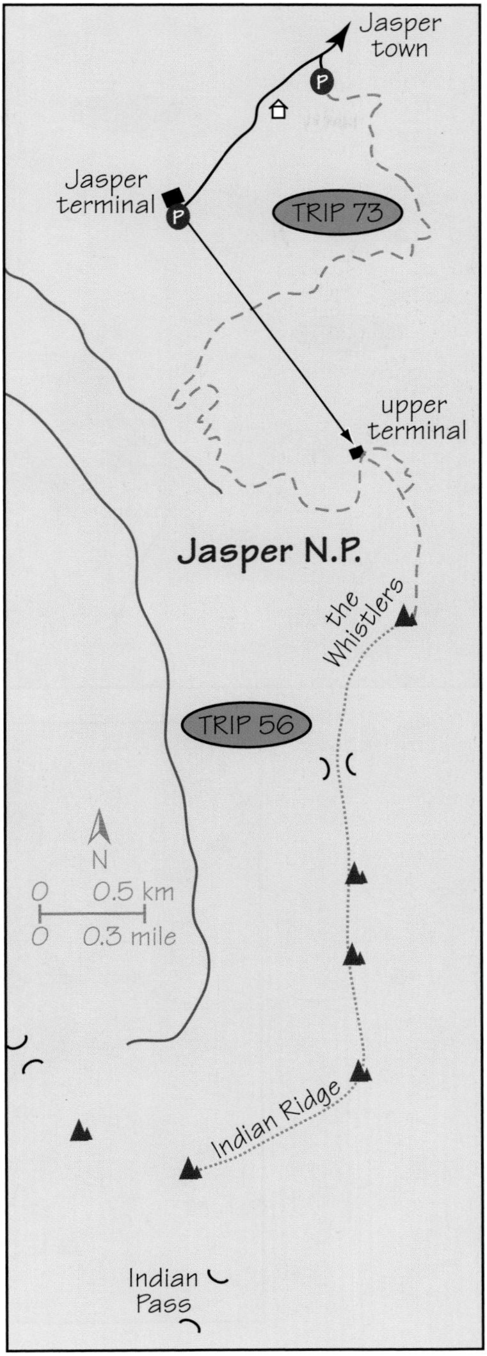
Jasper
town
Jasper
terminal
TRIP 73
upper
terminal
Jasper N.P.
the
Whistlers
TRIP 56
N
0 0.5 km
0 0.3 mile
Indian Ridge
Indian
Pass

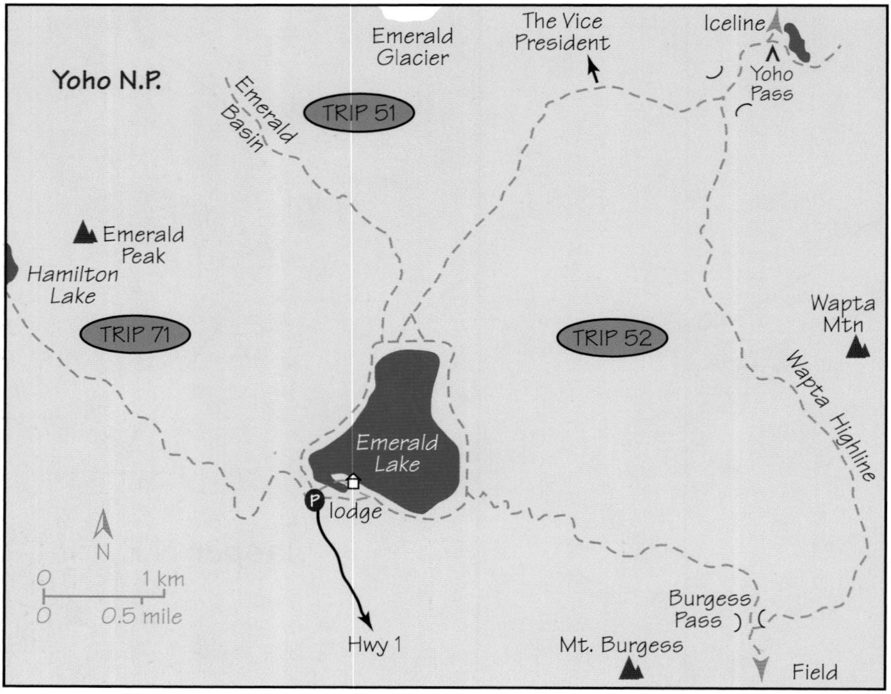

Yoho N.P.
Emerald Glacier
The Vice President
Iceline
Yoho Pass
Emerald Basin
TRIP 51
Emerald Peak
Hamilton Lake
TRIP 71
TRIP 52
Wapta Mtn
Wapta Highline
Emerald Lake
lodge
N
0 1 km
0 0.5 mile
Burgess Pass
Hwy 1
Mt. Burgess
Field

Jasper
Waterfowl
Mt. Chephren
Chephren Lake
Lakes
93
N
0 1 km
0 0.5 mile
Banff N.P.
TRIP 67
Lake Louise
Howse Peak
Cirque Lake
Mt. Synge
Mistaya Lake

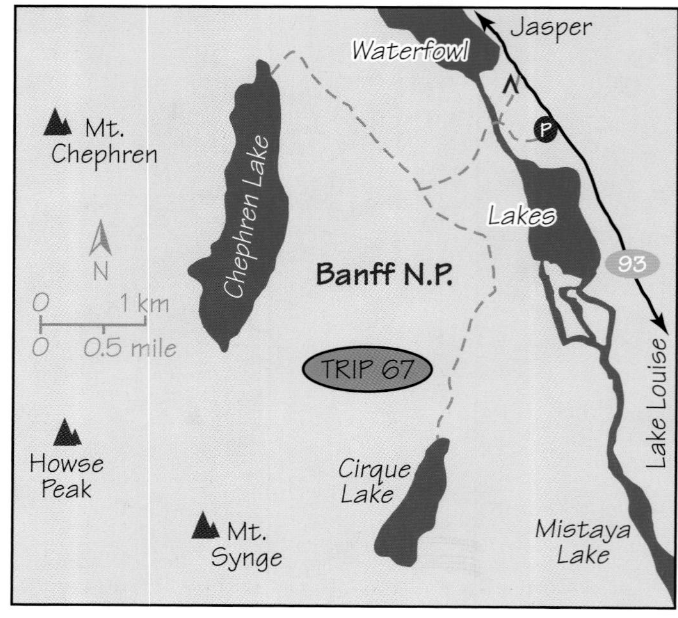

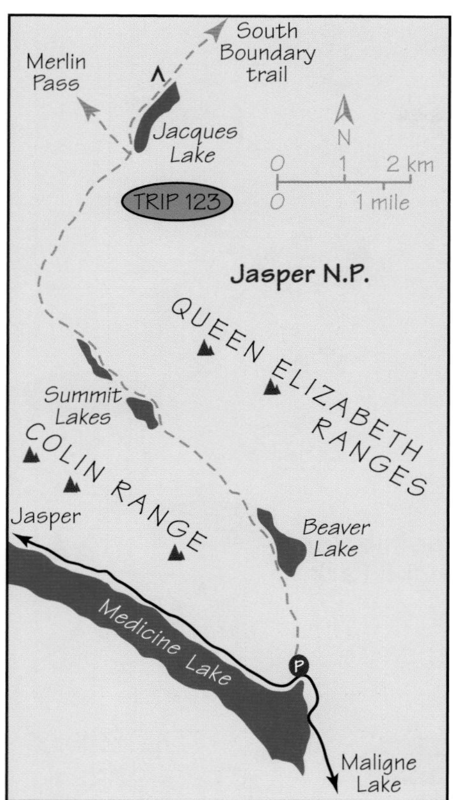
South
Boundary
trail
Merlin
Pass
Jacques
Lake
0 1 2 km
0 1 mile
TRIP 123
Jasper N.P.
QUEEN ELIZABETH
RANGES
Summit
Lakes
COLIN RANGE
Jasper
Beaver
Lake
Medicine Lake
Maligne
Lake

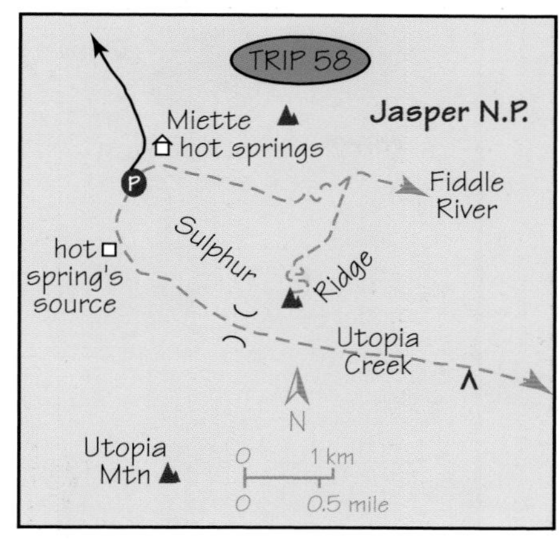
TRIP 58
Jasper N.P.
Miette
hot springs
Fiddle
River
hot
spring's
source
Sulphur
Ridge
Utopia
Creek
Utopia
Mtn
0 1 km
0 0.5 mile

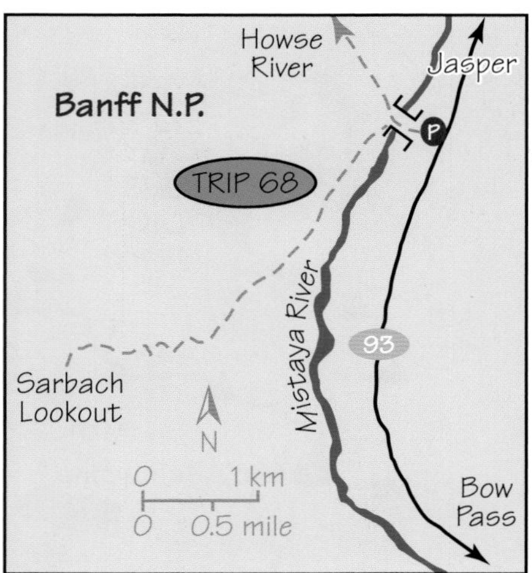
Howse
River
Jasper
Banff N.P.
TRIP 68
Mistaya River
93
Sarbach
Lookout
0 1 km
0 0.5 mile
Bow
Pass

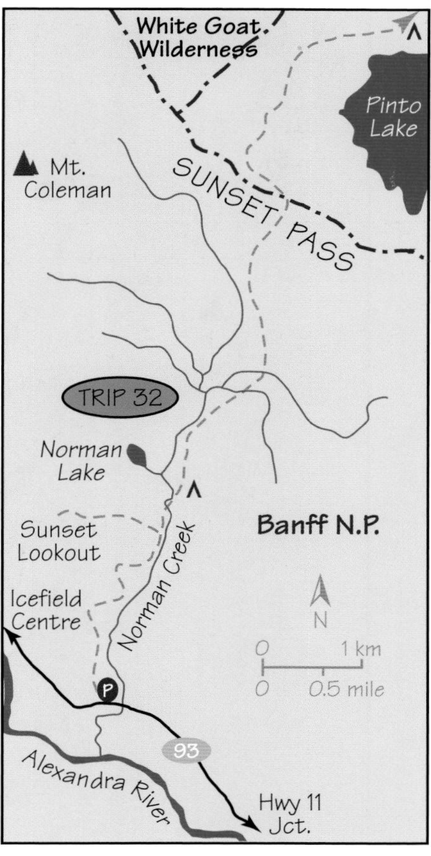
White Goat
Wilderness
Pinto
Lake
Mt.
Coleman
SUNSET PASS
TRIP 32
Norman
Lake
Sunset
Lookout
Banff N.P.
Icefield
Centre
Norman Creek
0 1 km
0 0.5 mile
93
Alexandra River
Hwy 11
Jct.

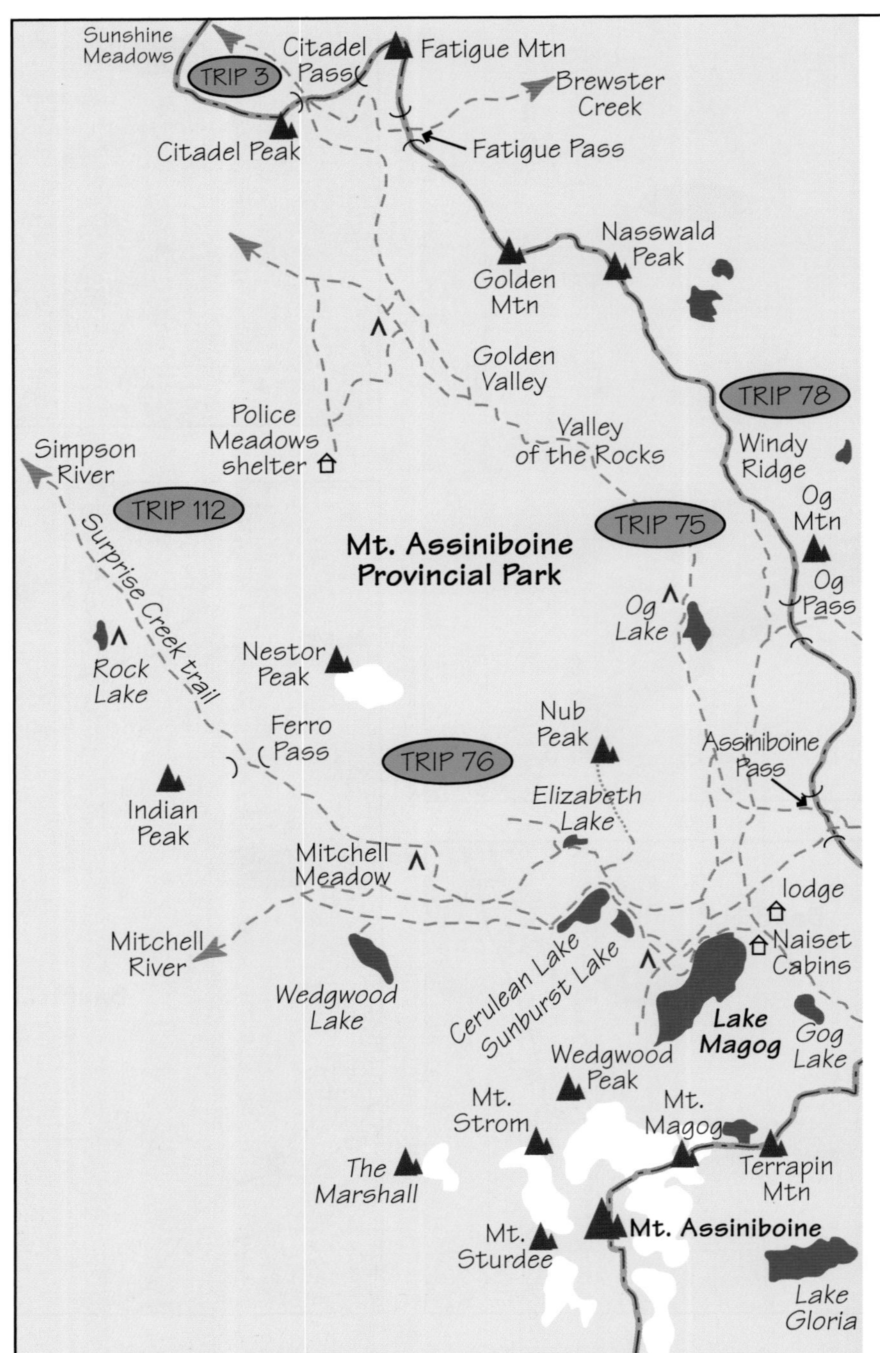
Sunshine Meadows
Citadel Pass
Fatigue Mtn
TRIP 3
Brewster Creek
Citadel Peak
Fatigue Pass
Nasswald Peak
Golden Mtn
Golden Valley
TRIP 78
Police Meadows shelter
Valley of the Rocks
Windy Ridge
Simpson River
TRIP 112
TRIP 75
Og Mtn
Mt. Assiniboine Provincial Park
Surprise Creek trail
Og Pass
Og Lake
Rock Lake
Nestor Peak
Nub Peak
Ferro Pass
TRIP 76
Assiniboine Pass
Indian Peak
Elizabeth Lake
Mitchell Meadow
lodge
Mitchell River
Naiset Cabins
Cerulean Lake
Sunburst Lake
Wedgwood Lake
Lake Magog
Gog Lake
Wedgwood Peak
Mt. Strom
Mt. Magog
Terrapin Mtn
The Marshall
Mt. Assiniboine
Mt. Sturdee
Lake Gloria

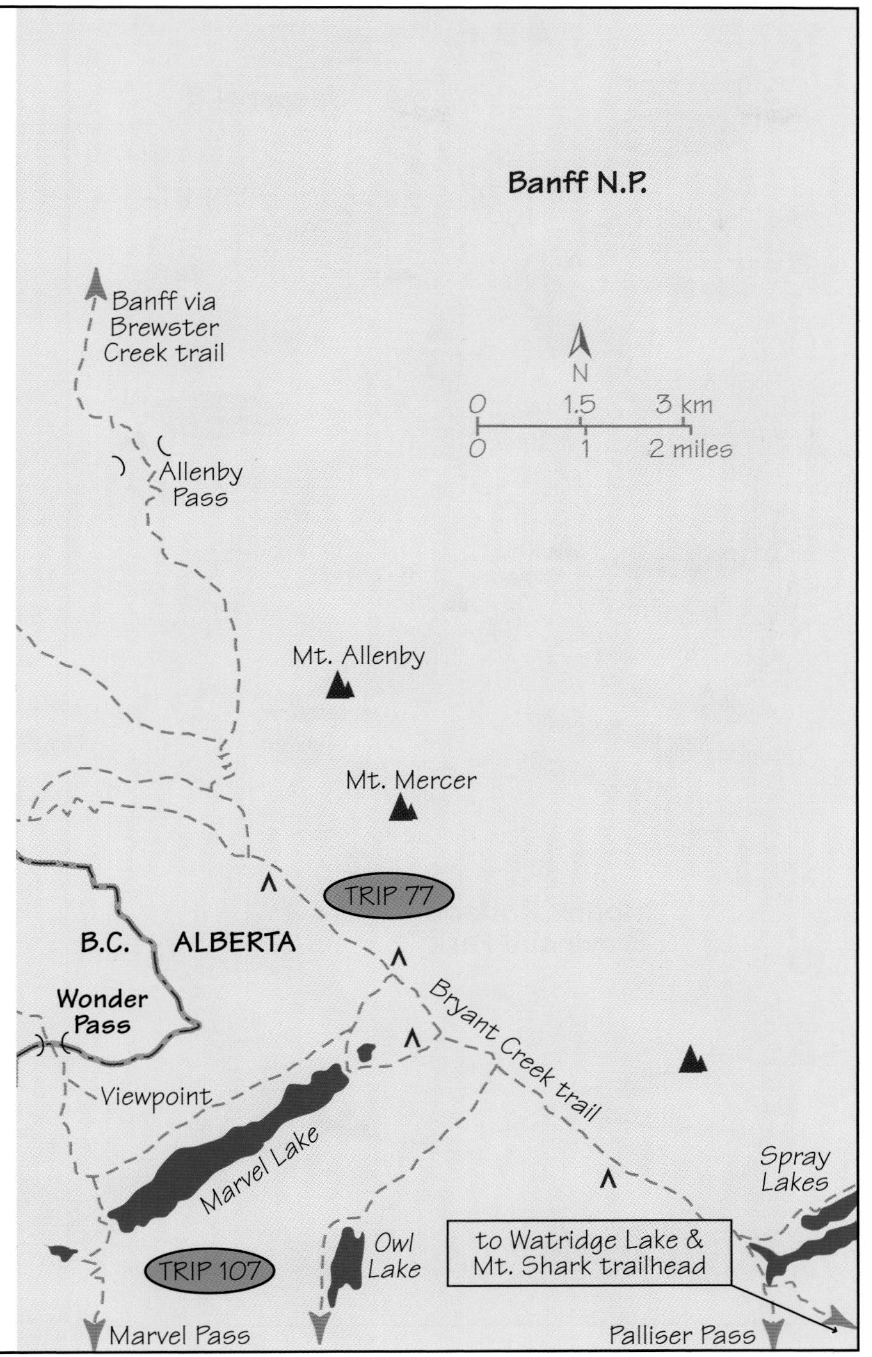
Banff N.P.
Banff via Brewster Creek trail
N
0 1.5 3 km
0 1 2 miles
Allenby Pass
Mt. Allenby
Mt. Mercer
TRIP 77
B.C.
ALBERTA
Wonder Pass
Bryant Creek trail
Viewpoint
Marvel Lake
Spray Lakes
Owl Lake
to Watridge Lake & Mt. Shark trailhead
TRIP 107
Marvel Pass
Palliser Pass

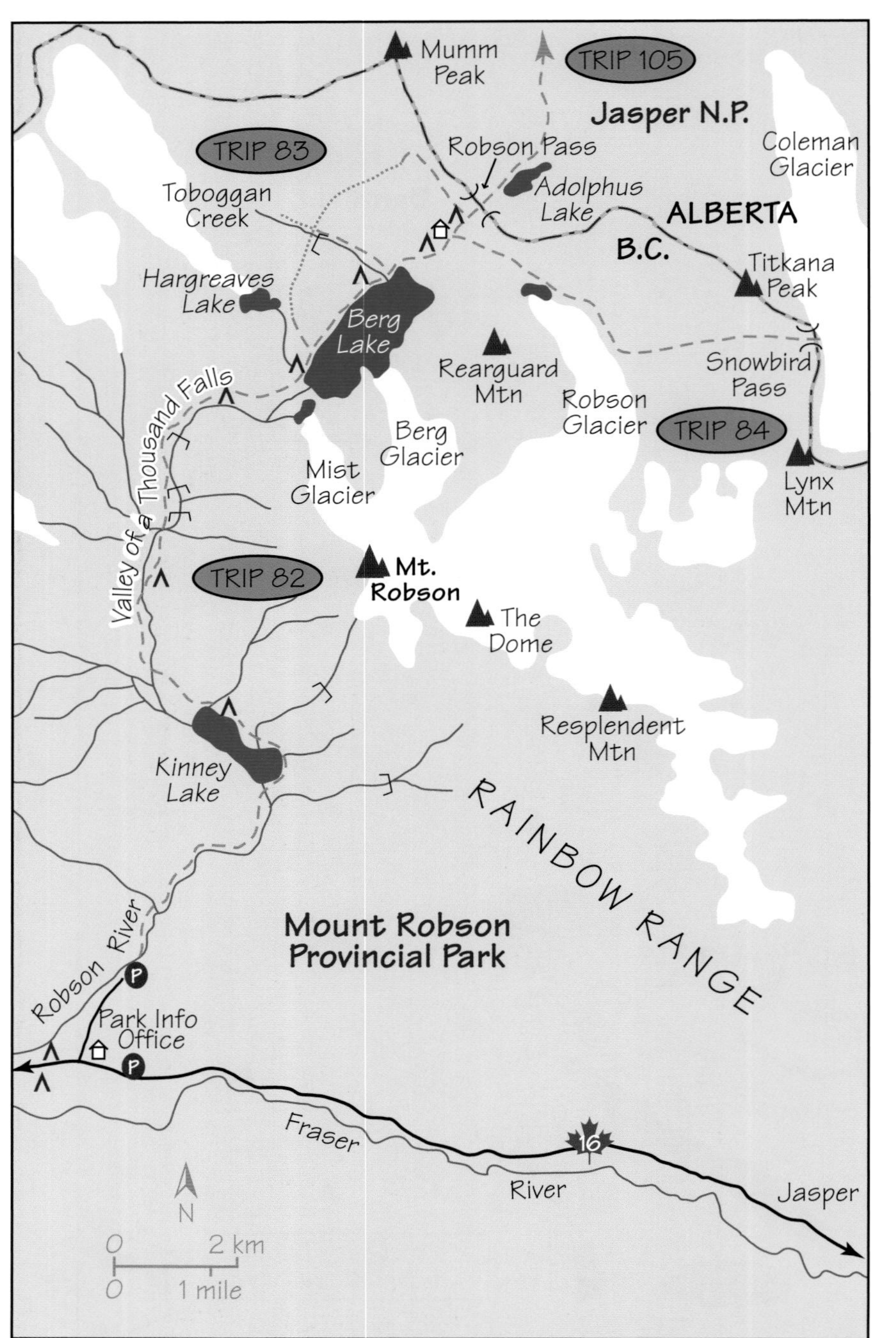
Mumm Peak
TRIP 105
Jasper N.P.
TRIP 83
Robson Pass
Coleman Glacier
Toboggan Creek
Adolphus Lake
ALBERTA
B.C.
Titkana Peak
Hargreaves Lake
Berg Lake
Rearguard Mtn
Snowbird Pass
Valley of a Thousand Falls
Robson Glacier
Berg Glacier
TRIP 84
Mist Glacier
Lynx Mtn
TRIP 82
Mt. Robson
The Dome
Resplendent Mtn
Kinney Lake
RAINBOW RANGE
Mount Robson Provincial Park
Robson River
Park Info Office
Fraser
River
16
Jasper
N
0 2 km
0 1 mile

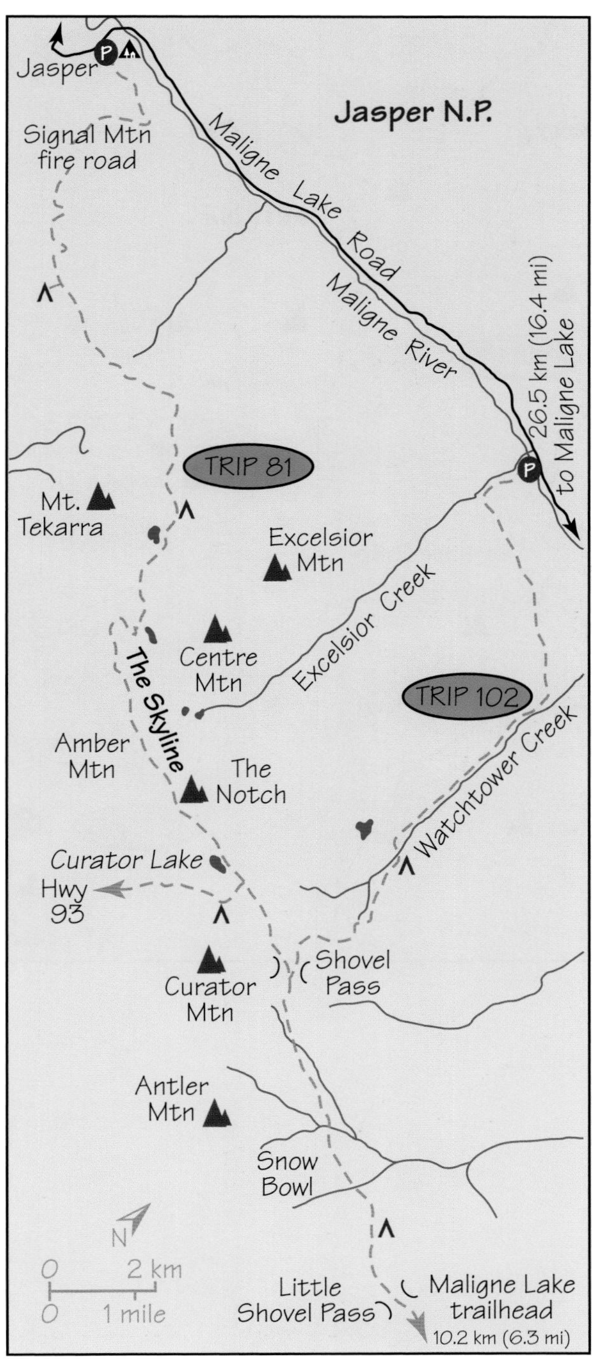
Jasper
Jasper N.P.
Signal Mtn
fire road
Maligne Lake Road
Maligne River
26.5 km (16.4 mi)
to Maligne Lake
TRIP 81
Mt.
Tekarra
Excelsior
Mtn
Excelsior Creek
Centre
Mtn
The Skyline
TRIP 102
Watchtower Creek
Amber
Mtn
The
Notch
Curator Lake
Hwy
93
Shovel
Pass
Curator
Mtn
Antler
Mtn
Snow
Bowl
N
0 2 km
0 1 mile
Little
Shovel Pass
Maligne Lake
trailhead
10.2 km (6.3 mi)

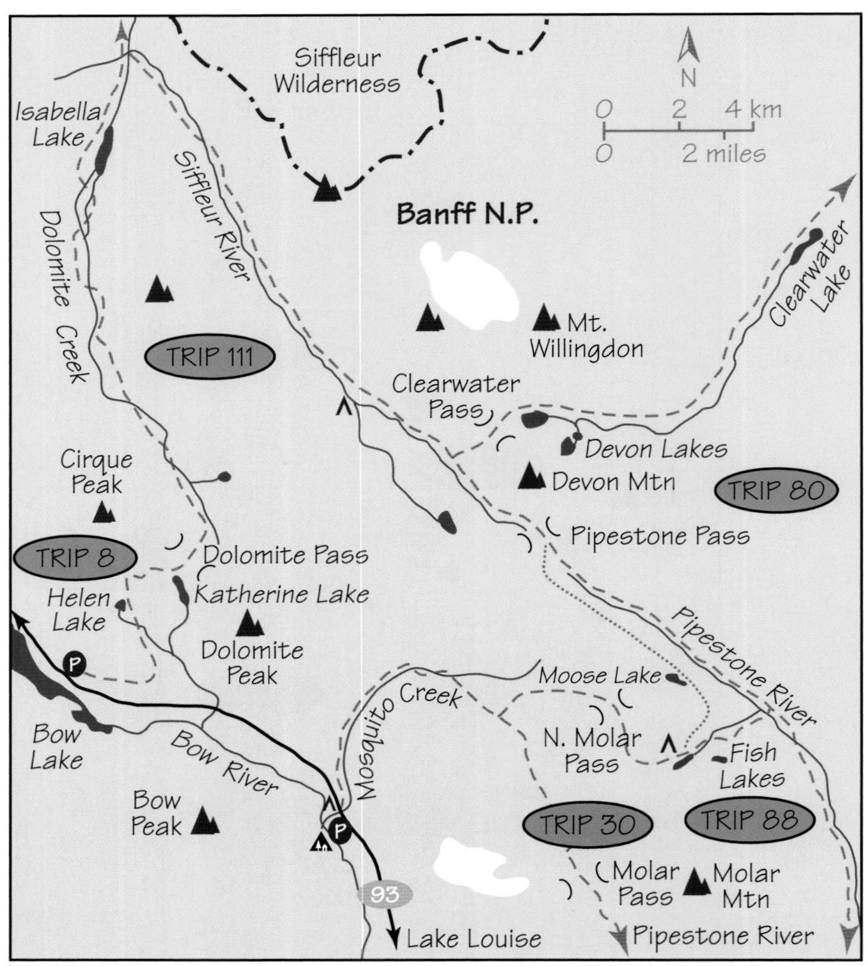
Siffleur Wilderness
N
0 2 4 km
0 2 miles
Isabella Lake
Siffleur River
Banff N.P.
Clearwater Lake
Dolomite Creek
Mt. Willingdon
TRIP 111
Clearwater Pass
Devon Lakes
Cirque Peak
Devon Mtn
TRIP 80
Pipestone Pass
TRIP 8
Dolomite Pass
Helen Lake
Katherine Lake
Dolomite Peak
Pipestone River
Moose Lake
Mosquito Creek
Bow Lake
Bow River
N. Molar Pass
Fish Lakes
Bow Peak
TRIP 30
TRIP 88
Molar Pass
Molar Mtn
93
Lake Louise
Pipestone River

Yellowhead Lake
Jasper
TRIP 104
16
P
Rockingham
Fitzwilliam Creek
Mt. Robson
Katka Mtn
Mt. Fitzwilliam
Creek
Mt. Robson Provincial Park
N
Frontier Peak
glacier
0 1 2 km
0 1 mile
Mt. Clairvaux

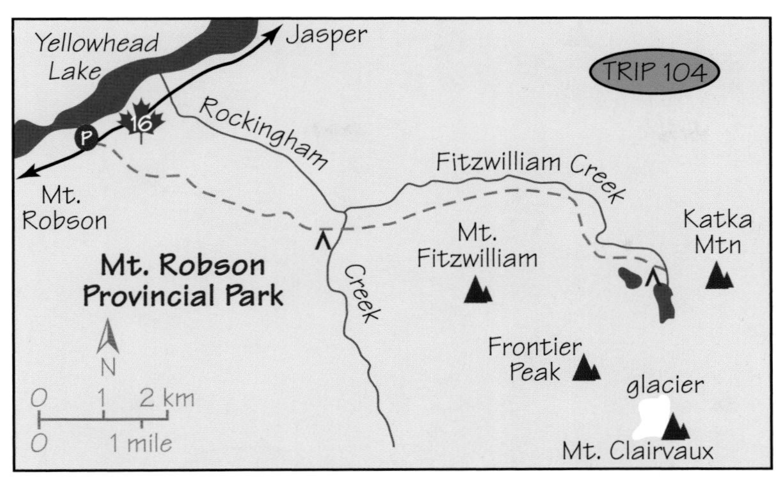

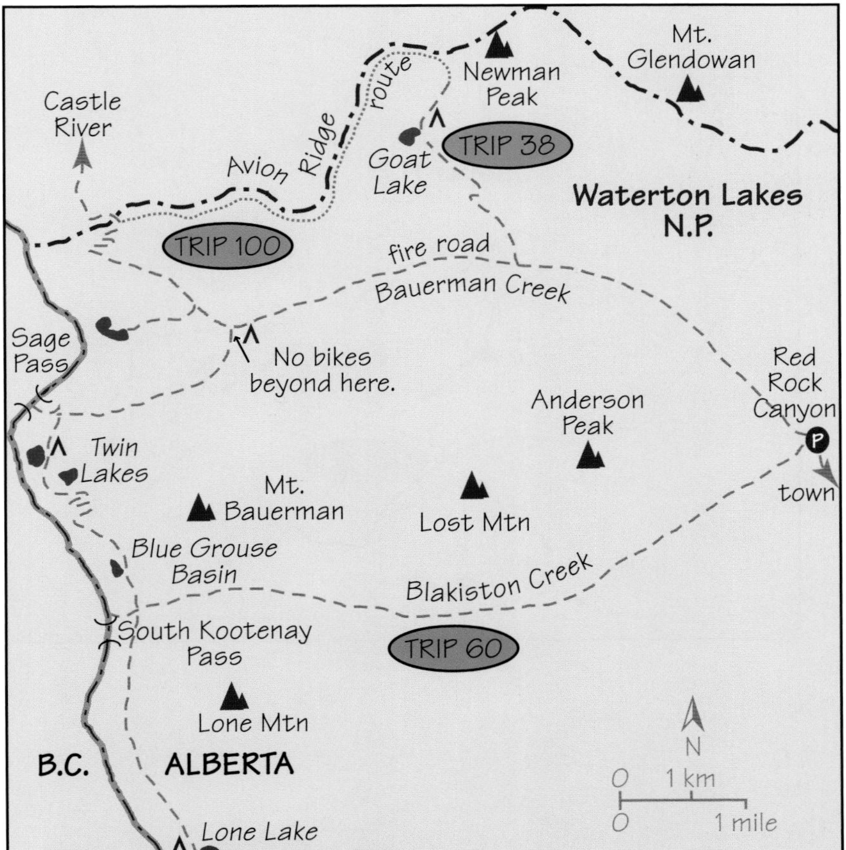

Mt. Glendowan
Newman Peak
route
Castle River
Ridge
TRIP 38
Goat Lake
Avion
Waterton Lakes N.P.
TRIP 100
fire road
Bauerman Creek
Sage Pass
No bikes beyond here.
Red Rock Canyon
Anderson Peak
P
Twin Lakes
town
Mt. Bauerman
Lost Mtn
Blue Grouse Basin
Blakiston Creek
South Kootenay Pass
TRIP 60
Lone Mtn
N
B.C.
ALBERTA
0 1 km
0 1 mile
Lone Lake
Lineham Ridge

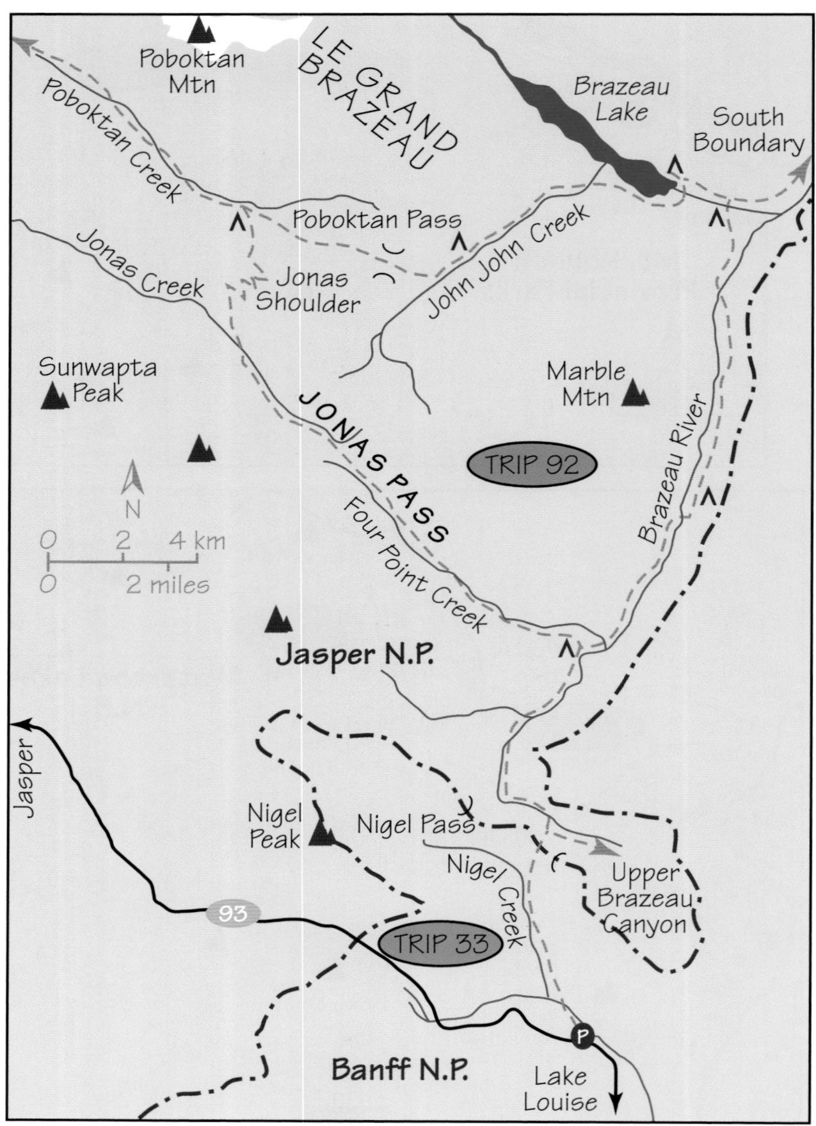
Poboktan Mtn
LE GRAND BRAZEAU
Brazeau Lake
South Boundary
Poboktan Creek
Poboktan Pass
John John Creek
Jonas Creek
Jonas Shoulder
Sunwapta Peak
Marble Mtn
JONAS PASS
TRIP 92
Brazeau River
N
0 2 4 km
0 2 miles
Four Point Creek
Jasper N.P.
Jasper
Nigel Peak
Nigel Pass
Nigel Creek
Upper Brazeau Canyon
93
TRIP 33
P
Banff N.P.
Lake Louise

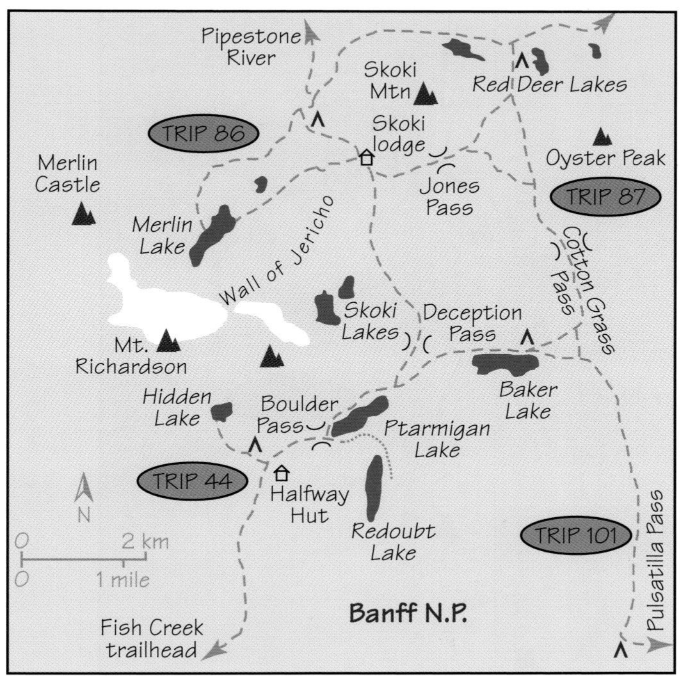
Pipestone River
Skoki Mtn
Red Deer Lakes
TRIP 86
Skoki lodge
Oyster Peak
Merlin Castle
Jones Pass
TRIP 87
Merlin Lake
Wall of Jericho
Cotton Grass Pass
Skoki Lakes
Deception Pass
Mt. Richardson
Hidden Lake
Boulder Pass
Baker Lake
Ptarmigan Lake
TRIP 44
Halfway Hut
N
0
2 km
0
1 mile
Redoubt Lake
TRIP 101
Pulsatilla Pass
Banff N.P.
Fish Creek trailhead

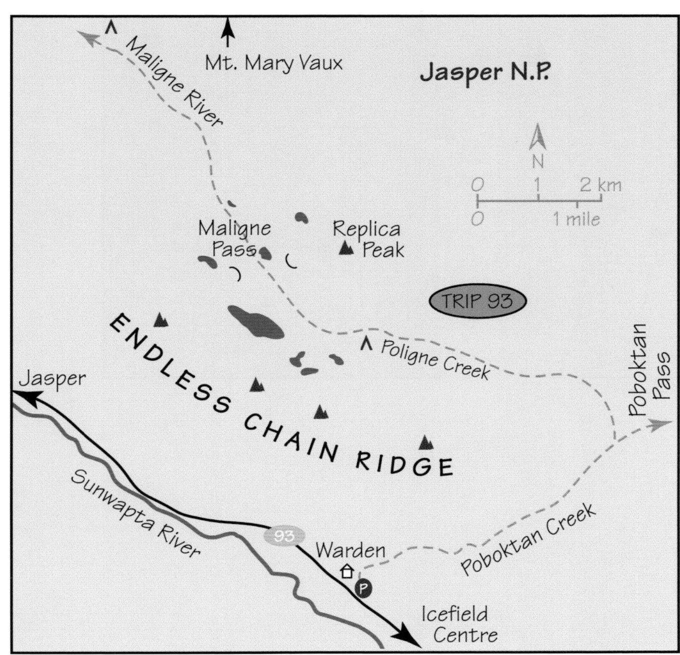
Maligne River
Mt. Mary Vaux
Jasper N.P.
N
0
1
2 km
0
1 mile
Maligne Pass
Replica Peak
TRIP 93
ENDLESS CHAIN RIDGE
Poligne Creek
Poboktan Pass
Jasper
Sunwapta River
93
Warden
P
Poboktan Creek
Icefield Centre

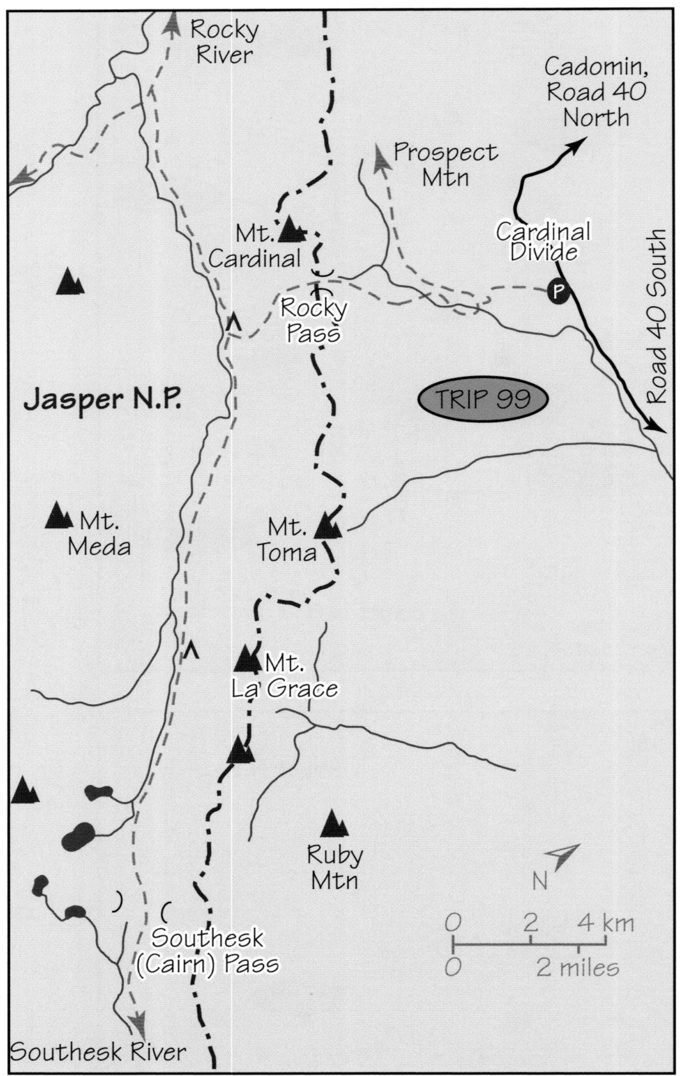
Rocky River
Cadomin, Road 40 North
Prospect Mtn
Mt. Cardinal
Cardinal Divide
Road 40 South
Rocky Pass
Jasper N.P.
TRIP 99
Mt. Meda
Mt. Toma
Mt. La Grace
Ruby Mtn
N
0 2 4 km
0 2 miles
Southesk (Cairn) Pass
Southesk River

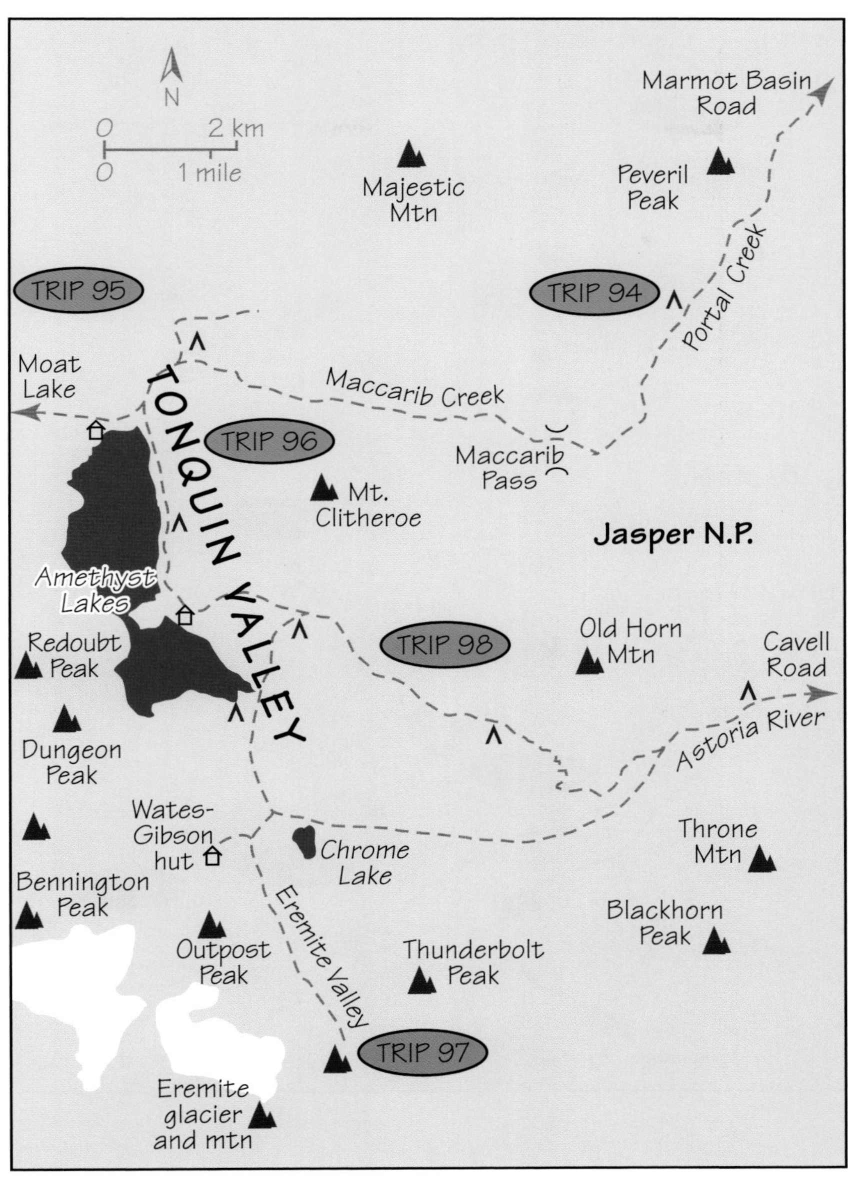
N
0 2 km
0 1 mile
Marmot Basin Road
Majestic Mtn
Peveril Peak
Portal Creek
TRIP 95
TRIP 94
Moat Lake
Maccarib Creek
TONQUIN VALLEY
TRIP 96
Maccarib Pass
Mt. Clitheroe
Jasper N.P.
Amethyst Lakes
Redoubt Peak
TRIP 98
Old Horn Mtn
Cavell Road
Astoria River
Dungeon Peak
Wates-Gibson hut
Chrome Lake
Throne Mtn
Bennington Peak
Eremite Valley
Blackhorn Peak
Outpost Peak
Thunderbolt Peak
TRIP 97
Eremite glacier and mtn

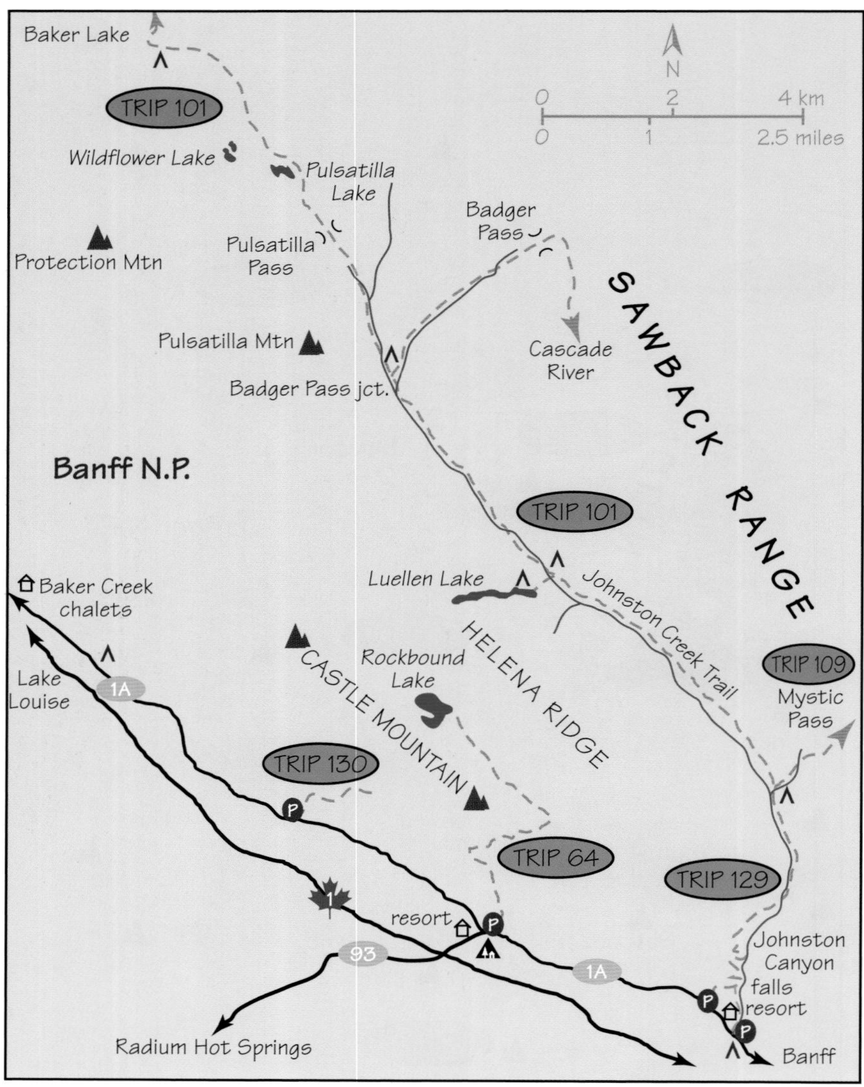
Baker Lake
TRIP 101
N
0 2 4 km
0 1 2.5 miles
Wildflower Lake
Pulsatilla Lake
Badger Pass
Protection Mtn
Pulsatilla Pass
SAWBACK RANGE
Cascade River
Pulsatilla Mtn
Badger Pass jct.
Banff N.P.
TRIP 101
Luellen Lake
Johnston Creek Trail
Baker Creek chalets
HELENA RIDGE
CASTLE MOUNTAIN
Rockbound Lake
TRIP 109
Mystic Pass
Lake Louise
1A
TRIP 130
TRIP 64
TRIP 129
1
resort
Johnston Canyon
falls
93
1A
resort
Radium Hot Springs
Banff

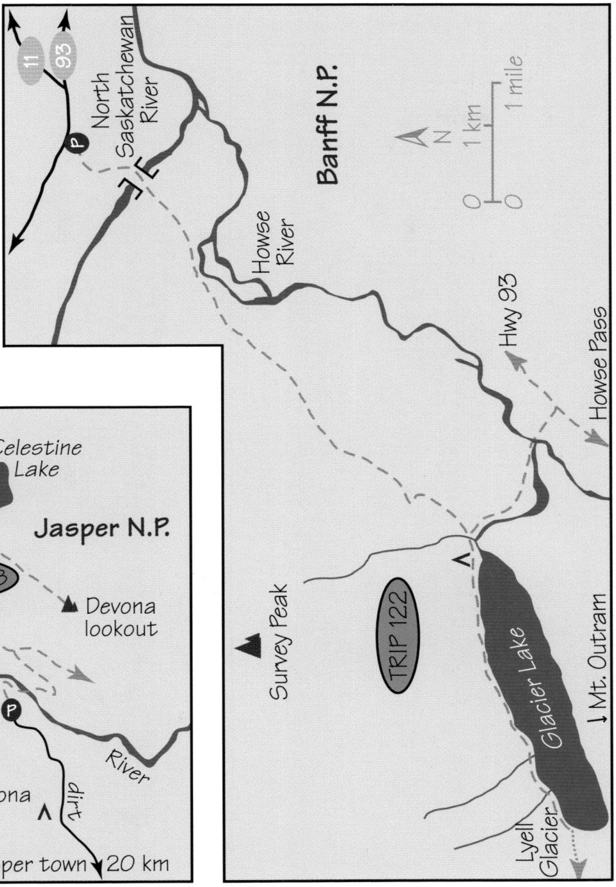

11
93
North Saskatchewan River
Banff N.P.
N
0 1 km
0 1 mile
Howse River
Hwy 93
Howse Pass
Survey Peak
TRIP 122
Glacier Lake
Mt. Outram
Lyell Glacier

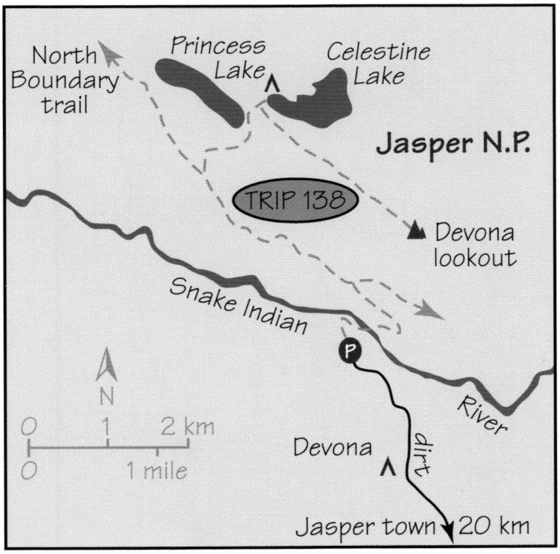

North Boundary trail
Princess Lake
Celestine Lake
Jasper N.P.
TRIP 138
Devona lookout
Snake Indian
River
N
0 1 2 km
0 1 mile
Devona
dirt
Jasper town 20 km

Old Fort
VALLEY OF FIVE LAKES
TRIP 137
First
Second
Third
Fourth
Fifth
N
0 1.5 km
0 1 mile
Jasper 9 km (5.6 mi)
93
Jasper N.P.
Wabasso Lake
TRIP 136

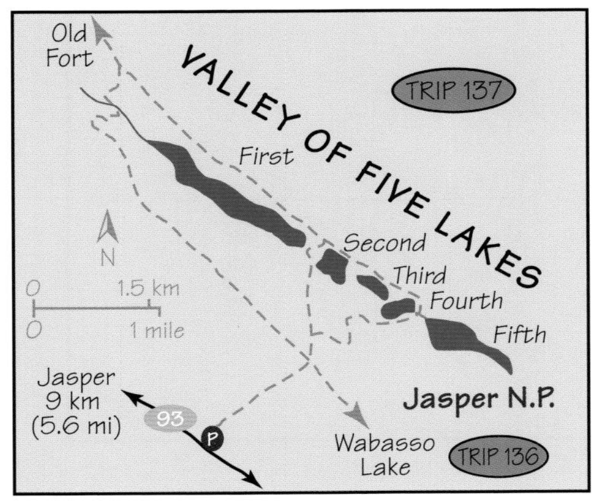

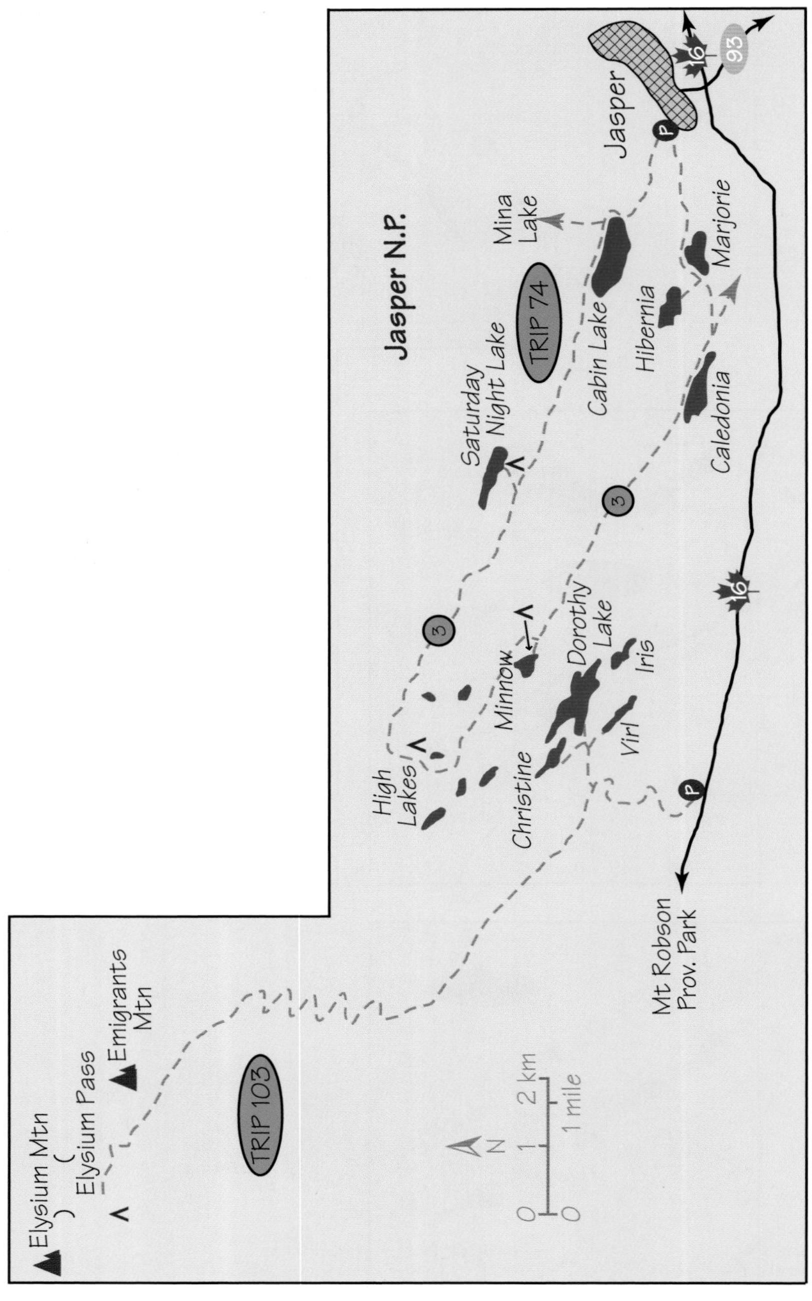
Jasper N.P.
Jasper
16
93
Mina Lake
TRIP 74
Saturday Night Lake
Cabin Lake
Marjorie
Hibernia
Caledonia
3
16
3
Minnow
Dorothy Lake
Iris
High Lakes
Christine
Virl
Mt Robson Prov. Park
Elysium Mtn
Elysium Pass
Emigrants Mtn
TRIP 103
N
0 1 2 km
0 1 mile

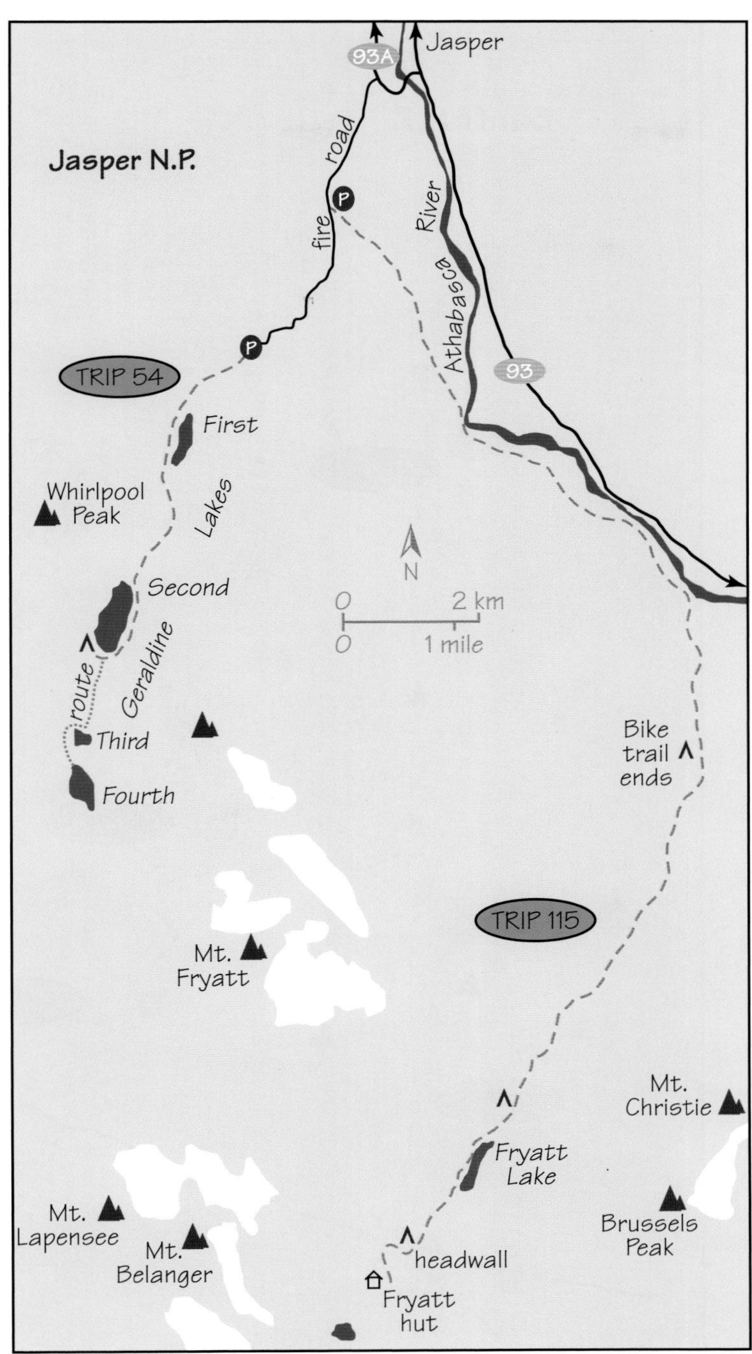
Jasper
93A
Jasper N.P.
fire road
River
Athabasca
93
TRIP 54
First
Whirlpool Peak
Lakes
Second
Geraldine
route
Third
Fourth
N
0 2 km
0 1 mile
Bike trail ends
TRIP 115
Mt. Fryatt
Mt. Christie
Fryatt Lake
Brussels Peak
Mt. Lapensee
Mt. Belanger
headwall
Fryatt hut

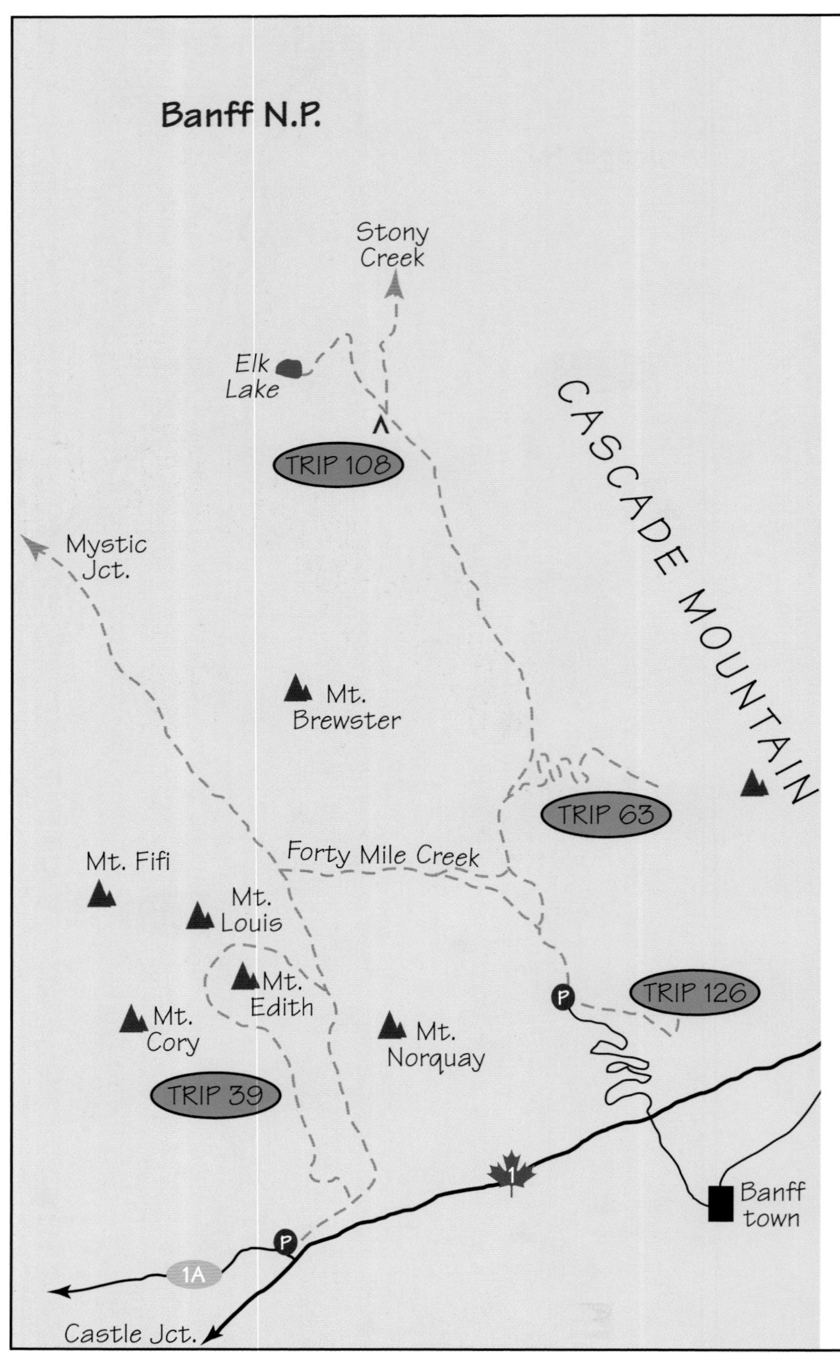
Banff N.P.
Stony Creek
Elk Lake
TRIP 108
CASCADE MOUNTAIN
Mystic Jct.
Mt. Brewster
TRIP 63
Forty Mile Creek
Mt. Fifi
Mt. Louis
Mt. Edith
TRIP 126
Mt. Cory
Mt. Norquay
TRIP 39
1
Banff town
1A
Castle Jct.

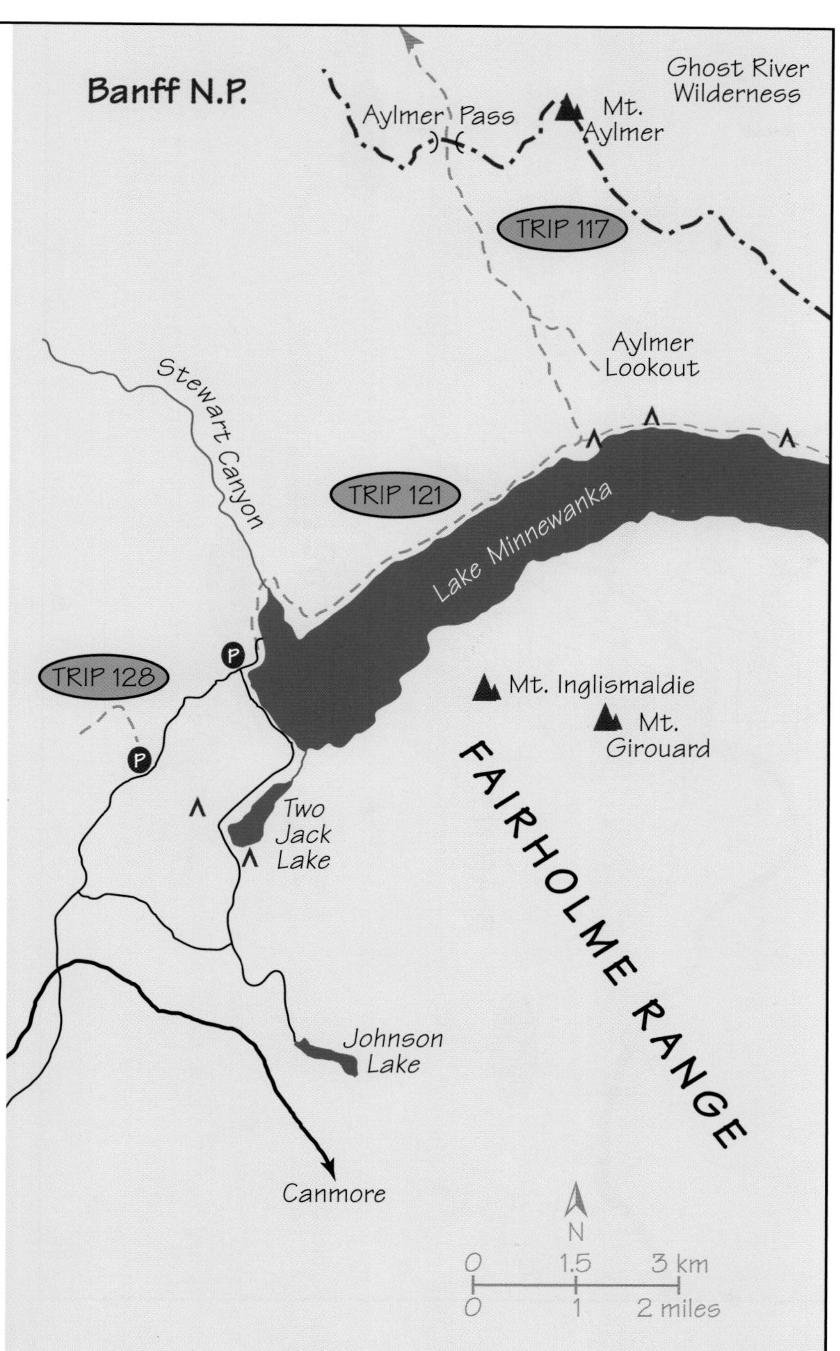
Banff N.P.
Aylmer Pass
Mt. Aylmer
Ghost River Wilderness
TRIP 117
Aylmer Lookout
Stewart Canyon
TRIP 121
Lake Minnewanka
TRIP 128
Mt. Inglismaldie
Mt. Girouard
Two Jack Lake
FAIRHOLME RANGE
Johnson Lake
Canmore
N
0 1.5 3 km
0 1 2 miles

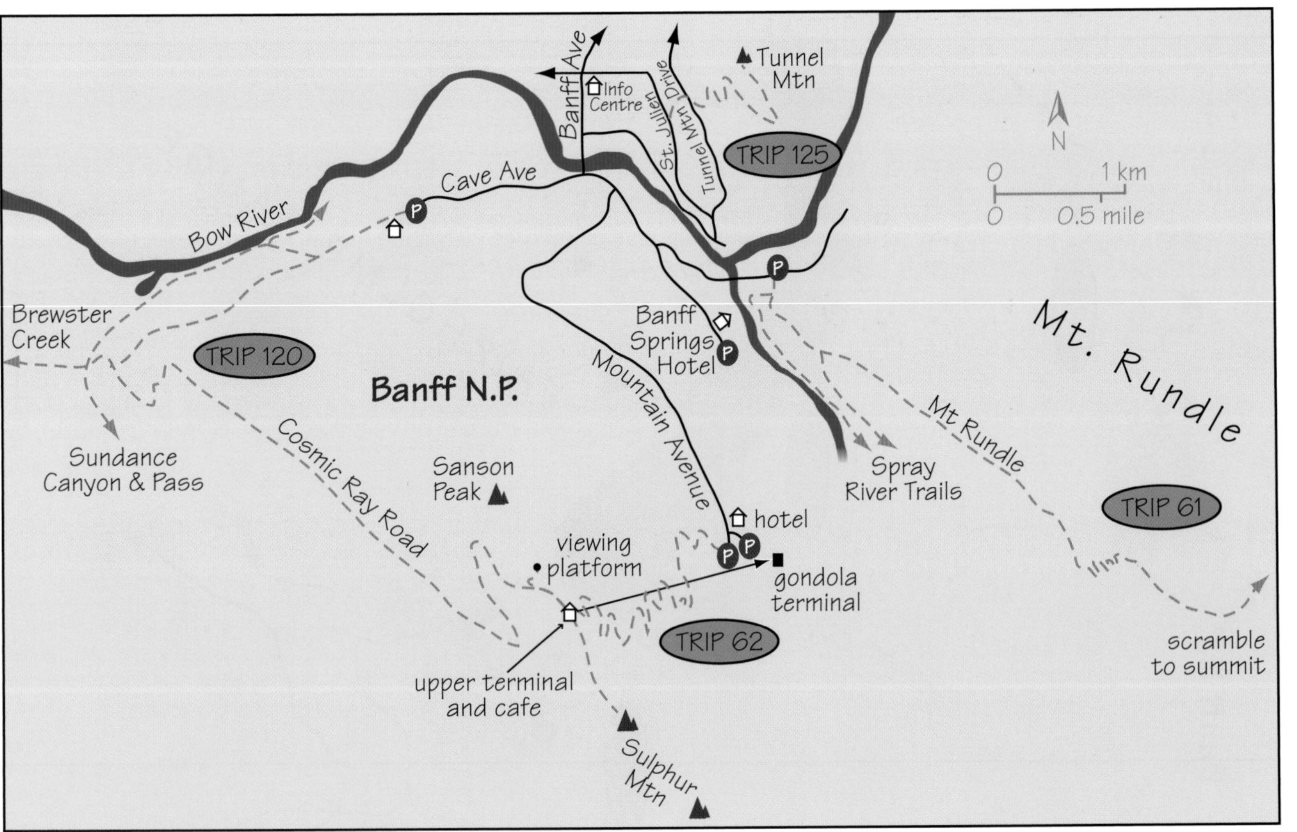
Banff Ave
Info Centre
St. Julien
Tunnel Mtn Drive
Tunnel Mtn
TRIP 125
N
0 1 km
0 0.5 mile
Cave Ave
Bow River
Brewster Creek
TRIP 120
Banff N.P.
Banff Springs Hotel
Mountain Avenue
Mt. Rundle
Mt Rundle
Spray River Trails
TRIP 61
Sundance Canyon & Pass
Cosmic Ray Road
Sanson Peak
hotel
viewing platform
gondola terminal
TRIP 62
scramble to summit
upper terminal and cafe
Sulphur Mtn

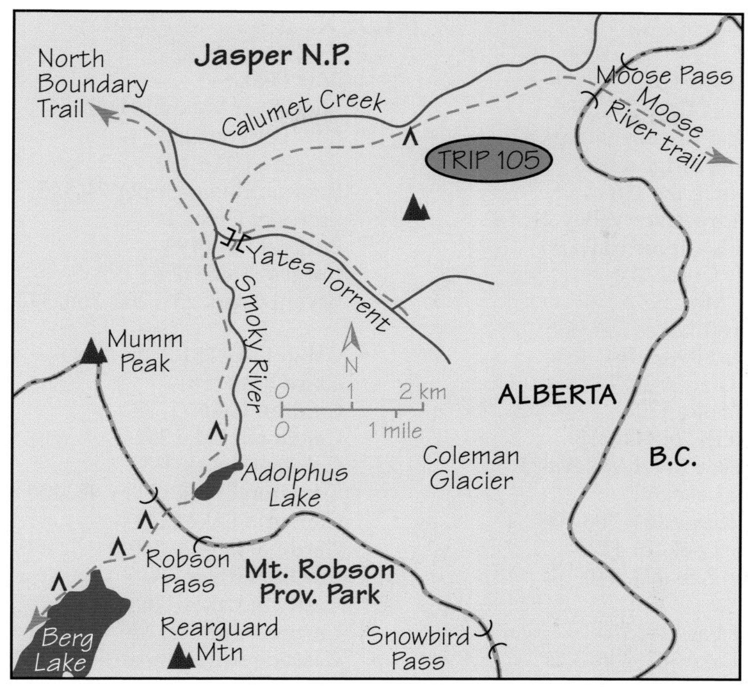
Jasper N.P.
North Boundary Trail
Calumet Creek
Moose Pass
Moose River trail
TRIP 105
Yates Torrent
Smoky River
Mumm Peak
N
0 1 2 km
0 1 mile
ALBERTA
B.C.
Coleman Glacier
Adolphus Lake
Robson Pass
Mt. Robson Prov. Park
Berg Lake
Rearguard Mtn
Snowbird Pass

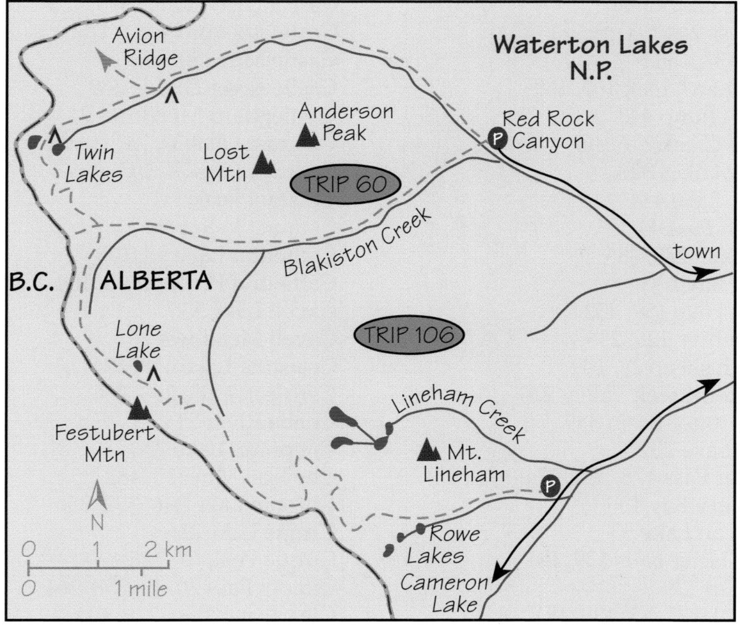
Avion Ridge
Waterton Lakes N.P.
Anderson Peak
Red Rock Canyon
Twin Lakes
Lost Mtn
TRIP 60
Blakiston Creek
town
B.C.
ALBERTA
TRIP 106
Lone Lake
Lineham Creek
Festubert Mtn
Mt. Lineham
N
0 1 2 km
0 1 mile
Rowe Lakes
Cameron Lake

INDEX

Moraine Lake, beneath Mounts Babel and Fay, from summit of Mt. Temple

THE AUTHORS

Kathy and Craig are dedicated to each other, and to hiking, in that order. Their second date was a 32-km (20-mile) dayhike in Arizona. Since then they haven't stopped for long.

They've trekked through much of the world's vertical topography, including the Himalayas, Patagonian Andes, Pyrenees, French Alps, Scottish Highlands, Dolomites, Sierra Nevada, North Cascades, Colorado Rockies, New Zealand Alps, and canyons of the American Southwest. In 1989, they moved from the U.S. to Canada, so they could live near the Canadian Rockies—the range that inspired the first of their refreshingly unconventional guidebooks.

While living in Vancouver, British Columbia, they explored the Coast Mountains and the North Cascades, then wrote hiking guidebooks on each of those ranges. Later, while living in a cabin on Kootenay Lake (between B.C.'s Purcell and Selkirk mountains), they researched and wrote two more hiking guidebooks: one on the West Kootenay, the other on the premier trails of southern B.C.

Kathy and Craig have since returned to the Canadian Rockies and now live in Canmore, Alberta. Their desire to hike, however, keeps them travelling constantly. For example, they migrate each spring and fall to the high-desert canyon country of southern Utah. Their guidebook *Hiking from Here to WOW: Utah Canyon Country* is especially stimulating and beautiful.

To complete the research for the first edition of *Don't Waste Your Time® in the Canadian Rockies*, Kathy and Craig hiked 2,500 km (1,550 mi) and ascended elevation equivalent to climbing from sea level to the summit of Mt. Everest eight times. For the all-new sixth edition, they re-hiked many of the trails, some for the third or fourth time.

But Kathy and Craig agree: no matter how arduous the trail, or how severe the conditions, hiking is the easiest of the many tasks necessary to create a guidebook. What they find most challenging is having to sit. They spend twice as much time at their computers—writing, organizing, editing, checking facts, rewriting, re-organizing, re-editing, re-checking facts—as they do on the trail.

The result is worth it. Kathy and Craig's colourful writing, opinionated commentary, and enthusiasm for the joys of hiking make their guidebooks uniquely helpful and compelling.

nomads@hikingcamping.com

by Ruedi Beglinger
New Zealand
Canadian Rockies
Exploring canyon country in 1978
Utah canyon country
Grateful to Gaia

The Authors

Other Titles from hikingcamping.com

The following titles—boot-tested and written by the Opinionated Hikers, Kathy & Craig Copeland—are widely available in outdoor shops and bookstores. Visit www.hikingcamping.com to read excerpts and purchase online.

Where Locals Hike in the Canadian Rockies

The Premier Trails in Kananaskis Country, near Canmore and Calgary

ISBN 978-0-9783427-4-6 The 55 most rewarding dayhikes and backpack trips within two hours of Calgary's international airport. All lead to astonishing alpine meadows, ridges and peaks. Though these trails are little known compared to those in the nearby Canadian Rocky Mountain national parks, the scenery is equally magnificent. Includes Peter Lougheed and Spray Valley provincial parks. Discerning trail reviews help you choose your trip. Detailed route descriptions keep you on the path. 320 pages, 180 photos, trail maps for each hike, full colour throughout. Updated 3rd edition July 2009.

Where Locals Hike in the West Kootenay

The Premier Trails in Southeast B.C. near Kaslo & Nelson

ISBN 978-0-9689419-9-7 See the peaks, glaciers and cascades that make locals passionate about these mountains. The 50 most rewarding dayhikes and backpack trips in the Selkirk and west Purcell ranges of southeast British Columbia. Includes Valhalla, Kokanee Glacier, and Goat Range parks, as well as hikes near Arrow, Slocan, and Kootenay lakes. Discerning trail reviews help you choose your trip. Detailed route descriptions keep you on the path. 272 pages, 130 photos, trail locator maps, full colour throughout. Updated 2nd edition April 2007.

Bears Beware!

Warning Calls You Can Make to Avoid an Encounter

Here's the 30-minute MP3 that could save your life. Download it from hikingcamping.com to your computer. Go to Guidebooks > Bear Safety. Listen to it at home, or on your iPod while driving to the trailhead.

You'll find out why pepper spray, talking, and bells are insufficient protection. You'll realize that using your voice is the only reliable method of preventing a bear encounter. You'll discover why warning calls are the key to defensive hiking. You'll understand how, where and when to make warning calls. You'll learn specific strategies for worry-free hiking and camping in bear country.

Bears Beware! was endorsed by the wardens at Jasper National Park, which has the biggest grizzly-bear population in the Canadian Rockies. It was also approved by the wardens at Waterton National Park, which has the highest concentration of grizzly bears in the Rockies.

Camp Free in B.C.

ISBN 978-0-9735099-3-9 Make your weekend or vacation adventurous and revitalizing. Enjoy British Columbia's scenic byways and 2WD backroads—in your low-clearance car or your big RV. Follow precise directions to 350 campgrounds, from the B.C. Coast to the Rocky Mountains. Choose from 80 low-fee campgrounds similar in quality to provincial parks but half the price. Find retreats where the world is yours alone. Simplify life: slow down, ease up. Fully appreciate B.C.'s magnificent backcountry, including the Sunshine Coast, Okanagan, Shuswap Highlands, Selkirk and Purcell ranges, Cariboo Mountains, and Chilcotin Plateau. 544 pages, 200 photos, 20 regional maps, full colour throughout. Updated 4th edition July 2009.

Heading Outdoors Eventually Leads Within

Thoughts Inspired by 30,000 Miles on the Trail

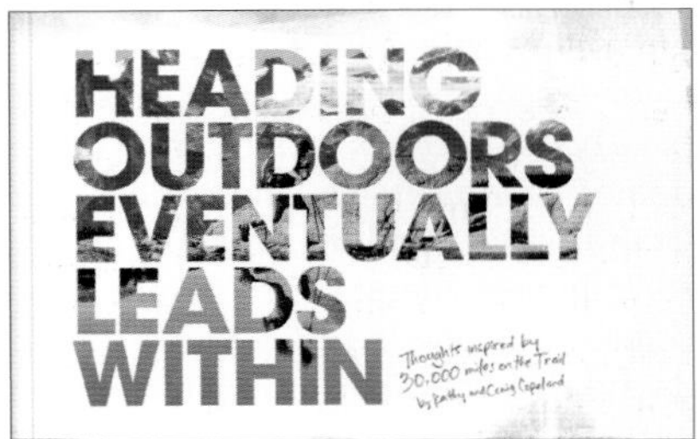

ISBN 978-0-9783427-6-0 Everyone walks. What distinguishes hikers is that walking does more than transport us, it transforms us. But nowhere is the thoughtful undercurrent of hiking celebrated. The wisdom we glean from the wilds is a match lit in the rain. That's why we created this book: to cup our hands around the flame. These journal entries are the mental waypoints we recorded while hiking 30,000 miles (more than the circumference of the Earth) through wildlands worldwide. Accompanying them are photos of the places (primarily the Canadian Rockies, Utah canyon country, and New Zealand) where we conceived and noted the initial ideas. We hope our words and images compel you to recognize, voice, own and honour the thoughts arising from within while heading outdoors. Doing so will deepen your fulfillment. A truly adventurous life is contemplative as well as vigourous. Hardcover, 96 pages, 72 full-colour photos. First edition January 2011.

Hiking from Here to WOW: North Cascades

50 Trails to the Wonder of Wilderness

ISBN 978-0-89997-444-6 The authors hiked more than 1,400 miles through North Cascades National Park plus the surrounding wilderness areas, including Glacier Peak, Mt. Baker, and the Pasayten. They took more than 1,000 photos and hundreds of pages of field notes. Then they culled their list of favourite hikes down to 50 trips—each selected for its power to incite awe. Their 264-page book describes where to find the cathedral forests, psychedelic meadows, spiky summits, and colossal glaciers that distinguish the American Alps. And it does so in refreshing style: honest, literate, entertaining, inspiring. Like all *WOW Guides*, this one is full colour throughout, with 180 photos and a trail map for each dayhike and backpack trip. First edition May 2007.

Hiking from Here to WOW: Utah Canyon Country

90 Trails to the Wonder of Wilderness

ISBN 978-0-89997-452-1 The authors hiked more than 1,600 miles through Zion, Bryce, Escalante-Grand Staircase, Glen Canyon, Grand Gulch, Cedar Mesa, Canyonlands, Moab, Arches, Capitol Reef, and the San Rafael Swell. They took more than 2,500 photos and hundreds of pages of field notes. Then they culled their list of favourite hikes down to 90 trips—each selected for its power to incite awe. Their 480-page book describes where to find the redrock cliffs, slickrock domes, soaring arches, and ancient ruins that make southern Utah unique in all the world. And it does so in refreshing style: honest, literate, entertaining, inspiring. Like all *WOW Guides*, this one is full colour throughout, with 220 photos and a trail map for each dayhike and backpack trip. First edition August 2008.

Done in a Day: Moab

The 10 Premier Hikes

ISBN 978-0-9735099-8-4 Where to invest your limited hiking time to enjoy the greatest scenic reward. Choose an easy, vigourous, or challenging hike. Start your adventure within a short drive of town. Witness the wonder of canyon country—including Arches and Canyonlands national parks—and be back for a hot shower, great meal, and soft bed. 160 pages, 110 photos, trail maps for each trip, full colour throughout. First edition February 2008.

Done in a Day: Banff

The 10 Premier Hikes

ISBN 978-0-9783427-0-8 Where to invest your limited hiking time to enjoy the greatest scenic reward. Choose an easy, vigourous, or challenging hike. Start your adventure within a short drive of town. Witness the wonder of Banff National Park and be back for a hot shower, great meal, and soft bed. 136 pages, 90 photos, trail maps for each trip, full colour throughout. First edition December 2007.

Done in a Day: Calgary

The 10 Premier Road Rides

ISBN 978-0-9783427-3-9 Where to invest your limited cycling time to enjoy the greatest scenic reward. Spring through fall, southwest Alberta offers cyclists blue-ribbon road riding: from alpine passes in the Canadian Rockies, to dinosaur-country river canyons on the edge of the prairie. And this compact, jersey-pocket-sized book is your guide to the crème de la crème: the ten most serene, compelling, bike-friendly roads in the region. Start pedaling within a short drive of Calgary. At day's end, be back for a hot shower, great meal, and soft bed. 120 pages, 80 photos, road maps for each ride, full colour throughout. First edition December 2007.

Done in a Day: Jasper

The 10 Premier Hikes

ISBN 978-0-9783427-1-5 Where to invest your limited hiking time to enjoy the greatest scenic reward. Choose an easy, vigourous, or challenging hike. Start your adventure within a short drive of town. Witness the wonder of Jasper National Park and be back for a hot shower, great meal, and soft bed. 128 pages, 75 photos, trail maps for each trip, full colour throughout. First edition December 2007.

Done in a Day: Whistler

The 10 Premier Hikes

ISBN 978-0-9735099-7-7 Where to invest your limited hiking time to enjoy the greatest scenic reward. Choose an easy, vigourous, or challenging hike. Start your adventure within a short drive of the village. Witness the wonder of Whistler, British Columbia, and be back for a hot shower, great meal, and soft bed. 144 pages, 80 photos, trail maps for each trip, full colour throughout. First edition December 2007.